Consumer Bankruptcy Law

This practical and invaluable textbook covers the principles and practice of U.S. consumer bankruptcy law, known as Chapter 7 and Chapter 13, for paralegals and legal studies students.

Consumer Bankruptcy Law provides step-by-step guidance on handling a bankruptcy case, from client interviews to preparing and filing the bankruptcy petition, as well as the issues which may arise after. Featuring practical examples throughout, the book ensures that you will become familiar not only with core legal concepts but also with the real-life issues and pitfalls that can occur. Screenshots of how to complete a bankruptcy petition are featured, along with flowcharts of the processes of consumer bankruptcy law in the U.S. and exercises to test your knowledge at the end of each chapter.

Including online resources for both students and instructors to benefit from, such as multiple-choice questions and PowerPoints summarizing each chapter, *Consumer Bankruptcy Law: A Practical Guide for Students and Professionals* will be an indispensable resource for anyone engaging in this important area of legal practice.

Alexander Hernandez earned his Bachelor and Master of Science degrees in Criminal Justice from Florida International University, USA, and Juris Doctor degree from Nova Southeastern School of Law, USA. His teaching career began at Millennia Atlantic University in 2013, where he taught Business Law I and II and received the honor of being the highest-ranked professor by students. Alexander teaches Family Law Practicum and Community Property at Concord Law School and is currently developing their bankruptcy course. He also teaches Bankruptcy Law in English and Spanish at Marconi International University and is developing their business law course. At the University of California at Riverside, he teaches the Paralegal Studies Program. He also teaches criminal justice and political science courses for Central State University and is a legal writer at Upsolve.org. Before teaching, he practiced law as a sole practitioner for more than two decades.

Consumer Bankruptcy Law

A Practical Guide for Students and Professionals

Alexander Hernandez

Routledge
Taylor & Francis Group
LONDON AND NEW YORK

Cover image: courtneyk (Getty Images)

First published 2022
by Routledge
4 Park Square, Milton Park, Abingdon, Oxon OX14 4RN

and by Routledge
605 Third Avenue, New York, NY 10158

Routledge is an imprint of the Taylor & Francis Group, an informa business

British Library Cataloguing-in-Publication Data
A catalogue record for this book is available from the British Library

Library of Congress Cataloging-in-Publication Data
Names: Hernandez, Alexander (Lawyer), author.
Title: Consumer bankruptcy law: a practical guide for students and professionals / Alexander Hernandez.
Description: Abingdon, Oxon; New York, NY: Routledge, 2022. | Includes bibliographical references and index. |
Identifiers: LCCN 2022002901 | ISBN 9781032066615 (hardback) | ISBN 9781032064697 (paperback) | ISBN 9781003203278 (ebook)
Subjects: LCSH: Bankruptcy–United States. | United States. Bankruptcy. Chapter 7, Liquidation. | United States. Bankruptcy. Chapter 13, Adjustment of debts of an individual with regular income. | LCGFT: Textbooks.
Classification: LCC KF1524.85 .H47 2022 | DDC 346.7307/8–dc23/eng/20220526
LC record available at https://lccn.loc.gov/2022002901

ISBN: 978-1-032-06661-5 (hbk)
ISBN: 978-1-032-06469-7 (pbk)
ISBN: 978-1-003-20327-8 (ebk)

DOI: 10.4324/9781003203278

Typeset in Bembo
by Deanta Global Publishing Services, Chennai, India

Access the Support Material: **www.routledge.com/9781032064697**

To Anny. Your unwavering support got me here. I'm forever indebted to you.

Contents

Acknowledgments

I wish to thank Russell George for his faith in this project and the kind staff at Routledge. Without your hard work and dedication, not only would this page not exist, but neither would this book. I look forward to one day crossing the pond to thank you all in person.

Introduction

The Need for Paralegals and the Future of Consumer Bankruptcy Law

Paralegals continue to be and always will be an integral part of a law office, even with technology, automated software programs, and answering services.

The benefits of a paralegal are numerous, whether for clients or the law firm. With the ever-increasing costs of legal representation, paralegals provide the opportunity for clients to save money by billing at a lower hourly rate. In flat-fee cases, which is the norm in bankruptcy, the paralegal reduces overhead costs. Bankruptcy paralegals will assist the attorney from beginning to end by providing support with the client intake, following up on requests for documents, preparing the bankruptcy petition, scheduling hearings, and helping draft motions. Post-filing, the paralegal will submit documents to the trustee, communicate with the trustee's office on issues concerning non-exempt property, and ensure Reaffirmation Agreement are completed correctly and filed timely. Paralegals serve as the right and left hand of the attorney and an extension of the client.

Like in all businesses, some clients will take more of one's time when compared to others, and the practice of law is not exempt. But a paralegal will serve as a buffer between the client and attorney. In a world of instant gratification, clients aren't always patient and willing to wait until the end of the day, sometimes not even a few hours, to have their concerns addressed. But, paralegals help facilitate communications between clients and lawyers, allowing the law firm to function smoothly and efficiently while simultaneously satisfying the client's needs. The success of a business depends on its employees, and a law office is no different. A good, competent paralegal with an outgoing personality will generate more income for the law firm, but a bad one will have the opposite effect. A happy client will result in ten referrals, while an unhappy one will speak ill of you to ten potential clients.

Practicing consumer bankruptcy law, while rewarding, is also time-consuming. Patience is required as clients may be indecisive. An organized client is rare, so organizational skills are necessary, especially when handling dozens, if not hundreds of cases simultaneously. But don't let this deter you. When clients schedule an appointment with a bankruptcy attorney, they are in a situation they never planned nor expected. No one looks forward to meeting with a lawyer, especially one that practices bankruptcy law. But with the client drowning in debt, as the client's financial struggles increase, so does their level of stress and anxiety. There's a direct link between financial difficulties and divorce, as well as an increase in

DOI: 10.4324/9781003203278-1

prescribed antidepressants and suicides during economic recessions.[1] The coronavirus pandemic has only exacerbated these issues. Studies show more than 70 percent of Americans consider the economy a significant source of stress, and more than one-third have experienced signs of clinical depression since the pandemic.[2] What once was an annual mental health report from the American Psychological Association is now published monthly.[3]

But when the client retains a bankruptcy lawyer and the harassing creditor calls end, the client is not only relieved psychologically and physically but attributes this newfound peace of mind to your efforts. Even if you have poor math skills, the formula is easy to calculate. Even more satisfying is the first question from the client after the Meeting of Creditors: "Is that it?" And when the client receives the *Order of Discharge*, there is that lengthy phone call thanking you endlessly for removing the weight of crushing debt off their shoulders.[4] The client feels whole again and has the opportunity to improve their credit score to buy another car or even their first home. They can and do get another bite at the apple, and it's because of you.

In my opinion, bankruptcy law is unique because it's gratifying on both ends. I call it "happy law" because happy lawyers and clients can be as elusive as Bigfoot. Remember, no one wants to meet with an attorney, so the dynamics of the relationship begin with pessimism. The hopelessness and despair of clients are evident in the first consultation, but with time, their attitude changes as they feel more confident and in control of their situation. The layman, even attorneys, think of bankruptcy as a depressing scenario where people are left destitute, or even worse, but my perception is different. I see an opportunity for a "fresh start."[5] We love movies and novels where the protagonist is given a second chance in life, only to succeed. Bankruptcy is that second chance.

Now we're facing the challenges of COVID-19, and the scars left behind from the coronavirus pandemic will financially impact the world for years, if not decades to come. In the first few months since the pandemic started, we have already witnessed record numbers of bankruptcy filings by popular brick-and-mortar businesses like J. Crew, J.C. Penney, Pier 1 Imports, and Hertz, leaving hundreds of thousands of employees without work. No industry was spared from the coronavirus. Millions of employees were furloughed or laid off, and tens of millions of Americans filed for unemployment benefits.[6]

The Coronavirus Aid Relief and Economic Security (CARES) Act, which provided stimulus checks for families and individuals, was not enough to keep families financially afloat.[7] Other attempts by Congress, such as the Paycheck Protection Program (PPP) and

1 Melanie Haikan, Suicide and Financial Crisis: How Real is the Risk? *Forbes*, August 10, 2011.

2 Naz Beheshti, 10 Eye Opening Statistics on the Mental Health Impact of the Coronavirus Pandemic. *Forbes*, May 28, 2020.

3 American Psychological Association, apa.org, retrieved on February 19, 2021.

4 Official Form B318, Discharge of Debtor in a Chapter 7 Case. 11 U.S.C. §727. Official Form 3180W, Chapter 13 Discharge. 11 U.S.C. §1328(a). Fed. R. Bankr. P. 9009.

5 *Wetmore v. Markoe*, 196 U.S. 68, 25 S. Ct. 172, 49 L. Ed. 390 (1904).

6 Jack Kelly, Nearly 50 Million Americans Have Filed for Unemployment: Here's What's Really Happening. *Forbes*, July 9, 2020. Retrieved February 11, 2021.

7 Coronavirus Aid, Relief, and Economic Security Act, PL 116-136, March 27, 2020, 134 Stat 281. U.S. Small Business Administration, sba.gov. Retrieved September 5, 2021.

low-interest loans from the Small Business Administration (SBA), will help businesses buy time.[8] Still, it will not stop the tsunami of bankruptcies headed our way. Bankruptcy attorneys and experienced paralegals will be in high demand as now, more than ever, people will need that second chance.

With this textbook, I hope to guide you through the ins and outs of consumer bankruptcy law not only from a legal perspective but also as a how-to guide with tips gained from my experiences as a bankruptcy attorney representing debtors for more than two decades. You will learn the basics of bankruptcy law, practice tips, and step-by-step explanations of the bankruptcy petition, as well as review sample documents and real cases and have access to important links related to the practice of bankruptcy. This textbook also provides extensive multiple-choice and essay questions to enhance the learning experience and improve critical thinking skills. This textbook should be helpful for paralegal programs, legal study majors, and the solo practitioner looking to jump-start a practice focusing on consumer bankruptcies. Established paralegals not familiar with bankruptcy law could also benefit from this text and use it as a training tool to learn Chapters 7 and 13 from the ground up.

My experiences in teaching paralegal programs, undergraduate courses, and law school have taught me that reviewing the subject matter and citing and dissecting cases based on the dreaded IRAC (issue, rule, application, conclusion) is not enough. For this reason, this text isn't solely about consumer bankruptcy law and procedure but also includes scenarios that any practitioner or paralegal is likely to encounter.

The common misperception is that the practice of law is just motions and pleadings, but it's not. Anyone can go online and find a motion to copy and paste. Likewise, anyone can also read and complete the bankruptcy forms without the help of a lawyer. If it were only that simple. Just ask any *pro se* debtor. The practice of law is real people with real problems. It requires looking into your legal crystal ball and seeing all the angles simultaneously while predicting the future and explaining the consequences to a client. It's three-dimensional chess with real consequences. That's why my goal is to not only teach you what you usually find in a textbook but also go beyond the four corners of the page. Early in my career, as an inexperienced lawyer, I found myself in situations where the answer to my questions was not in any textbook, case law, or guide. There is an abyss between education, practicality, and real-world experience, and I intend to fill in those gaps with this textbook.

I wish you the best of luck and success as you embark on your legal career.

REFERENCES

11 U.S.C. §727.

11 U.S.C. §1328.

American Psychological Association, apa.org.

Fed. R. Bankr. P. 9009.

8 Paycheck Protection Program and Health Care Enhancement Act, PL 116-139, April 24, 2020, 134 Stat 620.

Jack Kelly, "Nearly 50 Million Americans Have Filed for Unemployment: Here's What's Really Happening" *Forbes* (July 9, 2020).

Melanie Haikan, "Suicide and Financial Crisis: How Real is the Risk?" *Forbes* (August 10, 2011).

Naz Beheshti, "10 Eye Opening Statistics on the Mental Health Impact of the Coronavirus Pandemic" *Forbes* (May 28, 2020).

Official Form B318. Discharge of Debtor in a Chapter 7 Case.

Official Form 3180W. Chapter 13 Discharge.

Paycheck Protection Program and Health Care Enhancement Act, PL 116-139, April 24, 2020, 134 Stat 620.

S.3548-116th Congress (2019–2020): CARES Act. Coronavirus Aid, Relief, and Economic Security Act, PL 116–136, March 27, 2020, 134 Stat 281. www.congress.gov/bill/116th-congress/senate-bill/3548.

U.S. Small Business Administration, sba.gov.

Wetmore v. Markoe, 196 U.S. 68, 25 S. Ct. 172, 49 L. Ed. 390 (1904).

CHAPTER 1

The History of Bankruptcy Law

Imagine yourself at your graduation ceremony, surrounded by fellow graduates. Your friends, family, and loved ones are looking on with excitement. As the commencement ceremonies begin, you drift off into thoughts of the past few years.

You reflect on the difficult path and sacrifices you made, at times thinking this day would never come. At some point, you considered giving up. The struggle was real, and you questioned your decision to pursue an education. The finish line was nowhere in sight, and completing your education seemed like a distant dream. But, facing adversity, you continued to push forward, refusing to give up.

Your thoughts now switch to what the future holds. Soon you will be entering the workforce with your degree in hand, or maybe you already have a job lined up. You've taken that next step toward independence, personal success, and the achievement of your goals. It won't be long before you're shopping for a new car, then the perfect home in the perfect neighborhood.

Fast forward ten years. An economy weakened because of a pandemic, divorce, and a real estate crash left you heavily in debt. Arguably these are matters beyond your control, but since you can't afford to pay your debts, you will spend time in prison.

Don't worry; debtor's prison was abolished long ago, but clients still ask if they can go to jail for not paying their debts. The question is not as farfetched as it seems since there was a time in our history when there were more people in prison for not paying their debts than actual criminals.[1] As bad as that sounds, we can agree that a creditor seizing the corpse of a debtor to collect on the debt from heirs is far worse.[2] Still, debt collectors can be ruthless. Thankfully, the Fair Debt Collection and Practices Act restricts debt collectors' actions and provides legal remedies for debtors when violations occur.[3] But, debt collectors still have the right to pursue legal action against debtors, and that's when the passing thought of bankruptcy becomes a reality.

1 R. Ford, Imprisonment for Debt, 25(1) *Michigan Law Review* 24–49 (1926).

2 Vern Countryman, Bankruptcy and the Individual Debtor and A Modest Proposal to Return to the Seventeenth Century, 32 *Cath. U. L. Rev.* 809 (1983).

3 15 U.S.C. §1692.

DOI: 10.4324/9781003203278-2

The word bankruptcy comes from the Italian words *banca* and *rotta*, which translate into "broken bench" and the practice of creditors breaking the benches or destroying the trading places of those who failed to pay their debts.[4] In Spanish, the word *quiebra* is used for bankruptcy, but so is *bancarrota*.

Bankruptcy law in the United States is a direct descendent of English law. Under the U.S. Constitution, Congress had the authority to pass federal legislation, which could have included bankruptcy. Still, it wasn't until 1800 that Congress passed bankruptcy legislation and unfortunately for debtors, debt relief, historically, was temporary.[5]

The first laws related to bankruptcy came under the Bankruptcy Act of 1800, which barely came to be since it passed by only one vote. In addition, it only applied to merchant debtors, so there were no remedies for consumers.[6] Creditors initiated bankruptcy proceedings, and it required that two-thirds of the creditors agree to a settlement.[7] However, the Bankruptcy Act of 1800 was short-lived and was repealed in 1803 by Congress, citing mounting costs and corruption.[8] The discharge of debts was now a state issue. However, in 1819, the U.S. Supreme Court ruled that a state lacks the authority to discharge debts from citizens in other states.[9] At least debtors' prison was abolished for good in 1838.[10]

With the Bankruptcy Act of 1841, major changes went into effect with bankruptcy laws and procedures. District courts now had "jurisdiction in all matters and proceedings in bankruptcy."[11] There was even the appointment of commissioners and assignees.[12] The Bankruptcy Act of 1841 also prohibited debtors from using state exemptions and allowed for the recovery of fraudulent transfers. Also, for a debtor to receive a discharge, assets had to be surrendered. However, the most significant change that favored debtors was that bankruptcy filings were now voluntary, meaning that the debtor could file bankruptcy, unlike the Bankruptcy Act of 1800, where creditors initiated it.

But following the same path as the Bankruptcy Act of 1800, the Bankruptcy Act of 1841 was short-lived. It was repealed in 1843 by Congress, once again citing high administrative costs, lack of state exemptions for debtors, and frustration by creditors.[13]

The lack of permanency with bankruptcy laws may have been a result of Congress overreacting to financial disasters. The Act of 1800 was passed after the Panic of 1797, the Act of 1841 after the Panic of 1837, the Act of 1867 after the Panic of 1857 and the Civil War, and the Act of 1898 after the Panic of 1893.[14] Yet, Congress remains consistent after all these

4 Supra, note 1.
5 U.S. Const. Art. I, §8, Cl. 4.
6 Charles Jordan Tabb, The History of the Bankruptcy Laws in the United States, 3 *Am. Bankr. Inst. L. Rev.* 5 (1995).
7 The Evolution of U.S. Bankruptcy Law, A Time Line. Federal Judicial Center, fjc.gov (hereinafter The Evolution). https://www.fjc.gov/sites/default/files/2012/BKTimeLine2012.pdf.
8 The Evolution.
9 Supra, note 6, citing *Ogden v. Saunders*, 25 U.S. (12 Wheat.) 213 (1827).
10 The Evolution.
11 The Evolution.
12 The Evolution.
13 The Evolution.
14 Supra, note 6 at 14.

years. Because of the coronavirus pandemic, bankruptcy reform continues to be at the forefront. In December of 2020, U.S. Senator Elizabeth Warren and House Judiciary Chairman Jerrold Nadler introduced bankruptcy legislation known as the Consumer Bankruptcy Reform Act of 2020.[15] It was even supported by the National Association of Consumer Bankruptcy Attorneys.[16]

As in life, bankruptcy law continued to evolve, as evident with the Bankruptcy Act of 1867, which resembles bankruptcy law today.[17] District courts now "constituted courts of bankruptcy" and were given original jurisdiction.[18] A debtor could choose between state or federal exemptions, and corporations could also file for bankruptcy. Creditors and debtors could also reach a compromise with payment plans similar to today's Chapter 13.[19] However, creditors needed to agree to the discharge.

Non-judicial assistants known as "registers in bankruptcy" could be appointed by the Chief Judge. In 1874, an amendment allowed for the distribution of assets between debtors and creditors to settle debts.[20] But, the familiar pattern of repealing bankruptcy legislation happened again in 1878 due to, you guessed correctly, excessive administrative fees and abuses of the bankruptcy system.[21]

In 1898, the next Bankruptcy Act was passed, providing bankruptcy protection for the next three decades.[22] Referees were assigned two-year terms by the district judges and compensated with a percentage of the bankruptcy estate assets, the same as today's trustees.[23] The trustee's office was also created.[24] By 1910, corporations were allowed to file for bankruptcy voluntarily, and in 1937, the Municipal Bankruptcy Act passed, which became known as Chapter 9 and enables municipalities to seek bankruptcy protection.[25]

Bankruptcy reform was even studied between 1932 and 1934 by the National Bankruptcy Conference, and reorganization became possible for individuals, corporations, and railroad companies.[26]

Significant changes came three decades later with the Chandler Act of 1938, which overhauled the Bankruptcy Act of 1898. The bankruptcy "chapters" were created, including Chapter XIII, known as a wage-earner's plan.[27]

In 1960, the U.S. Supreme Court authorized an Advisory Committee on bankruptcy based on a request from Congress, resulting in the Commission on Bankruptcy Laws in the

15 Consumer Bankruptcy Reform Act of 2020. S.4991, 116th Congress, 2nd Session (2019–2020).

16 NACBA Encouraged by Senator Elizabeth Warren's Introduction of the Consumer Bankruptcy Reform Act. Retrieved May 31, 2021. https://judiciary.house.gov/news/documentsingle.aspx?DocumentID=3470.

17 The Evolution.

18 The Evolution.

19 11 U.S.C. Chapter 13 – Adjustment of Debts of an Individual with Regular Income.

20 The Evolution.

21 The Evolution

22 The Evolution.

23 The Evolution.

24 The Evolution.

25 The Evolution. See also 11 U.S.C. Chapter 9.

26 The Evolution.

27 The Evolution.

United States, whose purpose was to recommend changes that reflected "current social and economic conditions."[28]

Major reforms continued with the Bankruptcy Reform Act of 1978.[29] Bankruptcy judges were now appointed to 14-year terms by the President of the United States and confirmed by the Senate. The U.S. Trustee's Office was also established, and Chapter 11 replaced Chapters X, XI, and XII. Roman numerals were also replaced with Western numerals.[30]

Fast forward to 1994 with the Bankruptcy Reform Act. New provisions affected both consumers and businesses. Jury trials were permitted for certain proceedings, Bankruptcy Appellate Panels were encouraged, and Congress authorized the National Bankruptcy Review Commission.[31] But it seems the Commission was set up for failure from the beginning by Congress since

> the Commission should be aware that Congress is generally satisfied with the basic framework established in the current Bankruptcy Code. Therefore, the work of the Commission should be based upon reviewing, improving, and updating the Code in ways which do not disturb the fundamental tenets and balance of current law.[32]

Indeed, that seemed to be the result since the Committee's report submitted within two years of their first meeting as required by Congress was "shelved."[33] Meanwhile, creditors continued to lobby Congress to make filing for bankruptcy more difficult, leading us to the present day and the Bankruptcy Abuse Prevention and Consumer Protection Act of 2005 (BAPCPA).[34]

On April 20, 2005, President George W. Bush signed into law the Bankruptcy Abuse Prevention and Consumer Protection Act, known as BAPCPA.[35] With BAPCPA, Congress intended to make qualifying for Chapter 7 bankruptcy more difficult for consumers, pushing debtors to file Chapter 13.[36] Known as a reorganization, Chapter 13 requires debtors to make monthly payments toward their debt with a payment plan ranging in time from a minimum of three years (36 months) to a maximum of five years (60 months). The trustee is responsible for protecting the bankruptcy estate, which includes receiving the payments and disbursing them to creditors based on their pro-rata share.

Because of BAPCPA, numerous changes went into effect, starting with mandatory credit counseling and financial management classes for debtors in both Chapters 7 and 13

28 The Evolution.
29 The Evolution.
30 The Evolution. See also 11. U.S.C. Chapter 11 – Reorganization.
31 The Evolution.
32 §1:9. Bankruptcy Reform Act of 1994, 1; *Bankruptcy Law Manual* (5th ed.) §1:9. See footnote 13. Updated June 2021.
33 §1:10. Bankruptcy Reform Act of 1994, 1; *Norton Bankr. L. and Prac.* (3rd ed.) §1:10. Updated July 2021.
34 Pub. L. No. 109-8, 119 Stat. 23 (2005). www.congress.gov/bill/109th-congress/senate-bill/256.
35 Id.
36 11 U.S.C. Chapter 7 – Liquidation. Supra, note 19.

cases.[37] In addition, §111 of the Bankruptcy Code lists the requirements for agencies that provide credit counseling and financial management classes, including being a non-profit organization, an initial six-month probationary period, and annual approval by the U.S. Trustee's Office. Providers approved by the U.S. Trustee are listed on the U.S. Department of Justice website and can be filtered by district and language.[38]

Debtors must complete the credit counseling class within six months of filing for bankruptcy.[39] If the certificate has expired, the client must retake the course. The second class, also known as the debtor education course, is taken post–petition filing and must be completed and filed within 60 days of the first scheduled Meeting of Creditors in Chapter 7 cases to receive a discharge.[40] In Chapter 13 cases, the debtor must complete the second class and file the certificate before the last payment or discharge.[41] Failure to comply with these two new requirements results in a dismissal. Corporations and partnerships are exempt from the credit counseling and financial management requirements.[42] Both courses are available via telephone or online with an approved agency.

Other significant changes include:

- *Means testing*, a mathematical formula that calculates the debtor's average income six months before the filing date.[43] Means testing applies to consumers only. Disabled veterans who incurred the debt primarily during active duty or a homeland defense activity are exempt from the means test.[44] Other exclusions are listed in §707(b)(2). Means testing, no doubt, is the most controversial requirement of BAPCPA.
- If a debtor fails the means test, there is a *presumption of abuse*, and the case is subject to dismissal.[45] There is also a presumption of abuse for bad faith filings.[46]
- *Domestic support obligations* (alimony and child support) cannot be discharged in bankruptcy and are considered a *priority claim*.[47] Domestic support obligations are defined in §101(14)(A).
- The *automatic stay*, which temporarily stops certain lawsuits from proceeding because of a bankruptcy filing, was also changed to prevent abuse from repeat filers.[48]
- Attorneys are also required to certify there is no *presumption of undue hardship* for *Reaffirmation Agreement*.[49]

37 11 U.S.C. §111.
38 List of Credit Counseling Agencies Approved Pursuant to 11 U.S.C. §111. Retrieved on June 5, 2021. www.justice.gov/ust/list-credit-counseling-agencies-approved-pursuant-11-usc-111.
39 11 U.S.C.§109(h)(1).
40 11 U.S.C. §727(a)(11).
41 11 U.S.C. §1328(g)(1).
42 11 U.S.C. §109(h).
43 11 U.S.C. 707(b)(2)(A.)
44 11 U.S.C. §707.
45 11 U.S.C. §707(b)(1).
46 11 U.S.C. §707(b)(3).
47 11 U.S.C. §507(2).
48 11 U.S.C. §362(c)(3).
49 11 U.S.C. §524(c)(3).

- Cases are subject to dismissal if tax returns are not received timely by the trustee.[50]
- The time frame in which debtors could file additional bankruptcies after a discharge was increased.[51]
- Homestead exemptions were also limited.[52]

SUMMARY

French writer Jean-Baptiste Alphonse Karr is credited with the saying, "the more things change, the more they stay the same." He may have been thinking of creditors lobbying for stricter bankruptcy laws. The history of bankruptcy law has always favored creditors, and the passing of BAPCPA in 2005 is more of the same. BAPCPA was Congress's intent to make qualifying for Chapter 7 bankruptcy more difficult and force debtors into Chapter 13. Creditors, through lobbying efforts, have always argued that debtors abused the bankruptcy system and that fraud was prevalent.

Now, debtors must pass the means test, a calculation of the average income six months prior to filing. If the debtor fails the means test, there is a presumption of abuse, and debtors must file Chapter 13. With Chapter 13, known as a reorganization, the debtor makes monthly payments to the bankruptcy trustee for a minimum of three years and a maximum of five. The trustee disburses the payments to creditors based on a pro-rata share. In Chapter 7, known as a liquidation, creditors aren't likely to receive any compensation.

KEYWORDS AND TERMS

- *Bancarrota*
- Bankruptcy Abuse Prevention and Consumer Protection Act of 2005
- BAPCPA
- Chapter 9, Municipal Bankruptcy Act
- Consumer Bankruptcy Reform Act of 2020
- Debt collectors
- Debtor
- Debtor's prison
- Fair Debt Collection and Practices Act (FDCPA).
- National Association of Consumer Bankruptcy Attorneys
- *Quiebra*

50 11 U.S.C. §521(e)(2).
51 11 U.S.C. §727(a)(8).
52 11 U.S.C. §522.

DISCUSSION QUESTIONS

1. Under Article 3 of the U.S. Constitution, federal judges have lifetime appointments. However, bankruptcy judges serve renewable 14-year terms. What are the advantages and disadvantages of lifetime appointments versus lengthy but limited renewable terms?
2. Chapter 9 allows for cities and municipalities to seek bankruptcy protection. What options does a state have if it cannot afford to pay back its debts?
3. Has your city/municipality ever filed for Chapter 9? Have any cities in your state filed for Chapter 9 protection?
4. Which city filed the largest municipal bankruptcy in U.S. history?
5. Do you think credit counseling and financial management classes help reduce consumer indebtedness and bankruptcy filings?
6. Instead of having debtors take online credit counseling and financial management classes, what steps can creditors take to reduce the number of bankruptcy cases filed?
7. Would bankruptcy filings decrease if creditors were more selective in providing and extending credit to consumers?
8. To what extent do you believe there is fraud and abuse in bankruptcy filings?
9. How can fraud be proven against a debtor heavily in debt?

PRACTICE QUESTIONS AND EXERCISES

1. Besides cities and towns, what other government entities are protected under Chapter 9? Provide a summary.
2. A debt collection agency continues to call a client about an outstanding bill, even after being provided the bankruptcy attorney's contact information. Write an email to the debt collector requesting that the client not be contacted directly and cite the Fair Debt Collection and Practices Act.

REFERENCES

11 U.S.C. §101.

11 U.S.C. §109.

11 U.S.C. §111.

11 U.S.C. §362.

11 U.S.C. §507.

11 U.S.C. §521.

11 U.S.C. §522.

11 U.S.C. §524.

11 U.S.C. §707.

11 U.S.C. §727.

11 U.S.C. §1328.

11 U.S.C. Chapter 7 – Liquidation.

11 U.S.C. Chapter 11 – Reorganization.

11 U.S.C. Chapter 13 – Adjustment of Debts of an Individual with Regular Income.

15 U.S.C. §1692.

Bankruptcy Abuse Prevention Consumer Protection Act (BAPCPA), Public Law 109–8, 11 Stat. 23 (2005).

Bankruptcy Act of 1800, 2 Stat. 19.

Bankruptcy Act of 1841, 5 Stat. 440.

Bankruptcy Act of 1867, 14 Stat. 517.

Bankruptcy Act of 1898, 30 Stat. 544.

Bankruptcy Reform Act of 1978, 92 Stat. 2657.

Bankruptcy Reform Act of 1994, Public Law 103–394.

Chandler Act of 1938, 52 Stat. 840, 841.

Charles Jordan Tabb, "The History of the Bankruptcy Laws in the United States" (1995) 3 *Am. Bankr. Inst. L. Rev.* 5.

Consumer Bankruptcy Reform Act of 2020. S.4991, 116th CONGRESS, 2nd Session (2019–2020).

Fair Debt Collection Practices Act, 15 U.S.C.A. §1692.

Hon. Joan N. Feeney, Hon. Michael G. Williamson, and Michael J. Stepan, Esq., *Bankruptcy Law Manual* (5th ed.). December 2021 Update.

List of Credit Counseling Agencies Approved Pursuant to 11 U.S.C. §111. Retrieved on June 5, 2021. Available at www.justice.gov/ust/list-credit-counseling-agencies-approved-pursuant-11-usc-111.

Municipal Bankruptcy Act of 1937, 50 Stat. 653. 11 U.S.C. Chapter 9, Adjustment of Debt of a Municipality.

"NACBA Encouraged by Senator Elizabeth Warren's Introduction of the Consumer Bankruptcy Reform Act." Retrieved on May 31, 2021. Available at https://judiciary.house.gov/news/documentsingle.aspx?DocumentID=3470.

Norton Bankr. L. and Prac. (3rd ed.).

Ogden v. Saunders, 25 U.S. (12 Wheat.) 213 (1827).

Richard Ford, "Imprisonment for Debt" (1926) 25(1) *Michigan Law Review* 24–49.

The Evolution of U.S. Bankruptcy Law, A Time Line. Federal Judicial Center, fjc.gov.

U.S. Const. Art. I, § 8, Cl. 4.

Vern Countryman, "Bankruptcy and the Individual Debtor-and a Modest Proposal to Return to the Seventeenth Century" (1983) 32 *Cath. U. L. Rev.* 809.

CHAPTER 2

Overview of the Bankruptcy Code

This chapter will review the Bankruptcy Code, but a summarized version since the Code no doubt is lengthy; then again, no one has ever accused the legislature at the state or federal level of being brief. Our focus will be on the chapters and sections that will most likely apply to consumer bankruptcy cases. There will be references to the Code throughout the text as we delve deeper into the specifics of bankruptcy, especially when drafting a petition.

In Title 11 of the U.S. Code, the Bankruptcy Code is divided into chapters and lists six types of bankruptcy cases (see Figure 2.1).

- Chapter 7: Liquidations.[1]
- Chapter 9: Adjustment of Debts of a Municipality.[2]
- Chapter 11: Reorganization.[3]
- Chapter 12: Adjustment of Debts of a Family Farmer or Fisherman with Regular Annual Income.[4]
- Chapter 13: Adjustment of Debts of an Individual with Regular Income.[5]
- Chapter 15: Ancillary and Other Cross-Border Cases.[6]

Notice that Title 11 of the U.S. Code is not only divided into "chapters," but except for Chapter 12, the chapters are odd-numbered. The assumption was if Congress decided to add new chapters, an even number can be sandwiched in between two odd-numbered chapters. Senator Elizabeth Warren and House Judiciary Chairman Jerrold Nadler confirmed that assumption with their proposed legislation for Chapter 10.[7]

1 11 U.S.C. §701–784.
2 11 U.S.C. §901–946.
3 11 U.S.C. §1101–1195.
4 11 U.S.C. §1201–1232.
5 11 U.S.C. §1301–1330.
6 11 U.S.C. §1501–1532.
7 See Chapter 1. Consumer Bankruptcy Reform Act of 2020. S.4991, 116th Congress, 2nd Session, (2019–2020).

DOI: 10.4324/9781003203278-3

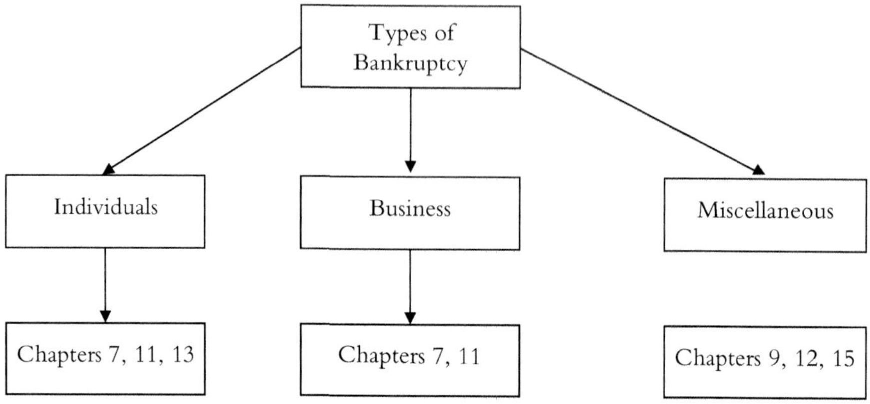

FIGURE 2.1 The different bankruptcy chapters.

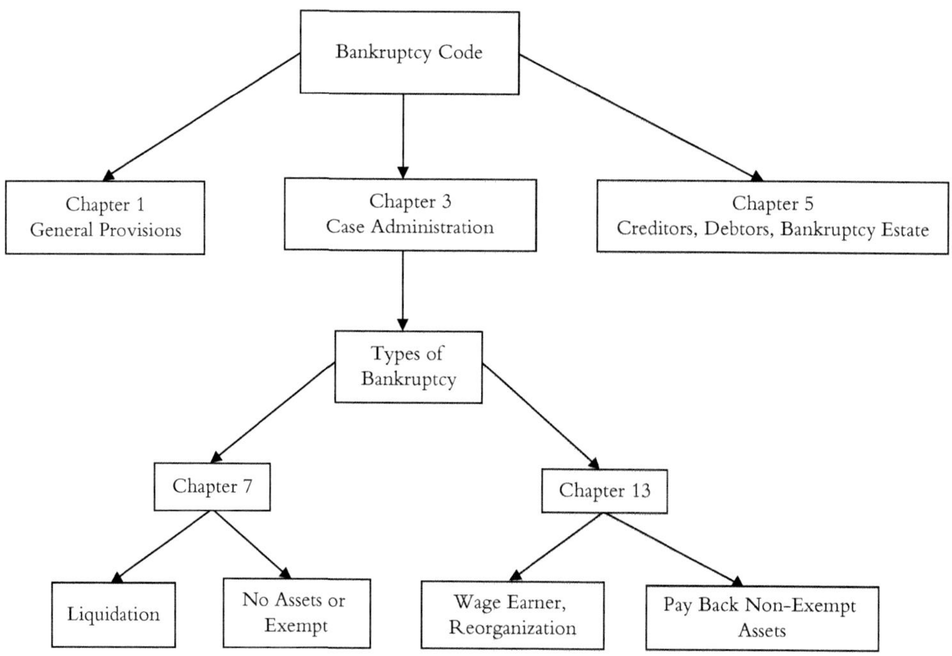

FIGURE 2.2 The bankruptcy code chart.

Chapters 1, 3, and 5 of the Bankruptcy Code are general provisions that apply to all bankruptcy proceedings, and the remaining chapters, such as 7, 9, 11, 12, 13, and 15, govern that specific type of bankruptcy. The chapters that focus on consumer bankruptcy are Chapters 7, 11, and 13. However, the focus of this textbook will be Chapters 7 and 13. The relevant parts of the Code applicable to Chapters 7 and 13, including a summary of each, will be in the following chapter (see Figure 2.2).

CHAPTER 1: GENERAL PROVISIONS

Chapter 1 of the Bankruptcy Code, "General Provisions," contains 12 sections in total. The following is a summary of the sections and terminology to focus on:

§101: Definitions

Section 101 provides a long list of definitions, but let's focus on and summarize the more important ones.

CLAIMS

(5)(A) defines the term "claim" as a right to payment liquidated, unliquidated, contingent, matured, unmatured, undisputed or disputed, secured or unsecured. Section (5)(B) also includes equitable remedies such as breach of performance.

Simply put, a creditor has a "right to payment" from the debtor, whether the debt is secured or unsecured. Unsecured debt is defined as debt with no property or collateral attached to it. Credit cards, medical bills, and student loans are examples of unsecured debt. An example of secured debt is a car loan since it is attached or "secured" by the vehicle. If payments cease, the creditor can repossess the car. Unlike unsecured debt, there is no property or collateral for the creditor to take back, so the creditor would have to pursue legal action.

An example of a claim that is "unmatured" is a debtor that borrows money from the bank, but the first payment isn't due until a future date. The bank has a claim even though the debt hasn't matured.

CREDITOR

Section (10)(A) defines a "creditor" as an "entity that has a claim against the debtor that arose at the time of or before the order for relief concerning the debtor." Who does the debtor owe money to? That's who the creditor is, whether it's the debtor's neighbor, dentist, or credit card company.

CURRENT MONTHLY INCOME

Section (10A) defines "current monthly income," also known as CMI, as the average monthly income from all sources that the debtor(s) receive during the six months before the bankruptcy petition is filed. The term "current monthly income" is a misnomer since it looks at past income. The debtor's current monthly income determines if the debtor qualifies for Chapter 7. Specific forms of income are excluded from the *means test*, such as benefits received under the Social Security Act and payments received by victims of crimes, including war crimes.[8]

8 11 U.S.C. §707.

DEBT RELIEF AGENCY

Section (12A) defines a debt relief agency as any person who provides "bankruptcy assistance," §101(4A), to an "assisted person," §101(3), in exchange for payment or other valuable consideration. In addition, the debts of the "assisted person" are primarily consumer debts, and the non-exempt property has a value of less than $204,425.[9]

Is a bankruptcy law firm a debt relief agency? When BAPCPA passed, I remember the panic and confusion this caused attorneys. Did BAPCPA result in law firms becoming "debt relief agencies" overnight? The word "attorney" is not mentioned in §101(12A), nor do attorneys fall within one of the five exempt categories, but lawyers and law firms scrambled to list "debt relief agency" on their letterhead and office doors for fear of violating the rule and being sanctioned by the U.S. Trustee. There were also economic concerns with a loss of walk-ins because potential clients would not associate a "debt relief agency" with a law firm, not to mention the added cost of obtaining new business cards, letterhead, signs, and changing advertisements. The concept and definition of a debt relief agency remain not only elusive but confusing to most practitioners, but to answer the original question – is a bankruptcy law firm a debt relief agency – the answer is yes, according to the U.S. Supreme Court in *Milavetz, Gallop & Milavetz, P.A. v. United States*, 559 U.S. 229 (2010).

In *Milavetz*, a bankruptcy law firm argued that §101(12A) doesn't apply to bankruptcy attorneys because it violates the First Amendment. Specifically, *Milavetz* argued that having to disclose under §528(a)(4) that a law firm is a debt relief agency and that under §526(a)(4), advising an "assisted person" not to incur more debt in contemplation of filing for bankruptcy violates the First Amendment. The Supreme Court disagreed and held that bankruptcy attorneys and law firms are a debt relief agency and that the regulation of speech contained in the debt relief agency provisions is otherwise constitutional.

This section also defines a bankruptcy petition preparer as a person other than one that works for the debtor's attorney or is under the supervision of a debtor's attorney, who prepares petitions for compensation. The same way a paralegal cannot give legal advice, neither can a bankruptcy petition preparer who faces potential fines and injunctive relief for violation of the Code under §110. You may wonder why this is referenced in the Code, but I have represented clients whose bankruptcy petition was prepared by a non-lawyer, resulting in the petition either being prepared wrong or fraudulently. For example, one debtor believed his monthly payments made directly to the petition preparer were being applied towards a Chapter 13 when in reality, Chapter 7 was filed. An emergency motion was filed and argued successfully to reverse the sale of his foreclosed property. Unfortunately, the petition preparer disappeared and was never to be seen or heard of again.

9 11 U.S.C. §101(3). Originally "$150,000," adjusted effective April 1, 2019. See 11 U.S.C. §104: Adjustment of Dollar Amounts.

DOMESTIC SUPPORT OBLIGATION

Section (14A) defines a *domestic support obligation* as a debt owed for alimony and/or child support, regardless of the unpaid amount before or after filing the bankruptcy petition. *Domestic support obligations* are not dischargeable in bankruptcy.

INSIDERS

Section 3(A) defines "insiders" as relatives or friends of the debtor or a company with which the debtor has a close relationship. You will become intimately aware of situations of clients transferring assets or paying back debts owed to insiders. Keep in mind that the trustee can go back as far as 12 months if there were payments to an insider.

LIENS

Liens are discussed in subsections 36 and 37 and are defined as a "charge against or a right to property to secure repayment of a debt or the performance of an obligation." Liens are divided into two groups: voluntary and involuntary. An example of a voluntary lien is a car loan, while an involuntary lien is imposed by the court (judicial lien). An example of an involuntary lien is a creditor that obtains a judgment against a debtor and seeks enforcement of the judgment by placing a lien on the debtor's car or any other asset.

§109: Who May Be a Debtor

To qualify as a debtor, a person must reside or have a domicile, a place of business, or property in the United States. In addition, under subsection (g), no individual can be a debtor if that individual was already a debtor in a case in the last 180 days if:

(1) The case was dismissed.
(2) The debtor failed to obtain credit counseling. Details regarding the credit counseling and financial management courses and the requirements of credit counseling agencies are in §111.

CHAPTER 3: CASE ADMINISTRATION

Chapter 3 of the Bankruptcy Code focuses on case administration, procedural steps, requirements for notices of hearings, closing and reopening cases, dismissing cases, converting cases from one chapter to another, and the role and powers of the trustee. Chapter 3 is divided into four subchapters.

Subchapter I: Commencement of a Case

Subchapter I of the Code contains rules about the administration of bankruptcy estates. It is a short chapter with eight sections focusing on single and joint filers and the U.S. Trustee. The sections to concern yourself with are as follows:

§307: United States Trustee

Section 307 authorizes the U.S. Trustee to appear at any hearing and be heard on any issue under this title. Therefore, if a U.S. Trustee wanted to appear at the Meeting of Creditors and question the debtor, they can. It's not common, but it does happen. U.S. Trustees will also sometimes request additional information from the debtor or debtor's attorney inquiring about the filing.

§308: Debtor Reporting Requirements

At first glance, §308 may seem applicable, but it applies to a debtor in a small business case and the requirement to file financial statements and reports periodically. Documents include proof of the debtor's profitability, tax returns, and paying taxes.

Subchapter II: Officers

Subchapter II focuses on the role and authority of the trustee. Sections to consider are as follows:

- §321 is the trustee's eligibility to serve.
- §322 requires the trustee to post a bond.
- §323 gives the trustee the authority to file lawsuits and to be sued.
- §326 refers to the trustee's compensation. For Chapter 7, the trustee is paid as follows:
  - 25 percent on the first $5,000 or less.
  - 10 percent on any amount between $5,000 to $50,000.
  - 5 percent on any amount over $50,000 but less than $1,000,000.
  - 3 percent over $1,000,000.
  - In a Chapter 13 case, the standing trustee fee varies, but it's typically 10 percent.
- §327 allows the trustee upon approval of the court to employ professionals such as attorneys, accountants, appraisers, and auctioneers to "assist the trustee in carrying out the trustee's duties under this title." Section 328 elaborates on how the professional retained by a trustee will be compensated.

§329: Debtor's Transactions with Attorneys

Section 329 requires a debtor's attorney to file a disclosure of compensation form.[10] In the bankruptcy petition, there are two sections where fees are listed. Note that per §329, the court does have the authority to cancel and return excessive attorney's fees to the debtor or the bankruptcy estate. In my experience, there was one trustee that routinely filed motions with the court for disgorgement of fees, but in my opinion, that trustee seemed biased against non-local attorneys. There was also a Chapter 13 trustee that issued fines routinely for documents provided late. If the debtor's attorney was not in agreement, then the matter was scheduled before the judge.

10 Official Form 2030B. Disclosure of Compensation of Attorney for Debtor.

Subchapter III: Administration

Subchapter III focuses on the handling of bankruptcy cases.

§341: Meetings of Creditors and Equity Security Holders

Known as the *341 Meeting*, that's the initial hearing before the bankruptcy trustee.

§342: Notice

Section 342 focuses on the notice imposed on the court clerk upon filing a bankruptcy petition, including a statement on fraud and perjury.

§343: Examination of the Debtor

Section 343 requires the debtor to appear at the Meeting of Creditors and be questioned under oath. Creditors are also allowed to appear at the meeting and question the debtor. However, while there is no mention of it in this section, a trustee will not allow a lengthy questioning process. Usually, a trustee will allow a few questions lasting two to three minutes at most since the creditor has the option of proceeding with a *2004 Examination*, which is similar to a deposition.[11]

§348: Effect of Conversion

Section 348 focuses on converting from one chapter to another, for example, converting from Chapter 7 to Chapter 13 or vice-versa. Conversion will not affect the original filing date of the petition or the relief the debtor is entitled to, nor a claim by the creditor against the debtor's estate.

§349: Effect of Dismissal

Under Section 349, a dismissal does not bar discharge. For example, if a case was dismissed because the debtor failed to file the financial management certificate, the debtor could seek permission from the court to set aside the dismissal. If approved by the court, the discharge will be entered.

§350: Closing and Reopening Cases

Section 350 requires that the trustee must be discharged and the case closed once a case has been finalized. Under subsection (b), a closed case can be reopened if assets remain to be administered, to accord relief to the debtor, or for other cause.

Subchapter IV: Administrative Powers

§362: Automatic Stay

Section 362 discusses the *automatic stay*, a powerful tool in the bankruptcy arsenal. We will discuss the *automatic stay* in detail in later chapters and how it's used to stop cases in state court

11 Fed. R. Bankr. P. 2004.

effectively, whether wage garnishments, car repossessions, or foreclosures. However, as this section confirms, the *automatic stay* does not apply to all cases. The *automatic stay* will not stop cases related to *domestic support obligations* such as paternity, child support, and alimony cases. Criminal cases and cases regarding suspensions of licenses such as a driver's license, professional or recreational, will also not be affected by the *automatic stay*.[12]

Part of the changes of BAPCPA was also to limit serial filers, meaning debtors who continuously filed for bankruptcy to take advantage of the *automatic stay*. Changes included the process for eviction proceedings. Before, it was common for debtors to file multiple bankruptcies to stop and slow down an eviction. BAPCPA made this more difficult. One case from the Southern District of Florida involving a serial filer will be analyzed later in the text. In that case, the court prohibited the debtor from filing bankruptcy in any district for five years because of multiple filings to stop eviction proceedings, a fact admitted by the debtor in open court.

§363: Use, Sale, or Lease of Property

This section gives the trustee authority to sell or lease property that is part of the bankruptcy estate. A common example is a debtor that surrenders a non-exempt vehicle. The trustee has the authority to sell the car and distribute the funds accordingly.

CHAPTER 5: CREDITORS, THE DEBTOR, AND THE ESTATE

Chapter 5 is divided into three subchapters and focuses on the rights of creditors and debtors. The sections to focus on are as follows.

Subchapter I: Creditors and Claims

§501: Filing of Proofs of Claims or Interests

Section 501 allows creditors to file a *proof of claim*, a formal notice by a creditor claiming money is owed by the debtor. Without a *proof of claim*, a creditor isn't entitled to non-exempt funds disbursed by the trustee.

§502: Allowance of Claims or Interests

Section 502 allows filing a *proof of claim* to proceed unless there's an objection that results in a hearing before the bankruptcy judge to determine the claim's validity.

§507: Priorities

Life is about priorities, and it's no different in the world of bankruptcy. Section 507 confirms this.

12 See *People of the State of New York v. The National Rifle Association of America, Inc., et al.*, Index No. 451625-2020.

For Chapter 7 cases, a trustee is guided by §507 and §726 to confirm which claims are paid first (prioritized). In Chapter 13, *priority claims* are paid in full through the plan. The priorities of claims are somewhat listed in order because *domestic support obligations* are at the top of the list. However, in subsection (c), the trustee's fees and expenses come first because, without the trustee, there would be no funds to distribute in the first place. Each claim in a category is paid in full before the next claim category receives any monies. Finally, note that this section only applies to unsecured creditors. Remember, secured creditors already have collateral.

Subchapter II: Debtor's Duties and Benefits

In Subchapter II, the obligations of debtors are spelled out.

§521: Debtor's Duties

Upon filing the bankruptcy petition, §521 provides a laundry list of obligations for debtors. Some of those obligations include providing the last 60 days of pay stubs, copies of tax returns, disclosure of all assets and liabilities, filing the credit counseling and financial management certificates, and appearing at the Meeting of Creditors.

§522: Exemptions

Exemptions, another way of saying protections of assets for debtors, are listed and discussed in §522. Exemptions are discussed in detail throughout this textbook, including when preparing a sample petition.

Since residency and domicile affect the exemptions claimed by a debtor, focus on two key dates: 730 and 180 days. For example, if the debtor has resided in Georgia for 730 days, that's the debtor's domicile, and the exemptions of the state of Georgia apply. But what if the debtor recently relocated to Florida, just two miles from the Florida–Georgia border, but since a creditor filed a lawsuit, the debtor can't wait 730 days? Then the issue is which state the debtor has resided in the most during the last 180 days. If the debtor resided in Florida for at least 91 days, the debtor could file in Florida, but Georgia's exemptions are applied.

Also, while exemptions apply to every bankruptcy filed, §522 focuses on federal exemptions. That's why the word "may" be exempt is used since some states have opted out of federal exemptions, while other states allow choosing between state or federal exemptions.

Section 522 lists additional exemptions that include prescribed health aids, Social Security benefits, welfare benefits, veterans' benefits, alimony, qualified pension and profit-sharing plans, disability, and unemployment benefits. Also, while personal injury awards are usually non-exempt, the award may be exempt if related to a crime victim's reparation law.

Section 522(d)(5) also includes the wildcard exemption that can be used towards non-exempt assets. The catch is that the wildcard exemption isn't applicable in every state, and the amount available also varies. For example, in some states, the unused portion of the homestead exemption could be applied to personal property. Other states have an increased exemption amount for filers without homestead property versus those are claiming a homestead exemption. Federal exemptions may also apply, depending on the state.

§523: Exceptions to Discharge

While the primary purpose of filing for bankruptcy is to eliminate debt, not all debts are dischargeable. Section 523 provides the following list of non-dischargeable debts:

- §523(a) income tax obligations are generally non-dischargeable. The exception is for tax returns filed more than three years ago that remain uncollected. For reasons that defy logical order, it's also important to look at section (14)(B), which makes debt non-dischargeable if incurred because of a non-dischargeable debt. Simply put, I've always paid my federal income tax and property taxes with my credit cards. That act in and of itself is not an issue, but if I turn around and file for bankruptcy, that portion of the debt is non-dischargeable.
- §523(a)(2) debts that were obtained by fraud.
- §523(a)(2)(B) and (C) include debts for luxury goods in excess of $500 incurred within 90 days of filing for bankruptcy and cash advances within 70 days of more than $750.
- §523(a)(3) debts that were not included in the petition.
- §523(a)(5) *domestic support obligations.*
- §523(6) damages that were willful and malicious and caused injury to another.
- §523(a)(7) government fines and penalties.
- §523(8) student loans backed by the government.
- §523(9) damages in a personal injury case caused by intoxication.
- §523(10) debts where a discharge was waived.
- §523(18) loans secured by retirement accounts.

It's important to distinguish between non-dischargeable debts and dischargeability under §727(a). Section 523 lists debts that aren't dischargeable, but the debtor can still receive a discharge. I know it sounds confusing, but just separate the two. For example, if the debtor has damages to pay from a car accident because of a D.U.I., but had filed bankruptcy to eliminate credit card debt, the credit card debt is discharged, but the debt related to the D.U.I. isn't.

§524: Effect of Discharge

While Section 523 focuses on debts that cannot be discharged, Section 524(a)(1) focuses on the effects of a discharge. In this case, a discharge voids any judgment, so the debtor is no longer liable for the debt. In §524(a)(2), collecting on a discharged debt is prohibited.

Section 524(k) relates to *Reaffirmation Agreements.* A debtor can choose to reaffirm (keep) an otherwise dischargeable debt. In this text, we will work on sample *Reaffirmation Agreements.* Generally, the reaffirmation of debt applies to secured debt such as a car or home that the debtor wishes to keep.

§526: Restrictions on Debt Relief Agencies

Section 526 imposes restrictions on debt relief agencies. If a debt relief agency fails to comply with §526, §527, and §528, the U.S. Trustee's Office has the authority to seek injunctive relief, an award for damages, and the refunding of fees. Most of the restrictions of §526 are logical such as failing to perform duties and misrepresentation to debtors, but what about advising debtors to incur more debt?

Section 526(a)(4) states that "a debt relief agency shall not...advise an assisted person or prospective assisted person to incur more debt in contemplation of such person filing" for bankruptcy protection. Clients routinely bring up the issue of maxing out their credit cards before filing for bankruptcy. It makes sense, doesn't it? If you are filing bankruptcy but still have $1,000 in available credit on your credit card, isn't now the perfect time to take that Caribbean cruise you've been thinking about? It only seems fair as you have been paying your credit cards timely for years, including a small fortune in interest. What's the difference at this point in filing for bankruptcy if the debt increased from $15,000 to $16,000? Is it a violation of §526(a)(4) for a bankruptcy lawyer to say, "Go ahead and enjoy yourself! You deserve it"?

What if a client consults with a bankruptcy attorney and, in reviewing their case, the attorney suggests refinancing their mortgage to avoid bankruptcy? The attorney even recommends buying a car through the refinance to save money on interest and lower the monthly payments since the client needs a new car. Isn't that advising an "assisted person" to incur more debt? If the client asks if they can co-sign a loan with their son or daughter, isn't that incurring more debt? The answer is yes, of course, but the advice given was not to abuse the bankruptcy system, which would be a violation of §526(a)(4). Whatever abusing the bankruptcy system is, is a question of fact to be determined on a case-by-case basis.

Suppose the "assisted person" is literally too broke to file for bankruptcy, and the only way the client can afford the services of a lawyer is by using a credit card to pay the retainer. Is that permissible? Doesn't hiring an attorney result in incurring more debt, anyway?

In *Cadwell v. Kaufman, Englett & Lynd, PLLC*, 886 F.3d 1153 (2018), the U.S. Court of Appeals in the Eleventh Circuit specifically dealt with those two issues. Per the court's ruling, hiring an attorney is not a violation of §526, but using a client's credit cards for fees is a big no-no! But, clients routinely ask to pay with credit cards. My response is always the same: if you can pay me with credit cards, instead of charging you $1,500, why not charge you $15,000 instead? From a practical standpoint, it's easy to determine if the client is using a credit card to make a payment when the client is in the office. But, issues may arise if payments are accepted over the phone, or the firm's website has a link for payments.

Throughout this text, I caution clients that consulted with a bankruptcy attorney in the past, and since then, their financial situation has changed, whether buying a new car, obtaining new credit cards, or maxing out debt limits. Because of the many loopholes of the *means test*, you will see firsthand how a client that didn't qualify for Chapter 7 does by getting into debt.[13] For example, the client finances a new car with a minimal deposit, and because of the rate of depreciation for cars, there's negative equity, and now the client passes the *means test*, has a shiny new car that's nicer than yours, and eliminates debt.[14] No one ever said life was fair. So how does this affect the bankruptcy practitioner? Here's what you need to know.

13 Supra, note 8.
14 Id.

Under §526(a)(1), the attorney shall not fail to perform their duties and, under subsection 2, make any false and misleading statements. In subsection 3, there shall not be any misrepresentations either. The assisted person's waiver of these sections is not enforceable against the client/debtor, but is against the debt relief agency.

In §526(2), the debt relief agency shall be liable to the assisted person for any fees and charges, including reasonable attorney's fees and costs, if the debt relief agency acted intentionally or negligently in failing to comply with §526, §527, or §528. This includes dismissal or conversion to another chapter because of the agency's intentional or negligent act.

§527: Disclosures

Section 342(b)(1) requires a debt relief agency to provide a brief written description of the different chapters available to consumers, the costs of proceeding under each of those chapters, and the services that are available from credit counseling agencies.

The debt relief agency must also provide written notice within three days of first offering assistance, a "clear and conspicuous written notice advising assisted persons that" all information required is to be "complete, accurate, and truthful" according to §527(2)(A). In addition, all assets and liabilities are to be disclosed, including the value of said assets per §527(2)(B), the current monthly income, and if Chapter 13 is being filed, the available disposable income per §527(2)(C). If that information is requested due to an audit and it's not provided, the case is subject to dismissal under subsection (D). Finally, §527(b) requires specific disclosures in writing. This notice is available in Chapter 28 of this text and will be discussed in detail in future chapters.

Section 527(c) can be referred to as the "how-to" section. This section requires additional information to be provided to assist the client with information gathering. In §527(c)(1), the attorney shall provide "in a clear and conspicuous writing" to the assisted person how to provide all the required information, how to value assets, determine current monthly income, and if it's a Chapter 13 case, how to determine disposable income. In §527(c)(2), information is required for the client's list of creditors, including determining the balance and creditor contact information. Section 527(c)(3) requires information on exempting property. Finally, §527(d) requires that a debt relief agency keep a copy of notices for two years after the date on which the notice was given to the client.

§528: Requirements for Debt Relief Agencies

The final requirements for a debt relief agency are listed in §528 and require that clients be provided with a written *Retainer Agreement* within five business days of being retained. The Retainer Agreement must clearly and conspicuously explain the services to be provided, the fees being charged, and the payment plan. A copy of the *Retainer Agreement* shall be provided to the client. A sample *Retainer Agreement* is available in Chapter 28.

Advertisements must be clear and conspicuous that the law firm provides bankruptcy relief and should include a statement to the effect of "we are a debt relief agency. We help people file for bankruptcy relief under the Bankruptcy Code." This informs debtors that they are in bankruptcy versus debt counseling, debt reduction plans, debt restructuring, or debt negotiations. Advertisements should also include a description of Chapter 13 plans, including wording such as a "federally supervised repayment plan" or "federal debt restructuring help." Please let me know if you figure out how to get all this information in a Google ad.

PRACTICE TIP

At the creditors' meetings, debtors are asked by the trustees if the petition was reviewed with the attorney. If the client is testifying via a translator, the trustee will also ask if the bankruptcy petition was translated. Also, by force of habit more than anything else, trustees continue asking if the debtor signed the petition, but signed declarations are no longer required.

As a practice tip, if the petition is reviewed at the office, the client should initial each page. If the petition is reviewed via telephone, the client should reply to an email confirming they reviewed the petition and that no additional changes are required. This prevents the client from denying responsibility, and the attorney is shielded from any issues regarding disclosures and disgorgement of fees.

Subchapter III: The Estate

§541: Property of the Estate

The estate, bankruptcy estate, and property of the estate are terms used interchangeably and will be used frequently throughout the text and in working on bankruptcy cases. Simply defined, the estate is whatever assets belong to the debtor, whether exempt or not exempt. If the property is exempt, then it's protected, and if non-exempt, then it's subject to distribution by the trustee for the benefit of creditors.

In combination with the term estate, is what is known as "turnover complaint." This is the right of the trustee to recover the property of the estate.[15] This works in conjunction with the trustee's avoidance powers that allow recovering assets that are part of the estate.

When does the estate begin? Upon the filing of a bankruptcy petition. However, what happens if assets are obtained after the bankruptcy petition has been filed? Section 541 lists specific situations post-petition. For example, an asset received within six months (180 days) after the petition has been filed becomes part of the bankruptcy estate. This includes gifts, transfers, inheritance, funds from a life insurance policy, or property received from a divorce settlement.

§544: Trustee as Lien Creditor and as Successor to Certain Creditors and Purchasers

Section 544 gives the trustee specific authority known as strong-arm powers or the strong-arm clause that provides the trustee with the authority to void transactions. The trustee also has lien authority over any other creditor. These sections allow for the trustee to protect creditors' rights.

15 §542: Turnover of Property to the Estate.

Of course, the trustee's powers are not infinite. Section 546 imposes time restraints by requiring a trustee to file a cause of action within two years after the order for relief or within one year of being appointed. The case could also not be closed or dismissed.

§547: Preferences; §548: Fraudulent Transfers and Obligations; §549 Post-Petition Transactions

Sections 547, 548, and 549 are lumped together since it's a continuation of the trustee's avoidance powers, but under different circumstances. These sections will be reviewed later, including examples from real cases. For now, just know that the trustee has the power under §547 to "avoid" certain transfers that are considered preferential, such as for the benefit of a creditor, transfers done fraudulently, and post-petition.

§554: Abandonment of Property of the Estate

The final of powers granted to the trustee is the power to abandon property. This is a common statement made by the trustee during the Meeting of Creditors where, simply, the trustee is not interested in certain property. Therefore, any interest is abandoned. For example, a common scenario is an over-exempt car, but the amount is minimal, so the trustee isn't interested and "abandons" any interest.

SUMMARY

In Title 11 of the U.S. Code, the Bankruptcy Code is divided into nine chapters, with six chapters devoted to the different types of bankruptcies. Chapters 7 and 13 are the most common type of bankruptcies filed by consumers and will be the focus of this text. Chapter 9 applies to municipalities, and Chapter 11 is a reorganization similar to Chapter 13. While an individual can file for Chapter 11, it usually applies to businesses. Chapter 12 applies to the farming and fishing industry, and Chapter 15 to cross-border cases.

Chapter 1 of the Code includes "General Provisions" and important definitions. Chapter 3 focuses on "Case Administration," the procedural requirements of a case including *341 Meetings* and *2004 Examinations*, and the administrative powers of the trustee. Chapter 3 also focuses on the automatic stay and limits imposed on serial filers. Chapter 5 focuses on creditor and debtor rights, exemptions, the bankruptcy estate, the trustee's power to void transactions, and the bankruptcy discharge.

Per the requirements of BAPCPA, bankruptcy attorneys and law firms are considered debt relief agencies. Thus, certain obligations are imposed on behalf of the attorney, including providing disclosures in writing to the debtor. These disclosures include written *Retainer Agreement* and a summary of bankruptcy chapters available to the debtor.

While debtors are no longer required to submit a signed declaration upon filing the petition, a debtor should still confirm in writing that the petition has been reviewed and approved. This can be done in one of two ways. The first and easiest method is to email the client the petition, review it over the phone, and require the client to respond to that email. The response can be kept as part of the client's file. The second method is if the review of the petition takes place in person, the client can initial each page of the petition or sign a statement to the effect that the petition was reviewed and approved. This was a common procedure before online filing.

KEYWORDS AND TERMS

- Assisted person
- Bankruptcy assistance
- *Cadwell* ruling
- Debt relief agency
- Disclosures of §527
- Bankruptcy estate
- Claims
- Creditors
- Current monthly income
- Debts (secured and unsecured)
- Debt relief agencies
- Discharge
- Domestic support obligations
- Exemptions
- Liens
- *Milavetz* ruling
- Proof of claim
- Trustee powers

DISCUSSION QUESTIONS

1. Using a credible source, find out what percentage of bankruptcy filings are Chapter 7 and 13.
2. What is the difference between the U.S. Trustee and the bankruptcy trustee?
3. A potential client is discussing a divorce case with the lawyer. During the consultation, the client mentions the substantial amount of debt that was incurred during the marriage. The attorney has more than a decade of experience and worked briefly for a bankruptcy law firm. Is the lawyer subject to the requirements of BAPCPA as a debt relief agency?
4. In reviewing the documents provided by the firm, the client asks, "What is a debt relief agency? I thought I was filing for bankruptcy? I'm not interested in a federal repayment plan!" How would you respond to the client?
5. Per the requirements of §528, an "assisted person" should be provided a written *Retainer Agreement* within five days. The potential client calls the office for the first time on Monday. When time permits, the attorney likes to consult briefly with clients on the

phone to screen cases. After their brief consultation, the attorney transfers the call to the receptionist to schedule an appointment with the client. The appointment is scheduled for two weeks from today. Did the attorney violate §528?

PRACTICE QUESTIONS AND EXERCISES

1. Look up the list of approved credit counselors in your area. Which agency offers the best pricing?
2. Look up a list of approved financial management course providers. Which agency offers the best pricing?
3. Does the agency that you chose provide both credit counseling and financial management courses? Make sure to save the links for future reference.

REFERENCES

11 U.S. Code Title 11 – Bankruptcy.
11 U.S.C. Chapter 1.
11 U.S.C. §101.
11 U.S.C. §104.
11 U.S.C. §109.
11 U.S.C. §110.
11 U.S.C. §111.
11 U.S.C. Chapter 3.
11 U.S.C. §307.
11 U.S.C. §308.
11 U.S.C. §321.
11 U.S.C. §322.
11 U.S.C. §323.
11 U.S.C. §326.
11 U.S.C. §327.
11 U.S.C. §328.
11 U.S.C. §329.
11 U.S.C. §341.
11 U.S.C. §342.
11 U.S.C. §343.
11 U.S.C. §348.
11 U.S.C. §349.
11 U.S.C. §350.
11 U.S.C. §362.

11 U.S.C. §363.

11 U.S.C. Chapter 5.

11 U.S.C. §501.

11 U.S.C. §502.

11 U.S.C. §507.

11 U.S.C. §521.

11 U.S.C. §522.

11 U.S.C. §523.

11 U.S.C. §524.

11 U.S.C. §526.

11 U.S.C. §527.

11 U.S.C. §528.

11 U.S.C. §541.

11 U.S.C. §542.

11 U.S.C. §544.

11 U.S.C. §546.

11 U.S.C. §547.

11 U.S.C. §548.

11 U.S.C. §549.

11 U.S.C. §554.

11 U.S.C. Chapter 7 – Liquidation.

11 U.S.C. §707.

11 U.S.C. §726.

11 U.S.C. §727.

11 U.S.C. Chapter 9 – Adjustment of Debts of a Municipality.

11 U.S.C. Chapter 11 – Reorganization.

11 U.S.C. Chapter 12 – Adjustment of Debts of a Family Farmer or Fisherman with Regular Annual Income.

11 U.S.C. Chapter 13 – Adjustment of Debts of an Individual with Regular Income.

11 U.S.C. Chapter 15 – Ancillary and Other Cross-Border Cases.

Cadwell v. Kaufman, Englett & Lynd, PLLC, 886 F.3d 1153 (2018).

Consumer Bankruptcy Reform Act of 2020. S.4991, 116th Congress, 2nd Session (2019–2020).

Fed. R. Bankr. P. 2004.

Milavetz, Gallop & Milavetz, P.A. v. United States, 559 U.S. 229 (2010).

Official Form 2030B. Disclosure of Compensation of Attorney For Debtor.

People of the State of New York v. The National Rifle Association of America, Inc., et al., Index No. 451625-2020.

CHAPTER 3

Summary of Chapter 7 versus Chapter 13

Chapter 7 is the most common type of bankruptcy case filed and will be most of the focus in this textbook. Usually, a Chapter 7 bankruptcy involves no assets or minimal assets, and the debts are unsecured such as credit cards and personal loans. While some assets are part of the bankruptcy estate, such as an automobile or even a home, those assets may be exempt. Bankruptcy exemptions are simply protections afforded to real or personal property. The exemption amounts vary by state and whether that state chooses federal and/or state exemptions.

For a debtor to proceed with a Chapter 7 bankruptcy, they must pass the *means test*, which requires that the debtor's income is at or below the median state income.[1] If so, the debtor can file Chapter 7, assuming there are no issues with non-exempt assets. However, calculating income for the means test is only step one.[2]

Step two requires calculating income again, this time for *Schedule I*.[3] In Schedule I, gross and net income are calculated for the month of filing, while only gross income is initially calculated for *the means test*.[4] Note I said "initially." Yes, there's a workaround of the means test if it's not passed "initially," however, it requires calculations with secured debt(s).[5] Calculations with and without secured debts will be worked on in our sample petitions, including calculations with income that's excluded from the means test, but required in Schedule I.[6] After calculating the net income in Schedule I and expenses in *Schedule J*, if there's minimal disposable income available, then the debtor qualifies for Chapter 7.[7]

If the client fails the means test, then the client has the option of filing for Chapter 13 and paying back a portion of their debt.[8] For this reason, Chapter 13 is commonly referred to as a "wage earner's plan" since income is required to qualify, while Chapter 7 is referred

1 11 U.S.C. §707(b)(2)(A).
2 Id.
3 Official Form 106I. Schedule I: Your Income (individuals).
4 Id. and supra note 1.
5 Supra, note 1, and Official Form 122A-2. Chapter 7 Means Test Calculation.
6 Supra, notes 1 and 3.
7 Supra, note 3. Official Form 106J. Schedule J: Your Expenses (individuals).
8 Supra, note 1.

DOI: 10.4324/9781003203278-4

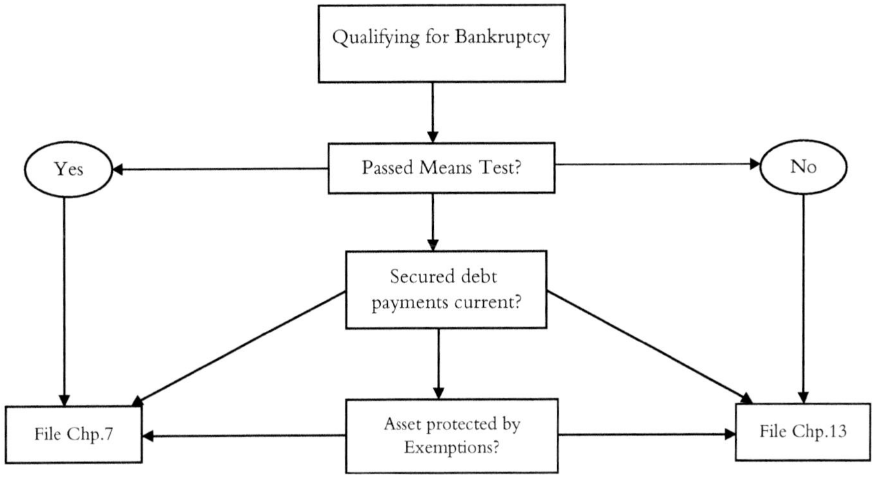

FIGURE 3.1 Qualifying for Chapter 7 or 13.

to as a liquidation (see Figure 3.1). Depending on the amount of available disposable income and value of non-exempt assets, a monthly amount is paid to the trustee who disburses a percentage of those funds to creditors.

Besides not qualifying for Chapter 7, Chapter 13 is likely when there are non-exempt assets that a debtor wishes to keep. If the debtor can afford to pay for the value of the non-exempt assets, the debtor can keep the property. In Chapter 13, the non-exempt amount is paid back over a 36- to 60-month period, while in Chapter 7, a lump sum payment is required, although trustees sometimes may agree to a payment plan of ten to 12 months. Regardless of which chapter a debtor files under, if the debtor can't afford to pay back the value of the non-exempt portion of an asset(s), the trustee will force the sale of the asset(s), and surplus funds are disbursed to creditors.

EXAMPLE

In Florida, the exemption amount for an automobile is $1,000.00 for a single filer.[9] If the debtor's car is worth $10,000.00 and the loan balance is $4,000.00, the equity is $6,000. Subtract the exemption amount, in this case, $1,000.00 from the equity, and the remaining amount is the non-exempt portion ($5,000.00) that the trustee is entitled to and belongs to the bankruptcy estate. If the debtor wishes to keep the car, the debtor must buy out the non-exempt portion from the trustee/bankruptcy estate, whether it's a Chapter 7 or 13. After administrative expenses and fees, the trustee disburses the remaining funds to creditors.

Finally, if the debtor wishes to keep secured debt (see Figure 3.2) such as a house or automobile, payments must be current at the time of filing a Chapter 7. If not, Chapter 13 allows

9 Fla. Stat. Ann. § 222.25(1).

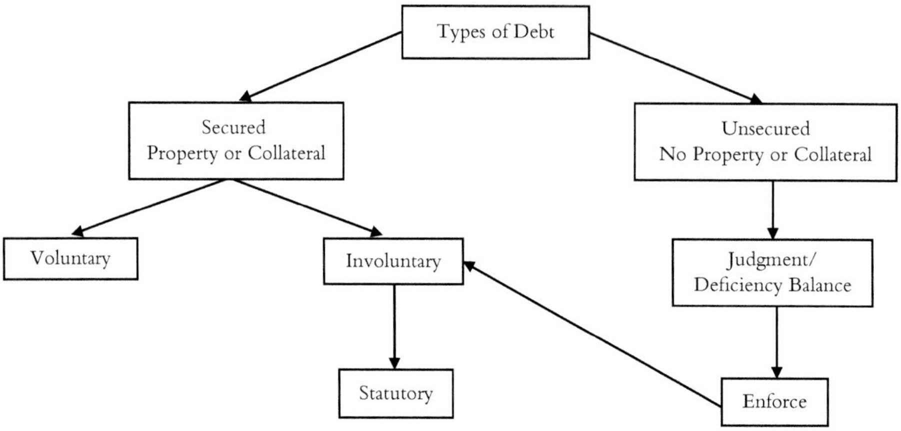

FIGURE 3.2 The different types of debt: secured and unsecured.

for the debtor to "catch up" with the arrears. A creditor may also require a *Reaffirmation Agreement* which is confirmed in writing that a debtor is keeping an asset. Reaffirmation agreements are discussed later in the text, including completing one.

Familiarize yourself with the following sections of Chapter 7: Liquidation.

SUBCHAPTER I: OFFICERS AND ADMINISTRATION

§701: Interim Trustee

Section 701 focuses on the appointment of a private trustee once a debtor files for bankruptcy. Depending on the size of the district, there could be several bankruptcy trustees.

§702: Election of Trustee

Section 702, while mentioned, is rare, to the point I've never encountered the situation or know of any of my colleagues that have. Regardless, creditors are given an opportunity to elect a trustee. If so, §702 provides the procedure. Just as rare would be a creditors' committee under §705.

§704: Duties of Trustee

Section 704 focuses on the duties of the trustee, such as collecting monies of the estate, investigating the debtor's financial affairs, objecting to improper proofs of claims, and a discharge when advisable.

In addition, the trustee is required to "review all materials filed by the debtor." Within ten days of the first Meeting of Creditors, the trustee is also responsible for filing with the court a statement if there's a *presumption of abuse* under §707(b). If there is a presumption of abuse, the trustee shall also proceed to file a motion to dismiss or convert to Chapter 13 within 30 days. Finally, the trustee is required to file a "final report and file a final account of the administration of the estate."

§706: Conversion

Section §704 gives the trustee the authority to file a motion for conversion from Chapter 7 to 13. The debtor also has the option under §706.

§707: Dismissal of a Case or Conversion to a Case under Chapter 11 or 13

Section 707 is lengthy since it includes the means test formula, but the summarized subparts are as follows.

In subsection (a), the court may dismiss a Chapter 7 case only after notice and a hearing. Reasons to dismiss a Chapter 7 filing include prejudicial delays to creditors caused by the debtor, failure to pay filing fees, or failure to file the required schedules within 15 days of filing the petition. In subsection (b)(1), the U.S. Trustee could file a motion to dismiss if there's abuse.

Subsection (b)(2)(A) contains the formula that is the means test to determine if a debtor qualifies for Chapter 7. This includes calculating the debtor's last six months of income according to §101(10)A.[10] The best way to learn the means test, as the calculations are extremely confusing if reading §707, is to complete the required forms or use bankruptcy software.

SUBCHAPTER II: COLLECTION, LIQUIDATION, AND DISTRIBUTION OF THE ESTATE

§721: Authorization to Operate Business

Section 721 is another situation that is rare since it won't apply to your average Chapter 7 case if the debtor owns a business. But, under §721, the court has the authority to have the trustee operate the debtor's business for a limited period if it's in the estate's best interest.

§722: Redemption

The debtor's option for keeping secured assets will be analyzed when reviewing secured debts and *Reaffirmation Agreement*. One of those options is to redeem the property under §722, which is paying the lienholder the amount owed. Normally, this is a unique situation as a debtor is not likely to have the funds to pay off a lien and will have to continue making monthly payments instead.

10 Official Form 122A-1, Chapter 7: Statement of Your Current Monthly Income.

§725: Disposition of Certain Property and §726: Distribution of Property of the Estate

Section 725 requires the trustee to provide notice and a hearing for the distribution of assets of the bankruptcy estate, and §726 details the pecking order on how unsecured claims are paid. This includes unsecured priority claims such as *domestic support obligations*, trustee administrative expenses, and other unsecured creditors such as credit cards.

§727: Discharge

Section 727 focuses on the debtor receiving a discharge and reasons that prohibit receiving a discharge, such as fraud or failing to complete the financial management course.

The following sections pertain to Chapter 13: Adjustment of Debts of an Individual with Regular Income.

SUBCHAPTER I: OFFICERS, ADMINISTRATION, AND THE ESTATE

§1301: Stay of Action against Codebtor

The *automatic stay* is also applicable in Chapter 13, but with a twist. In this case, codebtors are also protected by the automatic stay during the pendency of the case, which could be up to five years. For example, if the debtor filed for Chapter 13 but the codebtor spouse didn't, the automatic stay still protects the spouse.

§1302: Trustee

Just as a trustee is appointed in Chapter 7 cases, the same applies to Chapter 13. Known as the standing trustee, the duties and obligations are the same as in Chapter 7 cases, but the Chapter 13 trustee is also responsible for collecting plan payments and disbursing the funds to creditors.

§1305: Filing and Allowance of Post-Petition Claims

Since Chapter 13 requires plan payments and the funds are disbursed to creditors, any creditor or entity may file a proof of claim to protect their interest.

§1306: Property of the Estate

Like Chapter 7, the estate is the assets of the debtor; however, the difference is the debtor's post-petition income is also considered property of the estate. For example, suppose the debtor's income increased from the initial plan confirmation. In that case, the excess income belongs to the estate and requires that the plan be modified to distribute the excess funds to the creditors.

§1307: Conversion or Dismissal

Similar to §706, the debtor may convert the case from Chapter 13 to 7. Besides conversion, the case may also be dismissed if it's in the best interests of the creditors. Other reasons to dismiss are not paying the filing fees, not filing the required schedules or providing tax returns and other documents requested by the trustee, and failure to make plan payments or pay domestic support obligations.

§1308: Filing of Prepetition Tax Returns

Since plan payments are based on the debtor's income, the debtor must have filed tax returns for the previous four years. The trustee does have the authority to give the debtor additional time to file unfiled tax returns, but the maximum amount of time the trustee can extend the Meeting of Creditors is 120 days.

SUBCHAPTER II: THE PLAN

§1321: Filing of Plan

Section 1321 couldn't be more straightforward, especially when compared to the length of §707: "The debtor shall file a plan." That's it! It couldn't be more clear. The filing of a plan isn't optional.

§1322: Contents of Plan

Now that we know a plan is required, §1322 confirms what's required of the plan. The first provision is that the debtor's future income is used to fund the plan. The second requirement is that *priority claims* are paid in full. This will be reviewed later in the text. Note that while this section requires that claim holders within the same class be treated equally, a creditor can agree to a lesser amount. In addition, subject to §365, if there is a lease/executory contract, the debtor must assume or reject the lease.

The length of plan payments are based on the debtor's income, so the plan will range in time from three to five years. If the debtor's household income is at or below the state median income, the plan length is three years, although the court has the discretion to extend the plan payments, and if above the state median, then five years (maximum). Finally, if the debtor is seeking to cure arrears, that will be reflected in the plan.

§1323: Modification of Plan before Confirmation

Modifications to the plan are common and permissible under §1323. A common occurrence is the miscalculation of arrears, or a creditor was omitted. Modifying plans after confirmation is pursuant to §1329.

§1324: Confirmation Hearing

The Confirmation Hearing takes place after the Meeting of Creditors, but not earlier than 20 days before or 45 days after. Unlike the Meeting of Creditors where the bankruptcy judge isn't present, the Confirmation Hearing takes place before the judge. Typically, it's a brief hearing where the standing trustee recommends confirmation of the plan. A party in interest may object to confirmation.

§1325: Confirmation of Plan

There are several parts of §1325 to focus on. The first part is that unsecured creditors must receive the same amount as would have been received had the debtor filed Chapter 7. Next is that plan payments are received each month in equal amounts and that the debtor's disposable income be used to fund the plan.

Finally, §1325 discusses the *cramdown* or reducing the balance on secured debt. The debt must not have been incurred within the last 910 days for vehicles and 365 days for personal property.

§1326: Payments

Plan payments begin within 30 days of filing the petition and upon confirmation of the plan. The trustee is responsible for distributing the payments to creditors.

§1328: Discharge

Section 1328 focuses on a discharge and provides a list of reasons why a discharge may be denied such as fraud, Chapter 13 being filed within the prohibited dates discussed in Chapter 7 of this text, and failing to complete the financial management class. The court may also revoke the discharge under §1330.

SUMMARY

Chapter 7 is the most common type of bankruptcy filed by consumers and requires passing the means test which calculates the average gross income for six months before the filing date. If the six-month average is below the state median income level, the client passes the means test and qualifies for Chapter 7. The client should also have minimal disposable income available after calculating net income on Schedule I and expenses on Schedule J. If the client fails the means test, the client has the option of proceeding with Chapter 13.

Besides exceeding the income limits of the means test, Chapter 13 should be considered when the client wishes to keep non-exempt assets or wishes to cure the arrears on secured debt payments. However, to qualify for Chapter 13, the client must earn sufficient income to pay for the monthly plan which lasts a minimum of three years and a maximum of five (see Figure 3.3).

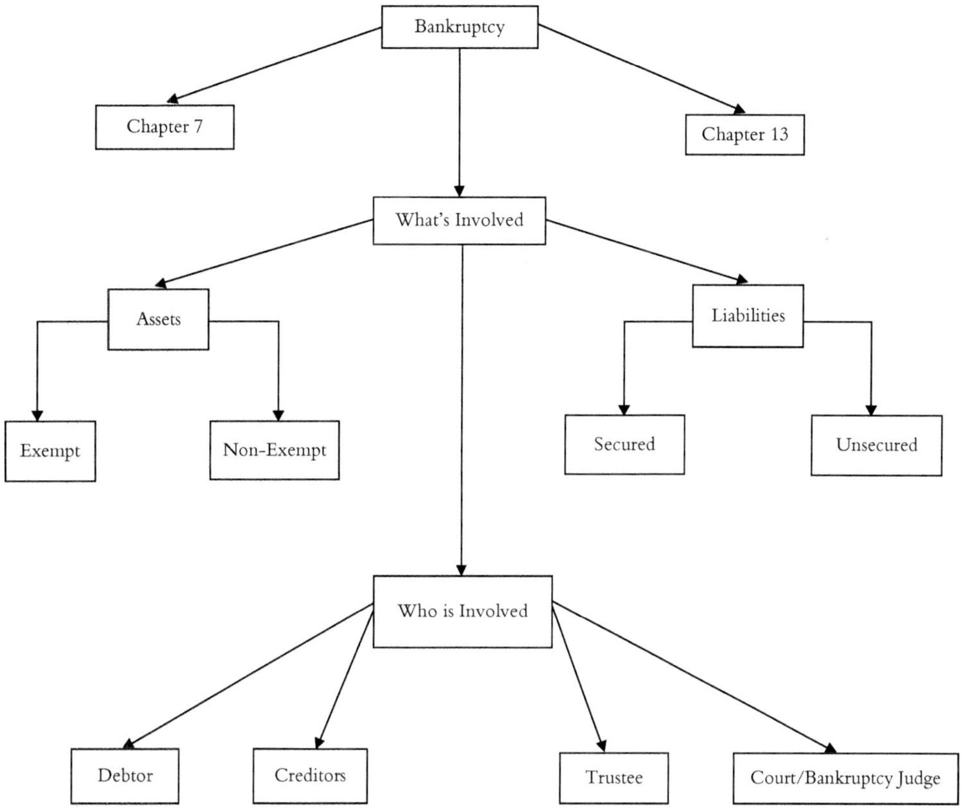

FIGURE 3.3 Issues, assets, debts, and parties involved in Chapter 7 and 13 cases.

KEYWORDS AND TERMS

- Assets
- Bankruptcy estate
- Current monthly income (CMI)
- Disposable income
- Equity
- Exemptions
- Gross income versus net income
- Liquidation
- Means test
- Non-exempt assets
- Personal versus real property
- Reorganization
- Schedule I
- Schedule J
- Secured debt

- Unsecured debt
- Wage earner's plan

DISCUSSION QUESTIONS

1. What is the purpose of an exemption?
2. What is the purpose of the means test?
3. Does your state use federal or state exemptions?

PRACTICE QUESTIONS AND EXERCISES

1. What amount can a debtor claim as the automobile exemption in your state?
2. In interviewing a client, you find out that the client's car is worth $10,000.00 and is secured by a $13,000.00 loan. How is the automobile exemption applied?
3. What is the exemption amount for homestead property in your state?
4. What is the exemption amount for personal property in your state?
5. What is the median income level in your state?
6. What is the difference between secured and unsecured debt?

REFERENCES

11 U.S.C. §101.
11 U.S.C. §365.
11 U.S.C. §701.
11 U.S.C. §702.
11 U.S.C. §704.
11 U.S.C. §705.
11 U.S.C. §706.
11 U.S.C. §707.
11 U.S.C. §721.
11 U.S.C. §722.
11 U.S.C. §725.
11 U.S.C. §726.
11 U.S.C. §727.
11 U.S.C. §1301.
11 U.S.C. §1302.
11 U.S.C. §1305.
11 U.S.C. §1306.

11 U.S.C. §1307.

11 U.S.C. §1308.

11 U.S.C. §1321.

11 U.S.C. §1322.

11 U.S.C. §1323.

11 U.S.C. §1324.

11 U.S.C. §1325.

11 U.S.C. §1326.

11 U.S.C. §1328.

11 U.S.C. §1329.

11 U.S.C. §1330.

Fla. Stat. §222.25.

Official Form 106I. Schedule I: Your Income (Individuals).

Official Form 106J. Schedule J: Your Expenses (Individuals).

Official Form 122A-1, Chapter 7 Statement of Your Current Monthly Income.

Official Form 122A-2. Chapter 7 Means Test Calculation.

CHAPTER **4**

The Court System and the Bankruptcy Rules and Procedure

> This Constitution, and the Laws of the United States which shall be made in Pursuance thereof; and all Treaties made, or which shall be made, under the Authority of the United States, shall be the supreme Law of the Land; and the Judges in every State shall be bound thereby, any Thing in the Constitution or Laws of any State to the Contrary notwithstanding.[1]

In the United States, we have a dual court system comprised of state and federal courts. Federal law is known as the "supreme law of the land," as just seen in the Supremacy Clause.[2] What this means is what it sounds like: federal laws are supreme, above state laws. Therefore, states are free to pass their laws so long as it doesn't conflict with federal law.

There are county and municipal courts, circuit courts, appellate courts, and the state Supreme Court at the state level. Note that states sometimes use different names for their court systems, but the structure is the same. At the lowest level in the court system are county and municipal courts that handle misdemeanors, traffic-related offenses, and small claims. Circuit court includes felonies and cases in civil court (lawsuits) that are over a specific dollar amount which the amount varies by state. There are also specialized courts such as juvenile and family courts. Cases appealed from the lower courts, also known as the trial courts, proceed to the appellate courts, then the state Supreme Court. See Figure 4.1.

At the federal level, the trial courts are known as the district courts, the U.S. Courts of Appeals are the appellate courts, and the highest court in the land is the United States Supreme Court. Federal courts have jurisdiction when either a case involves a federal issue or when a lawsuit is for more than $75,000, and there is diversity of citizenship, which means between citizens or corporations of two different states.[3] For example, suppose City A passes a law that is believed to violate the freedom of speech clause of the First Amendment.[4] In that case, the plaintiff could seek remedies in federal court since freedom of speech is protected

1 U.S. Const. Art. VI, Cl. 2.
2 Id.
3 U.S. Const. Art. III, §2, Cl. 1.
4 U.S. Const. Amend. I.

DOI: 10.4324/9781003203278-5

under the U.S. Constitution.[5] For a diversity of citizenship case, suppose the respondent resides in Georgia and the plaintiff in Florida. If the lawsuit is for at least $75,000, the case could be filed in federal court. The option of filing in state court also exists, depending on where the cause of action arose. See Figure 4.2.

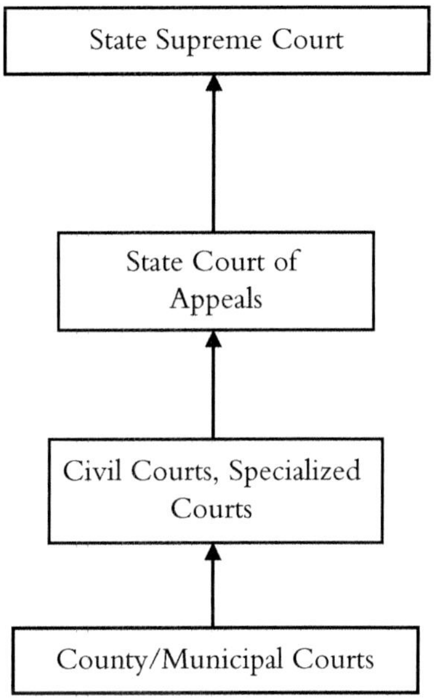

FIGURE 4.1 The state court system.

FIGURE 4.2 Federal court jurisdiction for civil cases.

5 Id.

The federal judiciary was created by Article III of the U.S. Constitution.[6] Per Article III, federal judges receive lifetime appointments subject to "good behavior" so long as acts of "treason, bribery, or other high crimes and misdemeanors" are not committed.[7] The power to impeach federal judges lies solely within the House of Representatives.[8] If impeached by the House, then a trial is held in the Senate with Senators playing the jury's role. A two-thirds majority is required to convict.[9] But, impeachment and conviction of federal judges are rare. Dating back to 1804, only 15 federal judges have been impeached and eight convicted.[10]

The President of the United States nominates federal judges. The President's power to appoint federal judges, known as the Appointment Clause, derives from Article II, Section 2, Clause 2. The Senate Judiciary Committee holds Confirmation Hearings, and a simple majority is required for confirmation. When compared to bankruptcy courts and judges, the steps and procedures are remarkably different.

The court of appeals appoints bankruptcy judges within that district to renewable 14-year terms.[11] The court of appeal will base its decision on recommendations by the Judicial Conference.[12] If a majority of the judges of any court of appeals cannot agree upon the appointment of a bankruptcy judge, then the chief judge of that court decides.[13] Congress determines the number of judges needed for a particular district.[14]

When considering the appointment of a bankruptcy judge, "the court of appeals shall consider the character, experience, ability, and impartiality of those to serve in the Federal judiciary."[15] The Judicial Council shall consider candidates that:

1. Are members in good standing of at least one State Bar, or the District of Columbia Bar, and are members in good standing of every other bar of which they are members.[16]
2. Possess and have a reputation for integrity and good character.[17]
3. Are in sound physical and mental health.[18]
4. Possess and have demonstrated a commitment to equal justice under the law.[19]
5. Possess and have demonstrated outstanding legal ability and competence, which is evidenced by substantial legal experience, have the ability to deal with complex legal issues,

6 U.S. Const. Art. III.
7 U.S. Const. Art. II, §4.
8 U.S. Const. Art. I, §2, Cl. 5.
9 U.S. Const. Art. I, §3, Cl. 6.
10 Impeachment of Federal Judges. www.fjc.gov/history/judges/impeachments-federal-judges. Retrieved April 10, 2020.
11 28 U.S.C. §152.
12 28 U.S.C. §152(a)(1).
13 28 U.S.C. §152(a)(3).
14 28 U.S.C. §152(a)(4). See for the current number of bankruptcy judges per state and district: www.law.cornell.edu/uscode/text/28/152#:~:text=28%20U.S.%20Code%20%C2%A7%20152%20-%20Appointment%20of,%20%202%20%2097%20more%20rows%20. Retrieved on March 6, 2021.
15 PL 98–353 §120(a)(1), appearing at 28 U.S.C.A. §152 note.
16 PL 98–353 §120(c)(2), 28 U.S.C.A. §152 note.
17 PL 98–353 §120(c)(3), 28 U.S.C.A. §152 note.
18 PL 98–353 §120(c)(4), 28 U.S.C.A. §152 note.
19 PL 98–353 §120(c)(5), 28 U.S.C.A. §152 note.

have an aptitude for legal scholarship and writing, and are familiar with the courts and court processes.[20]
6. Have the demeanor, character, and personality that would exhibit judicial temperament.[21]

The bankruptcy court system includes 90 districts, with some states having more than one district, and each district will have at least one bankruptcy court. For example, Florida has the Southern, Middle, and Northern Districts. The Southern District has three bankruptcy courts: Miami, Fort Lauderdale, and Palm Beach.[22] The Middle District, which is a larger district, has five bankruptcy courts.[23] The Northern District has four.[24] Colorado only has one district.[25] But by comparison, in 2019, the District of Colorado had 8,512 Chapter 7 cases filed, while the Middle District of Florida exceeded that amount by June.[26] The Middle District alone had 18,797 Chapter 7 cases filed.[27]

Bankruptcy courts have exclusive jurisdiction in what is known as "core proceedings" and may have jurisdiction for "non-core proceedings." Core proceedings are cases "arising under" the Bankruptcy Code, for example, an adversary proceeding or a creditor objecting to the dischargeability of debts. A list of examples is provided in 28 U.S.C. §157(b)(2). Non-core proceedings are "related to" bankruptcy cases and can be defined as a right that could exist outside of bankruptcy court. Generally, non-core proceedings are matters handled in state court. A bankruptcy court can hear a non-core matter unless objected to by one of the parties in the case. At that point, the bankruptcy court will refer the case to the district court.

Historically, bankruptcy courts did not always have exclusive jurisdiction. In the U.S. Supreme Court case *Northern Pipeline Construction Co. v. Marathon Pipe Line Co.*, the Supreme Court ruled that it was unconstitutional for Congress to grant Article III powers to non-Article III courts since bankruptcy judges served 14-year renewable terms versus Article III judges who have lifetime appointments.[28] With the Reform Act of 1978 now considered unconstitutional, Congress responded with the Bankruptcy Amendments and Federal Judgeship Act of 1984, also known as BAFJA or the 1984 amendments.[29]

Appeals from bankruptcy court may proceed to a district court, the Bankruptcy Appellate Panels (B.A.P.), or the U.S. Court of Appeals.[30] A Bankruptcy Appellate Panel has jurisdiction

20 PL 98–353 §120(c)(6), 28 U.S.C.A. §152 note.
21 PL 98–353 §120(c)(7), 28 U.S.C.A. §152 note.
22 Court Locations. Southern District of Florida. United States Bankruptcy Court. www.flsb.uscourts.gov/court/locations. Retrieved on July 10, 2021.
23 Court Hours and Locations. U.S. Bankruptcy Court Middle, District of Florida. www.flmb.uscourts.gov/thesource/divisions/default.asp. Retrieved on July 10, 2021.
24 Court Locations. Northern District of Florida, United States Bankruptcy Court. www.flnb.uscourts.gov/court-info/court-locations. Retrieved on July 10, 2021.
25 Court Location. District of Colorado. United States Bankruptcy Court. www.cob.uscourts.gov/court-info/court-locations. Retrieved on July 10, 2021.
26 Bankruptcy Filing Statistics. District of Colorado. United States Bankruptcy Court. www.cob.uscourts.gov/bankruptcy-filing-statistics. Retrieved on July 10, 2021.
27 United States Bankruptcy Court Middle District of Florida. Main Case Filing Analysis, December 2019. www.flmb.uscourts.gov/statistics/2019/December.pdf. Retrieved July 10, 2021.
28 *N. Pipeline Const. Co. v. Marathon Pipe Line Co.*, 458 U.S. 50, 102 S. Ct. 2858, 73 L. Ed. 2d 598 (1982).
29 PL 98–353 (HR 5174), PL 98–353, July 10, 1984, 98 Stat 333.
30 28 U.S.C.A. §158.

to hear an appeal if all parties consent and the district courts allow appeals to the B.A.P. The Bankruptcy Appellate Panels consist of three judges and five circuits: the First, Sixth, Eighth, Ninth, and Tenth Circuits. B.A.P. judges are appointed from the circuit district courts, but with the restriction that no judge can hear an appeal from their own district.[31] See Figure 4.3.

Besides the Bankruptcy Code and the Federal Rules of Bankruptcy Procedure, each district also has local rules published on the court's website. For example, the Local Rules for the Middle District of Florida versus the Southern District of Florida differ on how attorneys are admitted to practice. Besides being in good standing with the state bar association, there is a unique requirement that attorneys take at least 12 credit hours for every Continuing Legal Education (CLE) reporting period in the Southern District.[32] The attorney must also be a member of the U.S. District Court, which is the norm since there is no actual "bankruptcy bar." Always review the court's website for the most updated version of local rules, policies, and procedures.

For example, when I started this text, the Middle District of Florida required admission from either the Southern or Northern District. Alternatively, the attorney seeking admittance could submit a petition with affidavits from two local bar members attesting to the attorney's good moral character and competence.[33] I wondered to myself how a newly admitted attorney to the bar would find two sponsoring attorneys. Thinking outside of the box, I thought, why not become a member first of the Southern District since the 12 credits aren't required to be admitted to practice, only to remain a member of that district.

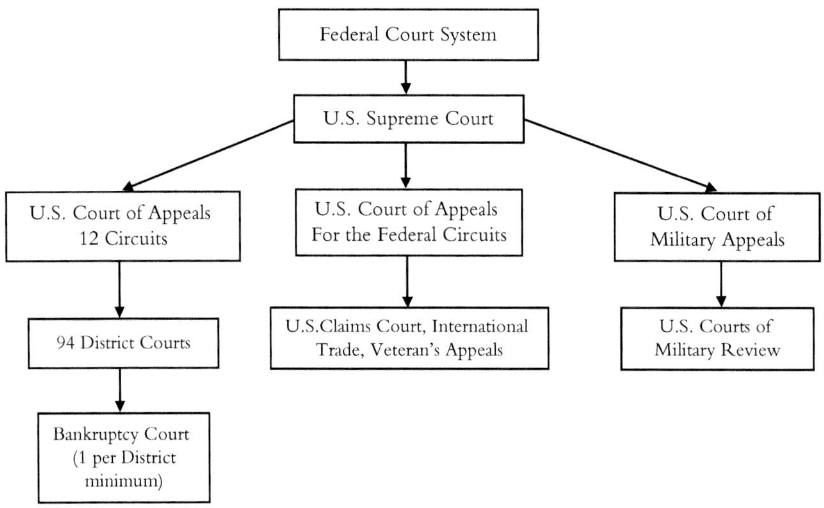

FIGURE 4.3 Federal court system.

31 Court Insider: What Is a Bankruptcy Appellate Panel. www.uscourts.gov/news/2012/11/26/court-insider-what-bankruptcy-appellate-panel. Retrieved on July 10, 2020.

32 Local Rule 2090-1(A)(3). Qualifications to Practice, Southern District of Florida. Retrieved on June 4, 2021. www.flsb.uscourts.gov/local-rule/attorneys

33 Local Rule 2:01(d) General Admission to Practice. Middle District of Florida. Revised March 5, 2021.

Then the practitioner could apply to the Middle District. Fast forward almost a year to the date, I discovered that two sponsoring attorneys are no longer required.[34] Even the filing fee increased from $196 to $203.[35]

Dating back to 2007, when I was admitted to the Middle District Fort Myers Division, I was required to attend a swearing-in ceremony. However, when I re-petitioned in 2018 for membership in the Middle District in Jacksonville, I only had to submit my petition with the required fee since I was a member of the Southern District. The swearing-in ceremony was via telephone, which is no longer a requirement either. Neither is the 75-question multiple-choice exam I took in 2000 to gain admittance to the Southern District.

Administrative Orders that may deal with an array of issues are also available on the court's website – for example, in the Southern District of Florida, an Administrative Order required wearing face masks inside the building, including practicing social distancing.[36]

In addition, there are likely to be separate policies created by judges that are also available on the court's website and that individual judge's page. These policies are usually administrative or procedural, such as scheduling hearings, submitting proposed orders to the court, and the preferred method of contact with the judge's office. See Figure 4.4.

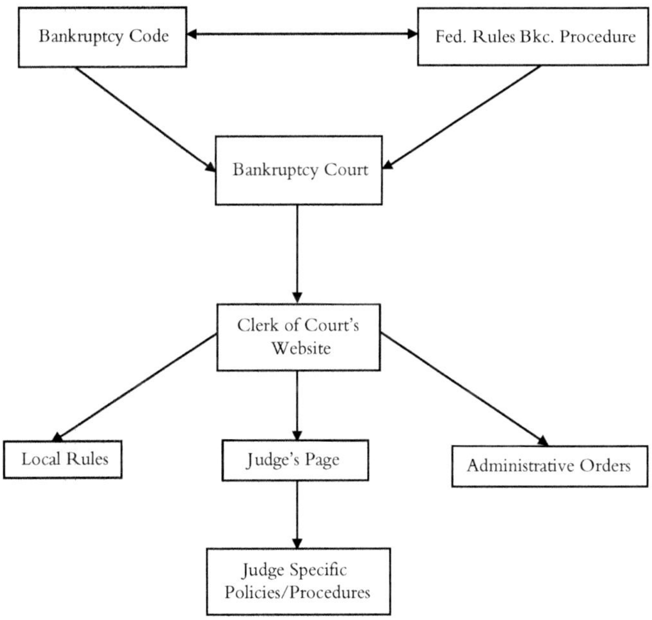

FIGURE 4.4 Rules and procedures applicable to bankruptcy cases.

34 Middle District of Florida Local Rule 2:01. https://www.flmd.uscourts.gov/sites/flmd/files/documents/flmd-attorney-admissions-and-e-file-registration.pdf. Retrieved on June 4, 2021.

35 Id., at www.flmd.uscourts.gov/local-rules/rule-201-practice-middle-district.

36 District Court Administrative Order 2020-33 In re: Coronavirus Public Emergency – Fourth Order Concerning Jury Trials and Other Proceedings. Southern District of Florida. United States Bankruptcy Court. www.flsb.uscourts.gov/news/district-court-administrative-order-2020-33-re-coronavirus-public-emergency-fourth-order. Retrieved on March 6, 2021.

CM/ECF AND PACER

Local rules also require registering with the court's online filing system and completing court-approved training sessions. The federal court system uses Case Management/ Electronic Case Filing (CM/ECF).[37] The login credentials for CM/ECF for bankruptcy court may be separate from the U.S. District Court.

PACER is the acronym for Public Access to Court Electronic Records, which allows public access to case and docket information for the federal court system, including bankruptcy courts.[38] The federal judiciary has also created Next Generation (NextGen), which combines PACER and CM/ECF into one account, avoiding having multiple usernames and passwords.[39] Note there is a fee of $0.10 per page with a maximum fee of $3.00 per document. Charges are billed quarterly but waived if the amount is less than $30.00.

Even for the experienced attorney or paralegal, PACER and CM/ECF can be of great benefit. For example, for issues that come up at the Meeting of Creditors for another attorney's case, I'll find the case on CM/ECF and review the docket. Then, I'll download the documents, whether it's a motion or the bankruptcy petition, and save them for a "just-in-case scenario" I may face with a future client.

SUMMARY

In the United States, there are two court systems: the federal system and the state system. State laws cannot conflict with federal laws, as federal law is the "supreme law of the land." If a county, municipal, or state law conflicts with federal law, that law is considered unconstitutional.

Federal judges are appointed by the President of the United States and confirmed by the U.S. Senate. Bankruptcy judges are chosen by the judges in the court of appeal and serve 14-year terms.

The paralegal should be familiar with the Bankruptcy Code, the Federal Rules of Bankruptcy Procedure, the local rules, and the administrative orders and policies of the bankruptcy judges. This information is readily available on the clerk of court's website.

PACER provides public access to cases in the federal court system. For filing in a U.S. District Court or bankruptcy court, CM/ECF is used. Registration and online training are required to use CM/ECF.

37 U.S. Courts. Electronic Filing (CM/ECF). www.uscourts.gov/court-records/electronic-filing-cmecf.

38 PACER: Federal Court Records. Public Access to Court Electronic Records. Pacer.us.courts.gov.

39 Get Ready for NextGen CM/ECF/PACER: Federal Court Records. https://pacer.uscourts.gov/file-case/get-ready-nextgen-cmecf. Retrieved on March 6, 2021.

KEYWORDS AND TERMS

- Administrative orders
- B.A.P. (Bankruptcy Appellate Panels)
- CM/ECF (Case Management/Electronic Case Filing)
- Core versus non-core proceedings
- District courts
- District Court of Appeals
- Diversity of citizenship
- Federal Rules of Bankruptcy Procedure
- Local rules
- Next Generation (NextGen)
- PACER (Public Access to Court Electronic Records)
- Supremacy clause
- Supreme law of the land

DISCUSSION QUESTIONS

1. Why would Article III of the U.S. Constitution include diversity of citizenship?
2. In reviewing a case you wish to schedule for a hearing, you realize a conflict exists between the local rule and the Federal Rules of Bankruptcy Procedure. Which one should you guide yourself by?
3. Look up the small claims division in the county you reside in.
   a. How are cases filed in that division? Online or hard copy?
   b. Is the process for filing a case explained on the court's website?
   c. Are there forms available? If so, how are those forms obtained?
   d. How are hearings scheduled?
4. What are the dollar amounts required to file where you reside for small claims court?
5. Review the website of the bankruptcy court in your district.
   a. Has your district merged with NextGen?
   b. How many bankruptcy districts are in your state?
   c. Which bankruptcy district are you located in?
   d. What is the courthouse address of your district?
   e. List the bankruptcy judges in your district.
   f. What are the local rules requiring admittance to your district?
   g. Which circuit are you in if you want to appeal to the Bankruptcy Appellate Panel?

PRACTICE QUESTIONS AND EXERCISES

1. Register for PACER and complete the CM/ECF online training program.

2. The law firm you are employed by needs to schedule hearings on a motion calendar for two cases, but each case is assigned to a different judge. Provide a summary of how each judge in your district prefers the scheduling of motions. Provide links as references.
3. What are the judges' preferred methods for receiving a proposed order? Provide the links.
4. Save or bookmark important links.

REFERENCES

28 U.S.C. §152.

28 U.S.C. §157.

28 U.S.C. §158.

Bankruptcy Amendments and Federal Judgeship Act of 1984.

Bankruptcy Filing Statistics. District of Colorado. United States Bankruptcy Court. Retrieved on July 10, 2021. www.cob.uscourts.gov/bankruptcy-filing-statistics.

Bankruptcy Reform Act of 1978.

Court Hours and Locations. U.S. Bankruptcy Court Middle, District of Florida. www.flmb.uscourts.gov/thesource/divisions/default.asp.

Court Insider: What is a Bankruptcy Appellate Panel. www.uscourts.gov/news/2012/11/26/court-insider-what-bankruptcy-appellate-panel.

Court Location. District of Colorado. United States Bankruptcy Court. www.cob.uscourts.gov/court-info/court-locations.

Court Location. Northern District of Florida. United States Bankruptcy Court. www.flnb.uscourts.gov/court-info/court-locations.

Court Locations. Southern District of Florida. United States Bankruptcy Court. www.flsb.uscourts.gov/court/locations.

District Court Administrative Order 2020-33 In re: Coronavirus Public Emergency – Fourth Order Concerning Jury Trials and Other Proceedings. Southern District of Florida. United States Bankruptcy Court. Retrieved on March 6, 2021. www.flsb.uscourts.gov/news/district-court-administrative-order-2020-33-re-coronavirus-public-emergency-fourth-order.

Get Ready for NextGen CM/ECF/PACER: Federal Court Records. Retrieved on March 6, 2021. https://pacer.uscourts.gov/file-case/get-ready-nextgen-cmecf.

Impeachment of Federal Judges. Retrieved on April 10, 2020. www.fjc.gov/history/judges/impeachments-federal-judges.

Local Rule 2:01. General Admission to Practice. Middle District of Florida.

Local Rule 2090-1(A)(3). Qualifications to Practice, Southern District of Florida. www.flsb.uscourts.gov/local-rule/attorneys.

N. Pipeline Const. Co. v. Marathon Pipe Line Co., 458 U.S. 50, 102 S. Ct. 2858, 73 L. Ed. 2d 598 (1982).

PACER: Federal Court Records. Public Access to Court Electronic Records. Pacer.us.courts.gov.

PL 98–353 §120.

United States Bankruptcy Court Middle District of Florida. Main Case Filing Analysis, December 2019. www.flmb.uscourts.gov/statistics/2019/December.pdf.

U.S. Const. Amend. I.

U.S. Const. Art. I.

U.S. Const. Art. II.

U.S. Const. Art. III.

U.S. Const. Art. VI.

U.S. Courts. Electronic Filing (CM/ECF). www.uscourts.gov/court-records/electronic-filing-cmecf.

CHAPTER 5

"Well, How Did I Get Here?"

If there's a song that would sum up the feelings of my clients and the realities of life, it would be "Once in a Lifetime" by the Talking Heads, ranked by the Rock and Roll Hall of Fame as one of the "500 Songs That Shaped Rock and Roll."[1] So, to borrow more than once from the Talking Heads, hopefully, bankruptcy is "once in a lifetime"; if not, it's the "same as it ever was."[2]

Let's review the steps that led to the client sitting nervously in the office's waiting area while tying it into the lyrics of "Once in a Lifetime." You didn't think you would get through this textbook without an 80s reference, did you?

Because of a million different reasons beyond the debtor's control, they are heavily indebted. While they struggled at times with the monthly payments, they managed to always pay on time. They had no choice. If they wanted to qualify for a mortgage and buy their family a home, they had to protect their credit score. However, the debtor has no choice but to skip this month's credit card payments. "My God! What have I done?"[3]

The debtor tries everything possible at this point to keep up with their debt payments, whether it's cutting back on unnecessary expenses or luxuries, selling personal items, or even negotiating with creditors. Still, all roads lead to a financial dead end. They may even try to obtain a personal loan with a lower interest rate and monthly payments, but borrowing money to pay off creditors is usually a losing proposition. When in a hole, stop digging.

Maybe the debtor tries the gig economy, but that only takes more time away from family and causes more problems than they already have, so frustrated and exhausted, they give up. Like the Talking Heads warn us, there is water dissolving, there is water under the rocks and stones, there is water at the bottom of the ocean and underground, but remove the water, carry the water, and there's still water. And so, there's still debt.

1 Once in a Lifetime (Talking Heads song). https://en.wikipedia.org/wiki/Once_in_a_Lifetime_(Talking_Heads_song). Retrieved on March 6, 2021.

2 Once in a Lifetime: The Best of.... http://talking-heads.nl/index.php/talking-heads-lyrics/22-once-in-a-lifetime-the-best-of. Retrieved on July 10, 2021.

3 Id.

DOI: 10.4324/9781003203278-6

At this point, the debtor realizes they-re "letting the days go by, let the water hold me down."[4] But it's not water that's holding them down; it's debt, an ocean of debt where the debtor struggles to stay above the surface of the water. But you can only tread "water" for so long. Can the debtor get "into the blue again, after the money's gone?"[5]

As predictable as the sunrise and sunset, the creditor calls begin. Because of technology, automated software programs dial the debtor's phone number endless times a day. When the debtor answers the call with "hello," they're transferred to a real person looking to collect past due payments. It won't be long before, again, no thanks to technology, the creditor starts calling from local numbers to deceive the debtor into answering the call. Finally, one call ends with the creditor offering to restructure the payment plan, but the offer is so ridiculous that if the debtor could afford that payment plan, he wouldn't be in this position in the first place.

But phone calls aren't enough in the pressure campaign to collect. So now it's letters, emails, and text messages reminding the debtor daily that they're late on their payments. How do you kick a good person while their down? Besides interest, the creditor adds late fees and penalties, so the debt continues to pile up. They may have stopped digging a while back, but they keep getting deeper and deeper into the hole.

For a while, it gets quiet, but that's just the calm before the storm. Next, the debt was "charged off," meaning the original creditor sold the debt to a third-party collection agency. After that, the debtor will continue to receive calls, letters, emails, and text messages with more intensity, just from a different company with fewer scruples.

But the debt collection agency only has so much patience, and threats aren't enough, so it's time to make good on those threats. The debt collector proceeds to hire an attorney to file a collection action. One day, the debtor hears a knock at the door and innocently enough, answers the door, only to hear, "you've been served."

If the debtor had money, they would hire an attorney to handle this, but they can't even afford a bankruptcy attorney. They're literally too broke to file for bankruptcy. The hearing date comes and goes, and it's been a while since they heard from the creditor. But Thursday afternoon, their employer receives a wage garnishment order. Tomorrow's paycheck will be minus a quarter of their pay as the employer is obligated by law to send the funds to the creditor. "*If I can't afford anything now, how can I afford it with 25 percent less? My rent is due Monday!*"

If it only ended there. Come one, come all. Creditors start coming out of the woodwork because they all want a piece of the pie. If that isn't enough, one creditor filed a motion, seeking a lien on their assets, plus freezing their bank accounts. "*When will it all end?*"

It's time to walk a mile in the debtor's shoes. If you were in this situation, it's right about now that you ask yourself, "am I right, am I wrong" as you grapple with the moral obligations of paying your debts on the one hand, but on the other hand, bankruptcy holds the solution to your problems.[6] It's time to replace the Band-Aid with a tourniquet.

4 Id.
5 Id.
6 Id.

"Where does that highway go to?"[7] There's only one way to find out. You call a bankruptcy lawyer and ask, "how do I work this," because the fact is "time isn't holding up."[8]

BEFORE MEETING WITH THE CLIENT

Bankruptcy has always been about money. The debtor needs money and borrows it from the creditor who wants it back. But the time comes that the debtor has no more money, and the creditor isn't willing to lend more. Now comes the delicate balancing act for the debtor of trying to protect what's left of income and assets while the creditor is looking to cash in.

When meeting with a potential client, it's essential to understand the client's position. The client may feel intimidated since this is the first time the client consults with an attorney. The client may be nervous and rambling about issues that may not be relevant to the case. Sometimes clients cry or are embarrassed that they are in this position to begin with. It is your job to put the client at ease. While everyone uses different techniques and methods, I always advise the client it's my job to help them get through this complicated process. I remind the client how many people have filed for bankruptcy before them and have continued with their lives. What else I say depends on the circumstances and facts surrounding that individual's case.

For example, we're now seeing the "graying of bankruptcy," a term meaning that the older generation is filing for bankruptcy at record numbers.[9] With figures obtained from the Consumer Bankruptcy Project, between 1991 and 2016, those aged 65 through 74 had a 200 percent increase in bankruptcy filings.[10] During the same time, for debtors over the age of 75, bankruptcy filings have tripled.[11]

The increase in bankruptcy filings for the older generation could result from several reasons, for example, insufficient health insurance coverage or substantial expenses for non-covered prescription medications. Others may have been impacted by the Great Recession of 2008 and could not bounce back after losing their homes to foreclosure, loss of income, and retirement accounts dwindling to almost nothing. But, that's the silver lining in the otherwise dark cloud of bankruptcy. The "graying of bankruptcy" in record numbers proves that the client is not at fault and their situation is not unique. Rarely, especially for an older client, is bankruptcy a result of misspending and financial irresponsibility. It's situational, meaning the situation the client is in is likely not their fault, especially if the bankruptcy is due to health-related illnesses or diminished retirement income because of a bad economy. There is strength in numbers, and that helps clients feel more at ease.

7 Id.
8 Id.
9 Deborah Thorne, Pamela Foohey, Robert M. Lawless, and Katherine Porter. Graying of U.S. Bankruptcy: Fallout from Life in a Risk Society. (August 2018). https://papers.ssrn.com/sol3/papers.cfm?abstract_id=3226574.
10 Id.
11 A. Soergel. Bankruptcy Soars Among Elderly as Inequality Deepens. *US News – The Report*. August 2018:C32. www.creditslips.org/consumerbankruptcyproject/news.html.

Likewise, even with the coronavirus pandemic, it goes without saying that there will be a surge of bankruptcy cases filed before this text is published. Major retailers such as J. Crew have filed for bankruptcy, and this is just the beginning.[12] Other businesses have taken different measures to avoid the fallout of bankruptcy. For example, the popular chain restaurant Cheesecake Factory stopped paying rent.[13] While businesses, whether in the food industry or retail, understand that bankruptcy may be the only solution and their situation resulted from acts beyond their control, clients may not. Business is business, but personal is personal. But again, I use this information to put clients at ease. There's no denying there's a certain level of comfort for a client when their situation is compared to that of a successful business. If a client is asked if they feel any different toward the business that filed for bankruptcy, the answer is always "no." Then why should it be any different for them? This helps put their situation into perspective. Yes, the practice of law is a service-oriented business, but it remains a noble profession. The most basic foundation of the law is to help clients right the wrongs and at times, that requires an empathetic ear.

Other situations leading to filing bankruptcy include divorce and long stretches of unemployment, for example, those furloughed because of COVID-19. In just about every consultation I've ever had, I remind clients of the fact that no one wants to file for bankruptcy. People don't wake up one day and think, "let me get in debt so I can file for bankruptcy in a few years." This wasn't planned! Even the consensus is that people abuse the bankruptcy system. Look no further than Congress, which went out of its way to include the word "abuse" in the title of BAPCPA and "presumption of abuse" within the body of the text if the debtor fails the means test. But after consulting with and representing thousands of clients, I can honestly tell you it's just not true.

The main reasons people file for bankruptcy are:

1. Lack of health insurance resulting in substantial medical bills or health-related illnesses that may have caused long stretches of unemployment.[14]
2. Unemployment.[15]
3. Divorce.[16]

12 Aimee Picchi. J. Crew files for bankruptcy after economic hit from coronavirus pandemic. *CBS News*. www.cbsnews.com/news/j-crew-bankruptcy-filing-chapter-11-coronavirus/.

13 Nathan Bomey. Cheesecake Factory Won't Pay April Rent as Coronavirus Hurts Restaurants. *USA Today*. www.usatoday.com/story/money/2020/03/26/cheesecake-factory-coronavirus-covid-19-rent/2914440001/.

14 Adrianna Belmonte. Medical Debt Is a "Uniquely American Problem" Caused by a "Very Broken" System Expert Explains. *Yahoo Finance*, June 21, 2021. https://finance.yahoo.com/news/medical-debt-uniquely-american-problem-155327746.html?.tsrc=fp_deeplink. See also R. Kluender, N. Mahoney, F. Wong, and W. Yin. Medical Debt in the US, 2009–2020. 326(3) *JAMA* (2021) 250–256. doi:10.1001/jama.2021.8694. https://jamanetwork.com/journals/jama/fullarticle/2782187?guestAccessKey=9e5fde5f-d5aa-410a-bbb3-bbe66a6b39fb&utm_source=For_The_Media&utm_medium=referral&utm_campaign=ftm_links&utm_content=tfl&utm_term=072021?ftag=YHFa5b931b.

15 Margaret Howard. The Fragile Middle Class: Americans in Debt Teresa A. Sullivan, Elizabeth Warren & Jay Lawrence, Westbrook Publisher, 2000. Pp. 380., 17 *Bankr. Dev. J.* 425 (2001).

16 Id.

With bankruptcy law, empathizing with and understanding the client's situation is what makes the practice rewarding. The fact is a majority of my clients have already tried alternatives to bankruptcy, such as a personal loan to consolidate debt and lower monthly payments. Some have used non-profit organizations for debt management strategies. Others have tried gig economy jobs, using the extra income to pay down their debt. Others sell whatever available assets they have, but bankruptcy is and will always be the last choice, but it's not for everyone and every situation. There are plenty of clients that I advise against filing for bankruptcy, even Chapter 13. But those that do qualify and have their debt eliminated because of bankruptcy are grateful.

With that being said, it's important to point out that if a client is reacting emotionally, you are guaranteed this is the first bankruptcy consultation for the client. It's important to know that you have to control the interview process because you don't want to spend too much time listening to their version. If 20 minutes are lost on that alone, after three clients, an hour of work is lost each day, and now you are behind on your other files. This also applies to phone calls where the client feels the need to explain their situation dating back to day one. Realistically, patients don't call a doctor's office, give an entire medical history, and expect the person that answered the phone to provide medical advice, who, in reality, isn't qualified to answer any medical-related questions. But the practice of law has and always will be different in the way clients react and respond. There is a closeness, a personal relationship between clients and attorneys that is lacking in other professions. While that is evidence that a client trusts you, you still have to be careful with your time, especially phone calls, because a few calls per day is enough to surpass an hour. It adds up quickly. Consider this: five hours lost per week amounts to 260 hours at the end of the year which equals more than six full-time weeks of work!

SCENARIOS YOU ARE LIKELY TO ENCOUNTER

Regardless of how prepared and thorough the consultation is, the client may have in mind to meet with several lawyers since the consultations are usually free. So after spending time with the client, the client says thank you, grabs a few business cards, and walks out the door, but doesn't retain the attorney. Unfortunately, this is common. Of course, with time, you will get better at interrupting a client to ask questions to take over the interview and speed up the process while not sacrificing quality.

The opposite is when the client meets with you for the first time but has already met with several attorneys. The client is either distrustful, indecisive, or shopping around for the lowest price, at the risk of sacrificing experience and quality. But, again, with time, you will be able to spot that client.

Some clients will be upfront and tell you they only want a price quote, and while that's understandable, there should still be a consultation. While this may be frustrating to clients, the attorney(s) they consulted with could have given the wrong advice or not mentioned the consequences of non-exempt assets or other issues clients are likely to encounter. That's why at the outset of the consultation, I confirm if there have been consultations with other attorneys. If they have, there is no need for a 30-minute-plus consultation to explain the entire process. Instead, I focus on specific issues.

If the client confirms they have consulted with another attorney, I'm usually able to add to the discussion by reviewing key issues that most likely weren't explained in detail. I do that for the obvious reason that when an issue wasn't discussed that affects the bankruptcy case, the client's reaction is always the same: "the other lawyer didn't mention that to me." Now there's a good chance the client will be retaining me instead. Sometimes a client abuses your time by using you as a sounding board. It's just the nature of the beast/business. Again, with time you'll get better at handling these situations.

Regardless of these issues, bankruptcy is a gratifying area of law in a profession that usually isn't. There's always stress involved when it comes to money and finances, and it's one of the major causes of divorce. But I promise you after a client attends their Meeting of Creditors, they are smiling and grateful for the work you have done. Remember, it's simple: before you, clients were overwhelmed, drowning in a sea of debt. Daily they were harassed with endless creditor robocalls. Some were served with lawsuits, while others had their wages garnished. But bankruptcy served as their life preserver. You provided them with the fresh start they needed to move forward with their lives. For this reason, I enjoy practicing and teaching bankruptcy law, and that's why I decided to write this book.

SUMMARY

As a paralegal, you will interact with clients daily. Clients have different personalities and styles, and how you handle each case and client will require that you adjust to the situation and be flexible. With some clients, you'll have to be patient. You'll have to hold their hands each step of the way. They may prefer to conduct transactions in person since they lack technological know-how or are distrustful of technology. Other clients may be experiencing difficult times personally, besides bankruptcy. You are that calming figure that guides them in the right direction, putting them at ease and reassuring them of the process. Other clients may be highly organized and follow directions to a T. In contrast, other clients are highly disorganized and fail to provide documents timely, repeatedly providing the same or wrong documents. However, part of your job is to make the process easier for clients and the firm. Remember, this is a learning process where you will continue to learn from each client interaction and adjust accordingly. Learn from the experience of others. Ask a paralegal or attorney if you can be their shadow so you can see how difficult clients and situations are handled.

KEYWORDS AND TERMS

- Common reasons debtors file for bankruptcy
- Debt consolidation
- Debt management
- Gig economy
- Graying of bankruptcy

DISCUSSION QUESTIONS

1. Because consulting with a lawyer on any matter is never easy, what steps can you take to make the client feel at ease, whether with the initial phone call and appointment setting or during the consultation and intake?
2. Do you know anyone that has filed for bankruptcy? What was their reason for filing for bankruptcy?
3. What experience(s) did that person share with you regarding the bankruptcy process?

PRACTICE QUESTIONS AND EXERCISES

1. You're discussing the case with the client. The client is nervous and begins to cry. What steps can you take to put the client at ease?
2. A walk-in comes into your office, and the following discussion takes place:

   "How much does the lawyer charge for a Chapter 7 bankruptcy? I just need a price. I already had a consultation with Larry the Lawyer (a well-known bankruptcy attorney). He said he will do it for $1,800. Can you beat that price? I don't want to take up the lawyer's time with a consultation. It's a simple bankruptcy. I can probably do it myself, but don't have the time. It's just easier to have a lawyer handle it."

   a. How do you respond?

   "Can you at least give me an idea of how much the lawyer usually charges for bankruptcy? Will he do it for $1,500? I can pay in cash, upfront."

   a. How do you respond?

REFERENCES

Adrianna Belmonte, "Medical Debt is a 'Uniquely American Problem' Caused by a 'Very Broken' System Expert Explains", *Yahoo Finance* (June 21, 2021). https://finance.yahoo.com/news/medical-debt-uniquely-american-problem-155327746.html?.tsrc=fp_deeplink.

Aimee Picchi, "J. Crew Files for Bankruptcy after Economic Hit from Coronavirus Pandemic", *CBS News*. www.cbsnews.com/news/j-crew-bankruptcy-filing-chapter-11-coronavirus/.

Andrew Soergel, "Bankruptcy Soars Among Elderly as Inequality Deepens", *US News – The Report* (August 2018:C32).

Deborah Thorne, Pamela Foohey, Robert M. Lawless, and Katherine Porter, "Graying of U.S. Bankruptcy: Fallout from Life in a Risk Society" (August 2018). https://papers.ssrn.com/sol3/papers.cfm?abstract_id=3226574.

Nathan Bomey, "Cheesecake Factory Won't Pay April Rent as Coronavirus Hurts Restaurants", *USA Today*. www.usatoday.com/story/money/2020/03/26/cheesecake-factory-coronavirus-covid-19-rent/2914440001/.

"Once in a Lifetime" (Talking Heads song). https://en.wikipedia.org/wiki/Once_in_a_Lifetime_(Talking_Heads_song).

"Once in a Lifetime: The Best of...." http://talking-heads.nl/index.php/talking-heads-lyrics/22-once-in-a-lifetime-the-best-of.

R. Kluender, N. Mahoney, F. Wong, and W. Yin, "Medical Debt in the US, 2009–2020" (2021) 326(3) *JAMA* 250–256. doi:10.1001/jama.2021.8694.

Margaret Howard. The Fragile Middle Class: Americans in Debt. Teresa A. Sullivan, Elizabeth Warren & Jay Lawrence, Westbrook Publisher, 2000. Pp. 380., 17 *Bankr. Dev. J.* 425 (2001).

CHAPTER 6

Office Protocols and Contact with the Client for the First Time

FIRST POINT OF CONTACT

The first interaction with a client is usually the initial phone call. Chances are the potential client asks about or is concerned with the following:

1. How much does the attorney charge?
2. Asks for legal advice after explaining their situation, usually in detail.
3. Requests a consultation over the phone.
4. If an appointment is scheduled, what documents should they bring to the consultation?

HOW MUCH DOES THE ATTORNEY CHARGE?

Most of the time, this will be the first question asked by a client, whether asked via a phone call, email, or in person. That, and if the consultation is free. Most attorneys will not provide legal advice or a price quote over the phone. Still, I know a colleague who prefers this method to avoid clients that will only take up his time if they're shopping around for prices, which is usually the case. My issue with that philosophy is simple enough: when you meet with the client, you may realize their case is more complicated, and the fee quoted should have been higher. The opposite also holds true. Some attorneys prefer to say or advertise "fees starting at," but that is the same difference, and if the fee quoted after the consultation is higher than the "starting at price," which it usually is, you'll have an upset client. This is especially true when the client finds out costs such as filing fees and the required bankruptcy classes are separate from attorney's fees.

Most clients consult with multiple attorneys since consultations are typically free. With time, you'll be able to filter out those clients immediately and shorten the amount of time devoted to a consultation.

DOI: 10.4324/9781003203278-7

REAL CASES

Talking shop with a colleague, he told me of one situation. After a lengthy consultation, he prepared the *Retainer Agreement*, but that's when the potential client, for the first time, mentioned he had already retained a bankruptcy attorney and wanted to confirm his attorney was doing his job correctly.[1] You can imagine the frustration and anger my colleague must have experienced. Even worse, the consultation took place after 5 p.m. on a Friday. After our conversation and sharing more legal war stories, I amended my *client intake* to include a section asking if other attorneys have been consulted on the same subject or if there's a pending case.[2] As stated in the prior chapter, I also ask the client the same question at the beginning of the consultation under the guise that I'm avoiding being repetitious. If the client states they have consulted with other attorneys, my consultation focuses on supplementing their already received information.

Like my colleague, I recently was in a similar situation where a potential client called my office regarding bankruptcy. It didn't take long to realize that the client would not be filing for bankruptcy any time soon, if ever. Her husband is a millionaire, and they were close to settling their divorce case. In reality, I believe the client was more interested in a free consultation on divorce because her focus shifted quickly to mediation, settlement, and if her attorney was doing a "good job."

When clients continue to pressure me for a quote over the phone, I advise the potential client that without analyzing their case, one of two things will happen: I may have quoted too high, which is unfair to the client, or the quote was too low, which is unfair to me, so someone isn't going to be happy.

I'll also advise the client that my fee structure varies per case and depends on numerous factors, such as how many creditors a client has and the value of non-exempt assets. In addition, if there are secured debts, *Reaffirmation Agreement* may be required which is a separate fee. Finally, if my response still isn't satisfactory to the client, even though my patience may be running thin at this point, I use two examples.

Since my brother is a dentist, I tell the client to imagine calling his office and asking him over the phone how much he charges for a procedure. Yes, my brother receives those calls too, but the answer is the patient may have dental insurance that covers the entire cost of the procedure, a portion, or maybe none at all. Perhaps the procedure isn't even needed. In addition, if after the initial consultation, my brother realizes more dental work is required, he's likely to lower his price.

It's no different from calling a mechanic and asking how much it will cost to fix your car. Yes, mechanics are on the receiving end of those questions as well. But, just like a dentist needs X-rays and the mechanic needs to get under the hood of the car, the attorney needs to consult with the client. At that point, remind the client that the *first* consultation is free. That's important because you will find clients that wish to meet with the attorney repeatedly.

1 A sample Retainer Agreement is available in Chapter 28.
2 See Chapter 28.

Therefore, it's essential to have a system that keeps track of consultations, especially to avoid conflicts of interest. If the client has returned for a second consultation, there should be a consultation fee unless the client is ready to start the case with an initial deposit. If the client is still unsure about proceeding, the consultation fee could be applied as a credit when the client is ready to begin. Remember, time is your most valuable asset.

PHONE CONSULTATIONS AND LEGAL ADVICE

There will always be potential clients who will say that they don't have time to meet in person for a consultation and request one over the phone due to a hectic schedule. Of course, if the client doesn't have time for a consultation, I'm unsure how the client will have time to provide all the necessary documents or attend the Meeting of Creditors. Whether a consultation should occur via telephone depends on the policy of the particular lawyer or law firm, but I advise against it.

If I commit to a telephonic consultation, it's because the client paid for the consultation, even though it's for a bankruptcy case. The fact is paying a minimal price for a consultation is likely cheaper than missing time from work, plus more convenient. Besides, if attorneys allow free telephone consultations, potential clients will consult with every attorney in town, ultimately choosing the one with the lowest fee.

Consultation fees or quotes over the phone usually result in the potential client saying "I don't have the money right now but will get back to you when I do." Sometimes potential clients also say that at the beginning or end of the consultation, which begs the question, why bother consulting with an attorney if you can't afford one? Do you go car shopping when you have no intention of buying a car?

Most attorneys do not provide legal advice to a stranger over the phone because of liability issues. Plenty of times, you will hear, "but it's just one question." For one, it's never one question. In my office, the paralegal will remind the potential client that the knowledge required to answer that one question cost me a king's ransom in student loans, not to mention time, and my time is valuable just like anyone else's.

As to liability, if an attorney answers that "one question," he/she just did so based on an incomplete picture. When the client acts accordingly and things go south, the blame falls on the attorney. At a minimum, it is a bar complaint in the making, if not malpractice. An attorney needs the complete set of facts to provide the correct legal advice. Would you feel comfortable if you called a doctor's office and explained to the doctor or whoever answered the phone that your shoulder hurts, and the recommendation was surgery?

I've even come across bar journal articles that argue it's ill-advised to give potential clients advice in settings that are not conducive to the attorney–client relationship or an environment not typical of a consultation. For example, there are endless articles published citing an example every attorney has encountered. The attorney is socializing at a party or event and hears the dreaded words, "let me ask you a question." The attorney and paralegal should avoid that situation, especially considering that person doesn't even respect the fact that work-related issues are being asked during time off, and there will be no compensation.

But, again, trust me, it happens in all professions, and no one likes to work for free. Even worse, rarely does that person retain the services of the professional. My dentist has told me of situations where she encounters patients in public settings and is asked if she can "take a quick look" as the patient is standing before her with their mouth open.

I also advise clients that I don't know who I am speaking with based on a phone call. It could be another lawyer trying to figure out what I charge or a paralegal trying to determine how to handle a situation. Even in family law cases, I've had the opposing party call me to either create a conflict of interest or to obtain information on their spouse's case. When my wife worked with me, she had the best response to clients. She would ask the voice at the other end of the call how they knew who they were talking to. It could be anyone, including non-office personnel, even the wrong phone number.

Ultimately, the decision on how to handle these situations depends on the attorney, but my advice is clear. I can't imagine any situation where it's worth facing a bar complaint and liability and not even being compensated. I fail to see how the headache(s) is/are worth it. Therefore, as the paralegal, always be careful what information you're releasing, especially if it's a phone call. When in doubt, either ask a senior paralegal or the attorney. More importantly, remember that as a paralegal, you are not to provide legal advice. That is the job of an attorney. When a client asks for legal advice, you will need to kindly defer to the lawyer, no different than the nurse who responds he/she is not allowed to give medical advice or opinions and to ask the doctor. At first, you may feel uncomfortable telling a client "no," but it's your job and income on the line.

Of course, when I first wrote this chapter, we were 50-plus days in with the nationwide quarantine due to the COVID-19 pandemic. As a result, more and more law firms have been switching to remote access for employees and clients. I've even attended *341 meetings* telephonically.[3] For the first time in my career, I offered telephone consultations to avoid person-to-person contact. Most clients understand and are appreciative. However, even with telephonic consultations, I make sure who I am consulting with. Clients must complete an intake form and have it returned to me via email before the consultation. My intake requests basic information such as name, address, contact information, and a copy of the client's driver's license to confirm their identity. If retained, the contract is signed digitally. State bars and the courts have already opined or ruled that digitally signed contracts are valid. Documents can be emailed, mailed, or dropped off at the office. In borderline cases, I'll request pay stubs immediately to confirm the client passes the means test.[4]

Surprisingly, many attorneys don't use intakes, but I always have since I save that information for my database. Usually, once or twice a year, especially during the Christmas holiday, I mail promotional materials. But regardless of my marketing techniques, again, it's to avoid multiple consultations with the same client and conflicts of interest. For example, I have witnessed situations where clients filed a joint bankruptcy, and the bankruptcy lawyer now represents one of the parties in a divorce case against the other. A conflict check would

3 11 U.S.C. §341.
4 11. U.S.C. §707.

have prevented that situation which could lead to a bar complaint. An astute and aggressive opposing counsel would even file for sanctions and likely be granted attorney's fees. For this reason, conflict checks should be routine.

Because of the coronavirus pandemic, the traditional way of consulting with clients will likely change if it hasn't already. For years I've been working remotely, and at one time, I had a bankruptcy paralegal that was 100 percent remote as well as a receptionist. Most of my colleagues have been practicing remotely for years, long ago having given up the traditional way of practicing law. Gone may be the day of being in the office all day dressed in business attire. Therefore, law firms, big and small, may be shifting toward a new norm. With each passing year, more lawyers enter the workforce which undoubtedly affects the way law is practiced. Younger clients that are comfortable with technology may also expect virtual consultations. So it's prudent that paralegals feel comfortable with the technology and be prepared to deal with clients in a non-traditional format.

With in-office consultations, I meet with the client initially to confirm they qualify for bankruptcy, then have the paralegal handle the specifics such as the *bankruptcy intake* which will be reviewed in the following chapters. Note that neither the paralegal nor the attorney should complete the bankruptcy intake on behalf of the client. The reason why will be explained later.

While the client is completing the bankruptcy intake, I'll meet again with the client if any new issues arise. As the paralegal, you will learn to spot those issues and bring them to the attorney's attention. In addition, the client has the option of completing the bankruptcy intake at home since there is a considerable amount of information required. For example, the client may not have access to the balance on a car loan or know how many miles are registered on the odometer. I also don't want the client to feel rushed.

Once retained, if another paralegal will be working on the file, it's recommended that the client be introduced to that paralegal. This helps establish the paralegal's role and limits any potential breakdown in communication between the office and the client. This simple act lays the foundation of mutual trust and respect necessary for a strong relationship between the client and the law firm. As support and guidance are provided to the client, the client's comfort level increases, which benefits everyone because it helps run the case/office smoothly. All it takes is one client to throw an office into chaos.

WHAT DOCUMENTS TO BRING

Since potential clients will ask what documents to bring to the consultation, the answer is whatever documents they feel are relevant and if possible, copies of their credit report and pending lawsuits. With lawsuits, remember that time can be of the essence. If a default has been entered, it's a matter of time before the creditor seeks to enforce the judgment, whether by wage garnishment and/or judicial liens.

One issue to be aware of is that some clients feel the urge to bring a large batch of documents to the consultation and expect the paralegal or the attorney to review it. Once, taking a Continuing Legal Education course, it was refreshing to find out I wasn't the only attorney to have experienced clients coming to the office with stacks of opened or closed envelopes stuffed into a grocery bag, and the client wants to review each document.

Besides being time-consuming and the fact that many of the documents will be from the same creditors, you shouldn't say over the phone, "don't bring any documents," as that will be looked upon negatively by the client. But I tell clients that the consultation focuses mainly on income and expenses and that usually, they would know the answer without the need for documentation. Unfortunately, that's not always the case, but that's why consultations are a fact-finding exercise. Later in this textbook, we will review the questions to ask clients and identify potential issues and pitfalls.

SUMMARY

There could be a host of reasons why clients consult with multiple attorneys. Some clients are indecisive or feel uncomfortable with the prior attorney's behavior, style, or demeanor. Other clients are simply shopping around for the best price, while some are not considerate of the time of others. Either way, this is expected and cannot be a source of distraction or frustration.

Paralegals wear many hats and juggle multiple tasks simultaneously, so time management and organizational skills are necessary. For example, a bankruptcy paralegal will be responsible for making and receiving dozens of calls daily, meeting with clients that are dropping off documents and always have more questions, preparing petitions, and submitting documents to the trustee. If the attorney is in court, the paralegal is also managing the office.

With time comes experience and how to deal with clients efficiently while at the same time providing excellent service and handling your caseload. However, understand that the practice of law is fluid. New issues and cases present themselves that require immediate attention, and since the paralegal usually works with minimal supervision, it's also essential to understand office policies, procedures, and protocols. When in doubt, seek the advice of a senior paralegal or the attorney, especially since not all lawyers and law firms provide in-depth training. Sometimes it's a learn-as-you-go process. Remember, it's better to err on the side of caution because mistakes cost the law firm, and could cost you your job.

Because a bankruptcy practice requires volume to be financially successful, systems must be developed to move cases along. Flexibility and the ability to adapt accordingly will increase efficiency and client satisfaction and contribute to the practice's success.

KEYWORDS AND TERMS

- Bankruptcy intake
- Client intake
- Conflict check
- Default
- Lawsuit

- Reaffirmation agreements
- Retainer agreements
- The three Ps:
  - Policies
  - Procedure
  - Protocol
- Wage garnishment

DISCUSSION QUESTIONS

1. How can a balance be struck between opening and closing files quickly while at the same time not having the client feel rushed?
2. Should bankruptcy attorneys charge a fee for the first consultation, regardless of how minimal that fee may be?
3. Whether because of the coronavirus pandemic or clients becoming more trustful of technology, should initial consultations be via phone or virtually with software such as Zoom? What are the advantages and disadvantages?
4. If clients can save money and time by avoiding in-office consultations and scheduling numerous consultations with multiple law firms, what steps can a bankruptcy law firm take to ensure that consultations conducted by phone or virtually are not a waste of time and resources?
5. What steps can be taken to avoid possible conflicts of interest?

PRACTICE QUESTIONS AND EXERCISES

1. After an initial deposit, the client refuses to work with the paralegal and wants to deal directly with the attorney. How should this situation be handled? What can be done at the initial consultation to prevent this scenario?
2. While consulting/interviewing the client, the client continually interrupts you and continues to pose hypothetical situations such as "what if" this happens or that happens? How do you handle this situation?
3. As you are consulting with the client on bankruptcy, the client shifts the conversation toward divorce since the law firm also handles family law cases. How would you handle this situation since the law firm charges a consultation fee for family law cases?
4. A potential client was referred to the office by a former client. The referral calls the office and says the following: "I've been doing research online, and I've spoken to some friends who either know about bankruptcy or already filed for bankruptcy, so to save everyone time, I would like my consultation by phone." How would you respond?
5. With the same facts from Question 4, the client responds: "To be honest, even if I qualify, I'm not sure if I would file for bankruptcy. I just want to know what my options are." How would you respond?

6. The conversation with the client continues. "Look, I'm very busy with my job, and honestly, your office is far away, so it's just easier for me if we can do this by phone." How do you respond?

REFERENCES

11 U.S.C. §341.

11 U.S.C. §707.

CHAPTER 7

The Bankruptcy Intake

INTRODUCTION

In this section, we will review the *bankruptcy intake*, the form that every client must complete. There's no exception to that rule! The bankruptcy intake is explained in detail and requires a considerable amount of information. But this is where the bulk of the information is obtained to complete the petition. Therefore, four chapters are devoted to the intake, with each chapter focusing on different sections. This chapter will focus on basic details of the debtor, while Chapter 8 focuses on assets and the trustee's avoidance powers. Chapter 9 is devoted to income and expenses, and Chapter 10 to liabilities and lawsuits. Once you complete these chapters, you'll be ready to begin preparing the petition.

A bankruptcy intake is available with the Best Case® program. However, I've modified my intake over the years, including a Spanish version for my non-English-speaking clients to avoid any miscommunication. Print the intake provided in Chapter 28 so that after each section, you can complete the corresponding section of the bankruptcy intake as if you were the client. This will help familiarize you with the form and identify issues.

When consulting with a client, most of my questions mirror the information requested in the bankruptcy intake and asked by the trustee. However, during the Meeting of Creditors, the trustee's questions tend to be broad in scope as it's the same set of standard questions for each debtor. On the other hand, the bankruptcy intake is more detailed, and depending on the facts of the case, my questions during the consultation land somewhere in between. My standard questions are as follows.

1. How much does the client owe?

There is no specific amount of debt that is required to file for bankruptcy. Each case is different. There could be a client that owes $100,000 or more that shouldn't file for any bankruptcy chapter, while another client is drowning in debt with $15,000 in credit cards. However, as a general rule, attorneys start at $10,000.

At this point, an estimate of the outstanding debt amount is okay. Just make sure to distinguish between secured and unsecured debt. For example, a client may say they owe $5,000, but by asking additional questions, you find out that the client wishes to surrender

DOI: 10.4324/9781003203278-8

their car that's secured by a $25,000 loan. So, don't be quick to dismiss a client without knowing the complete set of facts. Likewise, don't jump to the conclusion that a client qualifies because the debt total is $300,000. For example, if $250,000 is owed on a mortgage and $25,000 on a car loan, the issue may be the remaining $25,000, which could be credit cards. Instead, ask questions that will lead to more questions, and continue asking questions until you have a complete and clear picture of the client's case. As it turns out, maybe the remaining $25,000 is mainly student loans that are unlikely to be discharged. So, find out early not only how much the client owes but categorize the debt accordingly.

REAL CASES

Once I consulted with a client who owed less than $3,000 in credit cards. The client also had student loans, but it was in forbearance status, and she knew that it was unlikely to be discharged. I continued to ask questions to determine what other debt may be outstanding, such as a deficiency balance on a foreclosure, car repossession, or maybe a pending lawsuit. There wasn't. The client was an educated professional and married to a successful medical doctor who was debt-free, except for a mortgage that he could easily afford. My advice was to have her husband pay the debt, but she responded with an adamant "no" by shaking her head from side to side. I then suggested she borrow the money from her husband, same response.

Common sense should have led my client to conclude that attorney's fees would equal at least half her debt total, and that's assuming she could pass the means test.[1] Still not satisfied, the client then requested that I negotiate her debt, but that option made no sense either as that would only hurt her credit score, and since she was self-employed, she may need a business loan one day. So, ask questions, dig deep. Don't assume. The devil is in the details.

2. What is the client's income?

Remember, to qualify for Chapter 7, the client must pass the means test.[2] In some cases, it's obvious the means test is not an issue, but other times, the means test has to be calculated during the consultation.[3] Most clients will have access to their paystubs on their smartphones. If so, review the most recent paystub for the year to date (YTD) and divide by the number of months in the year so far to get an accurate monthly average. Also, confirm that the client did not receive a substantial bonus or overtime that will inflate their income during the six-month period. If the client is unsure of their income, then the means test can be calculated once paystubs are provided.[4] Since this can be time-consuming and there will be communications after the initial consultation, I sometimes charge for this service or request a deposit to proceed. If the client doesn't qualify, depending on the deposit amount, a portion

1 11.U.S.C. §707(b)(2)(A).
2 Id.
3 Official Form 122A-1. Chapter 7 Statement of Your Current Monthly Income.
4 Id.

may be refunded. Remember, if the client didn't sign a retainer or provide an initial deposit, the client would likely consult with another lawyer.

3. Are there any other issues that may affect the bankruptcy?

If there are no issues with the debt amount or income, I then ask specific questions that may affect the bankruptcy case. For example, are secured debts such as the home or car current? If not, and the client can't catch up soon or is at risk of a foreclosure or car repossession, the focus will shift to filing a Chapter 13 immediately.

Are there pending lawsuits, whether the client is being sued or suing a third party? If a creditor is suing the client, multiple issues need to be considered. If the case is nearing conclusion, then the creditor's next step is to garnish the client's wages and seek a judicial lien on the debtor's assets. If so, the bankruptcy needs to be filed soon. If the client was involved in a car accident, the funds received from that lawsuit are likely non-exempt and belong to the bankruptcy estate. Most clients prefer to receive the settlement and file for bankruptcy at a later date.

4. Is the client still using their credit cards?

Some clients may be current with their creditors, and while they will need to stop making payments on their credit cards once they start their case, the concern is the client that went on a recent shopping spree and spent thousands of dollars. Clients should be asked what purchases were made with credit cards. Was it luxury items such as furniture or electronics, or necessities? Depending on several factors, the client may be obligated to pay back a certain amount to the bankruptcy trustee or delay the bankruptcy filing.

5. What assets does the client have?

Does the client own a car, motorcycle, boat, WaveRunner, or home? What is the value of the asset minus the loan amount? Does the equity exceed the exemption limits?

REAL CASES

The client owes $50,000 in credit cards and has been unemployed for quite some time. Since the means test is based on the last six months of income, the client likely qualifies for Chapter 7.[5] However, taking nothing for granted, I continued asking questions. Does the client own or rent a home? One question leads to another. It turns out that while technically the client was unemployed, the proper term would be semi-retired. The client recently sold her business, including the real estate the business was located in. Naturally, this led to further questions.

Question: "Did you make any money from the sale of the business, and if so, how much?"
Answer: "After paying off some debt, I still have $250,000 in my bank account."

5 Supra, note 1.

Question: "Do you own any other real estate?"
Answer: "I have two condominiums, and both are rented."
Question: "What is the balance on each mortgage?"
Answer: "There is none. I also paid off the mortgage of my house with the money I received from the sale of the business."

At least the Porshe 911 wasn't paid off. At this point, neither Chapter 11 nor 13 would make sense. But if I had guided myself by the client, she was "broke" and couldn't afford to pay back her credit cards. So, of course, she called again a few months later. Now the properties were transferred to her daughter, who, apparently, was always the true owner. She also created an irrevocable trust believing that would shield her assets from creditors and the bankruptcy trustee. If it were only that simple. A trustee can undo a fraudulent transfer on an irrevocable trust dating back ten years.[6] See why I keep a client database?

This interaction is an excellent example of your role. Think of yourself as an investigator using the client's responses as clues to get to the bottom of the case. Question clients thoroughly to get a complete picture and use follow-up questions. However, don't sound adversarial, but inquisitive. The key is to ask, ask, and ask until you are comfortable that there are no more questions to ask. That will come with experience, but this is important since attorneys sometimes don't get into details with clients during consultations. If the client is honest, the bankruptcy intake will also facilitate the discovery of any issues.

Other Factors to Consider

The age of the client also results in specific questions. For example, the older the client, the more likely they own a cemetery plot which is considered real estate and not protected by an exemption. The bankruptcy intake has a section on cemetery lots.

As they say in the world of real estate: location, location, location. Now that I'm residing in Jacksonville, Florida, and my office is near the Naval Air Station, I ask clients if they are members of the military as there may be residency issues.

6. Is the client expected to receive a tax refund?

Finally, especially when nearing the end or the beginning of the year, I question clients about tax refunds. Trustees love going after tax refunds because it's easy money and, depending on the expected amount of the refund and the size of the bankruptcy estate, most of the funds could be non-exempt. A tax refund is an overpayment of taxes based on income, so the trustee is entitled to a portion depending on the size of the bankruptcy estate minus exemptions. If the client has a child(ren), the portion that pertains to the Child Tax Credit may be exempt under state law.

6 U.S.C. 11 §548(e)(1).

Remember, these are standard questions the client is likely to be asked by the trustee. These basic questions lead to more detailed questions and confirm whether bankruptcy is the right option for the client.

SUMMARY

When consulting with clients, you will learn to be inquisitive while at the same time being empathetic. Your interviewing skills will improve with each and every client until it becomes second nature to you. Ask questions to classmates so that you both become more comfortable with the fact-finding process. When you review the bankruptcy intake, you will see how the intake outlines the questions you'll be asking clients.

KEYWORDS AND TERMS

- Bankruptcy intake
- Forbearance
- IRS Living Standards
- Year to date (YTD)

DISCUSSION QUESTIONS

1. Does your state allow for exemptions for the Earned Income Child Tax Credit? If so, how much?

SECTION 1: MARITAL STATUS

Name, Married/Single, Spouse Filing, or Non-Filing

While most of the information in the intake is self-explanatory, it provides key information that could affect the bankruptcy case.

The first issue to consider is the marital status of the client. A married debtor must include spousal income as part of means testing, even if the spouse isn't filing for bankruptcy. This makes qualifying more difficult because of the combined incomes. If the parties are separated, only the filer's income is included. However, be careful of situations involving separation. For example, an astute client may have previously consulted with a bankruptcy attorney and confirmed he didn't qualify for Chapter 7 and the monthly payments for Chapter 13 were too high. So now the client is "separated," and the spouse's income is excluded. This is another reason I ask clients if there have been consultations with a prior attorney, and if so, was bankruptcy discussed or another legal issue. For example, if the client consulted with an attorney about divorce, the bankruptcy could likewise be affected.

Marital separation is fact-based. Some states recognize legal separation, and there may be a written agreement to that effect. Confirm the date of separation and evidence to support the claim, such as a change of address with bills, driver's license, voter registration, residential lease, etc. Expenses listed on the intake should be reflected in bank statements. Are there children born of the marriage? If so, is the client receiving/paying child support? Is the child support court ordered? Is the separation recent? It's not likely that a client that separated from a spouse a week ago would be consulting with a bankruptcy attorney instead of a divorce lawyer. These are just some of the questions that should be asked to confirm the separation and avoid potential issues with the trustee.

If the client is divorced, obtain a copy of the *final judgment* and *marital settlement agreement* since the trustee requests divorce-related documents dating as far back as five years. Next, review the agreement for how assets were divided, especially since assets may become non-exempt. If the client is married but will be filing for divorce, additional fact-finding is required.

Depending on the situation, it may be to the client's advantage to file for bankruptcy after divorce, and sometimes a joint filing needs to be considered. For example, if the parties are married, there may be no issues on exemptions for homestead property in their state. However, if the parties are getting divorced and the marital home will be sold, the net proceeds will likely exceed the exemption limits. As a result, the client may have to purchase a new home to protect the net proceeds under the homestead exemption or file for Chapter 13. Remember, just because an asset is exempt today, it doesn't mean it will be exempt tomorrow, especially if the form of that asset changes. Retirement accounts and 401ks are good examples. It's common for a client to have withdrawn money from a retirement account during times of financial difficulty, but once those funds are deposited into a personal account, the exempt status is lost.

If exempt assets are not an issue and the clients don't qualify for Chapter 7 as a married couple but do single, then the divorce should be finalized first. That's why timing is always critical when it comes to filing for bankruptcy. Sometimes the best course of action is the passage of time: the more time that has passed by, the better. Other times, a filing may have to be sooner than later.

From a strategical standpoint, if the divorce is litigated, it may also be to the client's advantage to file bankruptcy after the divorce is finalized. For one, litigated divorces aren't cheap. Outstanding fees owed to the debtor's divorce lawyer are dischargeable. However, fees owed to the ex-spouse's attorney are not dischargeable if the fees are related to litigation regarding child support and/or alimony. *Domestic support obligations* also aren't dischargeable, and neither is debt from a property settlement agreement in a Chapter 7 case. However, with Chapter 13, the debts from the property settlement agreement are unsecured and will be discharged at the end of the case. If the marital debt is an issue, but the debt is titled solely in the client's name, the client can offer to assume the debt, settle the case quicker, and proceed to file for bankruptcy, avoiding a lengthy and costly divorce.

Address Information

Compare the address listed on the intake to documents and photo identification provided by the client, as different addresses could lead to potential problems. Confirm why the mailing address differs from the residential address.

One common reason is that the client rented their homestead property. While the client may be claiming homestead for purposes of reduced real estate taxes and property insurance premiums, they shouldn't unless they are residing on the property. Only homestead property can be claimed exempt in bankruptcy, and the exemption amount is subject to the laws of that state. In this case, the debtor would have to file Chapter 13 to protect the equity in the property or return to the property after claiming homestead for that year. The client's bills should be received at their homestead property, and there should be no forwarding address.

The client may also have different addresses for purposes of convenience. For example, the client is renting temporarily and uses a family member's home as a mailing address. That's fine but again, confirm there is no real estate owned or transferred by the client.

Social Security Number

Mistakes do happen, so always compare the Social Security number listed on the intake and petition to the tax returns and original Social Security card. If the tax returns have the incorrect Social Security number, have the client amend the tax returns before filing.

At the creditors' meeting, the trustee will compare the original Social Security card to the Social Security number listed on the petition. If the numbers do not match, the hearing is continued in order to amend the petition. This requires the additional step of notifying the three major credit reporting bureaus that a bankruptcy was filed with an incorrect Social Security number. This small mistake will result in attending another hearing plus additional time spent working on the case that the law firm is unlikely to be compensated for.

Because of COVID-19, the Meeting of Creditors is taking place telephonically, although the trustee has the option of in-person hearings.[7] For telephonic/virtual hearings, the trustee will require copies of the debtor's driver's license and Social Security card between seven to ten days before the hearing. Some trustees prefer that attorneys confirm the Social Security number and debtor's address match.

Household Members

Members of the family, friends, and renters residing in the household should never be overlooked. Because we live in the age of the internet, trustees have access to mountains of information with a few strokes of the keyboard. Paralegals and attorneys should ask questions in detail more than ever because situations will arise that no one would have reason to know or guess in advance, and clients may not consider it an issue.

7 U.S. Department of Justice, Local 341 Meeting Status, retrieved March 9, 2021, www.justice.gov/ust/Local_341_Meeting_Status.

REAL CASES

The trustee asked the debtor who person "x" is who resides in his house. If that person lived in my client's home, financial contributions and expenses should be reflected in the schedules. In this case, it was the client's sister-in-law, but she never resided at the debtor's home even though she had an automobile registered to his address. The sister-in-law's car was actually driven by my client's son, who added the aunt as the policyholder to obtain a cheaper premium on his car insurance. Once the trustee mentioned insurance fraud, my client became nervous. It didn't take long for the trustee to figure out that my client provided the cash deposit to his son to purchase the car, resulting in a 2004 Examination.[8] The case settled quickly for the amount of the deposit, but my client also had to pay additional attorney's fees. Had I known of other members of the family registered to the same address, steps could have been taken in advance to remedy the situation, saving my client a substantial amount of time and money. As a result of that case, I started asking clients additional questions about everyone residing at their address, including those who don't but receive mail at their home.

Clients should always be asked about any financial contributions received, whether by someone residing in the home or not. Household contributions usually are from parents/in-laws, adult children, or renters. That's why reviewing the client's bank statements is imperative. For example, a client may list auto insurance as an expense on the intake for multiple cars. However, that expense isn't reflected in the bank statements because another household member pays the premiums. If the client is claiming a $200 monthly expense that's paid for by someone else, once that expense is removed from Schedule J, there's $200 in disposable income available.[9] While the client may have passed the means test, Chapter 13 would be required because of the $200 in disposable income.[10]

Besides expenses, review bank statements for consistent deposits that are non-work related. For example, the premium amount is deposited into the client's bank account instead of a household member paying the insurance premiums directly. Likewise, that would have to be reflected in the schedules. The same applies to a roommate situation. In this case, clients should list their actual expense(s). For example, if rent is $1,000, but the client is only responsible for half, then $500 is listed as the expense for rent.

Income and expenses are usually combined for married debtors, so the total amount of household expenses is calculated. Remember, even for a single filer that's married, the non-filing spouse's income is used in Schedule I and the means test.[11] However, domestic partnerships are treated differently. That's why clients should be asked if they are legally married. In domestic partnerships, the non-filing partner's income is not used in the means test but is for

8 Fed. R. Bankr. P. 2004.
9 Official Form 106J. Schedule J: Your Expenses (Individuals).
10 Supra, note 1.
11 Official Form 106I. Schedule I: Your Income (Individuals). Official Form 122A-1. Chapter 7 Statement of Your Current Monthly Income.

Schedule I because it's a household contribution.[12] How these adjustments are made and how they affect a bankruptcy will be reviewed later in the text.

Dependents

Always compare the dependents listed on the bankruptcy intake to those on the client's tax returns. For example, it's common for in-laws/parents to be listed as dependents on the intake and not the tax returns or vice-versa. Usually, the claimed dependents don't even reside in the household, a red flag. Unless the family members moved in recently, don't include the additional expense unless verified. Confirm the dependents' address on the driver's license matches that of the client. Other forms of proof include receiving mail and bills at the client's home. If there are transfers of money, even if the expenses are verified, the trustee could object because of the reduced amount of available disposable income. There could also be issues of preferential treatment and fraudulent transfers. Take my hometown as the perfect example.

In Miami, with a large Cuban population, many residents provide financial support to family members in Cuba by wiring money via Western Union. Usually, this wouldn't reflect in bank statements since the client has saved cash over time. But, if there are consistent and substantial withdraws, especially with services such as Western Union, filing should be delayed until the client can provide "clean" bank statements. Preferential treatments and fraudulent transfers will be discussed in a later chapter.

PRACTICE TIP AND REAL CASES

The majority of attorneys have paralegals complete the bankruptcy intake for the client because of productivity reasons, but that is a practice I advise against because of the potential for liability. The form by itself is simple enough to fill out, where it shouldn't be an issue for clients. But, there's a fine line between assisting the client and completing the intake. The latter could result in liability for the firm for any mistakes. Case in point, only one time in my career did I complete the intake for the client, a mistake I almost paid for dearly.

Concerned about making mistakes due to vision problems, my elderly client pleaded with me to fill out her intake. Of course, I rejected my client's request several times but, feeling sympathetic, I eventually caved in and completed the intake with the client at the office. Big mistake!

At the Meeting of Creditors, my client was questioned about real estate transferred to a family member two years earlier. Even though the property was mortgage-free, that alone would not have prevented my client from qualifying for bankruptcy because if the transfer had not taken place, my client still qualified for Chapter 7. However, my client was now residing in a second property that was also mortgage-free. The first property was not listed

12 Id.

in the *Statement of Financial Affairs* (SOFA) because I wasn't aware of it, and as a result, the trustee filed for a 2004 Examination.[13]

At that point, it became obvious to me that the client likely consulted with another attorney who advised to wait two years before filing bankruptcy, as that is the question asked in SOFA. But trustees routinely go past the two-year period if allowed by state law. Thus, while the case concluded favorably, I would not have been as concerned had the client completed the intake without my assistance. Pressed for time with other clients waiting, I even told my paralegal I would complete the form because I would get it done quicker. But that brief lapse in judgment and policy, at the minimum, could have resulted in a bar complaint, or worse, a malpractice suit.

My preference is and continues to be for the client to fill out the intake at home. My experience is that clients feel rushed and pressured when meeting with a bankruptcy attorney and to expect them to complete the intake correctly is wishful thinking. If anything, have the client complete the intake alone in the conference room and check in with the client to confirm if they have any questions.

When the potential for liability exists, the attorney and paralegal should take the necessary precautions, including requiring a written response from the client. If the answer is satisfactory, then proceed as usual. If not, the client should sign an acknowledgment.

REAL CASES

Once I represented a party in a divorce case whom I suspected transferred all of the marital assets to the spouse to qualify for bankruptcy. That advice should never be given to a client, but another law firm was handling the client's bankruptcy. All the business debts were in my client's name because the client had excellent credit. I advised the client that the future ex-spouse stood to eliminate all financial liabilities while at the same time leaving my client destitute. The client understood the situation and signed an acknowledgment that was prepared in the client's own words. The short acknowledgment stated that I had advised against signing the agreement as it was not in the client's best interests.

PRACTICE TIP

Experienced attorneys know to commence working on a file immediately upon being retained, and the reason why is simple: economics.

Refund requests are common, even if it's the client's fault the case hasn't progressed. For that reason, it's vital to stay in regular contact with clients. Emails are the best form of communication, in my opinion, because they remain in the sent box for years and can be easily accessed.

13 Official Form 107. Your Statement of Financial Affairs for Individuals Filing for Bankruptcy (Individuals). Fed. R. Bankr. P. 2004.

While every Retainer Agreement is explicit that fees are non-refundable, that's not true.[14] For example, suppose a client hired the attorney and initiated the case with a $1,000 retainer, only to call the following morning to cancel the case. Even though the bankruptcy is a flat-fee case and fees are non-refundable, the attorney did not do $1,000 worth of work. Otherwise, a bar complaint would focus on excessive fees. If work was done on the client's case, the attorney is entitled to compensation for the work performed. Sometimes clients have legitimate reasons to terminate their case. At other times they don't, such as finding a lower-priced attorney.

Other situations that may present themselves are beyond your control, such as the COVID-19 pandemic. Clients may not have received their stimulus checks or were furloughed, and now desperate for cash, they contact the office requesting a refund, stating they don't wish to proceed with their case. Again, just make sure to begin working on the file as soon as possible and document the work done. Clients aren't likely to understand the amount of work involved in preparing a bankruptcy petition, including additional time-consuming steps such as scanning and organizing documents, calculating the means test, and communicating with the client and creditors.[15]

It should become common practice to keep track of time spent on the case with a *billing statement*. If there is a reimbursement issue, the billing statement confirms the amount of time spent working on the client's file. Since bankruptcy cases are flat-fee cases, it's unlikely that a client will ever see the billing statement or even request one. Chances are, most lawyers don't even use one, even though it's common for other types of cases such as divorces because of hourly billing. However, a billing statement or another form of time-keeping provides instant feedback on the work performed to date. For example, a client may respond that document requests were complied with, but a quick review confirms that specific documents have been requested several times.

Note, it's important to distinguish between fees and costs. Costs are always refundable as that is not fees earned by the attorney. Costs are deposited into the trust account. If reimbursement includes a portion of fees and costs, the client should receive one check from the trust account (costs) and a second check from the firm's operating account (fees). Failure to keep adequate trust accounting records is why most attorneys get disbarred. Attorneys should never allow staff access to their trust accounts.

Bar rules require attorneys to keep a ledger of fees and costs paid by a client. However, there is no set format or accounting procedure on how this is done, just so long as it's done. For example, one attorney I know keeps track by writing it down on the client's intake. Another colleague has a separate file folder with ledgers of all clients. I prefer to simply create a table in Word and save it as part of the client's document folder.

In Table 7.1, fees and costs are in designated columns, including the date payments were made. As the paralegal, you will be handling payments received from clients, so it's

14 See Chapter 28 for a sample Retainer Agreement.

15 Supra, note 11, Official Form 122A-1.

TABLE 7.1 Client Ledger

Date	Fees $1,100.00	Costs $400.00
3/9/21	500/600	
3/19/21	600/0.00	
3/30/21		200/200
4/15/21		200/0.00

important to keep adequate records. A client's ledger also serves as a guide because once the balance has been paid, it serves as a reminder for the client to enroll in credit counseling.

SUMMARY

Each section of the bankruptcy intake should be reviewed carefully. If there is any doubt, seek clarification from the client. Also, to avoid issues, it's recommended the client complete the intake. Clients should also be given the option to complete the intake in their own handwriting or receive a copy via email in Word format if they prefer to type in the information.

Keeping track of billing or time spent working on a file is essential as it provides several key functions that assist the paralegal and attorney. For one, it gives a quick summary of the work performed. The attorney can make sure that cases are being worked on and keep track of files that have gone stagnant or are too time-consuming. It also helps organize cases for the paralegal who needs to move cases along quickly and efficiently. Finally, the lawyer can justify fees if there is a refund request.

KEYWORD AND TERMS

- Billing statement
- Child support
- Clean bank statements
- Dependents
- Domestic partnership
- Fees versus costs
- Final judgment
- Fraudulent transfer
- Homestead exemption
- Homestead property
- Household members

- Marital settlement agreement
- Preferential treatment
- Property settlement agreement
- Refund request
- Retainer Agreement
- SOFA (Statement of Financial Affairs)
- Trust account

DISCUSSION QUESTIONS

1. In the initial consultation, you remember the client stating he was in the process of divorce. However, in the bankruptcy intake, the client lists his marital status as "single." You have requested confirmation from the client of the divorce, but the client fails to provide a final judgment of dissolution of marriage or the marital settlement agreement. What steps should be taken to avoid any mistakes with the bankruptcy petition?
2. The client provides credit card statements and collection letters. The address on the credit card statement is different from the address listed on the intake and is also different from the address listed on the driver's license. What issues does this present, and what steps must be taken with the client to confirm their residence?
3. Your client states in the consultation that the bankruptcy is for him and his wife. No other household members are listed, but the credit report shows the client has three car payments. What questions should you ask the client?
4. The client is separated from her spouse and confirms that her ex-husband will soon file for divorce. However, the client appears at the office with someone you believe is the boyfriend. Is this relevant? How could the client's new relationship affect the case?

PRACTICE QUESTIONS AND EXERCISES

1. While software programs exist that help with billing, create your own billing statement, whether in a Word document or Excel. Include the following categories: date, work performed, and time spent.
2. Now that you've completed the billing statement, add work done on the client's file on five different dates and list any potential issues.
3. The client has decided not to file for bankruptcy and requests a full refund of $700. Based on the information in the billing statement, prepare a letter or email that will be sent to the client regarding the refund request.
4. Research the clerk of court's records in your county to find a final judgment of dissolution of marriage and a marital settlement agreement to supplement the client's file. Search for any information in the agreement that may affect the bankruptcy filing and highlight it for the attorney to review.

5. The client's marital status on the bankruptcy intake is "separated." Prepare an email requesting additional information from the client. In this exercise, forward the email to a classmate who should respond and vice-versa.

SECTION 2: RESIDENCY REQUIREMENTS

Residency requirements apply in every case in the law, and it's no different with bankruptcy. For this reason, you cannot assume because a client is consulting with you that they meet the residency requirements to file in that specific district.

For example, in the Southern District of Florida, rarely did I ever face a residency issue. However, residency is an issue in more than 50 percent of my cases in the Middle District of Florida, which includes Jacksonville. Clients have relocated from neighboring states, especially Georgia, or are in the military working at the Naval Air Station. With members of the military, they may be residing in Florida temporarily. Therefore the laws of their state may have to be applied. Sometimes, they own real estate in other states, so the homestead exemption doesn't protect their property. Depending on the equity in the house, Chapter 13 may be the best option unless the client wishes to surrender the property.

In what jurisdiction a debtor files for bankruptcy depends on the client's residence, domicile, principal place of business, or where assets are located. Two dates must be considered per 28 U.S.C.§1408. The first date is where the client has resided during the last 180 days (six months). The second date is the previous 730 days (two years).

To distinguish between residency and domicile, you must look at the debtor's intent, an important distinction. A client may reside in one place while their domicile is in another state. For example, consider a professional athlete who owns a home in the city where his team is located. This is where the athlete resides during the season, but he returns to his hometown in the off-season, which is located in another city, maybe even state. In this case, the athlete's hometown is his domicile, even if he has homes in multiple states. Therefore, residency could be in multiple states, but domicile can only be in one state. To simplify, domicile is where your permanent home is.

To determine which district is proper for the client to file the bankruptcy petition depends on where the client has resided during the last 180 days or most of that time. Once that has been established, the next step is to determine which state exemptions apply.

To avoid forum shopping, which means "shopping" for a favorable jurisdiction, BAPCPA requires that the debtor resides in that state for two years, known as the 730-day test, to claim the exemptions of that state. If the debtor has not resided in that state for at least 730 days, the debtor would have to apply the exemptions of the state he previously lived in.

For example, referring again to military service members, the client is now residing in Jacksonville, Florida, where he's stationed. The first question is, where has the client lived the most in the last six months or 180 days. If the client has resided in Jacksonville, Florida, for 91-plus days, the venue is appropriate in Florida's Middle District. If not, the case would have to be filed where the client resided previously. See Figure 7.1. Assuming the client meets the residency requirements, the next issue is which state exemptions are used. The answer to that question depends on where the client has resided for the last 730 days (two years). If the client was residing in North Carolina during this time period, even though the client is now residing in Florida, the exemptions of North Carolina are used. See Figure 7.2.

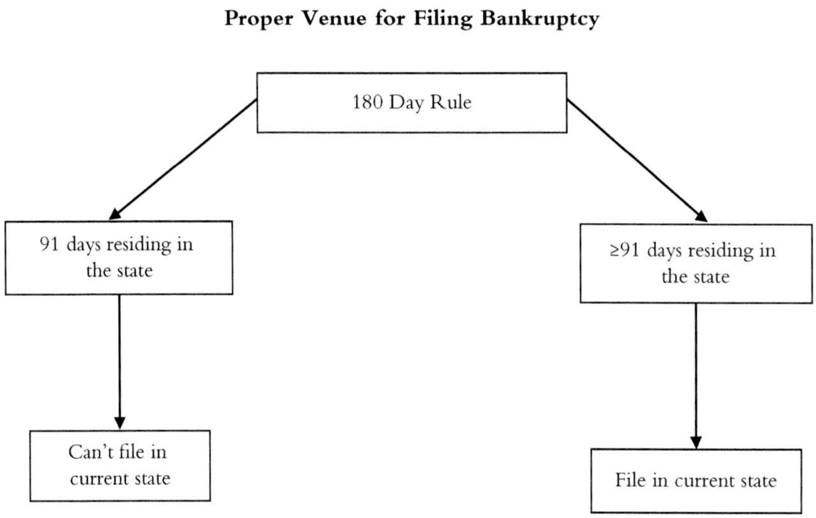

FIGURE 7.1 Determining venue based on the 180-day rule.

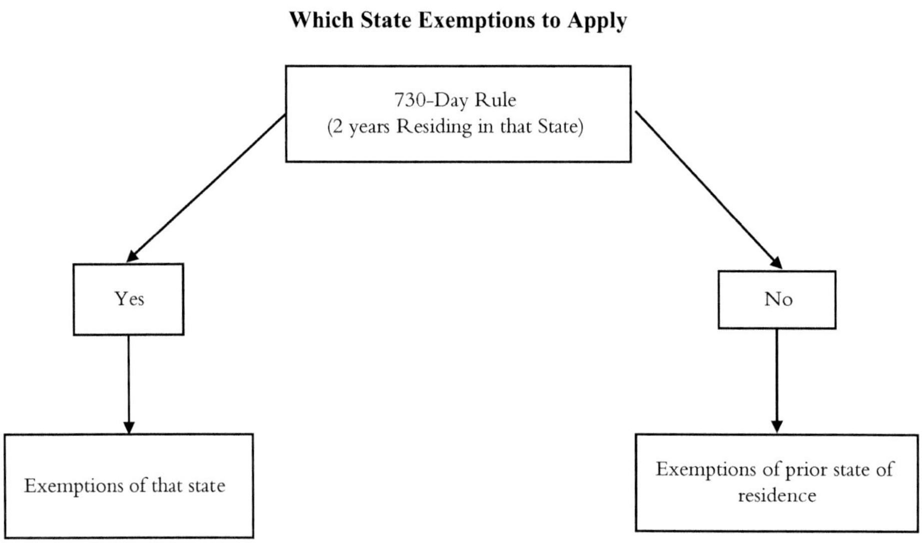

FIGURE 7.2 Applying exemptions based on the 730-day rule.

The final issue is: when does the client file for bankruptcy? The answer to that question depends on which state offers exemptions most beneficial to the client. For example, in Florida, there is no exemption provided for "tools of the trade," while in North Carolina, the exemption is a maximum of $2,000.[16] If the client owns a landscaping business and has equipment that may exceed the exemption limits, it would be more favorable to the client to file bankruptcy within the two-year period while living in Florida or file while still residing in North Carolina.

SUMMARY

Before any case is filed, the first question is what jurisdiction is appropriate? In bankruptcy, jurisdiction is based on where the client has resided mostly during the last six months. Once established, the next question is which state exemptions to apply. The answer to that question depends on where the client has resided for the last 730 days (domicile).

The distinction between residency and domicile is essential because a client can reside in multiple states but only have one domicile. Likewise, a client may have relocated to the jurisdiction recently or even temporarily. If so, a debtor may file for bankruptcy in the jurisdiction he has resided in most of the last six months but would have to apply the exemptions of the state he resided in previously because of the 730-day rule.

KEYWORDS AND TERMS

- 180-day rule (six-month rule)
- 730-day rule (two-year rule)
- Domicile
- Forum shopping
- Residency
- Venue

DISCUSSION QUESTIONS

1. What is the purpose of residency requirements?
2. Describe the difference between residency and domicile.

PRACTICE QUESTIONS AND EXERCISES

1. Carla the Celebrity hasn't made a movie in years and is now considering filing for bankruptcy. Carla resides in Spearfish, South Dakota, during the summer months, and winters in Daytona Beach, Florida. What questions would you ask Carla to confirm her residency and domicile?

16 N.C. Gen. Stat. Ann. § 1C-1601.

2. Carla's only asset of substantial value is her car, valued at $15,500.00, for which the loan was paid off last year. Which state offers a higher exemption amount to protect her vehicle? Florida? South Dakota? Or your state? Summarize the amounts for each state.
3. If Carla owned a home in Florida, South Dakota, or your state, which state provides a higher exemption for homestead property? Summarize the amounts for each state.

SECTION 3: DOMESTIC SUPPORT OBLIGATIONS

Domestic support obligations (DSO) relate to alimony and child support obligations.[17] They include debt accrued before, on, or after the bankruptcy petition has been filed and are recoverable by the spouse, former spouse, the debtor's child, legal guardian, or governmental unit.[18] Domestic support obligations are non-dischargeable debts.[19]

Domestic support obligations are given priority status in relation to payments of claims.[20] This means if non-exempt assets belong to the bankruptcy estate, before unsecured creditors such as a credit card company are paid, a priority claim is paid first. Also, the *automatic stay* does not apply to support obligations.[21]

If a client has a pending domestic support obligation, request documentation to confirm the amount being paid and the balance, if any, since it may affect the case. Whether the debtor pays or receives child support and/or alimony, it's included in Schedule I.[22] See Figure 7.3.

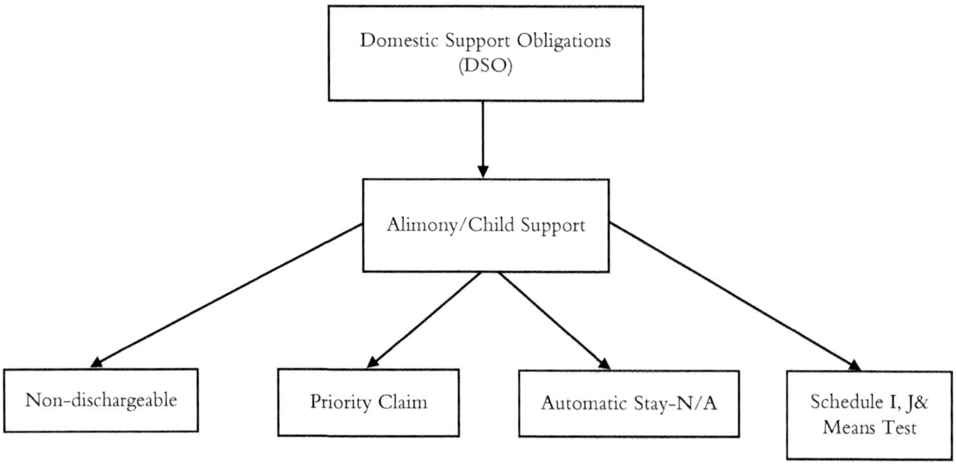

FIGURE 7.3 Domestic support obligations (domestic support obligations are non-dischargeable and the automatic stay doesn't apply. DSO are listed in Schedule I, J, and the means test).

17 11 U.S.C. §101(14)(a).
18 Id.
19 11 U.S.C. §523(a)(5).
20 11 U.S.C. §507(a)(1).
21 11 U.S.C. §362(b)(2).
22 Supra, note 11.

KEYWORDS ANDTERMS

- Alimony
- Child support
- Domestic support obligations (DSO)
- Priority claims

DISCUSSION QUESTIONS

1. Why would the automatic stay not apply to cases related to family court?
2. What is a priority claim?
3. In reviewing the bankruptcy intake, the client listed $400 per month in child support as an expense. What documentation should you request from the client?

PRACTICE QUESTIONS AND EXERCISES

1. Complete a domestic support obligation form.
2. Upon separation from his spouse, the client started paying child support each month. The client's bank statements confirm this expense. However, no case has been filed, and the $400 is an informal agreement between the parties. Is this an issue? Write an email to the client regarding this situation.
   a. Explain how this affects the domestic support obligation order form.
3. Summarize the different types of priority claims under §507.
4. You receive an email from your client that includes a copy of two garnishment orders. One court order is for child support, and the other one is from a credit card company. The client wishes to file for bankruptcy to stop the garnishment. Write back your response to the client.

SECTION 4: PRIOR BANKRUPTCIES

If the client filed for bankruptcy previously, confirm the date and outcome of the case. Clients rarely have the date correct, so it's best to perform a quick search on PACER with the client's Social Security number, which should be done anyway as part of due diligence.

Review the court docket. Confirm if the case was dismissed or discharged, as this will affect a subsequent filing. If the case was dismissed, the first question is when, and the second question is why? A dismissed case requires a 180-day waiting period (prejudice period) before filing a subsequent bankruptcy.[23] However, the six-month prejudice

23 11 U.S.C. §109(g).

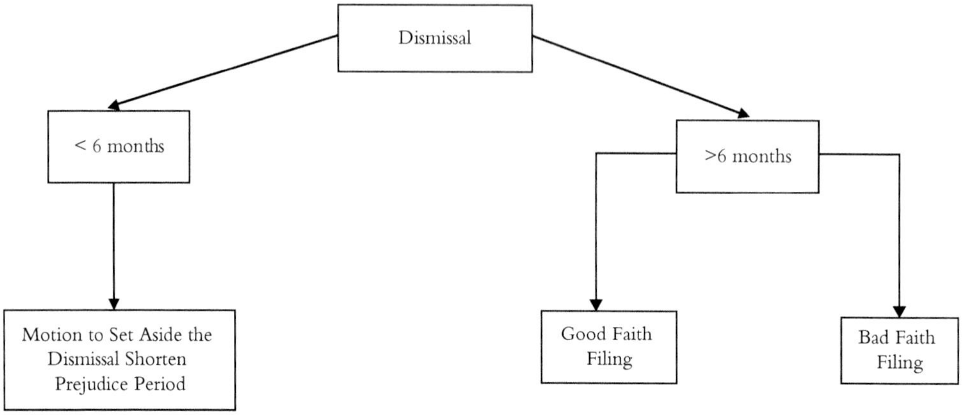

FIGURE 7.4 Dismissals and the six-month prejudice period (dismissals last for six months unless a shorter time period is approved by the court, so long as it is a good faith filing).

period can be shortened upon a motion and hearing before the bankruptcy judge. If granted, the original case continues.

The "why" is important because the issue is a good faith versus bad faith filing. For example, the debtor failed to complete the financial management course or never filed the certificate. For Chapter 13 cases, it's usually because the debtor stopped making payments. These are examples of a good faith filing, but if the debtor is taking advantage of the *automatic stay*, that's a bad faith filing. See Figure 7.4.

With BAPCPA, the waiting period increased for a debtor to refile for bankruptcy. Therefore, the following date restrictions apply for subsequent bankruptcy filings.

Chapter 7

1. The discharge couldn't have been received for a Chapter 7 within eight years.[24]
2. The discharge was received in a Chapter 13 case within six years with the following exceptions:
   a. The debtor paid 100 percent of the unsecured creditors.[25]
   b. The debtor paid back 70 percent of the unsecured debt and
      (1) the proposed plan was done in good faith and
      (2) best efforts were made to comply with the plan.[26] See Figure 7.5.

24 11 U.S.C. §727(a)(8).
25 11 U.S.C. §727 (a)(9).
26 11 U.S.C. §727 (a)(9)(B)(i) and (ii).

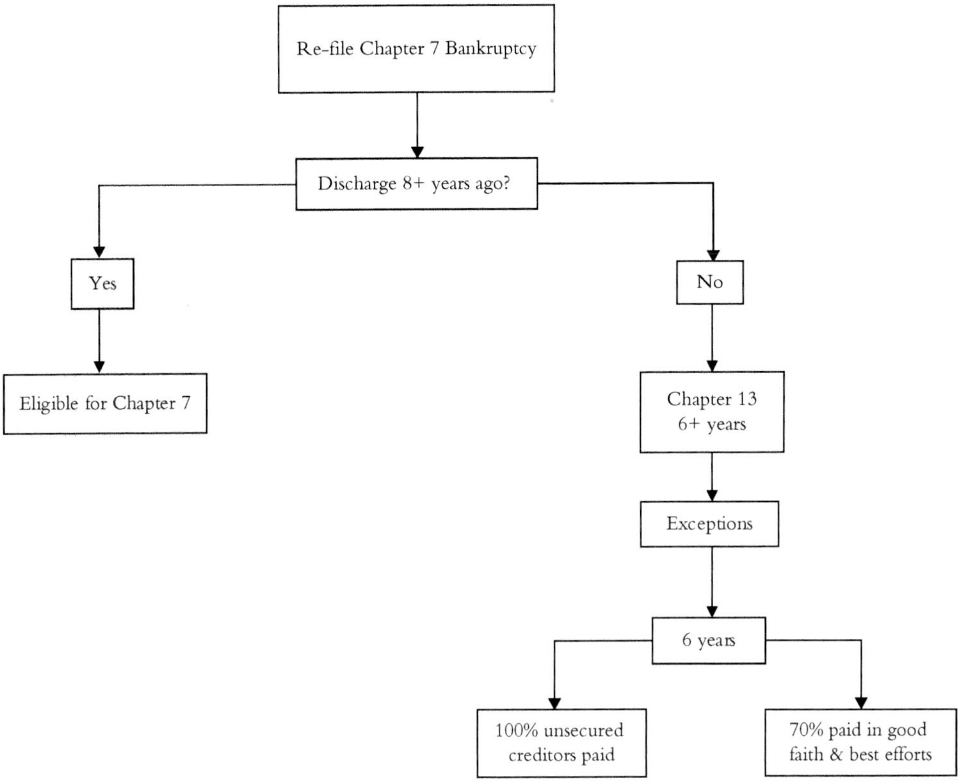

FIGURE 7.5 The time period to refile a Chapter 7 after a discharge has been granted (a debtor can file subsequent bankruptcies, depending on the date of discharge).

Chapter 13

1. To be eligible for a second discharge in Chapter 13, the previous Chapter 13 discharge was received more than two years ago.[27]
2. There wasn't a prior discharge in Chapter 7, 11, or 12 within four years.[28] See Figure 7.6.

27 11 U.S.C. §1328 (f).
28 11 U.S.C. §1328 (f).

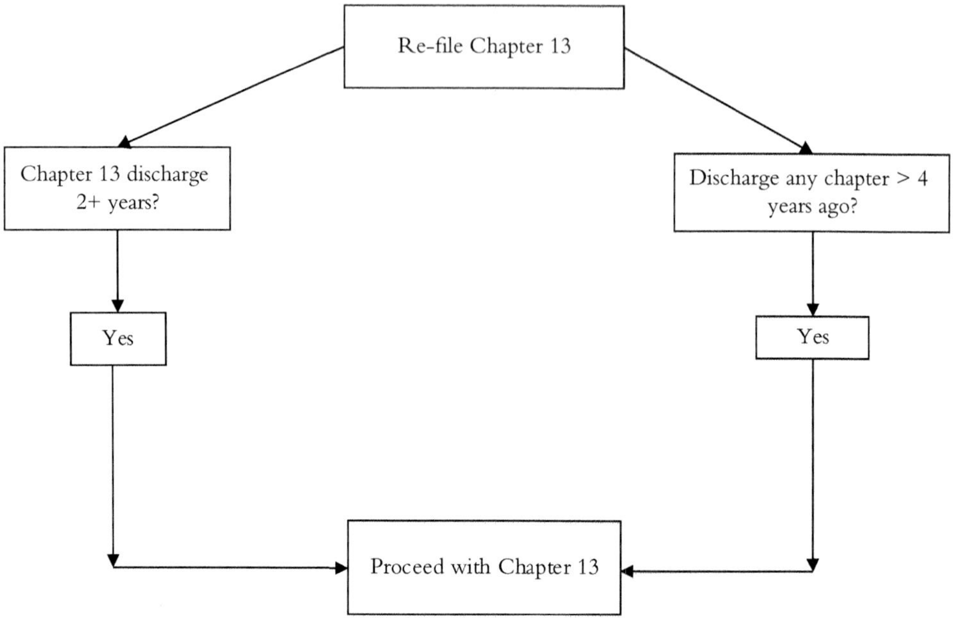

FIGURE 7.6 Time restrictions to file Chapter 13 (a debtor can file a subsequent Chapter 13 if the first one was more than two years ago).

SUMMARY

When qualifying a client for bankruptcy, confirm if there have been prior bankruptcies. If so, when was the case closed? Was the case dismissed or an *Order of Discharge* received?

If dismissed, there is a six-month waiting period before the debtor can refile unless the bankruptcy judge shortens the prejudice period. This would depend on the facts of the case and whether the subsequent filing was done in good or bad faith. If the debtor received a discharge, then the specific time frames of BAPCPA must be complied with since there is no judicial discretion to shorten the waiting period.

KEYWORDS AND TERMS

- 180-day rule for dismissals
- Bad faith filing
- Good faith filing
- Prejudice period

DISCUSSION QUESTIONS

1. What is the difference between a dismissal, a discharge, and non-dischargeable debt?
2. If a Chapter 7 case was dismissed on December 15th, 2015, when can the debtor refile for Chapter 7 and 13? What if it was discharged?

PRACTICE QUESTIONS AND EXERCISES

1. Search for either a Chapter 7 or 13 case in your district using PACER. Review the docket; was a discharge entered?
2. If a discharge was entered, when can the client refile for Chapter 7 and Chapter 13?
3. Danny the debtor failed to appear for the *341 Meeting of Creditors* because he was confused about the dates. Prepare a motion to set aside the dismissal and shorten the prejudice period for a Chapter 7 bankruptcy.

a. Same set of facts as in Question 3, but Danny the debtor's Chapter 13 was dismissed for failing to make a payment. However, Danny now has sufficient funds to bring the plan current. Prepare a motion to set aside the dismissal.

4. Provide a brief explanation based on the local rules in your district on how to schedule a motion to set aside the dismissal.

SECTION 5: CRIMINAL HISTORY

While it may seem odd to worry about someone's criminal history for bankruptcy purposes, debts related to a criminal act are not dischargeable. Even if this section is left blank by the client, in reviewing the creditors listed at the end of the intake, look for individuals listed as creditors, auto insurance companies, or government agencies. The following list includes non-dischargeable debts related to criminal acts:

1. Debts related to a fraudulent tax return.[29]
2. Debts incurred by false pretenses or false representation.[30] This includes debts incurred to a single creditor for more than $500 in luxury goods or services incurred within 90 days of filing for bankruptcy or cash advances that total more than $750 within 70 days of filing for bankruptcy.[31] This is why clients should always be asked about recent credit card use and cash advances.

29 11 U.S.C. §523(a)(1)(C).
30 11 U.S.C. §523(a)(2)(A).
31 11 U.S.C. §523(a)(2)(C).

3. Debts related to embezzlement, theft, or fraud while acting in a fiduciary capacity.[32]
4. Debts related to a "willful and malicious injury by the debtor to another entity or to the property of another entity."[33]
5. Debts related to any "fine, penalty, or forfeiture" that is owed to a governmental unit that "is not "compensation for actual pecuniary loss."[34] If the due date is more than three years old, the return was filed within two years, and the assessment was more than 240 days ago, then the taxes are dischargeable.[35]
6. Debts related to personal injuries or death caused by driving under the influence, including motorboats and planes.[36]
7. Debts that were a final judgment, unreviewable order, consent order, or decree issued by a federal depository agency resulting from fraud, and where the debtor was acting in a fiduciary capacity.[37]
8. "Malicious or reckless failure to fulfill any commitment by the debtor to a Federal depository institutions regulatory agency to maintain the capital of an insured depository institution."[38]
9. Debts related to violations of security laws.[39]

KEYWORDS AND TERMS

- DUI
- Embezzlement
- Forfeiture
- Fraud
- Willful and malicious injury

DISCUSSION QUESTIONS

1. While reviewing the list of creditors, your client lists a debt with an individual and an insurance company. What questions should you ask the client?
2. Ten years ago, John was convicted of felony burglary. Once out of prison, he started his own business that was thriving, but due to the pandemic, he had no choice but to file for bankruptcy. Does his felony conviction prevent him from receiving a discharge?

32 11 U.S.C. §523(a)(4).
33 11 U.S.C. §523(a)(6).
34 11 U.S.C. §523(a)(7).
35 11 U.S.C. §523(a)(7)(B).
36 11 U.S.C. §523(a)(9).
37 11 U.S.C. §523(a)(11).
38 11 U.S.C.§523(a)(12).
39 11 U.S.C.§523(a)(19).

PRACTICE QUESTIONS AND EXERCISES

1. Based on the facts listed in Discussion Question 1, write an email to the client asking what the debts are related to.
2. The client responds that the debts are related to a car accident. Respond with follow-up questions.

REFERENCES

11 U.S.C. §101.

11 U.S.C. §109.

11 U.S.C. §362.

11 U.S.C. §507.

11 U.S.C. §523.

11 U.S.C. §548.

11.U.S.C. §707.

11 U.S.C. §727.

11 U.S.C. §1328.

28 U.S.C. §1408.

Fed. R. Bankr. P. 2004.

N.C. Gen. Stat. Ann. § 1C-1601.

Official Form 106I. Schedule I: Your Income (Individuals).

Official Form 106J. Schedule J: Your Expenses (Individuals).

Official Form 107. Your Statement of Financial Affairs for Individuals Filing for Bankruptcy (Individuals).

Official Form 122A-1. Chapter 7 Statement of Your Current Monthly Income.

Official Form 122A-2. Chapter 7 Means Test Calculation.

U.S. Department of Justice, Local 341 Meeting Status. Retrieved on March 9, 2021. www.justice.gov/ust/Local_341_Meeting_Status.

CHAPTER **8**

Bankruptcy Intake Continued

SECTION 6: REAL ESTATE

A debtor must list all assets and liabilities in the petition, including all forms of real property. As previously mentioned, compare the addresses listed on the debtor's identification and documents. Confirm the client resides in the homestead property and that the exemption protects the equity. So, the date of purchase, mortgage balance, and property's fair market value are required. Remember, exemptions don't protect additional real estate, so Chapter 13 is required unless the client plans to surrender the property.

Besides residing in the property, it's essential to know what type of property the client owns. For example, a duplex or vacant lot isn't protected, nor is a converted home to produce rental income. If the conversion was done legally and the client obtained permits, that information is available publicly and likely known by the trustee.

If there was a recent sale of real property, confirm the amount of the net proceeds. As discussed in the previous chapter, if there is a divorce case pending, net proceeds aren't likely to be exempt unless the client uses the funds to purchase a new home within the same state.[1] Even if the new property is mortgage-free, the client's property is protected if the total equity amount is below the exemption limits. Otherwise, the client would be obligated to proceed with Chapter 13 and pay back the unexempt amount within 36 to 60 months.

If a prior home was sold and another one purchased, confirm the sale and purchase dates and the equity in the second home. For example, Florida offers unlimited homestead protection, but there are domicile requirements.[2] To prevent persons from moving to Florida simply to shield their assets and take advantage of Florida's generous homestead exemption, BAPCPA requires owning the property for at least 1,215 days (40 months), and the equity is capped at $170,350 unless state exemptions allow for a greater amount.[3] Therefore, in Florida, even if the home is mortgage-free and worth $300,000, so long as the purchase date

1 11 U.S.C.§522(p)(2)(B).

2 Fla. Const. Art. X, § 4(a)(1) limited to ½ acre within a municipality or 160 acres of contiguous land if outside of a municipality.

3 11 U.S.C.§522(b).

DOI: 10.4324/9781003203278-9

exceeds 1,215 days before filing for bankruptcy, the homestead exemption protects the total amount of equity. If the equity is less than the exemption limits, the home's equity is protected. The exemption amounts are adjusted on April 1 every three years.[4]

SUMMARY

An important fact to always consider is that exempt property can become non-exempt if the asset changes form. Therefore, if the client is considering selling the house or a divorce case is pending, the net proceeds determine the next step.

KEYWORDS AND TERMS

- Capital gains taxes
- Homestead protection
- Net proceeds

DISCUSSION QUESTIONS

1. What are the homestead exemption limits in your state?
2. Your client moved out of the marital home during a litigated divorce and purchased a new home with $35,000 in funds from a recent inheritance. Her husband continues to reside in the marital property and has been making the mortgage payments. Mediation is scheduled for next month, and the client believes the case will settle. What questions should you ask your client?

PRACTICE QUESTIONS AND EXERCISES

1. The client owns a timeshare and cemetery plot. How does this affect the case? Prepare an email to send to the client regarding these issues.
2. Draw a diagram similar to Figure 8.1, with your state's homestead exemption requirements.

4 11 U.S.C.§104.

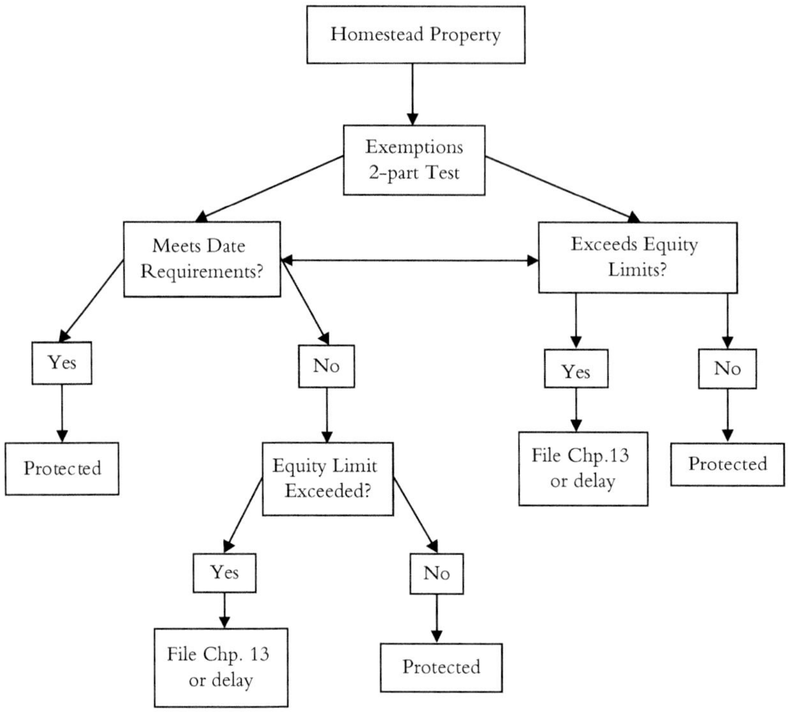

FIGURE 8.1 Homestead exemptions (for homestead property to be protected, depending on the state's exemption limits and when the property was purchased).

SECTION 7: MORTGAGES

With mortgages, first, confirm the client is current with payments. If not, Chapter 13 will allow for the client to catch up with the arrears. Remember, with Chapter 7, secured debts must be current unless the client is surrendering the property.

Next, confirm creditor contact information. Upon filing a bankruptcy petition, the clerk sends notice to all creditors listed in the schedules. If an address is incorrect, the clerk will require that it be updated. This is significant because the lender may require a *Reaffirmation Agreement* yet didn't receive notice of the bankruptcy filing.

Since exemptions vary by state, compare the mortgage balance to the home's fair market value to determine the equity. The most recent mortgage statement will provide the loan balance and the monthly payment amount and state whether taxes and insurance are escrowed.

If the debtor has a second mortgage or home equity line of credit (HELOC), confirm the amount borrowed and how the funds were used. For example, a client may have used the second mortgage or HELOC funds to pay off credit cards and other debt, but the client now owes x amount in credit cards and unsecured loans. If that's the case, the issues are when the previous debts were paid off, during what period of time the new debt was incurred, and how the funds were spent. While there is no specific amount of debt or time frame by statute or otherwise to determine when to file, I may advise a client to wait x amount of time. The same would apply to a refinance of a first mortgage. Note that if the second mortgage results in the house being worth less than what is owed, Chapter 13 may reduce the balance on the second mortgage. So, even if a client wasn't considering Chapter 13, the pros and cons should be discussed. Strategies involving lien stripping will be reviewed later in the text.

If the client is elderly, inquire about non-traditional mortgages such as the popular reverse mortgage. Again, the issues are when the funds were received and how the funds were spent. For example, during the real estate boom of the early 2000s, homeowners were cashing out with second or reverse mortgages and purposefully going into foreclosure. Since this may be considered fraud, question the client and request additional documentation if need be. Finally, be cautious of situations where clients became indebted because of home remodeling.

SUMMARY

A mortgage is a secured debt that cannot be eliminated with bankruptcy unless the client surrenders the property. This needs to be explained since clients sometimes believe all debt is eliminated. Clients are confused because they have heard of "lien stripping," which can reduce or eliminate a second mortgage with a Chapter 13, an option not available in Chapter 7.

With HELOC loans, second mortgages, and reverse mortgages, review how the funds were spent, and within what time frame.

KEYWORDS AND TERMS

- Home equity line of credit (HELOC)
- Lien stripping
- Mortgage
- Reverse mortgage

DISCUSSION QUESTIONS

1. The client filed for Chapter 7 three years ago and included the second mortgage on his homestead property in the petition. The client was recently served with a complaint for foreclosure by the second mortgage company. Explain to the client why.
2. Research the laws in your state. Can a mortgage lender sue a homeowner on a deficiency judgment because of foreclosure?

PRACTICE QUESTIONS AND EXERCISES

1. In consulting with the client, you find out the following:
   a. The homestead property has approximately $125,000 in equity.
   b. The client used the funds from a HELOC to pay off his car and $15,000 in credit card debts six months ago.
   c. The client is considering Chapter 7 bankruptcy and owes $17,000 in credit cards.
2. In writing a case summary for the attorney, mention the issues listed above and answer the following questions.
   a. Is the equity in the homestead property protected in your state?
   b. Is the equity in the car protected?
   c. What is required to strip the HELOC?
   d. Any issue(s) regarding the credit cards being paid off six months earlier and the current amount owed on credit cards?
   e. Would it matter if the client was paying off medical bills?
   f. Mention any other issues you consider relevant.

SECTIONS 8 AND 9: TAXES AND INSURANCE

Reviewing the most recent mortgage statement will determine if the taxes and insurance are escrowed, meaning included in the mortgage payment. If not, make a notation so that the taxes and insurance are calculated separately in *Schedule J*.[5] Request the client's insurance and property tax bill. Note the property tax bill is usually available online through the county property appraiser's website.

If the client pays property taxes and insurance annually, divide the total amount by twelve for a monthly total. If the client pays insurance quarterly, four times per year, divide the total amount by three to calculate the monthly amount or multiply by four and divide by twelve. Failure to do so will result in incorrect figures on Schedule J.[6]

Examples

Property taxes equal $1,000 annually.

$1,000/12 = $83.33 monthly.

Quarterly insurance payments of $250.

$250 × 4 = $1,000/12 = $83.33 or $250/3 = $83.33.

5 Official Form 106J. Schedule J: Your Expenses (Individuals).
6 Id.

Also, depending on the location of the property, there may be flood insurance as well. While flood insurance premiums are relatively low and paid annually, it's still an expense listed on Schedule J.[7]

Note that for purposes of the *means test*, when a client's income exceeds the state median level, additional information is required on secured debts that may help a client pass the means test.[8] Therefore, exact figures on the mortgage, property taxes, and insurance are needed. For example, how many months/years are remaining on the loan, and what's the balance? Most of the time, taxes and insurance are escrowed, but if they are not, and the expenses aren't included in the calculations, the debtor's expenses are underreported, which would not only affect Schedule J, but may prevent the client from passing the means test.[9] Examples with and without secured debt will be worked on in our sample petition later in the text.

SUMMARY

When the client owns a home and lists a mortgage on the bankruptcy intake, review the most recent mortgage statement to determine if taxes and insurance are escrowed and calculate accordingly. Whether an automobile or mortgage loan, secured debt will help a debtor pass the means test, so exact figures are needed.

KEYWORDS AND TERMS

- Escrow
- Insurance premiums
- Mortgage statement
- Property taxes

DISCUSSION QUESTIONS

1. When reviewing the client's documents, you notice the taxes and insurance aren't escrowed, and the client is behind on his property taxes. How does this affect bankruptcy?
2. Because of a robust real estate market, the client's property increased substantially in value, and the mortgage statement reads an escrow shortage of $3,000. How does this affect bankruptcy?
3. Because of a weak economy, property values have plummeted 50% in the last year. If the client has an escrow, how does this affect the case?

7 Id.
8 Official Form 122A-2. Chapter 7 Means Test Calculation.
9 Supra, note 5 and id., note 8.

4. Harriet the Homeowner is paying $810 per month for her interest-only mortgage. What concerns should you have, and any follow-up questions for Harriet?

PRACTICE QUESTIONS AND EXERCISES

1. Harriet the Homeowner pays $1,175 per month for her mortgage, which doesn't include $2,824 in annual property taxes, $622 in quarterly insurance, and $569 in annual flood insurance. Calculate the total monthly expense that belongs on Schedule J.

SECTION 10: HOMEOWNER'S ASSOCIATION

Homeowner's associations or HOAs are important for several reasons when it comes to bankruptcy. For one, there is a monthly expense associated with an HOA, and that expense is listed in Schedule J.[10] Two, clients are often surprised that an HOA can initiate foreclosure proceedings. When facing financial difficulty, it's common for clients to pay their mortgage(s) timely since they are afraid to lose their home, but they stop paying their HOA dues. The HOA proceeds with a foreclosure action and now the client that qualified for Chapter 7 is left with no other choice but to file a Chapter 13 to cure the arrears.

Since an HOA or any other creditor for that fact can place a lien on real property, a lien search may be warranted prior to filing bankruptcy. It should also be noted that even though bankruptcy was filed, a lien will not be removed unless a successful motion to remove lien is argued before the bankruptcy judge or a stipulation is reached with the creditor. Sometimes a creditor that has already been paid in full has inadvertently left a lien on the property. This is common with roofing companies and contractors, and it's not until years later that the client finds out when selling the property or refinancing their mortgage. So be prepared as the paralegal to explain to past clients that the lawyer did not commit any mistakes by not removing the lien, especially since additional fees are required.

Also, note homeowners believe the myth that their homes are protected and, thus, judgment-proof. The typical response is, "they can't take away my home." That is correct, but that is a partial truth, and I experienced that personally.

On the day of closing on a house I was buying, the seller was convinced he was going to receive "x" amount in funds. Typically, the title company will perform a lien search on the day of the closing to confirm no last-minute liens have been placed on the property. In this case, the seller had tens of thousands of dollars in liens on his homestead property. The seller had county tax liens, utility liens, credit card judgments, and even one lien from the county for failing to renew his dog's rabies tag. The client stated he was canceling the sale of his house, and I had no choice but to remind him this would result in a breach of

10 Supra, note 5.

contract suit. In a rush, most of the liens were negotiated for a reduced amount, and the closing took place.

Clients fail to understand that maybe they won't lose their homestead property because of a lien in their state, but the debt doesn't magically disappear unless the client filed for bankruptcy. In addition, the lien accrues interest which is what happened to the seller in my case. Creditors do seek to enforce judgments. I only handled one probate case in my career as a favor to the client, and the utility company had filed a claim for $80 on the decedent's estate. I've also had clients who have had liens placed on their automobiles, bank accounts frozen, and even business assets seized, then sold at auction to pay off the judgment. Even one colleague of mine froze the assets of a well-known music band. He showed up just before a concert to seize the assets/equipment of the band. If there's no equipment, there's no concert, not to mention millions lost in a breach of contract lawsuit. He was paid on the spot. So never tell a client that a creditor is unlikely to enforce a judgment.

PRACTICE TIP

Being a paralegal or practicing attorney requires thinking outside of the box. As such, a successful paralegal or attorney will spot issues and work around those issues to the client's benefit since conventional wisdom won't always apply. Case in point, when the foreclosure crisis hit south Florida during the Great Recession, the courts couldn't keep pace with the number of case filings regardless of what actions they took. This included having retired judges assist in proceedings, increasing filing fees by thousands of dollars, and even having law students intern in the newly created foreclosure division.

The foreclosure process slowed considerably, to the point that homeowners resided in their homes between one to three years before the case was finalized. Meanwhile, not one payment was made on the mortgage, so homeowners lived for free in their homes. Even better, creditors rarely pursued a collection action against the client, and some states passed legislation prohibiting seeking deficiency judgments related to foreclosures. Hence, there was no motivation for homeowners to vacate their property.

However, even though the client stopped paying the mortgage, I always advised the client to continue to pay their HOA dues timely to avoid speeding up the foreclosure process. As long as the associations were receiving their monthly dues, whether the mortgage was being paid or not was of no concern to them. That's important because an association will initiate and finalize a foreclosure much faster than a lender. As a result of the foreclosure crisis, a new law was implemented in Florida that favored homeowner's associations, so it's important to remain current on the law and trends. A recent example is the CARES Act passed by Congress to provide financial relief during the COVID-19 pandemic. The stimulus checks were not counted as income for purposes of the means test or for Schedule I (Income).[11] This is important because not every client was furloughed. Many of my clients continued to work

11 S.3548-116th Congress (2019–2020): CARES Act. www.congress.gov/bill/116th-congress/senate-bill/3548.

as normal, so their income was not impacted, but at the same time, they received the $1,200 stimulus check. Had the stimulus funds been included in their calculations, a client would have been given the erroneous advice that they didn't qualify for Chapter 7 unless the filing was delayed or the plan payments for Chapter 13 are increased.

Since homeowner's associations depend on dues to maintain the property, when owners stopped paying the dues during the foreclosure crisis, the upkeep of the property wasn't possible, and it wasn't long before the properties were in disrepair. There were endless media reports of associations that included utilities such as water in their monthly dues but could no longer afford to pay the utility fees. So condominium owners were left without access to water, penalizing the homeowners that were paying their monthly association dues and mortgages. Meanwhile, landlords were receiving rent but not paying the mortgage or association, and the tenant was unaware of the foreclosure until they received an order from the sheriff's office to vacate the premises. Some sheriffs faced contempt hearings for taking a moral stand against the court orders, arguing it was unjust to forcibly remove tenants that had no prior knowledge of the foreclosure and had a moment's notice to vacate the property or face trespassing charges. Initially, mortgage lenders would serve homeowners at their registered address, not the address of the foreclosed home, so the tenant wasn't aware of the lawsuit. Life isn't always fair, especially in the world of creditors and debtors.

As a result, lenders started serving tenants as well, but there was still the issue of the property owner collecting rent while associations went bankrupt and tenants were forcibly removed from the property. In response, some states passed legislation to protect lenders, associations, and tenants.

For one, lenders began to visit properties to confirm if there were tenants or if the property was abandoned. Lenders also sought that the rent monies were paid directly to them versus the landlord, and the lease was honored. Therefore, if six months remained on the lease, the tenant would continue to rent the premises as usual, and instead of rent payments being sent to the landlord, it was sent to the lender. If the foreclosure remained pending, lenders extended the lease. HOAs were also given special consideration under the Bankruptcy Code under 11 U.S.C. §523(a)(16).[12]

If the client owns a condominium, a cooperative corporation, or a lot with a homeowner's association, the client can discharge all debt accrued pre-petition. However, whether it's the debtor or the trustee that has a "legal, equitable, or possessory ownership interest in such unit, such corporation, or such lot," the debtor continues to be liable for association fees post-bankruptcy. Reread that last sentence and let that sink in.

If a client files for Chapter 7, all dischargeable debts are eliminated. If the client is in foreclosure proceedings and files for bankruptcy, we know that the *automatic stay* kicks in and stops the foreclosure, but the creditor can file a motion to lift the stay. During the foreclosure crisis, clients remained in their home until the lender took possession of the property." But upon receiving a discharge, the debtor was no longer responsible for the balance due on the mortgage. However, imagine if the mortgage lender took their time in foreclosing on the

12 11 U.S.C. §523 (a)(16).

property and sued the client for each month of the mortgage after the bankruptcy was filed. Sounds possible? Of course not, unless it's a homeowner's association.

Under §523(a)(16), a debtor is not responsible for the accrued pre-petition debt, but is post-petition. So even if the client filed for bankruptcy on January 1, come February 1, one month of association dues are owed even if the client no longer resides in the property. If the lender is delayed in finalizing the foreclosure for whatever reason, every month that passes, the client is responsible for another month of dues. Does this sound fair or logical? Not at all. But when advising the client, the potential pitfalls with homeowner's associations need to be explained.

However, the debtor still has options, and that's when thinking outside of the box is helpful. While I did receive calls from attorneys representing HOAs that demanded payment for post-petition accrued fees, I had two arguments I made on behalf of my clients. First, the amount owed was usually minimal, so I would advise the HOA attorneys it wouldn't make financial sense to file lawsuits to collect the balance. In addition, a collection action would make even less financial sense if there were no assets to seize. My final argument was that in the worst-case scenario, I could reopen the bankruptcy to include the debt. To my knowledge, no HOA proceeded against my clients.

SUMMARY

Remember to advise debtors that homeowner's associations are given special treatment under the bankruptcy code and that HOAs also have the power to initiate foreclosure proceedings. Debtors should be advised to continue paying their association dues whether they are residing in the property or not.

If a tenant is served with a foreclosure action, the tenant should consult with an attorney and confirm the lender will honor the lease terms.

KEYWORDS AND TERMS

- Deficiency judgment
- Homeowner's association
- Mechanic's lien
- Motion to remove lien
- Probate
- Underwater mortgage

DISCUSSION QUESTIONS

1. In consulting with the client, he states he is surrendering his home since the mortgage is "underwater." The lender already began foreclosure proceedings, and the client moved

out of the property and into a rental. What issues need to be addressed with the homeowner's association?

PRACTICE QUESTIONS AND EXERCISES

1. Draft a motion to remove lien, citing a lien by a collection agency and a mechanic's lien placed by a roofing company for work completed nine years ago. The roofing company was paid in full at the time, and the business is no longer in existence.
2. Summarize the law on homeowner's associations and foreclosures in your state.

SECTION 11: OTHER PROPERTIES AND REAL ESTATE

Other than homestead property, interest in other real estate is not protected (non-exempt property). Therefore, any other property, including vacant land, timeshares, and cemetery plots, are listed in Section 11 of the bankruptcy intake. Take the time to explain to clients that this is non-exempt property as clients are usually surprised that timeshares and cemetery plots are considered real property.

Note, whether it is a vacant lot, timeshare, or cemetery plot, so long as the client agrees to surrender it to the trustee, the client can proceed with Chapter 7. If the client can afford to purchase the non-exempt portion outright or the trustee agrees to a ten-to-12-month payment plan, then Chapter 7 is possible, if not Chapter 13. Surrendering a cemetery plot(s) is usually an issue for elderly clients. However, clients are generally eager to surrender timeshares, and trustees usually abandon their interests since timeshares rarely have value or equity.

PRACTICE TIP

Time to think outside of the box. During the real estate boom of the early 2000s, many homeowners refinanced and cashed out their equity and bought a second property for investment purposes. However, the foreclosure crisis produced underwater mortgages, so homeowners let the second property go into foreclosure and then filed for bankruptcy. Since the means test includes calculations of all secured debt, clients earning \$100,000 plus per year easily qualified for Chapter 7 even though one or more houses were in foreclosure.[13] One of the flaws of means testing is the more secured debt a debtor has, the better, in essence, penalizing the debtor with less or no secured debt. I know, it doesn't make sense. Bankruptcy can be cruel. Regardless, even though the house was in foreclosure and clients weren't interested in retaining the property/properties, the secured debts resulted in debtors passing the means test when otherwise they wouldn't.[14] However, once the foreclosure process has been finalized, the secured debt becomes unsecured and serves no purpose for means testing. So, if a

13 Supra, note 8.
14 11 U.S.C. §707(b)(2)(A.)

client has one or more properties in foreclosure, calculate the means test with and without the secured debt.[15] If the secured debt is needed to pass the means test, file the bankruptcy before the completion of the foreclosure.[16] But, like the go-to line in infomercials, "but wait, there's more."

At the Meeting of Creditors, when a trustee questions the debtor about secured debt, whether an automobile or real property, the trustee will ask if the payments are current. Remember, if the client wants to keep an asset secured by a lien and the payments are in arrears, the client must file Chapter 13. Because the property was underwater, there's no equity, so the trustee abandons any interest. At this point, the property reverts to the mortgage holder. Here's where it gets interesting.

The housing market crash created surplus inventory. Banks are in the business of loaning money, not selling homes. Since the banks didn't want the property either, they negotiated with debtors to keep the house(s) by reducing the mortgage balance at or near the property's market value. Now, the client eliminated not only unsecured debts but also kept non-homestead property. As a result, another area of law became saturated overnight, however brief.

Attorneys were now modifying mortgages, an option that was rarely available before the mortgage crisis. Lenders were so desperate to avoid foreclosure that lawyers even routinely negotiated a deed in lieu of foreclosure, which meant that the mortgage holder was now paying homeowners to vacate the property. It was cheaper than litigating a case for two years or more. Suffice to say, this scenario had never presented itself before, and time will tell if it happens again.

SUMMARY

Timeshares and cemetery lots are considered real estate, so it's non-homestead/non-exempt property. Since timeshares rarely have equity and are difficult to resell, trustees generally abandon any interest unless the timeshare is paid off. On the other hand, cemetery plots usually have value and are commonly surrendered to the trustee. If the client wishes to keep either, Chapter 13 may be necessary. Note that it's difficult to assign a value to either one, and timeshare companies and the funeral service providers usually are of no help.

KEYWORDS AND TERMS

- Cemetery plots
- Deed in lieu of foreclosure
- Mortgage modification
- Timeshares

15 Supra, note 8.
16 Supra, note 15.

DISCUSSION QUESTIONS

1. Why are timeshares and cemetery lots considered real estate?
2. In reviewing your elderly client's bank statements, you see an automatic withdrawal each month in the amount of $50 for J.B.'s Funeral Home. The client also has a timeshare in the Dominican Republic. What questions should you ask your client?
3. The client you consulted with for Question 2 returns two years later and is ready to file for bankruptcy because of a lawsuit filed by a creditor. What questions do you ask the client now about the timeshare and cemetery plot?
4. With the same set of facts, the client states that the cemetery plot was sold. The timeshare was returned to the lender. What are your follow-up questions?
5. If the cemetery plot was sold to a family member, what additional questions should the client be asked? What if the cemetery plot was sold back to the funeral service provider?

PRACTICE QUESTIONS AND EXERCISES

1. Prepare an email to send to the client regarding the value of the timeshare and cemetery plot.
2. Explain to the client how the value of the cemetery plot and timeshare may affect the bankruptcy case.

SECTION 11(A): AVOIDANCE POWERS AND TRANSFERS OF PROPERTY

Remember the client that transferred real estate to a family member within two years of filing bankruptcy? Because of the trustee's avoidance powers, a *2004 Examination* was scheduled to investigate the issue further.[17] This section will focus on the power of the bankruptcy trustee in these situations.

The Avoiding Powers of the Trustee

The bankruptcy trustee has what is known as avoiding powers. Simply defined, the trustee has the power to "avoid" certain transactions that, but for bankruptcy, are generally valid. For example, imagine two proud parents deciding to transfer the family car to their daughter as a graduation gift. That seems innocent enough and normal in the real world, but it's a problem in the world of bankruptcy. In that case, the trustee has the power to "avoid" the transfer. The concept is simple enough: fairness in protecting creditors. It wouldn't be fair that a debtor can simply transfer an asset to a family member or trusted individual to protect

17 Fed. R. Bankr. P. 2004.

it from creditors. That's the purpose of exemptions, to protect assets to a certain extent and give debtors the opportunity for a fresh start.

The avoiding powers of the bankruptcy trustee are as follows:

- Strong-arm clause
- Preferential transfers
- Fraudulent transfers
- Post-petition transfers

Strong-Arm Clause

Under 11 U.S.C., §544, known as the strong-arm clause, refers to the trustee's power over the bankruptcy estate.

1. §544(a)(1): The trustee has lien authority above any creditors.
2. §544(a)(2): The trustee has the authority to avoid transfers pre-filing even if there is an actual creditor who would also have that same power.
3. §544(a)(3): The trustee has the power of a bona fide purchaser of real property, and thus the interest to "buy" assets from the estate that is superior to that of any other bona fide purchaser.

Preferential Treatment

When comparing the different types of transfers, consider that a preferential transfer is considered innocent. In contrast, a fraudulent transfer is deemed sinister since there is an intent to hide assets. A preferential transfer may be regarded as valid, depending on when the transfer took place. The value of the asset is also of significance.

Preferential transfers are governed by 11 U.S.C. §547, giving trustees the power to avoid payments or pre-petition transfers made to a creditor during the probationary period. Under §547(b), a preference occurs when:

- There is a transfer of property that belonged to the debtor.
- The transfer was for the benefit of a creditor
- On the account or debt of the debtor.
- The transfer occurred within 90 days of the petition filing or one year if the transfer is to an insider.
- The transfer occurred while the debtor was insolvent.
- The creditor received a greater return on the debt had there been a distribution of assets.

Because of the potential issue of preferential treatment, clients should list payments made to creditors within the last 90 days of $600 or more.[18] But this is based on the date of filing. So,

18 11 U.S.C. §547(b).

if the debtor files bankruptcy four months later, then a total of seven months has passed since the last payment. However, if the client paid back a personal loan to his friend, in this case, the 90-day rule doesn't apply. Instead, it's one year since the friend is considered an "insider." An insider is defined as a relative of the debtor or general partner of the debtor.[19] Preferential treatments with insiders are common during tax season, where the client uses the refund to pay back a friend or family member. Transfers are detailed in the *Statement of Financial Affairs* (SOFA) and include domestic support obligations.[20]

Fraudulent Transfers

With fraudulent transfers, the trustee will avoid or undo the transfer since there is an intent to hide assets.[21] A simple example was a client who "forgot" to mention the transfer of his boat that was worth a substantial amount of money. Everything seemed fine since not even the trustee knew about it. At the end of every Meeting of Creditors, a trustee will always ask if any creditors are present, which is rare if there are. If no one is present, the trustee adjourns the meeting and proceeds to the next case.

However, in my case, when the trustee asked if there were any creditors present, a woman stood up and nervously approached the trustee. "Who is she?" I asked my client. When I heard his answer, I knew my client was in trouble. "My ex-girlfriend."

She advised the trustee a few months earlier that he transferred the boat to his best friend. She showed the trustee photos on her phone that the client had posted on Facebook the day before. Of course, it looked like he was having the time of his life on the boat with a female companion. At that point, the trustee shifted his focus to me, and before he had a chance to make a statement, I said I knew what to do.

I stepped outside the hearing room to discuss with my client his options, which were none in reality since he had just committed bankruptcy fraud, a federal offense. Before starting every calendar, this particular trustee even had the habit of pointing at the signs behind him on the wall that provided bullet points on the penalties for fraud. He would then mention cases he was involved in where debtors were imprisoned for fraud. My client was advised to deliver the boat and title to my office by the end of the day. Luckily, my client only lost the boat and avoided criminal prosecution.

As a general rule, preferential treatment dates back two years. But, I wouldn't depend solely on that time frame because it depends on the asset's value. For example, if the client transferred his car to his son and the car is worth $700, it's not a concern. But, if he transferred a Ferrari, I'm very concerned.

19 11 U.S.C. §101(a)(31).
20 Official Form 107. Your Statement of Financial Affairs for Individuals Filing for Bankruptcy (Individuals).
21 11 U.S.C. §548(a)(1)(A).

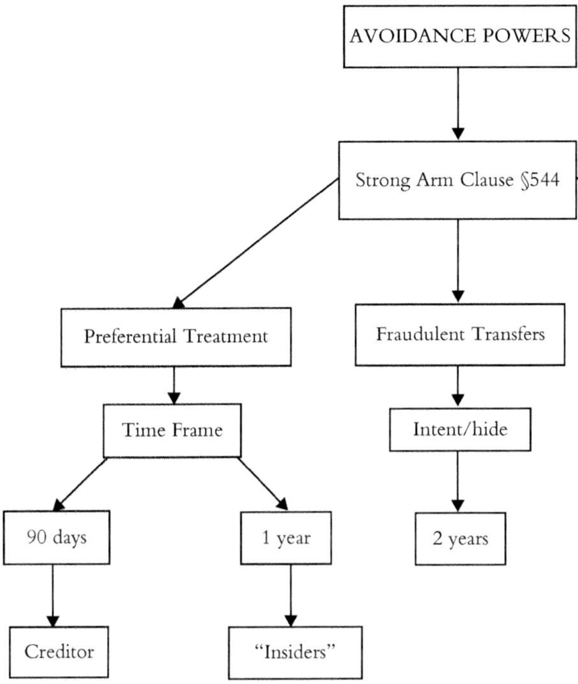

FIGURE 8.2 The trustee's avoidance powers (the bankruptcy trustee has the power to void transactions that are fraudulent, or when preferential treatment was given to a creditor or insider, including post-petition transfers).

Post-Petition Transfers

Post-petition transfers are governed by 11 U.S.C. §549 and apply in three situations. The first type of post-petition transaction that can be avoided is when the bankruptcy court does not previously approve it.[22] The second type is for involuntary bankruptcies and cites 11 U.S.C. §303(f).[23] The third and final type of post-petition transfer applies to a bona fide purchaser of real estate who had no prior knowledge of the bankruptcy.[24] See Figure 8.2.

SUMMARY

Trustees have the power to void transactions to protect the bankruptcy estate from being depleted. The strong-arm clause lists three scenarios: preferential transfers, fraudulent transfers, and post-petition transfers.

22 11 U.S.C. §549(a)(2)(B).
23 11 U.S.C. §549(a)(2)(A).
24 11 U.S.C. §549(c).

For preferential transfers, trustees look at transactions within 90 days of the filing date and one year if the transfer involved an "insider." With fraudulent transfers, there is an intent to hide or defraud. Finally, post-petition transfers apply after the bankruptcy filing. Situations include transfers without court approval, in an involuntary bankruptcy proceeding, or a bona fide purchaser of real estate who did not know of a bankruptcy filing.

KEYWORDS AND TERMS

- Avoidance powers
- Fraudulent transfers
- Post-petition transfers
- Preferential transfers
- Strong-arm clause

DISCUSSION QUESTIONS

1. Upon receiving a tax refund, your client paid back his brother $3,000, funds he had received to use as a deposit to buy a car. The tax refund was received on February 5 and his brother cashed the check on February 15. Discuss any issues.
2. With a divorce pending, your client sold his motorcycle to a friend, valued at $15,000, for $13,500, needing the money to move out of the marital home, hire a divorce attorney, and pay three months of child support in advance. Six months later, he's at the office. Discuss any issues.
3. Use the same set of facts as for Question 2, except that the motorcycle was sold for $2,000.

PRACTICE QUESTIONS AND EXERCISES

1. Write a short exam question involving preferential treatment that includes three creditors. Then, have a student in the class answer your question and vice-versa.

SECTION 12: AUTOMOBILES

All automobiles owned or leased will be listed in this section, even if the client isn't making payments since the client may be a co-borrower or co-signer. Owned and financed vehicles are listed in Schedule A/B as an asset and exempted on Schedule C.[25] Since there

25 Official Form 106 A/B-Schedule A/B: Property (Individuals), Official Form 106C-Schedule C: The Property You Claim as Exempt (Individuals).

isn't an ownership interest in a leased vehicle, it's listed in Schedule G as an executory contract.[26]

To determine a car's equity, compare the loan balance to the vehicle's fair market value. Kelley Blue Book (KBB) is a free online service that bankruptcy attorneys commonly use for vehicle valuations.[27] The National Automobile Dealers Association (NADA) is another excellent source.[28] If the car's value is too high, a client should consider an appraisal at a reputable local dealership since a detailed inspection will likely result in a lower value.

If the car will be surrendered (voluntary repossession), there should not be a monthly expense listed on the bankruptcy intake as that will affect calculations for Schedule J (expenses).[29] If the vehicle has been repossessed, the deficiency balance is listed as an unsecured debt.

If the client does not own or lease a vehicle, there could still be automobile-related expenses. For example, the client had a friend or family member obtain a car loan because of bad credit, but the client makes the monthly payments and pays for the insurance and maintenance costs. The expenses are listed in the petition with a notation that the client does not own the vehicle. Note that the client must be listed on the insurance policy and make sure there are no potential fraud issues by having the driver of the vehicle listed at the same address as the client if they don't reside together.

The opposite situation is when the client is responsible for the debt as a co-signer but a third party is making the payments. In that case, it's no different as if the client owns the car, except there is no expense to list, but the creditor's information is still listed. Calculations with multiple scenarios will be reviewed when you begin working on petitions.

SUMMARY

Before filing the bankruptcy petition, make sure to have the most recent statement for the client's car loan. Find out the value of the car with online resources such as Kelley Blue Book or NADA. If need be, have the client appraise the vehicle onsite at a reputable dealership.

Confirm if the debt is titled in the client's name, even as a co-borrower or co-signer. Distinguish between a third party making the payments versus the client making the payments but is not listed on the debt. If the vehicle is leased, remember there is no ownership interest. If the car has or will be repossessed, there is no monthly expense. If the client is still in possession of the car, the car is listed as secured debt, but if the client is no longer in possession of the vehicle, it's an unsecured debt.

26 Official Form 106G-Schedule G: Executory Contracts and Unexpired Leases (Individuals).

27 Kelley Blue Book. Retrieved June 16, 2021. Kelley Blue Book | New and Used Car Price Values, Expert Car Reviews. kbb.com.

28 NADA. Retrieved on June 16, 2021. www.nadaguides.com/.

29 Supra, note 5.

KEYWORDS AND TERMS

- Co-borrower
- Co-signer
- Executory contract
- Kelley Blue Book
- Lease
- NADA Guidelines
- Repossession
- Voluntary repossession

DISCUSSION QUESTIONS

1. The client has $7,500 worth of equity in the vehicle and responds: "but I need my car. They can't take my car. That's what I use to go to work. If I can't go to work, then I lose everything. If I file for bankruptcy, you are telling me I'm worse off than I am right now." How do you respond?

PRACTICE QUESTIONS AND EXERCISES

1. Appraise your car using both online sites mentioned in this chapter. What is the difference in value? Does the equity exceed the exemptions in your state?

SECTION 13: PERSONAL PROPERTY

The final section on assets focuses on personal property. Here, personal property is categorized, and like all other assets, the approximate purchase date and fair market value are listed. Clients typically struggle to assign a value to their assets, but a guesstimate is appropriate. A good barometer is garage sale value or popular sites such as Craiglist.com. However, be careful in undervaluing personal property. Some trustees use data analysis to determine the value of personal property based on the debtor's residential area.

Bank Accounts

When reviewing bank statements, skim through the transactions, looking for any substantial deposits, withdrawals, and/or expenses. Clients must provide at the minimum the last six months of bank statements and trustees request between six and 12 months. Note that the balance at the time of filing the petition is required. For this reason, petitions are reviewed the day before or the same day as the filing date. For bank account(s) closed within one year, ask about the amount of funds in the account at the time of closing and how the funds were used. Usually, the funds are transferred to the new account.

Don't leave the "cash on hand" section blank even if it's a minimal amount, as that only increases the trustee's skepticism. Be aware of clients paid in cash or that cash their checks, or work off tips, as the cash on hand amount should be higher than normal.

Jewelry

For the most part, clients don't possess expensive jewelry but have "costume jewelry" with minimal value. In that case, not every single piece of costume jewelry needs to be listed, just a combined value. Note that some trustees will require photos of the jewelry as part of the document request. If the client is married, confirm if there is a wedding ring and list the approximate value. Too many times at the creditor's meeting, trustees will start asking additional questions because the wedding ring wasn't listed, but the debtor is wearing one. The result is the trustee asking, "what else did you fail to list on the petition?"

PRACTICE TIP

Clients routinely list as creditors jewelry stores such as Kay Jewelers. When reviewing the credit report, confirm the date the debt was incurred. Also, compare the current balance to the original balance. Ensure the client made payments on the debt and not simply purchased an expensive piece of jewelry only to default on the payments immediately. In addition, confirm if the jewelry is still in the client's possession, if so, it's listed on Schedule A/B and exempted on Schedule C.[30] Remember, some trustees require credit reports as part of the original document request and will be analyzing the payment history.

For example, the client lists a $3,000 debt with a jewelry store, but the original debt amount was $15,000. In this case, substantial payments were made, but now the issue is the current value of the jewelry in case it's non-exempt. If the jewelry was sold, the trustee would inquire to whom, when, and the sale price to ensure there wasn't preferential treatment or a fraudulent transfer. Whether it's jewelry or any other asset, always inquire about when the asset was sold, the amount received, and how the monies were spent. Finally, remember that balances may increase artificially because of late fees and penalties.

IRA/Retirement Accounts

Even though a retirement account is exempt, it's an asset listed in the bankruptcy petition. Review recent statements to confirm funds weren't withdrawn, causing it to lose its exempt

30 Supra, note 26.

status. If the client borrowed against a retirement account, it's a secured debt and not dischargeable. Remember to deduct the expense.

Investment/Stocks/Bonds

A bankruptcy client is unlikely to have money invested in stocks and bonds, except for retirement accounts. However, clients sometimes do have a certificate of deposits (CDs) or mutual funds, and regardless of the amount, it needs to be listed, especially since this is non-exempt property.

Interests in a Corporation

Clients may have an interest in a corporation even though they are not active in the corporation. A typical example is a spouse who owns a business and lists the client as an officer of the corporation. Is the client merely an officer on paper or also assigned shares in the corporation? Since the corporation is an asset, what is the value of the client's share?

For example, the husband owns a landscaping business that includes a truck, trailer, and other equipment. If the client was issued shares that equal 50 percent of the business, what are the shares worth? Are the assets of the landscaping business secured by a lien that reduces the company's value, or is the business debt-free, pushing the bankruptcy estate past the exemption limits?

Other forms of a corporation, even informal, includes transactions, especially sales with online companies such as Poshmark, PayPal, Amazon, and eBay. Confirm the volume of sales and monies generated. Ask about social media accounts and posts showing the inventory. Just ask 50 Cent what happens when you boast about making $8 million in bitcoin, take photos with millions in cash, and post it on Instagram.[31]

SUMMARY

Always review the bankruptcy intake carefully as it provides a roadmap to potential issues with the bankruptcy. Documents should aid in filling in the blanks. If there is any doubt, the client should be asked to clarify.

The value of jewelry, household goods, and furnishings are based on fair market value. The client shall provide statements for all financial accounts, whether open or closed, even for exempt accounts such as retirement accounts, since withdrawn funds become non-exempt. At the time of filing, update the current balance on all financial accounts.

Financial accounts closed within one year of filing usually aren't an issue, but the client is required to provide the name of the bank, account number, the type of account, when

31 Jennifer Deutschmann. 50 Cent Denies Bankruptcy Fraud, Claims He Posed With Fake Money. March 10, 2016. *The Inquisitr*. Retrieved August 17, 2021. www.inquisitr.com/2874487/50-cent-2/.

the account was closed, and the balance. When possible, obtain bank statements from closed accounts.

KEYWORDS AND TERMS

- Craigslist.com
- Garage sale value
- Personal property

DISCUSSION QUESTIONS

1. Your client, the wife, tells you that she has signatory authority on her husband's business checking account and is listed in his corporation as an officer. What further questions should be asked of your client?
2. Your client passes the means test but withdraws his entire paycheck from his checking account every two weeks. What issues does this present?

PRACTICE QUESTIONS AND EXERCISES

1. The client stopped making payments two years ago on a debt with a current balance of $3,500. The creditor is a department store that also sells expensive jewelry. At the consultation, the client stated he sold his Rolex and used the proceeds to catch up on his mortgage. Prepare an email to the client regarding this situation.
2. Complete the corresponding sections in your bankruptcy intake. Include information with an online sales account.

REFERENCES

11 U.S.C. §101.

11 U.S.C. §104.

11 U.S.C. §303.

11 U.S.C. §522.

11 U.S.C. §523.

11 U.S.C. §544.

11 U.S.C. §547.

11 U.S.C. §548.

11 U.S.C. §549.

11 U.S.C. §707.

Fed. R. Bankr. P. 2004.

Fla. Const. art. X, § 4(a)(1) limited to ½ acre within a municipality or 160 acres of contiguous land if outside of a municipality.

Jennifer Deutschmann, "50 Cent Denies Bankruptcy Fraud, Claims He Posed with Fake Money", *The Inquisitr* (March 10, 2016). Retrieved on August 17, 2021. www.inquisitr.com/2874487/50-cent-2/.

Kelley Blue Book | New and Used Car Price Values, Expert Car Reviews. kbb.com.

NADA. www.nadaguides.com/.

Official Form 106 A/B-Schedule A/B: Property (Individuals).

Official Form 106C-Schedule C: The Property You Claim as Exempt (Individuals).

Official Form 106G-Schedule G: Executory Contracts and Unexpired Leases (Individuals).

Official Form 106J. Schedule J: Your Expenses (Individuals).

Official Form 107. Your Statement of Financial Affairs for Individuals Filing for Bankruptcy (Individuals).

Official Form 122A-1. Chapter 7 Statement of Your Current Monthly Income.

Official Form 122A-2. Chapter 7 Means Test Calculation.

S.3548-116th Congress (2019–2020): CARES Act. www.congress.gov/bill/116th-congress/senate-bill/3548.

CHAPTER 9

Bankruptcy Intake: Employment, Income, and Expenses

SECTION 14: EMPLOYMENT

In the employment section of the bankruptcy intake, confirm the employer information and that the income amount(s) match the last six months of pay stubs. If the client worked part-time jobs or gig economy jobs like Uber, Lyft, etc., likewise obtain the pay stubs and have the client complete the information, no matter how brief the employment was.

With gig economy jobs, there could be an issue with qualifying for bankruptcy. The extra income may not be an issue for purposes of the means test, but increases the disposable income available for Schedule I.[1] If so, the client will either have to file Chapter 13, use the extra funds to pay down the debt, or quit the gig economy job to qualify for Chapter 7. Usually, it's not going to make any sense for a client to file Chapter 13 just because of a gig economy job.

Similar issues present themselves when the client sells items online, as discussed in the previous chapter. If the client has accounts with popular sites such as Amazon, eBay, Poshmark, PayPal, Square, or CashApp, seek clarification to confirm if the client is selling items. Review the client's transaction history and ask about the inventory. For example, my sister-in-law recently started an online store, but sales are few and far between. However, she has substantial inventory and expensive products from when she worked for a high-end retailer. So, in her case, while there are no income issues, there are exemption issues. Likewise, if a corporation has been formed, review the business bank accounts.

Income Taxes

Tax returns present several issues, starting with when to file bankruptcy. It's common for trustees to begin asking about tax refunds at *341 meetings* in December.[2] Remember, a tax

1 Official Form 122A-1, Chapter 7 Statement of Your Current Monthly Income. Official Form 106I, Schedule I: Your Income (Individuals).
2 11 U.S.C. §341.

DOI: 10.4324/9781003203278-10

refund is based on income and an overpayment of taxes. The funds belong to the bankruptcy estate. Tax refunds typically push clients over the personal property exemption amounts. If the client expects to receive a large refund, the best option is to delay filing for a few months and spend the funds slowly on reasonable, ongoing expenses. If the filing can't be delayed, notify the client in writing that the trustee will likely keep the tax refund. Using prior returns as a guide will determine if the client is expecting a refund this time around.

Prior tax filings also provide a snapshot of the client's financial past. For example, if the client's income has remained consistent for the last three years, there's likely no concern for purposes of the means test.[3] However, what if the client has earned a six-figure income several years in a row and now there is a substantial drop in income, to the point the client's income is below the state median? There could be multiple valid reasons for the significant change in income, but ask the client for clarity as always.

SECTION 15: MONTHLY INCOME AND EXPENSES

Exact calculations with Schedule I and Schedule J will be reviewed in detail later when we prepare a bankruptcy petition, but for purposes of the intake, only an estimate of the client's income and expenses are needed.[4] Again, it is recommended that the client completes this section and the entire bankruptcy intake to avoid liability issues. Another reason is that as a paralegal, you will start to develop habits and patterns that will reflect in the bankruptcy petition. For example, you may begin listing $200 a month in fuel expenses for every client. When several bankruptcies are filed simultaneously and scheduled before the same trustee, the trustee will notice this and ask the attorney, "why do all your clients spend the same amount of money for gas?"

Note that clients tend to over- or under-exaggerate their expenses, so don't guide yourself solely by the amount the client lists. For example, you might see a client list $200 per month in clothing, yet $400 monthly for food for a family of three. Instead, use the IRS living standards built into the bankruptcy program to determine the maximum allowable amounts if need be.[5]

The expenses listed in the intake are not exhaustive but cover most household expenses. Note that there is no expense listed for credit cards. That's because the debtor should have ceased making credit card payments if proceeding with bankruptcy. During the initial consultation, confirm if there's disposable income available if the debtor stops making credit card payments. For example, suppose the debtor is currently making payments that total $500 per month. If the debtor stops making those payments, $500 per month would be available in disposable income, forcing the debtor towards Chapter 13. But as always, keep asking

3 Supra, note 1, Official Form 122A-1.
4 Supra, note 1, Schedule I. Official Form 106J, Schedule J: Your Expenses (Individuals).
5 U.S. Department of Justice. Census Bureau, IRS Data and Administrative Expenses Multipliers. www.justice.gov/ust/means-testing.

questions until you get a full picture. Maybe the debtor is receiving financial assistance from family to make up the difference or withdrew funds from a retirement account to make the payments.

Real Estate Taxes and Insurance

As discussed throughout this text, review the client's most recent mortgage statement to confirm if the mortgage payment is escrowed and if the payments are made monthly, quarterly, or annually to calculate the correct amount. Ask about other types of insurance as well, such as flood insurance.

Repairs and Upkeep on the Home

In this section, clients tend to exaggerate the actual cost of maintaining their homes. For example, a client may list $200 per month, but it's unlikely that amount is spent consistently. What typically happens is the client spent $200 recently and includes that as a regular monthly expense. Regardless of the expense, if it seems too high, it probably is. The reverse also holds true. Clients don't always know how much is spent monthly on household expenses, so guide yourself by the bank statements, the means testing tables on the Department of Justice website, and common sense.[6]

Health-Related Expenses and Insurances

Health-related expenses such as medical and dental out-of-pocket expenses are not to be confused with debt settlement payments or insurance. For example, even though a client has insurance, co-payments and prescriptions may not be covered under the policy. In addition, confirm the monthly expense is not medical debt based on a settlement. If the client has reached an agreement with a creditor regarding medical bills, payments should cease like any other unsecured debt. Medical debt like credit cards is unsecured debt and is listed in Schedule F.[7] Finally, confirm that insurance is not already deducted from the client's paycheck to avoid doubling the expense.

Installment Payments

Installment payments usually relate to secured debt such as a car but could apply to unsecured debts like personal and student loans. While student loans are generally non-dischargeable, payments on an unsecured personal loan should stop immediately.

6 Id.
7 Official Form 106E/F. Schedule E/F: Creditors Who Have Unsecured Claims (Individuals).

Domestic Support Obligations (Alimony and Child Support)

Even though alimony and child support obligations are non-dischargeable, the debt and the expense are listed in the petition. In addition, because of its priority status, the trustee's "avoidance powers" don't apply to the transfer of asset(s) made "to the extent such transfer was a bona fide payment of a debt for a domestic support obligation."[8]

Distinguish between court-ordered support and agreed-to support. For example, what if the parties agreed to an amount that exceeds the child support guidelines? Does it exceed the recommended amount by $25 or $500, and now the client has eliminated disposable income? Potentially, that could be the case, which goes back to confirming if the parties are separated and are not pretending they are for bankruptcy purposes.

SUMMARY

Clients must provide the last six months of paystubs, including any part-time work or gig economy job. Look for months where the client earned more income, whether because of bonuses, commissions, or overtime that may affect the means test or Schedule I.

With tax refunds, you're guaranteed that everyone who is expecting one has already made plans on how to spend it. Don't overlook this issue! If need be, either the client is willing to lose the tax refund because the filing can't wait, or it should be delayed to avoid being over-exempt. Remember, bankruptcy is about time; sometimes there's plenty of it, sometimes there isn't. Therefore, the facts of the case dictate best when the filing should occur.

Upon comparing the client's income to expenses and excluding credit card debt, is there disposable income available? If so, review the intake again and consult with the client to ensure all expenses have been included. Sometimes, clients inadvertently leave out certain expenses such as lawn maintenance, babysitting/daycare, pet-related costs, etc.

Finally, look for expenses that seem too low or high. While the expense may be accurate, err on the side of caution and discuss any possible issue with the client.

KEYWORDS AND TERMS

- Gig economy jobs
- IRS living standards

DISCUSSION QUESTIONS

1. The client's medical expenses seem high. What questions would you ask the client?

8 11 U.S.C.A. § 547(c)(7).

2. Each month, the client has withdrawn $200 from a checking account by a third-party debt collector. The debt is related to medical bills. What steps can the client take to stop making payments on unsecured debt?

PRACTICE QUESTIONS AND EXERCISES

1. While reviewing the intake, you notice the client received a tax refund last year of $4,400, and the year before $6,200. The client continues to work for the same employer. Draft an email that you will send to the client regarding this year's tax refund.
2. While reviewing the client's bank statements, you noticed two deposits last month; one deposit was for $75 and the other for $130, both from PayPal. Prepare an email addressing your questions or concerns.
3. Complete a domestic support obligation worksheet.
4. Complete the corresponding sections of the intake.

REFERENCES

11 U.S.C. §341.

11 U.S.C. §547.

Official Form 106I. Schedule I: Your Income (Individuals).

Official Form 106J. Schedule J: Your Expenses (Individuals).

Official Form 106E/F. Schedule E/F: Creditors Who Have Unsecured Claims (Individuals).

Official Form 122A-1. Chapter 7 Statement of Your Current Monthly Income.

U.S. Department of Justice. Census Bureau, IRS Data and Administrative Expenses Multipliers. www.justice.gov/ust/means-testing.

CHAPTER 10

Liabilities

SECTION 16: LIABILITIES

Section 16 focuses on specific information related to credit cards. Clients should provide recent credit card statements to compare to the credit report. This avoids overlooking information regarding specific purchases and transactions that aren't available on a credit report. For example, cash advances while on statements will not be in the credit report. Since cash advances may affect a bankruptcy, the intake requests the withdrawal date, the amount, and how the funds were used. Per the Code, cash advances cannot exceed $1,000 in the last 70 days.[1] In addition, the debtor could not purchase luxury goods or services in the previous 90 days where the value exceeds $725.[2]

Whether it's on vacations, cash advances, or major purchases, rather than consult with a bankruptcy attorney first, clients accept legal advice from friends and relatives or continue practicing Google Law and decide to max out their credit cards. To what extent the filing date is affected depends on how much was spent and when. If there has been a substantial increase in debt, the next question is why? Was the client unemployed, went on a shopping spree, or finally took that dream Caribbean cruise? Subsection (ii) defines "luxury goods or services" to exclude "goods or services reasonably necessary for the support or maintenance of the debtor or a dependent of the debtor."[3] By definition, that seems to exclude the latest 60-inch flatscreen television with surround sound, but note the debt is "presumed" non-dischargeable. What if the client purchased a new laptop? If the laptop is required for work, it's most likely "reasonably necessary for the support or maintenance of the debtor," therefore, the debt associated with the laptop might be dischargeable, but there might be over-exempt issues. Likewise, a cash advance to buy the television is likely an issue, but not if the client used it for necessities such as paying for food and utilities.

1 11 U.S.C. §523(a)(2)(c)(i)(II).
2 11 U.S.C. §523(a)(2)(c)(i)(I).
3 11 U.S.C. §523(a)(2)(c)(ii).

DOI: 10.4324/9781003203278-11

Get into the details of the purchase. Sometimes the answer is for the client to return at a later date, but to continue making payments on the debt. Other times, the client may have to proceed with Chapter 13.

KEYWORDS AND TERMS

- Cash advances
- "Goods or services reasonably necessary for the support or maintenance of the debtor or a dependent of the debtor"
- "Luxury goods or services"

PRACTICE QUESTIONS AND EXERCISES

1. The lawyer recently started handling consumer bankruptcy cases and requests from you a summary of §523 based on the following facts:
   a. The client withdrew $5,000 in the form of a cash advance less than two months ago. The funds were spent and confirmed on funeral expenses for the unexpected death of a family member.
   b. Can the client proceed to file bankruptcy this week to avoid an upcoming garnishment? What are the best and worst-case scenarios?
2. Three months ago, another client's $3,500 cash advance was spent as follows:
   a. $1,000 as a gift to their daughter who leaves for college next month.
   b. $1,000 on household expenses.
   c. $1,500 for the bankruptcy attorney.

   Provide a summary for the attorney of any potential issues and the likely outcome.

SECTION 17: LAWSUITS

Lawsuits are potentially an issue whether the client is being sued by a creditor(s) or is suing someone. If a creditor is suing the client, is the debt secured or unsecured? If a foreclosure or car repossession is pending, the bankruptcy may have to be filed soon to take advantage of the *automatic stay*. If the client intends on keeping the asset, Chapter 13 is required to bring the arrears current.

If it is an unsecured debt, time may be on the client's side, depending on the jurisdiction. For example, a credit card lawsuit in a large metropolitan city could easily take a year or more to finalize. Hearing dates are scheduled months in advance. By then, it's likely the bankruptcy was filed and the discharge received before the creditor even had the opportunity to obtain a final judgment. If the asset was taken back by a creditor or surrendered voluntarily, it could exceed a year or more before the lawsuit is filed, if ever, to collect on a deficiency balance. However, if time is not on the client's side, the client should retain a lawyer to litigate the matter.

REAL CASES

The client could not account for spending more than $40,000 within a few months and defaulting on payments shortly after. Since the client didn't qualify for Chapter 13 and Chapter 7 required filing in the distant future, instead I was retained to represent the client in the suit filed by the collection agency.

After filing an answer and affirmative defenses, more than a year passed before the creditor's attorney requested a motion for summary judgment. The judge's office scheduled the hearing nine months later. One week before the hearing, Chapter 7 was filed. By then, the only issue with the bankruptcy was the non-exempt equity in the vehicle, but a settlement was reached quickly with the trustee's office.

Depending on the jurisdiction, pre-trial conferences or mediation may be scheduled automatically, and because of the coronavirus pandemic, it's most likely a virtual hearing. Whether at the pre-trial conference or mediation, a payment arrangement will halt the lawsuit, and when appropriate, the bankruptcy is filed.

If the client is suing a third party, then other issues come into play. For example, is it a worker's compensation claim where the settlement proceeds are exempt or a personal injury lawsuit where most if not all of the settlement proceeds will belong to the bankruptcy estate? If the latter, the trustee will require the personal injury attorney's contact information. After all liens are satisfied and attorney's fees paid, the remainder belongs to the bankruptcy estate.

When asked about a personal injury case, clients know few details. So, if the client decides to continue with the bankruptcy case, the likely consequences should be detailed in writing, even if the client believes the settlement proceeds will be minimal. If the client chooses to proceed, the bankruptcy filing date depends on the amount received. However, the larger the settlement, the longer the delay in proceeding with Chapter 7, unless Chapter 13 is filed. Another option is to use the injury award to settle the debts with creditors.

KEYWORDS AND TERMS

- Affirmative defenses
- Answer
- Mediation
- Motion for summary judgment
- Pre-trial conference
- Settlement proceeds

DISCUSSION QUESTIONS

1. The debtor was served with a lawsuit, and mediation is scheduled in 30 days. If the debtor cannot file for bankruptcy immediately, what steps should the debtor take?
2. Search with the clerk's office in your county for a motion for summary judgment.

PRACTICE QUESTIONS AND EXERCISES

1. Write an email to the client regarding a case listed on the petition. Confirm if the case is a worker's compensation case or a personal injury lawsuit. Explain the difference to the client.
2. Complete the corresponding sections of the bankruptcy intake.

SECTION 18: LIST OF CREDITORS AND CREDIT REPORTS

With the *list of creditors*, clients are simply listing their debts. Clients tend to skip this section out of laziness or not wanting to duplicate accounts, but unfortunately, the credit reporting system isn't perfect. At times, debts listed with one credit reporting agency aren't listed with another. Besides mistakes, with some types of debt, such as medical bills, it may be months, even years, before it appears on a credit report, if at all. Finally, if the creditor doesn't report to the credit bureaus, the debt will never make it to the credit report in the first place. Perfect examples are debts with a dental office or law firm. My business loans don't appear on my credit report, even though I am a solo practitioner and personally guaranteed the loan. Finally, money owed to an individual isn't going to reflect in a credit report either.

The list of creditors works to supplement the credit report, statements, and collection letters. Clients should make an effort to provide as much information as possible about creditor(s). This covers all the bases and avoids omitting creditors and unnecessary complications. Note the notation on the bottom of the page of the intake. While that statement seems self-explanatory, clients sometimes don't list secured debt such as their car or home because they believe only the debt they are trying to eliminate should be included. Clients also tend to ask if they can pick and choose which creditors to include in bankruptcy.

The creditor's correct address is also imperative since the clerk's office sends notice of the bankruptcy filing. If the address is incorrect, the clerk sends an email notification to the law firm's registered email with an attachment requesting an updated address. Trust me, the last thing a practitioner wants to hear is that the case has been finalized and a creditor was omitted from the petition. For this reason, clients' credit card statements and collection letters are sought, then compared to the creditors on the credit report and the list of creditors. Remember, an attorney cannot be responsible for an unknown debt. From a practical standpoint, that's why it's important to mark off each creditor once listed in the bankruptcy petition. However, most courts have taken the approach that if the outcome remains the same because there are no assets to distribute, the debt is still dischargeable even if the creditor was omitted from the schedules and failed to receive notice. If a creditor argues that the debtor is still liable, a motion to reopen can be filed to seek the court's permission to amend the petition and add the creditor. Worst-case scenario, an adversary proceeding is filed.

The credit report also provides valuable information such as the date the account was opened. Look for accounts that were opened recently, and the credit limit is already reached. Of course, this depends on the amount. A few hundred dollars normally won't be an issue, but if a client opened an account six months ago and maxed out the $5,000 credit limit, further questions need to be asked to avoid an objection to the dischargeability of the debt by either the trustee or creditor. Confirm what purchases were made with the credit card. Sometimes, the client transferred old debts to a new creditor because of a lower interest rate or more flexible monthly payments. Under those circumstances, that's fine since new debt wasn't incurred, but this is fact-specific.

REAL CASES

Typically, a client who incurs a substantial amount of debt within a short time should hold off on filing Chapter 7. However, one client incurred a debt of more than $24,000 and defaulted after two payments. But upon further review, the client obtained a personal loan to pay off multiple creditors, including hospital bills. The client never even received the funds as the lender paid off the debt directly. But because of the coronavirus lockdown, the client's employer closed the business for a few months, resulting in the client being furloughed. Since the client easily qualified for bankruptcy, there were no issues because the client did not incur "new debt" nor received any loan proceeds.

Some credit reports show the debt total each month. Watch for a spike in debt near the time the client consulted with the office. Again, the passage of time is your friend in these circumstances, and decisions are based on a case-by-case basis.

REAL CASES

A client's credit card debt increased by approximately $70,000 in less than two months, and yet during the consultation, this was never mentioned even though clients are asked to provide a timeline of their debt balance over the last six months. For example, if a client states they have $35,000 in debt, I ask how fast did you get to the $35,000? Was it in a few months or has the debt been accumulating for years?

After reviewing my client's credit report, my advice was to try again in two years since my client had no explanation on how the debt was incurred, other than to say her boyfriend used to assist her with the household expenses, but he was now in prison. While that's possible, maybe even true, neither the boyfriend's nor my client's expenses equaled that amount of debt. The numbers simply did not add up. However, referring to the previous example, if the majority of the debt resulted from hospitalization, there would be no need to delay the filing. But, that wasn't the case since I could trace at least one-third of the debt to plastic surgery, which of course, is distinct from a medical emergency that would be considered "reasonably necessary for the support or maintenance of the debtor or a dependent of the debtor."[4] Therefore, the client was advised to make minimal payments for at least a year, and then we can revisit the issue of filing bankruptcy.

Another client spent approximately $30,000 in one week, but the debt resulted from excessive gambling and no doubt feeding his gambling addiction on a trip to Las Vegas, Nevada. I rejected his case, which upset the client. He even stated I was obligated to take his case and help him since it's not his fault he got into debt. I'm not sure whose fault it was, it definitely wasn't mine, but there is no need to accept a case like that. It's not worth the time and effort unless the client is willing to file for Chapter 13, and even then, it's probably still not worth it as problematic clients never are. Remember, with Chapter 13, there will be regular contact with the client for the next 36 to 60 months. When faced with these situations, point it out to the lead paralegal or lawyer as most lawyers avoid difficult clients.

When it's time to obtain the credit report, I prefer for clients to get it themselves. I email the link provided at the end of this chapter and advise the client to return the credit report via email in PDF format or print it and drop it off at my office. The reason being is that sometimes the security questions are difficult to answer. Even in obtaining my own credit report, I've had to answer questions about prior phone numbers that were several years old, and I didn't remember the information. If the questions aren't answered correctly, access is denied, and the request will have to be done via mail, which usually takes 30 days or more to receive. Whether you are on the phone or in the office with the client, answering three to five security questions per credit provider – Equifax, Experian, and Transunion – could result in a substantial amount of time. As a result, our policy changed to having clients get their credit reports to save time. Of course, always confirm what the firm's policy is.

If credit reports can't be accessed, Best Case® does provide a service to obtain a basic credit report or a merged credit report from Equifax, Experian, and Transunion. There's even a premium service that includes related addresses of the debtor, vehicle registrations, real estate owned, and work history. In addition, there is the added convenience that creditors are downloaded automatically into the petition. This saves time, especially for firms with a voluminous practice, but it does increase client costs.

Finally, credit reports should be accessed as close as possible to the filing date, after the documents have been provided, the balance paid in full, and the credit counseling class completed. One reason is to include an accurate balance on the petition. With each passing month, interest and late fees increase the balance. Another reason is cases can be delayed for multiple reasons, whether the client lost contact with the office, extended payment plans, or a change in circumstances. Creditor information also changes routinely with debts sold to third parties. That's why collection notices are requested.

4 11 U.S.C. §523(a)(2)(c)(ii).

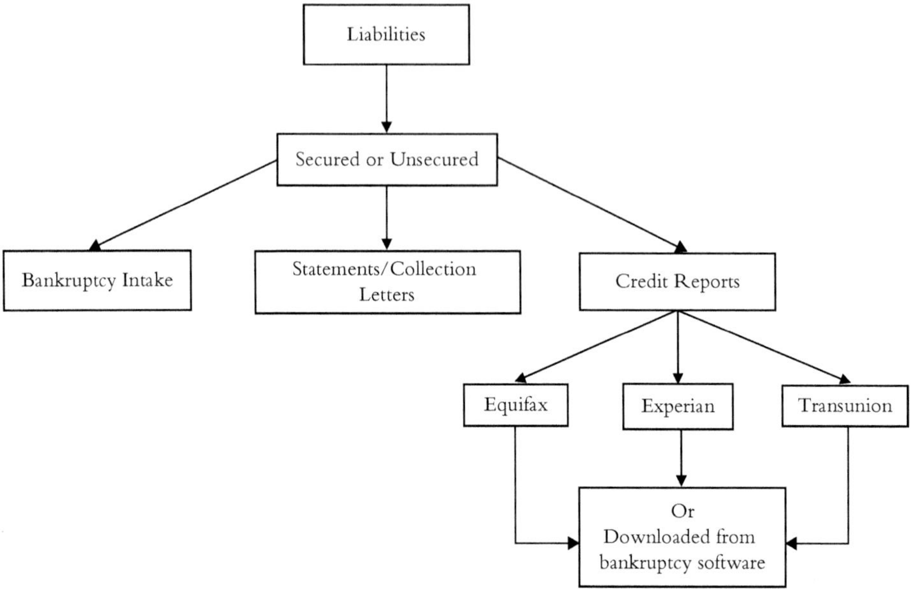

FIGURE 10.1 Sources to use to verify the client's liabilities (use multiple sources to confirm the client's liabilities, including the bankruptcy intake, collection notices, and credit reports from the three major credit reporting bureaus).

To expedite the process, clients should have several options to deliver documents, whether in person or by mail or email. Some creditors will forward statements directly to the attorney if the client has provided the contact information.

To obtain a free copy of a credit report, visit Annualcreditreport.com. Every 12 months, free copies are provided by the three major reporting bureaus. See Figure 10.1

SUMMARY

By having credit card statements, collection letters, the list of creditors, and credit reports, it's unlikely creditors will be omitted inadvertently from the petition. Credit reports should be obtained as close as possible to the filing date. If the client is suing a third party, obtain a copy of the lawsuit and confirm if the proceeds are exempt. For lawsuits by secured creditors, if the client intends on keeping the asset and is in arrears, Chapter 13 is required.

KEYWORDS AND TERMS

- Charged-off
- Equifax

- Experian
- List of creditors
- Transunion

DISCUSSION QUESTIONS

1. Obtain your credit report from all three credit reporting bureaus and add it to your client file. Were the security questions easy to answer?
2. Review your credit report(s). Are all your debts listed? Is all the information in your credit report correct and current?
3. How are errors in a credit report corrected?
4. If you are filing for bankruptcy and find a debt that is not yours, do you include it in the bankruptcy or dispute the debt?

PRACTICE QUESTIONS AND EXERCISES

1. In reviewing your client's credit report, you notice that an account was opened four months earlier, and the $2,000 credit limit was reached in one month. Write an email to the client requesting further information on that credit card.
2. The client responded to your email and stated that $1,000 was used to pay off a creditor. The remaining $1,000 was used to purchase a laptop for their child. Write a summary of how §523 may affect this case.
3. In reviewing the bankruptcy intake, the client seemed only to provide a partial list of creditors. Prepare an email to the client regarding this issue.
4. Complete the corresponding sections in the bankruptcy intake.

REFERENCES

11 U.S.C. §523.

Annualcreditreport.com.

CHAPTER 11

Required Documents

In this chapter is the list of documents required for every bankruptcy case, whether Chapter 7 or 13. While this list is not exhaustive, it includes most documents needed to complete a bankruptcy petition successfully. The list of required documents should be provided to the client upon being retained, along with the bankruptcy intake, disclosures under Sections 342 and 527, and the Retainer Agreement. Also, clients should provide copies, not originals. The documents to be provided are as follows.

INCOME TAX RETURNS FOR THE LAST THREE YEARS

Besides issues with tax refunds being non-exempt, look for discrepancies that may result in a 2004 Examination.[1] Here's what to look for.

Marital Status

Did the client file tax returns as "single," "married filing jointly," "married filing separately," "head of household," or "qualifying widow?"

In the bankruptcy intake, marital status is asked on the first page and it's listed in Schedule I and SOFA of the petition.[2] Spousal income is included in Schedule I and Form 122 (means test), even if it's a single filing.[3] If there is a discrepancy, it's usually because a client files under the wrong category for purposes of receiving a larger tax refund. Other times clients are not legally married but file as they are. Plain and simple, that is tax fraud.

If there are discrepancies, the client should amend the tax return(s). Once the amended return has been filed and accepted by the IRS, then proceed to file the bankruptcy. Have the client provide a signed copy of the amended return since some trustees require a signature.

1 Fed. R. Bankr. P. 2004.
2 Official Form 106I. Schedule I: Your Income (Individuals); Official Form 107. Your Statement of Financial Affairs for Individuals Filing for Bankruptcy (Individuals).
3 Id., Schedule I. Official Form 122A-1. Chapter 7 Statement of Your Current Monthly Income.

DOI: 10.4324/9781003203278-12

Remember that a domestic partner's income is excluded from the means test, but household contributions are listed on Schedule I.[4] If not, there will be a negative balance when comparing income to expenses. For example, if the difference between income and expenses results in a negative balance of $500.00, then that amount is listed as a domestic spouse contribution. However, remember to review the client's bank statements to confirm which household expenses the client is actually and consistently paying for each month, as sometimes spouses and partners pay specific expenses.

REAL CASES

A married couple had multiple discrepancies with their tax returns, documents, and bankruptcy intake. For months, I was requesting documents that the clients failed to provide. In addition, we were short on time because of a pending lawsuit and wage garnishment order. If the bankruptcy was not filed by Thursday, the wife would lose 25 percent of her pay because of the garnishment.

The tax returns were provided Thursday morning. I had already thoroughly reviewed the bank statements, which was another issue, but the address on the tax returns did not match the address on their lease, bank statements, or driver's licenses. Nothing matched! There could be a valid explanation as to why, but as it turns out, the husband had been using a separate address for years to claim head of household even though they were married and both working full-time. I advised the clients that it was tax fraud unless they were separated for at least six months every year. Of course, the wife, who had an answer for everything, stated they were having marital problems. Fact is, they weren't separated for that amount of time each year except once years earlier. Bottom line: they just wanted a larger tax refund.

In addition, the last two pages of the wife's tax returns had separate attachments which listed more than $11,000 in benefits paid to each child from the Social Security Administration. This was the first time I had seen or heard of this, even though I had been retained seven months earlier. None of this information was listed on the bankruptcy intake. Now see why clients should complete the intake on their own?

The wife advised me that the $11,000 was death benefits paid to her children from another marriage. My next question was whether the funds were commingled with her accounts, and how the funds were used. The answer to the first part of that question was no, and that the children used the funds for their expenses. One child was 17 years old, the other 11. "What expenses?" I asked. Cell phones, new sneakers, and miscellaneous was the response. That doesn't amount to $900 each month. Mind you, the client had spoken with another attorney before and was advised those funds were separate from the bankruptcy estate. That is true to a certain extent unless she was using that money. The wife had the habit of referring to the prior bankruptcy attorney, which caused me to be suspicious. It was as if she always implied that I was wrong and I should guide myself by the other attorney.

4 Supra, notes 3 and 2.

My next question: "Have you used at least $1 from that money?" The client responded by saying, "I can't say I haven't." The obvious reality is that the clients have been using those funds, and probably most of it, based on my guess. You don't have to be a forensic accountant to notice that the bank statements did not square up with their income and that money was coming from another source. Because the clients were using the children's death benefits, it would not have been any different from a family member residing in the house making household contributions.

Having been rushed the entire time with this case and needing to file bankruptcy to avoid the wage garnishment, had I simply looked at the front page of the husband's tax returns and listed his gross income on Section 4 of SOFA, I would have had a major problem on my hands.[5] While the red flag was waving high in this case, especially since the client wasn't providing every page of the tax returns, it's still my reputation on the line at the end of the day. At the minimum, had I filed the petition, I would have been seen as incompetent, maybe worse.

As the paralegal, you must keep track of cases and notify the senior paralegal or attorney of problematic cases and clients. That's why it's important to make notations in the file of the steps you have taken, check off what has been done, and ensure that the case is ready for filing.

PRACTICE TIP

Avoid filing bankruptcy until every requested document and page has been received. Do not take a client at their word or assume anything! That should be evident in the case just cited. There could be issues with large deposits or withdrawals from bank accounts just before filing. In this case, there were multiple issues, especially with the tax returns.

You'll always see red flags. Simply put, when two plus two equals five, you know you have a problem. Note the issue in the file and discuss it with the attorney. In my case, every time I requested a document, the wife always replied with frustration, saying it was previously provided. She even told me that she owed money to the Internal Revenue Service, yet documentation was never provided or put in writing as I required. Since my numerous requests were never complied with and the clients weren't honest, I terminated my representation. The lesson to be learned is that not all clients are truthful; it's a small percentage, but keep that in mind. Curiosity did get the best of me while working on this textbook. They eventually filed for bankruptcy and seemed to be more truthful with their third attorney.

Dependents

If dependents are claimed on tax returns, remember to confirm that the dependents reside with the client since household contributions are listed on Schedule I.[6] But whatever the contributing amount is, there has to be an equal amount of expenses matching Schedule J.[7]

5 Supra, note 2.
6 Supra, note 2.
7 Official Form 106J, Schedule J: Your Expenses (Individuals).

Otherwise, there would be excess disposable funds available, and the client will not qualify for Chapter 7. This will be reviewed later in the text.

PAYCHECK STUBS FOR BOTH SPOUSES FOR THE LAST SIX MONTHS

Because of means testing, paychecks from the last six months are needed, including pay stubs for the month of filing. With pay stubs, there are several issues to focus on.

First, every job has to be listed, including part-time employment, gig economy jobs, and income from selling products online. So even if the client worked at a job for one day five months ago, that job and income are listed on *Form 122*.[8]

Schedule I income focuses on the month of filing, but there aren't always pay stubs available.[9] For example, a petition may be filed during the first week of the month, but the next paycheck is not until the following week. In those situations, there's an educated guess as to income for that month. Use prior pay stubs as a guide. However, confirm there won't be substantial changes that will increase the amount of disposable income. For example, dozens of overtime hours are expected, or the client is paid time and a half for working on a legal holiday or cashing out paid time off (PTO). As discussed in the real case example below, these issues are common and easily resolved by delaying the filing.

For borderline cases, even though the bankruptcy may not be filed for a few months and the pay stubs will be outdated, it's a good idea to calculate the six-month average as soon as possible to make sure there are no income issues.

Note that clients sometimes won't provide pay stubs because bank statements show the employer's deposited amount. However, a bank statement cannot substitute for a pay stub. The deposited amount is net income, and Schedule I requires line-by-line deductions.[10] If the client is a 1099 employee, then tax deductions are estimated.

REAL CASES

A car salesman averaged $4,000 per month in income, primarily commissions. Therefore, the client easily qualified for Chapter 7. However, one month, the client earned more than $10,000 in commissions. Fortunately for him, every salesperson at the dealership was fired, leaving him alone to earn all the commissions. But, that one month prevented the debtor from passing the means test.[11]

8 Supra, note 3.
9 Supra, note 2.
10 Supra, note 2.
11 Supra, note 3.

In calculating the last six months of income, the $10,000 month was in month three. The bankruptcy was delayed four months to eliminate that month from means testing. Remember, the means test focuses on past income, not future income.[12] That's why it's essential to receive every single pay stub from the client, as one paycheck is enough to result in failing the means test or increasing the disposable income for Schedule I.[13]

401k, IRA, and Pension Deductions

Review deductions for 401ks and retirement plans from the client's pay stubs. If the deductions are too high, say more than $100 per month, contributions may have to be reduced until the bankruptcy is finalized to avoid an objection by the trustee. However, this varies per district. For example, a trustee may not object if the deductions have remained consistent but may object if the deductions started recently. It also has to be considered if the debtor's income is below the state median income. If so, the issue is likely moot. Regardless, the answer is not in the Code. The unwritten rule is that deductions between 5 and 15 percent are okay, but I've come across articles and blog posts where trustees haven't allowed any amount to be deducted. So, it's likely that if you ask ten lawyers from ten different districts, you will get ten different answers. The courts are also divided on this issue. That's where using PACER or CM/ECF can be beneficial by researching petitions filed by local bankruptcy attorneys.[14]

PRACTICE TIP

Clients will provide the last six months of pay stubs, but the filing won't be for another three months, so the first three months of paystubs are outdated. To save time, money, space, and paper, clients can be advised to provide the last two to three months of paystubs with the initial batch of documents and continue updating their records monthly. If the case is "borderline," request all six months of paystubs at once to confirm there are no means test issues.[15]

VEHICLES

For cars, the following documentation is required:

1. A copy of the title if paid off.
2. If financed, a copy of the most recent statement that reflects the current balance and arrears, if any.

12 Id.
13 Supra, notes 2 and 3.
14 PACER. Public Access to Court Electronic Records. https://pacer.uscourts.gov/file-case/court-cmecf-lookup.
15 Supra, note 3.

3. If the car is leased, a copy of the lease agreement and the most recent statement.
4. Proof of insurance and vehicle registration. Make sure the addresses match on all documents.

For vehicles, the issue is non-exempt equity versus executory contracts or leases, where there's no ownership interest. Leasing a car is no different than renting an apartment. The only difference with the car is that there is an option to buy the car upon the lease expiration. Leases are listed on Schedule G, even though some jurisdictions may also want the car loan information listed on *Schedules A*/B and given a value of zero dollars.[16] Personally, I don't think that makes any sense. If you are renting your residence, there is no interest in the home, and therefore, you wouldn't list the rental property on Schedules A/B and then exempt it on Schedule C.[17] However, if that makes the trustee happy or is common in that jurisdiction, list it accordingly.

Proof of insurance and vehicle registration is also required. Again, take note of the addresses. If other persons are listed on the insurance policy, find out why and their relation to the client. For example, a son or daughter won't be an issue, but if it is someone else, there may be financial contributions to the household expenses that should be reflected in Schedule I.[18]

REAL ESTATE

If the client owns real estate, the following documents should be provided:

1. Deed.
2. Proof of homestead (tax bill or homestead application/approval submitted to the county).
3. Recent mortgage statement that includes balance, arrears, and escrow, if any.
4. Homeowner's insurance policy.
5. Recent utility bills.
6. Documentation regarding homeowner's association.

Trustees generally require copies of the deed and proof of homestead or tax bill to confirm the homestead exemption applies. Request utility bills to ensure it's not listed in another party's name. If so, confirm why in case it's a renter. Usually, the reason is that the utility company required a large deposit, so the client used someone else's credit. As long as all the other documents indicate the client resides at the homestead property, there shouldn't be an issue.

16 Official Form 106G. Schedule G: Executory Contracts and Unexpired Leases (Individuals); Official Form 106A/B. Schedule A/B: Property (Individuals).

17 Id., Official Form 106 A/B. Official Form 106C. Schedule C: The Property You Claim as Exempt (Individuals).

18 Supra, note 2.

The mortgage statement, homeowner's insurance policy, and tax statements are standard documents. Note that trustees ask if there are pending or recent insurance claims, especially for high-prone areas of natural disasters, for example, Florida with hurricanes. If an insurance claim was filed, the trustee will request proof that the funds were spent to fix the home. The client should provide receipts, invoices, contracts, and canceled checks. Finally, confirm the HOA fees are current.

NON-HOMESTEAD PROPERTY

As you know from Chapter 8, Section 11 of the intake, timeshares, cemetery plots, and vacant land are non-homestead properties. For reasons unknown, timeshare companies tend not to cooperate with the request of documents. Hence, clients have difficulty obtaining information about their timeshare, whether it's the balance due on the note or the timeshare's value. The same issue occurs with cemetery plots. Unless paid off, timeshares usually have a minimal value, and trustees will abandon their interest in the timeshare unless it's paid off, and even then, sometimes trustees aren't interested because it's difficult to resell the timeshare. The same cannot be said about cemetery plots and vacant land.

BANK ACCOUNT STATEMENTS AND CANCELED CHECKS FOR THE LAST SIX MONTHS

Review transactions on bank statements. Request clarification on large withdrawals and deposits and expenses that are likely to be objected to.

REAL CASES

A client had the habit of withdrawing her entire paycheck from her bank account and paying for all her expenses in cash. The rent was split with her mother, and her portion was deposited into the mother's account. Usually, this isn't an issue, especially since my client earned minimal income. However, a $5,000 check was cashed earlier in the year, so the trustee requested a copy of the canceled check. The check was in the exact amount of my client's tax refund. She made the check out to herself.

The trustee made this an issue and requested a settlement of the bankruptcy estate for $5,000. I advised the attorney from the trustee's office that the funds were spent on regular ongoing expenses and that there was no way of proving whether she had the funds or not. The bankruptcy was filed more than seven months after the withdrawal. With this particular trustee, he has the habit of asking few questions at the Meeting of Creditors, but then, a few weeks later, an email is sent requesting additional information and/or documentation. Most of the time, nothing comes of it. The overwhelming majority of trustees will ask relevant questions at the creditors' meeting, including about the withdrawal and how the funds were spent. In addition, most trustees would have requested a copy of the check in advance.

When reviewing bank statements, look for any transaction that simply doesn't belong. An occasional expense is not an issue, but regular expenses can be. For example, in a joint filing, the bank statements revealed a substantial amount of money being spent dining out. When I averaged their dining out expenses for every month after they retained my office, they were spending between $800 and $1,000. When questioned about this extraordinary expense, my clients advised me that they led busy lives, so there was little time available to prepare dinner for the family. I reminded her that her husband leaves work at 4 p.m. and she leaves work at 5 p.m., so they have regular hours. In this case, the clients believed it was necessary to increase their expenses to qualify for a Chapter 7.

While the IRS Living Standards work well as a guide to determine if an expense is too high or low, remember it's only a guide. For example, a client may have a special diet, thus, spending more on groceries and exceeding the standards, while another client spends several hundred dollars monthly on medications. A client's job may also result in higher expenses. For example, police officers eat out more, increasing their expenses, but may spend less on fuel if they drive home in their patrol car. However, when possible, avoid exceeding the allowable amounts. Also, use bank statements to compare expenses listed on the bankruptcy intake since clients may underreport their expenses. If you guide yourself solely by a client's figures, you may conclude they don't qualify for bankruptcy because the disposable income is too high.

Charitable donations, up to 15 percent, are permitted under 11 U.S.C. §548(a)(2). The issue here is if the client is claiming the expense for purposes of qualifying for bankruptcy. For example, in a joint filing, the clients listed in the bankruptcy intake monthly donations of approximately $500 per month to their church. However, nowhere was that reflected in the bank statements. The clients claimed the donations were made in cash, but there weren't any withdrawals in the bank statements. Yes, being a bankruptcy paralegal or attorney sometimes requires being a part-time detective and accountant. The expenses were adjusted accordingly, and the $500 charitable donation was excluded from Schedule J.[19]

Another client was retired and earning $800 per month in Social Security. Living solely off Social Security is a virtual guarantee of qualifying for bankruptcy – sometimes. The client resided with her daughter and advised me that her entire Social Security benefit was used to help with the household expenses. Her bank accounts told another story.

When her Social Security benefits were deposited each month, the client withdrew the full amount at once. Again, usually, this isn't an issue, especially since the client only earns $800 per month. However, where the withdrawals were made was the issue. It wasn't at the bank but from an ATM at a casino. The client was advised to return in six months with clean bank statements, and at that time, I would reevaluate her case.

Note, withdrawing money from a casino ATM doesn't mean the client doesn't qualify for bankruptcy either, but appearances are everything, and the optics with this case were opaque at best. In reviewing the client's credit card statements, there was never any use of her credit cards at that casino. This was as simple as a Chapter 7 bankruptcy could be, and

19 Supra, note 7.

the idea was to keep it that way instead of complicating it unnecessarily. In an abundance of caution and to avoid unnecessary issues, it was just easier to delay the bankruptcy.

RETIREMENT ACCOUNTS

Retirement accounts are exempt but focus on withdraws that will cause the funds to be non-exempt. Deductions for 401k loans are listed in Schedule D as secured debt.[20] The most recent statement will provide the loan balance. Remember, retirement/pension loans are non-dischargeable.

LAWSUITS

Provide copies of lawsuits to the trustee and make sure to list the lawsuit in *Line 9* of *Form 107* (SOFA).[21] This includes lawsuits whether the client is being sued or suing a third party. If a creditor is suing the client, clients should cease direct deposits into accounts known by the creditor and open a new account. However, if the bankruptcy will be filed soon, there's no need to change accounts. The debt associated with the lawsuit is listed on Schedule E/F and includes the creditor's attorney for notice.[22]

IDENTIFICATION

The original Social Security card and driver's license are used to confirm the debtor's identity at the creditors' meeting. A copy of the client's identification should be kept on file, preferably a laptop or tablet, and taken to the Meeting of Creditors as sometimes clients forget to bring their identification. Without identification, the hearing will be rescheduled, but sometimes if the attorney can provide clear color copies, the trustee may be willing to proceed. This, of course, assumes we will "return to normal" with 341 meetings taking place in person.[23] If not, the driver's license and Social Security card is submitted to the trustee with the required documents and the debtor's identity will be confirmed during the telephonic hearing.

Unfortunately, I've represented multiple clients who filed for bankruptcy because their identity was stolen. Between endless lawsuits and harassing creditor calls, bankruptcy was the simpler solution. I've even had two cases where the victim of identity theft was the son, and the perpetrator was the father. Providing multiple forms of identification such as copies of a U.S. Passport, Resident Alien Card, or birth certificate reduces the chances my office

20 Official Form 106D. Schedule D: Creditors Who Hold Claims Secured By Property (Individuals).
21 Supra, note 2.
22 Official Form 106E/F. Schedule E/F: Creditors Who Have Unsecured Claims (Individuals).
23 11 U.S.C. §341.

makes a mistake. In addition, since all names used in the past are listed in the petition, other forms of identification may have deviations not listed in the credit report.

PRACTICE TIP

It's recommended that a search be performed on CM/ECF with each client's Social Security number.[24] In the same way a victim of identity theft files for bankruptcy, so can the perpetrator. A search on CM/ECF will confirm bankruptcies previously filed and should be done as part of due diligence.[25]

It's also important to determine if prior bankruptcies were filed to take advantage of the automatic stay. To avoid issues with the bankruptcy court and, more importantly, for reputation purposes, I do not file the second bankruptcy if it seemed the first one was filed for purposes of delay. It's not worth the potential hassle or aggravation. If I filed the first bankruptcy and it was dismissed, depending on why the case was dismissed, will determine if I file a motion to set aside the dismissal or refile after the prejudice period ends.

For example, if the dismissal is because the client failed to appear, the debtor can move to set aside the dismissal or refile in six months. If other counsel represented the debtor, I ask why not use the same attorney since I have no guarantees that the client will appear the second time around. Since the potential exists for a bad faith filing, it's not worth the extra work needed to attend any hearings scheduled by the trustee or the judge. But as always, each firm has its own policy and procedures that should be learned in case the attorney isn't immediately available.

If I do represent the same debtor for a second filing, it's because the foreclosure has been finalized, and all that remains pending is the deficiency balance. Trust me when I say that little acts such as this build a strong reputation with the trustees, resulting in receiving the benefit of the doubt and making for easier negotiations in future cases.

Note that for Chapter 13, it's common for cases to be dismissed because the debtor failed to make the monthly payment. But any motions to set aside the dismissal are based on continuing with the original case, and rarely is there an issue of a serial filer and bad faith filings with Chapter 13.

CHILD SUPPORT ORDER, MARITAL SETTLEMENT AGREEMENT, AND/OR DOMESTIC SUPPORT OBLIGATIONS

Child support orders and marital settlement agreements are provided to the trustee for two reasons. The first reason is to confirm the debtor is current on his/her domestic support obligations. The second reason is to ensure the correct amount is deducted on Schedule I

24 Supra, note 14.
25 Id.

or Schedule J.[26] If the support is withdrawn automatically via an income deduction order, this would be reflected in the client's paystubs and deducted in Schedule I.[27] If payments are made directly to the custodial parent, the deduction is listed on Schedule J.[28] Make sure not to duplicate the expense.

The marital settlement agreement is reviewed in case assets will become non-exempt because of a divorce. A common example is that the marital home is/was sold, and the net proceeds received by the client exceed the exemption amount.

Copies

Clients typically don't want to invest the time or money to provide copies of documents. But remember, if an original is provided, then the office becomes responsible for it. If there are originals, they can be returned to the client at the Meeting of Creditors. However, if the hearing is virtual, additional time is spent meeting with the client and scanning documents, or money spent if the documents are returned via mail (see Figures 11.1 and 11.2).

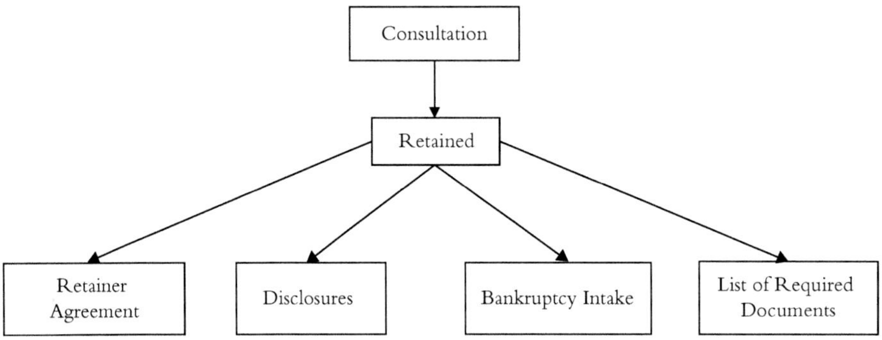

FIGURE 11.1 Documents to be given to the client upon being retained (once the client retains the office, provide the Retainer Agreement, disclosures, the bankruptcy intake, and the list of required documents).

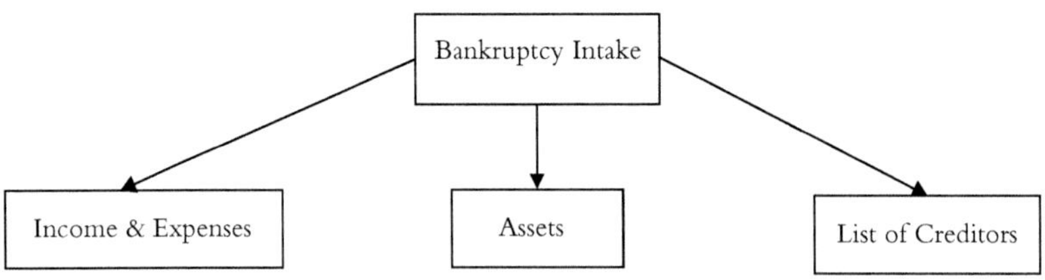

FIGURE 11.2 How the bankruptcy intake is divided (the bankruptcy intake can be divided into three parts: income and expenses, assets, and liabilities).

26 Supra, notes 2 and 7.
27 Supra, note 2.
28 Supra, note 7.

SUMMARY

Failure to provide documents timely to the trustee may result in a dismissal. Documents should be submitted at least ten days in advance of the 341 Meeting of Creditors. Avoid accepting originals from the client and definitely don't forward originals to the trustee.

Finally, as the paralegal, you will likely spend more time working on a file and communicating with the clients than the attorney. As such, it's your role to put your superiors on notice if there are any issues with documents, the filing, or the client is problematic or not cooperating. Remember to make notes of any potential issues.

KEYWORDS AND TERMS

- 1099 employee
- Abandon interest
- Clean bank statements
- Income deduction order

DISCUSSION QUESTIONS

1. Why is it important to know the date a client was served with a lawsuit and the current status of the case?
2. How many days does a defendant or respondent have to respond to a lawsuit in your state?

PRACTICE QUESTIONS AND EXERCISES

1. There was a substantial deposit and withdrawal from the client's bank account four months earlier. Send the client an email regarding this issue.
2. The same month the law firm was retained, there was a withdrawal of $2,500 from the client's retirement account. Draft an email to be sent to the client regarding the withdrawal.

REFERENCES

11 U.S.C. §341.

11 U.S.C. §342.

11 U.S.C. §527.

11 U.S.C. §548.

Fed. R. Bankr. P. 2004.

Official Form 106A/B – Schedule A/B: Property (Individuals).

Official Form 106C – Schedule C: The Property You Claim as Exempt (Individuals).

Official Form 106D – Schedule D: Creditors Who Hold Claims Secured by Property (Individuals).

Official Form 106E/F – Schedule E/F: Creditors Who Have Unsecured Claims (Individuals).

Official Form 106G – Schedule G: Executory Contracts and Unexpired Leases (Individuals).

Official Form 106I. Schedule I: Your Income (Individuals).

Official Form 106J. Schedule J: Your Expenses (Individuals).

Official Form 107. Your Statement of Financial Affairs for Individuals Filing for Bankruptcy (Individuals).

Official Form 122A-1. Chapter 7 Statement of Your Current Monthly Income.

PACER. Public Access to Court Electronic Records. https://pacer.uscourts.gov/file-case/court-cmecf-lookup.

CHAPTER 12

The Bankruptcy Petition

Note that the sections are as they appear in Official Form 101.[1] It would appear the same with bankruptcy software when the petition is printed or saved in PDF format. The corresponding figures are as the petition appears in the bankruptcy software Best Case®. Therefore, use the official forms and software to compare both formats. Note that Best Case® offers a free downloadable version as well as other software companies.

OFFICIAL FORM 101: VOLUNTARY PETITION FOR INDIVIDUALS FILING FOR BANKRUPTCY

Part 1

Sections 1–3

The identity portion of Part 1 of the bankruptcy petition is self-explanatory. However, make sure to list all names used in the last eight years. Credit reports also list name variations. For example, *Johnathon Smith*, *John Smith*, *John P. Smith*, *Johnathan P. Smith*. Use the name listed on the driver's license and Social Security card first, and then variations in the "Other Names" section.

1 Official Form 101. Voluntary Petition for Individuals Filing for Bankruptcy.

DOI: 10.4324/9781003203278-13

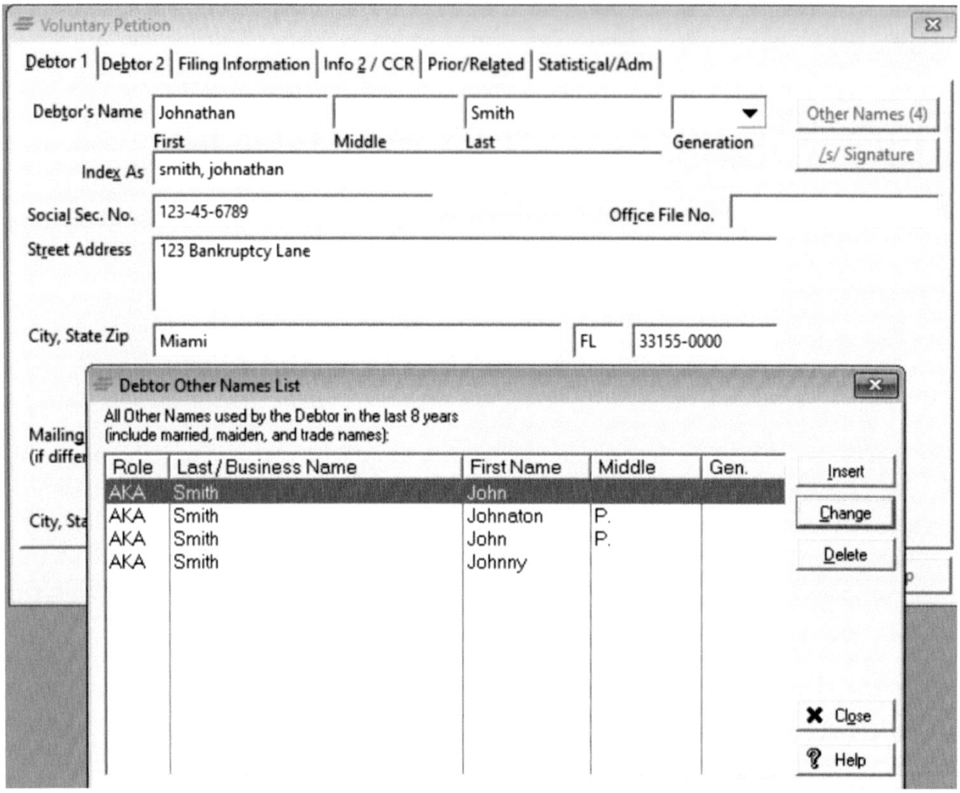

Best Case®

If the debtor's identification does not match the name(s) on the petition or the Social Security number, the Meeting of Creditors is rescheduled even though it's a simple typographical error. An amended petition is filed, and if the Social Security number was incorrect, notice is sent to the three major credit reporting bureaus of the error since the bankruptcy was filed under someone else's Social Security number.

For this reason, clients must approve the petition before filing. Since additional work is required, plus attending another hearing, additional fees and costs can be charged to the client. While the Social Security number is masked on the petition for security purposes, the client can confirm it's correct by looking at Official Form 121.[2] Note, access to Social Security numbers is restricted in CM/ECF.[3]

2 Official Form 121. Your Statement About Your Social Security Numbers.

3 PACER – Public Access to Court Electronic Records. https://pacer.uscourts.gov/file-case/court-cmecf-lookup.

Section 4

Businesses registered to the client are listed in Section 4. If the business is active, depending on the company's size, further inquiries by the trustee are likely, especially with a 2004 Examination.[4] However, in most cases, a business owner that has filed for personal bankruptcy is unlikely to have substantial assets. If there are, the debtor can sell the assets and use the funds to settle with creditors, surrender the assets to the trustee, or proceed with Chapter 13. As always, remember that depending on the facts, time may be your friend or your worst enemy.

If the business is closed, additional information is required, such as the date of closure, the sale or transfer of assets, and the balance in financial accounts at the time of closing.

Section 5

Confirm the addresses match with the documentation provided by the client, whether it's a single or joint filing. Note, some trustees require that driver's licenses be updated within a few days after the Meeting of Creditors. Therefore, clients should update addresses before filing.

Section 6

This section focuses on the residency requirements. If the client meets the residency requirements by living in the district for more than 180 days or has resided mainly in that district during that time frame, then proceed to the next section.

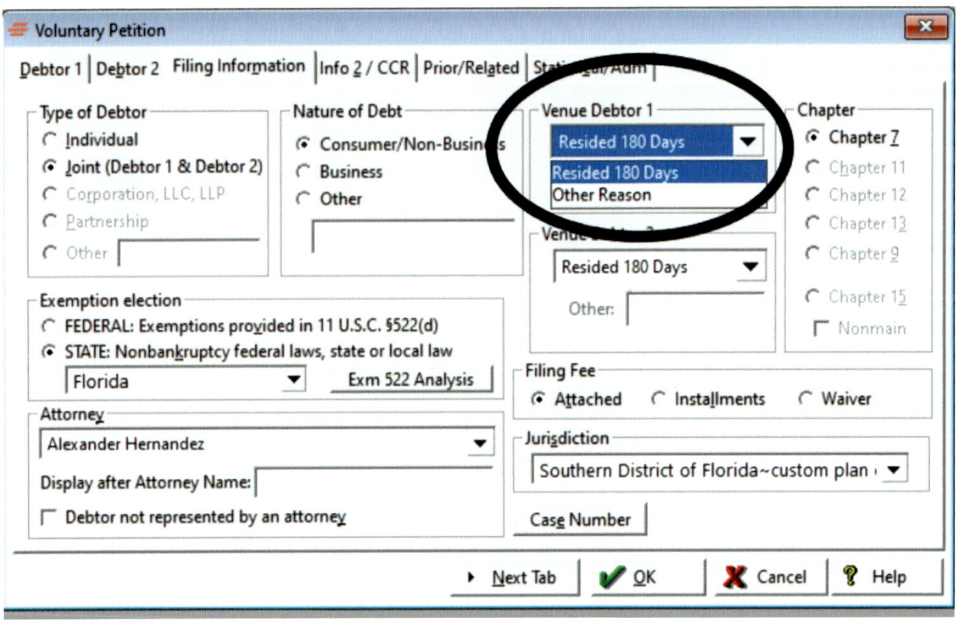

Best Case®

4 Fed. R. Bankr. P. 2004.

Besides the appropriate venue, the exemptions are applied based on domicile and the 730-day rule.[5] In the figure below, the debtor's domicile is in Florida. The drop-down menu allows for the exemptions of other states to be applied if the debtor did not meet the domicile requirements.

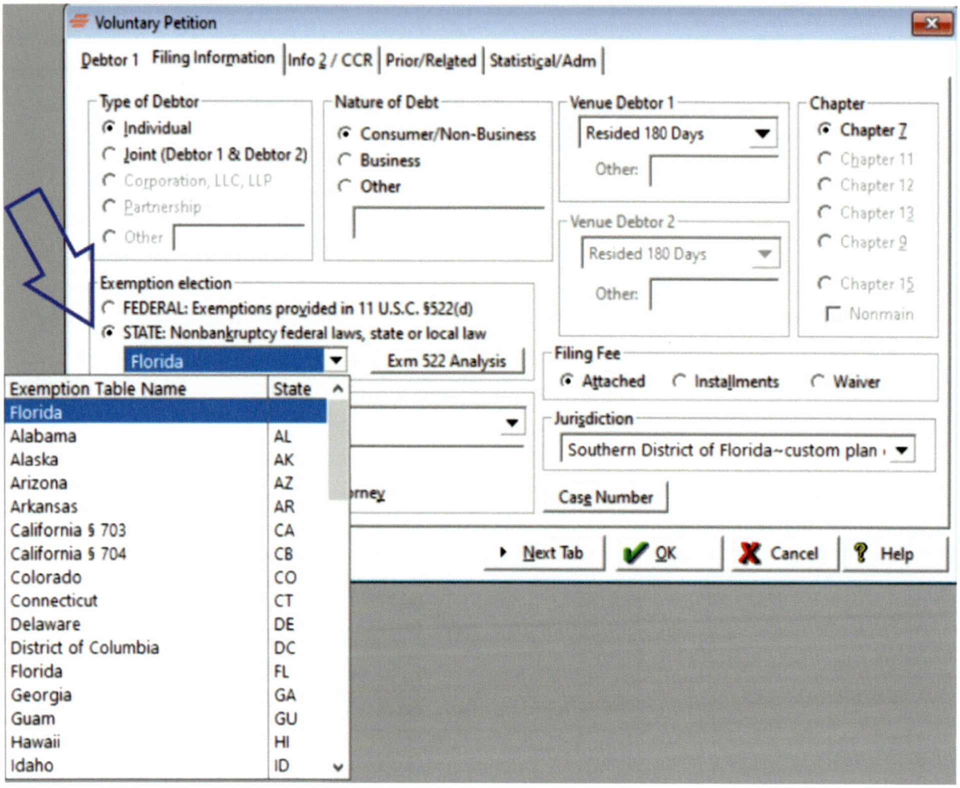

Best Case®

The Best Case® software also provides the opportunity to confirm the correct exemptions are applied. In this figure, when the federal exemptions option was elected, the pop-up window confirms that Florida has opted out of federal exemptions.

5 11 U.S.C. §522(b)(3)(A).

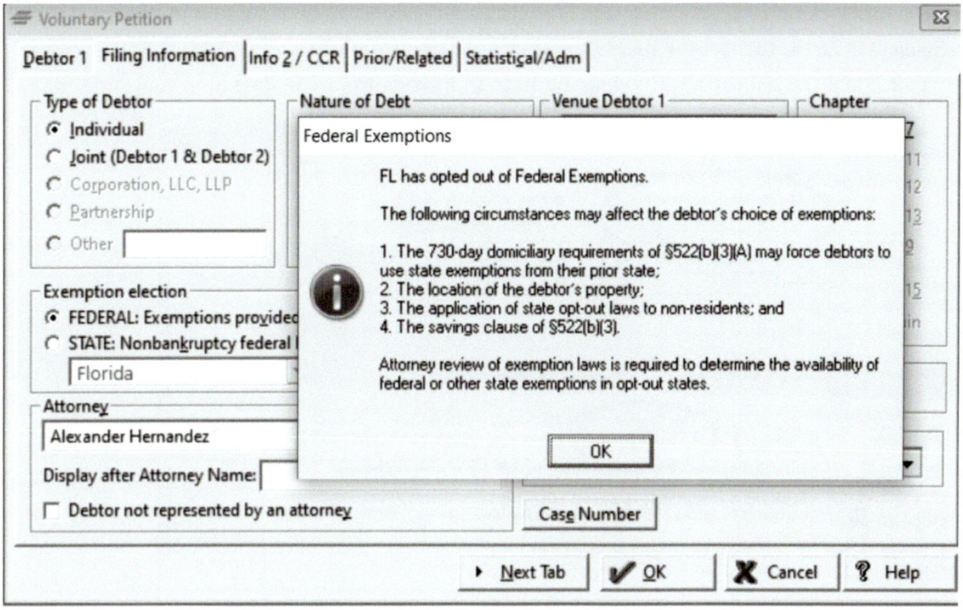

Best Case®

Domicile and exemption issues are resolved by clicking the "Exm 522 Analysis" button and entering the dates in question.

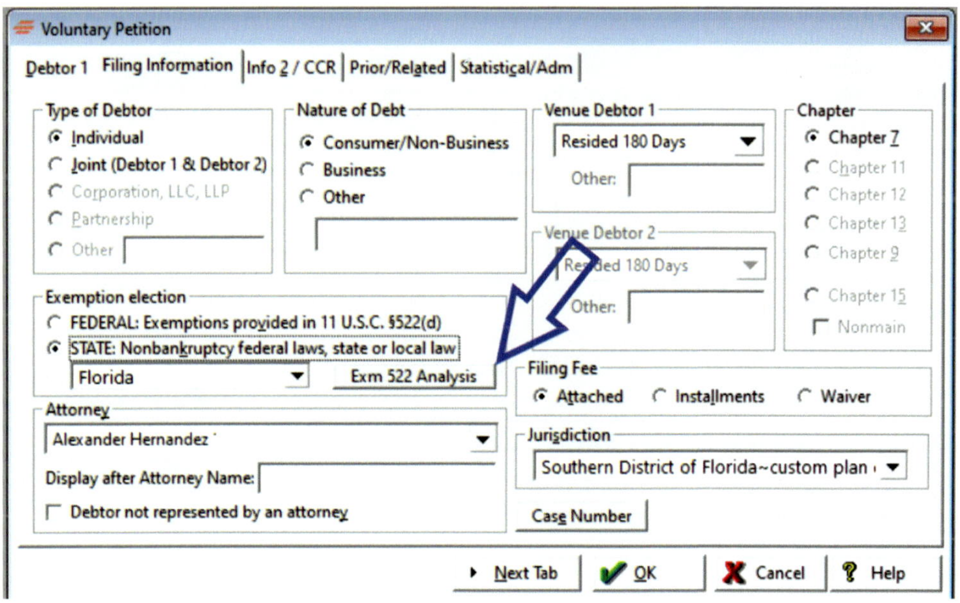

Best Case®

In our example, based on a current date of March 17, 2021, and a move-in date of February 1, 2018, the debtor meets the domicile requirements and complies with the 730-day rule since the debtor has lived in the state of Florida for 1,141 days.[6]

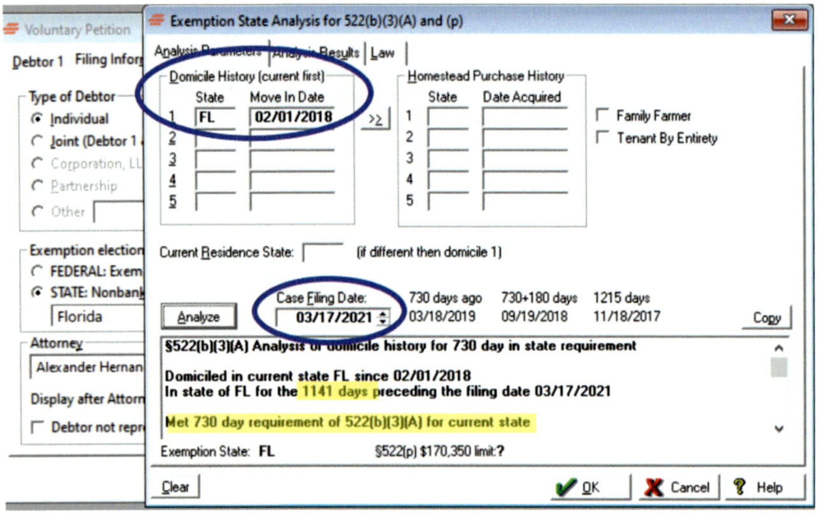

Best Case®

Likewise, a homestead exemption analysis can be performed. Here, the debtor acquired the property three months after relocating to Florida.

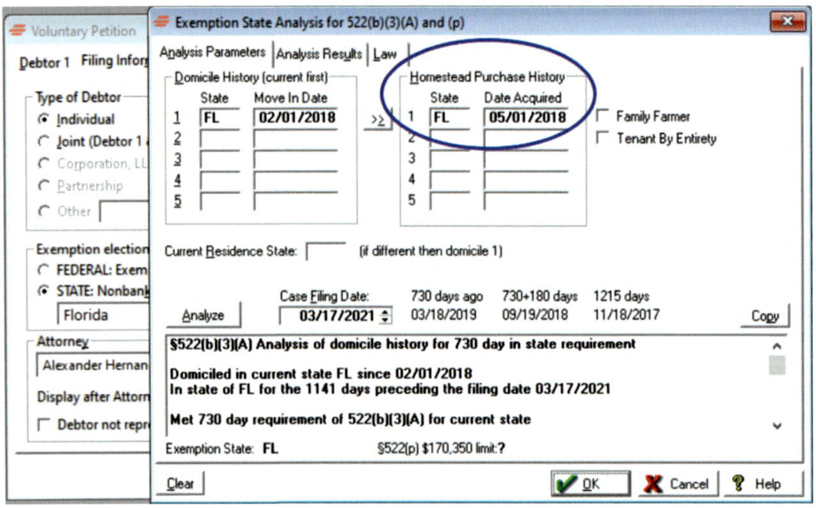

Best Case®

6 Id.

Use the "Analysis Results" tab to confirm if the 1,215-day rule for homestead property exemption has been met.[7] In this case, the debtor is 164 days short, but the debtor could still file for bankruptcy. Option one, of course, is to wait another 165 days. However, if the equity in the property doesn't exceed $170,350, the debtor can proceed to file.

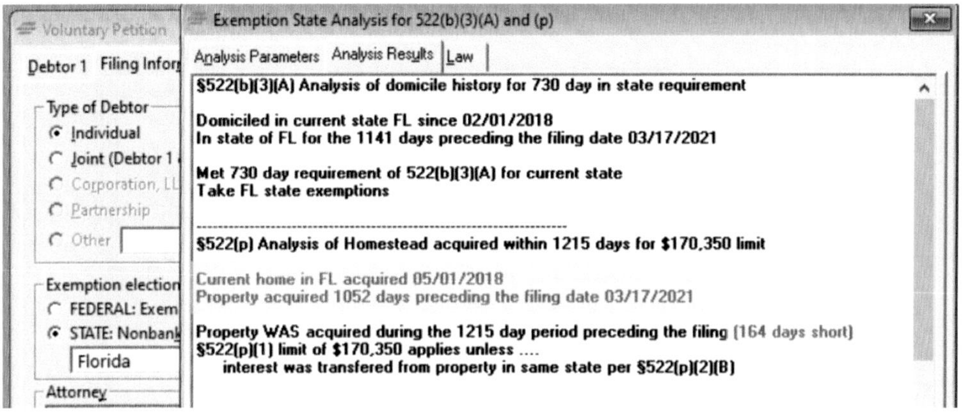

Best Case®

The relevant parts of the Code are summarized by choosing the "Law" tab.

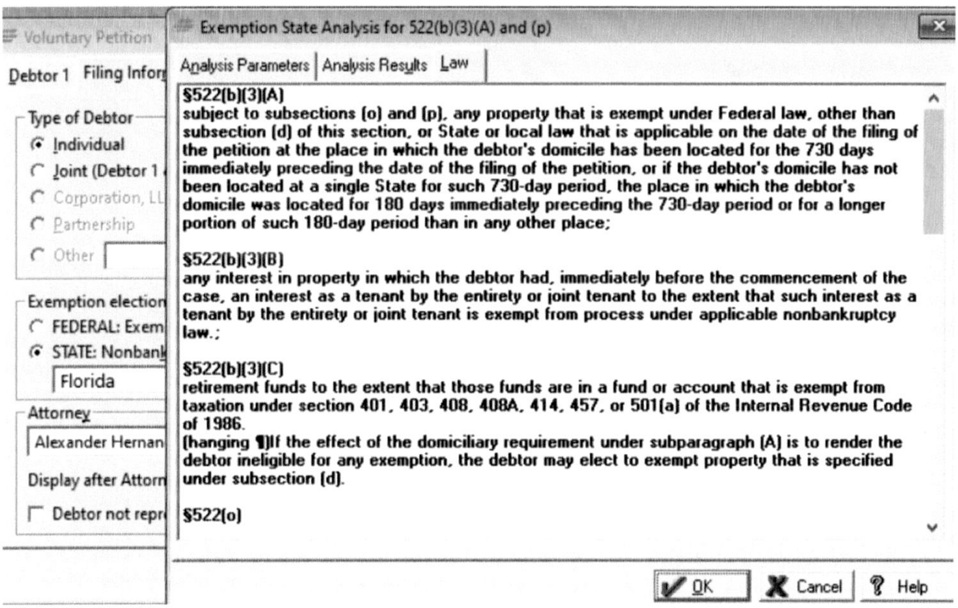

Best Case®

7 11 U.S.C. §522(p)(1).

Note, while the bankruptcy program files the petition based on the debtor's zip code, it's worth taking a few extra seconds to confirm the correct district is chosen if the firm files in multiple districts.

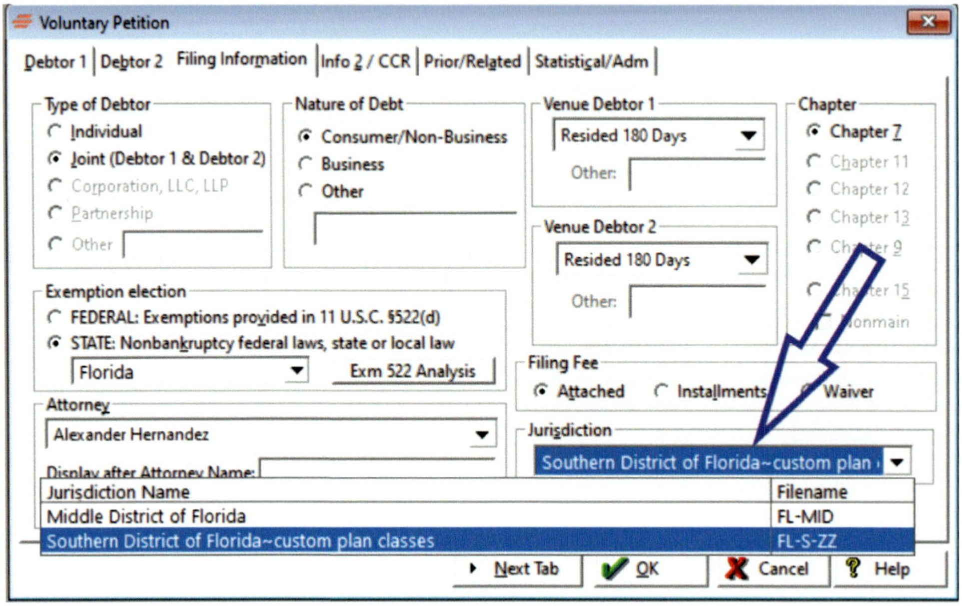

Best Case®

Part 2

Section 7

Which bankruptcy chapter the debtor is filing under will be checked in this section. Bankruptcy programs will provide a notification if the debtor does not pass the means test.[8] For example, with Best Case®, it couldn't be simpler. If there is a bright yellow and red unhappy face, that warns there is a presumption of abuse at.[9] If the happy face is green, there is no issue.[10]

8 Official Form 122A-1. Chapter 7 Statement of Your Current Monthly Income.
9 Id.
10 Id.

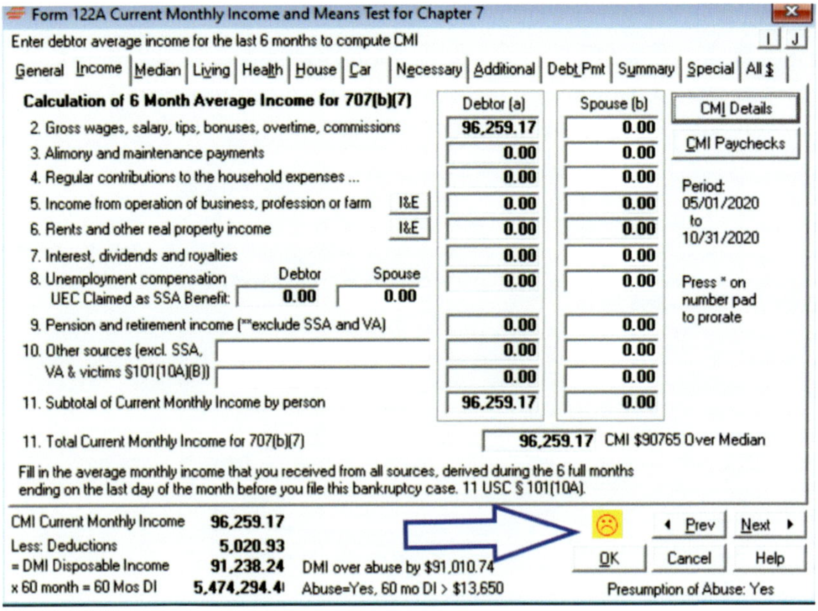

Best Case®

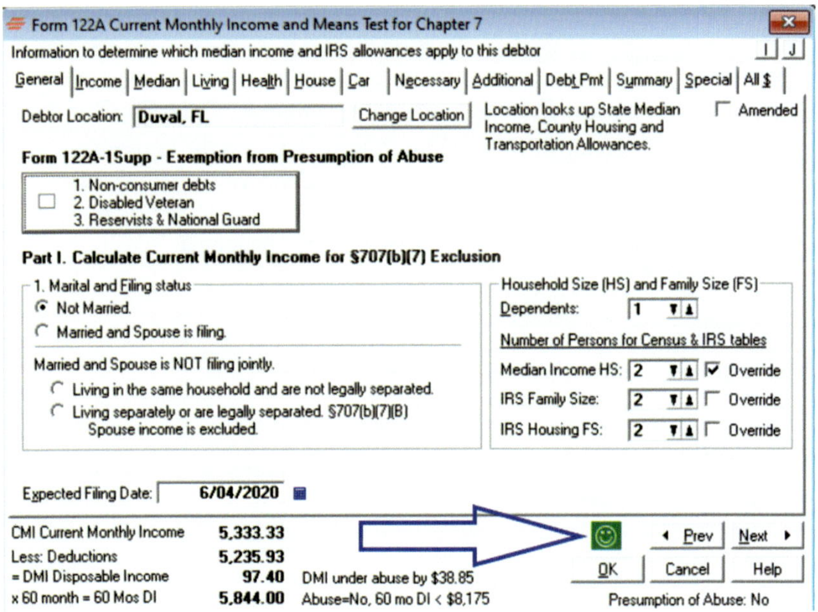

Best Case®

Section 8

Section 8 is completed automatically, but there is the option to request that the filing fee be paid in installments or waived. However, if the debtor can afford an attorney, this request is rarely made, especially since it costs more time for the firm.

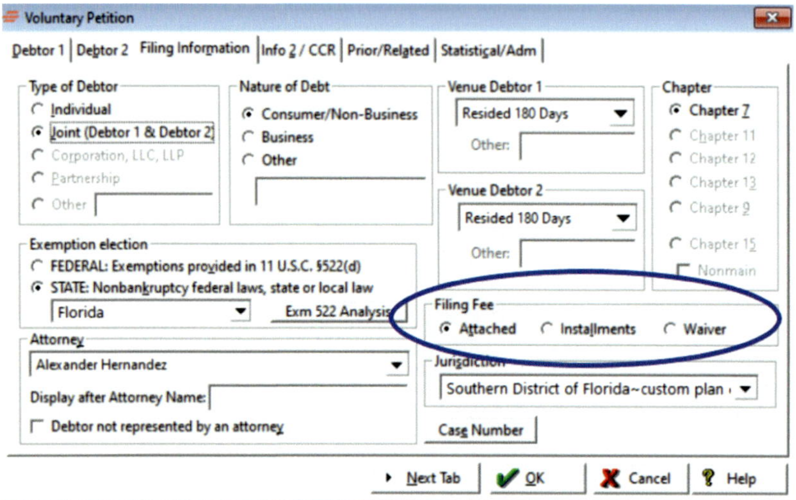

Best Case®

Section 9

With the automated software, inserting the date of a prior bankruptcy will confirm if the debtor can proceed to file. For example, in the figure below, because the bankruptcy was filed more than eight years ago, the debtor can file another Chapter 7.

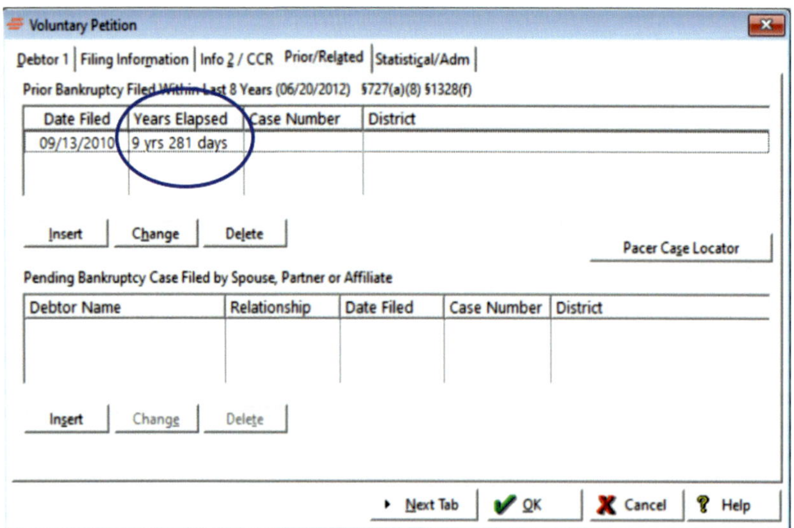

Best Case®

Cases filed more than eight years ago can be excluded, but since most trustees tend to ask questions about prior filings anyway, they can be included since they won't affect the outcome.

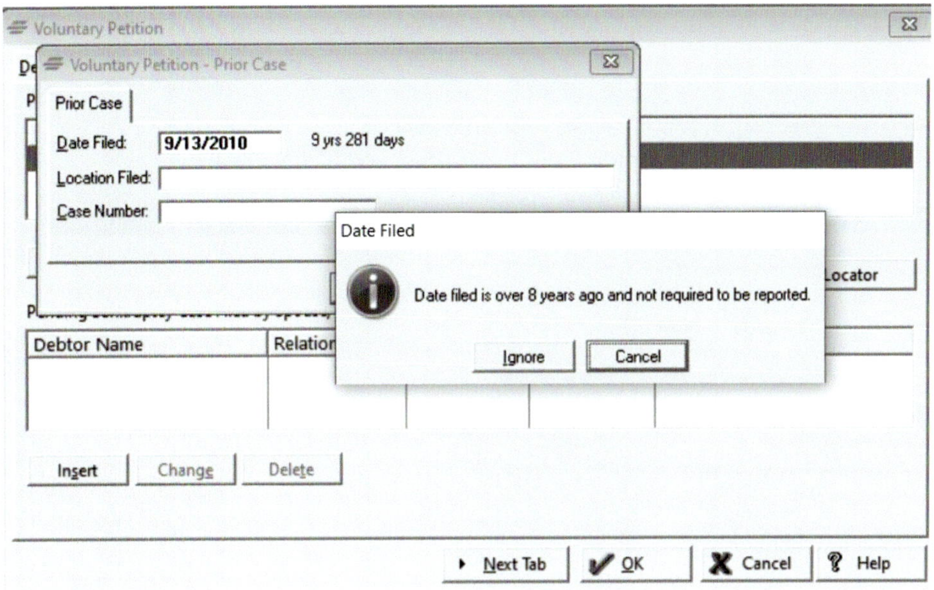

Best Case®

If the filing is within eight years, as in this figure, the number of days between the original and current filing dates is calculated. In this case, it's three years and 300 days.

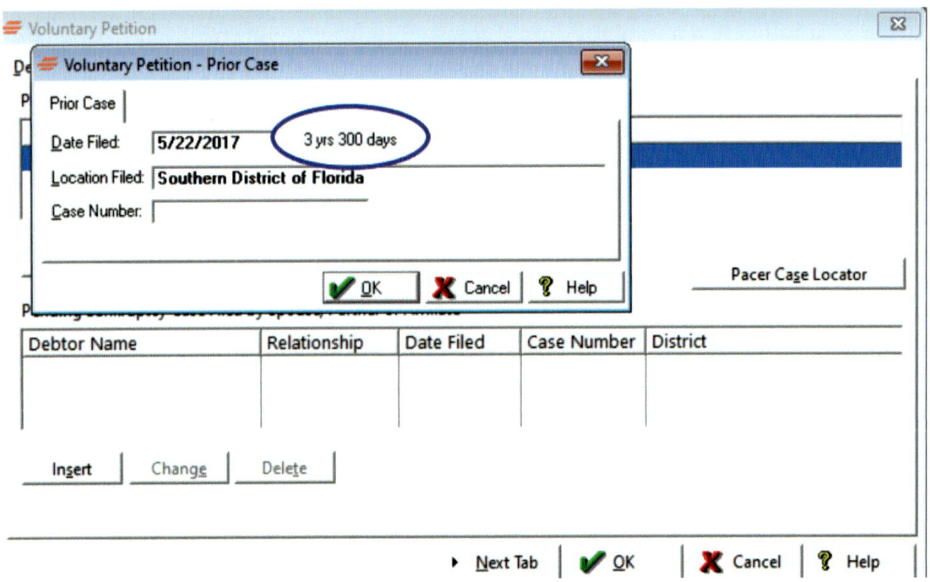

Best Case®

Once the window is closed, the amount of time elapsed since the bankruptcy was filed is highlighted. The top heading provides the date the bankruptcy should have been filed, in this case, March 18, 2013. Also, if research is required, the relevant section of the Code is included. Remember, this only applies if a discharge was entered. If the case was dismissed, then there is a six-month prejudice period.[11]

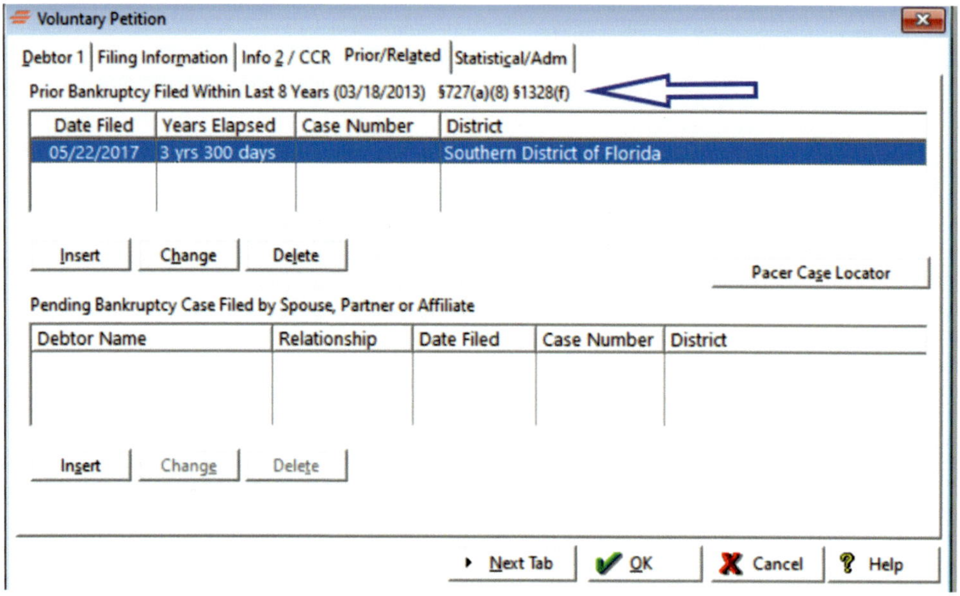

Best Case®

Each district is different, and in the Middle District of Florida, upon filing, the court's system automatically references a prior bankruptcy, even from another district. In this case, the debtor previously filed for bankruptcy in the Southern District of Florida.

Section 10

This section is self-explanatory but again goes to the issue of pending divorces and the division of assets that could affect the bankruptcy case if assets are over-exempt.

Section 11

BAPCPA introduced new provisions regarding evictions to curb the abuse of serial filing.[12] Like a foreclosure, an eviction proceeding halts (temporarily) because of the automatic stay. Before this provision, serial filing seemed common, especially with technology lacking. When I gained admittance to the federal bar in 2000, the internet was still in its infancy, especially in the legal world. Therefore, if a client had filed multiple bankruptcies, an attorney

11 11 U.S.C. §109(g).
12 11 U.S.C. §362(b)(22).

was unlikely to know unless advised by the client or the attorney had previously represented the debtor. Again, you can see the importance of having clients complete the intake on their own. The figure below illustrates how it has become more difficult for serial filers to take advantage of the automatic stay.

Bankruptcy Adversary Query Reports Utilities Search Logout

#	Docket Text
1 (56 pgs)	Voluntary Petition under Chapter 7. (Fee Paid.). Schedules and Summary of Assets. Statement of Financial Affairs. Statement of Intentions. Disclosure of Compensation. Statement of Income and Means Test Calculation. Filed by Alexander Hernandez on behalf of [redacted] (Hernandez, Alexander) [redacted]
2	Statement of Debtors Social Security Numbers Filed by Alexander Hernandez on behalf of Debtor [redacted] (Hernandez, Alexander) (Entered: [redacted]
	Receipt of Filing Fee for Voluntary Petition (Chapter 7) [redacted]) [misc,volp7a2] (335.00). Receipt Number [redacted] Amount Paid $ 335.00 (U.S. Treasury) (Entered [redacted]
3 (1 pg)	Certificate of Credit Counseling. Date Course was Completed: [redacted] Filed by Alexander Hernandez on behalf of Debtor [redacted] (Hernandez, Alexander) (Entered: [redacted]
→	Prior Bankruptcy Case(s) for debtor [redacted] Case Number [redacted] Chapter 7 filed in Florida Southern Bankruptcy Court on [redacted], Standard Discharge on [redacted]

REAL CASES

A client had filed multiple bankruptcies *pro se* without my knowledge. *Pro se* debtors typically file a bare-bones petition, meaning most of the petition is left blank because the debtor has no intent on receiving a discharge. Instead, the debtor lists secured creditors such as the mortgage lender, but unsecured creditors are omitted. Why bother doing all the work a petition requires if the goal is to delay a foreclosure.

At the Meeting of Creditors, I became aware for the first time of multiple filings. The landlord had been trying to evict the debtor for months. Each time the landlord was ready to finalize the eviction, the tenant filed for bankruptcy. However, this case took another unexpected turn. The office called minutes before the hearing to advise me that the retainer check was returned for insufficient funds. That terminated the attorney–client relationship!

The day before, the client consulted with my former law partner and called me for my advice on accepting the case last minute. He said he trusted her, and since he was a good judge of character, considering he had more than 20 years of experience at the time, I left the decision to him, although I was concerned about accepting a check last minute. So, lesson number one, checks shouldn't be accepted for any case that has to be filed on an emergency basis. The same applies to debit cards because clients may dispute the transactions later on. Of course, with a bankruptcy case, credit card payments cannot be accepted but can for other areas of law, so be wary of office policy and the forms of acceptable payments in emergency cases. Regardless of the trend toward a cashless society, cash is still king.

In this case, what made this situation even worse is the lack of technology. At the time, bankruptcy petitions were filed in person or sent via regular U.S. mail to the clerk's office. Because new filings required the original bankruptcy petition plus four copies, a substantial amount of paper was used, so the best practice was to drop off petition(s) at the clerk's office and pick up stamped copies a few days later. Because we were short on time, we sent a paralegal downtown to file the petition, so more time and money were wasted. Lesson learned!

Section 362(b)(22) is Congress's attempt to limit such acts by debtors and hopefully protect attorneys like myself that were duped. Actually, I wasn't the one duped. Regardless of the semantics involved, Section 362(b)(22) allows the landlord to proceed with the eviction if a judgment for possession of the residential property has been obtained prior to filing the bankruptcy.

In this figure, since the debtor rents, that option is marked, and nothing else is required. But, if the debtor is in eviction proceedings and the landlord has obtained a judgment, then the landlord's information is required.

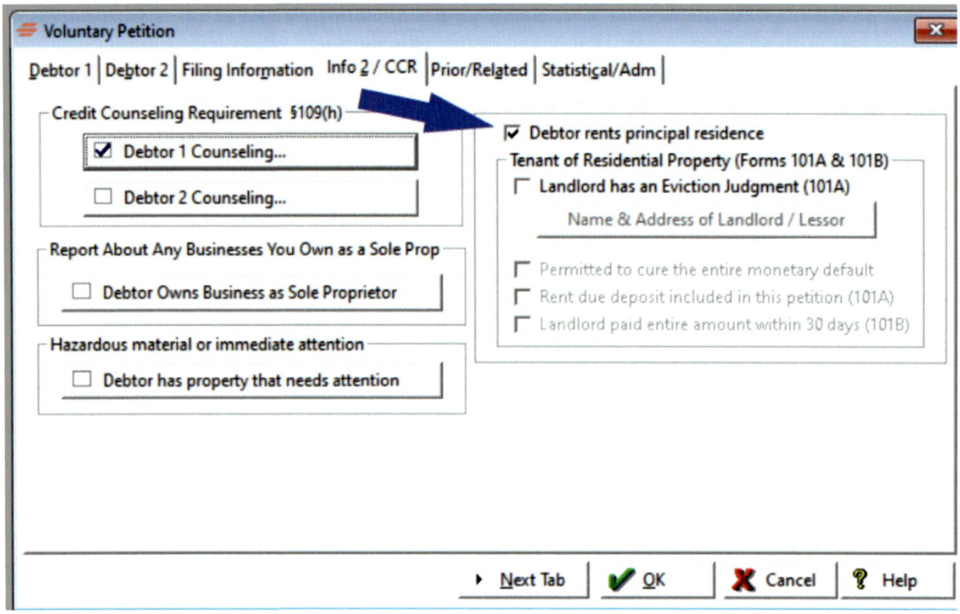

Best Case®

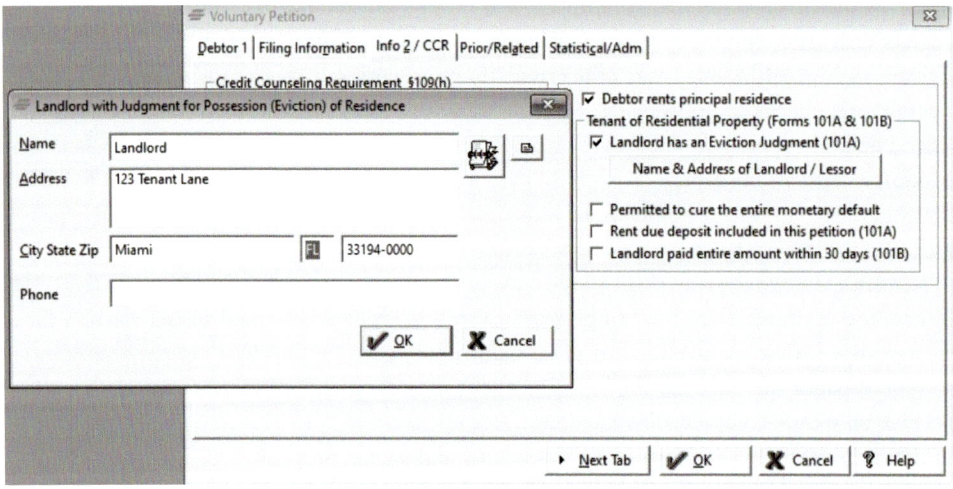

Best Case®

The steps in the eviction case at this point mirror the process in state court. The debtor/renter can remain in the leased property if the rent amount plus arrears are deposited in the court registry. This is a winner takes all scenario because the winner gets the funds, whether it's the landlord or the tenant. Most of the time, renters fail to deposit the funds in the court registry, and evictions are finalized relatively quickly. Because of BAPCPA, the power of the automatic stay has now been considerably weakened with evictions. However, at least with §362(l), the eviction is delayed for another 30 days.[13]

In Section 11 of the petition, if the landlord has obtained an eviction judgment against the debtor, *Form 101A* is completed.[14] The first section requires completing the form if the landlord has a judgment for possession. The second section is completed if the debtor intends on staying in the property. Finally, the landlord is served with a copy of Form 101A and paid the delinquent amount to keep the protection of the automatic stay.[15]

Besides my case, another excellent example of a serial filer is the case of Maurice Symonette, who received political infamy and 15 minutes of fame as the founder of "Blacks for Trump." Symonette was seen regularly in the audience behind former President Trump at rallies.

Symonette was barred from filing bankruptcy for five years in any district in the United States since he had filed bankruptcy a total of eight times, with each case dismissed.[16] In the instant case, Symonette testified that the purpose of filing the bankruptcy was to stop the eviction. He also appealed with the Third District Court of Appeal (state appellate court in Miami-Dade County) to further delay the eviction.[17]

Chief Bankruptcy Judge Laurel M. Isicoff's ruling outlined that, per Symonette's testimony, there was no point in proceeding with the bankruptcy case once the eviction was complete.[18] As a result, Judge Isicoff ruled against Symonette, stating that "a case that is filed solely for the purpose of triggering the automatic stay and for no other purpose is a bad faith filing."[19] Symonette even tried removing Judge Isicoff from the case by accusing her of being a racist.[20] Read the article on HuffPost.com to learn more about Symonette's colorful past.[21]

13 11 U.S.C. §362(l).
14 Official Form 101A. Initial Statement about an Eviction Judgment against You.
15 Id., 11 U.S.C. §362(a)(3). See also Official Form 101B. Statement about Payment of an Eviction Judgment against You (Individuals).
16 In Re: Maurice Symonette, Case 18-15891 BKC-LMI.
17 Id., page 2, paragraph 1.
18 Id., page 3, paragraph 3.
19 Id. See In Re: Curtis L. Stuart@UCCI-207, 2005 WL 3953894 at *4 (Bankr. ND. Ga 2005) (Concluding Bad Faith Exists Where the Debtor Files for Bankruptcy for the "Sole Purpose of Invoking the Automatic Stay.").
20 Id. page 4, paragraph 3.
21 Id. at footnote 5. Supra, note 16. The Real Story Behind That "Blacks for Trump Guy" at the Arizona Rally. HuffPost.com. Retrieved on March 11, 2020. www.huffpost.com/entry/blacks-for-trump-man-rally-maurice-symonette_n_599db434e4b0d8dde99aa7d2.

Part 3

Section 12

Any business owned by the debtor as a sole proprietor will be listed in this section and in Section 5 of Schedules A/B and exempted in Schedule C.[22]

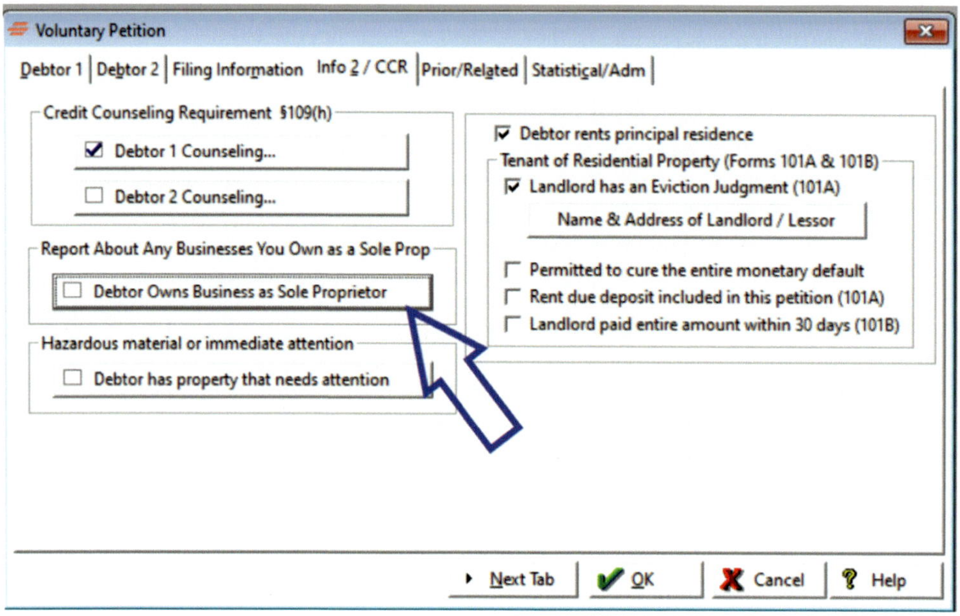

Best Case®

If a client lists a business, get details on the assets of the company. For example, a client employed as a handyman, mechanic, etc., may own several thousands of dollars worth of tools. Since clients rarely know how to appraise their business correctly, start by asking general questions. Is there inventory, tools, or a warehouse that is owned or rented? What would be a fair sale price for the business? A client may suggest reviewing the tax returns, but tax returns are never an accurate portrayal of a business' value.

Also, depending on the type of business, there may be large deposits and withdrawals. For example, there's a $6,000 deposit, but an immediate withdrawal of $5,000. Usually, that's an issue, but if $5,000 was for materials paid for by the homeowner, then the client's income is the remaining $1,000. If necessary, request receipts. Also, the client should provide additional documentation regarding the business, like bank statements and tax returns.

22 Official Form 106A/B. Schedule A/B: Property (Individuals); Official Form 106C. Schedule C: The Property You Claim as Exempt (Individuals).

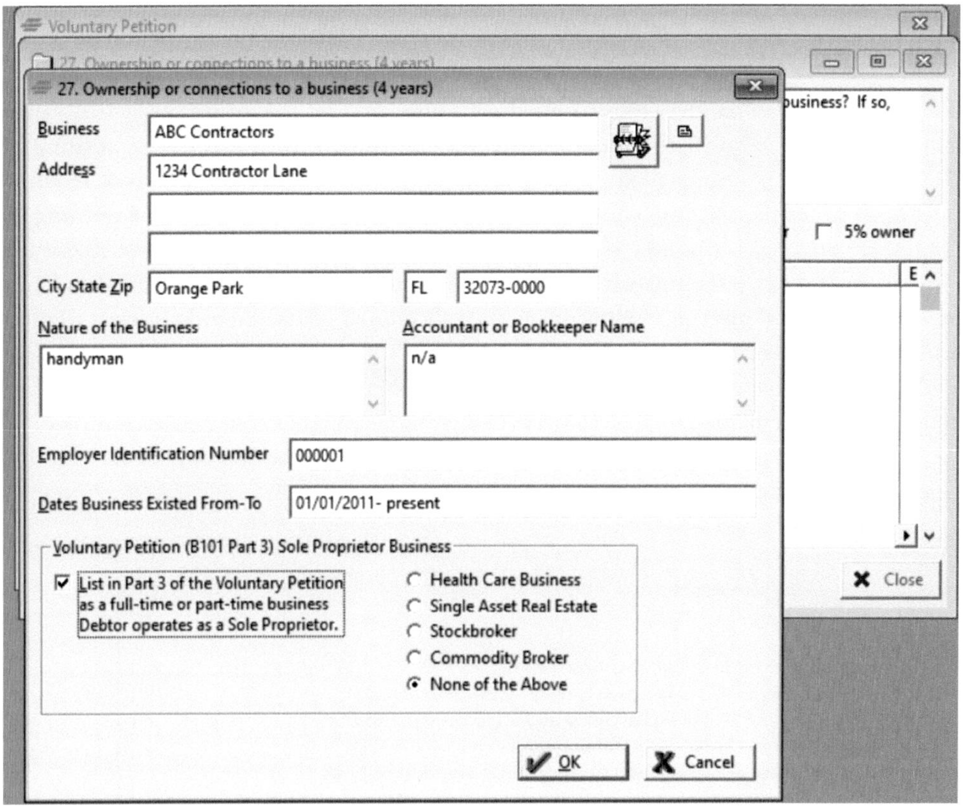

Best Case®

Section 13

Chapter 11 could apply to an individual subject to the debt limits of Chapter 13.[23] Chapter 11 relates typically to businesses, but even then, it's rare since it's less than 1 percent of all bankruptcies filed.[24] However, Chapter 11 filings did increase substantially in 2020, and that trend will likely continue due to the coronavirus pandemic. Chapters 11 and 13 are similar in the sense that it is a reorganization. Note there are no debt limits to file Chapter 7.

Part 4

Section 14

This section is likely to apply to business bankruptcy and, therefore, is inapplicable for a Chapter 7 consumer bankruptcy.

23 11 U.S.C §109(e).

24 U.S. Dept. of Justice, U.S. Trustee's Program, Preliminary Report on Chapter 7 Asset Cases 1994–2000.

Part 5

Section 15

The completion date of the credit counseling course ensures the certificate is still valid. Some jurisdictions require listing the completion date in CM/ECF at the time of filing as well.[25] Note, if the petition is filed the same day the class was completed, Best Case® requires confirmation that the class was completed before the filing. There may also be a warning in CM/ECF.[26] So long as it is, even if less than an hour before, §111 has been complied with.[27]

The certificate for the financial management course must be filed within 60 days from the initial creditors' meeting.[28] Confirm with your chosen course provider if they file the second certificate as a courtesy.

In the figure below, credit counseling was completed on April 5, 2020, 60 days before "today," so there remains a total of 120 days before the certificate expires. Therefore, adding the "60 days prior to today" and the "120 days to file" equals the 180 days or six months, which is the length of time the certificate is valid for.

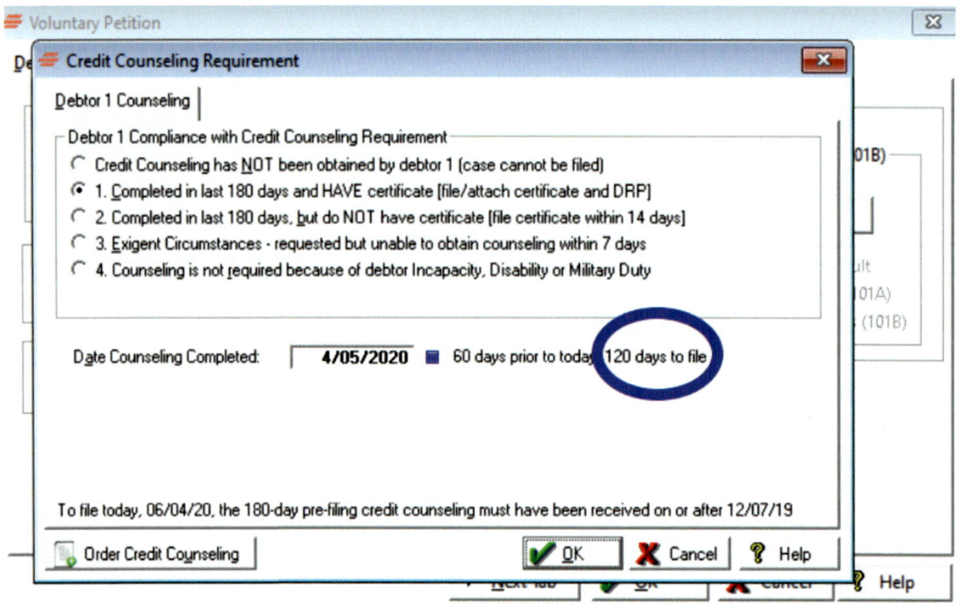

Best Case®

25 PACER – Public Access to Court Electronic Records. https://pacer.uscourts.gov/file-case/court-cmecf-lookup.

26 Id.

27 11 U.S.C. §111.

28 Fed. R. Bankr. P. 1007(b)(7)(c).

Exceptions to Credit Counseling

Like with every rule, there are always exceptions, and credit counseling is no different. First, the U.S. Trustee may decide that the credit counseling agencies in that district are unable to "provide adequate services to the additional individuals."[29] You can foresee that issue in a rural area, but since credit counseling occurs mostly by phone or internet these days, it's unlikely. The trustee also has the authority to revoke approval of the credit counseling agency at any time.[30] I would be the first to admit that practitioners aren't in the habit of researching the agencies for compliance, but maybe we should. That extra minute or two spent could save us a fortune in headaches.

Credit counseling can be waived under "exigent circumstances."[31] The statute provides an example, such as when the debtor requests credit counseling services from an approved non-profit budget and credit counseling agency but was unable to obtain the services during the seven-day period beginning on the date on which the debtor made that request.[32] This explanation must be "satisfactory to the court."[33] Even if the court is satisfied, the debtor still has to complete the course within 30 days of filing the petition, or with a showing of good cause, extend the deadline by another 15 days.[34] Again, since credit counseling takes place online, it would be difficult to imagine this scenario.

Another set of exceptions exists for a debtor that is either incapacitated, disabled, or on active military duty in a combat zone.[35] This section defines "disability" as a person who is "physically impaired as to be unable, after reasonable effort, to participate in an in-person, telephone, or internet briefing."[36] Incapacity is defined as "impaired by reason of mental illness or mental deficiency so that he is incapable of realizing and making rational decisions with respect to his financial responsibilities."[37]

Because of the relative ease of taking a credit counseling class, it's not recommended to depend on an exception. Courses are available 24/7 online and don't have to be completed in one sitting. Since the judge has discretion, it's an unnecessary risk to file a motion to seek a waiver or delay of the credit counseling class.

29 11 U.S.C. §109(h)(2)(A).
30 11 U.S.C §109(h)(2)(B).
31 11 U.S.C §109(h)(3)(A)(i).
32 11 U.S.C. §109(h)(3)(A)(ii)
33 11 U.S.C. §109(h)(3)(A)(iii)
34 11 U.S.C. §109(h)(3)(B)
35 11 U.S.C. §109(h)(4).
36 Id.
37 Id.

☐ **I certify that I asked for credit counseling services from an approved agency, but was unable to obtain those services during the 7 days after I made my request, and exigent circumstances merit a 30-day temporary waiver of the requirement.**

To ask for a 30-day temporary waiver of the requirement, attach a separate sheet explaining what efforts you made to obtain the briefing, why you were unable to obtain it before you filed for bankruptcy, and what exigent circumstances required you to file this case.

Your case may be dismissed if the court is dissatisfied with your reasons for not receiving a briefing before you filed for bankruptcy.
If the court is satisfied with your reasons, you must still receive a briefing within 30 days after you file. You must file a certificate from the approved agency, along with a copy of the payment plan you developed, if any. If you do not do so, your case may be dismissed.

Any extension of the 30-day deadline is granted only for cause and is limited to a maximum of 15 days.

☐ **I am not required to receive a briefing about credit counseling because of:**

Best Case®

☐ **I am not required to receive a briefing about credit counseling because of:**

☐ **Incapacity.**
I have a mental illness or a mental deficiency that makes me incapable of realizing or making rational decisions about finances.

☐ **Disability.**
My physical disability causes me to be unable to participate in a briefing in person, by phone, or through the internet, even after I reasonably tried to do so.

☐ **Active duty.**
I am currently on active military duty in a military combat zone.

If you believe you are not required to receive a briefing about credit counseling, you must file a motion for waiver credit counseling with the court.

Best Case®

PRACTICE TIP

When a client is quoted a fee, it should include the costs of the credit counseling and financial management courses and the court filing fee. Costs are paid at the end except for Chapter 13, where fees may be paid through the plan. Once costs are paid, the client is enrolled in credit counseling. It's not done sooner because if the course is completed too early, there's the risk the client will not be able to pay the balance on time or provide documents timely, resulting in the certificate expiring. Clients are never excited about retaking the class or paying for it again.

Some law firms will have the client enroll and pay for the course independently, but this only slows down the case. It is far more efficient to have collected the costs from the client and enroll the client automatically. A firm can register for an account with the debt relief agency that provides a unique user code and password that is given to the client upon the final payment of fees and costs. When a client enrolls and completes the class, the credit counseling agency will notify the firm via email to prevent fraud. In addition, there's usually access to the client dashboard to confirm the status. Note that classes are offered in multiple languages as well.

Part 6

Sections 16 through 20 are self-explanatory and are completed automatically by the bankruptcy program.

Part 7

Because petitions are filed online, the debtor's signature appears automatically because of the software. Since signed declarations aren't required when filed online through an attorney, remember to receive confirmation from the client that the petition has been approved.

SUMMARY

Official Form 101 requires basic information about the debtor such as name, current address, and Social Security number. At this stage, residency and domicile need to be analyzed to avoid dismissal or exemption issues. If the debtor has filed bankruptcy previously, confirm the date of dismissal or discharge to avoid a situation of a bad faith filing. If the debtor is in eviction proceedings and the landlord has obtained a judgment for possession, Official Form 101A is filed as well as Official Form 101B if the debtor wishes to remain in the rental property for an additional 30-plus days.

KEYWORDS AND TERMS

- Bare-bones petition
- Eviction judgment

- Eviction proceedings
- Exceptions to credit counseling
- Exigent circumstances
- Form 101 Voluntary Petition for Individuals Filing Bankruptcy
- Form 101A Initial Statement about an Eviction Judgment against You (Individuals)
- Form 121 Your Statement about Your Social Security Numbers
- Judgment for possession
- Serial filer
- Sole proprietor

DISCUSSION QUESTIONS

1. The debtor filed for bankruptcy four years ago. What additional information would you need to confirm if the debtor can file bankruptcy again?
2. If there is an eviction pending, how is it affected by the filing of bankruptcy?

PRACTICE QUESTIONS AND EXERCISES

1. The client cannot complete the credit counseling class before filing for bankruptcy but possibly meets the conditions of an exception. Complete the appropriate form/section.
2. Based on Question 2, prepare an email to the client stating the risks involved in seeking an exception to credit counseling.
3. Complete Forms 101, 101A, and 101B of the petition.

REFERENCES

11 U.S.C. §109.

11 U.S.C. §111.

11 U.S.C. §362.

11 U.S.C. §522.

Fed. R. Bankr. P. 1007.

Fed. R. Bankr. P. 2004.

In Re: Curtis L. Stuart@UCCI-207, 2005 WL 3953894 at *4 (Bankr. ND. Ga 2005) (Concluding Bad Faith Exists Where the Debtor Files for Bankruptcy for the "Sole Purpose of Invoking the Automatic Stay").

In Re: Maurice Symonette, Case 18-15891 BKC-LMI.

Official Form 101. Voluntary Petition for Individuals Filing for Bankruptcy.

Official Form 101A. Initial Statement about an Eviction Judgment against You.

Official Form 101B. Statement about Payment of an Eviction Judgment against You (Individuals).

Official Form 106A/B. Schedule A/B: Property (Individuals).

Official Form 106C. Schedule C: The Property You Claim as Exempt (Individuals).

Official Form 121. Your Statement about Your Social Security Numbers.

Official Form 122A-1. Chapter 7 Statement of Your Current Monthly Income.

PACER – Public Access to Court Electronic Records. https://pacer.uscourts.gov/file-case/court-cmecf-lookup.

"The Real Story Behind That 'Blacks for Trump Guy' at the Arizona Rally." HuffPost.com. Retrieved on March 11, 2020. www.huffpost.com/entry/blacks-for-trump-man-rally-maurice-symonette_n_599db434e4b0d8dde99aa7d2.

U.S. Dept. of Justice, U.S. Trustee's Program, Preliminary Report on Chapter 7 Asset Cases 1994–2000.

CHAPTER 13

Assets and Liabilities

OFFICIAL FORM 106DEC: DECLARATION ABOUT AN INDIVIDUAL DEBTOR'S SCHEDULES

Because of bankruptcy software like Best Case®, the debtor's and attorney's signatures appear on the petition automatically/digitally. However, the declaration of the debtor's schedules is still part of the forms filed with the bankruptcy.[1] Previously, a separate form was required to be signed by the debtor and filed with the bankruptcy petition. While this requirement no longer exists, it does for bankruptcy petition preparers who must sign and file Form 119.[2]

The debtor's declaration is simply a statement that the petition is true and correct. Also, the debtor is acknowledging that bankruptcy fraud is subject to criminal fines and penalties of up to $250,000 and 20 years in federal prison under 18 U.S.C., sections 152, 1341, 1519, and 3571 for any false statements, concealing property, or obtaining money or property by fraud.[3]

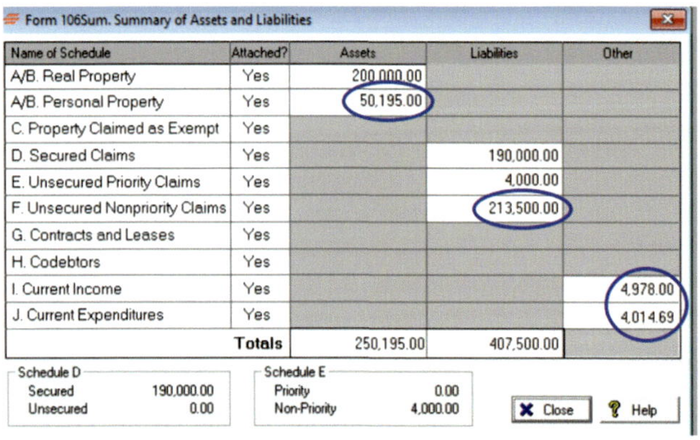

Form 106Sum. Summary of Assets and Liabilities

Name of Schedule	Attached?	Assets	Liabilities	Other
A/B. Real Property	Yes	200,000.00		
A/B. Personal Property	Yes	50,195.00		
C. Property Claimed as Exempt	Yes			
D. Secured Claims	Yes		190,000.00	
E. Unsecured Priority Claims	Yes		4,000.00	
F. Unsecured Nonpriority Claims	Yes		213,500.00	
G. Contracts and Leases	Yes			
H. Codebtors	Yes			
I. Current Income	Yes			4,978.00
J. Current Expenditures	Yes			4,014.69
	Totals	250,195.00	407,500.00	

Schedule D		Schedule E	
Secured	190,000.00	Priority	0.00
Unsecured	0.00	Non-Priority	4,000.00

Close Help

Best Case®

1 Official Form 106Dec. Declaration About an Individual Debtor's Schedules
2 Official Form 119. Bankruptcy Petition Preparer's Notice, Declaration and Signature.
3 18 U.S.C.A. § 152, §1341, §1519, §3571.

DOI: 10.4324/9781003203278-14

OFFICIAL FORM 106SUM: SUMMARY OF ASSETS AND LIABILITIES AND CERTAIN STATISTICAL INFORMATION

Official Form 106 is a snapshot of the debtor's assets and liabilities and helps spot anything that may seem out of place.[4] At this stage, the petition is incomplete, but we'll briefly review it to remain consistent with the order in which the forms are published. Note that the figures update automatically when changes are made to the schedules.

In the figure below, the personal property and unsecured debt figures seem high, as well as the disposable income. It may be a typographical error. Maybe an extra "zero" was added by mistake to an asset. Still, that simple mistake will require amending the bankruptcy petition, costing time and money. Once the petition is complete, we'll review the summary to see if any errors were committed.

Schedules A/B

Part 1: Real Property

Schedule A/B is where the debtor's assets are listed. In the next figure, the different categories available for assets are shown.[5]

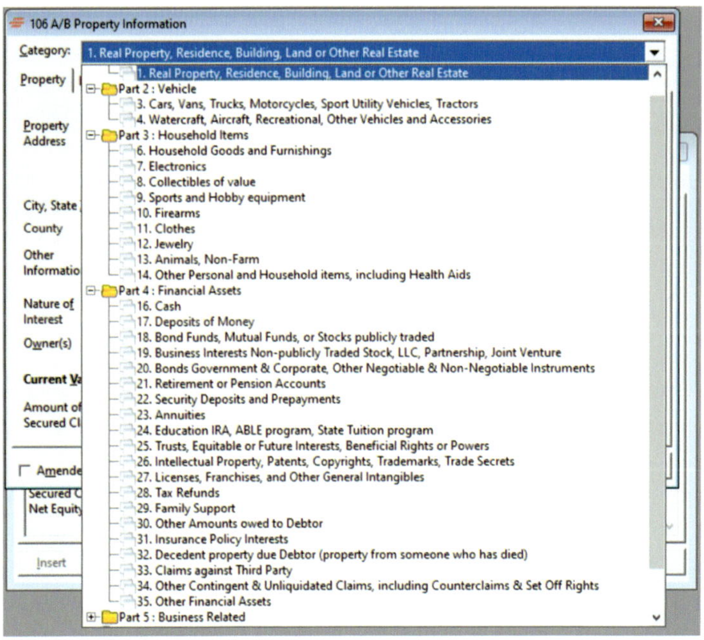

Best Case®

4 Official Form 106Sum. A Summary of Your Assets and Liabilities and Certain Statistical Information (Individuals).

5 Official Form 106A/B. Schedule A/B: Property (Individuals).

The County Property Appraiser's Office will have relevant information related to the debtor's real property. Since it's a government website, it's a credible source and has information such as market value, lot size, purchase date, and sale/transfer dates. Note that county websites usually value homes much lower than commercial websites, so use multiple sources if there are exemption issues. In the "Other Information" section, reference the source of the valuation.

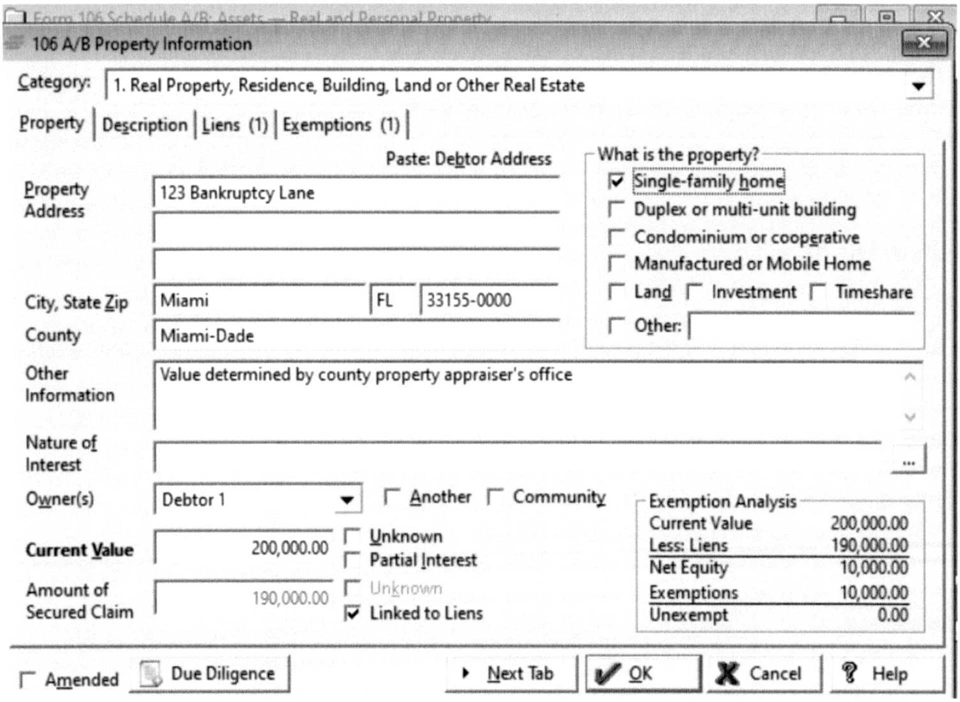

Best Case®

Since creditors receive notice of a bankruptcy filing, creditor information is listed in the "Liens" tab. Additional information such as "Claim Amount" (mortgage balance) is included, as well as the "Nature of Lien," in this case, a first mortgage. The outstanding balance and account number are available on the most recent mortgage statement; sometimes, credit reports list the full account number as well. Note that the account number can be "masked." The date the debt was incurred is not likely to be on the mortgage statement but will be on the credit report. With time, as more creditors are added, a time-saving feature saves creditor contact information, so the creditor's address is filled in with one click.

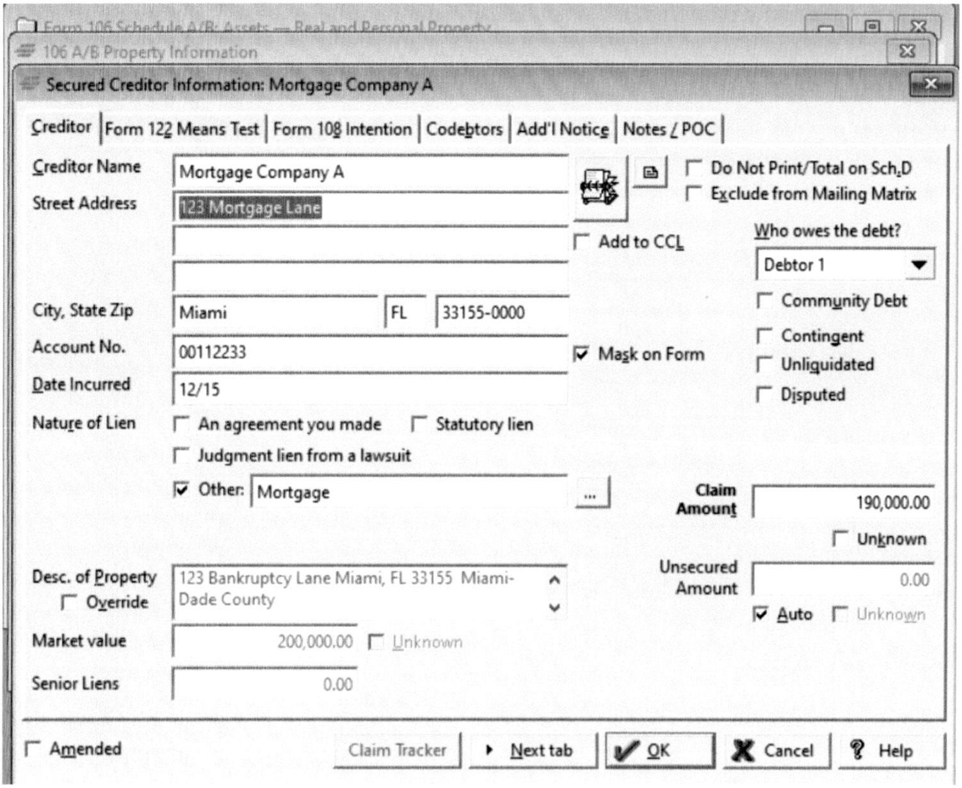

Best Case®

If the client does not pass the means test, the "Form 122 Means Test" tab requires details on the monthly payment, including escrow, and the number of months left on the loan.[6] Note that the maximum amount of months is 60, the same as Chapter 13. If the client passes the means test initially, then this section is left blank.[7] How secured debt affects the means test will be reviewed later.[8] The convenience of using bankruptcy software is that this information transfers automatically to the means test section.[9]

6 Official Form 122A-1. Chapter 7 Statement of Your Current Monthly Income.
7 Id.
8 Id.
9 Id.

The mortgage payment is $662.99 and the escrow amount is $180.25. These figures need to match the amounts listed in Schedule J.

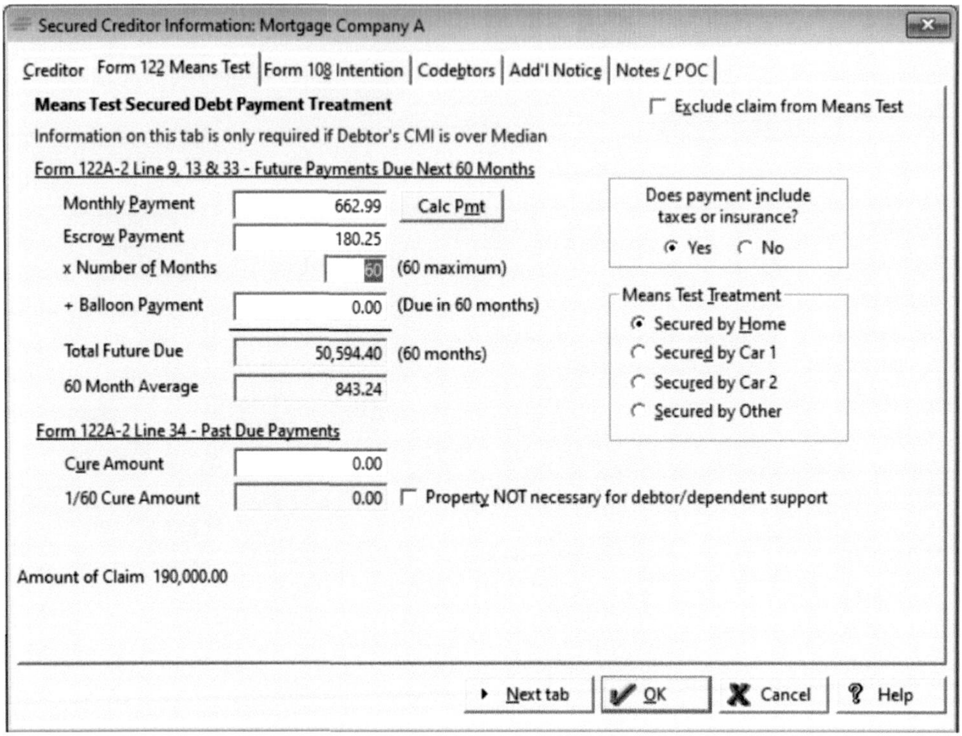

Best Case®

The mortgage payment is $662.99, and the escrow amount is $180.25. These figures need to match the amounts listed in Schedule J.[10]

The debtor's intent (Form 108 Intention) is the next tab, and that is simply what the debtor plans to do with the property.[11] If the debtor is surrendering real property, whether voluntary or because of a foreclosure, "surrendered" is marked. If the creditor already took back the property, the debt is listed as a deficiency balance on Schedule F as an unsecured creditor, not on Schedule A/B.[12]

10 Official Form 106J. Schedule J: Your Expenses (Individuals).

11 Official Form 108. Statement of Intention for Individuals Filing Under Chapter 7.

12 Official Form 106E/F. Schedule E/F: Creditors Who Have Unsecured Claims (Individuals); supra, note 5.

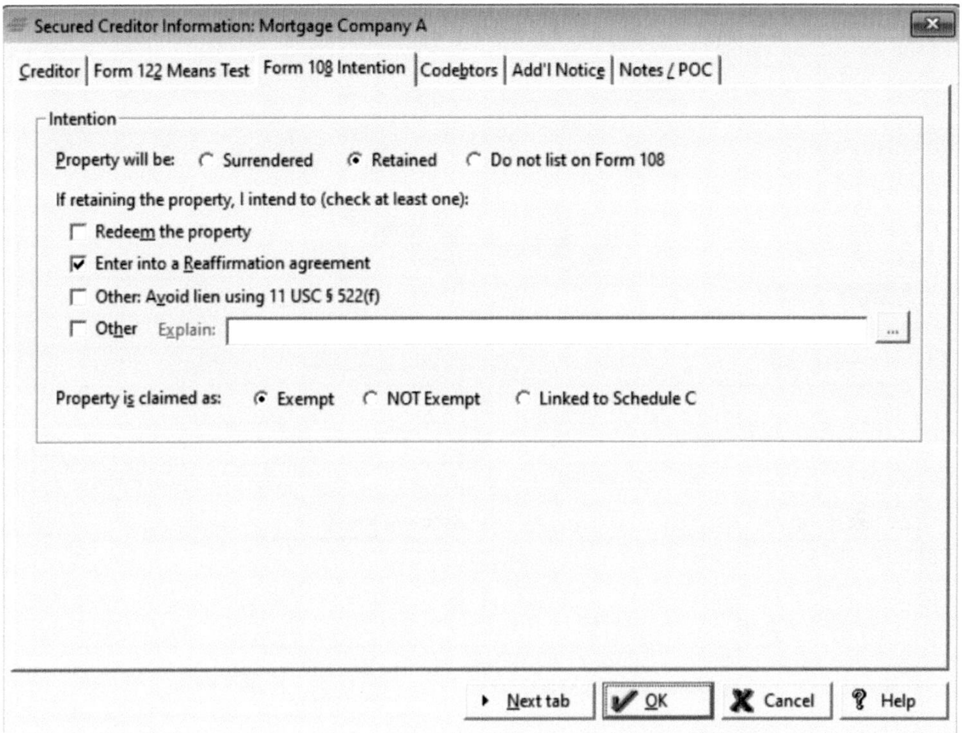

Best Case®

If the debtor is keeping the house, mark "Retained" and then choose whether the debtor will redeem, reaffirm the debt, or avoid the lien under §522.

If the debtor is redeeming the property, this means the debtor will automatically pay off the mortgage, which is rarely, if ever, the case. Otherwise, choose "enter into a Reaffirmation Agreement" and check "exempt." "Not exempt" will be chosen if the debtor has a non-homestead property such as an investment property, timeshare, cemetery lot, or homestead property that is being surrendered.

The final option is §522, "avoid the lien."[13] However, this doesn't apply to a voluntary or consensual lien such as a mortgage, but a judicial lien so long as it is not a domestic support obligation.[14] An example of a judicial lien is a judgment from an unsecured creditor. While rare, unsecured creditors sometimes do seek to enforce a judgment with a lien. With most county websites, a search can be performed for outstanding judgments and liens. This prevents returning to court after the discharge has been entered to argue a motion to remove lien. Note that under §522(e), the exemption can't be waived.

13 11 U.S.C. §522.
14 11 U.S.C. §523(a)(5).

Co-debtors are listed in the proceeding tab. This is common when the client is divorced, and the ex-spouse remains on the loan, or the debtor is married and filing alone. Another reason could be there's a co-signer.

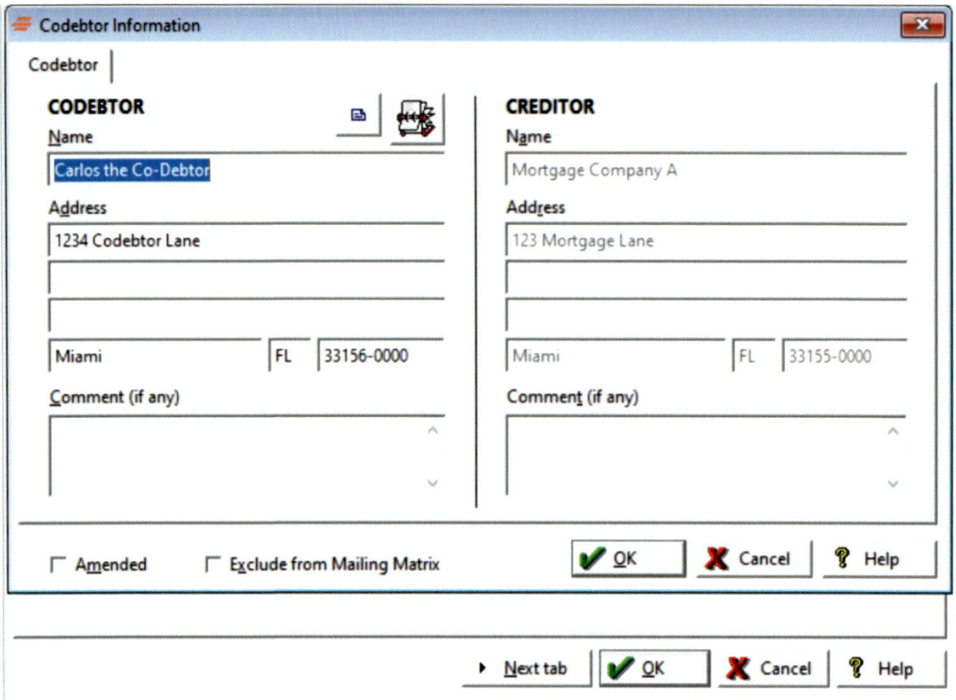

Best Case®

The next step is applying the exemption by choosing the property type and applicable statute. The calculations are automatic.

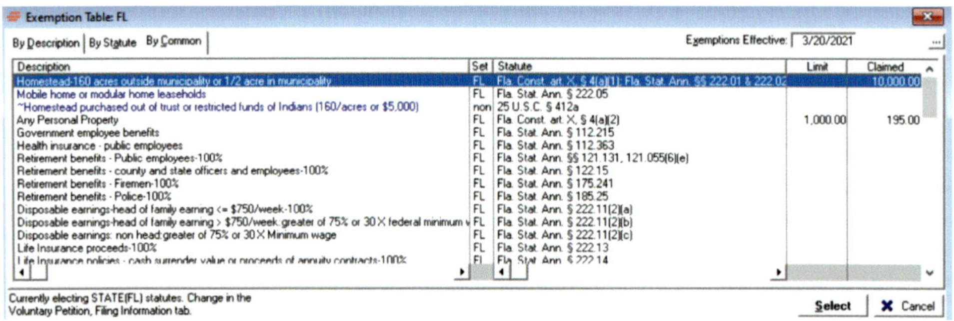

Best Case®

Note at the bottom of the figure below, the grayed/shaded area states that the debtor must have been residing in Florida for no less than 1,215 days to have more than $170,350 in equity exempt. Any amount above that figure is non-exempt. In this example, there is only $10,000 in equity, far below the maximum equity limits. Similar to the Summary of Assets and Liability, a snapshot shows the unexempt portion, in this case, $0.00.[15]

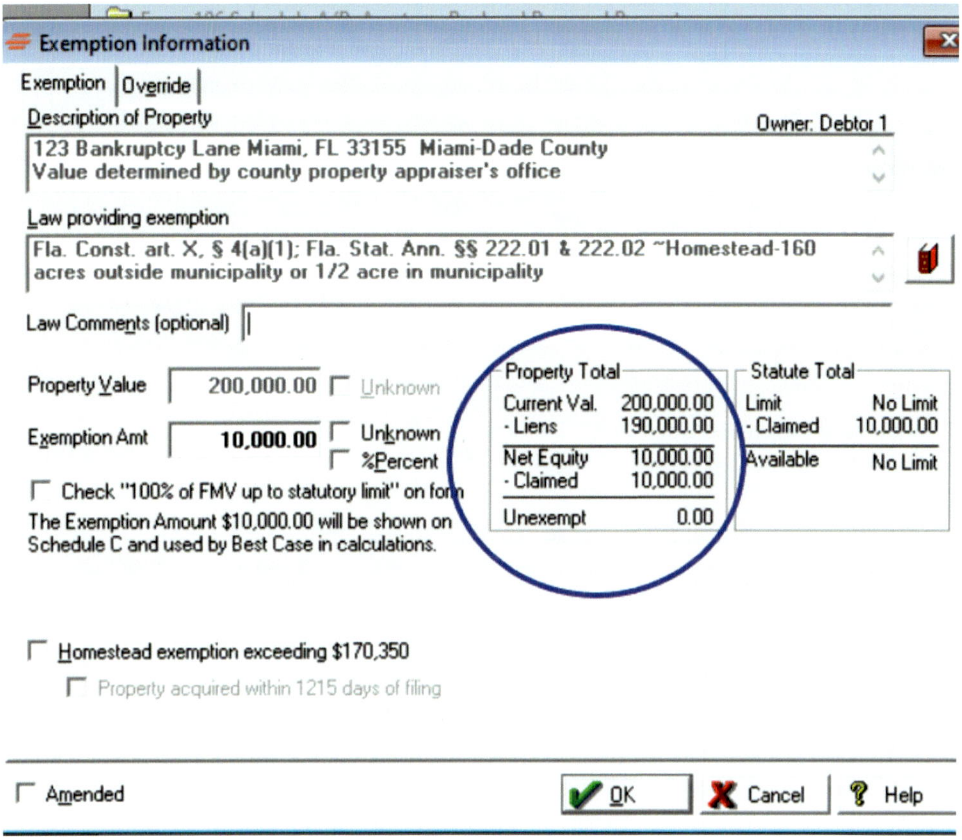

Best Case®

Part 2: Describe Your Vehicles

The tabs to enter vehicle information are the same as for real property. This includes a detailed description of the year, make, model, and mileage of the vehicle. In the "other information" section, list the source of the appraised value. Apply the exemption after including the creditor's information, lien amount, and the debtor's intent.

15 Supra, note 4.

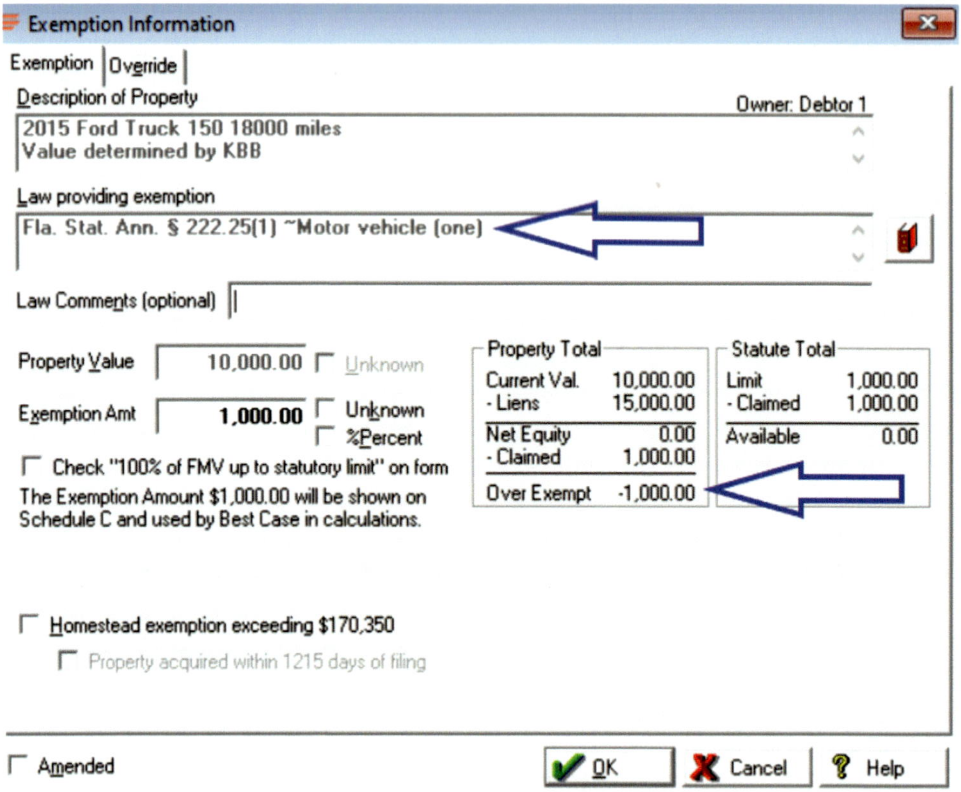

Best Case®

In this case, notice the equity is negative. That's because the value of the Ford truck ($10,000) is less than the lien amount ($15,000). So, since there is $5,000 in negative equity, there is no net equity or unexempt amount.

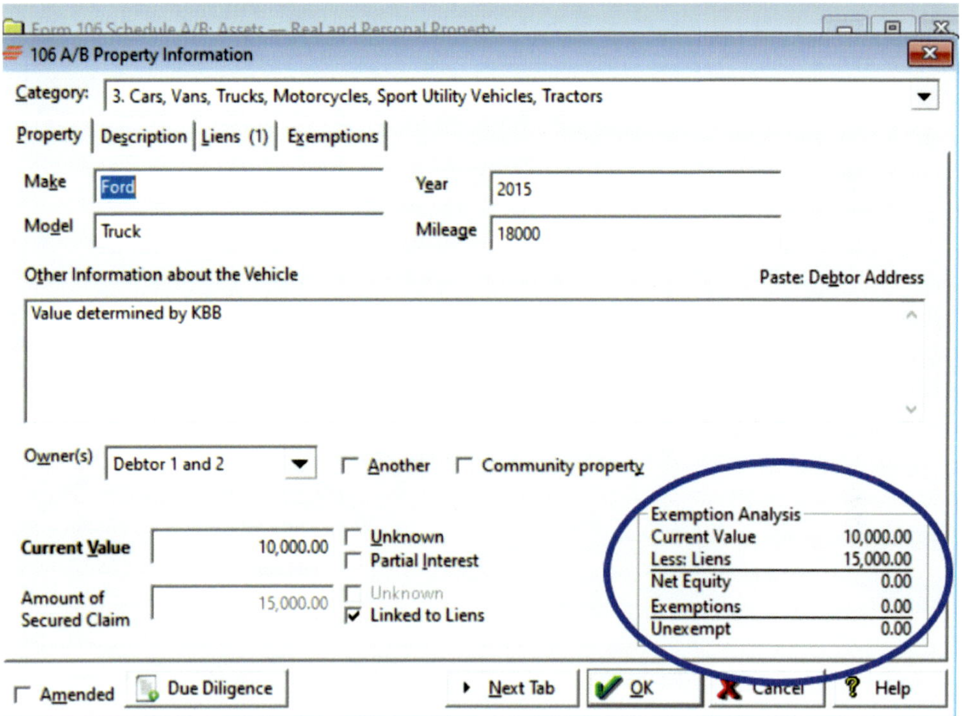

Best Case®

If the figures are reversed, and now the value of the Ford truck is $15,000, and the lien amount remains the same, the net equity would be $5,000. After applying the $1,000 vehicle exemption (Florida/single filer), the unexempt portion is $4,000.[16] That is the amount that the trustee could require to settle the bankruptcy estate.

16 Fla. Stat. §222.25(1).

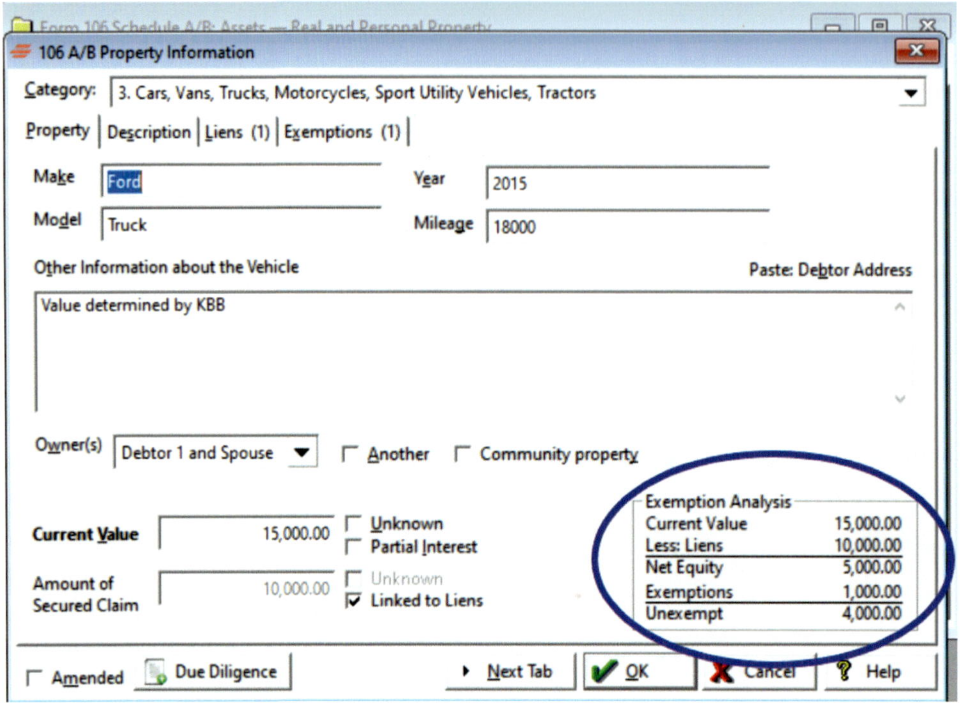

Best Case®

SUMMARY

Real or personal property is listed on Schedules A/B. For information on the debtor's real property, use the county property appraiser's website and online sources for vehicle valuation. Use recent statements and credit reports to obtain information about the debt and the creditor. Confirm if the assets are exempt or non-exempt. Also, make sure that co-debtors are listed in the petition.

For secured debt, the debtor must confirm whether the property will be kept or surrendered. If kept, the debtor must be current on payments to file Chapter 7. The lender will likely require a Reaffirmation Agreement. If the creditor has already taken back the property, the debt is unsecured and listed on Schedule F.

KEYWORDS AND TERMS

- Avoid the lien §522
- Co-debtors
- County property appraiser

- Official Form 106Sum: Summary of Assets and Liabilities and Certain Statistical Information
- Official Form 106 A/B. Schedules A/B (Individuals)
- Form 108 Intention
- Homestead property
- Motion to remove lien

PRACTICE QUESTIONS AND EXERCISES

1. The debtor has two properties: one homestead property and the other investment property. List the first mortgage for the homestead property and both mortgages for the investment property. Note the investment property is being surrendered. Also, list the co-debtor for the investment property.
2. Look up an address using your county's property appraiser website. Are there any liens on the property? Transfers?
3. Research the value of your car using Kelley Blue Book.
4. List your car in Schedule A/B and include any outstanding loan in Schedule D. Also, apply the exemptions allowed in your state.
5. If your car is "upside down," add another vehicle that has non-exempt equity.
6. Prepare a motion to remove lien.

REFERENCES

11 U.S.C. §522.

11 U.S.C. §523.

18 U.S.C. §152.

18 U.S.C. §159.

18 U.S.C. §1341.

18 U.S.C. §1519.

18 U.S.C. §3571.

Fla. Stat. §222.25.

Official Form 106A/B. Schedule A/B: Property (Individuals).

Official Form 106Dec. Declaration about an Individual Debtor's Schedules.

Official Form 106Sum. Summary of Your Assets and Liabilities and Certain Statistical Information (Individuals).

Official Form 106E/F. Schedule E/F: Creditors Who Have Unsecured Claims (Individuals).

Official Form 106J. Schedule J: Your Expenses (Individuals).

Official Form 108. Statement of Intention for Individuals Filing under Chapter 7.

Official Form 119. Bankruptcy Petition Preparer's Notice, Declaration and Signature.

Official Form 122A-1. Chapter 7 Statement of Your Current Monthly Income.

CHAPTER 14

Schedules A/B: Personal Property and C: Exemptions

PART 3: DESCRIBE YOUR PERSONAL AND HOUSEHOLD ITEMS

Household Goods and Furnishings

Since assets are listed in Schedules A/B, that includes other types of assets like furniture, household goods, financial accounts, jewelry, and electronics such as televisions and computers.[1] While these sections seem self-explanatory, clients struggle with appraising their personal belongings, usually by over-valuating personal property. But personal property, like all other assets, is based on fair market value. Therefore, personal property is based on garage sale value, not what was paid for it or what is owed. For example, how much should the item be listed for on popular sites like Craigslist.com? If the client wanted to buy the same item, how much are they willing to pay for it?

In addition, to avoid clients lumping all their personal property together and providing an overall price, clients should list the household goods and furnishings per room. For example, the first bedroom has a bed/mattress, dresser, and two nightstands purchased in 2016 and has an approximate value of $200. The second bedroom has bunk beds, one dresser, one nightstand, and an armoire. It was purchased approximately in 2014, and the estimated value is $300.

1 Official Form 106A/B. Schedule A/B: Property (Individuals).

DOI: 10.4324/9781003203278-15

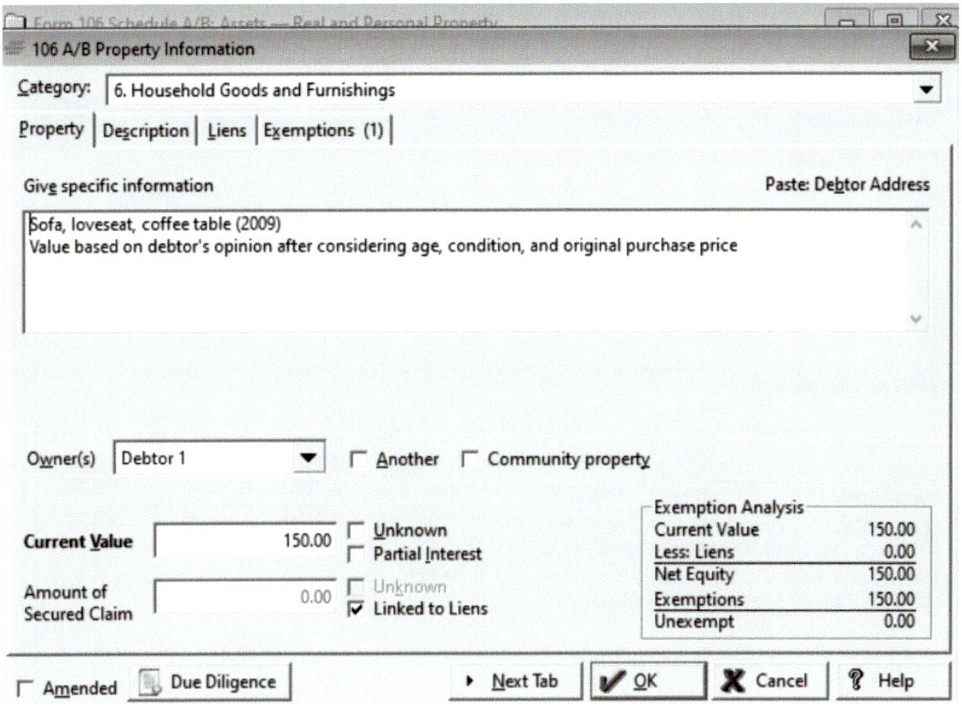

Best Case®

Household items are categorized as "any personal property" when applying exemptions.

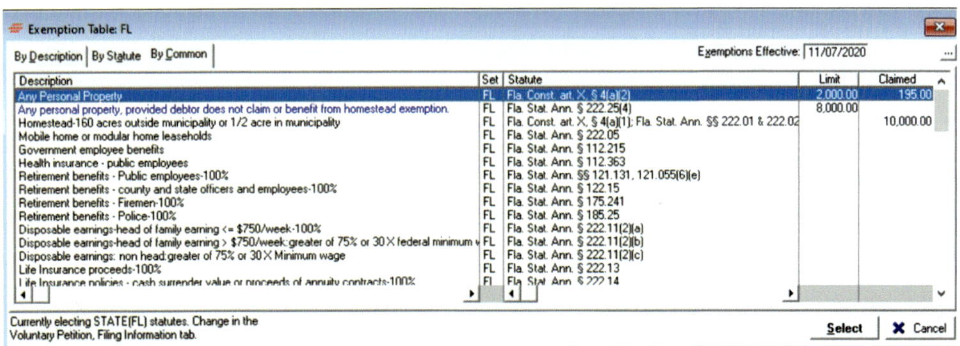

Best Case®

In this example, since the debtor is in Florida, the exemption for personal property is $1,000 for a single filer if there is homestead property and $4,000 without.[2] The amounts are doubled for a joint filing. The applicable statute is programmed into the software. Note,

2 Fla. Const. Art. X, §4(a)(2).

make sure the correct exemption is chosen each time, if not, all the property exemptions moving forward will be wrong.

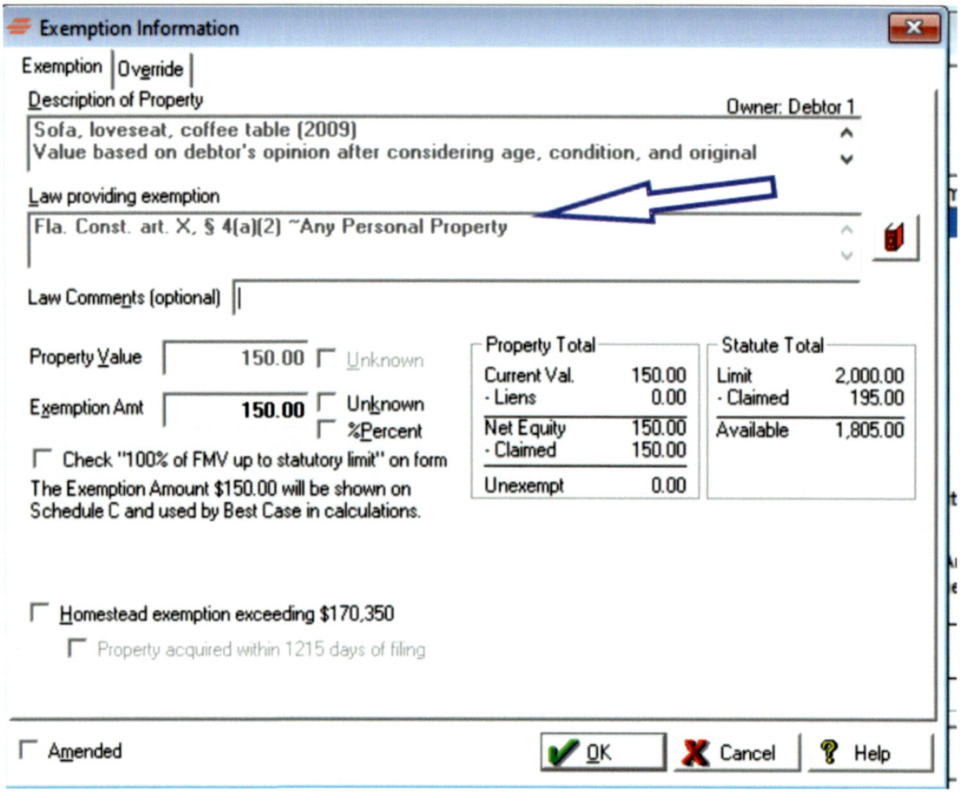

Best Case®

In the figure below, the "Property Total" is the value of the personal property minus any liens. The "Statute Total" section provides a quick summary of the exemption limits ($2,000), the amount "claimed" ($195.00), and the amount still available ($1,805).

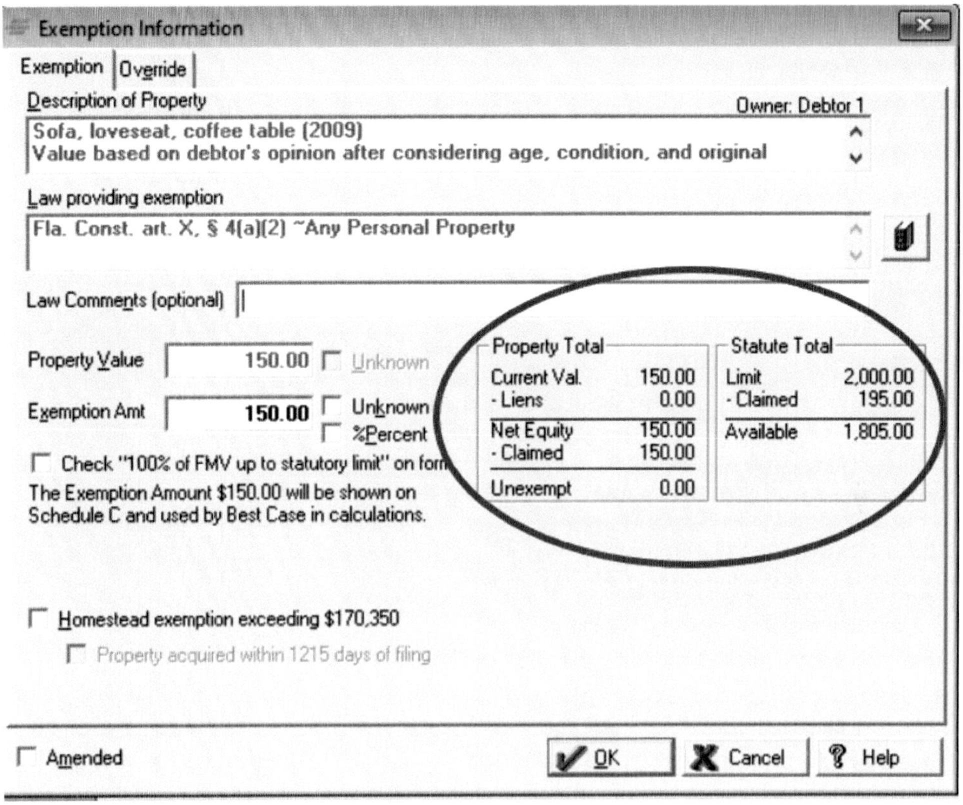

Best Case®

Electronics

The electronics section lists televisions, computers, fax machines, printers, DVD players, etc. For televisions, include the screen size, and for computers, sometimes the brand should be listed. For example, an Apple computer can be worth several thousand dollars. Note in this figure that the available amount of exempt property continues to update.

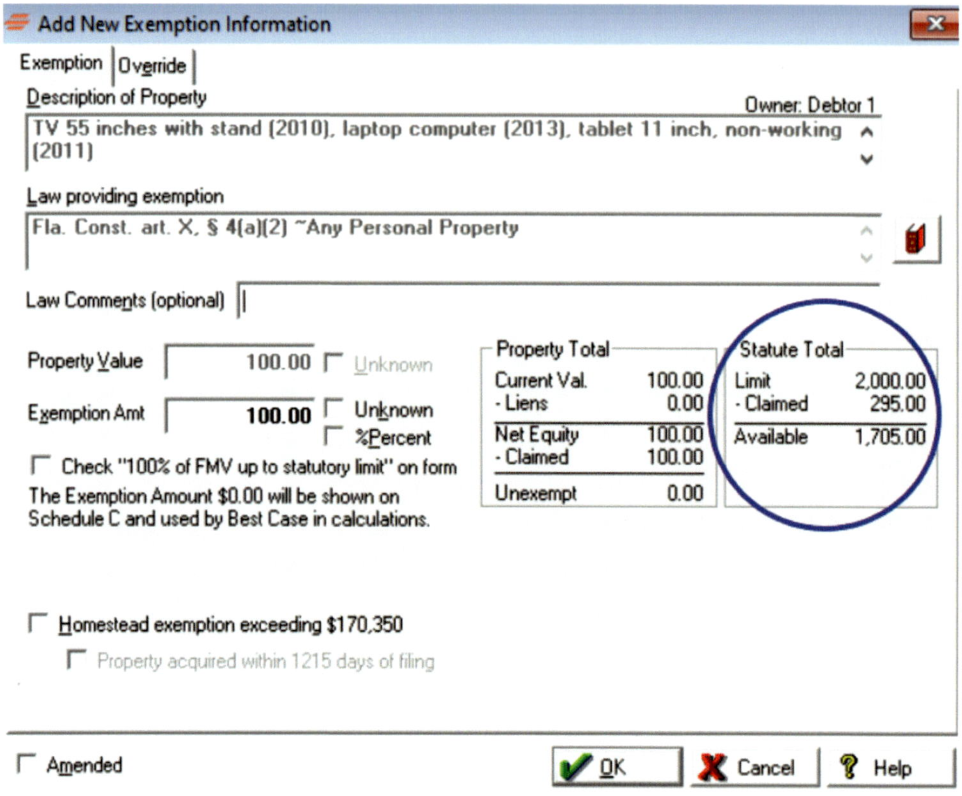

Best Case®

Equipment for Sports and Hobbies

Clients owning home gym equipment or equipment for hobbies has most likely increased because of COVID-19. Interactive home gyms are expensive and have monthly subscription fees. Confirm the purchase date and how many payments were made. The creditor will likely require a Reaffirmation Agreement.[3]

Since the trustee will request at least six months of bank statements, review transactions carefully. For example, regular visits to the local golf course will result in more questions, especially if golf clubs weren't listed as personal property.

REAL CASES

A client listed a music store as a creditor. When I questioned what equipment was purchased, the client told me he had a side gig as a disc jockey. That information was not listed in his

3 See Chapter 28.

bankruptcy intake, and the bank statements did not reflect additional income. Therefore, his monthly income as a disc jockey was estimated and included on Schedule I, Line 8h as "other income."[4] Had the trustee discovered that information at the Meeting of Creditors, it most likely would have resulted in a 2004 Examination.[5]

Clothes

Clients typically overlook this section, but of course, they have clothes. Clients are in the habit of saying "I have nothing of value," but everything has value regardless of how minimal it may be. Each article of clothing doesn't have to be included, but a description such as "used shoes and clothing." Again, the amount is usually minimal, between $100 to $200.

Jewelry

Jewelry is another section routinely ignored by clients. Clients will state they don't have any jewelry, yet they wear a watch, earrings, and/or necklace at the initial consultation. It may not be expensive jewelry, maybe costume jewelry, but still list it, including smartwatches. It's better to list personal property and be over-exempt versus not listing an item since it may result in further inquiries. Clients are easily unnerved, and this only causes more problems. I have represented clients where nervousness alone resulted in a 2004 Examination because the trustee didn't believe the debtor was being truthful.[6]

Non-Farm Animals

This section is ignored not only by clients but also by bankruptcy attorneys and trustees. Trustees aren't concerned about Fluffo, the family cat, but it's an expense that should be listed. The few extra dollars spent on a family pet could be the difference between Chapter 7 and 13.

PART 4

Cash

Even though a client may be paid via direct deposits, there may be ATM withdrawals or clients who cash their employment checks. It's easy to overlook "cash in hand," but don't. Remember, clients being sued may fear having their bank accounts frozen, so they leave little to no cash in their financial accounts. If the client made cash advances, focus on the amounts and when.

4 Official Form 106I. Schedule I: Your Income (Individuals).
5 Fed. R. Bankr. P. 2004.
6 Id.

Deposits of Money

All open bank accounts are listed in this section, and closed bank accounts are in SOFA.[7] Confirm the balance in the account(s) on the date of filing. If the balance seems high, ask why. For example, maybe the client deposited funds from a retirement account or recently got paid, pushing them past the exemption limits. The fact that those funds will be used to pay the rent or the mortgage in a week is irrelevant to the trustee because, at the time of filing, the funds are non-exempt and belong to the bankruptcy estate. The solution is to delay the filing until those expenses are paid, and the balance is reduced.

Also, note some banks automatically open a savings account when a checking account has been opened. Regardless of the balance, the account is listed in the schedules, and bank statements are provided to the trustee. Note, only include the last four digits of the account number.

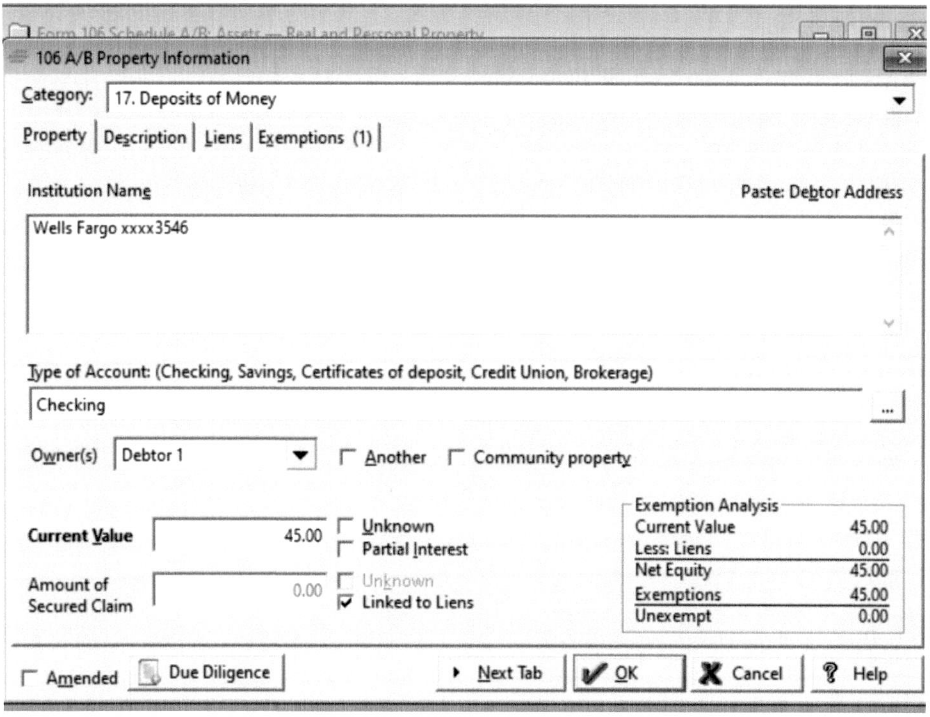

Best Case®

Bonds, Mutual Funds, or Publicly Traded Stocks

Any non-checking accounts such as certificates of deposits, mutual funds, and stocks/bonds are included in this section. Note that if the client is listed as a beneficiary on a financial account, there is no ownership interest, and thus, the account should not be listed.

7 Official Form 107. Your Statement of Financial Affairs for Individuals Filing for Bankruptcy (Individuals).

Businesses

For businesses, obtain the corporate documents to confirm the client's ownership share. What is the business's fair market value, divided by the number of shares? Typically, the client or non-filing spouse's company has few assets, but clients are concerned that they will "lose the business and" suggest transferring or selling the business, but this results in issues of fraudulent transfers with insiders.[8]

Retirement or Pension Accounts

With retirement and pension accounts, multiple scenarios are possible. The first is the account is an asset that will be reflected in Schedules A/B.[9] Two are ongoing contributions that may apply to Schedule I if deducted by the employer or Schedule J if the client pays directly.[10] Finally, if the client borrowed against the retirement account, it's a secured debt listed on Schedule D.[11]

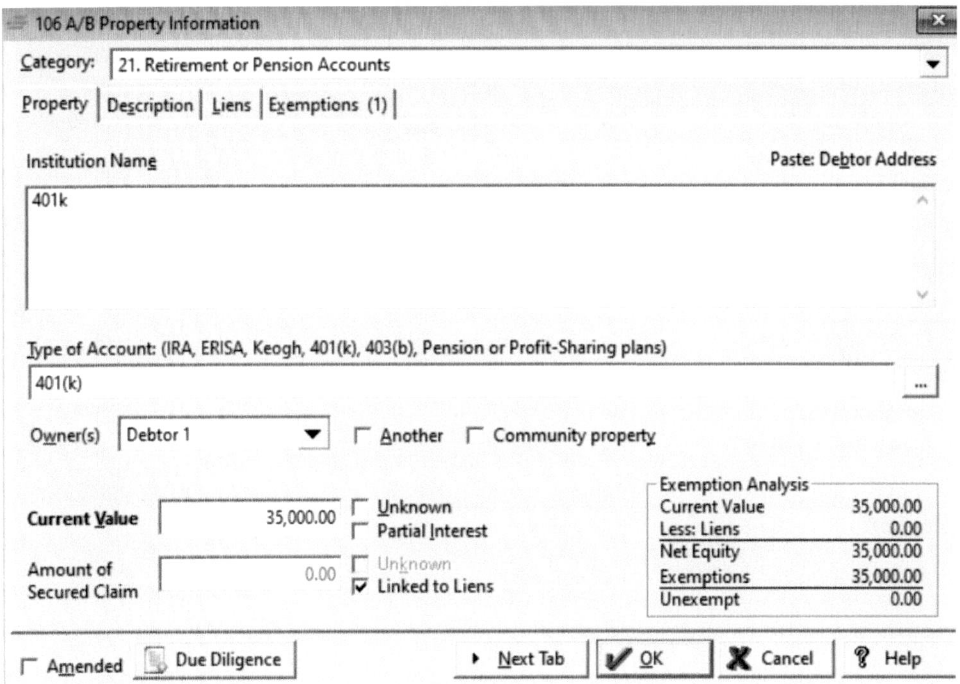

Best Case®

8 11 U.S.C. §101(3)(A).
9 Supra, note 1.
10 Supra, note 4. Official Form 106J. Schedule J: Your Expenses (Individuals).
11 Official Form 106D. Schedule D: Creditors Who Hold Claims Secured By Property (Individuals).

PRACTICE TIP

It's normal for clients to take action(s) without consulting with an attorney. Retirement accounts serve as a perfect example. Even though a retirement account is exempt, its protected status is lost if the funds comingle with non-exempt funds, such as a checking/savings account. That's why reviewing bank accounts is imperative and asking for the balance on checking and savings accounts on the day of filing. For example, it's not likely an issue if the funds were withdrawn near the filing date to use to catch up on the arrears of a mortgage. But if the funds were spent on a family vacation, you have a problem. Remember, time is both your ally and enemy.

Now, let's return to the summary of assets and liabilities from Chapter 13 and view the figure below again.[12] Since the approximate balance on the IRA is $35,000, plus the value of the Ford truck, that explains why the personal property valuation seemed high. Since the retirement/pension account is exempt, there are no mistakes for now by glancing at the summary of assets and liabilities.[13]

Form 106Sum. Summary of Assets and Liabilities

Name of Schedule	Attached?	Assets	Liabilities	Other
A/B. Real Property	Yes	200,000.00		
A/B. Personal Property	Yes	50,195.00		
C. Property Claimed as Exempt	Yes			
D. Secured Claims	Yes		190,000.00	
E. Unsecured Priority Claims	Yes		4,000.00	
F. Unsecured Nonpriority Claims	Yes		213,500.00	
G. Contracts and Leases	Yes			
H. Codebtors	Yes			
I. Current Income	Yes			4,978.00
J. Current Expenditures	Yes			4,014.69
	Totals	250,195.00	407,500.00	

Schedule D		Schedule E	
Secured	190,000.00	Priority	0.00
Unsecured	0.00	Non-Priority	4,000.00

Close Help

Security Deposits

In my experience, trustees rarely ask about security deposits unless the debtor recently moved. If so, the trustee is focused on the source of the funds. For example, a friend or family

12 Official Form 106Sum. A Summary of Your Assets and Liabilities and Certain Statistical Information (Individuals).

13 Id.

member provided the deposit, and the debtor paid back the debt to the "insider." Remember, family is family, and blood may be thicker than water, but in debtor/creditor law, family members are creditors just like American Express. Therefore, one creditor cannot be given preference over another. Although, clients do ask if a specific creditor can be excluded from the bankruptcy. As always, the answer is: it depends. If the balance on the account is zero, yes, but again, what was the original balance, and when was it paid off?

REAL CASES

The debtor filed for bankruptcy, and part of the estate was a motorcycle titled solely in the debtor's name. That's another issue with debtors who believe an asset isn't theirs, even if titled solely or partially in their name, since it "belongs" to someone else. The law looks at the title, not why the debtor is listed.

At the Meeting of Creditors, the debtor became nervous and testified that friends were paid back with the tax refund, which is "funny" because that's not true. In fact, the tax refund was simply spent. After the hearing, I asked the debtor the obvious question of what happened? The debtor admitted that being nervous, froze, and chose to improvise. The debtor believed that admitting to spending the tax refund on the child's birthday party seemed frivolous, so she concluded that a better response was that the funds were spent to pay back friends. The debtor's logic does make sense, just not legally. The debtor's off-the-cuff statement resulted in a 2004 Examination.[14]

At this point, the best way to describe this situation is that all bets are off. Something that wasn't an issue before now is, and that included the security deposit. I've never listed a security deposit nor requested to do so. Even if listed and it results in over-exempt funds, it's not likely worth the trustee's efforts to pursue it. For one, the trustee isn't entitled to it automatically. The landlord could contest the bankruptcy estate's interest because there is unpaid rent or damages to the property. Also, how much is the client over the exemption limits? Again, most likely, it's not worth it for the trustee. However, now that there were transfers to "insiders," the security deposit became of interest to the trustee.

14 Supra, note 5.

WHEREAS, the Debtor filed a voluntary petition under Chapter 7 of Title 11 of the U.S. Code (the "***Bankruptcy Code***") on [redacted] (the "***Petition Date***");

WHEREAS, the Debtor's First Meeting of Creditors (the "***§341 Meeting***") was held and concluded [redacted];

WHEREAS, [redacted] is the duly appointed Chapter 7 Trustee of the Debtor's bankruptcy estate (the "***Estate***");

WHEREAS, under Schedule B, Item 3, the Debtor lists her interest in a rental security deposit valued at [redacted] (the "*Rental Deposit*"), and the Trustee has asserted the Estate's interest in this asset;

WHEREAS, under Schedule B, Item 4, the Debtor lists her interest in household goods and furnishings valued at [redacted] which the Trustee believes may be undervalued (the "*Household Goods*"), and the Trustee has asserted the Estate's interest in this asset;

In the figure below, note the term "transfers to insiders," in this case friends of the debtor that received a portion of the tax refund. The rental security deposit increased the bankruptcy estate by $3,500. Remember, the trustee's job is to pursue non-exempt funds. Therefore, the more the bankruptcy estate increases in value, the more the creditors and the trustee receives.

WHEREAS, the Debtor may be entitled to a federal tax refund for [redacted] (the "*Tax Refund*"), and the Trustee has asserted the Estate's interest in this asset;

WHEREAS, the Trustee asserts that the Debtor made avoidable transfers of funds to an insider, [redacted] in excess of [redacted] within the applicable avoidance period (the "*Transfers to* [redacted]), and the Trustee has asserted the Estate's interest in recovery of the Transfers to [redacted]

WHEREAS, the Trustee asserts that the Debtor made avoidable transfers of funds to an insider, [redacted], in excess of [redacted] within the applicable avoidance period (the "*Transfers to* [redacted]" and with Transfers to [redacted], the "*Transfers to Insiders*"), and the Trustee has asserted the Estate's interest in recovery of the Transfers to [redacted]

WHEREAS, the Rental Deposit, Household Goods, Tax Refund, and Transfers to Insiders are collectively referred to as the "***Property***";

WHEREAS, based on the Debtor's testimony during the §341 Meeting of Creditors held July [redacted] (where the Debtor was represented by counsel), conference with Debtor and counsel prior to the scheduled Rule 2004 Examination of the Debtor on [redacted]

Sections 23–27

These sections are self-explanatory.

Money or Property Owed to You

While these sections are self-explanatory, it's worth reviewing possible scenarios. Trustees do ask if money is owed to the debtor by friends, family, or third parties. For example, a pending personal injury case or a judgment against a third party, even if the third party is judgment proof. Depending on the facts of the case, the trustee may pursue collecting on behalf of the bankruptcy estate.

Section 28: Tax Refunds Owed to You

Tax season is always busy for bankruptcy attorneys because clients typically use the refund as a deposit to start their case. But if bankruptcy attorneys are busy, then so are trustees. Review past tax returns to estimate the refund amount. If it is a substantial amount, discuss the issue with the client to determine if the bankruptcy will be delayed. Clients should not hear about losing their tax refund for the first time at the creditors' meeting.

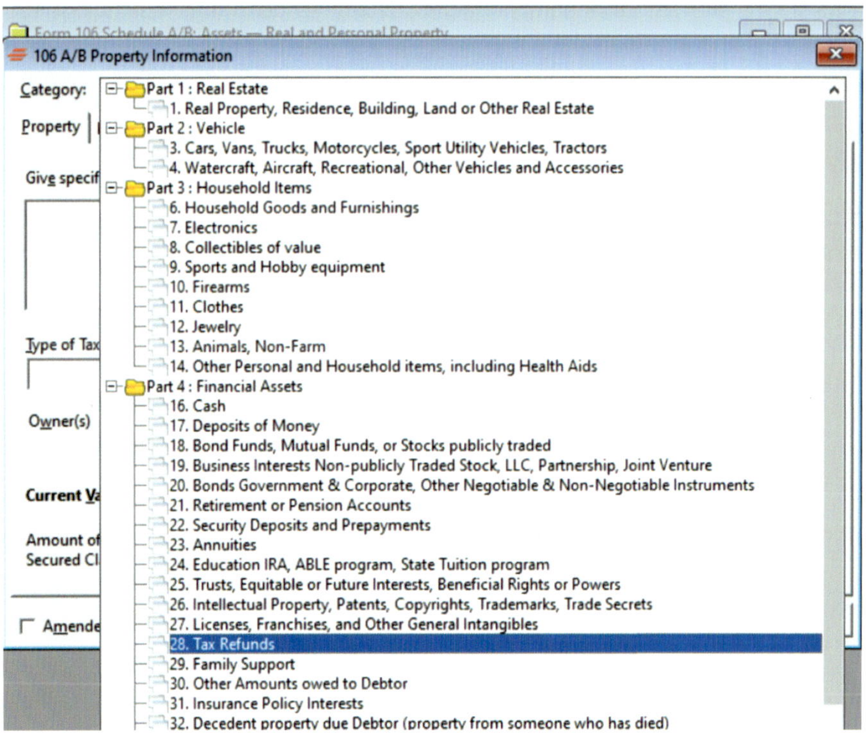

Best Case®

Family Support

Review the marital/property settlement agreement for possible non-exempt assets such as the pending sale of real estate or other assets.

Interests in Insurance Policies

If the client lists life insurance as an expense, confirm it's not a whole life policy that has a "cash surrender value." If so, it's an asset listed on Schedule A/B.[15] A term life policy has no current value until the time of death of the insured, but the expense is still listed.

Trustees will ask at the Meeting of Creditors if the debtor is a beneficiary of a life insurance policy. While it may be common to be a beneficiary of a spouse's policy or other family members, the trustee's focus is if the insured recently passed away or is about to. So, as uncomfortable as the subject may be, confirm the client isn't a beneficiary of a life insurance policy and the insured is on his/her deathbed. If so, the bankruptcy is either delayed, Chapter 13 is filed, or the funds are used to settle with creditors.

Any Interest in Property That Is Due You from Someone Who Has Died

Besides life insurance policies, confirm if the debtor is a beneficiary of a will. While the answer is usually yes, the issue is if there is a pending or soon-to-be probate case.

Claims against Third Parties, Whether or Not You Have Filed a Lawsuit or Made a Demand for Payment

Distinguish between a lawsuit that is or will be filed versus pre-trial claims. Most claims against third parties will be personal injury lawsuits. Car accidents and slip and fall cases are common examples of pre-trial claims.

15 Supra, note 1.

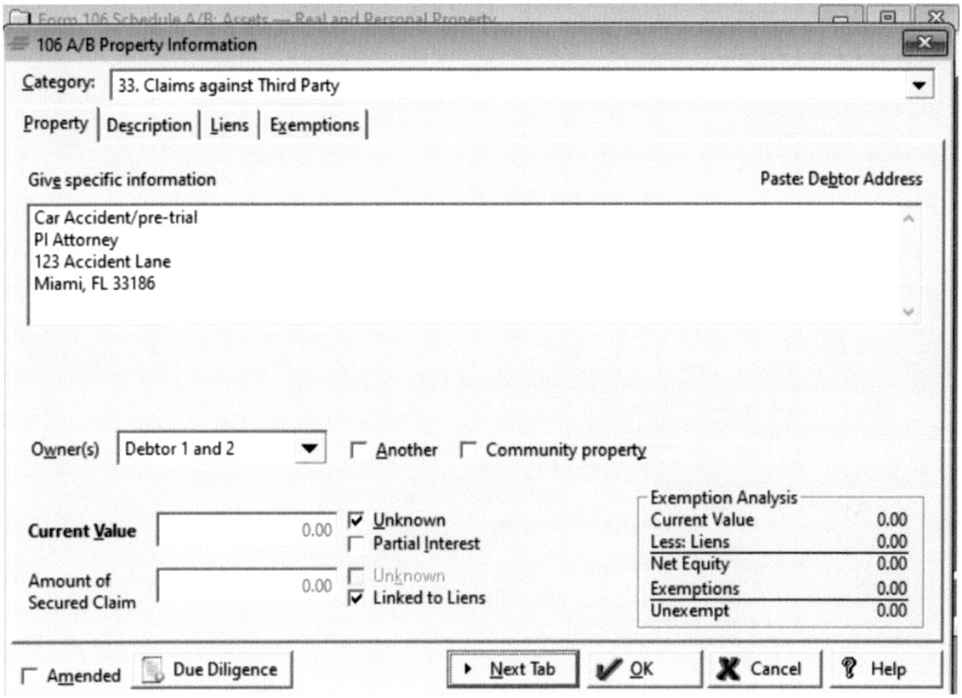

Best Case®

It's virtually impossible to determine in advance the settlement amount in a personal injury case, so "unknown" can be checked off as to the amount. It's not necessary to list the contact information of the client's attorney in the petition, but the trustee will request that information anyway. Whether a case or pre-trial claim is pending, the client continues with the case as normal, except when the case settles, the client's portion belongs to the bankruptcy estate.

Note that pending lawsuits, not pre-trials, are disclosed on line 9 of the Statement of Financial Affairs.[16] See the figure below. If the client is being sued, also list the debt as unsecured.

16 Supra, note 7.

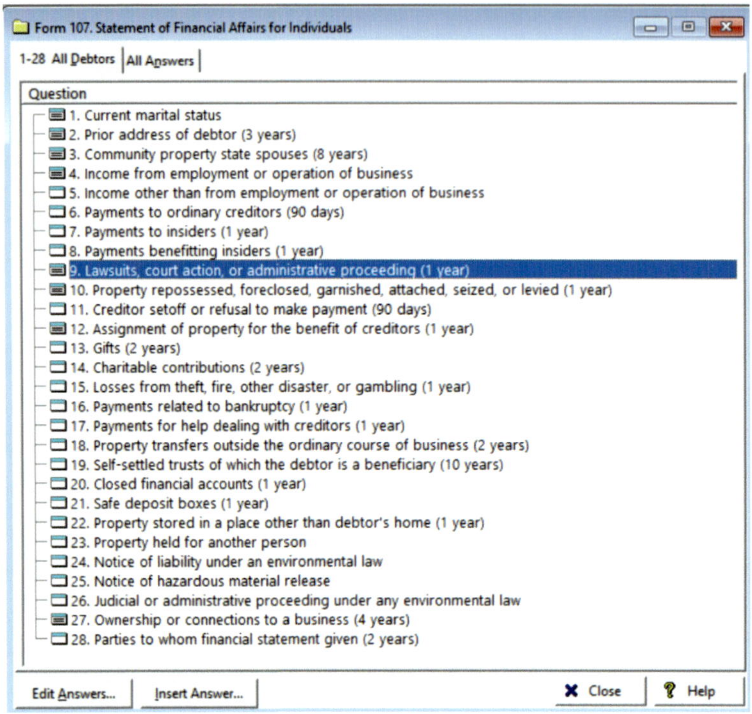

Best Case®

Worker's compensation settlements are protected under §522.[17] But, let's review why, as that can be confusing when compared to personal injury settlements. On its face, there seems to be no difference between a personal injury award and a worker's compensation claim. In a personal injury case, there was an injury based on a third party's fault/negligence. For worker's compensation, there is also an injury because of an accident but while employed. Personal injury claims are based on compensation for losses, while worker's compensation claims are based on replacing future income, and they're categorized as disability benefits, so they're exempt.[18] However, even though federal and state court cases seem to confirm that worker's compensation funds are protected, steps should be taken to avoid unnecessary complications.

For example, suppose there is $1,000 in a checking account from a worker's compensation settlement and $1,000 because of a gift from a family member. Even though the funds are comingled, the worker's compensation monies are protected. However, to make life easier and avoid an evidentiary hearing having to trace the source of the funds, clients should keep the exempt funds in a separate account. In addition, if a creditor tries to freeze a bank account, if the bank can confirm that one hundred percent of the funds are exempt such as Social Security income, the bank will reject the freeze.

17 11 U.S.C. §522(d)(10).
18 11 U.S.C. §522(d)(10)(c).

PART 5

Businesses owned by the debtor or a spouse generally have limited assets and will most likely depreciate quickly. As with personal property, valuate assets based on the fair market value.

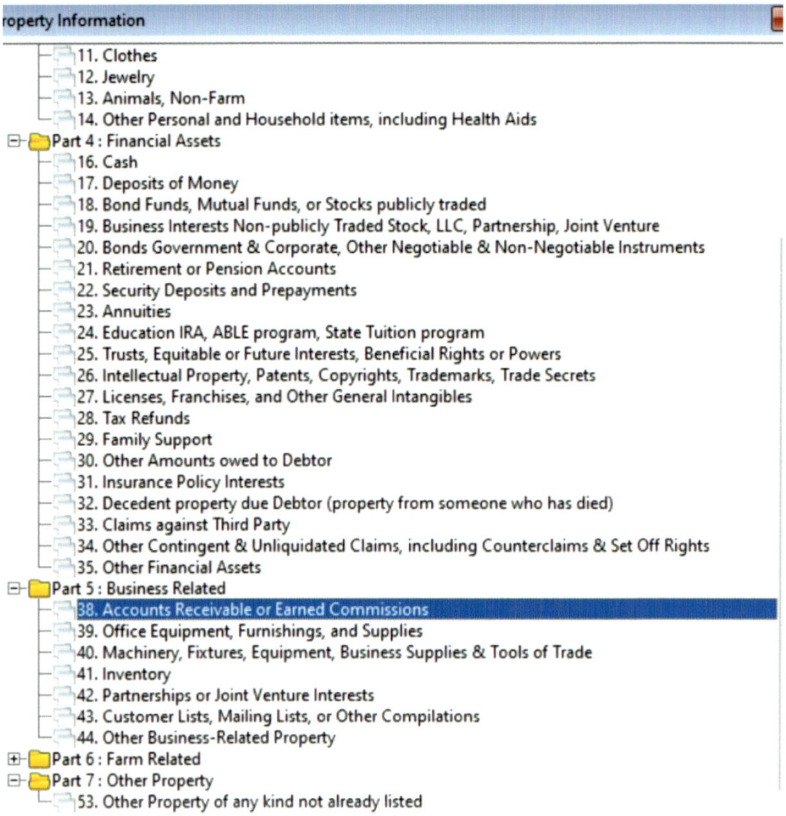

Best Case®

SUMMARY

The bankruptcy petition has assets categorized into seven different sections. Part 1 is for real property, and Part 2 is for automobiles. Part 3 includes household items such as furniture, clothes, jewelry, and electronics. Part 4 focuses on financial assets such as cash, bank accounts, retirement accounts, and tax refunds. Part 5 is related to businesses, and Part 6 is farm-related/commercial fishing, while Part 7 is other assets not previously listed.

Personal property is valued at the fair market value, another way of saying "garage sale" value. Clients tend to skip this section or provide limited information, either because they don't know how to value their personal property or are concerned the trustee will "take it away."

Review the credit report for secured debt to determine when the account was opened and compare it to the original balance. In addition, certain items require further inquiry, such as expensive jewelry. The same applies to electronics such as televisions and computers, and furniture.

Because the balance on bank accounts varies, confirm the balance the day before or day of filing. It's common for trustees to require the petition to be amended to reflect the bank account balance on the filing date, even if amending the petition results in the client being protected by exemptions. In addition, a minor omission or mistake such as bank account balances could lead to unnecessary and extensive questioning by the trustee, which at a minimum, will increase the client's nervousness.

Retirement accounts, like all assets, even if exempt, must be listed in Schedule A/B. Review the client's paystubs for any deductions which indicate the client borrowed against the retirement account. Confirm the amount of the funds borrowed and how the funds were used. Loans borrowed against a retirement account are secured debts and are listed in Schedule D.

Tax refunds are always an issue depending on the amount and the time of year. Regardless of when the initial client interview takes place, tax refunds should be discussed to determine when the petition should be filed. If the debtor's portion of the tax refund includes the Child Tax Credit, it may be exempt per state law.

Finally, lawsuits are listed, even pre-trial suits, whether the client is the plaintiff or respondent. If the client is a respondent in a lawsuit, list the case on SOFA and the debt on Schedule F. If the case is close to being finalized, consider filing sooner to avoid garnishment. If the client is the plaintiff and settlement proceeds are expected, the funds are likely non-exempt and belong to the bankruptcy estate.

KEYWORDS AND TERMS

- Craigslist.com
- Garage sale value
- Schedules A/B
- Section 522
- Negligence
- Personal injury cases
- Pre-trial suits
- Transfers to insiders
- Worker's compensation claims

DISCUSSION QUESTIONS

1. As you begin working on the client's petition, you notice minimal personal property and expenses, especially rent, which is far below market value. Your client responds that he moved in with a friend after the divorce and rents a room. How could this potentially affect the bankruptcy?
2. The client has not provided all the requested documents but did provide the bankruptcy intake, which doesn't include information on earnings from prior years. In addition, the client has not filed taxes for the last two years. How should the client be advised?
3. The client expects a $4,000 tax refund this year. What issues need to be addressed if the client wishes to keep the tax refund?

PRACTICE QUESTIONS AND EXERCISES

1. Continue working on your client's file. Complete Schedules A/B by listing your personal property. Feel free to make up facts if need be.
2. Include an armoire in the bedroom that was a gift from a family member in your petition. How would the armoire be listed and valued?
3. Don't forget to include in the petition additional household goods such as items in your kitchen, including appliances.
4. List your sofa in the petition that was purchased at a garage sale three years ago. See Figure 14.1.

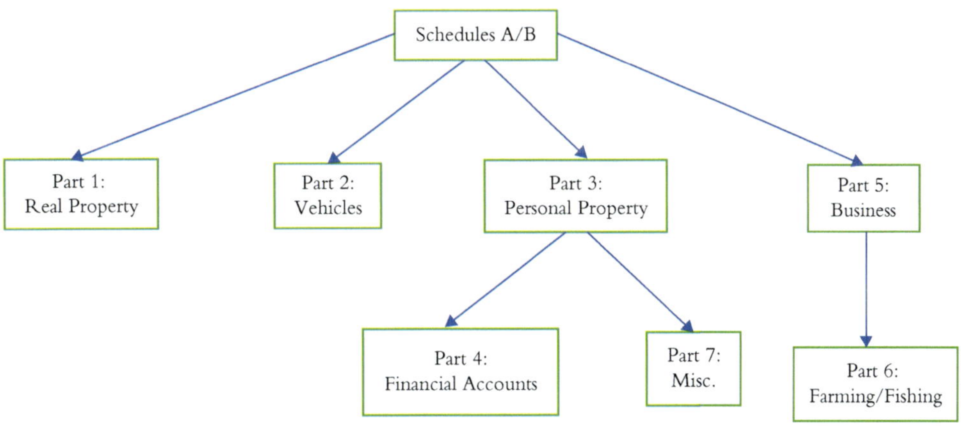

FIGURE 14.1 An overview of Schedueles A/B.

OFFICIAL FORM 106C – SCHEDULE C: THE PROPERTY YOU CLAIM AS EXEMPT

Schedule C (Form 106C) summarizes Schedules A/B and divides it into four sections: exemption detail, property summary, statute summary, and liquidation analysis.[19] Schedule C provides a more detailed analysis than the summary of assets and liabilities since the assets are listed.[20]

In the figure below, the "Property Summary" tab shows the assets listed in Schedules A/B, including the equity in the property, the amount exempted, and any unexempt portion.[21] The "Exemption Detail" is the applicable statute.

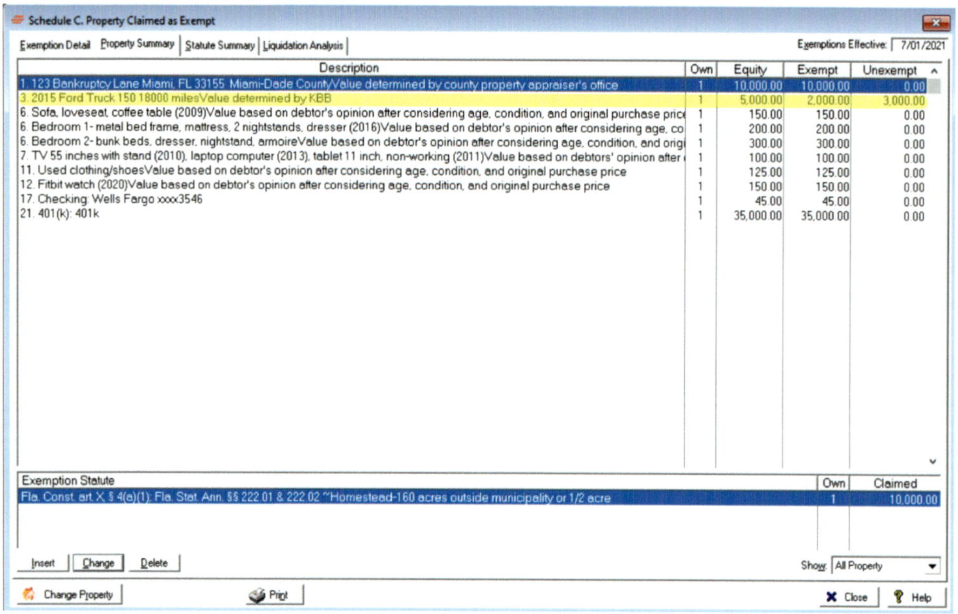

Best Case®

The "Liquidation Analysis" tab provides valuable information regarding over-exempt property. Because the Ford truck was valued at $15,000 and the lien was $10,000, there is $5,000 in equity minus the Florida automobile exemption of $2,000 (joint filing), leaving $3,000 in non-exempt equity.[22] Whether Chapter 7 or 13, that is the amount that belongs to the bankruptcy estate and would have to be paid back if the debtor wishes to keep the

19 Official Form 106C. Schedule C: The Property You Claim as Exempt (Individuals).
20 Id., and supra, note 12.
21 Supra, note 1.
22 Fla. Stat. Ann. § 222.25(1).

vehicle. If not, the car is surrendered to the trustee, who will sell/auction the car, and the net proceeds will be distributed among the creditors based on claim priority.

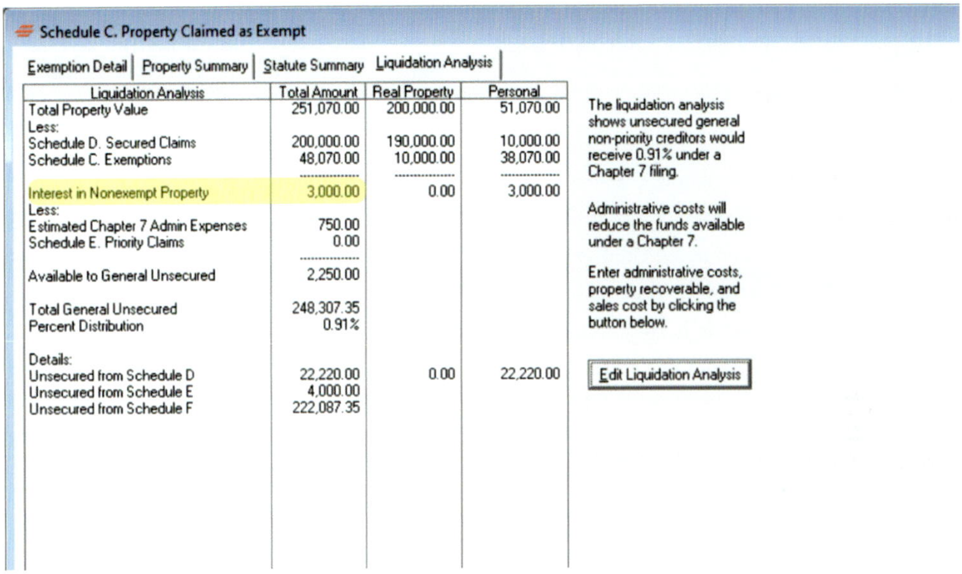

Schedule C. Property Claimed as Exempt

Exemption Detail | Property Summary | Statute Summary | Liquidation Analysis

Liquidation Analysis	Total Amount	Real Property	Personal
Total Property Value	251,070.00	200,000.00	51,070.00
Less:			
Schedule D. Secured Claims	200,000.00	190,000.00	10,000.00
Schedule C. Exemptions	48,070.00	10,000.00	38,070.00
Interest in Nonexempt Property	3,000.00	0.00	3,000.00
Less:			
Estimated Chapter 7 Admin Expenses	750.00		
Schedule E. Priority Claims	0.00		
Available to General Unsecured	2,250.00		
Total General Unsecured	248,307.35		
Percent Distribution	0.91%		
Details:			
Unsecured from Schedule D	22,220.00	0.00	22,220.00
Unsecured from Schedule E	4,000.00		
Unsecured from Schedule F	222,087.35		

The liquidation analysis shows unsecured general non-priority creditors would receive 0.91% under a Chapter 7 filing.

Administrative costs will reduce the funds available under a Chapter 7.

Enter administrative costs, property recoverable, and sales cost by clicking the button below.

Edit Liquidation Analysis

Best Case®

SUMMARY

Similar to the summary of assets and liabilities, Schedule C provides a synopsis of the assets listed in Schedule A/B, equity, exemptions, secured and unsecured debt totals, and the corresponding exemption statutes. Use Schedule C as a quick guide to review any issues with over-exempt property.

KEYWORD AND TERMS

- Official Form 106C/Schedule C

DISCUSSION QUESTIONS

1. Based on the initial preparation of your bankruptcy petition, review Schedule C. Does anything specific stand out that could be of concern?
2. Based on Question 1, return to Schedule A/B and confirm the assets and liabilities were properly listed.

REFERENCES

11 U.S.C. §101.

11 U.S.C. §522.

Fed. R. Bankr. P. 2004.

Fla. Const. Art. X, §4(a)(2).

Fla. Stat. Ann. § 222.25(1).

Official Form 106A/B. Schedule A/B: Property (Individuals).

Official Form 106C. Schedule C: The Property You Claim as Exempt (Individuals).

Official Form 106D. Schedule D: Creditors Who Hold Claims Secured by Property (Individuals).

Official Form 106I. Schedule I: Your Income (Individuals).

Official Form 106J. Schedule J: Your Expenses (Individuals).

Official Form 106Sum. A Summary of Your Assets and Liabilities and Certain Statistical Information (Individuals).

Official Form 107. Your Statement of Financial Affairs for Individuals Filing for Bankruptcy (Individuals).

CHAPTER 15

Schedules of Secured and Unsecured Creditors

OFFICIAL FORM 106D. SCHEDULE D: CREDITORS WHO HAVE CLAIMS SECURED BY PROPERTY

Secured creditors listed on Schedules A/B will transfer automatically to Schedule D with automated software.[1] In our sample petition, the secured assets were the homestead property and truck. The Statement of Intention accompanies Schedule D.[2]

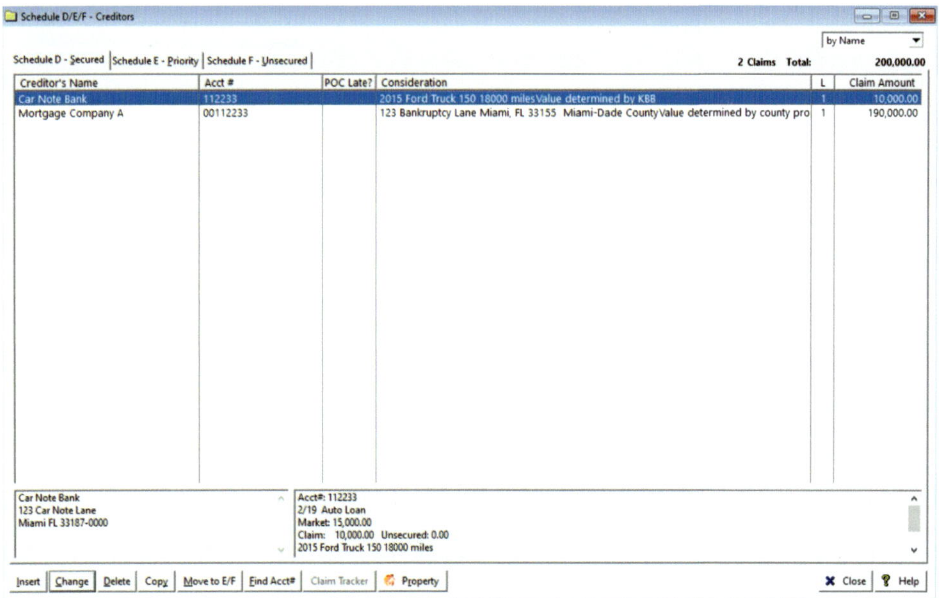

Best Case®

1 Official Form 106 A/B. Schedule A/B: Property (Individuals). Official Form 106D. Schedule D: Creditors Who Hold Claims Secured By Property (Individuals).

2 Official Form 108. Statement of Intention for Individuals Filing Under Chapter 7; id., Schedule D.

DOI: 10.4324/9781003203278-16

Next to the Schedule D tab is the Schedules E and F tab, which provides the convenience of jumping from one schedule to another without closing the current window.[3] Take a moment to click through your sample petition and confirm that no information is missing from Schedule D or the Statement of Intention.[4] If all the information is correct, proceed to the remaining schedules. However, remember that debt amounts increase or decrease each month, so obtain the most recent mortgage and card statement if the client's file has been pending for quite some time.

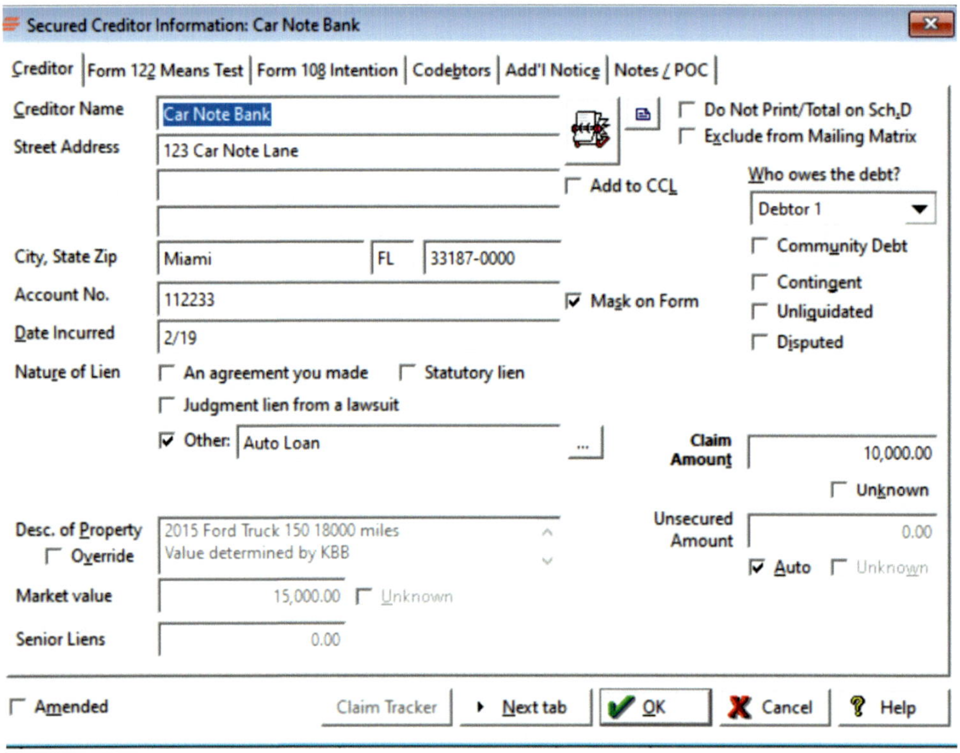

Best Case®

OFFICIAL FORM 106 E/F. SCHEDULE E/F: CREDITORS WHO HAVE UNSECURED CLAIMS

Part 1: Priority Unsecured Claims

Priority unsecured debts are usually taxes or domestic support obligations and are listed on Schedule E.[5] In the figure below, the different types of unsecured priority claims are shown.

3 Official Form 106E/F. Schedule E/F: Creditors Who Have Unsecured Claims (Individuals).

4 Supra, note 1, Official Form 106D; supra, note 2.

5 Supra, note 3.

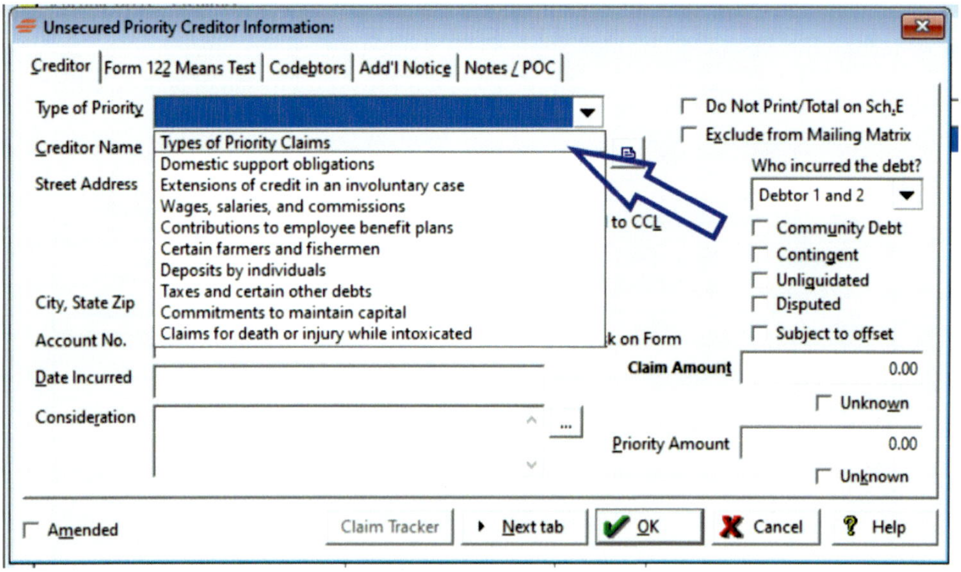

Best Case®

In this case, the debtor owes $4,000 to the Internal Revenue Service.

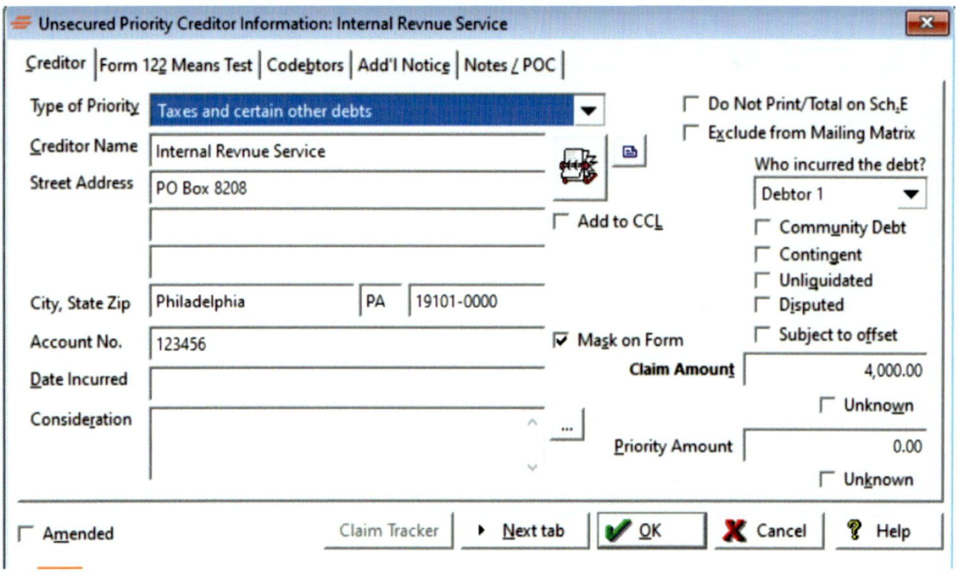

Best Case®

If payments to a priority unsecured creditor are deducted from the debtor's wages, list the deduction in Schedule I.[6] It's also common for domestic support obligations to be withdrawn from a debtor's pay stub. If so, the deduction is listed on Line 5h of Schedule I.[7]

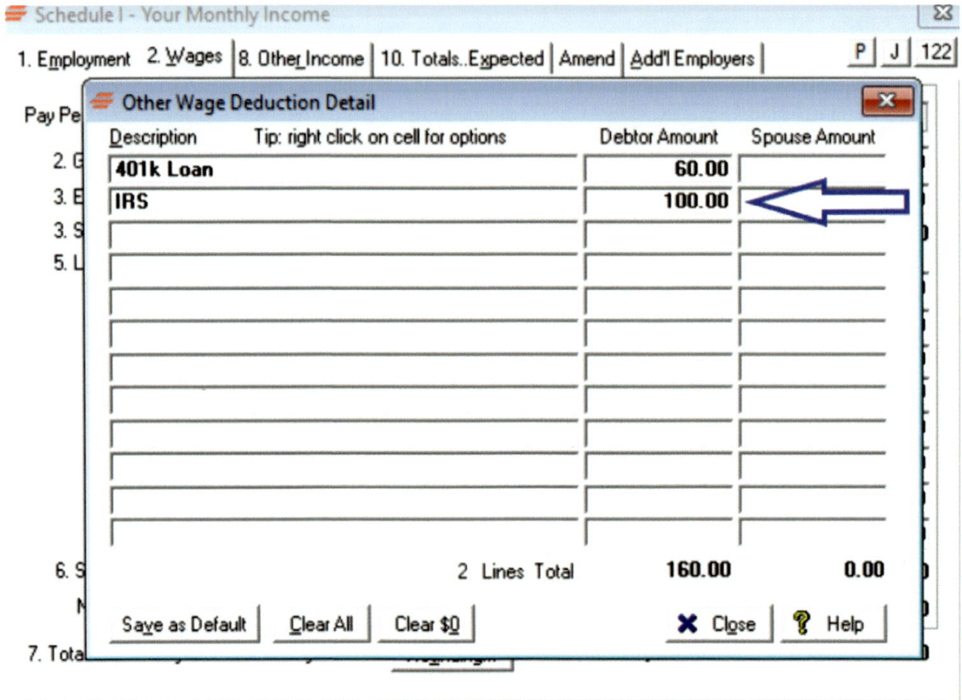

Best Case®

If payments are made directly to a priority creditor, the expense is listed on Schedule J, Line 16.[8] Make sure the client hasn't listed the expense of a priority claim twice, and it's carried over to the petition.

Note the "excess" funds or disposable income is $22.69, as shown in the figure below. If the IRS debt/expense is not listed, the client would have $122.69 in disposable funds, potentially resulting in Chapter 13 instead of Chapter 7. Clients by default may not include nondischargeable debts, but you see how it affects the case. That's why it's essential to confirm all debts, whether or not the debt is dischargeable.

6 Official Form 106I. Schedule I: Your Income (Individuals).

7 Id.

8 Official Form 106J. Schedule J: Your Expenses (Individuals).

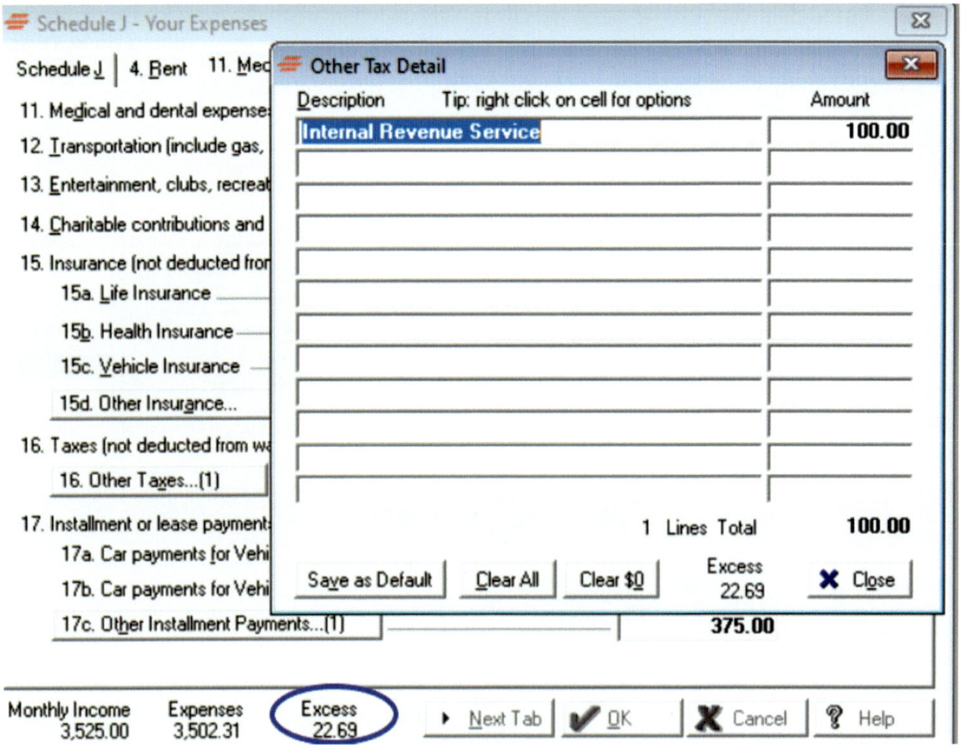

Best Case®

Also, clients may have ceased payments or received a forbearance on priority claims, but the payments need to continue to reduce the availability of disposable funds to qualify for Chapter 7. Student loans in default or forbearance status are a good example of payments that may need to resume to increase the client's expenses on Schedule J.[9] This became a common issue during the coronavirus pandemic when lenders allowed mortgages to go into forbearance status.

Part 2: Nonpriority Unsecured Claims

Credit cards and other unsecured creditors are listed in Schedule F.[10] Confirm the address is correct to avoid having to file an updated address. If an address is no longer valid, remember to remove it from the addresses book.

Credit reports list the date accounts were opened. As the paralegal, you're looking for a pattern where credit cards were opened recently and maxed out within a short period of time. Depending on the facts, the bankruptcy filing may have to be delayed.

9 Id.
10 Supra, note 3.

Unsecured debt can also be categorized. In this case, because of a foreclosure, from the drop-down menu, in the "Consideration" window, "deficiency balance" is highlighted. Once the "Consideration" window is closed, additional information is required. In this case, the property address of the foreclosed property.

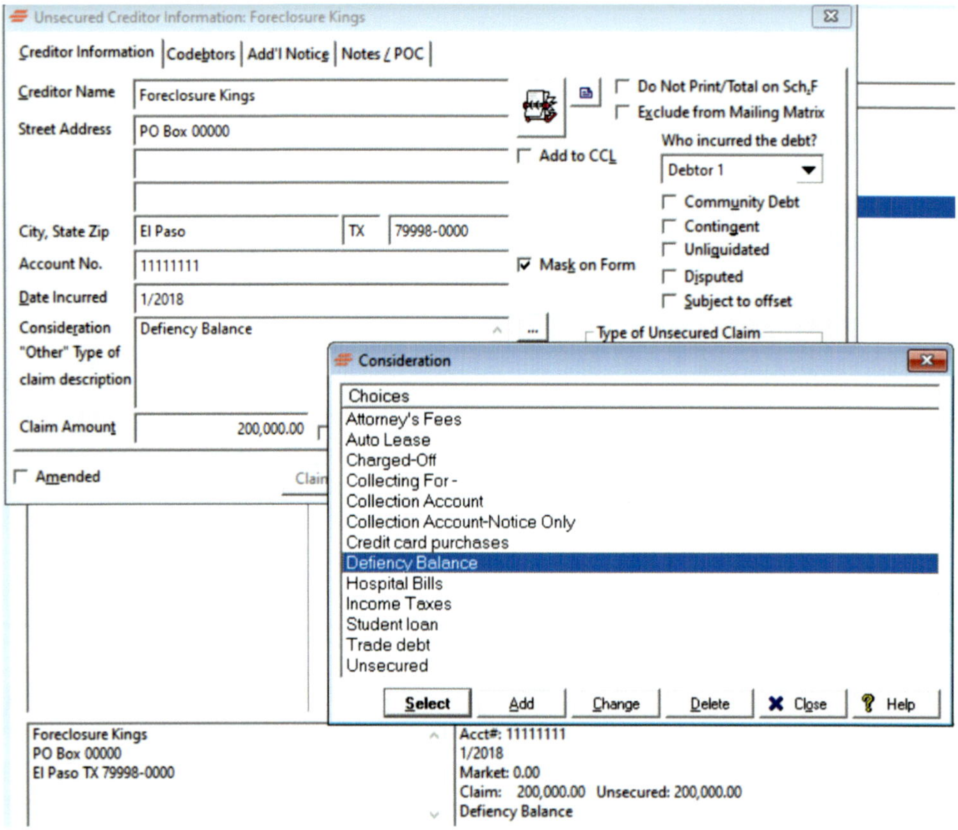

Best Case®

One reason categorizing the debt is essential is to avoid inquiries. For example, suppose the foreclosure was labeled as credit card debt. In that case, it's likely that before the creditor's meeting, additional information would be requested from the bankruptcy trustee and the U.S. Trustee's Office as $200,000 in credit card debt is substantial, and there exists the likelihood of fraud. But, by making it clear the debt is real property, unnecessary complications are avoided, not to mention time saved by not having to amend the petition.

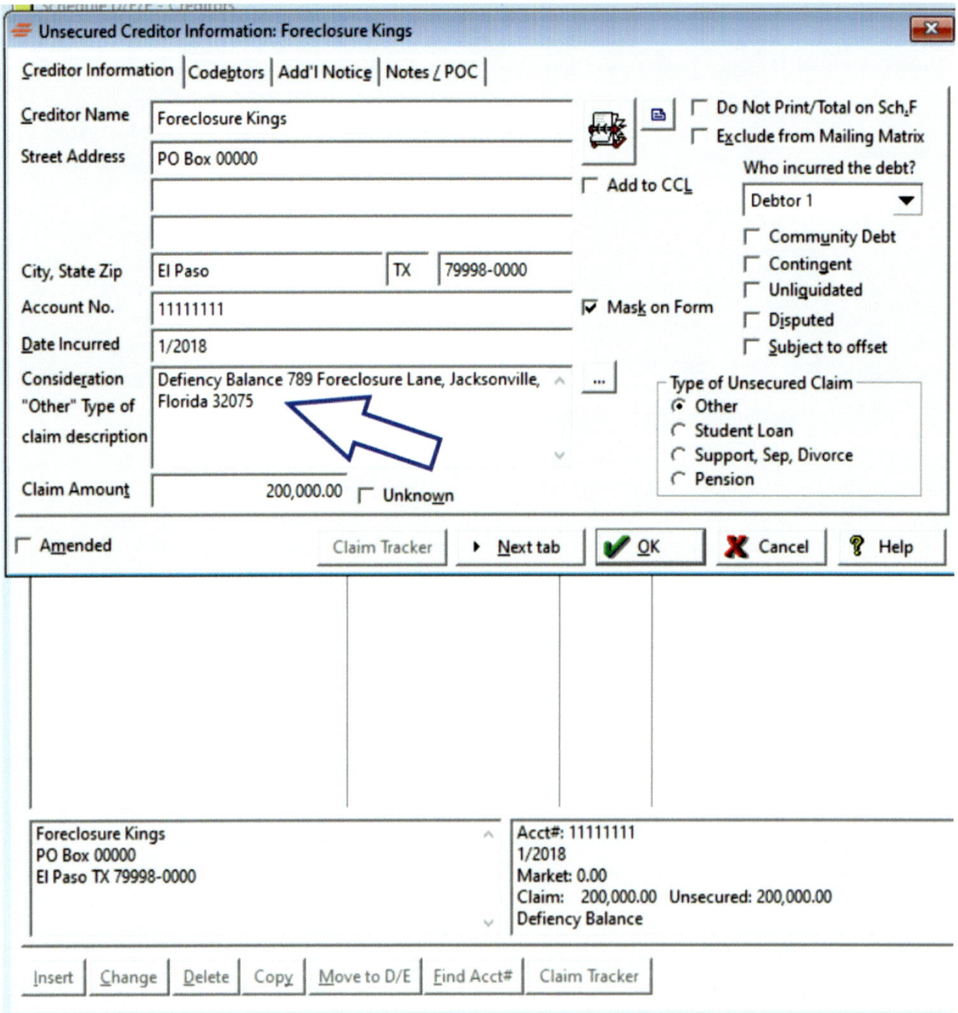

Best Case®

To categorize credit card debt, mark "other" as the "type of unsecured claim" and then choose "credit card purchases" from the drop-down menu.

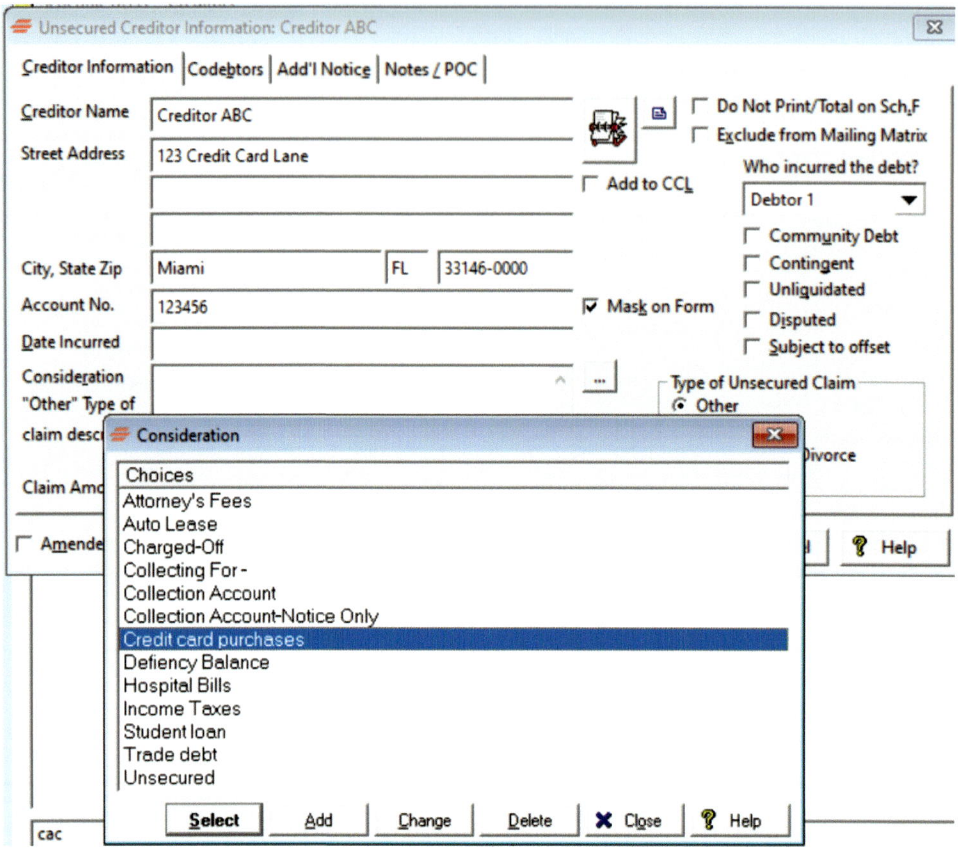

Best Case®

Once the window is closed, "credit card purchases" is placed in the "consideration" window. Remember to add the "claim" amount or balance on the debt, close the window, and proceed to add the subsequent creditor.

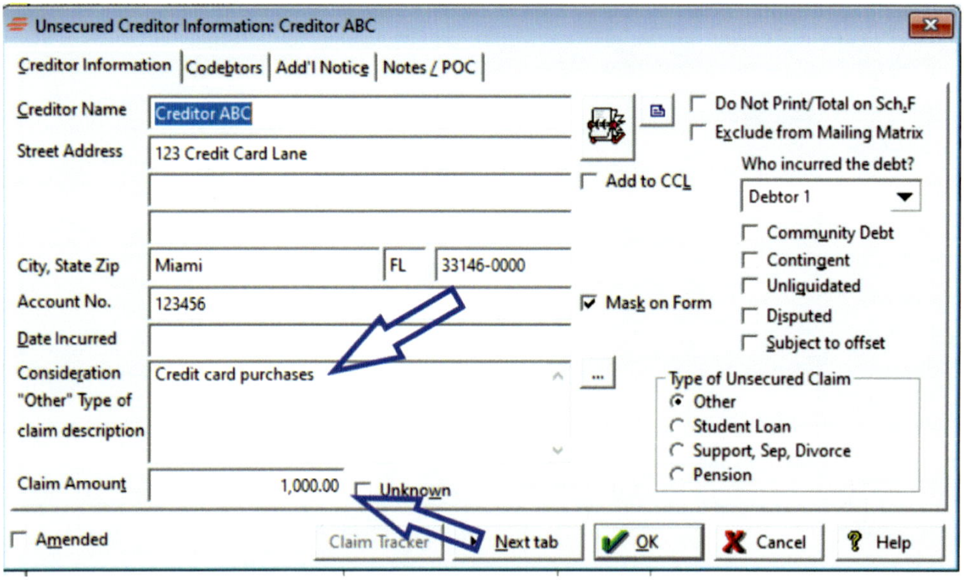

Best Case®

The next creditor is a medical bill. In interviewing the client, always ask if there are hospital bills and why. Are the medical bills related to an accident or illness?

Like all debt, the creditor's contact information, account number, and approximate balance are required. It's easy for clients to remember credit card debt, but not hospital bills, and since medical debt is rarely listed on a credit report, medical bills may inadvertently be excluded. Clients may have to contact the hospital directly, but it has been my experience that obtaining information on pending medical bills isn't easy. Therefore, clients should never mention that the information is needed for their bankruptcy but rather to schedule or make payments. Of course, no payments will be made.

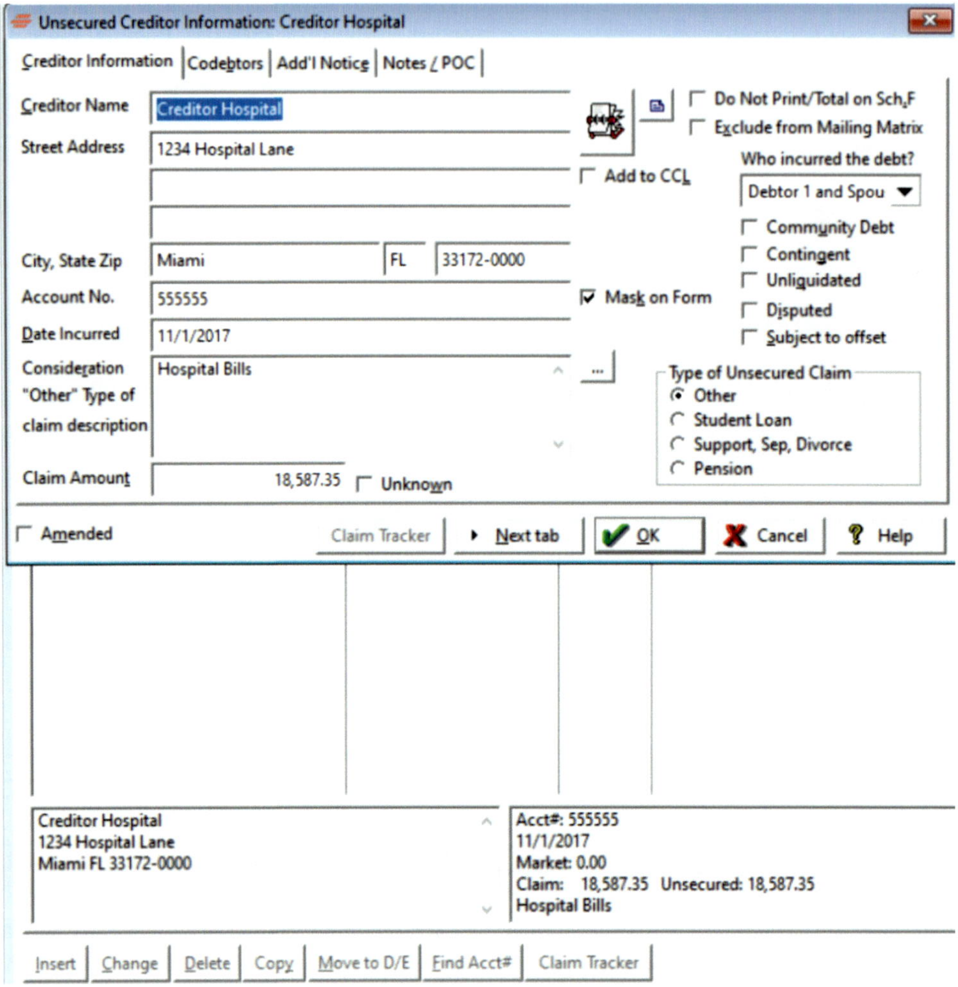

Best Case®

PRACTICE TIP

One issue that debtors have experienced is hospitals trying to "collect" at the moment. The hospital may request payment or a deposit and will swipe the credit card for the available credit limit. If the client was already contemplating bankruptcy, it's not an issue, but imagine the client with a high credit score and a substantial line of credit that gets maxed out immediately at a hospital. Even worse, if a bank account is wiped out clean from a debit card. While there is nothing that can be done legally after the fact, in consulting with clients, I let them know it's rare but has happened before just so that it doesn't happen to them. Hopefully, they spread the word and advise others.

Note when listing collection agencies or debt collectors, the date the account was purchased from the original creditor isn't relevant since it's not new debt. If the debt collector has not filed a lawsuit, describe the claim as "collection account – notice only." Since the debt collection agency is only attempting to collect on the debt, the claim amount is zero, especially if the original creditor is listed. If not, the debt total is doubled.

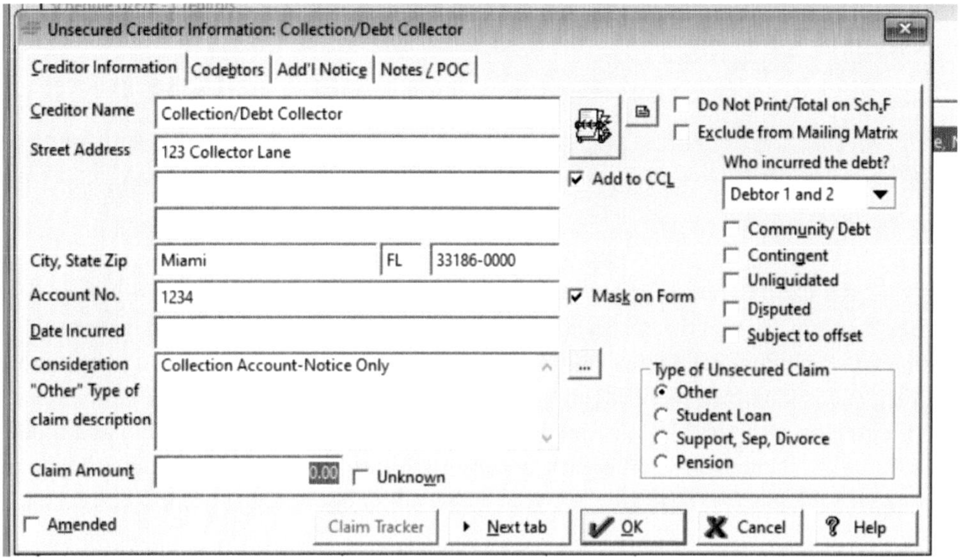

Best Case®

Sometimes it's challenging to identify the original creditor, and it's common for debt collectors to have multiple companies and addresses. If there is confusion as to whether an original creditor is being repeated, a notation can be included in the "Consideration" window such as "possible repeated creditor." If the same debt has been sold or transferred to multiple collection agencies, a common occurrence, to err on the side of caution, list each collection agency, not just the most recent one.

In the figure below, notice the total amount of debt is $163,803.30, and 27 claims or creditors are listed. The unwritten rule is that the U.S. Trustee's Office may get involved when the debt total exceeds $50,000, but that depends on the type of debt. In this case, there's no denying the unsecured debt total is substantial. However, approximately 80 percent of the debts are hospital bills, so it's not an issue if the debt is categorized correctly. Although, the bankruptcy trustee will ask at the Meeting of Creditors for confirmation that the medical bills are health, not accident-related.

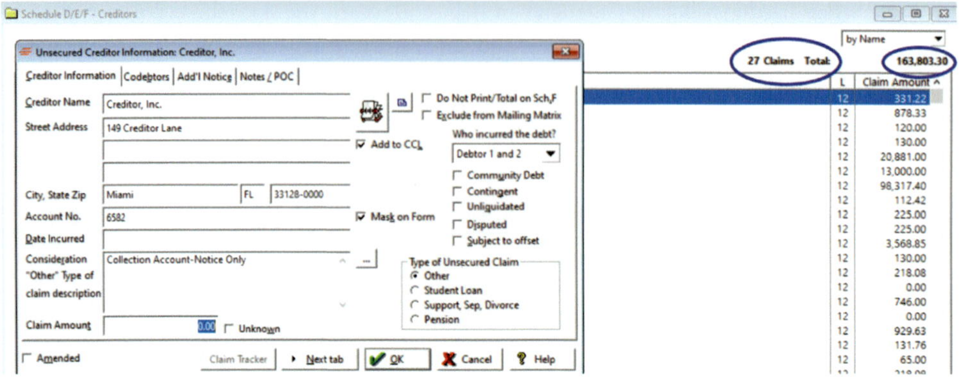

Best Case®

Note, the U.S. Trustee's Office does random audits, and for the record, when they call, it might be a conversation that leaves you scratching your head since the U.S. Trustee may be looking for something that doesn't exist; it's a shot in the dark. But if you happen to be on the receiving end of that call, pass the call on to the attorney. Do not engage in a conversation with them. However, the U.S. Trustee's Office has temporarily stopped random audits due to COVID-19.[11] Note, this is different from communicating with the bankruptcy trustee's office, which is common, especially between paralegals of both offices.

REAL CASES

Once I received a call from the U.S. Trustee's Office because of my motion to set aside a dismissal. The client failed to appear at the Meeting of Creditors and the case was dismissed. Compared to serial filers, there was nothing sinister about this case. A simple review of the petition would lead any reasonable person to the same conclusion. The client simply missed his hearing.

The staff attorney from the U.S. Trustee's Office started the conversation by asking me if he knew who I was. How am I supposed to know the answer to that question? I answered honestly: I would have no idea who he would know or not know, but I did say that I had never dealt with him before, whether personally or professionally. Then for the second time, he tried to confirm if he knew who I was. This conversation was already weird, so I responded as sometimes I do, with an example. In this case, I said that's like asking me if I know Tiger

11 Department of Justice. Office of Public Affairs. *U.S. Trustee Program Acts Quickly to Protect Public Health and Ensure Effective Functioning of the Bankruptcy System During COVID-19 Emergency*. April 13, 2020.

Woods. I do know Tiger, but I don't know Tiger, at least not personally, so I would have to conclude he doesn't know who I am either. At least he chuckled at my sarcasm.

The U.S. Trustee shifted his focus towards the motion, asking why it had been filed. The title seemed sufficiently self-explanatory. As I'm shaking my head in disbelief and rolling my eyes, the U.S. Trustee let me know he would object to my motion. I assume my sarcasm had something to do with his decision. I then asked: "you are objecting to setting aside a dismissal on a debtor who lives in a studio apartment with his daughter because his wife died unexpectedly, and he can't afford to live anywhere else, doesn't even own a car, which is part of the reason why he missed his hearing?" I noticed the assigned bankruptcy judge, and let's just say his level of sarcasm far exceeds mine. Even better, the judge is considered pro-debtor. I've often witnessed him respond to a creditor's objection to a Chapter 13 plan and ask if he should hang the debtor upside down and shake him to see if any loose change falls out of his pockets. I mentioned the judge's name and that I looked forward to meeting him for the first time. He never did appear at the hearing, which was even odder, but the motion was granted and that's all that matters. And if a bankruptcy attorney asks for the name of a U.S. Trustee that happens to be at a creditors' meeting, expect shock as a response. But again, when faced with this situation, rather than discuss details of the case with the U.S. Trustee's Office, let the attorney handle it.

Returning to the subject of random audits from the U.S. Trustee's Office, pre-BAPCPA, I regularly received inquiries. After BAPCPA, I doubt I even get one a year, and I can't remember the last time I saw a U.S. Trustee at the Meeting of Creditors, whether on my case or that of another bankruptcy attorney. The fact is cases that should be flagged aren't, and cases that shouldn't be flagged are. However, out of an abundance of caution, if the client's debt exceeds the invisible line drawn in the sand, clients should be advised the potential exists that they may be the next "lucky one." Regardless, it's not likely to change the result of their case, except to cause more work for you.

Returning to the figure above (see p. 206), besides 27 creditors and a substantial amount of debt related to medical bills, there is also a car repossession resulting in a deficiency balance exceeding $15,000. When the medical bills and car repossession are deducted from the debt total, the client owes approximately $17,000 in credit cards. Since payments have not been made for a considerable amount of time, the debt total has increased by several thousands of dollars due to interest and late fees. While $17,000 in credit card debt is unlikely to result in an inquiry from the U.S. Trustee's Office, it does happen from time to time. If that's the case, the response to the inquiry would be as explained above, giving a breakdown of the debt.

In the figure below, besides being able to add manually other types of consideration, additional parties can be noticed by clicking "Additional Notice."

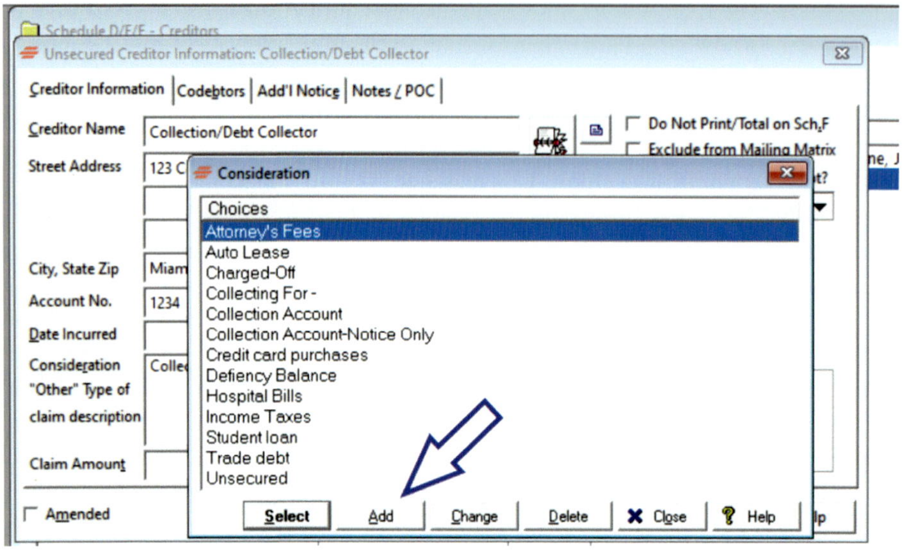

Best Case®

In this figure, the "claim amount" is listed even though the debt is with a collection agency. The difference this time is that there is a pending lawsuit. The case number can be used as the account number and include the creditor's attorney in the "Additional Notice" section. If the original creditor is known, choose "collecting for," which was added manually in case the original creditor was counted separately, doubling the debt total.

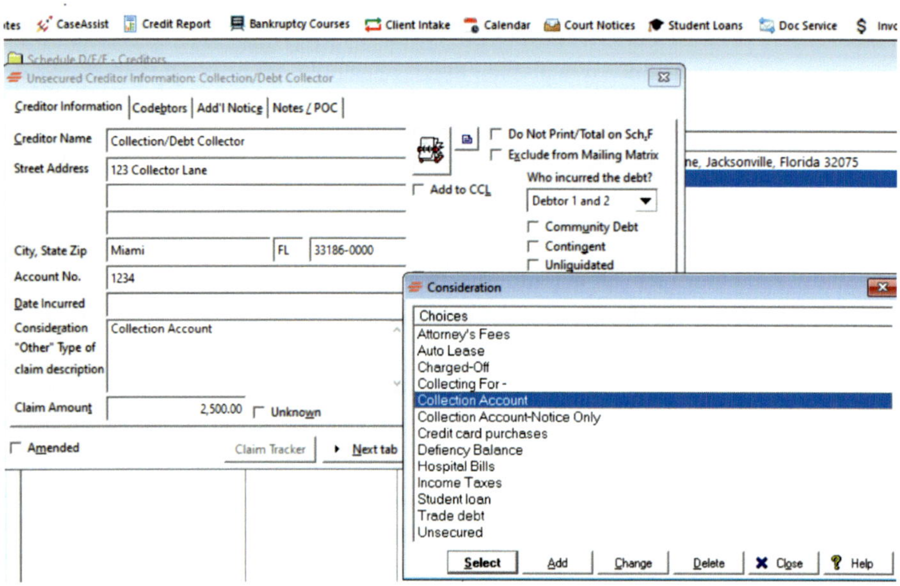

Best Case®

Remember, lawsuits are included on Line 9 of the Statement of Financial Affairs.[12]

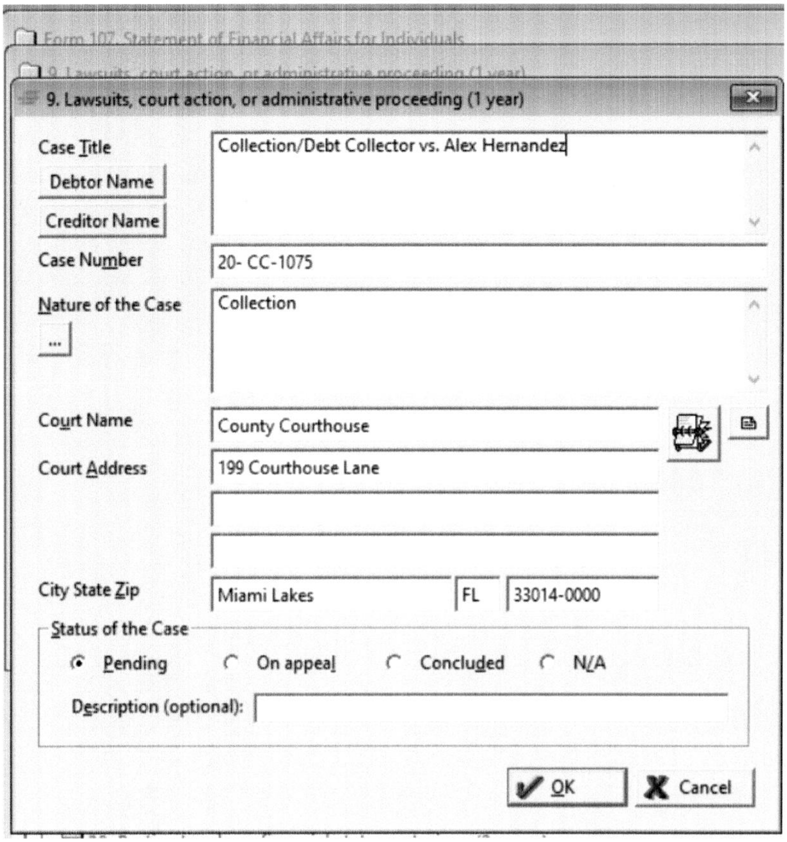

Best Case®

Even though student loans are primarily non-dischargeable, list the creditor information even if there is no intent to discharge the debt. Sometimes filing bankruptcy works to the client's advantage, who may be granted a forbearance or lower monthly payments by the lender because of the filing. Payments on student loans are listed on Schedule J line 17c "Other Installment Payments" or Line 21 "Other Expenses."[13]

12 Official Form 107. Your Statement of Financial Affairs for Individuals Filing for Bankruptcy (Individuals).
13 Supra, note 8.

SUMMARY

Adding creditors to the petition can be time-consuming since information is obtained from credit reports, credit card statements, collection letters, and the bankruptcy intake. However, the process is relatively simple since it's just copying creditor information.

Whether dischargeable or not, all debts are listed and categorized as secured or unsecured and belong on Schedules D, E/F, or G. Secured debts are detailed in Schedule D, and the debtor's intent is listed on Form 108. Unsecured debt, Schedule E/F, is separated into priority or non-priority claims. Examples of priority claims are tax obligations and domestic support obligations, and non-priority claims are credit cards and personal loans. Schedule G, Official Form 106G is for leases and executory contracts.

Each debt listed must include the creditor's address, account number, current balance, and the date the debt was incurred.

KEYWORDS AND TERMS

- Executory contracts
- Leases
- Official Form 106D. Schedule D: Creditors Who Have Claims Secured by Debt
- Official Form 106 E/F. Schedule E/F: Creditors Who Have Unsecured Claims (Individuals)
- Official Form 106G. Schedule G: Executory Contracts and Unexpired Leases (Individuals)
- Official Form 108. Statement of Intention for Individuals Filing Under Chapter 7

DISCUSSION QUESTIONS

1. A debt with an insurance company is listed on the bankruptcy intake. What questions should you ask the client?
2. In reviewing the bankruptcy intake, an outstanding debt to a local chiropractor is listed. What further information do you need from the client?

PRACTICE QUESTIONS AND EXERCISES

1. Include the following creditors in your petition:
   a. Hospital Lien, LLC,123 Hospital Lane, Biloxi, Mississippi 39530.
   b. Car Repossession, Inc., 987 Repo Lane, Los Angeles, California 90014.
   c. Credit Card Company A, 456 I Owe Lane, Laredo, Texas 78042.

d. Collection Depot, 345 Debtor Collector Lane, Boise, Idaho 83702. Note the debtor has received collection letters that a lawsuit is imminent.
e. Lawsuit, Inc. 100 Lawsuit Avenue, PO Box 811, Denver, Colorado 80202. This creditor has filed a lawsuit against the debtor. Also, notice the creditor's attorney: Jack Law, 89 Courthouse Lane, Suite 22, Naples, Florida 34110.
f. Add categories to the "Consideration" section.
g. Write a response to the trustee's inquiry about a debtor with more than $200,000 in unsecured credit card debt. Note the debt is related to a failed business of the client that has been closed for more than one year. Add facts as need be.

OFFICIAL FORM 106G. SCHEDULE G: EXECUTORY CONTRACTS AND UNEXPIRED LEASES

An executory contract can best be described as a contract that has yet to be completed, meaning performance is required by both parties. An executory contract is nothing other than a lease, for example, a residential lease.

Leases are in §365 of the Bankruptcy Code and belong on Schedule G.[14] For the typical Chapter 7 case, Schedule G applies to residential leases and leased cars.[15] Note, as a bankruptcy practitioner, I've never listed a residential lease in Schedule G, nor do I know of any other bankruptcy lawyers that do.[16] I've also never been asked to by the trustee either. But, since practices and customs change from one district to another, confirm what's the norm in your district.

Auto leases aren't listed in Schedule A/B since there isn't an ownership interest, so there is nothing to exempt on Schedule C.[17] However, the expense of the lease is listed on Schedule J, Line 17.[18]

14 11 U.S.C., §365. Official Form 106G. Schedule G: Executory Contracts and Unexpired Leases (Individuals).
15 Id.
16 Id.
17 Supra, note 1; Official Form 106C, Schedule C: The Property You Claim as Exempt (Individuals).
18 Supra, note 8.

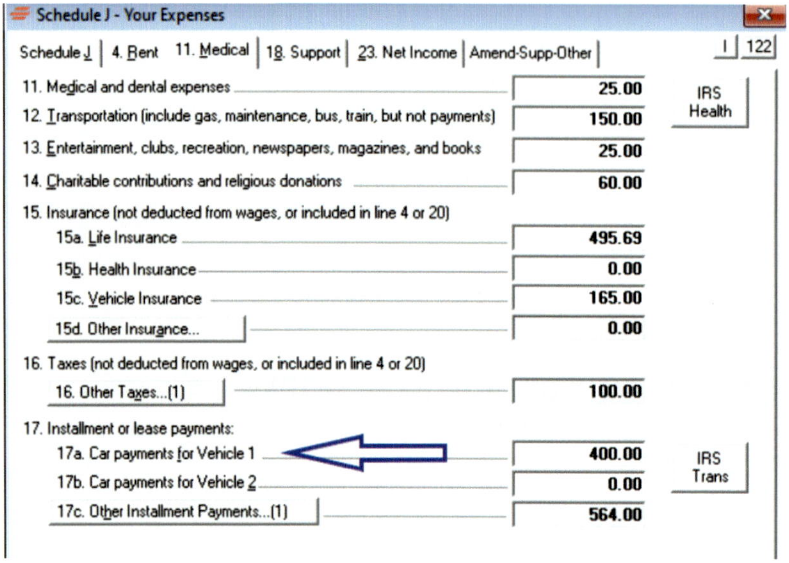

Best Case®

Remember to include the intent of the debtor whether to assume or reject the lease. If the debtor rejects the lease and surrenders the vehicle, the debt is listed on Schedule F as an unsecured creditor with a deficiency balance.[19] If the deficiency balance is unknown, the current balance can be listed.

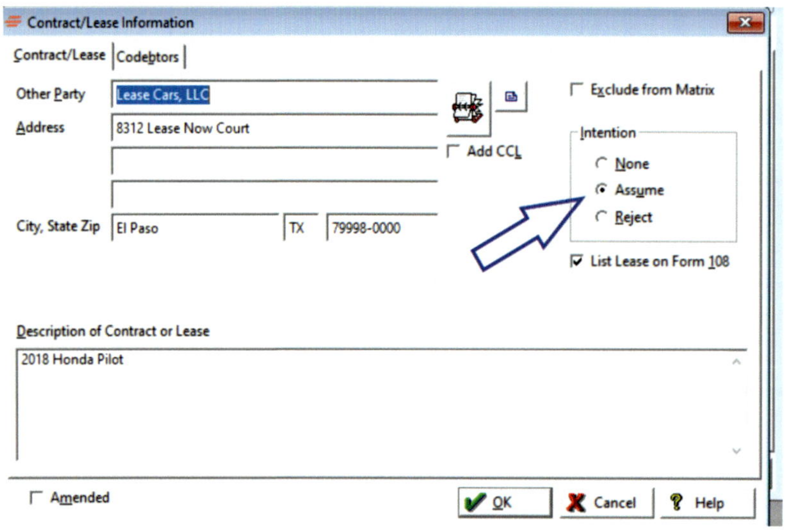

Best Case®

19 Supra, note 3.

SUMMARY

Leases and executory contracts are mentioned in §365 of the Code and are listed in Schedule G. Form 108 Intention is also required to conclude if the lease will be assumed or rejected. Terminated leases belong on Schedule F as an unsecured non-priority debt, and the monthly payment of an assumed lease is listed in Schedule J, Line 17.

KEYWORDS

- Assume
- Executory contract
- Lease
- Reject
- Section 365
- Voluntary repossession/voluntary repo

DISCUSSION QUESTIONS

1. The debtor intends on surrendering his vehicle as he is already two months behind on payments. How does this affect the bankruptcy filing?
2. When the debtor completed the bankruptcy intake six months earlier, the car was leased. The client expressed his concern about obtaining a car loan post-bankruptcy. The current lender on the car lease is offering a low-interest rate, and the dealership has agreed to substantially reduce the purchase price of the car, so the client intends to proceed with the option to buy clause of the lease. How does this affect the bankruptcy?

PRACTICE QUESTIONS AND EXERCISES

1. List the information required for Schedule G for a cell phone and car lease.
2. The client has decided to surrender a leased vehicle because the monthly payments are too high. Complete the necessary information for Schedule G and other schedules.
3. The debtor has found a new apartment to rent that is closer to work. The rental amount of $1,200 remains the same, but six months remain on the current lease. Add the landlord as a debtor.

OFFICIAL FORM 106H. SCHEDULE H: YOUR CODEBTORS

Co-debtors are listed in Schedule H.[20] The co-debtor could be a parent or family member that co-signed an auto loan or any other type of debt with the client. This has become more common with student loans as lenders try to figure out different ways to collect on the debt. Ex-spouses are commonly listed as co-debtors as well. For example, the debtor kept the car in a divorce. Another common situation is the client who is making payments on the debt, but the debt belongs to someone else, whether an ex-spouse or family member. Even though it's arguable if the client owns the asset, list the asset on Schedule A/B and the expense on Schedule J, Line 17.[21] Make a notation that the debt belongs to another individual to avoid confusion since there's no debt to list on Schedule D.[22]

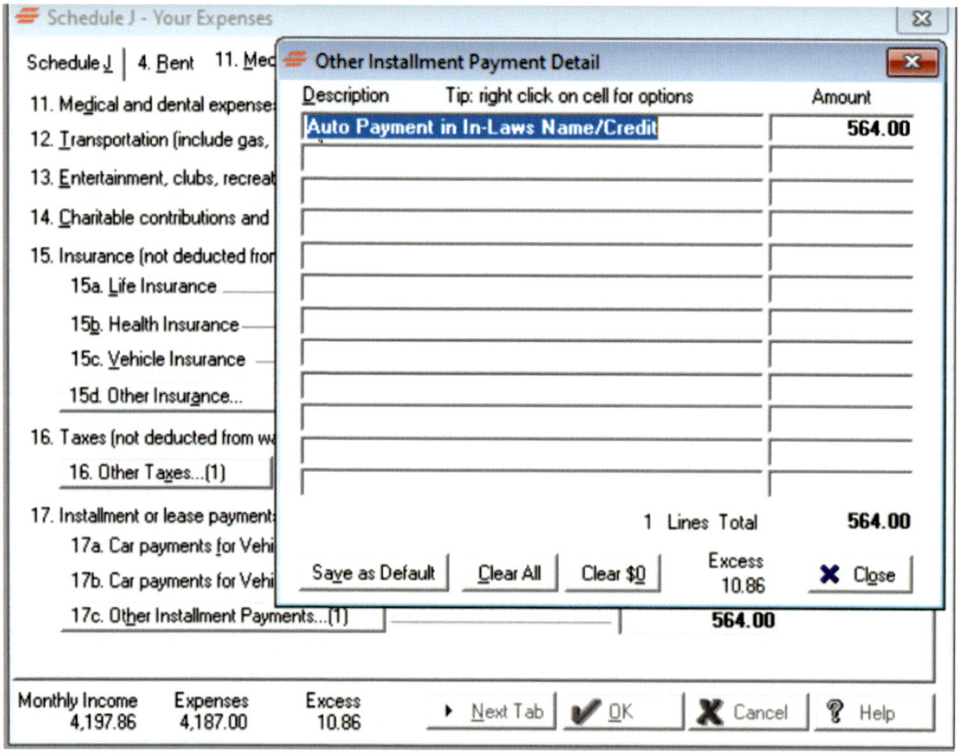

Best Case®

Of course, verify how the client is making payments. If the client pays the third party in cash, it's preferred to make payments with a check to better track the expenses. Note even

20 Official Form 106H. Schedule H: Your Codebtors (Individuals).

21 Supra, notes 1 and 8.

22 Supra, note 1, Official Form 106D.

with bankruptcy, co-signers remain liable for the debt. This sometimes results in the client deciding to keep the vehicle. For joint filings, there is no need to list the second debtor as a co-debtor.

SUMMARY

Co-debtor is the term used in the bankruptcy petition, but it's synonymous with co-borrower and co-signer. This is different from an authorized user who has the authority to use a credit card but is not responsible for the debt. Co-debtors are as responsible for the debt as the debtor. Bankruptcy does not discharge the debt for a co-debtor.

KEYWORDS AND TERMS

- Authorized user
- Co-borrower
- Co-signer
- Co-debtor

DISCUSSION QUESTIONS

1. The client and the domestic partner are in the office completing the bankruptcy intake. Only the client is filing for bankruptcy, but both parties have several credit cards together as co-borrowers and authorized users. How can you confirm which debt the client is responsible for?
2. The client has dropped off the bankruptcy intake along with three credit reports. The client disputes several of the debts as not belonging to him. The client believes two debts belong to his brother who has a similar name and Social Security number, and multiple credit cards belong to his wife, who is not filing for bankruptcy. Are those debts listed in the petition?

PRACTICE QUESTIONS AND EXERCISES

1. List two co-debtors in your bankruptcy petition, one with secured debt and the other unsecured.
2. The bankruptcy petition has to be filed this week to avoid wage garnishment. In the credit report, there is a car repossession and two foreclosures. However, neither of those three debts belongs to the client. It appears to be a mistake by the credit reporting bureaus. Add the debts along with any notations you feel are necessary. See Figure 15.1.

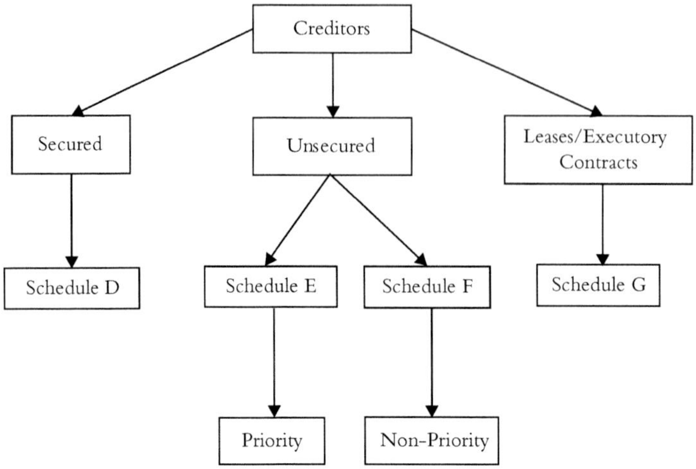

FIGURE 15.1 An overview of creditors.

REFERENCES

11 U.S.C. §365.

Department of Justice. Office of Public Affairs. *U.S. Trustee Program Acts Quickly to Protect Public Health and Ensure Effective Functioning of the Bankruptcy System during COVID-19 Emergency*. April 13, 2020. Available at www.justice.gov/opa/pr/us-trustee-program-acts-quickly-protect-public-health-and-ensure-effective-functioning.

Official Form 106 A/B. Schedule A/B: Property (Individuals).

Official Form 106C. Schedule C: The Property You Claim as Exempt (Individuals).

Official Form 106D. Schedule D: Creditors Who Hold Claims Secured by Property (Individuals).

Official Form 106E/F. Schedule E/F: Creditors Who Have Unsecured Claims (Individuals).

Official Form 106G. Schedule G: Executory Contracts and Unexpired Leases (Individuals).

Official Form 106H. Schedule H: Your Codebtors (Individuals).

Official Form 106I. Schedule I: Your Income (Individuals).

Official Form 106J. Schedule J: Your Expenses (Individuals).

Official Form 107. Your Statement of Financial Affairs for Individuals Filing for Bankruptcy (Individuals).

Official Form 108. Statement of Intention for Individuals Filing under Chapter 7.

CHAPTER 16

Schedule I

Income

OFFICIAL FORM 106I. SCHEDULE I: YOUR INCOME

The debtor's income is calculated and listed on Schedule I.[1] Unlike the means test, which is based on the debtor's last six months of income, income for Schedule I is for the month of filing.[2]

Part 1: Describe Employment

In this section, the client's employer information is listed, and that of the spouse. Spousal income is also included even if the spouse is not filing for bankruptcy.

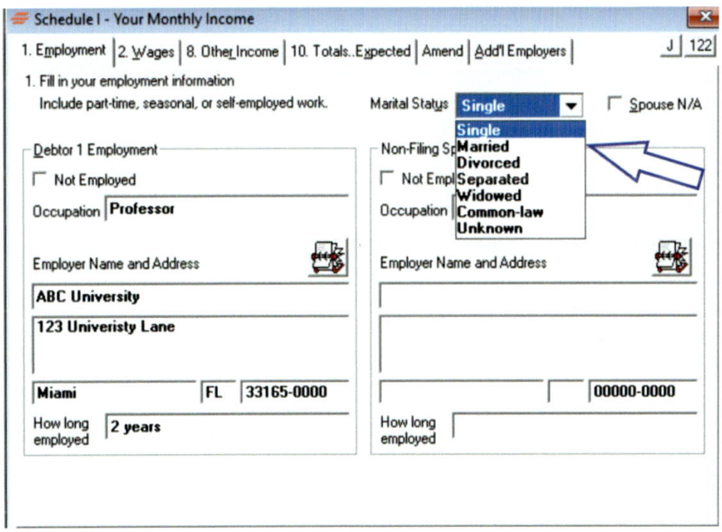

Best Case®

1 Official Form 106I. Schedule I: Your Income (Individuals).
2 Official Form 122A-1, Chapter 7 Statement of Your Current Monthly Income; id.

DOI: 10.4324/9781003203278-17

If the client is not legally married, the domestic partner's employment information is excluded from Schedule I and the means test.[3] However, household contributions from the domestic partner are listed in Schedule I, Line 8h.[4]

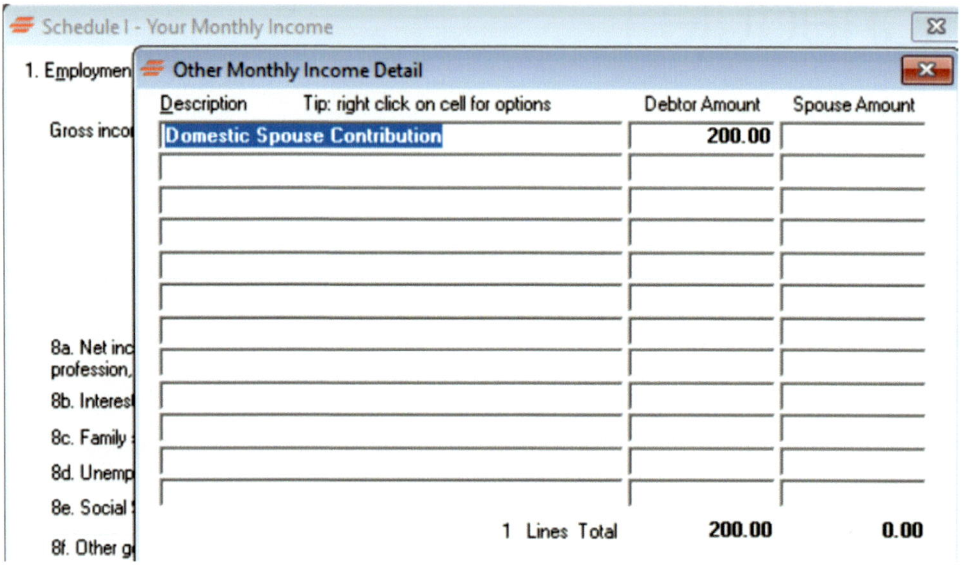

Best Case®

Calculating the last six months of income for the means test is straightforward.[5] However, Schedule I calculations are trickier.[6] For example, if the filing occurs on the last day of the month, there's no guesswork as to that month's income. But, if the petition is filed early in the month, say March 5, a calculated guess is made as to income earned for the remainder of the month. Past pay stubs help serve as a guide but confirm a possible increase in pay that month, whether because of overtime, bonuses, commissions, etc. If the possible increase results in substantial disposable income, delay filing. Note that most trustees require copies of pay stubs up to and past the filing date.

3 Id.
4 Supra, note 1.
5 Supra, note 2, Official Form 122A-1.
6 Supra, note 1.

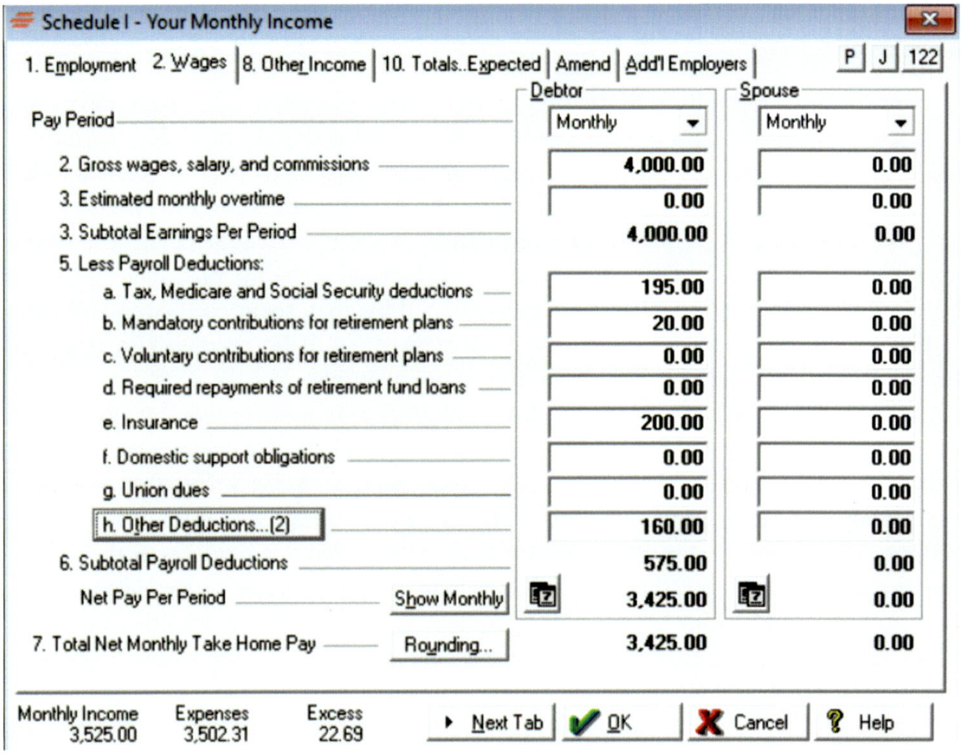

Best Case®

8. Other income. Other streams of revenue are listed in this section, including:

8a. Net income rental property and operating a business, profession, or farm.

8b. Interest and dividends; investment income received by the client.

8c. Family support (child support/alimony). Include alimony or child support payments received, whether court-ordered or not, on Line 8c. However, note there is a difference between court-ordered support and actually receiving it. If the obligor is not complying with the court order, so the client isn't receiving support, this section is left blank. If support is inconsistent, then average out the amount received.

Finally, make sure this section isn't confused with Line 5f (domestic support obligation), where the client is paying support, and payments are deducted from pay stubs. If support payments are made directly to the ex-spouse, list the expense on Schedule J, Line 18.[7]

7 Official Form 106J. Schedule J: Your Expenses (Individuals).

8d. Unemployment compensation. List any ongoing unemployment compensation payments received.

8e. Social Security. Even though unemployment compensation and Social Security are included in Schedule I, it's not in the means test.[8] This is one of the issues, criticisms, and confusion created by BAPCPA where certain sources of income are excluded from the means test, but not for Schedule I.[9] As a result, it's common to have a client pass the means test, but there's disposable income available when comparing Schedules I and J, resulting in Chapter 13.[10] Likewise, a debtor may have minimal disposable income but still fails the means test.[11] This may seem confusing and contradictory, not to mention unfair, but each scenario will be reviewed in detail in future chapters. For now, consider the following example.

To avoid filing for bankruptcy, the client took steps to reduce expenses by moving to a lesser expensive apartment so that more funds were available to pay down debt. However, with time the client realizes bankruptcy is the only solution. As we know, the client must stop paying unsecured creditors before filing. But by reducing expenses and not paying creditors, the amount of disposable income has increased, and as a result, even though the client passed the means test, the increased availability of disposable income prevents the client from proceeding with a Chapter 7.[12] In essence, the client is being penalized for saving money and avoiding having to file for bankruptcy. Even worse is that the means test benefits debtors with secured debt.[13]

The astute client realizes this and takes steps to qualify by reducing income, increasing expenses, or increasing secured debt. A common tactic is buying a new car. For this reason, a trustee is likely to ask when the attorney was retained and the car purchased. Again, you can see the importance of asking clients if they met and/or consulted with a prior bankruptcy attorney.

8f. Other government assistance. Food stamps, Section 8 housing vouchers, etc., will be listed in this section. Note clients may list their rent obligation but forget to include that housing assistance is received, resulting in incorrect figures for Schedule I.[14] For example, in the figure below, if tab 8f is clicked, additional details can be included

8 Supra, note 2.
9 Id.
10 Supra, notes 1, 2, and 7.
11 Supra, note 2.
12 Supra, note 2.
13 Id.
14 Supra, note 1.

in the pop-up window. Here, Section 8 housing vouchers were added in the amount of $612.

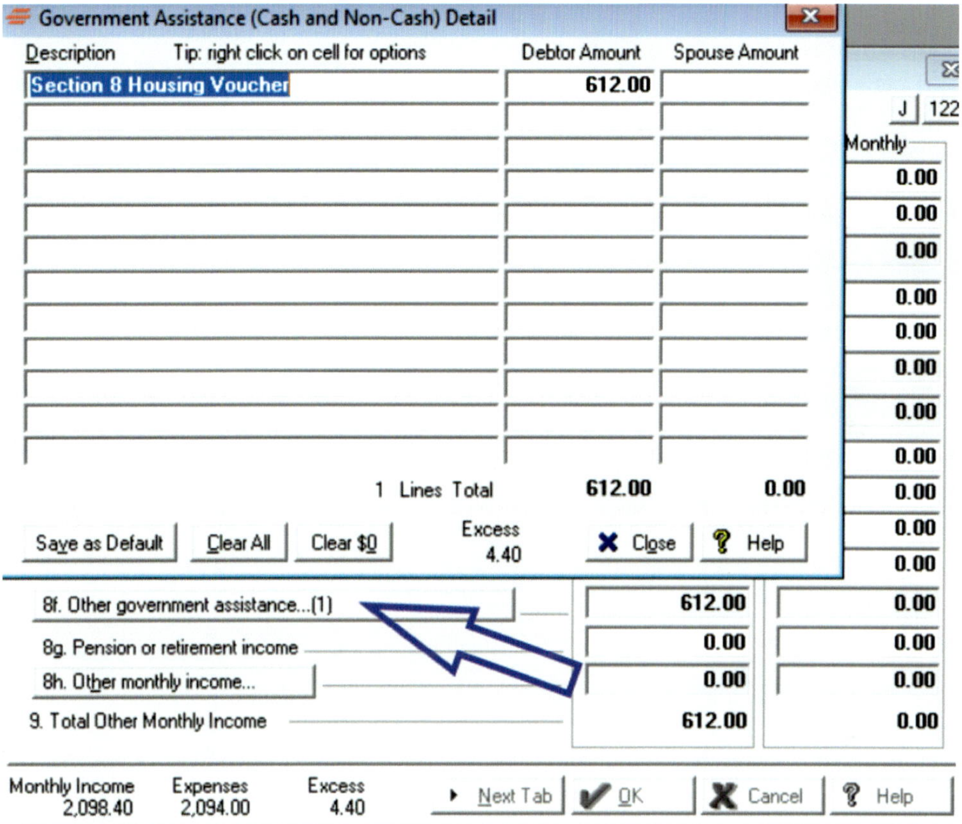

Best Case®

In the next figure, the rent obligation is listed at $790. In reality, the client pays $178 in rent, which is the difference between the $790 rent obligation and the $612 received in housing assistance. However, if $178 is listed as the rent amount, the client's total expenses are reduced to $1,482, leaving excess funds in the amount of $616.40, resulting in Chapter 13. However, by adding the housing assistance and total rent obligation, the figures square up.

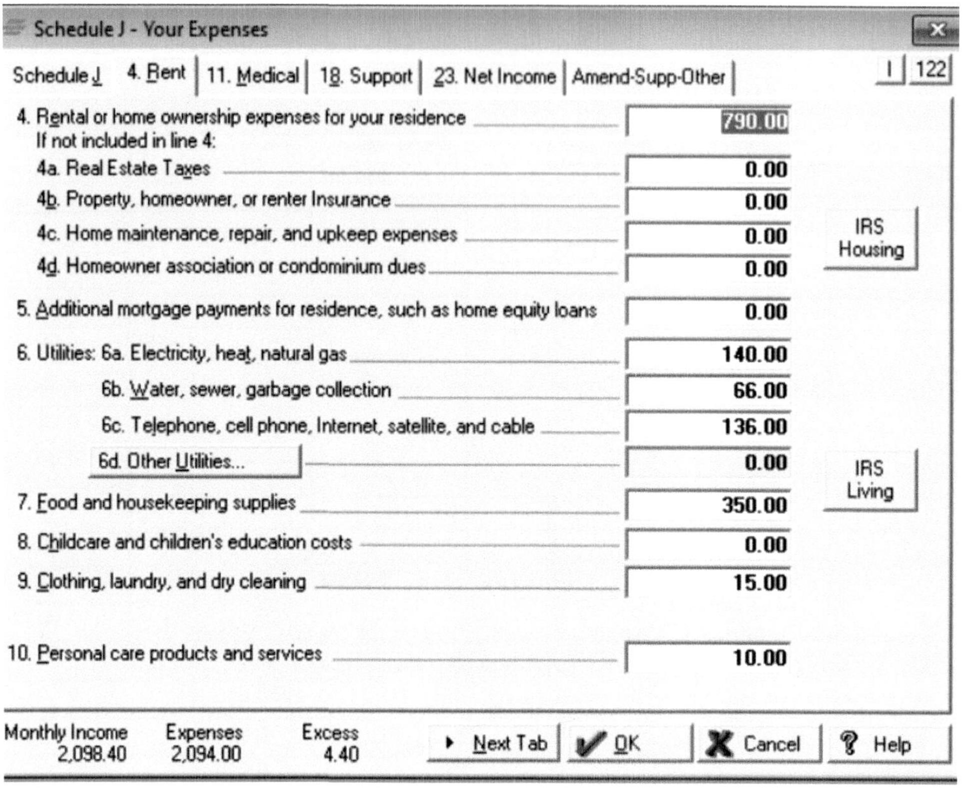
Schedule J - Your Expenses

Schedule J | 4. Rent | 11. Medical | 18. Support | 23. Net Income | Amend-Supp-Other | I | 122

4. Rental or home ownership expenses for your residence	790.00
If not included in line 4:	
4a. Real Estate Taxes	0.00
4b. Property, homeowner, or renter Insurance	0.00
4c. Home maintenance, repair, and upkeep expenses	0.00
4d. Homeowner association or condominium dues	0.00
5. Additional mortgage payments for residence, such as home equity loans	0.00
6. Utilities: 6a. Electricity, heat, natural gas	140.00
6b. Water, sewer, garbage collection	66.00
6c. Telephone, cell phone, Internet, satellite, and cable	136.00
6d. Other Utilities...	0.00
7. Food and housekeeping supplies	350.00
8. Childcare and children's education costs	0.00
9. Clothing, laundry, and dry cleaning	15.00
10. Personal care products and services	10.00

IRS Housing

IRS Living

Monthly Income	Expenses	Excess
2,098.40	2,094.00	4.40

Next Tab | OK | Cancel | Help

Best Case®

8g. Pension or other retirement income. If the amount is minimal, clients may forget to list their pension benefits but review bank statements, tax returns, and W-2s for inconsistencies.

8h. Other income. Contributions by a domestic spouse or household members are included in Line 8h.

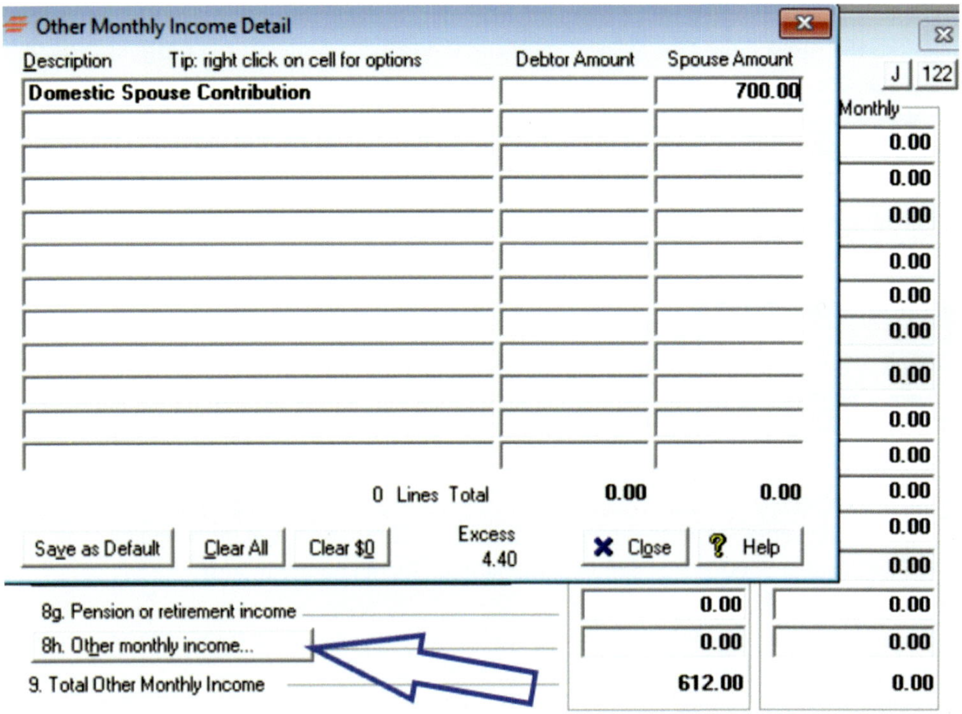

Best Case®

PRACTICE TIP

A couple of issues present themselves when calculating income for Schedule I.[15] The first is separating income that belongs on Schedule I and the means test.[16] For example, if a pay stub received on the sixth day of the month is included in Schedule I calculations, those six days of income were actually earned in the prior month and belong in the means test.[17] Therefore, it's essential to use a calendar or other system to calculate the applicable pay periods accordingly.

The next issue is calculating income correctly. Most people calculate their bi-weekly income by multiplying their paycheck times two for the monthly amount and times 24 for the annual amount. However, multiplying times two is only applicable when pay periods are semi-monthly on the fifteenth and thirtieth of the month. Besides carryover days, with bi-weekly pay periods, some months have more than two pay periods equaling 26 to 27 pay periods per year. Therefore, the bi-weekly formula is determined by multiplying the income

15 Id.
16 Id., supra note 2.
17 Supra, note 2.

amount by 26 and dividing by 12. Disposable income is likely for months with an extra paycheck, so the filing should be delayed until the following month. When filing towards the end of the year, be aware of year-end bonuses and tax refunds for the upcoming year.

When pay periods are weekly, clients may multiply their income times four to determine the monthly amount. However, that results in 48 pay periods when there are 52 weeks in a year. The correct formula is multiplying the weekly amount times 52 and dividing by 12 for the monthly figure.

Formula Comparisons

Example 1 (bi-weekly):

- (Incorrect) \$500 × 2 = \$1,000.00 per month × 12 months = \$12,000.00 annually.
- (Correct) \$500 × 26 / 12 = \$1,083.33 × 12 months = \$13,000.00 annually.

Example 2 (weekly):

- (Incorrect) \$500 × 4 = \$2,000 per month × 12 months = \$24,000 annually.
- (Correct) \$500 × 52 = \$26,000 annually or \$2,166.66 per month.

In Example 1, note the difference when multiplying a pay period times two to arrive at \$1,000 per month. But when calculated correctly by multiplying the bi-weekly amount times 26 pay periods and dividing it by 12, the difference is an increase of \$83.33 per month or \$1,000 per year.

In Example 2, income increased by \$166.66 per month when multiplied by the number of weeks per year. However, note these formulas should be used as a quick estimate only to determine Schedule I income since each paycheck must be calculated.[18] If not, the incorrect amount of income is shown on Schedule I since carryover days, overtime, paid time off, and bonuses weren't included.[19]

Let's review examples to illustrate further how income is calculated for Schedule I.[20] Suppose the bankruptcy is filed in March. Review the pay stubs to confirm the dates the client is paid for, not the date pay was received. For example, if the client is paid on March 3, the pay period is from February 17 through February 28. Just because the paycheck was received in March, it doesn't mean it's for workdays in March because the pay is for work performed in February. That pay period is included in the means test, not Schedule I.[21] Therefore, when calculating income for the current month, days are added or subtracted accordingly.

In the figure below, if the pay date is April 10, the last three days of March aren't included in Schedule I.[22] In this case, the calculations for April begin on the first of the month.

18 Supra, note 1.
19 Id.
20 Id.
21 Supra, note 2.
22 Supra, note 1.

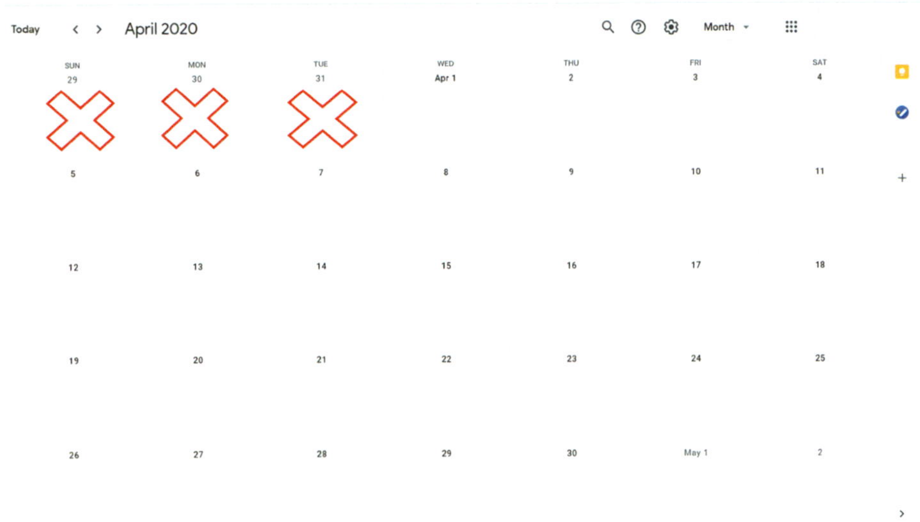

Best Case®

If that paycheck is included for April, an extra seven days from March were added (see dates highlighted in red in the figure below). The pay period is from March 23 through April 3, so only the first three days in April are used in Schedule I.[23]

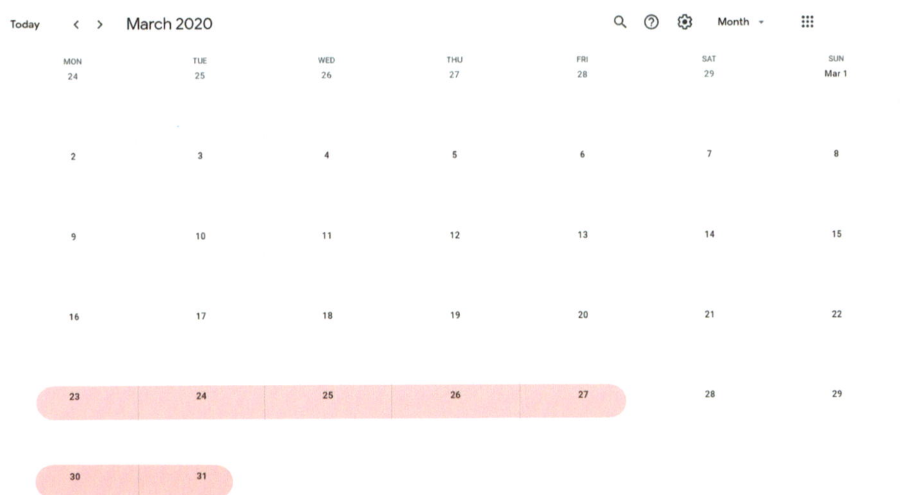

23 Id.

Likewise, in the next figure, the next pay date is April 24, and after that, May 8. April's income includes April 27–30 but May 1–8 is excluded.

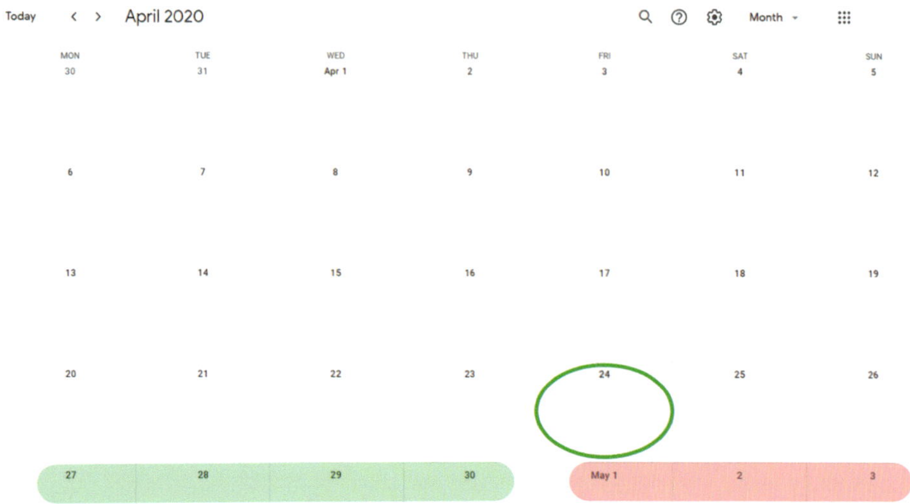

Also, make sure to count workdays, not calendar days. Therefore, Monday through Friday has been included in this example, which equals five days, so for a bi-weekly pay stub, that equals ten days. When adding carryover dates, the average daily income must be calculated. Divide the gross income by the number of workdays, ten in this example, then multiply that figure times the number of carryover days. The same calculations are performed for deductions. Remember to include the remaining days from the prior month in the means test.[24]

In the figure below, the dates highlighted in green are the dates included in Schedule I.[25]

24 Supra, note 2.
25 Supra, note 1.

Note that daily calculations are not necessary for the first five months of the means test even though there is an overlap of dates.[26]

Example Calculations

Using the example above to calculate income for April, the client earns $1,275 bi-weekly with $191.25 in tax deductions, $75 in health insurance, $5.75 in dental insurance, and $2.50 in vision insurance. The pay dates are April 10, 24, and May 8.

1. For the April 10 pay date, the pay period is from March 23 through April 3. Therefore, April 1, 2, and 3 are included in Schedule I.[27] The client's workdays are Monday through Friday, equaling ten days, so all figures are divided by ten (days).
   - Pay: 1,275.00/10 = 127.50 × 3 = 382.50
   - Deductions: 191.25/10 = 19.12 × 3 = 57.36
   - Health insurance: 75/10 = 7.5 × 3 = 22.50
   - Dental insurance: 5.75/10 = 0.57 × 3 = 1.71
   - Vision insurance: 2.50/10 = 0.25 × 3 = 0.75

26 Supra, note 5.
27 Supra, note 1.

2. For the pay period of April 6 through 17, the pay date is April 24, so there are no carryover days. For the pay period of April 20 through May 1, the client is paid on May 8, so April 20–24 (five days) is included, and 27–30 (four days). So May 1 is excluded.
   - Pay: 1,275.00/10 = 127.50 × 9 = 1,147.50
   - Deductions: 191.25/10 = 19.12 × 9 = 172.08
   - Health insurance: 75/10 = 7.5 × 9 = 67.50
   - Dental insurance: 5.75/10 = 0.57 × 9 = 5.13
   - Vision insurance: 2.50/10 = 0.25 × 9 = 2.25

Category	(3/23–4/3) paid 4/10	4/6–4/17 paid 4/24	4/20–5/1 paid 5/8	Total
Income	382.50	1,275.00	1,147.50	2,805.00
Deductions	57.36	191.25	172.08	420.69
Health insurance	22.50	75.00	67.50	165.00
Dental insurance	1.71	5.75	5.13	12.59
Vision insurance	0.75	2.50	2.25	5.50

Total income	2,805.00
Total deductions	603.78
Net income	2,201.22

Net income (Schedule I)[a]	2,201.22
Monthly expenses (Schedule J)[b]	2,190.00
Monthly excess	11.22

[a] See note 1.

[b] See note 7.

For the first table shown above, the gross income is \$2,805.00, and with deductions of \$603.78, the net income is \$2,201.22. For purposes of this example, if the client's monthly expenses (Schedule J) are \$2,190.00, the disposable income is \$11.22.[28]

28 Id.

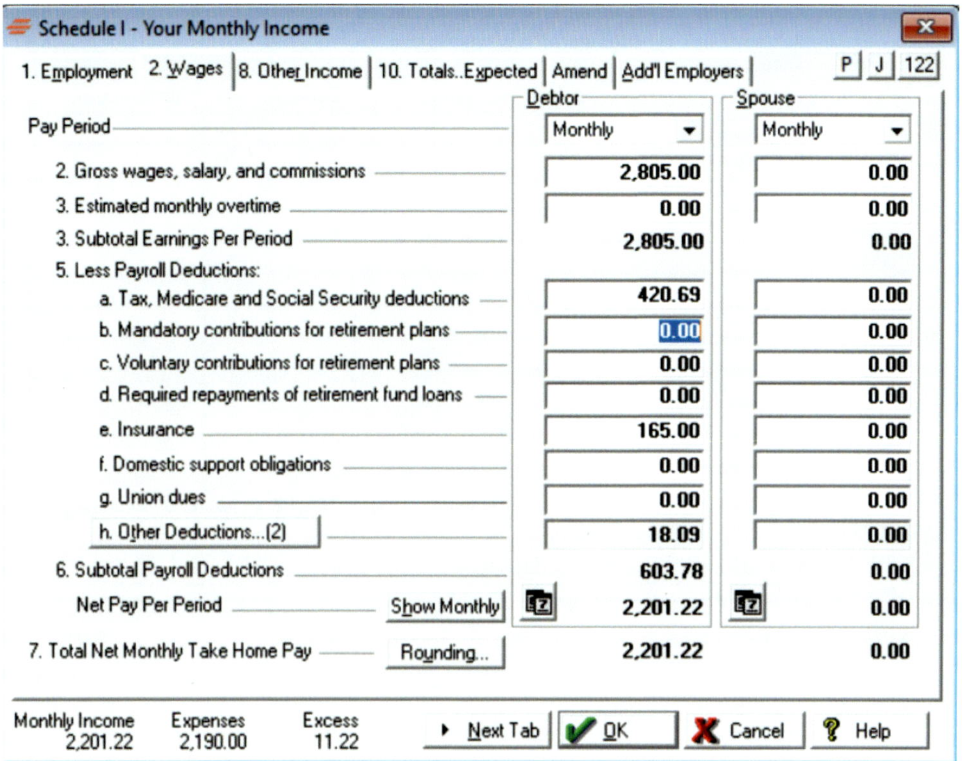

Best Case®

Note in Line 5h, "Other Deductions" totals $18.14, which is dental insurance ($12.64) plus vision insurance ($5.50).

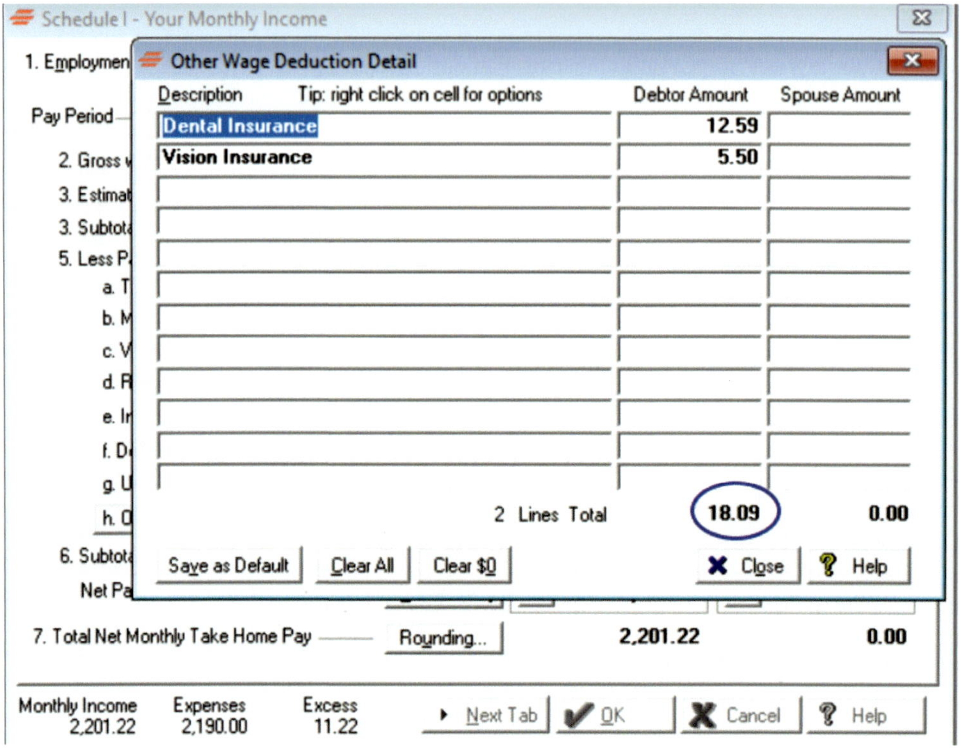

Best Case®

While similar deductions can be lumped together, my preference is to separate deductions since it keeps it visually clear and straightforward for the bankruptcy trustee. It also guarantees that all deductions were included and calculated correctly.

Assuming the client passed the means test, the client can proceed with Chapter 7 because of the minimal disposable income.[29] However, suppose by mistake, May 1 was included in the calculations.

Category	One day	Prior totals	Total
Pay	127.50	2,805.00	2,932.50
Taxes	19.12	420.69	439.81
Health insurance	7.50	165.00	172.50
Dental insurance	0.57	12.59	13.16
Vision insurance	0.25	5.50	5.75

29 Supra, note 5.

Total income	2,932.50
Total deductions	631.22
Net income	2,301.28

In the first table shown above, the extra day of income and deductions was added to the "prior totals" column, resulting in a "net income" of $2,301.28 (see the second table above). If the monthly expenses remained the same, the excess funds would amount to $111.18. See the table below.

Net income	2,301.28
Monthly expenses	2,190.00
Monthly excess	111.18

With more than $100 in disposable income available, the client could end up in Chapter 13 because of the simple mistake of including one extra day of income.

PAYROLL DEDUCTIONS

In Section 5 of Schedule I, deductions are calculated.[30] Compare previous pay stubs for alternating deductions per pay period. For example, some clients may have deductions for uniforms, meals, or 401k loans alternated or deducted between different pay periods or even at the end of the month for commission-based jobs where the paycheck is higher than base paychecks.

PRACTICE TIP

There are situations where monies aren't included in either the means test or Schedule I.[31] For example, when Congress passed the CARES Act for coronavirus relief, 11 U.S.C. was amended to exclude the stimulus check as income for both Chapters 7 and 13.[32] However, if the employer provides a disaster relief payment, that's included.

30 Supra, note 1.
31 Supra, note 2.
32 Notice to Chapter 7 and 13 Trustees Regarding Recovery Rebates Paid to Consumer Bankruptcy Debtors Under the Cares Act of 2020. Available at www.justice.gov/ust/file/cares_act_recovery_rebate_notice.pdf/download.

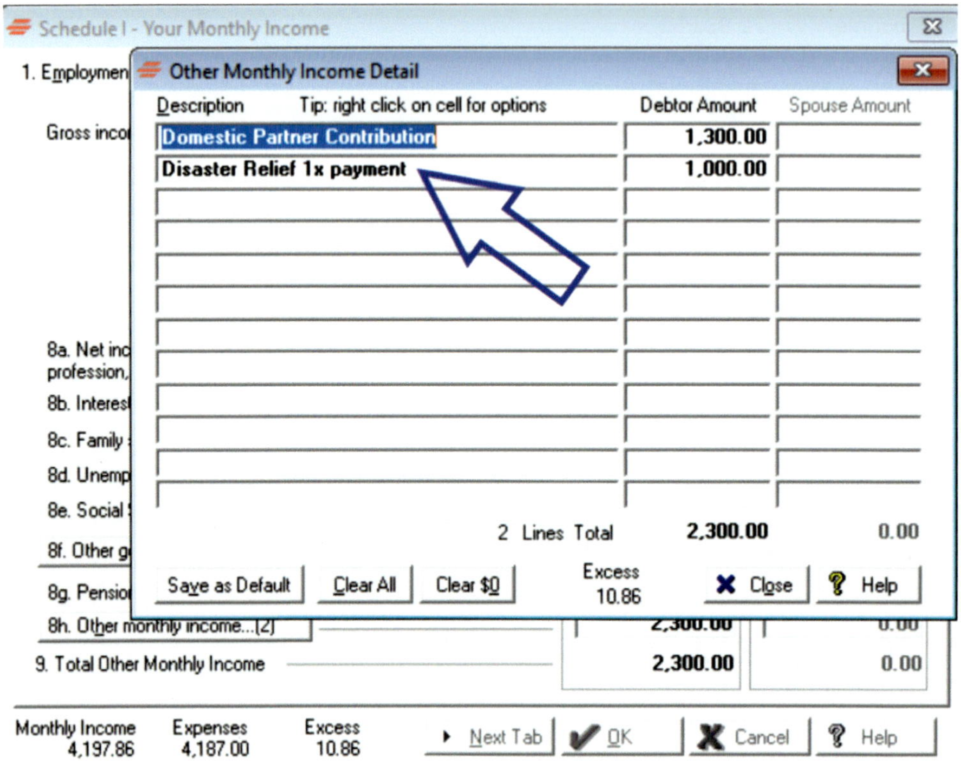

Best Case®

In this case, it was a one-time payment provided by the employer because of COVID-19. However, since the debtor's domestic partner was also earning less, the figures remained the same, so there was no need to delay the filing until the following pay period or month.

Finally, be aware of employer reimbursements such as fuel and mileage costs and gig economy jobs that will affect income and expense calculations.

SUMMARY

Schedule I requires calculating gross and net income. Other forms of income or financial assistance are also included, whether government assistance, child support, alimony, or financial contributions from family members and domestic partners. Domestic support obligations are also deducted or added to Schedule I.

Since pay periods may include days from the prior and following month, remember to calculate accordingly any carryover days. If the filing occurs early in the month, confirm any possible increases in income due to overtime, bonuses, and commissions.

KEYWORDS AND TERMS

- CARES Act
- Carryover days
- Deductions
- Official Form 106I. Schedule I: Your Income (Individuals)
- Paid time off
- Pay periods
- Schedule I

DISCUSSION QUESTIONS

1. For the last pay period of the year, your client's employer always provides a gift, usually for $1,500 which is reflected in the pay stub. How does this affect the client's case?
2. The client works for a major corporation that has filed for Chapter 11. Since the corporation is liquidating many of its assets, your client has been working fifteen to twenty hours of overtime per pay period. What impact does this have on Schedule I, and how can this issue be resolved?
3. When the client retained the office, he qualified for Chapter 7 because he was reduced to part-time hours. However, after two months, the client started claiming his paid time off (PTO) benefits, so now his paychecks reflect 40 hours per week. What action should be taken?

PRACTICE QUESTIONS AND EXERCISES

1. Below are your client's paystubs. In the first paystub, the client's pay period is from April 25 through May 8. The second pay stub is for the pay period of May 9 through May 22. The final paystub is from May 23 through June 5. Calculate income in May for Schedule I (see Figures 16.1, 16.2, and 16.3).

	Rate	Hours/Units	Current Period	Year To Date	
Earnings					
Regular	30.01	68.03	2041.58	20378.29	
Weighted OT	45.01	0.00	0.00	1454.00	
FOP85A PTO	30.01	12.00	360.12	2160.72	
Holiday Pay	30.01	0.00	0.00	1500.50	
Personal Holiday	30.01	0.00	0.00	300.10	
COVID 19 Stipend			0.00	250.00	
Holiday OT Worked	45.02	0.00	0.00	11.71	
Holiday Worked	45.02	0.00	0.00	1809.81	
Holiday Worked Differential	1.50	0.00	0.00	24.85	
Shift Diff Reg	1.50	21.47	32.21	424.52	
Excess Life GTL			1.32	13.20	In/Out
Gross		**101.50**	**2435.23**	**28327.70**	
W/H Taxes					
Federal W/H(M)			118.81	1889.85	
Medicare			31.37	371.35	
Social Security			134.14	1587.85	
Deductions					
BlueChoice 0727			252.75	2527.50	
BlueDental- Lo			9.43	94.30	
FOP 85A Union Dues			17.50	175.00	
Florida Retirement Pension EE%			73.02	841.93	
Valic Employee Contribution $			20.00	200.00	
Vision			9.54	95.40	
Net Pay			**1767.35**	**20531.32**	Voucher No. 247127065DD
Net Pay Distribution					
Direct Deposit Net Check			1667.35	19931.32	A/C:7404
Direct Dep. Distribution 1			100.00	600.00	A/C:6890

Employee Benefits, Allowances, and Other	Current Period	Year To Date	YTD Taken	Available
FRS Regular ER *	206.15	2377.06	*Memo Only	
Group Ins AD&D *	0.73	7.30	*Memo Only	
Group Insurance Memo *	8.72	87.20	*Memo Only	
LTD Memo *	12.96	129.60	*Memo Only	
Medical Employer Contribution *	739.36	7393.60	*Memo Only	
Valic Memo $ *	10.00	100.00	*Memo Only	
FOP85A PTO Hours	9.91	360.65	52.00	308.65

FIGURE 16.1 Pay stub 1.

	Rate	Hours/Units	Current Period	Year To Date	
Earnings					
Regular	30.01	70.00	2100.70	22478.99	
Weighted OT	45.01	0.00	0.00	1454.00	
FOP85A PTO	30.01	10.00	300.10	2460.82	
Holiday Pay	30.01	0.00	0.00	1500.50	
Personal Holiday	30.01	0.00	0.00	300.10	
COVID 19 Stipend			0.00	250.00	
Holiday OT Worked	45.02	0.00	0.00	11.71	
Holiday Worked	45.02	0.00	0.00	1809.81	
Holiday Worked Differential	1.50	0.00	0.00	24.85	
Shift Diff Reg	1.50	21.53	32.30	456.82	
Excess Life GTL			1.32	14.52	In/Out
Gross		**101.53**	**2434.42**	**30762.12**	
W/H Taxes					
Federal W/H(M)			118.71	2008.56	
Medicare			31.36	402.71	
Social Security			134.09	1721.94	
Deductions					
BlueChoice 0727			252.75	2780.25	
BlueDental- Lo			9.43	103.73	
FOP 85A Union Dues			17.50	192.50	
Florida Retirement Pension EE%			72.99	914.92	
Valic Employee Contribution $			20.00	220.00	
Vision			9.54	104.94	
Net Pay			**1766.73**	**22298.05**	Voucher No. 249541201DD
Net Pay Distribution					
Direct Deposit Net Check			1666.73	21598.05	A/C:7404
Direct Dep. Distribution 1			100.00	700.00	A/C:6890

Employee Benefits, Allowances, and Other	Current Period	Year To Date	YTD Taken	Available
FRS Regular ER *	206.08	2583.14	*Memo Only	
Group Ins AD&D *	0.73	8.03	*Memo Only	
Group Insurance Memo *	8.72	95.92	*Memo Only	
LTD Memo *	12.96	142.56	*Memo Only	
Medical Employer Contribution *	739.36	8132.96	*Memo Only	
Valic Memo $ *	10.00	110.00	*Memo Only	
FOP85A PTO Hours	9.91	370.56	62.00	308.56

FIGURE 16.2 Pay stub 2.

	Rate	Hours/Units	Current Period	Year To Date		
Earnings						
Regular	30.01	65.98	1980.06	24459.05		
Weighted OT	45.01	0.00	0.00	1454.00		
FOP85A PTO	30.01	14.00	420.14	2880.96		
Holiday Pay	30.01	10.00	300.10	1800.60		
Personal Holiday	30.01	0.00	0.00	300.10		
COVID 19 Stipend			0.00	250.00		
Holiday OT Worked	45.02	0.00	0.00	11.71		
Holiday Worked	45.02	0.00	0.00	1809.81		
Holiday Worked Differential	1.50	0.00	0.00	24.85		
Shift Diff Reg	1.50	21.07	31.61	488.43		
Excess Life GTL			1.32	15.84	In/Out	
Gross		**111.05**	**2733.23**	**33495.35**		
W/H Taxes						
Federal W/H(M)			153.49	2162.05		
Medicare			35.69	438.40		
Social Security			152.61	1874.55		
Deductions						
BlueChoice 0727			252.75	3033.00		
BlueDental- Lo			9.43	113.16		
FOP 85A Union Dues			17.50	210.00		
Florida Retirement Pension EE%			81.96	996.88		
Valic Employee Contribution $			20.00	240.00		
Vision			9.54	114.48		
Net Pay			**1998.94**	**24296.99**	Voucher No. 251646841DD	
Net Pay Distribution						
Direct Deposit Net Check			1898.94	23496.99	A/C:7404	
Direct Dep. Distribution 1			100.00	800.00	A/C:6890	
Employee Benefits, Allowances, and Other			**Current Period**	**Year To Date**	**YTD Taken**	**Available**
FRS Regular ER *			231.39	2814.53	*Memo Only	
Group Ins AD&D *			0.73	8.76	*Memo Only	
Group Insurance Memo *			8.72	104.64	*Memo Only	
LTD Memo *			12.96	155.52	*Memo Only	
Medical Employer Contribution *			739.36	8872.32	*Memo Only	
Valic Memo $ *			10.00	120.00	*Memo Only	
FOP85A PTO Hours			9.91	380.47	76.00	304.47

FIGURE 16.3 Pay stub 3.

REFERENCES

Notice to Chapter 7 and 13 Trustees Regarding Recovery Rebates Paid to Consumer Bankruptcy Debtors under the Cares Act of 2020. Available at www.justice.gov/ust/file/cares_act_recovery_rebate_notice.pdf/download.

Official Form 106I. Schedule I: Your Income (Individuals).

Official Form 106J. Schedule J: Your Expenses (Individuals).

Official Form 122A-1. Chapter 7 Statement of Your Current Monthly Income.

Official Form 122A-2. Chapter 7 Means Test Calculation.

Official Form 106E/F. Schedule E/F: Creditors Who Have Unsecured Claims (Individuals).

S.3548 – CARES Act, 116th Congress (2019–2020), Coronavirus Aid, Relief, and Economic Security Act or the CARES Act.

CHAPTER 17

Schedule J

Expenses

OFFICIAL FORM 106. SCHEDULE J: YOUR EXPENSES

The debtor's expenses belong on Schedule J.[1] Since expenses vary per case, separate what the debtor is responsible for versus what is paid since expenses may be divvied up between a domestic partner, spouse, roommate, or lumped together. For example, suppose the client resides in an apartment, and the rent is $1,000 per month, but the client is responsible for half. If that is the case, then $500 is listed as the client's rent. If the client lumps the household expenses together with a spouse, then the total amount of expenses is listed since spousal income is included in Schedule I and the means test.[2] However, since income isn't included with a domestic partner, the expenses are added up, and the difference (negative balance) is made up with a household contribution.

In the previous chapter, in the figure on p. 232, the debtor included a disaster relief payment from the employer as a household contribution. Usually, the domestic partner paid the rent; however, it was listed as an expense paid for by the debtor in Schedule J.[3] Since the domestic partner was earning less because of the coronavirus shutdown, the debtor paid the rent the month of filing with the surplus funds. While the trustee made an issue of this, it was a proper deduction since Schedules I and J are based on the current month.[4] But as always, if need be, delay the filing.

Part 1: Describe Your Household

Sections 1 and 2 of Schedule J focus on the number of household members as this affects the expense amounts and the figures for the means test.[5] The larger the household and more

1 Official Form 106J. Schedule J: Your Expenses (Individuals).
2 Official Form 106I. Schedule I: Your Income. Official Form 122-A1, Chapter 7 Statement of Your Current Monthly Income.
3 Supra, note 1.
4 Supra, notes 1 and 2.
5 Supra, notes 1 and 2.

DOI: 10.4324/9781003203278-18

dependents a debtor has, the higher the costs of living. If the parties are separated, then an additional schedule is required.[6]

If the debtor has dependents, the age of the dependent and the relationship to the debtor is included. Dependents can reside in or outside of the home.

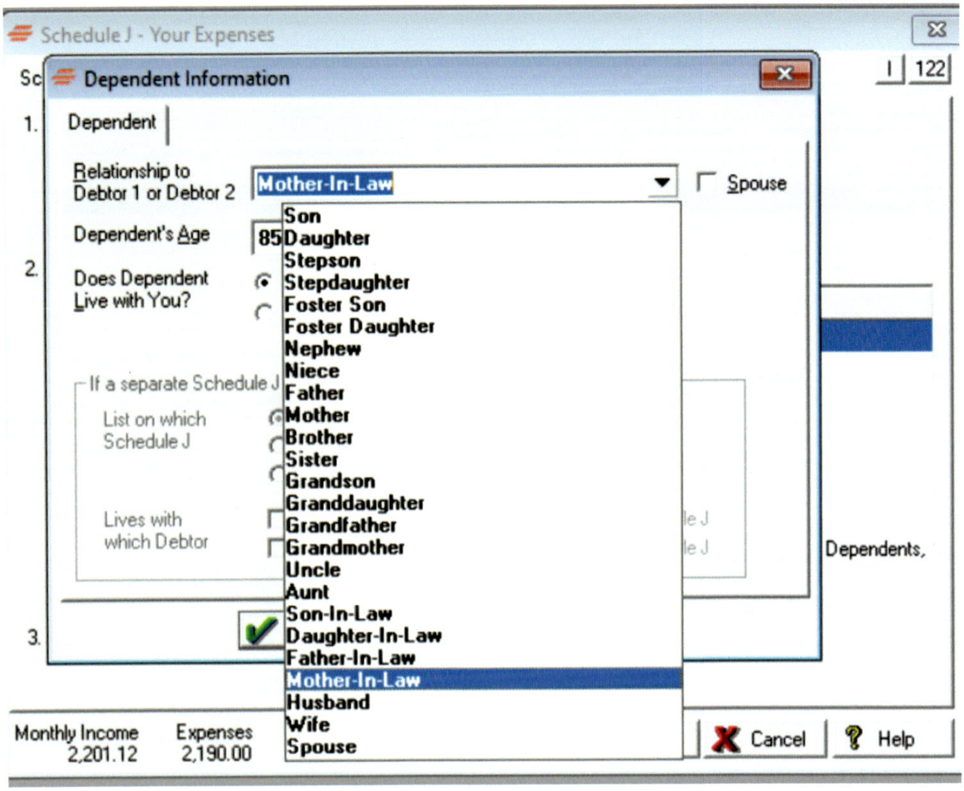

Best Case®

6 Official Form 106J-2, Expenses for Separate Household of Debtor 2.

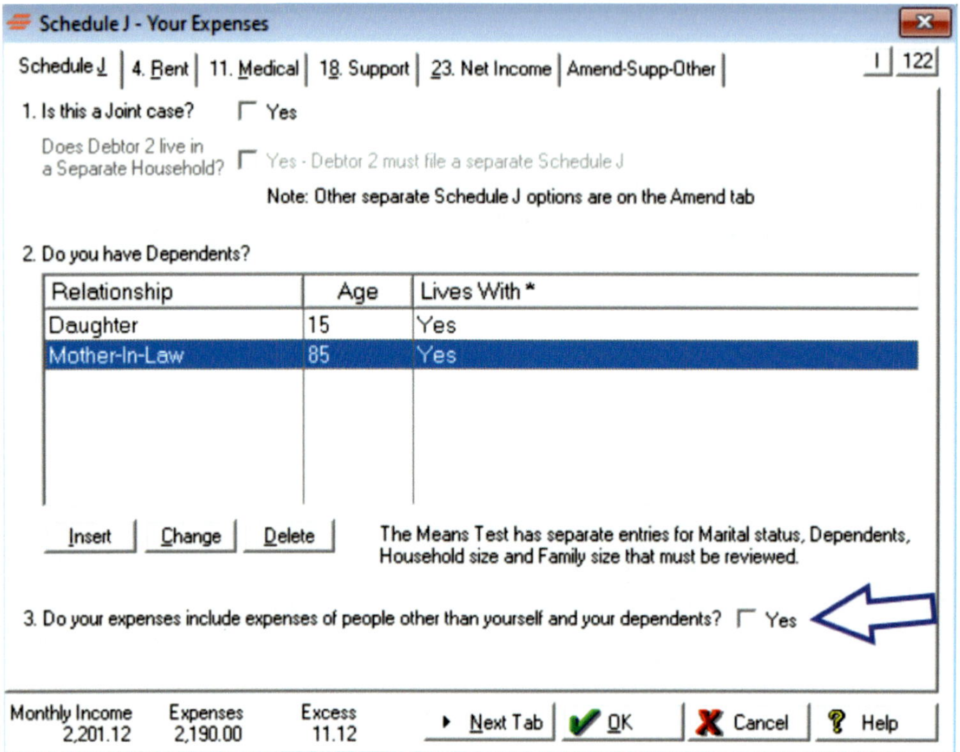

Best Case®

PRACTICE TIP

Verify dependents are claimed on the client's tax returns. Occasional support isn't enough to qualify as a dependent, but there could still be associated expenses. The option to include expenses for a non-household member is seen in the figure below

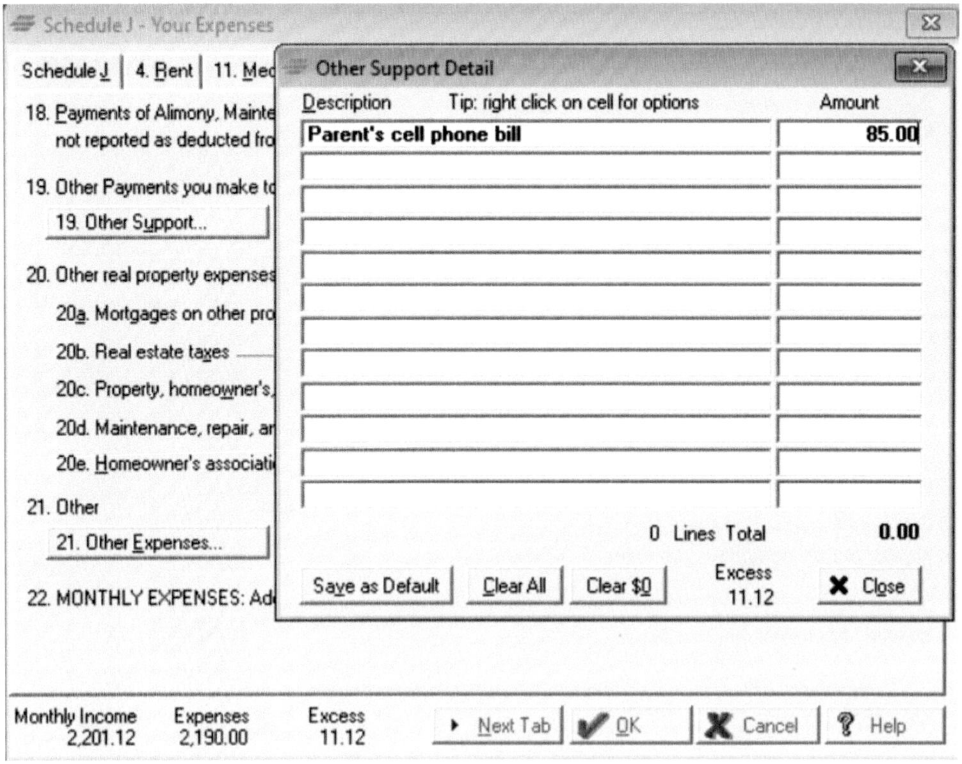

Best Case®

Part 2: Estimate Your Ongoing Monthly Expenses

Sections 4 and 5 focus on residential expenses, whether the residence is owned or rented, including separate categories for real estate taxes and insurance if the mortgage is not escrowed. Remember, the client must be current on the mortgage and association dues to file Chapter 7.

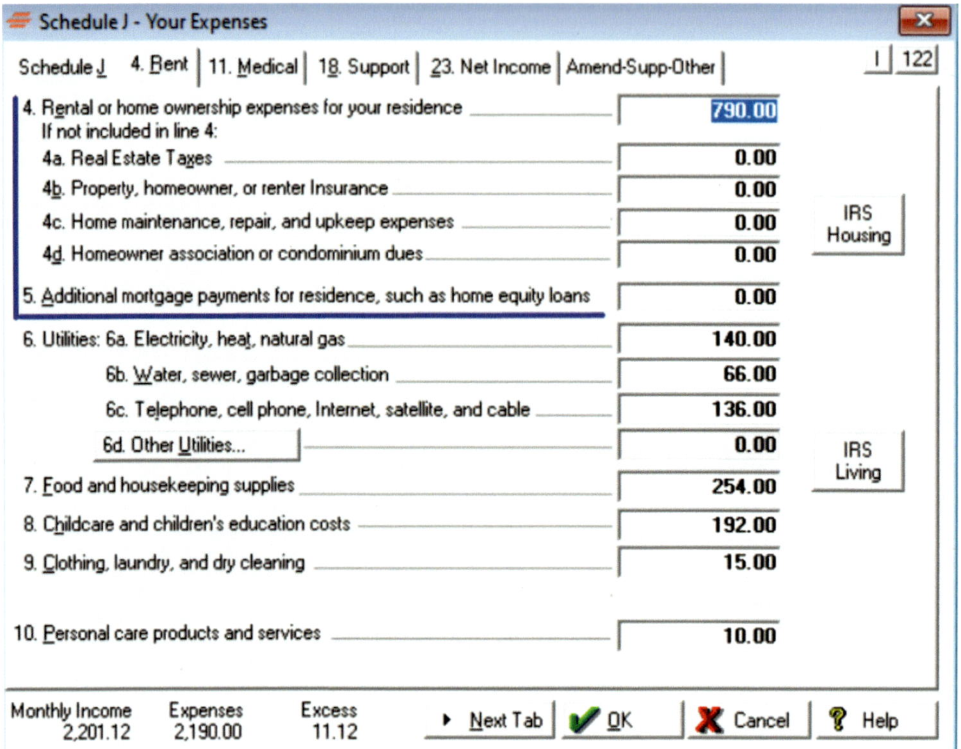

Best Case®

Line 6: Utilities

For utilities, the expense varies depending on the time of year. For example, in southern states like Florida, utility bills will be higher in the summer versus northern states where they're higher during the winter. But remember that the debtor's expenses are based on the current month, so use a recent utility statement.

Note that the IRS Living Standards vary per county and state.[7] Become accustomed to using the IRS Living Standards not only because it's used for means testing, but it also serves as a guide to determine if clients are under or overreporting expenses. With Best Case®, hyperlinks to the Department of Justice website provide a breakdown by date and county.

7 Census Bureau, IRS Data and Administrative Expenses Multipliers. Updated April 30, 2021. www.justice.gov/ust/means-testing.

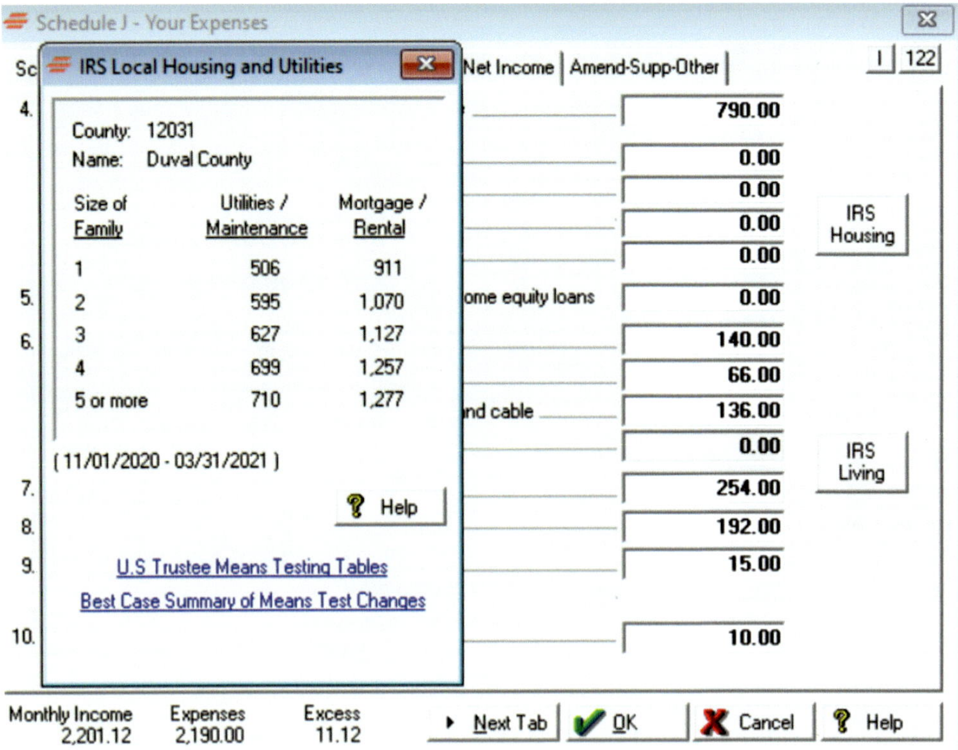

Best Case®

Line 7: Food and Housekeeping Supplies

The amount spent on groceries tends to be an expense that clients over or underestimate. The average costs can be determined by reviewing bank and credit card statements and using the IRS National Standards for Living Expenses as a guide.[8] Note that while situations warrant exceeding the national standards, it's recommended to avoid doing so. For example, in the next figure, the allowable expense is $715 for two people, but as noted in prior chapters, clients may live a healthier lifestyle, buy organic foods or have a special diet due to health reasons.

8 Id.

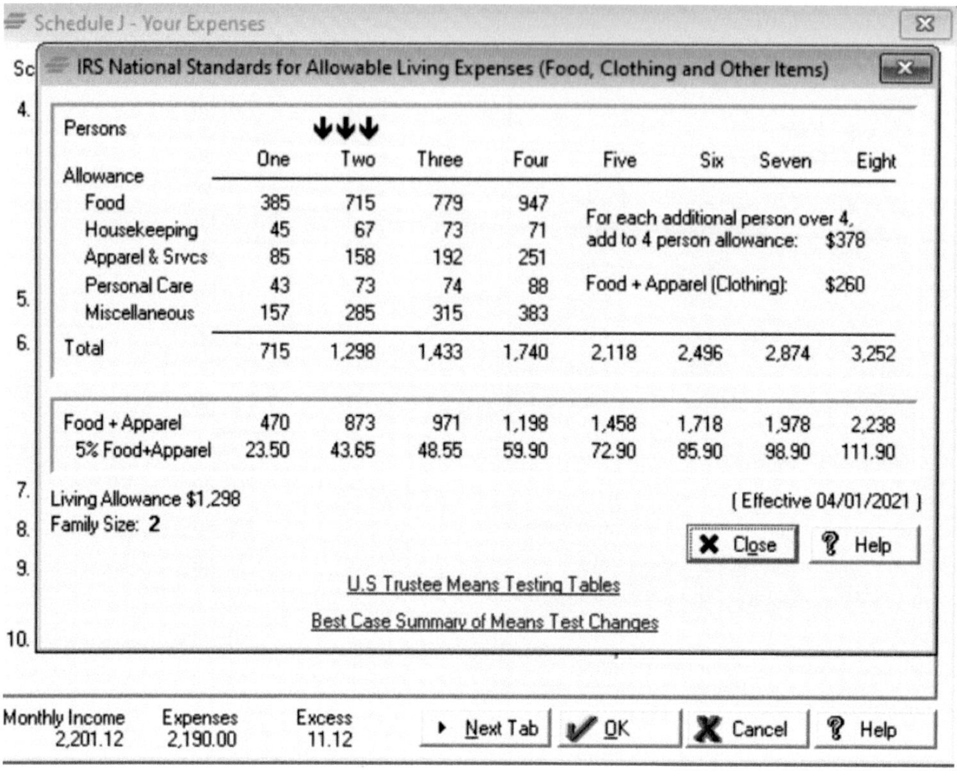

Best Case®

Line 8: Childcare and Children's Educational Costs

Childcare costs are consistent each month but are distinguished from educational expenses. In the figure on p. 240, the mother-in-law and 15-year-old daughter were listed as dependents. At 15 years of age, barring exceptional circumstances, the $192 expense is unlikely related to childcare and should be a red flag.[9] If the education-related costs are for private schooling, it's likely to be objected to by the trustee. Make a note as a reminder to discuss the expense with the client.

9 See the figure on p. 242, Line 8.

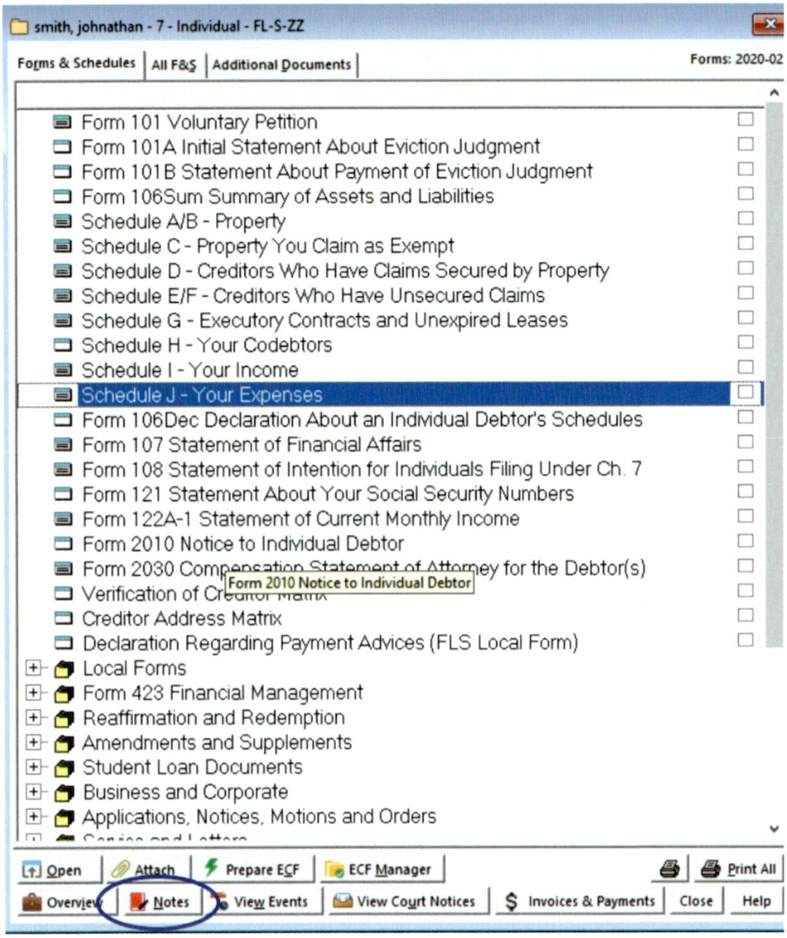

Best Case®

Making notations within the case is preferable to notes in a physical file since files get misplaced for one reason or another. For example, the attorney took the file home, or paralegals are working on files remotely. With this time-saving feature, if the paralegal working on a specific case isn't available, but the client calls, the notes can be accessed to determine any issues that need to be communicated to the client.

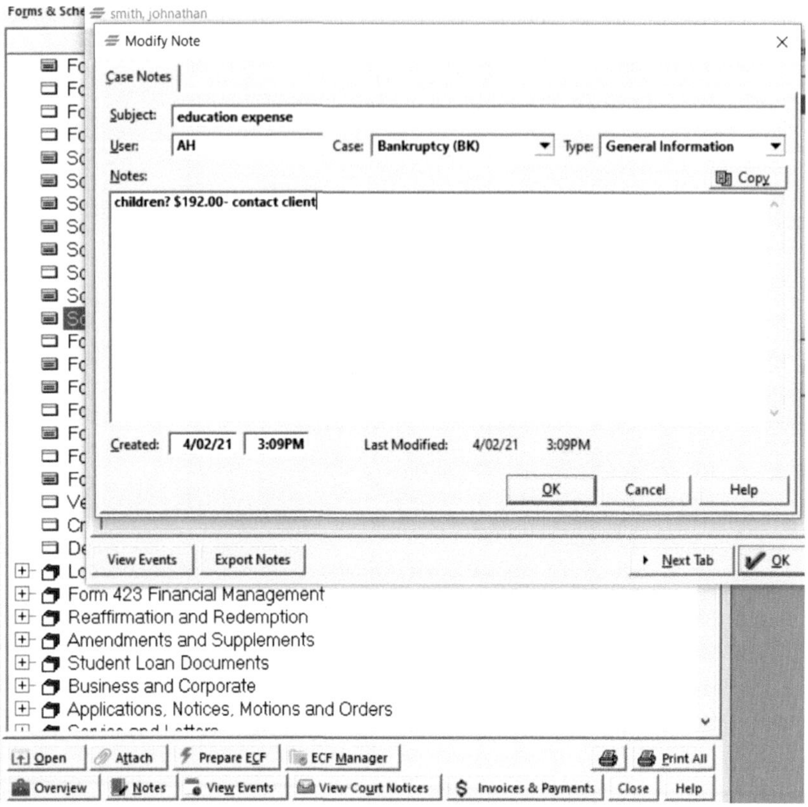

Best Case®

Line 9: Clothing, Laundry, and Dry Cleaning

Section 9 is self-explanatory, just be aware of exaggerated expenses.

Line 10: Personal Care Products and Services

Personal care and products include haircuts, hair and nail salon visits, etc. Again, be careful with exaggerated expenses, which is common since some clients feel the need to increase expenses to qualify for bankruptcy.

Line 11: Medical and Dental Expenses

On Line 11, include healthcare-related costs, but not insurance premiums deducted from the client's wages which belong in Schedule I.[10] If the client pays the insurance premiums directly, list the expense on Line 15. Include the average cost of medical and dental expenses such as out-of-pocket payments, co-payments, medications, etc. Note the figures may be

10 Supra, note 2, Official Form 106I.

higher for clients that are elderly or ill. Unfortunately, it's common for debtors to spend several hundred dollars per month on non-covered prescription medications, and it's most likely the reason why they're filing for bankruptcy.

Some clients pay for prescription medications and/or co-payments in cash, concerned that their health insurance provider will find out and increase their premiums. When faced with that situation and the expense is substantial, future payments should be made via their checking account to track the expense and avoid the trustee objecting.

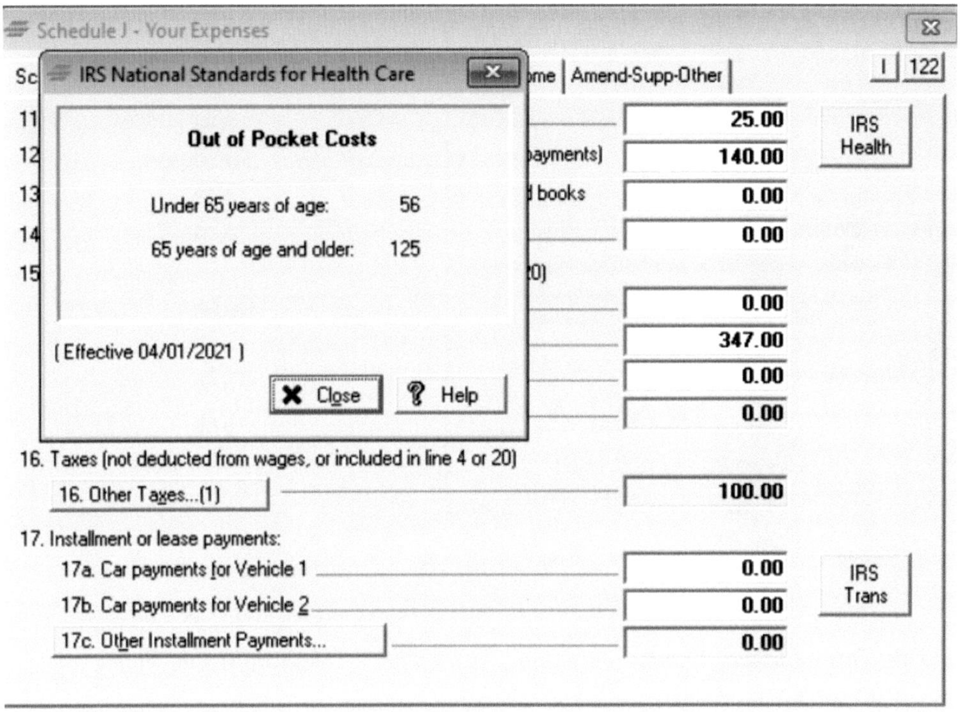

Best Case®

Line 12: Transportation

For transportation expenses, list the average fuel costs, vehicle maintenance, and public transportation costs. Don't list car payments in this section. Note, use local transportation expense standards as a guide.[11] However, those figures may be higher or lower depending on the circumstances. For example, if the client is divorced and has child visitation rights, he may reside a considerable distance from the ex-spouse, thus resulting in more fuel costs and tolls. The client may also have a gig economy job such as Uber and Lyft that increases costs,

11 Supra, note 7.

but remember the extra income is added to Schedule I and the means test.[12] The opposite situation is the client who works remotely and has minimal transportation costs.

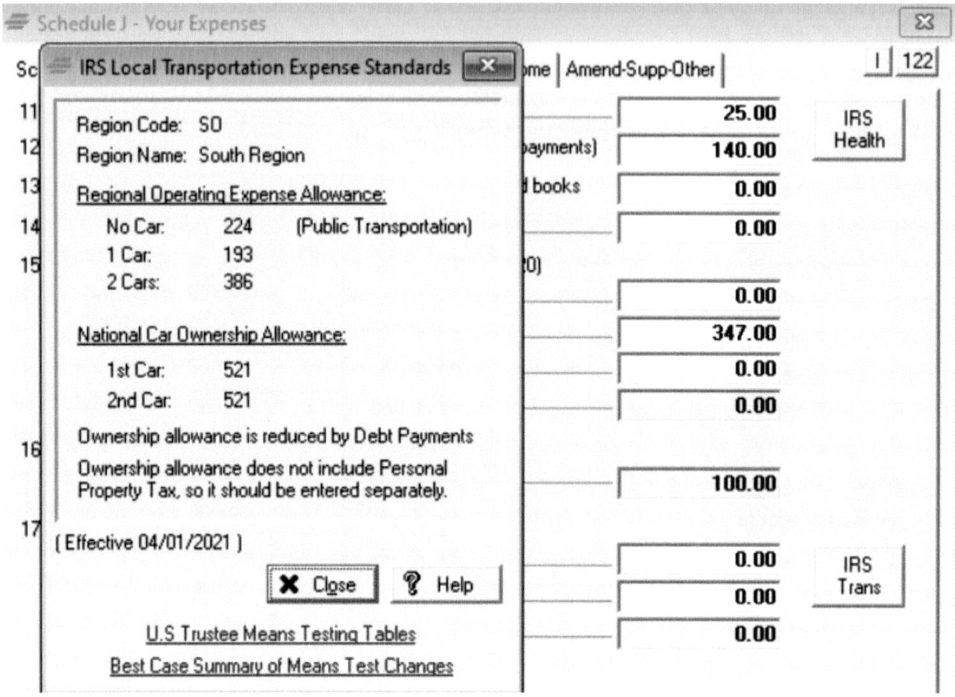

Best Case®

Line 13: Entertainment Clubs, Recreation, Newspapers, Magazines, and Books

For entertainment costs, again, watch for excessive amounts.

Line 14: Charitable Contributions and Religious Donations

Under the Code, charitable and religious donations up to 15 percent of the client's income are permitted, but it should be a consistent practice by the debtor.[13] Verify the expense with bank statements, canceled checks, or receipts provided by the church/organization.

Line 15: Insurance

Confirm that insurance premiums are not already withdrawn from the client's paystub. Always compare Schedule I deductions to expenses on Schedule J to avoid duplicated transactions.[14]

12 Supra, note 2.
13 11 U.S.C. §548(a)(2).
14 Supra, note 2, Official Form 106I. Supra, note 1.

Line 16: Taxes

Taxes not related to income taxes that are already listed as a deduction on Schedule I or for real estate in Line 4a of Schedule J will be listed here.[15] Include tax liabilities from Schedule E.[16]

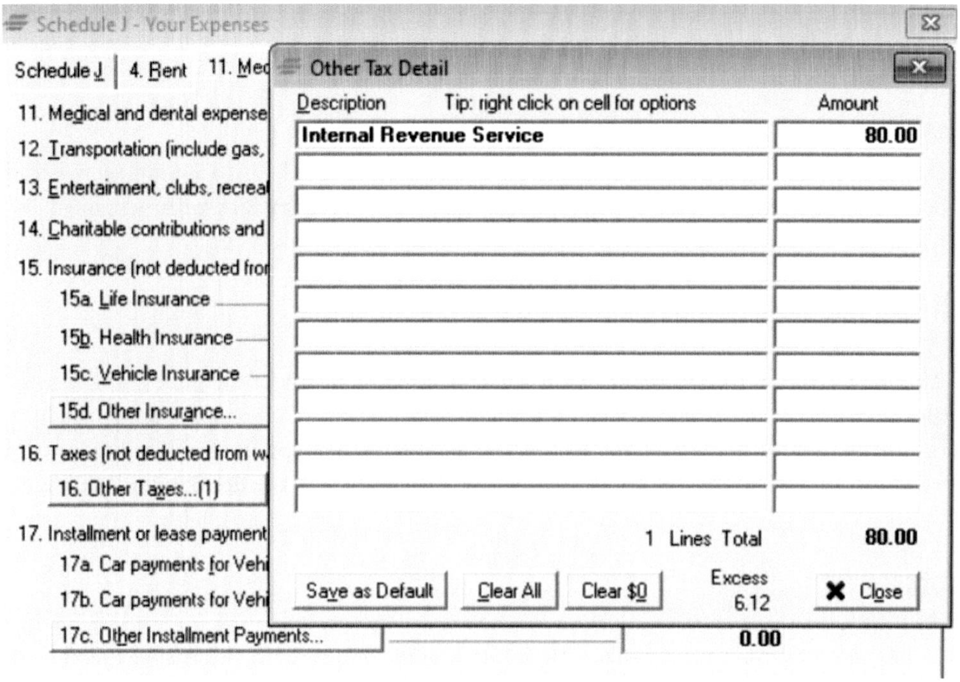

Best Case®

Line 17: Installment or Lease Payments

Car payments for purchased or leased vehicles are listed on Line 17.[17] Financed vehicles are secured debts listed on Schedules A/B and exempted on Schedule C, and leased vehicles belong on Schedule G.[18]

15 Id.

16 Official Form 106E/F. Schedule E/F: Creditors Who Have Unsecured Claims (Individuals).

17 Supra, note 1.

18 Official Form 106A/B. Schedule A/B: Property (Individuals). Official Form 106C. Schedule C: The Property You Claim as Exempt (Individuals). Official Form 106G. Schedule G: Executory Contracts and Unexpired Leases (Individuals).

Line 18: Alimony, Child Support, Domestic Support Obligations

If domestic support obligations aren't deducted from the client's paystubs, list the expense on Line 18.[19] Remember that cases initiated within one year before filing are also listed in SOFA.[20]

Line 19: Other Payments You Make to Support Others Who Do Not Live with You

See Part 1: Describe Your Household and the figure on p. 240.

Line 20: Other Real Property Expenses

Lines 4 and 5 pertain to homestead property, but Line 20 should be used for non-homestead property, whether an investment property, second home, cemetery plot, or timeshare.[21]

PRACTICE TIP

If the client has renter's insurance, the trustee will request a copy of the policy. The trustee will compare the value of assets listed in the policy compared to the value listed on Schedules A/B.[22] If the values differ substantially, either the assets were undervalued for bankruptcy purposes or overvalued for insurance purposes. Either result is to the detriment of the client.

SUMMARY

The debtor's expenses are listed on Schedule J and compared to disposable income on Schedule I. Whether expenses will be lumped together or listed individually depends on the facts of the case. Certain household expenses are paid quarterly or annually, such as real estate taxes, property insurance, and auto insurance, and should be calculated accordingly. If expenses seem excessively high or low, compare them to the IRS National Standards, but keep in mind that allowable expenses can be exceeded depending on the facts of the case.

KEYWORD AND TERMS

- Department of Justice/DOJ
- IRS Living Standards
- IRS National Standards
- Local transportation expenses
- Schedule J and Schedule J-2

19 Supra, note 1.
20 Official Form 107 Your Statement of Financial Affairs for Individuals Filing for Bankruptcy (Individuals).
21 Supra, note 1.
22 Supra, note 18.

DISCUSSION QUESTIONS

1. The client has a pending child support order for $400 per month but is five months in arrears. What should the client be advised, and how does this affect Schedule J?
2. After the client initiated his case, he received a promotion at work and earns approximately $500 more per month. However, the client's home has roof damage, and the roofing company will charge $6,000 to be paid at the rate of $500 per month for 12 months. Can the client proceed with a Chapter 7 bankruptcy?
3. On which schedule is the debt with the roofing company listed?
4. Will the debt with the roofing company be eliminated in bankruptcy?

PRACTICE QUESTIONS AND EXERCISES

1. Complete Schedule J. What is the amount of disposable income available? Can the client proceed with Chapter 7?
2. Include household contributions from a domestic partner and two minor dependents that reside with the client.
3. Research the IRS Living Standards applicable to your area, and update the petition based on those figures. Compare the expenses and disposable income from Questions 1 and 2.

REFERENCES

11 U.S.C. §548.

Census Bureau, IRS Data and Administrative Expenses Multipliers. Updated April 30, 2021. www.justice.gov/ust/means-testing.

Official Form 106A/B. Schedule A/B: Property (Individuals).

Official Form 106C. Schedule C: The Property You Claim as Exempt (Individuals).

Official Form 106E/F. Schedule E/F: Creditors Who Have Unsecured Claims (Individuals).

Official Form 106G. Schedule G: Executory Contracts and Unexpired Leases (Individuals).

Official Form 106I. Schedule I: Your Income.

Official Form 106J. Schedule J: Your Expenses (Individuals).

Official Form 106J-2. Expenses for Separate Household of Debtor 2.

Official Form 107. Your Statement of Financial Affairs for Individuals Filing for Bankruptcy (Individuals).

Official Form 121A-1. Chapter 7 Statement of Your Current Monthly Income.

CHAPTER 18

Statement of Financial Affairs

OFFICIAL FORM 107: STATEMENT OF FINANCIAL AFFAIRS FOR INDIVIDUALS FILING FOR BANKRUPTCY

Form 107, the Statement of Financial Affairs, also known as SOFA, reviews the debtor's financial history.[1] SOFA is divided into 12 parts and 28 sections, and the information required is self-explanatory. While the questions and information requested seem similar to prior schedules, that information was based on the debtor's current situation, while SOFA is based on the past. Bringing the past and the present together gives a complete picture of the debtor's financial situation.

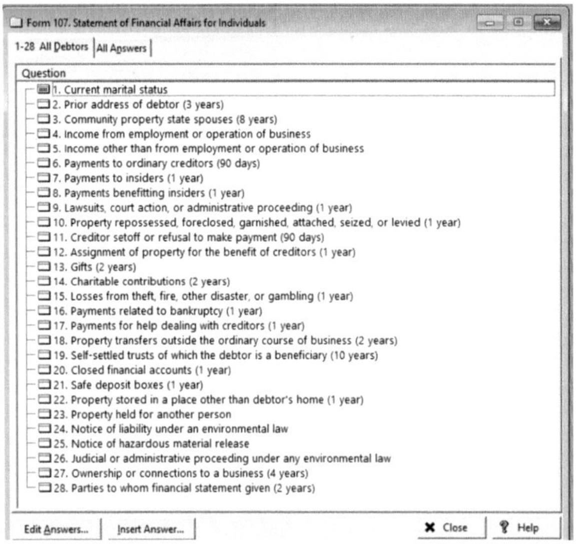

Best Case®

1 Official Form 107. Your Statement of Financial Affairs for Individuals Filing for Bankruptcy (Individuals).

DOI: 10.4324/9781003203278-19

PART 1: MARITAL STATUS AND PRIOR ADDRESSES

1. In Part 1, the current marital status of the client is chosen. Remember that spousal income is included in Schedule I and the means test, but financial contributions by a domestic partnership are only considered in Schedule I.[2]
2. Former addresses are available on credit reports, including dates. This section serves as a reminder of potential residency and domicile issues or the sale of real estate and unexempt funds.

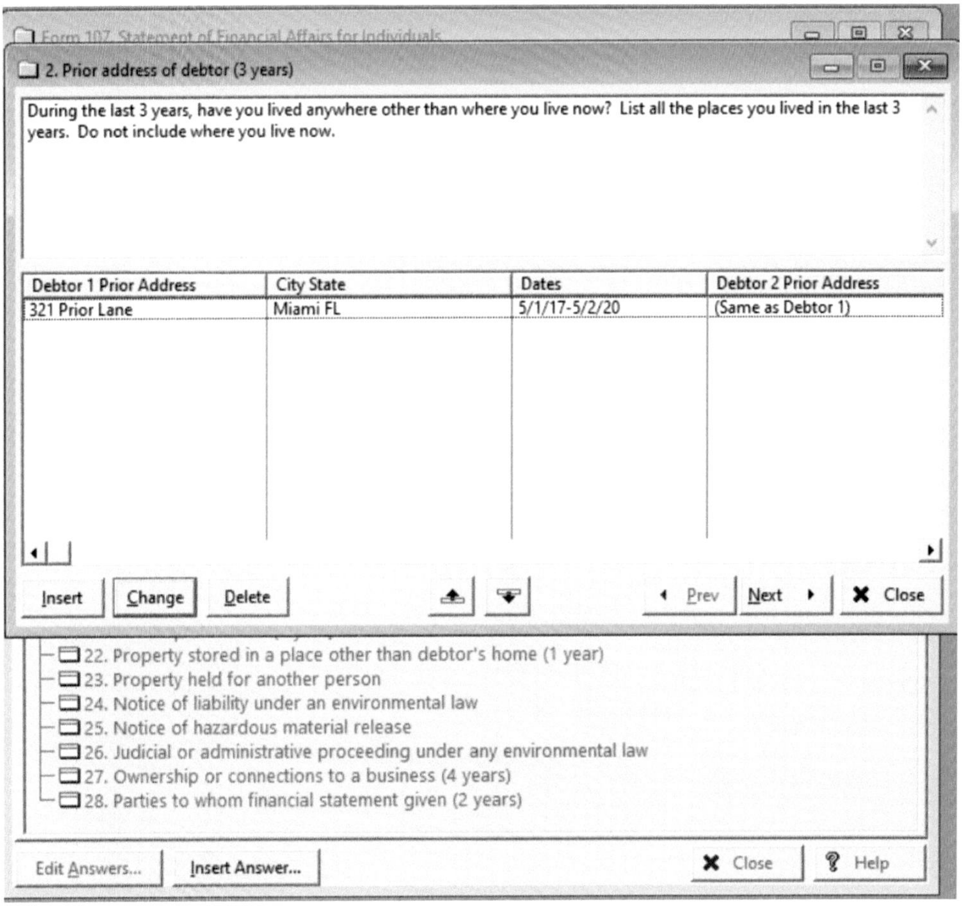

Best Case®

2 Official Form 106I. Schedule I: Your Income (Individuals), Official Form 122A-1. Chapter 7 Statement of Your Current Monthly Income.

Section 3 lists the community property states (Arizona, California, Idaho, Louisiana, Nevada, New Mexico, Texas, Washington, Wisconsin).[3] Again, this is to confirm any property interest a debtor may have or exemption issues.

PART 2: SOURCES OF INCOME

Section 4 requires the client's income for the last two years. Review the client's tax returns for an exact figure and the client's most recent pay stub for the year to date (YTD). This is a good time to double-check for any substantial changes in income and tax refunds that may be unexempt.

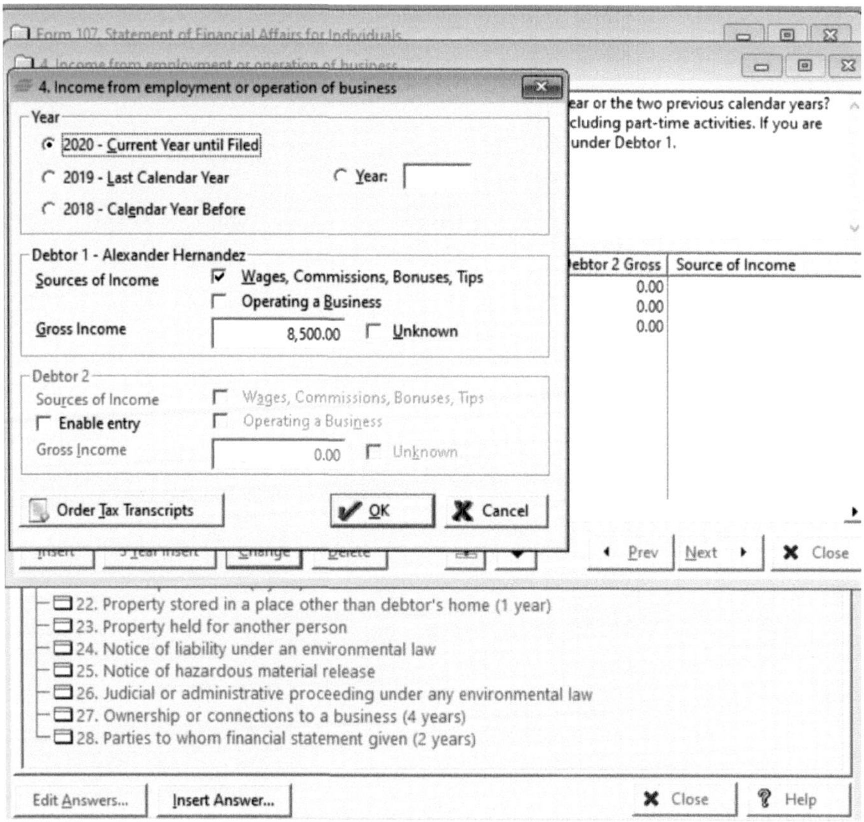

Best Case®

3 IRS. "25.18.1 Basic Principles of Community Property Law: Community Property Law." Accessed June 24, 2020.

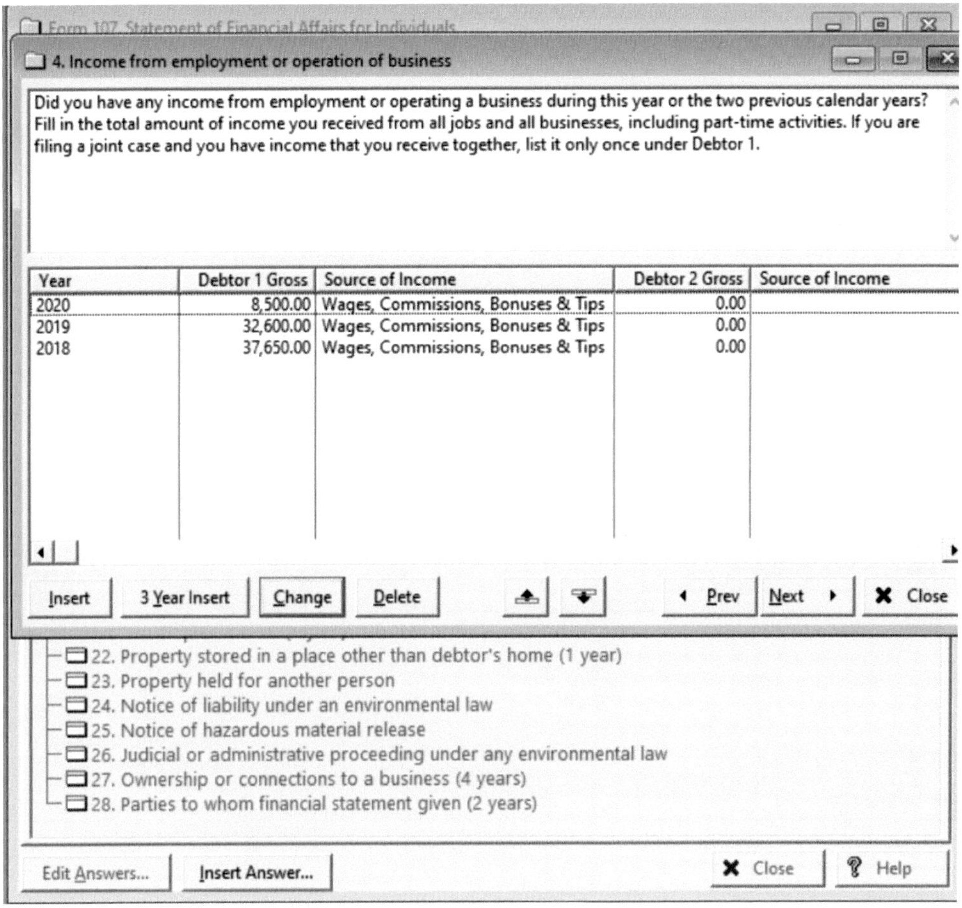

Best Case®

Additional sources of income such as child support or alimony, lawsuits, Social Security income, unemployment, and rental receipts are listed in Section 5, whether or not it's taxable income.

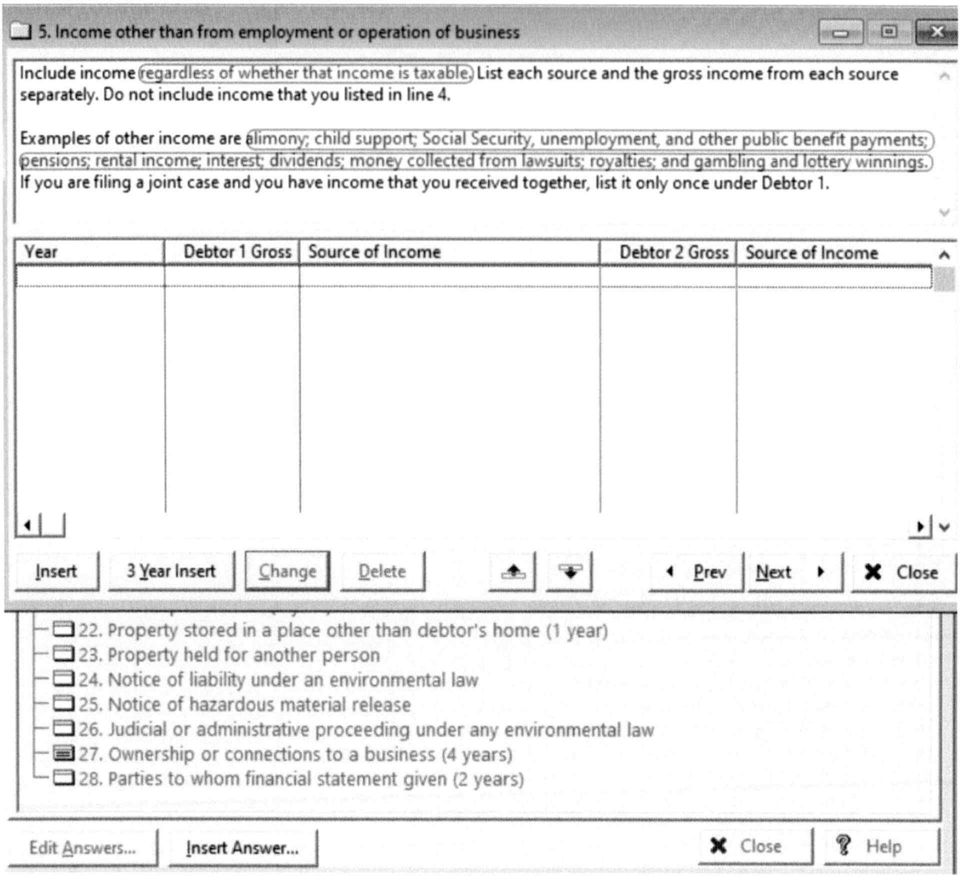

Best Case®

PART 3: LIST CERTAIN PAYMENTS YOU MADE BEFORE YOU FILED FOR BANKRUPTCY

Section 6

Part 3 focuses on payments to creditors exceeding $600 that were made 90 days before filing. At the Meeting of Creditors, the trustee asks when the debtor stopped using credit cards. If payments were made, the trustee might seek those funds as part of the bankruptcy estate, but this depends not only on the type of debt but also the amount.

The purpose of this section is to reveal any fraudulent transfers or preferential payments. Mortgage and car payments are usually listed in this section, but since the debt is secured and likely to be reaffirmed, the trustee won't take any action, but may for unsecured debt. Note that domestic support obligations and attorney's fees are excluded.

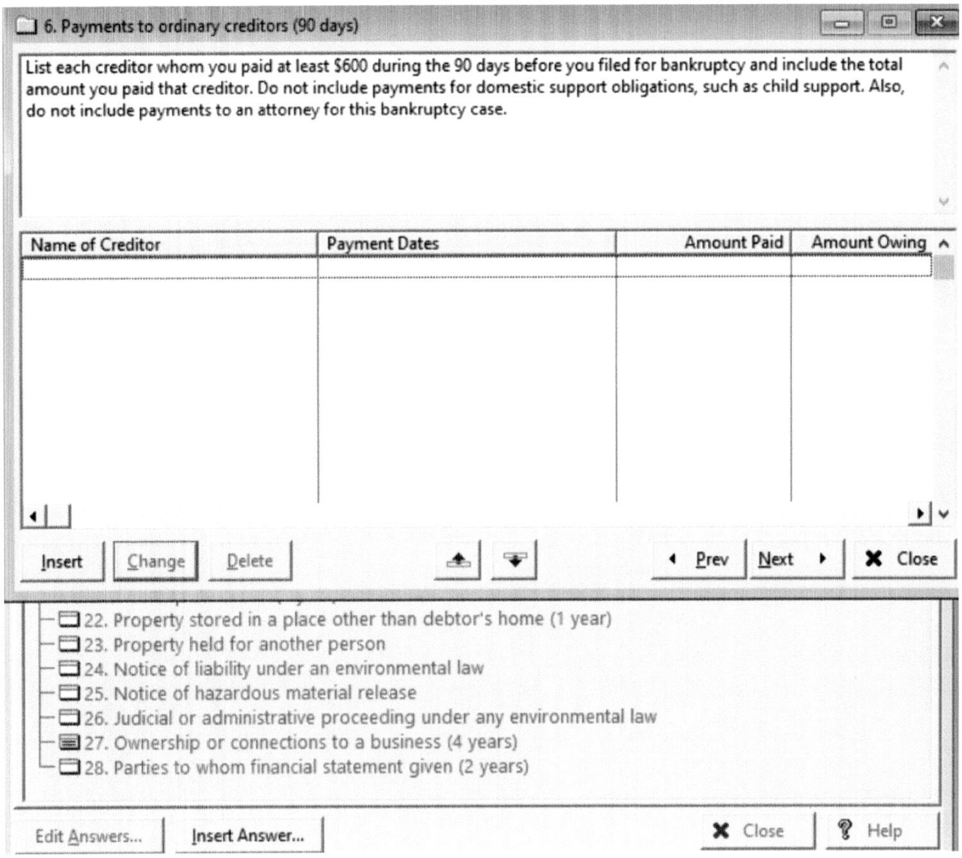

Best Case®

Section 6 also serves as an example of how the practices of jurisdictions vary. I'd be the first to admit I don't list secured debt payments in Section 6, and my experience has been sometimes lawyers do, and sometimes they don't. But as I have stated before, each jurisdiction is different, and what is required is learned over time. Regardless, there is no harm in listing secured creditors as it's required anyway. When in doubt, research petitions filed by other attorneys in your district.

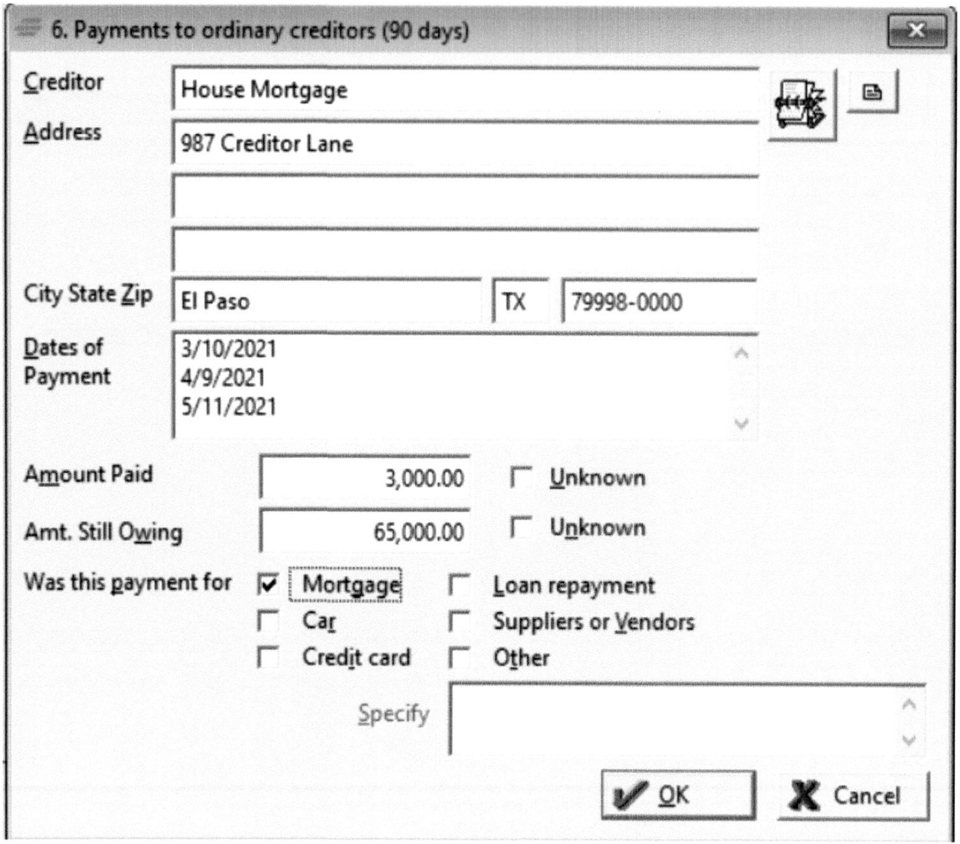

Best Case®

Section 7

In Chapter 2, §101(31)(A), we learned the definition of an "insider." Bankruptcy trustees do inquire about payments made to "insiders," especially friends and family. In comparison, Section 6 focuses on creditors in the traditional sense of the word, while Section 7 focuses on someone close to the debtor, someone on the "inside."[4] Therefore, domestic support obligations such as alimony and child support are listed in Section 7, unlike Section 6.[5]

Here, at issue again are tax refunds. While the refund amount could result in over-exempt funds, the other concern is the debtor using the funds to pay back friends and family. There is no distinction between a creditor such as a credit card company and a friend or relative in creditor-debtor law. Therefore, while it's understandable that loyalty means paying Uncle Larry instead of the credit card company, both are creditors under the Code,

4 Supra, note 1.
5 Id.

regardless of how uncomfortable the client will feel at Uncle Larry's house on Thanksgiving. It also answers the inevitable question: "can the petition be filed now, and I promise to pay later?" No, because the attorney is a creditor and would like to get paid.

If the client reimbursed an insider, especially after receiving a tax refund, the best course of action is to delay filing. There is no specific timeframe or magical date as to when to file as that decision is based on experience and decided on a case-by-case basis, but the general rule is the more time that has passed, the better. If it's necessary to file the petition urgently, such as with a wage garnishment, notify the client in writing of the issue and the likelihood that the trustee will seek the funds as part of the bankruptcy estate.

Section 8

Section 8 is similar to Section 7 but goes a step further by inquiring about property transfers to an insider.[6] If there was a transfer, if it's an issue depends on the facts. For example, did the client transfer a boat worth $200 to his brother within a year of filing for bankruptcy? That may lead to further inquiries by the trustee and a request for additional information such as the year, make, and model of the boat, photos, maybe even an appraisal. But if the boat is worth $200, the trustee will most likely abandon any interest. Would it make a difference if the boat was worth $2,000? Maybe the trustee is interested, but there's always the option of delaying the filing or considering Chapter 13 if the boat's value is substantial.

PART 4: LEGAL ACTIONS, LAWSUITS, COURT CASES

Section 9

This section requires listing lawsuits the debtor is involved in within the last year. Most suits listed in this section relate to collection matters, repossessions, or foreclosures but could be other types of cases such as personal injury or worker's compensation claims. If the lawsuit is debt-related, confirm the creditor was listed on Schedule E/F, and the law firm representing the creditor is included in the "Additional Notice" section.[7]

6 Id.
7 Official Form 106E/F. Schedule E/F: Creditors Who Have Unsecured Claims (Individuals).

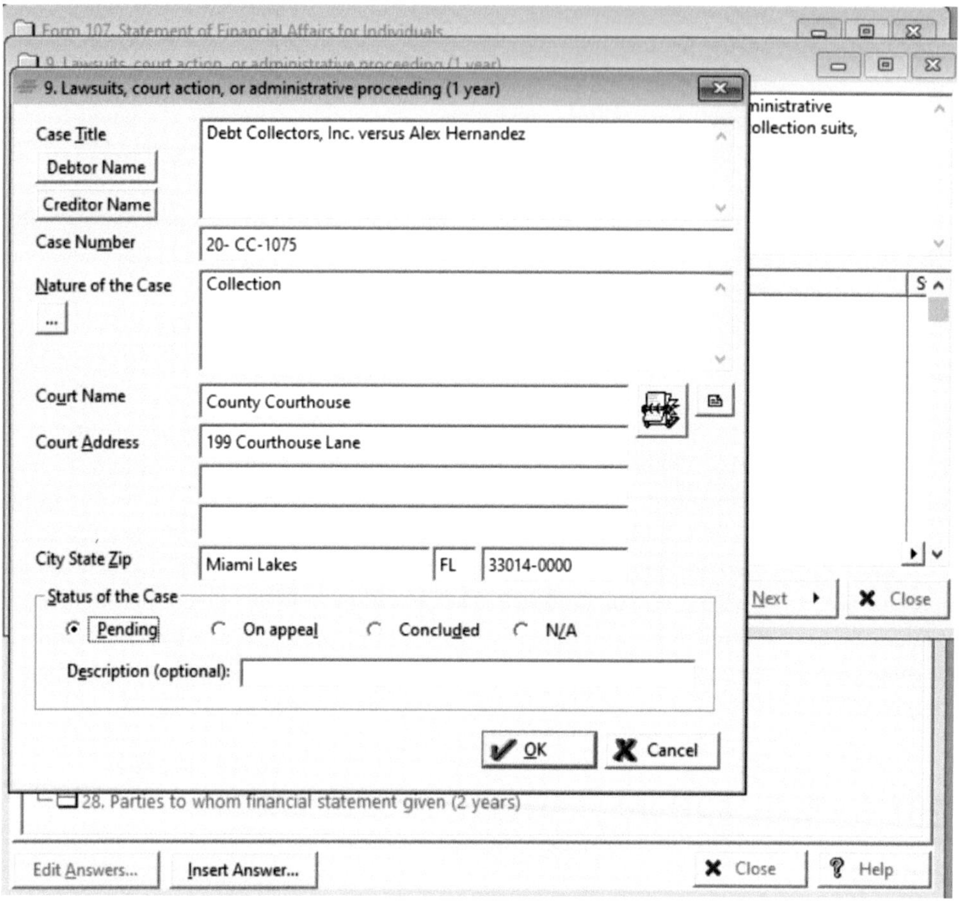

Best Case®

Section 10

Section 10 could relate to Section 9 but also be independent of it.[8] For example, a foreclosure lawsuit was listed in Section 9, and the lender took the property back.[9] But there could have also been a lawsuit from years earlier, and within the last 12 months, the creditor has taken steps to enforce the judgment. This is a common scenario with bank accounts that have been frozen. Again, make sure to list the debt on Schedule F.[10]

8 Supra, note 1.
9 Id.
10 Supra, note. 7.

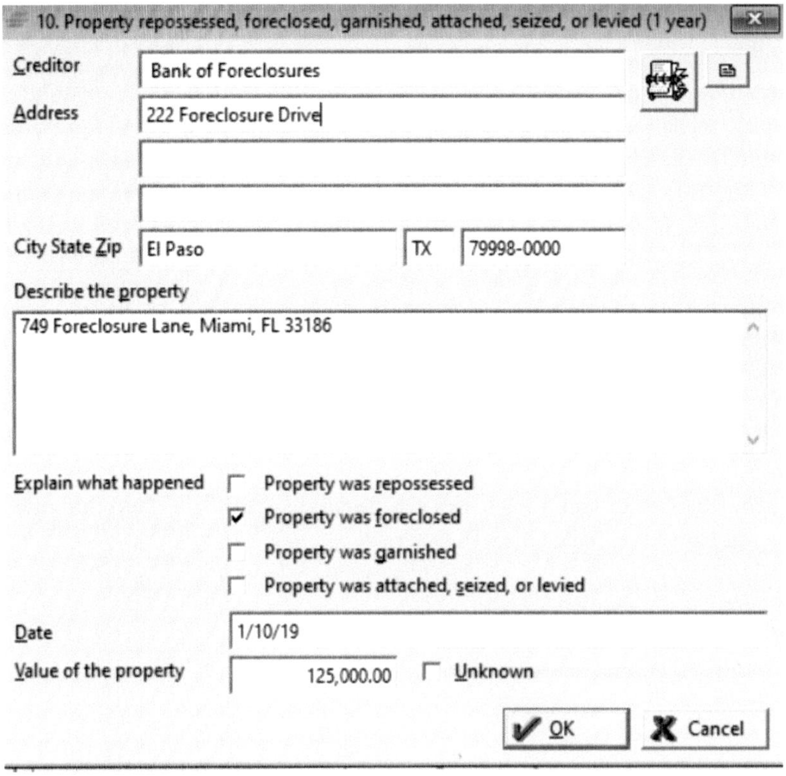

Best Case®

Sections 11 and 12

These two sections require listing information on any assets set off by a creditor or held by a court-appointed receiver.

PART 5: GIFTS AND CONTRIBUTIONS

Sections 13 and 14

Sections 13 and 14 focus on gifts and charitable contributions with a value of $600 or more. Provide the recipient's name and address, the contribution amount or value, and the date. A typical scenario is transferring an automobile to a family member such as a son or daughter. If there are religious or charitable contributions on an ongoing basis, remember to include that as an expense on Line 14 in Schedule J.[11] Documentation should be obtained to confirm if the amount is substantial.

11 Official Form 106J. Schedule J: Your Expenses (Individuals).

PART 6: LOSSES

Losses related to gambling, theft, or insurance are listed in this section. If an insurance claim was filed and proceeds were received within the last year, the client should provide receipts. For example, if the client had water damage in the kitchen and the insurance company provided a $5,000 settlement, then the client will need to prove those funds were used to fix the kitchen. Suppose the client did not hire a professional and did the repairs himself; receipts of materials purchased need to be provided. Any excess funds should have been spent over time as they will likely be claimed non-exempt by the bankruptcy trustee. In south Florida, insurance claims are common because of hurricane damages. But when the policy is insufficient to pay for the damages, the client may accumulate more debt to fix or upgrade their home. If so, confirm the debt increase amount, during what time period, and the amount paid toward the debt. Pending claims are listed on Schedules A/B.[12]

In Chapter 10, the client with gambling losses was discussed. Had I accepted that case, that information would have been included in this section.

PART 7: PAYMENTS AND TRANSFERS

Section 16

Section 16 focuses on bankruptcy-related fees and costs. Individual payments can be listed or the total amount received. Attorney's fees are also listed in Form 2030, Attorney Disclosure of Compensation Statement.[13] With Best Case®, if Form 2030 has been completed, then by clicking "Attorney Fee," all the information transfers automatically.[14]

12 Official Form 106AB. Schedule A/B: Property (Individuals).
13 Official Form 2030. Disclosure of Compensation of Attorney for Debtor.
14 Id.

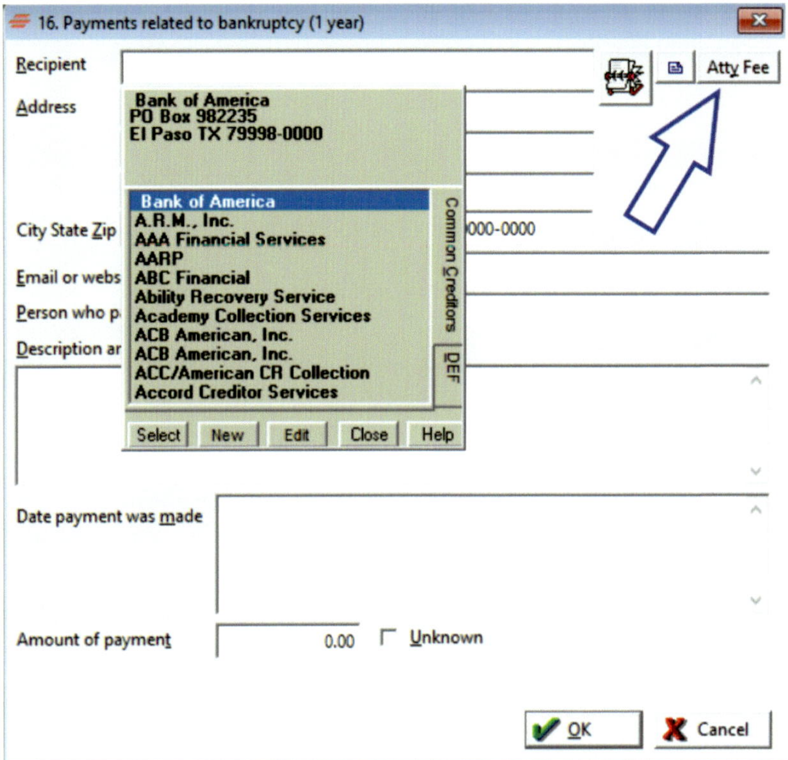

Best Case®

Remember that fees and costs are separate. If there are additional fees such as motions or Reaffirmation Agreement, SOFA doesn't have to be amended.

PRACTICE TIP

It's common for a client to have attempted to reach settlement agreements with creditors before proceeding with bankruptcy. The client may have even enrolled in a credit counseling service or a debt management program where a payment plan was agreed to. If so, include that information in this section. Any outstanding fees due to the agency are an unsecured debt which is listed in Schedule F.[15]

If the client is still enrolled in a payment plan with creditors, payments must be canceled immediately. It doesn't make any sense to pay any amount if the client is filing for bankruptcy. Most of the time, payments are withdrawn automatically from the client's checking account, so the client should notify the bank immediately to prohibit further withdraws. This sometimes requires a written request to the agency and the bank, and even then, it's

15 Supra, note 7.

common for clients to close the account and open a new one since payments continue to be withdrawn. Have the client obtain the bank statements before closing the account.

Section 17

This section focuses on any other transfers not previously listed, including potential fraud committed by a third party.

Section 18

Any transfers of property within the last two years are listed in Section 18.[16] Again, the fact there was a transfer does not prohibit a client from filing bankruptcy. It would depend on the facts, especially the value of the asset, to whom, why, and when.

For example, if a client sells a car, even if below market value, it's not likely to be an issue if the purchaser was not known to the client as it's common for someone in dire straits to sell an asset below the fair market value. What is at issue is how much was received and the use of those funds.

Section 19

Trusts are used as a form of asset protection. The cut-off is ten years because after that, depending on state law, the trust may be protected from creditors. However, it's unlikely that you will come across this situation. Remember the client with the Porsche? Eventually, she created a trust and transferred all her assets to her daughter. Of course, in that scenario, the trust was not going to protect the assets from the trustee, especially with transfers to an "insider" a few months earlier.

PART 8: CLOSED FINANCIAL ACCOUNTS

Section 20

Clients routinely close bank accounts when there are pending lawsuits, fearful of their accounts being frozen. If applicable, list the banking institution, the last four digits of the account (xx1234), the date the account was closed, and the balance at the time of closing. Usually, funds are easily traced since it's transferred to a new account. If the account has a negative balance, list it as an unsecured creditor.

16 Supra, note 1.

Section 21

Safe deposit boxes are sometimes opened automatically with new accounts. Usually, it's not an issue since most bankruptcy clients have limited funds and assets, but the trustee will inquire about the contents if a safe deposit box is listed.

Section 22

Storage units sometimes charge quarterly, so it's an expense a client may forget to list, but that's why a quick review of bank statements is necessary. Confirm with the client why there is a storage unit and what is being stored. If the client is self-employed, corroborate the value of tools or inventory. Depending on the state, the client may have a "tools of the trade" exemption.

PART 9: PROPERTY HELD FOR ANOTHER PERSON

Line 23

While rare, a client may be in possession of property that belongs to a third party. An example is when money is owed to the client, so the client holds title to an asset in return. Trustees do ask debtors if any money is owed to them.

PART 10: NOTICE OF LIABILITY UNDER AN ENVIRONMENTAL LAW

Lines 24–26 require information related to hazardous material and liability under environmental laws.[17] These sections aren't likely to apply in a consumer bankruptcy case.

PART 11: BUSINESS OWNERSHIP AND INTERESTS

Line 27

If the client's spouse owns a business, double-check the client isn't listed in the corporate documents as an owner.

17 Id.

Section 28

Clients rarely have financial statements. However, sometimes one is prepared to obtain a loan or settle a tax debt with the Internal Revenue Service. If there's a pending divorce or the divorce was finalized recently, review the filed financial affidavit for any inconsistencies.

PART 12: SIGNATURE

With an automated bankruptcy software program, the client's signature is digital. However, as discussed before, the prudent cause of action is to have the client initial each page of the bankruptcy petition or reply via email with the approval.

SUMMARY

Official Form 107, Statement of Financial Affairs for Individuals Filing for Bankruptcy, also referred to as SOFA, is divided into 11 parts focusing on past transactions and the debtor's financial history. SOFA can be summarized as follows:

- Part 1: asks about the debtor's marital status and prior addresses, whether the property was owned or rented.
- Part 2: requires listing income earned during the last two years, including the current year.
- Part 3: reviews payments made to creditors and insiders, including transfers, but excludes domestic support obligations.
- Part 4: details legal actions the debtor is involved in, including repossessions and foreclosures.
- Part 5: gifts and charitable contributions are listed.
- Part 6: insurance claims or losses.
- Part 7: payments or transfers made to a bankruptcy attorney or petition preparer.
- Part 8: includes closed financial accounts, safe deposit boxes, and storage units.
- Part 9: assets held by the debtor belonging to another person.
- Part 10: the status of cases pertaining to environmental law.
- Part 11: business interests within the last four years.
- Part 12: the debtor's signature.

KEYWORDS AND TERMS

- Attorney's fees and costs
- Community property states
- Official Form 107

- Operating account versus trust account
- SOFA/Statement of Financial Affairs
- YTD/year to date

DISCUSSION QUESTIONS

1. The client's car was stolen, and since the insurance policy had lapsed, the insurance company rejected the claim. Where should this information be listed?
2. If a client makes a final payment of $750, how are the fees and costs separated in SOFA, including deposits into the operating and trust account?

PRACTICE QUESTIONS AND EXERCISES

1. The client has an outstanding judgment in the amount of $4,000 owed to We Sue and Collect, Inc. The client confirmed that yesterday, the creditor seized $1,400 from a savings account. List that information where required.
2. Create a ledger system that separates fees from costs. Include those payments on SOFA.
3. Complete all the information requested in the Statement of Financial Affairs.

REFERENCES

11 U.S.C. §101.

IRS. "25.18.1 Basic Principles of Community Property Law: Community Property Law." www.irs.gov/irm/part25/irm_25-018-001#idm140332592923296.

Official Form 106AB. Schedule A/B: Property (Individuals).

Official Form 106E/F. Schedule E/F: Creditors Who Have Unsecured Claims (Individuals).

Official Form 106I. Schedule I: Your Income (Individuals).

Official Form 106J. Schedule J: Your Expenses (Individuals).

Official Form 107. Your Statement of Financial Affairs for Individuals Filing for Bankruptcy (Individuals).

Official Form 122A-1. Chapter 7 Statement of Your Current Monthly Income.

Official Form 2030. Disclosure of Compensation of Attorney for Debtor.

CHAPTER 19

Statement of Intention for Individuals Filing Under Chapter 7

Remember Schedule A/B?[1] Of course, you do! Let's go back in time, or at least a few chapters, and tie it together with the Statement of Intention.[2]

When it comes to secured debts listed on Schedule A/B, the debtor has two options: keep the asset and pay for it or surrender it and not pay anything.[3] If the debtor decides to keep a secured asset, there are three choices: redeem/retain the property, enter into a Reaffirmation Agreement, or avoid the lien.[4] Of course, there's the fourth option… "*Wait, what fourth option? You never mentioned a fourth option.*" Great, you've been paying attention.

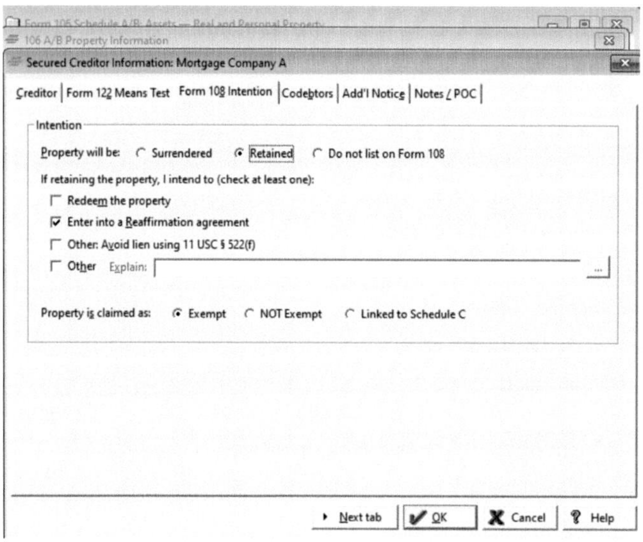

Best Case®

1 Official Form 106A/B. Schedule A/B: Property (Individuals).
2 Official Form Form 108. Statement of Intention for Individuals Filing Under Chapter 7.
3 Supra, note 1.
4 11 U.S.C. §521(a)(6). Official Form 2400 A/B. Reaffirmation Agreement.

DOI: 10.4324/9781003203278-20

In the figure above, assets secured by debt are listed on Schedules A/B transfer automatically to the Statement of Intention.[5] Note there's no fourth option shown. "*Here he goes mentioning the fourth option again.*"

Ready to ride through the three options and proceed to the mysterious fourth option? Well, you just did. The fourth option is known as the "ride-through" option. Let me save you time; don't bother looking for it in the Code because it doesn't exist. That explains how you didn't know about it, but then again, how is something non-existent an actual option? The answer to that is simply that the ride-through option has been created by case law.

In Chapter 5, I asked, "how did I get here?" The same can be said of the ride-through option, but a historical perspective will provide insight, but unfortunately, not even the legal crystal ball will tell us where we will go from here.

Even pre-BAPCPA, the Statement of Intention was required, but Congress, in its infinite wisdom, failed to conclude what would happen if a debtor didn't file a statement of intention or failed to comply with it.[6] As a result, this huge loophole exists. Basically, Congress is saying, "*you must tell creditors what you are doing with the secured debt, if not, the consequences are...Well, there are no consequences, but just do what we tell you.*" But bankruptcy lawyers are a stubborn bunch and ignored Congress. As a result, the courts got involved and ruled there was the ride-through option. So, if the debtor didn't sign a Reaffirmation Agreement but was timely on the payments and a discharge was received, the debtor still got to keep the property. However, the ride-through option seemed to apply only to personal property such as a car. Hence the term "ride through." Frequently it's also referred to as "pay and drive." Either term makes sense if you think about it, continue making payments, and you can "ride through" to next month or your next destination, or "pay," and you continue to "drive." To summarize, the ride-through option means if you keep sending checks, the creditor will keep cashing those checks as if the bankruptcy never happened. If you don't, invest in a good pair of walking shoes.

Congress wasn't happy with these results. Better yet, creditors told Congress they weren't happy with these results. The lack of consequences failed to protect creditors, and as we know, lobbyists for creditors don't work for you. This loophole meant that a debtor, for whatever reason, could stop making payments, have their car repossessed, and there were no consequences. Meanwhile, the creditor assumes all the risk, especially because vehicles depreciate quickly in value. Of course, there's an inherent risk in any business transaction, but creditors want to limit that risk while increasing the debtors' responsibility. So with BAPCPA, Congress specifically mentioned personal property in §521(a)(6) to eliminate the ride-through option.[7] But, the ride-through option has more twists and turns than the famous US 129 and NC 28, known as the "Tail of the Dragon," an 11-mile stretch of road with 318 turns. Since §521 doesn't specifically exclude real estate, it now seems the "pay and drive" option also exists for the debtor's home, so maybe we have "pay and stay." Note that the ride-through option varies per district.

5 Supra, notes 1 and 2. Listed under section Part 1 when petition converted to PDF format.

6 Supra, note 2.

7 U.S.C. §521(a)(6).

PRACTICE TIP

Several states passed laws prohibiting lenders from seeking a deficiency judgment against a homeowner during the mortgage foreclosure crisis. Of course, this gave little to no incentive for homeowners to move out during a foreclosure because there were no consequences. Other states limited the time frame in which to enforce a deficiency judgment, while Florida passed a law allowing lenders to use the bankruptcy petition as evidence that the property was being surrendered, thus, getting around the automatic stay and subjecting the homeowner to perjury.[8]

PART 2: LEASES

Leases listed on Schedule G, also transfer automatically with Best Case® software.[9] However, note the difference between the information required for an auto lease versus a financed vehicle. Since there's no ownership interest in the lease, the mileage and value of the car aren't required, and the "intention" is based on assuming or rejecting the lease. Whether the vehicle is financed or leased, remember to include the expense on Schedule J.[10]

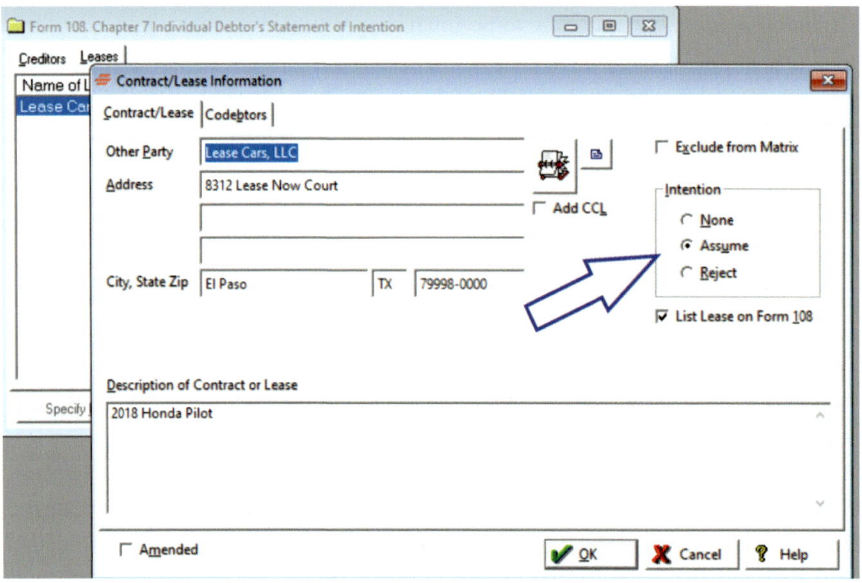

Best Case®

8 Fla. Stat. §702.12.
9 Official Form 106G. Schedule G: Executory Contracts and Unexpired Leases (Individuals).
10 Official Form 106J. Schedule J: Your Expenses (Individuals).

PART 3: SIGN BELOW

Remember, signatures are no longer required unless the forms are being completed manually. But as advised previously, obtain approval from the client in writing.

SUMMARY

With secured debt, debtors have to decide between the three R's (retain, reaffirm, or redeem) and, depending on the jurisdiction, the fourth "R" (ride-through). Form 108, the Statement of Intention, alerts creditors on the "intent" of the debtor regarding secured assets. Normally, a Reaffirmation Agreement will be prepared by the creditor, signed by the debtor and the creditor, and filed with the court. If the ride-through option is accepted in that jurisdiction, as long as the debtor is not in default and continues to make monthly payments, the debtor will be allowed to keep the property. However, with BAPCPA, Congress's intent was to eliminate that option with personal property, but the ride-through option still exists in some jurisdictions with not only cars but also real property.

KEYWORDS AND TERMS

- Ride-through option
- Official Form 108 (Statement of Intention)

DISCUSSION QUESTIONS

1. Research your current district. Does the ride-through option exist for personal property?
2. Is there a ride-through option in your district for real property?

PRACTICE QUESTIONS AND EXERCISES

1. Complete the necessary information in the Statement of Intention for a financed and leased vehicle, including real estate.
2. Include another asset that is secured in the Statement of Intention. Don't forget to include the secured asset in the appropriate schedules.
3. Summarize the law on deficiency judgments related to homestead property in your state (see Figure 19.1).

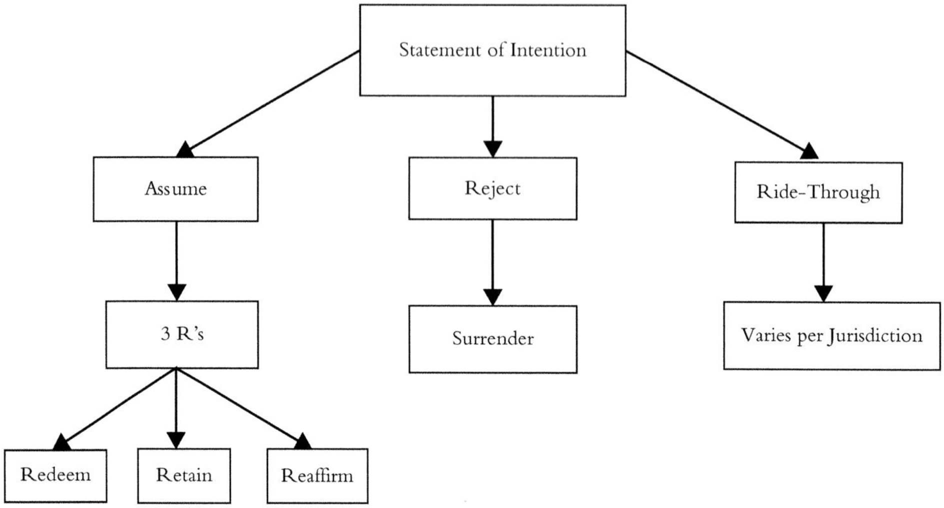

FIGURE 19.1 An overview of the Statement of Intention.

REFERENCES

11 U.S.C. §521.

Fla. Stat. §702.

Official Form 106A/B. Schedule A/B: Property (Individuals).

Official Form 106G. Schedule G: Executory Contracts and Unexpired Leases (Individuals).

Official Form 106J. Schedule J: Your Expenses (Individuals).

Official Form Form 108. Statement of Intention for Individuals Filing Under Chapter 7.

Official Form 2400 A/B. Reaffirmation Agreements.

CHAPTER 20

Statement of Current Monthly Income

OFFICIAL FORM 122A-1: CHAPTER 7 STATEMENT OF CURRENT MONTHLY INCOME

Even though we're nearing the end of the petition, this is where the fun begins; the means test, the centerpiece of BAPCPA.[1]

The Statement of Current Monthly Income (CMI) was introduced with BAPCPA and requires calculating the last six months of all gross income for debtors, including non-filing spouses.[2] This includes gig economy jobs or any other employment regardless of how brief as long as it was during the six-month period.

If the debtor's six-month average is below the state median income, there is no presumption of abuse under §707(b)(2), and the debtor can proceed with Chapter 7.[3] In the figure below, the last six months are from October 1 to March 31. The total amount of income is $12,260.00, an average of $2,043.33 per month. Income earned in April belongs on Schedule I.[4]

1 11 U.S.C. §707.
2 Official Form 122A-1. Chapter 7 Statement of Your Current Monthly Income.
3 Supra, note 1.
4 Official Form 106I. Schedule I: Your Income (Individuals).

DOI: 10.4324/9781003203278-21

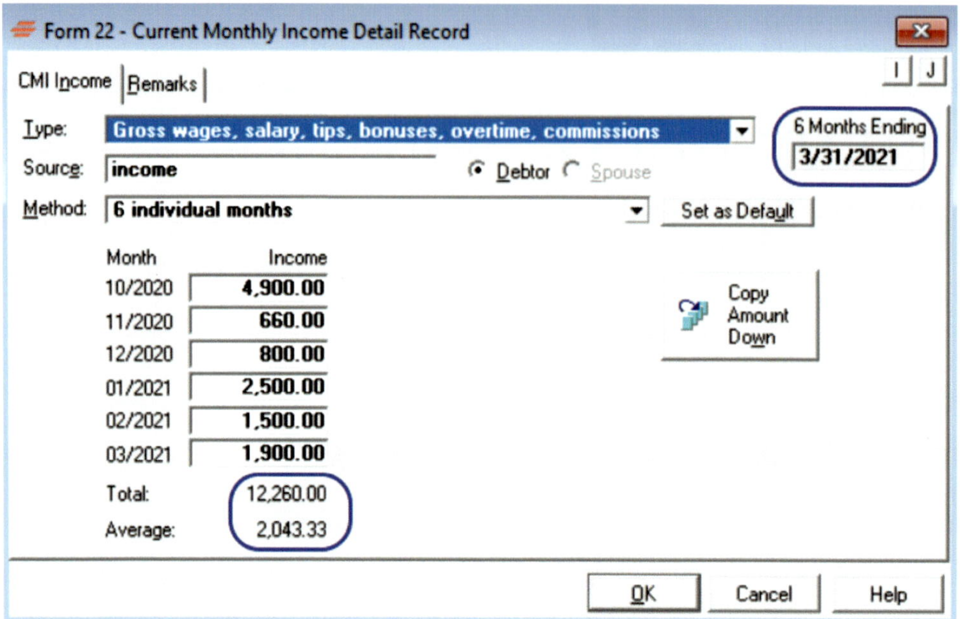

Best Case®

In the next figure, Line 12b calculates the debtor's income over a 12-month period using the amount listed on Line 12a. In this case, the debtor will earn $24,519.96 which is below the State Median Household Income ($66,748.00) shown on Line 13. For two persons in the same household, that's the maximum amount of income allowed to qualify for Chapter 7 and skip the means test calculation.[5] Highlighted in green is confirmation that the client can proceed since there is no presumption of abuse under §707(b)(7).[6]

5 Supra, note 1.
6 Supra, note 1.

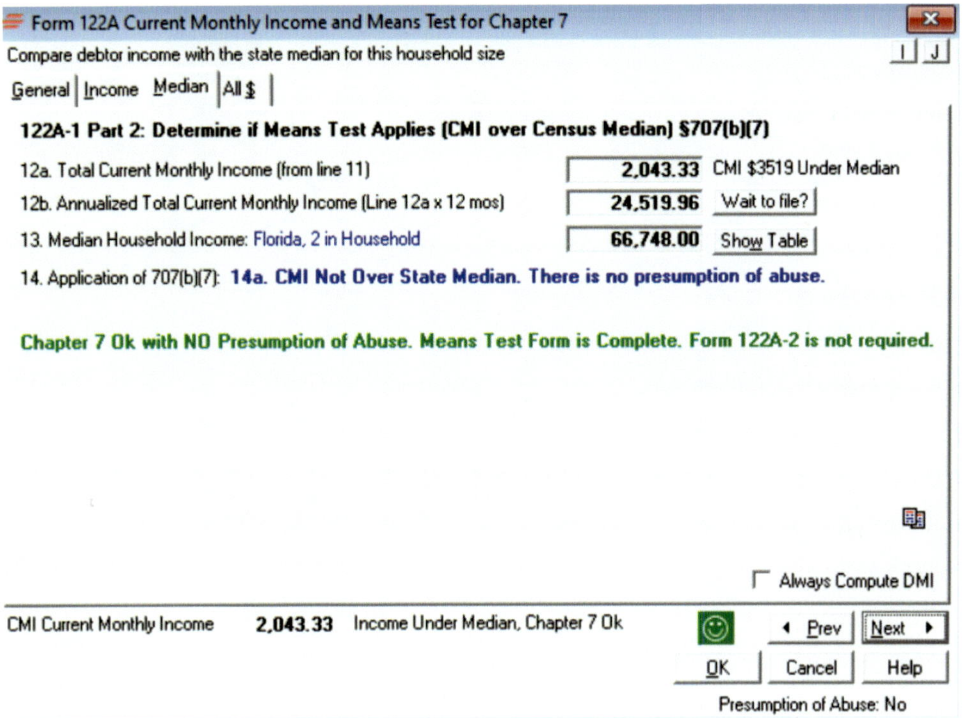

Best Case®

In the figure below, by increasing the client's income for October, the six-month average is now $7,043.33 (see also Line 12a, of the figure on the bottom of p. 276). Calculated over 12 months, the client will earn $84,519.36 (Line 12b), while the median household income (Line 13) is $66,748.00. In this scenario, the client may have to proceed with Chapter 13, but Form 122A-2 must also be completed before that determination is made.[7] Form 122A-2 will be reviewed in the next chapter.[8]

7 Official Form 122A-2. Chapter 7 Means Test Calculation.
8 Id.

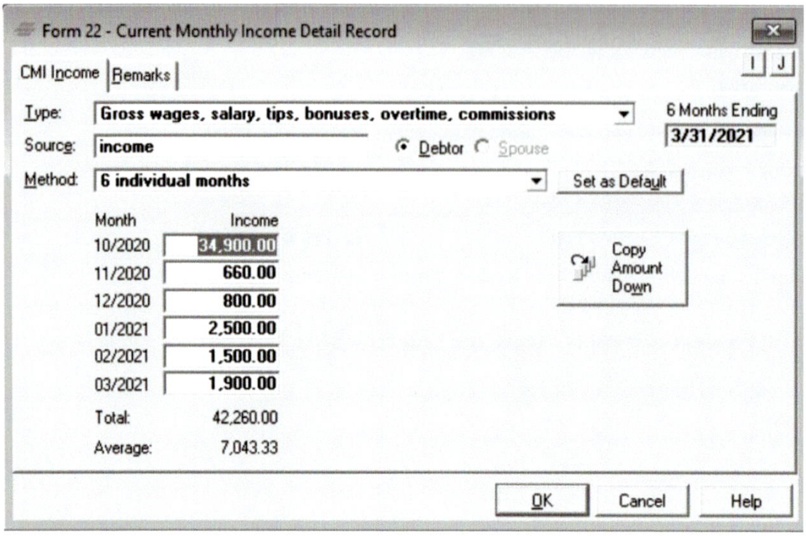

Best Case®

Since the Disposable Monthly Income (DMI) is $3,249.82 (see bottom of figure below), the debtor would make payments in the approximate amount of $194,989.20 over 60 months in Chapter 13. This is not an exact figure as that depends on additional factors that will be discussed when we focus on Chapter 13. However, the client may still qualify for Chapter 7.

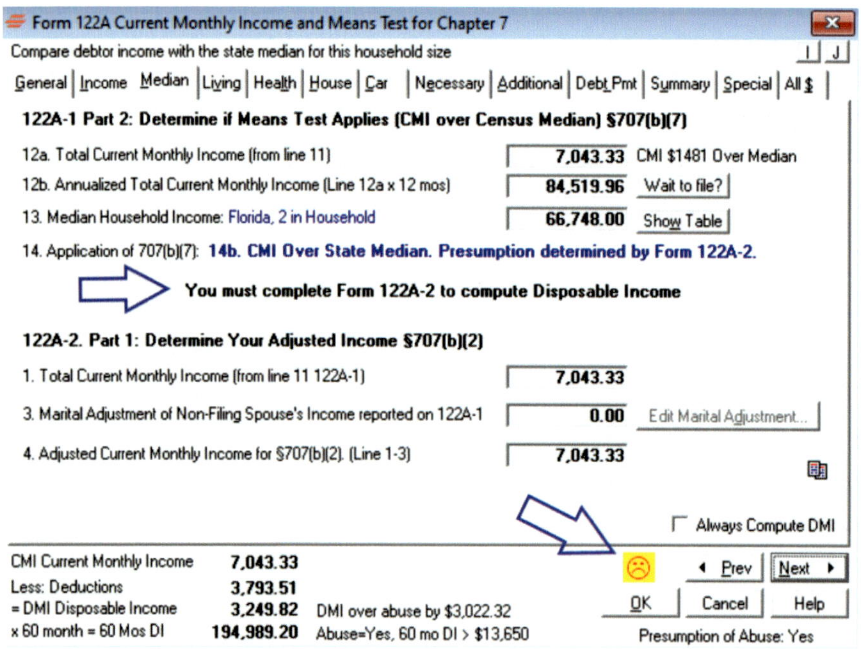

Best Case®

By exaggerating the income for October, we see that the debtor did not pass the means test.[9] With Schedule I using April's income, if filing is delayed by one month, where now April becomes part of the means test and May's income is used in Schedule I, the new six-month calculation for the means test will be from November 1 through April 30.[10] Since October is no longer included in the means test, assuming the client's income remained the same, the client now qualifies for Chapter 7 by simply delaying the bankruptcy for one month.[11] This is similar to the example I provided in Chapter 11 with a debtor who failed the means test because of $10,000 in commissions earned in one month. The coronavirus lockdown is another example of how delays in filing resulted in clients qualifying for Chapter 7. Since clients were furloughed or unemployed, with each passing month, their average six-month income decreased.

In the figure below, the six-month average was reduced to $148 (Line 12a) over the median income. Since the debtor is close to passing the means test, notice Line 12b the "Wait to File" button.[12]

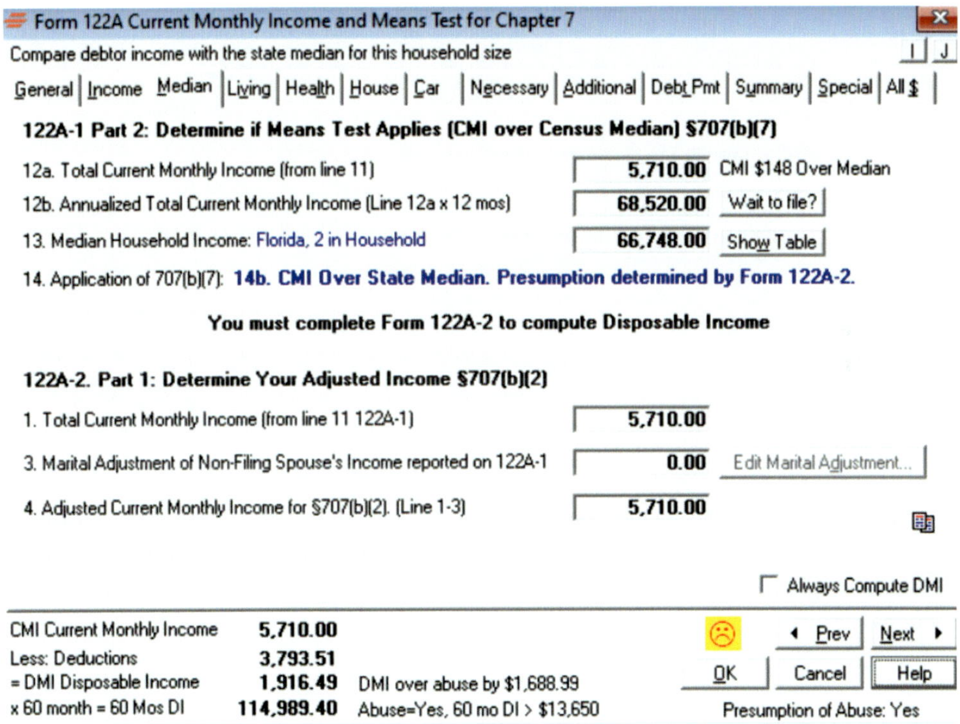
Form 122A Current Monthly Income and Means Test for Chapter 7

Compare debtor income with the state median for this household size

General | Income | Median | Living | Health | House | Car | Necessary | Additional | Debt Pmt | Summary | Special | All $

122A-1 Part 2: Determine if Means Test Applies (CMI over Census Median) §707(b)(7)

12a. Total Current Monthly Income (from line 11)	5,710.00	CMI $148 Over Median
12b. Annualized Total Current Monthly Income (Line 12a x 12 mos)	68,520.00	Wait to file?
13. Median Household Income: Florida, 2 in Household	66,748.00	Show Table

14. Application of 707(b)(7): **14b. CMI Over State Median. Presumption determined by Form 122A-2.**

You must complete Form 122A-2 to compute Disposable Income

122A-2. Part 1: Determine Your Adjusted Income §707(b)(2)

1. Total Current Monthly Income (from line 11 122A-1)	5,710.00	
3. Marital Adjustment of Non-Filing Spouse's Income reported on 122A-1	0.00	Edit Marital Adjustment...
4. Adjusted Current Monthly Income for §707(b)(2). (Line 1-3)	5,710.00	

Always Compute DMI

CMI Current Monthly Income	5,710.00	
Less: Deductions	3,793.51	
= DMI Disposable Income	1,916.49	DMI over abuse by $1,688.99
x 60 month = 60 Mos DI	114,989.40	Abuse=Yes, 60 mo DI > $13,650

Prev | Next | OK | Cancel | Help

Presumption of Abuse: Yes

Best Case®

9 Supra, note 1.
10 Supra notes 4 and 2.
11 Supra, note 2.
12 Id.

By clicking "Wait to File," the debtor's income is reduced each month to calculate the amount of income needed to pass the means test.[13] For debtors with variable income, this is an excellent tool for guidance for when a debtor can proceed with Chapter 7.

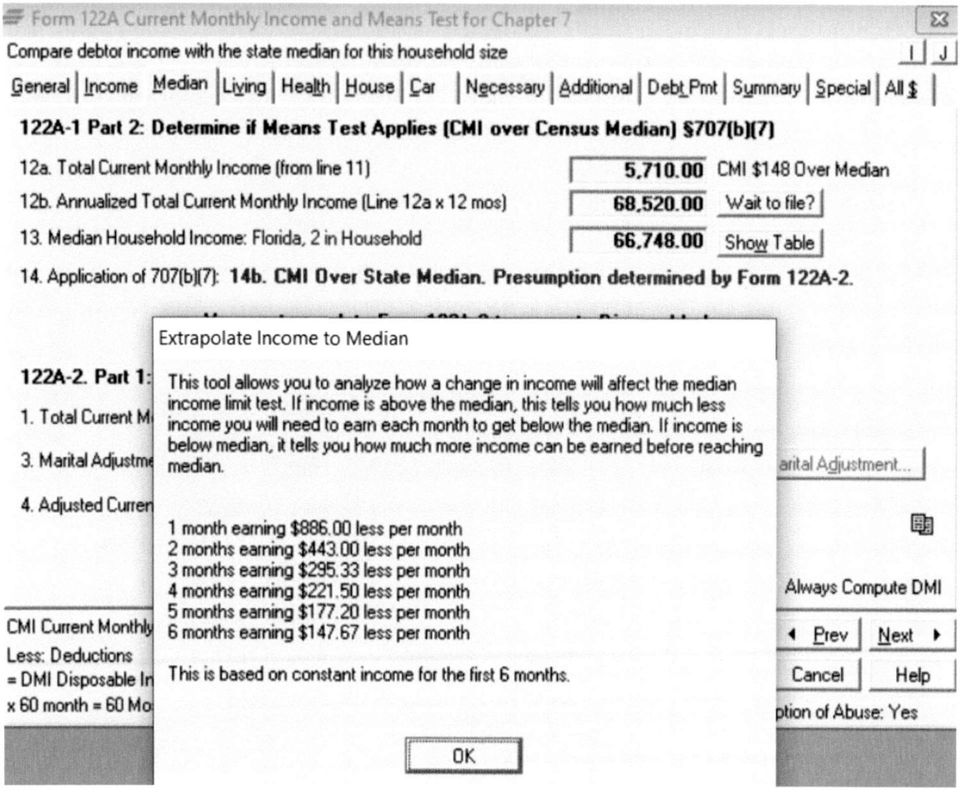

Best Case®

The "Show Table" option on Line 13 provides median income levels monthly and annually depending on the household size. By using this feature, other situations that may affect household size, such as a divorce case, could be used to determine if there will be issues with the means test.[14]

13 Supra, note 1.
14 Id.

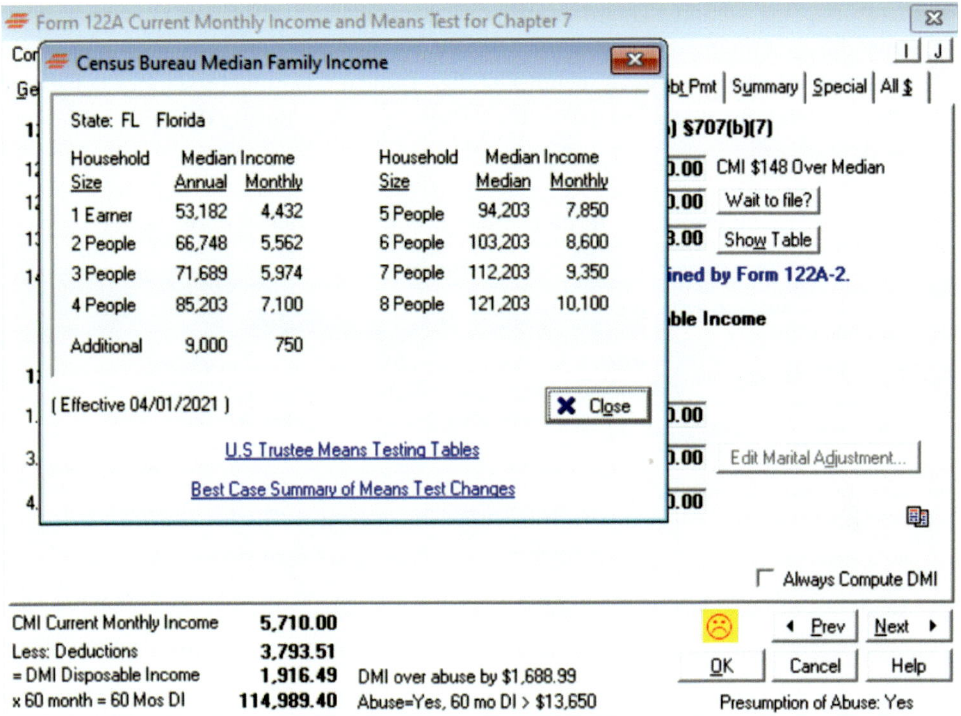

Best Case®

The means test isn't required if the debtor meets the following criteria:[15]

- If the debts aren't primarily consumer debts, defined as "debt incurred by an individual primarily for a personal, family, or household purpose."[16] Therefore, if more than 50 percent of the debt is related to business, the debtor can skip the means test.[17]
- Disabled veterans who have a disability rating in excess of 30 percent or were discharged because of a disability that occurred in the line of duty may also be exempt.[18] However, the debts must have been incurred primarily while on active duty or performing a homeland defense activity.[19]

15 Id.
16 11 U.S.C. §101(8).
17 Supra, note 1.
18 38 U.S.C. §3741(1).
19 10 U.S.C. §101(d)(1), 32 U.S.C. §901(1).

- Members of the National Guard or military reserve may qualify for an exemption if on active duty after September 11, 2001.[20] However, there are time restrictions. The first is that the military reservist or member of the National Guard be on duty or homeland defense activity for at least 90 days.[21] If so, they are exempt during that time frame and 540 days after that.[22]

Debtors that are exempt from the means test should complete Official Form 122-A-1Supp.[23]

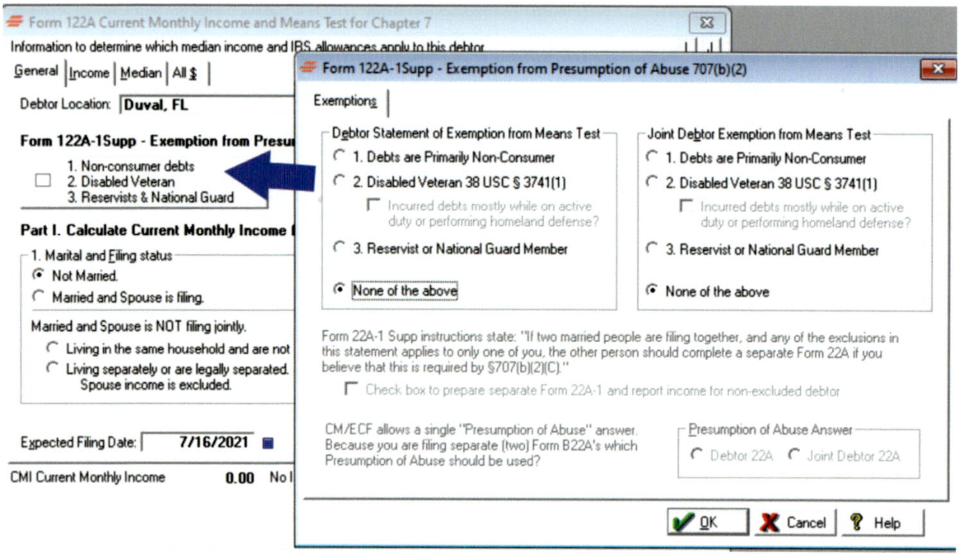

Best Case®

In addition, some forms of income are excluded from the means test.[24] Note that it's important to distinguish between being exempt from means testing and having income that is excluded.

20 Id.
21 11 U.S.C. §707(b)(2)(D)(ii).
22 Id.
23 Official Form 122A1-Supp. Statement of Exemption from Presumption of Abuse Under §707(b)(2).
24 Supra, note 1.

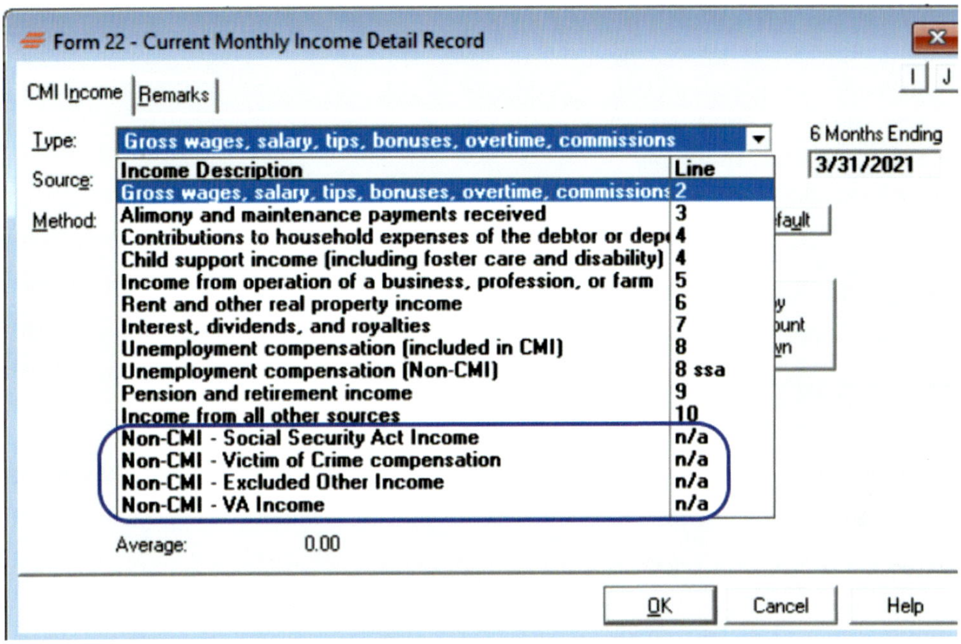

Best Case®

PRACTICE TIP

If there is one thing that law schools fail to teach is just because something can be done, it doesn't mean it should. I can fill an entire book on this one subject alone. But, one simple question should always be asked: is this in the client's best interests? That question applies to all clients, especially those in specific careers.

Members of the military might have security clearance issues if they filed for bankruptcy. They should always receive advice and guidance through the proper channels. On the other hand, I've had clients advised by superiors to file for bankruptcy to avoid security clearance issues. Yes, it's a topsy-turvy world, but the theory is someone heavily in debt may be susceptible to bribes.

SUMMARY

Form-122A-1 (means test), requires calculating the last six months of income without deductions (gross). Whether for Schedule I or the means test, verify no pay periods have been omitted. If the debtor's income is over the state median, there is a "presumption of abuse" and the debtor will need to complete the second part of the means test.

KEYWORDS AND TERMS

- Exemptions to the means test
- Official Form 122A-1
- Official Form 122A-1 Supp
- CMI/Statement of Current Monthly Income
- Median household income
- State median income
- Presumption of abuse

DISCUSSION QUESTIONS

1. The client wishes to exclude his wife from bankruptcy because of her excellent credit. Is her income used for purposes of the means test?
2. How does a divorce affect the means test?
3. What is the state median income in your state?

PRACTICE QUESTIONS AND EXERCISES

1. Add six months of income to the means test. Is the average above or below the state median?
2. What is the total annual income?
3. Calculate income so that there is a presumption of abuse. What are the six-month calculations if the client was to wait to file?
4. What are the income amounts monthly and annually for two, three, and four members of the household?
5. Calculate the means test with three household members, then recalculate with one. Does the client still qualify? What is required to qualify? See Figure 20.1.

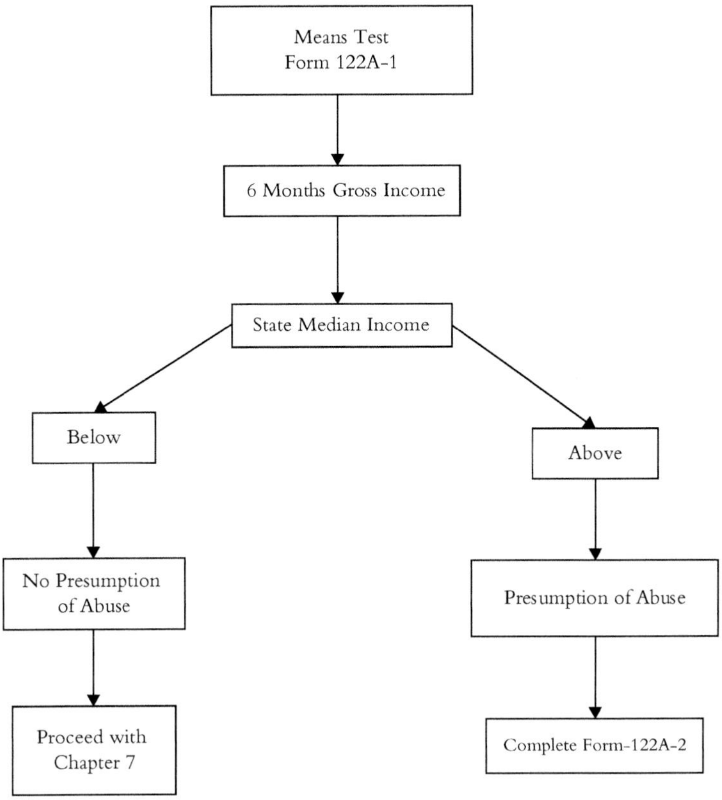

FIGURE 20.1 An overview of the means test Form 122A-1.

REFERENCES

10 U.S.C. §101.

11 U.S.C. §101.

11 U.S.C. §707.

32 U.S.C. §901.

38 U.S.C. §3741.

Official Form 106I. Schedule I: Your Income (Individuals).

Official Form 122A-1. Chapter 7 Statement of Your Current Monthly Income.

Official Form 122A-1-Supp. Statement of Exemption from Presumption of Abuse under §707(b)(2).

Official Form 122A-2. Chapter 7 Means Test Calculation.

CHAPTER

21

Means Testing Official Form 122A-2

In the previous chapter, the debtor's Current Monthly Income was calculated.[1] Since the debtor passed the first part of the means test, in this case, by delaying filing by one month, the debtor can proceed to file Chapter 7.[2] Of course, this assumes there are no disposable income issues. But if the debtor fails the first part of the means test because the state median income is exceeded, there's a presumption of abuse, but the debtor still gets a second bite at the bankruptcy apple.[3] Sounds complicated? It should, but by breaking this down into smaller digestible parts, it's actually relatively easy and straightforward. So, let's tame the beast that is the means test.[4]

Suppose the client has consistent income that is still above the state median income and using the "wait to file" button on Line 12b on Form 122A is of no help since the client is paid a salary versus per hour.[5] Can the client still qualify for Chapter 7? The answer depends on the amount of secured debt the client has and the amount of unsecured debt the client can afford to pay back. I know it still sounds confusing, but the answer lies hidden in §707(b)(2).[6]

This second part of the means test focuses on disposable income, basically, how much can the debtor afford to pay back.[7] How disposable income is determined is quite simple to calculate, but first, let's focus on the "magical numbers" and figure out how we got here.

In the figure below, by hovering the cursor over the DMI section, the yellow popup box tells you everything you need to know under §707(b)(2).[8] If the debtor has less than $8,175.00 ($136.25 per month) in disposable income over a 60-month period (a hypothetical Chapter 13), the debtor can proceed with Chapter 7. If the disposable income exceeds $13,650.00 or $227.50 per month, there is a presumption of abuse, and the debtor will proceed with Chapter 13. Note these figures do adjust, but updates are provided automatically

1 Official Form 122A-1. Chapter 7 Statement of Your Current Monthly Income.
2 11 U.S.C. §707(b)(2).
3 Supra, note 1.
4 Supra, note 2.
5 Supra, note 1.
6 Supra, note 2.
7 Id.
8 Id.

DOI: 10.4324/9781003203278-22

by Best Case®. What if the debtor falls in between those two figures? Then the question is whether the debtor can afford to pay back twenty-five percent of the unsecured non-priority creditors.

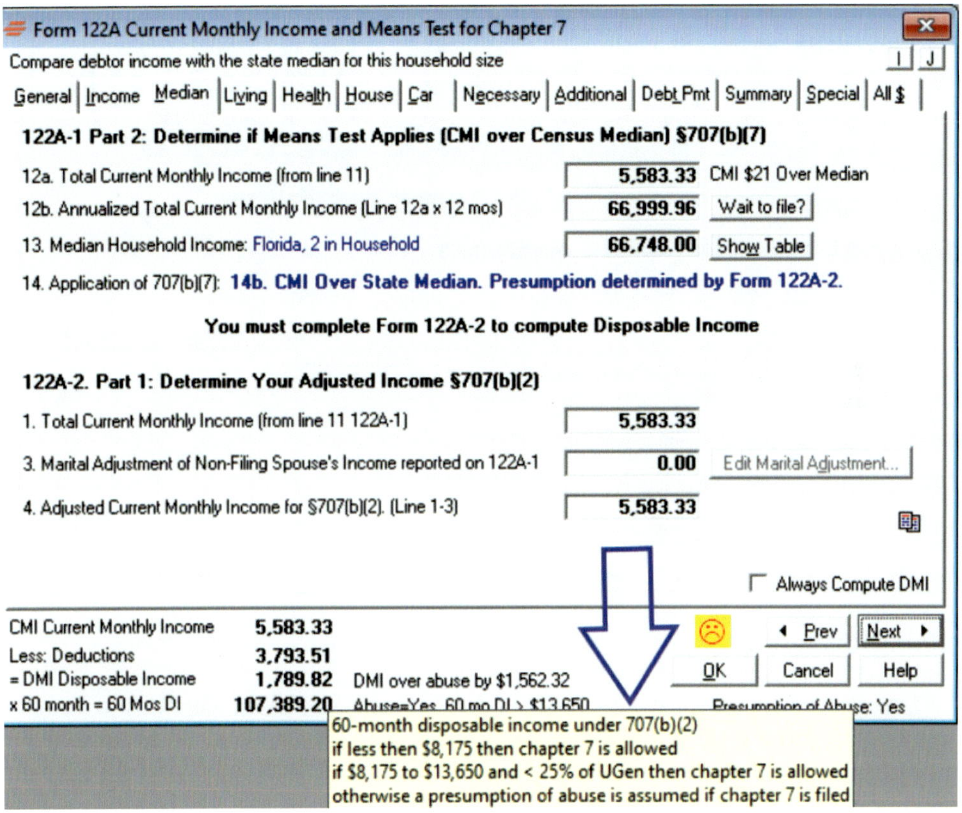

Best Case®

In the next figure, the CMI is $21 over the median state income. Thus, the debtor doesn't qualify for Chapter 7 and must proceed to the second part of the means test to determine if the debtor can stay with Chapter 7 or proceed with Chapter 13.[9]

9 Supra, note 1.

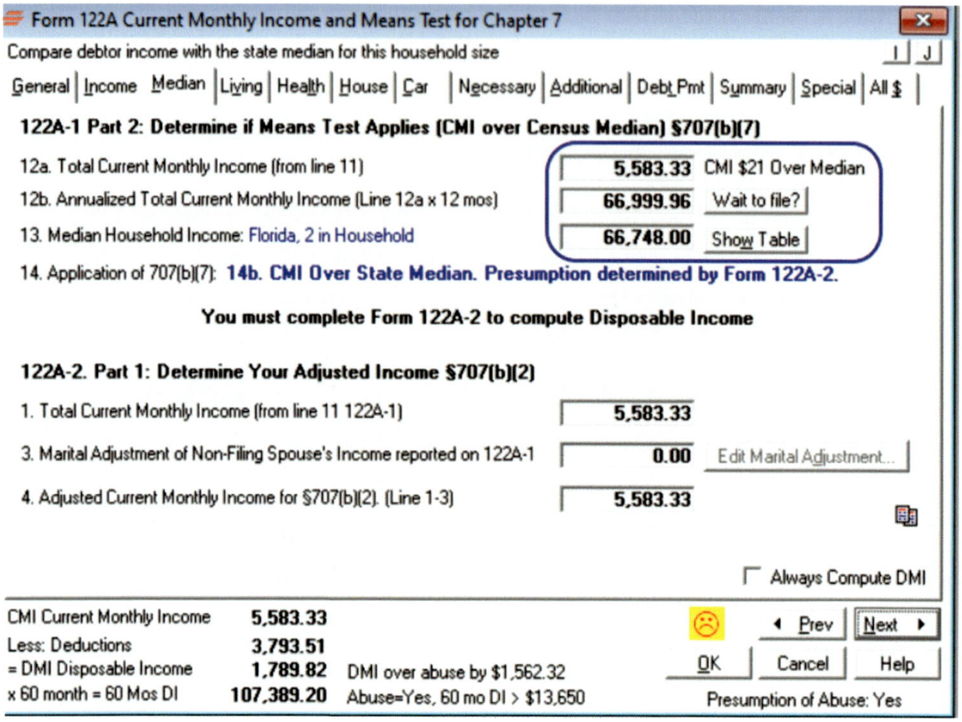

Best Case®

The median household income is $66,748.00 (Line 13), and the client is on pace to earn $66,999.96 (Line 12b). The difference between Line 12b and Line 13 equals $251.96 which divided by 12 months equals $21.00 (rounded up from $20.99). That's the amount that exceeds the Current Monthly Income and is reflected on Line 12a. However, notice the CMI and the deductions of $3,793.51 leave $1,789.83 in disposable income. Are those the same expenses and deductions in Schedule I and J?[10] No! I can tell by your reaction that I confused you even more, but again, trust me, it will make sense, and by the time we're done, you'll be a means test expert.[11]

When completing Form 122A-2, expenses are now based on IRS allowable expenses, which may or may not be the same amount as listed in Schedule J.[12] As a matter of fact, the

10 Official Form 106I. Schedule I: Your Income (Individuals). Official Form 106J. Schedule J: Your Expenses (Individuals)

11 Supra, note 2.

12 Official Form 122A-2 Chapter 7 Means Test Calculation. Supra, note 10, Official Form 106J.

IRS allowable expenses may even exceed the debtor's actual expenses.[13] This could result in the client passing the means test and qualifying for Chapter 7![14]

"*What? How does that make any sense?*" you ask. The answer is it doesn't, but at least it gives our client one more shot at proceeding with Chapter 7. Now, let's figure out the debtor's disposable income.

- $1,789.82 (disposable income) × 60 months = $107,389.20. This of course is greater than the $13,650.00 threshold.
- $1,789.82 (disposable income) – $227.50 (monthly threshold) = $1,562.32.

"*So, it's over, right? We have nothing else to do as this is an obvious presumption of abuse, and the debtor should proceed with Chapter 13.*" Not so fast!

When a debtor fails the second part of the means test, even after IRS allowable expenses, secured debts must also be deducted.[15] Before we review the effect of secured debt on the means test, let's review the different sections of the IRS allowable expenses.[16]

Starting with the "Living" tab in the figure below, the different categories for household expenses according to the IRS National Standards are provided. The convenience of the hyperlinks at the bottom of the popup window directs you to the U.S. Trustee's website on means testing.

13 Means Testing. Census Bureau, IRS Data and Administrative Expense Multipliers. Retrieved on July 17, 2021. www.justice.gov/ust/means-testing.

14 Supra, note 2.

15 Supra, note 12.

16 Id., and supra note 13.

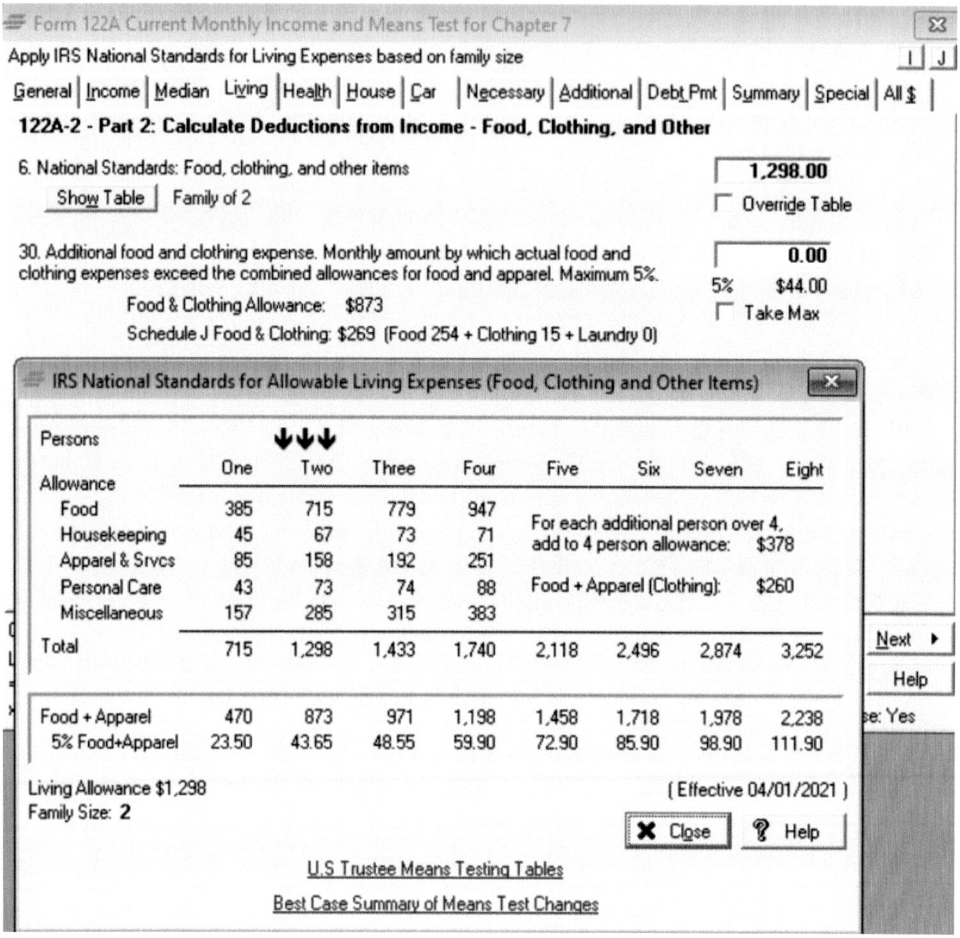

Best Case®

In this example, the food allowance is $715. Can a debtor exceed the IRS food allowance? Yes. Remember prior examples of clients that were on special diets? Each tab reflects the allowable expenses for "Health Care," "Housing," "Car," and "Necessary" expenses such as tax deductions and "Additional" expenses not previously listed.

Now, ready to have the client still pass the means test?[17] Click the "Debt Payment" tab as shown in the figure below and then click "View/Edit Secured Claims."

17 Supra, note 2.

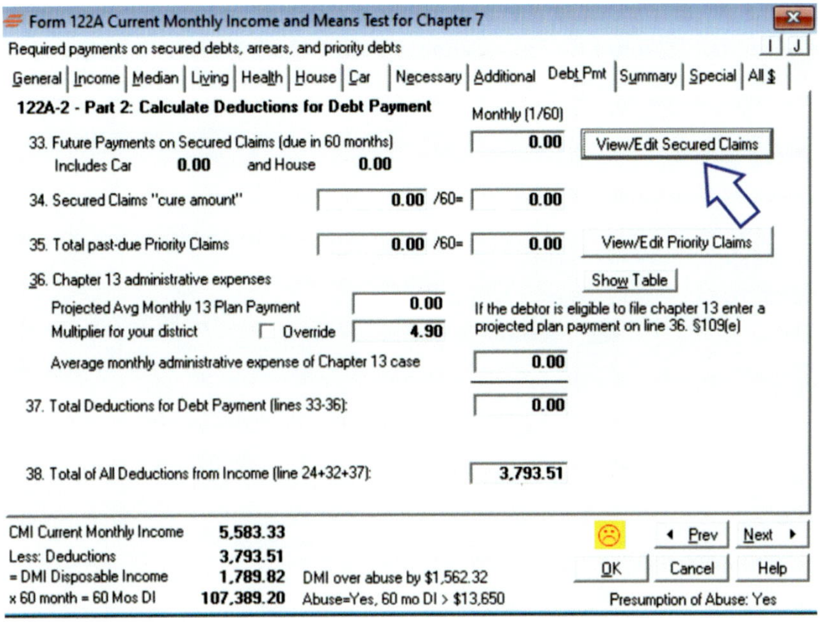

Best Case®

Remember the car and house listed on Schedules A/B?[18]

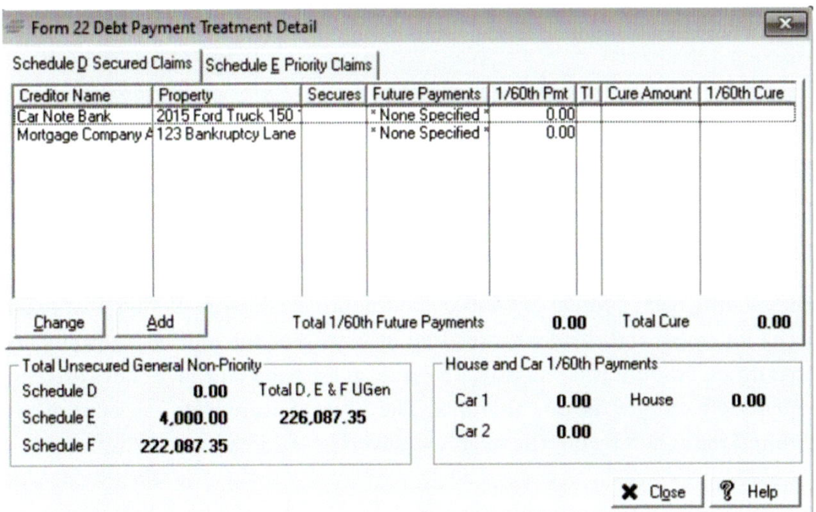

Best Case®

18 Official Form 106A/B. Schedule A/B: Property (Individuals).

Double-click the Ford truck, and the next screen has additional information that's required for the means test.[19] Notice the information is blank. That's because it's not needed if the debtor initially passes the means test.[20]

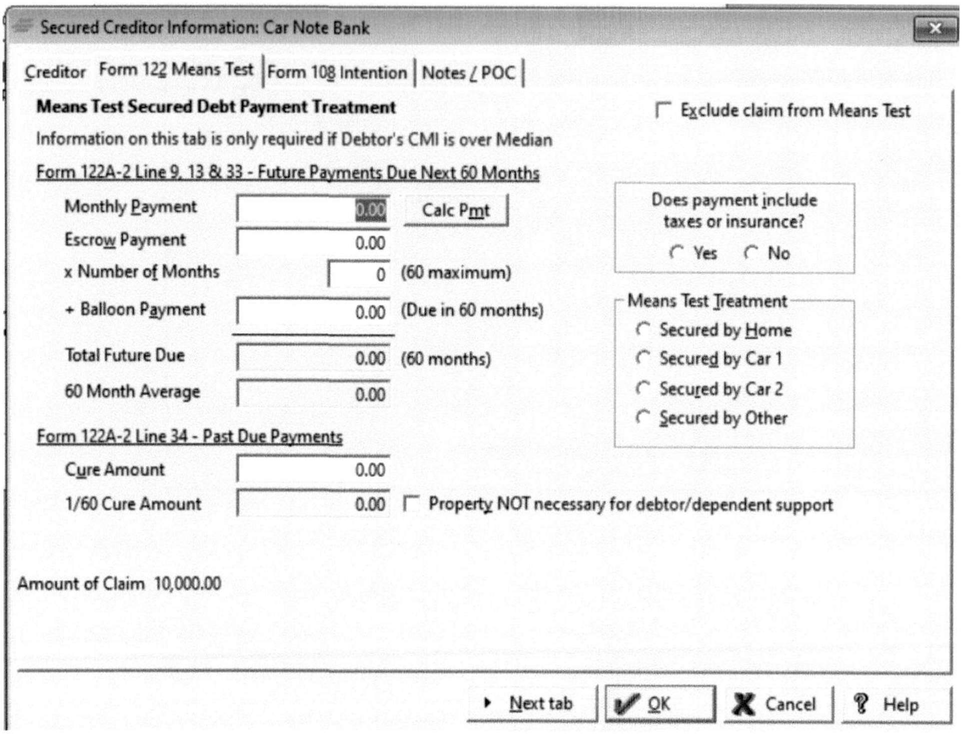

Best Case®

This whole time with the means test, we've been looking at the past.[21] Now, we are looking into the future! But don't worry, you don't need psychic legal ability to answer these questions.

Start with the monthly car payment of $400.00 per month. Make sure to click that taxes and insurance aren't included, and the debt is secured by a car. For the number of payments left, notice the maximum amount is 60 months, the same as a Chapter 13 plan. Let's pretend there are 45 payments left and no past due amounts. The "Total Future Date" amount due is $18,000. By dividing $18,000.00 by 60, the 60-month average is $300.00.

19 Supra, note 12.
20 Supra, note 2.
21 Supra, note 1.

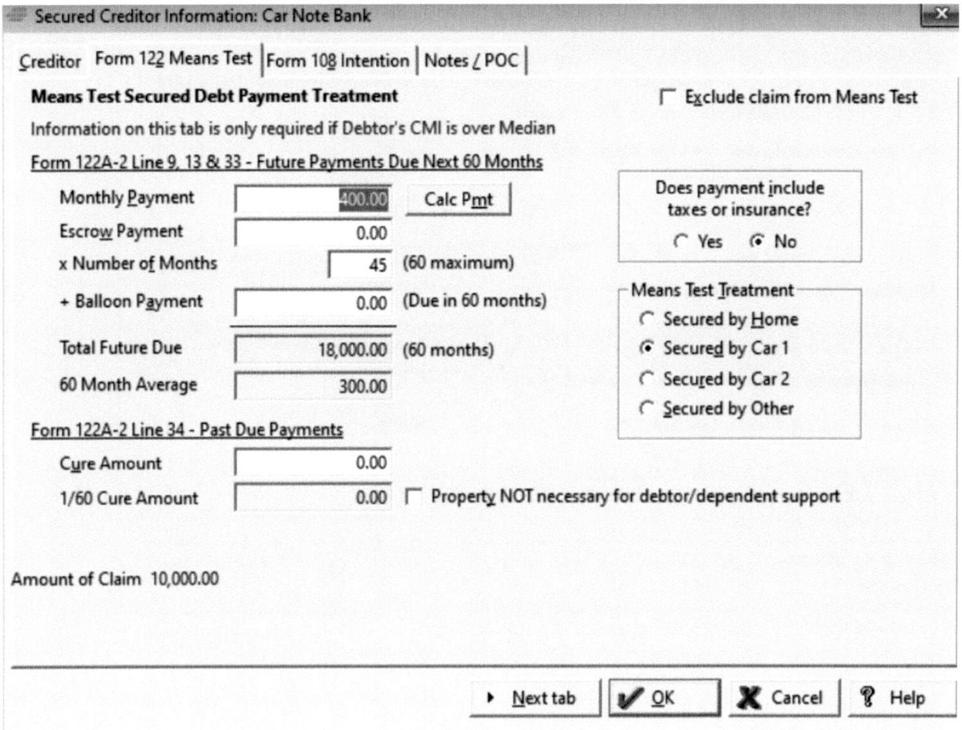

Best Case®

Close the windows and return to Form 122A-2.[22] Compare the figure below to the figure at the top of p. 289. See the difference now between the deductions and disposable income? Unfortunately, the client isn't out of the woods yet, but we aren't done either as the mortgage still needs to be included.

22 Supra, note 12.

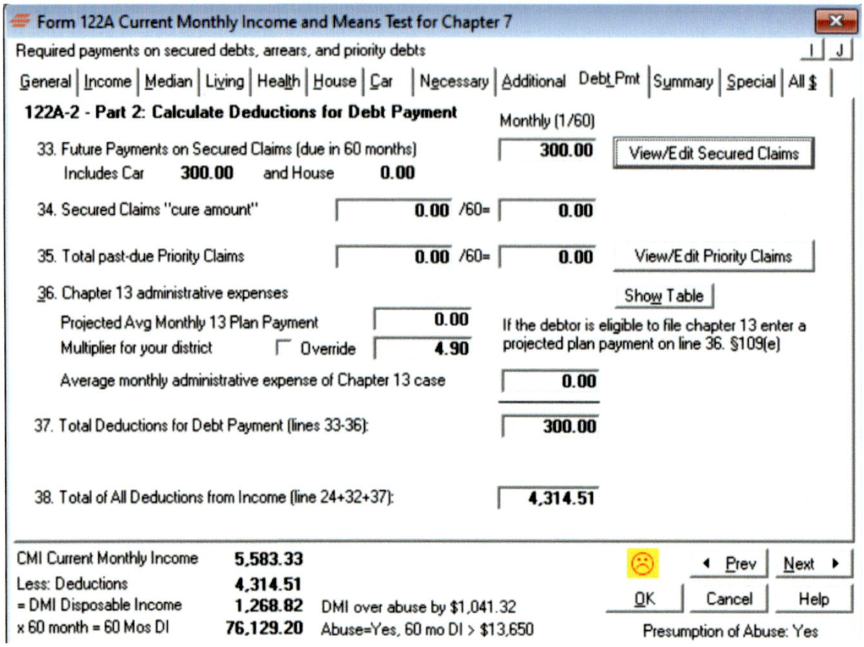

Best Case®

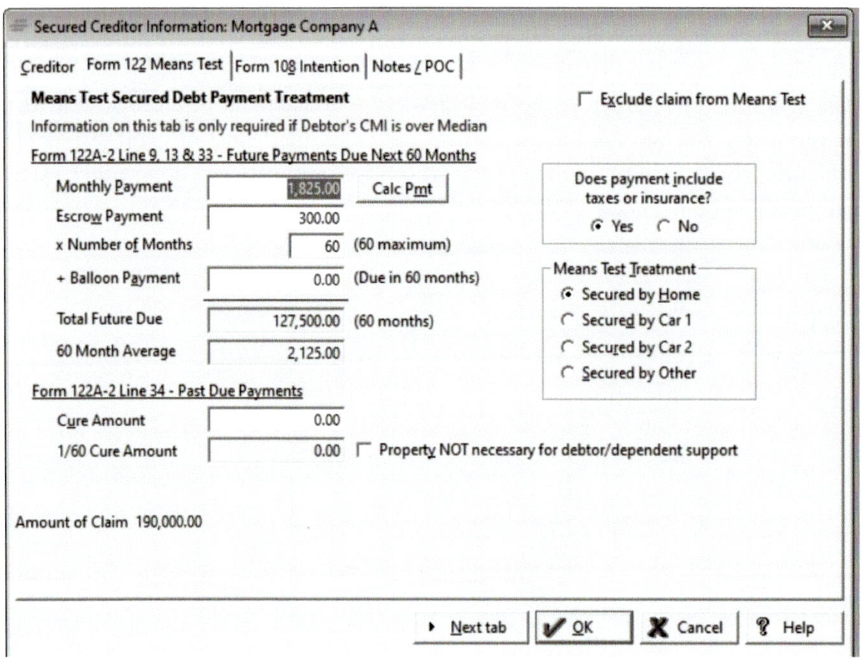

Best Case®

The monthly payment on the mortgage is $1,825, and taxes and insurance are escrowed at $300 per month. Since the client has more than 15 years left on the mortgage, the maximum amount is five years or 60 months. Return to Form 122A-2.[23]

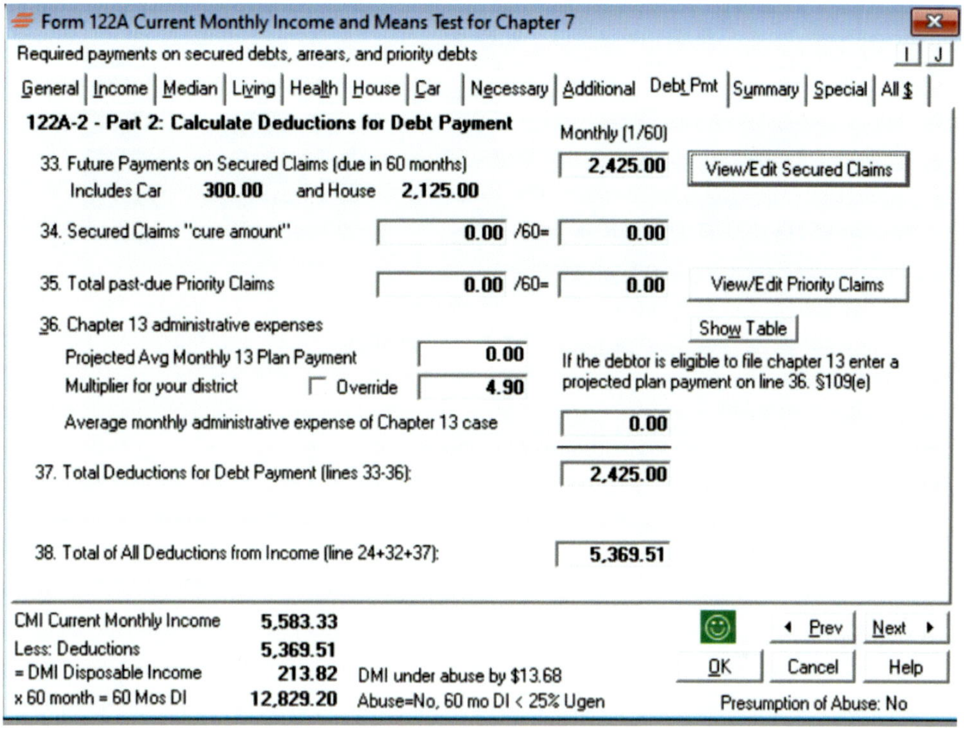
Form 122A Current Monthly Income and Means Test for Chapter 7

Required payments on secured debts, arrears, and priority debts

General | Income | Median | Living | Health | House | Car | Necessary | Additional | Debt Pmt | Summary | Special | All $

122A-2 - Part 2: Calculate Deductions for Debt Payment Monthly (1/60)

33. Future Payments on Secured Claims (due in 60 months) **2,425.00** View/Edit Secured Claims

Includes Car **300.00** and House **2,125.00**

34. Secured Claims "cure amount" **0.00** /60= **0.00**

35. Total past-due Priority Claims **0.00** /60= **0.00** View/Edit Priority Claims

36. Chapter 13 administrative expenses Show Table

Projected Avg Monthly 13 Plan Payment **0.00** If the debtor is eligible to file chapter 13 enter a projected plan payment on line 36. §109(e)

Multiplier for your district Override **4.90**

Average monthly administrative expense of Chapter 13 case **0.00**

37. Total Deductions for Debt Payment (lines 33-36): **2,425.00**

38. Total of All Deductions from Income (line 24+32+37): **5,369.51**

CMI Current Monthly Income	**5,583.33**	
Less: Deductions	**5,369.51**	
= DMI Disposable Income	**213.82**	DMI under abuse by $13.68
x 60 month = 60 Mos DI	**12,829.20**	Abuse=No, 60 mo DI < 25% Ugen

Prev | Next | OK | Cancel | Help

Presumption of Abuse: No

Best Case®

Voila! And just like that, the debtor has passed the means test and can proceed with Chapter 7 even though there appears to be $213.82 left in disposable income.[24] How is that possible? Again, we must return to the threshold figures.

23 Id.

24 Supra, note 2.

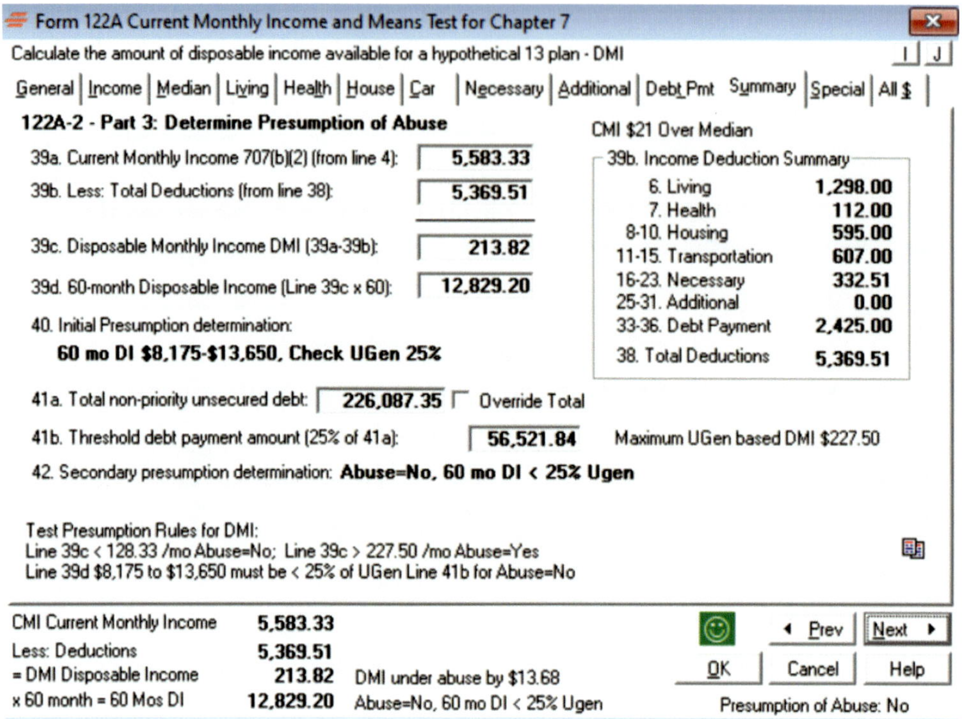

Form 122A Current Monthly Income and Means Test for Chapter 7

Calculate the amount of disposable income available for a hypothetical 13 plan - DMI

General | Income | Median | Living | Health | House | Car | Necessary | Additional | Debt Pmt | Summary | Special | All $

122A-2 - Part 3: Determine Presumption of Abuse

CMI $21 Over Median

39a. Current Monthly Income 707(b)(2) (from line 4): **5,583.33**

39b. Less: Total Deductions (from line 38): **5,369.51**

39c. Disposable Monthly Income DMI (39a-39b): **213.82**

39d. 60-month Disposable Income (Line 39c x 60): **12,829.20**

40. Initial Presumption determination:

60 mo DI $8,175-$13,650, Check UGen 25%

39b. Income Deduction Summary

6. Living	**1,298.00**
7. Health	**112.00**
8-10. Housing	**595.00**
11-15. Transportation	**607.00**
16-23. Necessary	**332.51**
25-31. Additional	**0.00**
33-36. Debt Payment	**2,425.00**
38. Total Deductions	**5,369.51**

41a. Total non-priority unsecured debt: **226,087.35** Override Total

41b. Threshold debt payment amount (25% of 41a): **56,521.84** Maximum UGen based DMI $227.50

42. Secondary presumption determination: **Abuse=No, 60 mo DI < 25% Ugen**

Test Presumption Rules for DMI:
Line 39c < 128.33 /mo Abuse=No; Line 39c > 227.50 /mo Abuse=Yes
Line 39d $8,175 to $13,650 must be < 25% of UGen Line 41b for Abuse=No

CMI Current Monthly Income	**5,583.33**	
Less: Deductions	**5,369.51**	
= DMI Disposable Income	**213.82**	DMI under abuse by $13.68
x 60 month = 60 Mos DI	**12,829.20**	Abuse=No, 60 mo DI < 25% Ugen

Prev | Next | OK | Cancel | Help

Presumption of Abuse: No

Best Case®

On Line 39d, the debtor's disposable income is $12,289.20, below the $13,650.00 threshold. But there is still the issue of can the debtor afford to pay back 25 percent of the unsecured non-priority creditors. On Line 41a, the total non-priority unsecured debt is $226,087.35, and 25 percent of that figure is $56,521.84 (Line 41b), which is greater than the $12,829.20 shown on Line 39d.

Now take a well-deserved deep breath. Hold it. Okay, exhale. You can now tell the client he can proceed with Chapter 7. But ask yourself this: what if the debtor was a renter instead of a homeowner, or if the mortgage amount was less? Better yet, what if the client in an effort to avoid bankruptcy, reduced expenses, sold the house for a minimal amount of profit, and moved into an apartment? Or, moved into an apartment because of a divorce since the client could not afford the mortgage by himself? Then the client would not have qualified for Chapter 7. Is this fair? Not at all, but bankruptcy and the means test are all about dollars and cents, and there will be situations that you will come across where the debtor is being penalized for lacking secured debt.[25] That's why it's essential to know all the facts regarding a client's financial situation. For example, if a client is considering giving up the house with bankruptcy, use the means test and calculate figures with and without the home.[26] The client

25 Id.
26 Supra, note 12.

may need to file for bankruptcy first to receive the benefit of the mortgage deduction and then sell the house at a later date. If there are no income issues, but the client plans on selling the home prior to bankruptcy, then the issue is the amount of the net proceeds.

Let's continue analyzing different situations you are likely to encounter. In the figure below, the client's six-month average income is far below the median state income. Since the client passes the first part of the means test, there's nothing else to do. Or is there?[27]

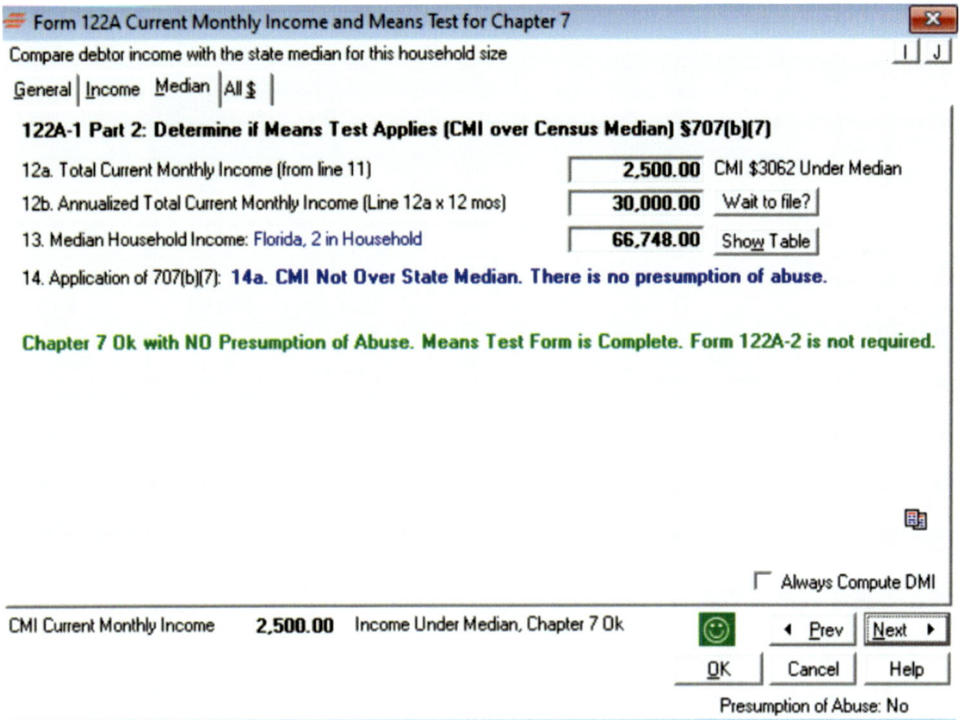

Best Case®

The next day after retaining the firm's services, looking for a "side hustle," the client got a gig economy job. He just received his first payment of $500.00, so now there are excess funds in the amount of $555.00 when comparing Schedule I to Schedule J.[28] The client will have to earn $500.00 less per month at his current job or quit his gig economy job.

27 Supra, note 1.
28 Supra, notes 10 and 12.

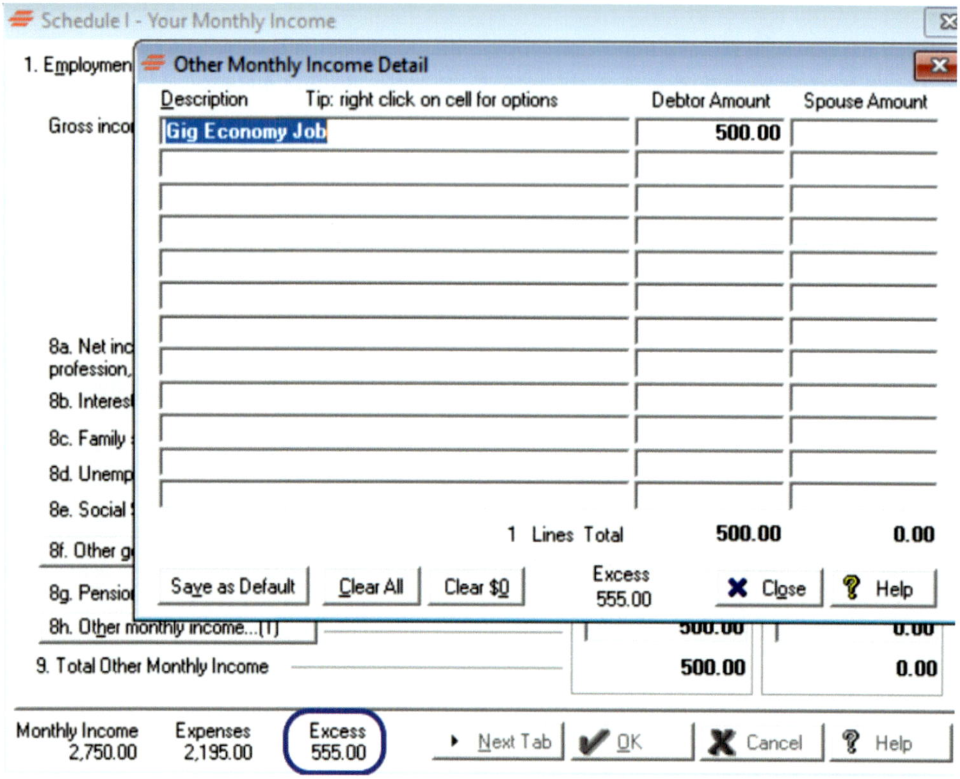

Best Case®

As a result, infinite scenarios can play out between Schedules I and J and the means test.[29] As you can see, a client may pass the means test, but Schedule I becomes an issue because of a part-time job.[30] If not, imagine that a client moves in with family during a divorce to save money. Now the reduction of expenses creates disposable income issues. The same goes for a client with an older model car whose value is below the exemption amount. Since the car is paid off and the client stopped making credit card payments, there's disposable income. However, if the client purchased a newer, more expensive car, the secured debt may result in passing the means test and eliminating disposable income.[31] Now the client has wiped out his credit card debt while driving a brand-new car that's nicer than yours! For this reason, bankruptcy judges, lawyers, and scholars have been critical of means testing, and after reviewing both parts of the means test, you see why BAPCPA remains controversial.[32] But, as long as there are laws, there will be loopholes, and bankruptcy is no different. Of

29 Id., and supra note 2.
30 Supra, notes 2 and 10.
31 Supra, note 2.
32 Supra, notes 1 and 12.

course, trustees are aware of this, and if a client recently purchased a car, the trustee will inquire about when the car was purchased and when they first consulted with the attorney. So, the key always lies in your ability to spot these issues. Even though calculating income and expenses can be a financial highwire act, the good news is that most clients will pass the first part of the means test.[33]

SUMMARY

When a client does not pass the initial means test, Form 122A-1, proceed to step two and complete Form 122A-2. This gives the debtor one more opportunity to qualify for Chapter 7 bankruptcy.

Form 122A-2 allows "IRS allowable expenses" which may exceed the debtor's actual expenses. If the client doesn't qualify for Chapter 7 and there are secured debts, complete the required information for Schedule D and the means test.

Remember also to confirm the threshold amounts. If the debtor is below the threshold amounts, he can proceed with Chapter 7. If above, then proceed with Chapter 13. Suppose the debtor lands in-between the threshold amounts. Then calculations are made to confirm if the debtor can afford to pay back 25 percent of the unsecured non-priority creditors.

KEYWORDS AND TERMS

- 25 percent unsecured non-priority creditors
- DMI (disposable monthly income)
- Official Form 122A-2
- IRS allowable expenses
- Threshold amounts

DISCUSSION QUESTIONS

1. Now that you have completed all parts of the means test, what are the pros and cons?
2. The means test does not apply to business bankruptcies. Should it?

PRACTICE QUESTIONS AND EXERCISES

1. Complete Form 122A-2, making sure the client passes the first part of the means test.

33 Supra, note 1.

2. Complete Form 122A-2, but increase the client's income so that you have to add secured debt. Also, increase the household size. Once completed, analyze if the client can afford to pay back 25 percent of the unsecured non-priority creditors?
3. Also, complete Form 122A-2 manually by downloading them off the court's website in your district.

REFERENCES

11 U.S.C §707.

Means Testing. "Census Bureau, IRS Data and Administrative Expense Multipliers." Available at www.justice.gov/ust/means-testing.

Official Form 106 A/B. Schedule A/B: Property (Individuals).

Official Form 106I. Schedule I: Your Income (Individuals).

Official Form 106J. Schedule J: Your Expenses (Individuals).

Official Form 122A-1. Chapter 7 Statement of Your Current Monthly.

Official Form 122A-2. Chapter 7 Means Test Calculation.

CHAPTER 22

Chapter 13 Basics

Since the client did not qualify for Chapter 7, the next step is considering Chapter 13. But, before we get there, let's review the nuts and bolts of Chapter 13.

While Chapter 7 is known as a liquidation, Chapter 13 is known as a reorganization because individuals with regular income can create a plan to pay back their debts or at least a portion. Consider it a restructuring of finances to get back on track.

Chapter 13 requires a monthly payment plan, known as "the plan," which lasts between three and five years. Generally, if the debtor's current monthly income is less than the state median income, the plan will be for 36 months. However, the bankruptcy judge has the discretion to extend the plan past three years. If the debtor's current monthly income exceeds the state median, it's a five-year plan, the maximum amount allowed under §1322(d).[1] As with Chapter 7, the automatic stay also applies to Chapter 13 and continues until the case is discharged or dismissed, including for co-signers.

REQUIREMENTS TO FILE CHAPTER 13

Chapter 13 is commonly referred to as a "wage earner's plan" because it requires that individuals have "regular income" to fund the plan. Note that a business cannot file for Chapter 13, but a self-employed individual can.[2]

Besides regular income, there are debt limits per §109(e).[3] Unsecured debts must be less than $419,275.00 and secured debts less than $1,257,850.00.[4] These figures are adjusted every three years to reflect changes in the consumer price index. Note, while researching for this textbook, many of the popular legal websites had figures that had not been updated in years. Therefore, it's recommended that the Code is accessed directly through your bankruptcy district's website.

1 11 U.S.C. §1322(d).
2 11 U.S.C. §109(e).
3 Id.
4 Id.

DOI: 10.4324/9781003203278-23

If the debt total exceeds these amounts, Chapter 11 should be explored, which is similar to Chapter 13. However, a discussion on Chapter 11 is beyond the scope of this text, on purpose, since it makes up for a small percentage of bankruptcies filed. In 2019, of the approximately 733,000 bankruptcies filed, 62 percent were Chapter 7, 38 percent Chapter 13, and one-tenth of 1 percent were Chapter 11.[5]

Compared to Chapter 13, notice that for Chapter 7, income isn't required to qualify. If anything, income is used to disqualify a debtor from filing Chapter 7. With Chapter 7, a reduction in income or no income at all may be the best time to file, but that same scenario most likely prevents a debtor from proceeding with Chapter 13. Also, with Chapter 7, there are no debt limits.

Time restrictions also apply with the refiling of bankruptcies. Since dismissals are "with prejudice," if Chapter 13 was dismissed within the last 180 days, the debtor can't refile unless the bankruptcy judge shortens the prejudice period.[6] Credit counseling and financial management classes are also required.[7] However, since Chapter 13s last between three and five years, the debtor has more time to complete the second course, but it should be filed as soon as possible to avoid a dismissal simply because it was forgotten.

Finally, the forms used for Chapters 7 and 13 are the same, but additional forms are required to calculate the debtor's disposable income and the plan amount.[8] In addition, if there are domestic support obligations, debtors will certify compliance with Official Form B2830, but local rules may have adopted a different version of the form.[9]

WHY FILE FOR CHAPTER 13

Besides failing the means test, there are multiple reasons that a debtor may file for Chapter 13.[10] One reason is to keep non-exempt assets. For example, if the debtor is over-exempt by $20,000.00, with Chapter 7, the debtor at most will have 12 months to pay back that amount and may even be facing a lump-sum payment, while with Chapter 13, the debtor can extend the payments over three to five years.

Another reason to file Chapter 13 is that the debtor has fallen behind on payments of secured collateral. Facing a car repossession or foreclosure, Chapter 13 allows the debtor to cure the arrears/catch up through the plan and keep the asset. With Chapter 7, the debtor must be current with secured debts if the intent is to reaffirm/keep the debt.

5 BAPCPA Report, retrieved May 2, 2021. www.uscourts.gov/statistics-reports/bapcpa-report-2019
6 11 U.S.C. §109(g).
7 11 U.S.C. §109(h), §1328(g).
8 Official Form 113. Chapter 13 Plan; Official Form 122C-1. Chapter 13 Statement of Your Current Monthly Income and Calculation of Commitment Period; Official Form 122C-2. Chapter 13 Calculation of Your Disposable Income.
9 Official Form B2830. Chapter 13 Debtor's Certifications Regarding Domestic Support Obligations and Section 522(q).
10 11 U.S.C. §707(b).

Another significant advantage of Chapter 13 is reducing the amount owed on certain secured assets to the actual value, known as a cramdown.[11] For example, if a car loan has a balance of $15,000.00, but the car's value is $10,000.00, the debt is "crammed down," and the $5,000.00 difference becomes unsecured debt like a credit card. At the end of the bankruptcy plan, the balance on the car loan has been paid off, and the debtor owns the car free and clear. Cramdowns are also possible with secured personal property such as household appliances, furniture, and even investment property. However, it's common for a debtor to opt out of a cramdown with investment property because it's unlikely the mortgage can be paid off in three to five years.

While the cramdown is a useful tool, time restrictions prevent a debtor from purchasing a new car and filing for bankruptcy to reduce the loan amount to the depreciated value. For car loans, there is a 910-day limit and one year for personal property.[12] Also, notice in the prior paragraph that mortgages on investment property were mentioned, not the principal residence. However, not all is lost for debtors and their homestead property.

Liens work on a priority basis, meaning the first lien/mortgage takes precedent over a second mortgage, and a second mortgage takes precedent over a third. During the mortgage foreclosure crisis, mortgages were "underwater," meaning the balance on the mortgage was more than the actual value of the home. Lien stripping allows the debtor to reduce junior liens down to the home's fair market value. For example, if the house is valued at $350,000.00 and there is a $250,000.00 first mortgage and a $100,000.00 second mortgage, there is nothing to "strip" as the mortgage amounts equal the home's value. However, if the balance on the second mortgage is $150,000.00, then $50,000.00 from the second mortgage can be stripped. If there was a third mortgage, then the full amount would be stripped, and the debt becomes unsecured. However, the debtor would still be responsible for the total amount on the first mortgage and $100,000.00 from the second mortgage. Unfortunately, lien stripping or cramdowns doesn't apply to Chapter 7 cases.

WHY FILING FOR CHAPTER 13 IS A BAD IDEA

So far, it seems to the debtor's financial advantage to proceed with a Chapter 13, but you will encounter plenty of scenarios where waving the Chapter 13 magical wand isn't likely to be of much help. First is the debtor that can't afford to fund the plan. Usually, the debtor owns a home. For example, suppose the debtor is now divorced and is responsible for the mortgage payments. If the debtor fell behind on payments, Chapter 13 is a consideration, but remember, the arrears don't magically disappear, it's just paid back through the plan. So, clients need to understand that the plan payment includes the current mortgage amount plus the arrears. Thus, if the debtor can't afford a $1,000.00 mortgage payment, they can't afford a mortgage payment that is $1,001.00. One bankruptcy judge in the Southern District

11 11 U.S.C. §506(a)(2); Fed. R. Bankr. P. 3012.
12 11 U.S.C. §1325(a).

of Florida would say it best when he realized confirming a plan meant funds were tight and there was little room for error. The judge would ask the debtor what if they developed a bad habit that would cause the debtor to default on the plan. The debtor, of course, would flash a look of confusion, only for the judge to say, "yes, a bad habit like eating." While everyone in the courtroom always shared a laugh with the judge's analysis no matter how many times they heard the same punchline before, it did illustrate the point.

Another reason is simple mathematics. Imagine a debtor struggling with plan payments to keep a home that doesn't have equity, and therefore, financially, it's not worth it. Any change in circumstances can create financial chaos. Something as simple as a car breaking down and having to be fixed or replaced means the debtor is in jeopardy of failing to make plan payments. There's a reason clients are met with a look of surprise when I find out they have received a discharge previously in Chapter 13. In 2017, an article published by the American Bankruptcy Institute concluded that a discharge was received in 42 percent of Chapter 13 cases, but only 2 percent for pro se debtors.[13] The fail rate is an issue, especially when bankruptcy attorneys push debtors into Chapter 13, knowing the likely outcome, but since fees can be triple the amount of a Chapter 7 case, well, you do the simple math. Even worse, a study conducted by *The Atlantic* concluded that a disproportionate amount of black Americans are pushed into Chapter 13 versus white Americans. Since some attorneys offer zero money down to file a Chapter 13 and include fees in the plan, zero money down sounds like a good deal when you are too broke to file for bankruptcy.[14] Debtors will be in denial and come up with irrational if not impossible ways to save their car or home, whether it's getting rid of cell phones, using public transportation exclusively, or even living without electricity. Some people are willing to spend two dollars to make one dollar back. The convenience of one monthly payment is another selling point for bankruptcy attorneys. If it seems, after calculating the monthly payments, the debtor is unlikely to succeed, and the retainer was minimal, make a notation in the file for the attorney to review.

Regardless of factors beyond our control, there's common sense. A lot can happen between three to five years: health issues, divorce, loss of job/income, even a global pandemic. If there's a dismissal, the debtor may be worse off between interest accumulating and the protection of the automatic stay gone. We have all heard that the divorce rate is more than 50 percent, and I routinely compare Chapter 13 to marriage to give clients perspective. If married, you shouldn't go out and buy a new car without discussing this issue first with your spouse. Bankruptcy is no different. Do you want or need a new car? Do you think you can go to the dealer and walk out with the latest model that has all the bells and whistles while a Chapter 13 is pending? Of course not, because that affects the amount received through the plan. Think about it. If at the time of filing, the debtor

13 Ed Flynn. Bankruptcy by the Numbers. August 2017, retrieved April 30, 2021. https://s3.amazonaws.com/abi-org-corp/journals/numbers_08-17.pdf.

14 Paul Kiel with Hannah Fresques. How the Bankruptcy System Is Failing Black Americans. September 27, 2017, *Propublica* co-published with *The Atlantic*. https://features.propublica.org/bankruptcy-inequality/bankruptcy-failing-black-americans-debt-chapter-13/.

had no car payment, or say a $200 car payment, and now the debtor has to buy a new car because their car has literally fallen apart, but the new car is $500.00 per month, the trustee is guaranteed to object. Why? For one, a debtor cannot incur new debt during bankruptcy.[15] Also, the trustee wants more money available to pay creditors, and guess who else does too? Creditors! In addition, how do you think trustees get paid? Trustees receive a percentage of plan payments. So, reducing a debtor's monthly payment is taking money out of the trustee's pocket!

THE CHAPTER 13 PROCESS

Like every bankruptcy, the case begins with the debtor filing the petition, proof of the credit counseling class, and paying the required filing fee of $310.[16] Like Chapter 7, certain documents are provided to the trustee, such as proof of income and tax returns. Unlike Chapter 7 where there may be multiple trustees per district, there's usually one trustee per district for Chapter 13 cases. The Chapter 13 trustee, known as the standing trustee, is obligated to collect the monthly payment and disburse the funds to creditors.

Approximately one month after filing, the creditors' meeting is scheduled. The first payment under the plan is due within 30 days, even if the creditor's meeting hasn't been held. If need be, the plan payment amount can be adjusted.[17] Unlike Chapter 7 cases where unsecured creditors rarely file a proof of claim, for Chapter 13, creditors will have to file their claims within 90 days after the first date set for the Meeting of Creditors.[18] Government entities have 180 days.[19] Creditors are paid according to how they are categorized, whether as a secured creditor (car or home), priority unsecured (taxes), or unsecured (credit cards, personal loans). The plan will indicate how secured creditors are paid and if arrears are to be cured. Unsecured creditors are rarely paid in full but should receive the same amount that would have been received in a hypothetical Chapter 7 case if non-exempt assets were liquidated.[20]

By the time the debtor attends the Meeting of Creditors, the trustee would have reviewed the payment plan that was filed within 14 days of the petition.[21] The plan payments are collected either biweekly or monthly and can be withdrawn from the debtor's paystubs. Next is the Confirmation Hearing.

15 11 U.S.C. §1305(c), §1322(a)(1), §1327.
16 28 U.S. Code §1930.
17 11 U.S.C. §1326(a)(1).
18 Fed. R. Bankr. P. 3002(c)
19 11 U.S.C. §502(b)(9).
20 11 U.S.C. §1325.
21 Fed. R. Bankr. P. 3015

CHAPTER 13 CONFIRMATION HEARINGS

Within 45 days of the Meeting of Creditors, the Confirmation Hearing is held to decide if the plan complies with 11 U.S.C. Sections 1324 and 1325. Creditors can object to confirmation of the plan under Fed. R. Bankr. P. 2002(b). Objections are common and are usually because the creditor argues more disposable income is available, the creditor is receiving less than in the Chapter 7 liquidation test, or the debt amount listed in the plan is incorrect. Note that it's common to have multiple Confirmation Hearings, unlike the Meeting of Creditors that's usually once. Upon confirmation, the trustee distributes the funds to creditors. If the plan isn't confirmed, then an amended/modified plan is submitted. This is also a common occurrence.

MOVING FORWARD

Now that the plan was approved, the monthly payments shall continue throughout the pendency of the case. If not, the case is subject to dismissal or converted to a Chapter 7 for liquidation.[22] The case may also be dismissed or converted if the debtor fails to pay domestic support obligations or file tax returns.[23]

PLAN COMPLETION AND DISCHARGE

As long as the debtor continues with plan payments, the debtor will receive a discharge upon completing the plan. Don't forget the financial management certificate! Secured debts that were not discharged, such as ongoing car and mortgage payments, shall continue as normal (pre-bankruptcy filing). Besides the discharge upon completion of the plan, there is also what's known as a *hardship discharge*.

A hardship discharge isn't automatic as it has to be requested by the debtor.[24] To qualify for a hardship discharge, the debtor must prove (1) that failure to complete plan payments is due to circumstances beyond the debtor's control and through no fault of the debtor; (2) that creditors have received at least as much as would have been received in a Chapter 7 liquidation case; and (3) that modification of the plan is not possible. Injury or illness that precludes employment sufficient to fund even a modified plan may serve as the basis for a hardship discharge. The hardship discharge is more narrowly focused than a standard discharge and doesn't apply to non-dischargeable debts.[25]

22 11 U.S.C. §1307(c).
23 11 U.S.C. §1307(c) and (e), §1308, §521.
24 11 U.S.C. §1328(b).
25 11 U.S.C. §523.

SUMMARY

Filing Chapter 13 requires the petition, proof of the credit counseling certificate, the filing fee, and the proposed payment plan, which must be filed within fourteen days of the petition, or the case is subject to dismissal. Because income is required to fund a Chapter 13, it's commonly referred to as a wage earner's plan. The monthly payment amount depends on various factors and requires approval by the court at a Confirmation Hearing.

The length of the plan is a minimum of three years, and a maximum of five and is determined based on the debtor's income. If the debtor's income is below the state median, it's a 36-month plan and 60 months if above. However, the bankruptcy judge does have the discretion to extend a three-year plan, but not a five-year plan.

There are several reasons why a debtor may file for Chapter 13 instead of 7. For one, the debtor may have failed the means test or wish to keep non-exempt property. Another reason is that the debtor fell behind on secured debt payments and can use Chapter 13 to catch up with the arrears, unlike Chapter 7 which requires that the debtor be current on secured debt payments. However, it's worth noting that the debtor has to continue the current monthly obligations plus the arrears, so their total monthly expenses will increase.

Chapter 13 also allows for a cramdown, which is the reduction of secured debt to the asset's fair market value. This is common with car loans but also applies to loans secured by personal property and investment property. A cramdown is not an option for the first mortgage on a primary residence, but lien stripping is for junior liens. Neither a cramdown nor lien stripping is available for Chapter 7 cases.

After filing a Chapter 13 petition, a 341 Meeting of Creditors is scheduled, and the first plan payment is due within 30 days, even if the plan has yet to be approved. Within 45 days of the 341 meeting, a Confirmation Hearing is held to approve the bankruptcy. Unless dismissed, there may be multiple Confirmation Hearings.

Once the plan has been confirmed, the debtor shall continue making payments directly to the trustee, or payments may be withdrawn from the debtor's paycheck. The trustee will disburse the funds to creditors according to the plan. Upon completing the plan, the discharge is granted, but the debtor must have filed the certificate for the financial management course. If the debtor is unable to complete the plan, the debtor may qualify for a hardship discharge.

A hardship discharge requires that the debtor prove that failure to complete the plan was due to reasons beyond the debtor's control. Also, the debtor must demonstrate that creditors received at least the same amount as would have been received in a Chapter 7 case. Finally, the debtor must show that modifying the plan isn't possible.

KEYWORDS AND TERMS

- Chapter 7 liquidation test
- Cramdown
- Hardship discharge

- Junior liens
- Lien stripping

DISCUSSION QUESTIONS

1. Briefly summarize Chapter 13.
2. Differentiate what happens with non-exempt assets in Chapter 7 versus Chapter 13.
3. After reviewing the client's file, you believe the debtor qualifies for a cramdown. After notifying the attorney, who agrees, what's the next step?
4. Does your district have a local form for domestic support certification? Download the form and complete the required information.

PRACTICE QUESTIONS AND EXERCISES

1. Draft a motion to cram down the debtor's vehicle.
2. Draft a motion for stripping a junior lien on the debtor's homestead property.

REFERENCES

11 U.S.C. §109.
11 U.S.C. §502.
11 U.S.C. §506.
11 U.S.C. §521.
11 U.S.C. §522.
11 U.S.C. §523.
11 U.S.C. §707.
11 U.S.C. §1305.
11 U.S.C. §1307.
11 U.S.C. §1308.
11 U.S.C. §1322.
11 U.S.C. §1324.
11 U.S.C. §1325.
11 U.S.C. §1325.
11 U.S.C. §1326.
11 U.S.C. §1327.
11 U.S.C. §1328.
28 U.S.C. §1930.

Ed Flynn, "Bankruptcy by the Numbers" (August 2017). Retrieved April 30, 2021. https://s3.amazonaws.com/abi-org-corp/journals/numbers_08-17.pdf.

BAPCPA Report. Available at www.uscourts.gov/statistics-reports/bapcpa-report-2019.

Fed. R. Bankr. P. 2002.

Fed. R. Bankr. P. 3002.

Fed. R. Bankr. P. 3012.

Fed. R. Bankr. P. 3015.

Paul Kiel and Hannah Fresques, "How the Bankruptcy System Is Failing Black Americans" (September 27, 2017). *Propublica* co-published with *The Atlantic*. https://features.propublica.org/bankruptcy-inequality/bankruptcy-failing-black-americans-debt-chapter-13/.

Official Form 113. Chapter 13 Plan.

Official Form 122C-1. Chapter 13 Statement of Your Current Monthly Income and Calculation of Commitment Period.

Official Form 122C-2. Chapter 13 Calculation of Your Disposable Income.

Official Form B2830. Chapter 13 Debtor's Certifications Regarding Domestic Support Obligations and Section 522(q).

CHAPTER 23

The Chapter 13 Plan

Here's the part where I say you kids have it easy today: automated software. Calculating a Chapter 13 plan is as easy as listing creditors in Schedule F.[1] When I first started handling Chapter 13 cases, the calculations were done manually, the same for child support guidelines in family law cases. You may think that's not a big deal, but when the judge says to step outside of the courtroom for a few minutes and complete a new plan before the confirmation calendar ends, the pressure is on. I even carried an electronic device known as a calculator. No, not the app on your phone, but an actual calculator! At least I didn't say I had to walk to school uphill in the snow; then again, Florida is flat, and there's no snow.

The first step in a Chapter 13 case is categorizing the debt. Is it secured, unsecured, or a priority debt? If the debt isn't classified correctly, you can imagine the monthly payment amount if a foreclosed home with a deficiency balance of $150,000.00 is miscategorized as secured debt. But there is no need to panic because you will know something isn't right when you see the payment plan amount.[2]

Let's begin with setting up and reviewing the basics. Start with the Setup menu, scroll down to "Edit Case Jurisdiction," and choose "13 Plan." In the figure below, "Standard Treatment of Claim" shows that debts are categorized as follows:

- Schedule D (secured creditors) = SPR.[3]
- Schedule E (unsecured priority creditors) = UPR.[4]
- Schedule F (unsecured creditors) = UGEN, including unsecured portions from lien stripping or a cramdown.[5]
- Schedule G (leases/executory contracts) = AEL.[6]

1 Official Form 106 E/F. Schedule E/F: Creditors Who Have Unsecured Claims (Individuals).
2 Official Form 113. Chapter 13 Plan.
3 Official Form 106D. Schedule D: Creditors Who Hold Claims Secured By Property (Individuals).
4 Supra, note 1.
5 Id.
6 Official Form 106G. Schedule G: Executory Contracts and Unexpired Leases (Individuals).

DOI: 10.4324/9781003203278-24

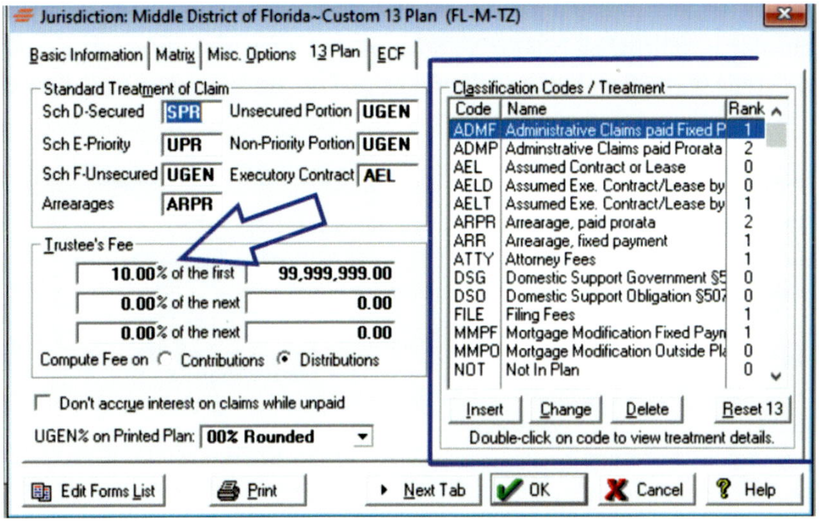

Best Case®

In the figure above, the trustee's fees are listed at the standard 10 percent, but that amount could vary per district. Additional classification codes can be seen by scrolling down the list. There are three options for payment methods, whether attorney's fees, secured, or unsecured debt. "Fixed" is a pre-determined length of time, say ten months. "Pro-rata" means spread out through the length of the plan, and "not in plan" means the payment is excluded from the plan. An example is attorney's fees paid prior to filing or a current mortgage. Note that pro-rata is the default setting and if the correct payment method isn't chosen, it will affect plan payment amounts.

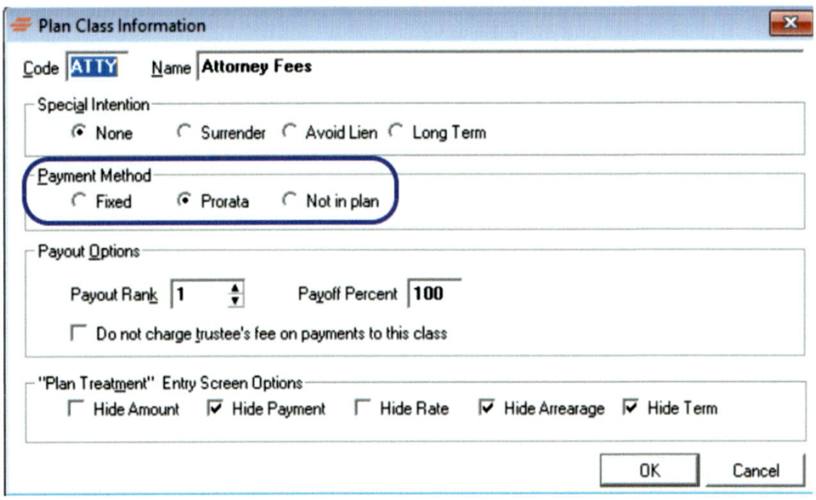

Best Case®

Now, let's begin with a typical Chapter 13 filing. In this case, the debtors have $1,429.00 in disposable income when comparing Schedule I to J.[7] The mortgage is current and is being paid outside of the plan, but the debtor is behind on the car payments, and since the loan balance exceeds the value, it could be crammed down.

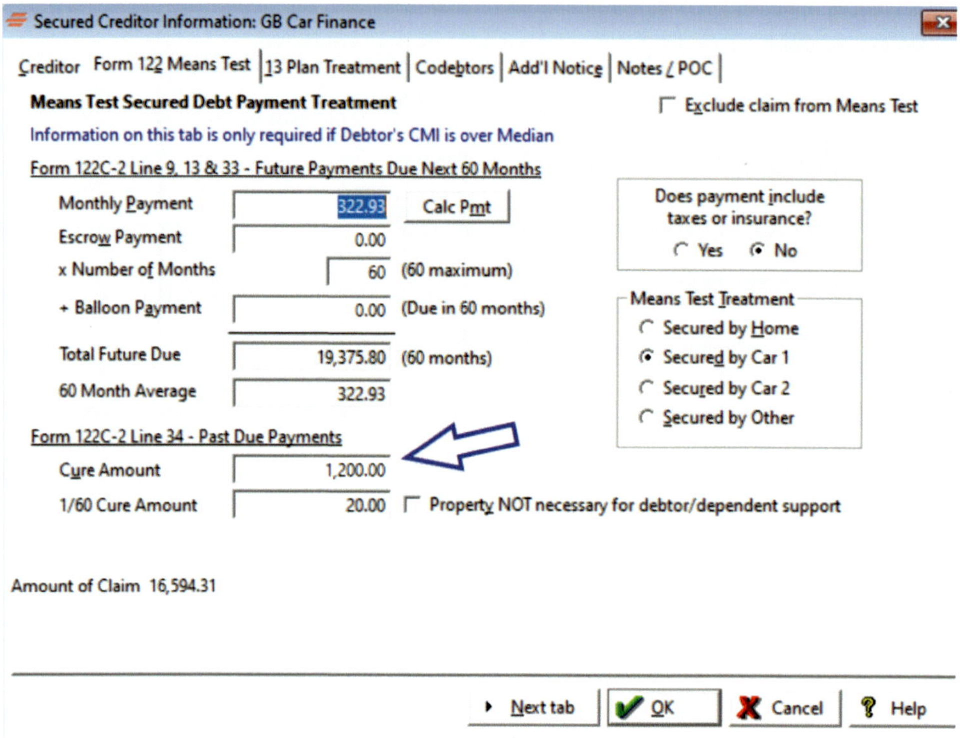

Best Case®

For purposes of means testing, detailed information is required in Form 122.[8] In this case, we see the arrears are $1,200.00. Click over to the next tab of Chapter 13 treatment, and the interest rate of 9.450 is added.

7 Official Form 106I. Schedule I: Your Income (Individuals). Official Form 106J. Schedule J: Your Expenses (Individuals).

8 Official Form 122A-1. Chapter 7 Statement of Your Current Monthly Income.

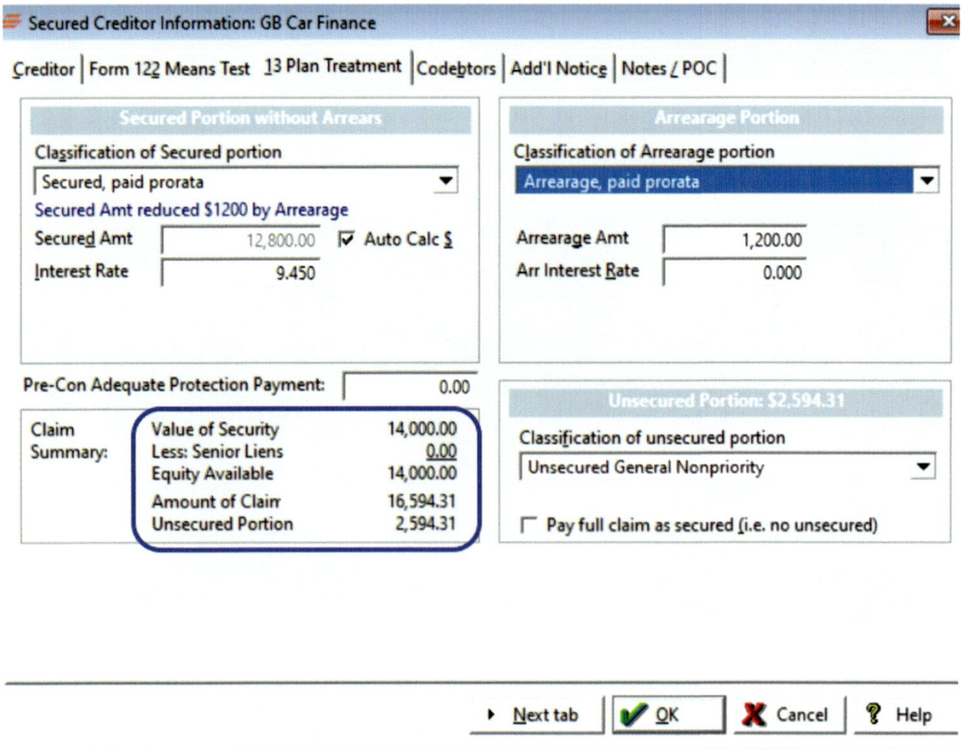

Best Case®

In the claim summary, notice the car's value is $14,000.00, but the loan balance is $16,594.31, so there is $2,594.31 in negative equity. With a cramdown, that portion becomes unsecured. Depending on the plan, maybe all or a small percentage of that amount gets paid back. Remember, there is a pecking order in bankruptcy with creditors, starting with secured creditors at the top, unsecured priority claims, and finally, unsecured claims.

This scenario also serves as an example of why plans are modified regularly. We will review an actual Chapter 13 case where multiple plans were submitted. Rarely is a plan going to be confirmed the first time around for a host of reasons. For example, additional proof of claims could have been filed, or the arrearages on secured debt were incorrect. Another reason is the cramdown isn't automatic as it requires approval by the bankruptcy judge. Since the plan is filed within 14 days of the petition, the motion may not be scheduled for another month or more.[9]

In the figure below, a summary of the plan is provided. All the figures are calculated automatically, including the total amount of claims, the actual payout each month with the pending balance, and the amount of principal and interest paid.

9 Fed. R. Bankr. P. 3015.

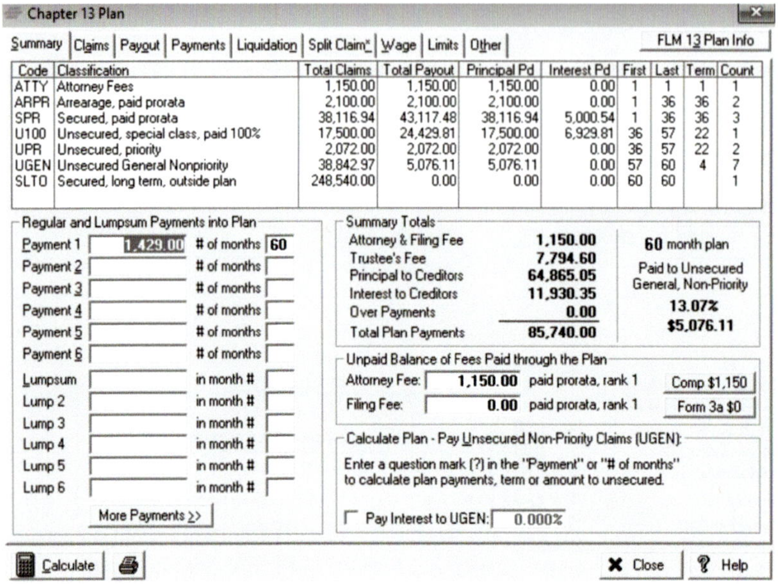

Best Case®

Most of the time, the monthly payment amount is known in advance because of the available disposable income, as well as the length of the plan, however, that doesn't mean that adjustments don't have to be made. For example, suppose the initial calculation was for a 55-month plan. Once you click "calculate," a notification states the plan is underfunded by $1,409.07.

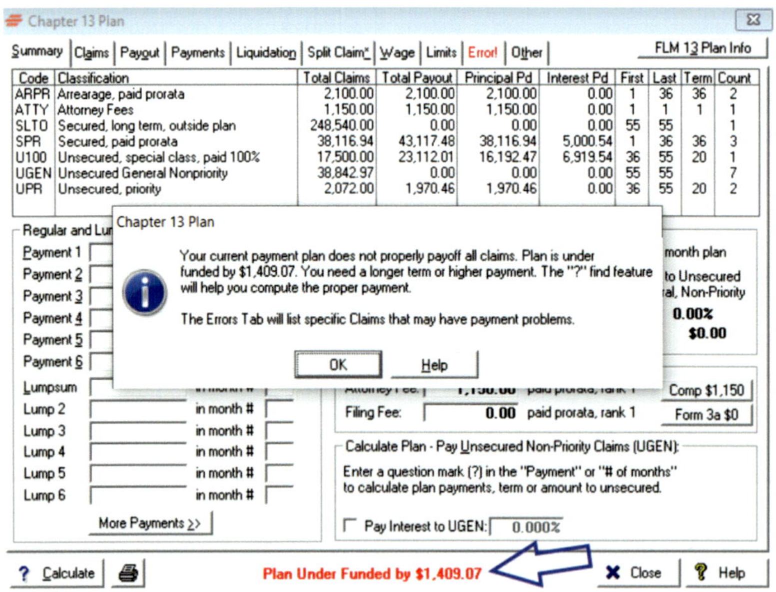

Best Case®

Chapter 13 is always about crunching numbers. In our example, attorney's fees were paid in full in the plan's first month, but that isn't always the case. The norm is to receive a portion of the fees upfront and the balance paid throughout the plan. For example, one colleague always had attorney's fees paid in the first ten months of the plan, or he wouldn't accept the case. Could the debtor had qualified if fees were stretched out for another ten months? Most likely, and number crunching would answer that question, but that was this particular attorney's preference, and he made it clear to clients it wasn't worth it to him financially to accept the case. His decision was based on the fact that he had a busy and successful practice. But, since he didn't practice bankruptcy law exclusively, he couldn't afford to put forth the time and effort in attending multiple Confirmation Hearings, only to have the case dismissed a few months later because of lack of payments. If he accepted a minimal monthly payment on fees throughout the plan and the case gets dismissed, he would have done more work than he was paid for, which is never good for business.

Another colleague who only practiced consumer bankruptcy law rarely filed motions to set aside dismissals even though additional fees are allowed. But, since the meetings of creditors are held simultaneously for Chapter 7 and 13 cases, including Confirmation Hearings and motion calendar, it's impossible to be at four places at once. If an attorney is on the first floor attending a 341 meeting, but the bankruptcy judge on the fourteenth floor calls a Chapter 13 case, and the attorney isn't present, it's common for the judge to dismiss the case.[10] Now it's even worse since, in the Southern District of Florida, Confirmation Hearings are held in another courthouse several blocks away. Also, consider that in a large district like the Southern District of Florida, a Confirmation Hearing scheduled at 9 a.m. may not be called until 1 p.m. as there could be 100 plus cases on the court's docket. Actually, what's worse is that cases in the northern part of the county get pushed over to the next county. You can see the scheduling chaos this creates and why a law firm may reject certain cases. However, COVID-19 restrictions have resulted in virtual appearances and have made handling multiple hearings at once easier.

Besides attorney's fees, cramdowns also serve as the perfect example of number crunching since the secured debt must be paid in full before the plan ends. If the debtor cannot afford to do so, then the regular monthly payments and arrears are paid through the plan. When the bankruptcy ends, the regular monthly payments continue.

Before we get into another type of plan known as a "step plan," let's review the importance of categorizing the debt and how this affects the plan amounts. In our case, the debtor was current on the mortgage, and there was no second mortgage that may require lien stripping. However, if "secured long term, in the plan" is chosen, that means that the regular monthly mortgage payment is added to the payment plan.

10 11 U.S.C. §341.

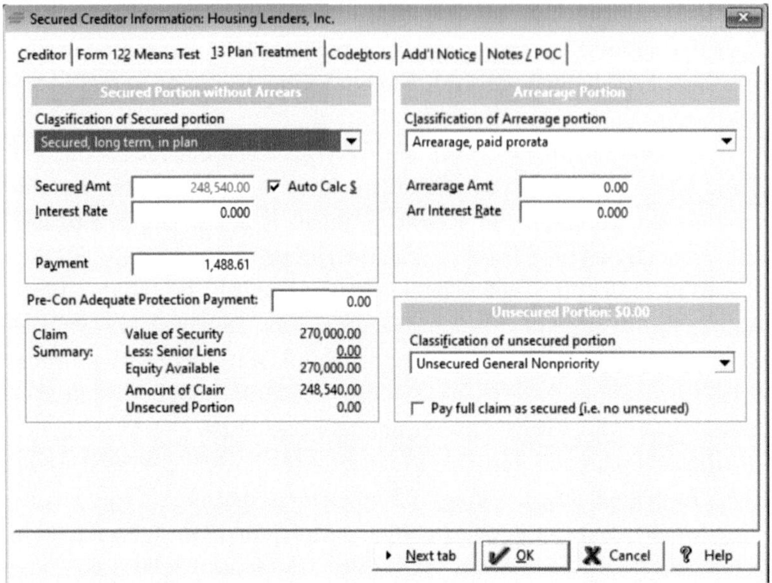

Best Case®

When the plan is recalculated, the monthly plan payment is increased to $3,066.49, yet, we only have $1429.00 in disposable income. But again, when number crunching, exaggerated figures most likely mean a simple mistake was made in categorizing the debt.

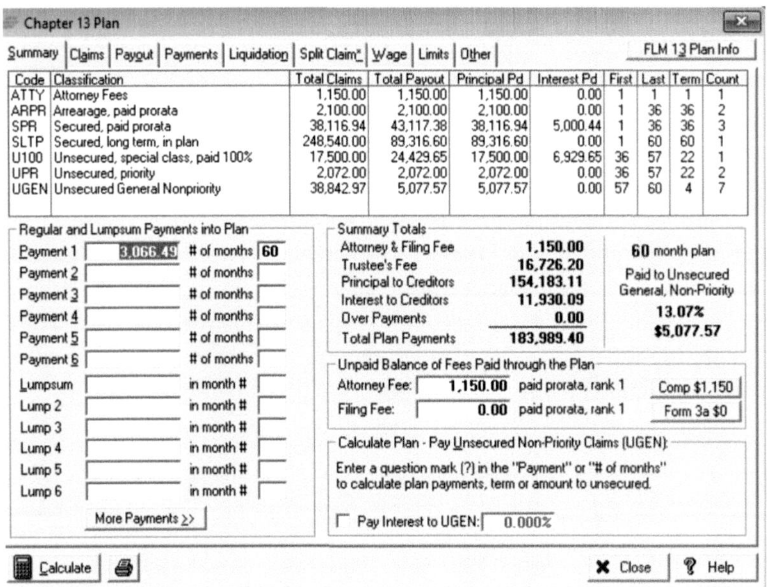

Best Case®

Also, remember to recalculate the plan each time so that figures remain accurate. But again, any errors will be highlighted. In the figure below, the plan wasn't recalculated, so the debtor is overpaying into the plan.

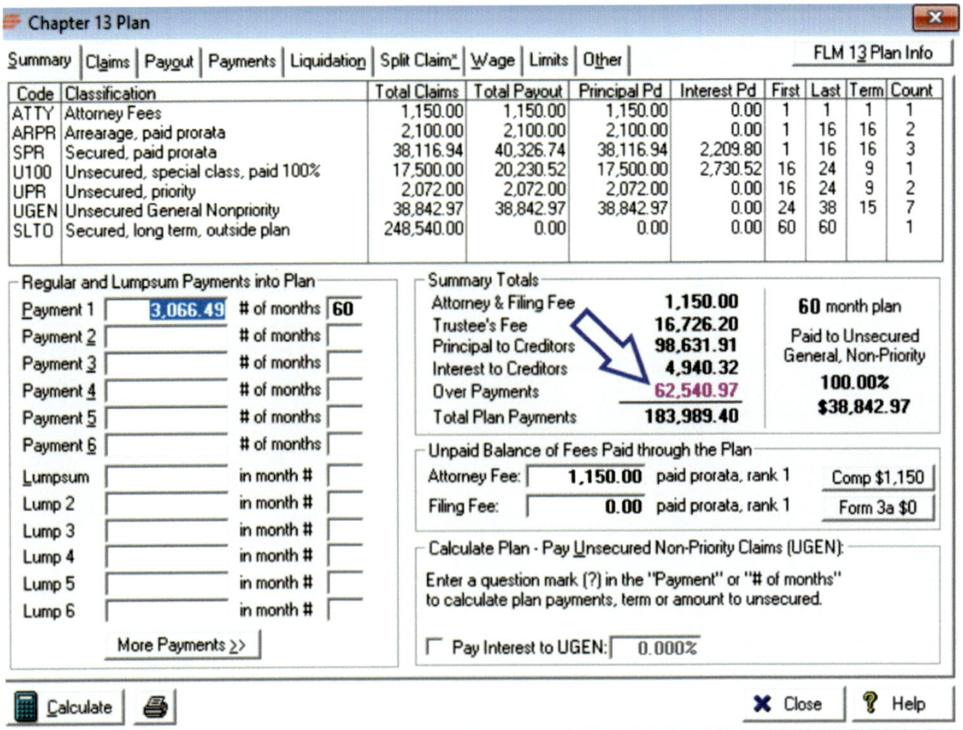

Best Case®

As we continue to crunch numbers, let's review the step plan. Chapter 13 requires flexibility, hence why plans are routinely modified, but a plan could also be increased over time to qualify a debtor. This is known as a step plan and how it works is pretty simple; just think of climbing steps to get to the top. In this case, the end of the plan is the top of the stairs.

A case I handled is a perfect example of a step plan. The debtor was self-employed and struggling to make plan payments because business revenue decreased. Facing dismissal, the bankruptcy judge recommended the step plan, which would lower her current payments, but future payments would increase. The idea was that hopefully, the debtor's business would pick up, allowing her to pay for the higher amount, or with the mortgage arrears paid off and equity in the property, the mortgage lender would allow a refinance, which would include paying off any pending unsecured creditors.

Using your number-crunching skills, you can try multiple ways of increasing future payments, and the plan is calculated automatically.

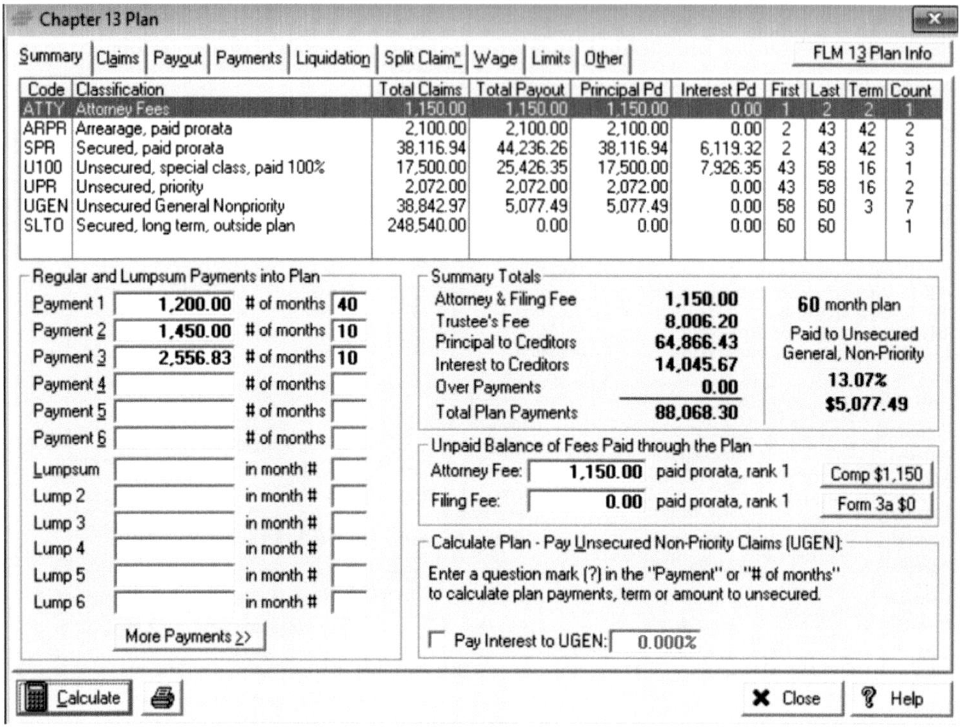

Best Case®

Another scenario where a step plan might work is where there is an expected increase in household income such as a spouse returning to work, whether part-time or full-time. Lump-sum calculations can also be tested if the debtor receives quarterly or year-end bonuses.

As you can see, Chapter 13 plans require flexibility and imagination. To further illustrate this, let's review two cases chosen from the Southern District of Florida that will also show the steps taken in a typical Chapter 13 case.

In the first case, the debtor had approximately $200 per month in disposable income. The debtor had negative DMI, and yes, that is possible since the means test is based on allowable IRS expenses that may exceed actual expenses.[11] Also, a debtor may pass the means test but still have disposable income available and vice-versa.[12] This is a common issue since some forms of income, such as Social Security disability income, are excluded from the means test.[13]

Here, the debtor had $6,466.64 in non-exempt property, most of which came from a paid-off vehicle. At the minimum, that is the amount that the unsecured creditors would

11 11 U.S.C. §707.
12 Id.
13 11 U.S.C. §522(d)(10)(A).

receive in liquidation with a Chapter 7. The unsecured creditors may receive more through Chapter 13, but that depends on the disposable income.

Notice that the attorney's fees are paid within 18 months, meaning this case would have been rejected by my colleague, but it was mathematically impossible to pay fees in a shorter time period. Anything shorter would have resulted in calculations exceeding the $200.00 per month available in disposable income. With the fees paid in 18 months, payments equal $192.50 per month, but $200.00 is paid since that is the amount of available disposable income, which, of course, benefits the unsecured creditors.

With the summary total in the previous figure, note that the unsecured creditors are receiving more than the value of non-exempt property. That's why this straightforward case was confirmed quickly. In total, $12,000.00 is paid into the plan, including $1,090.80 as the trustee's fee and the $3,150.00 in attorney's fees. The unsecured creditors receive $7,759.20, which is $1,292.56 more than would have been received in a Chapter 7 liquidation ($6,466.64).

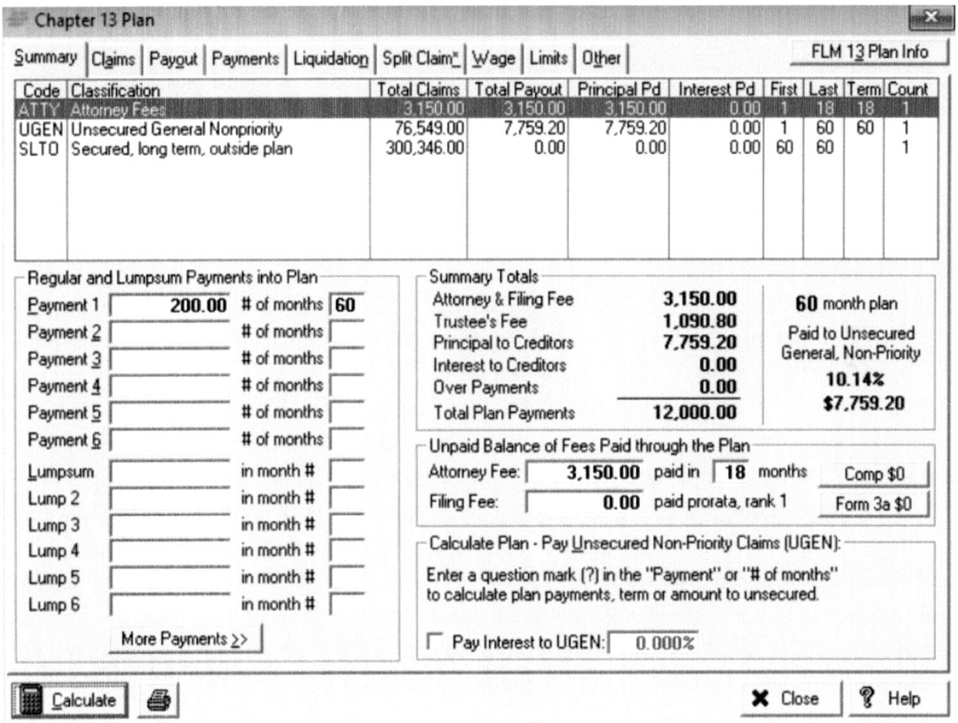

Best Case®

The total pro-rata share received by each creditor can be seen by clicking on the "claims" tab, and the "payout" tab shows the pro-rata monthly amount. Note the difference between the claim amount and the amount actually received through the plan.

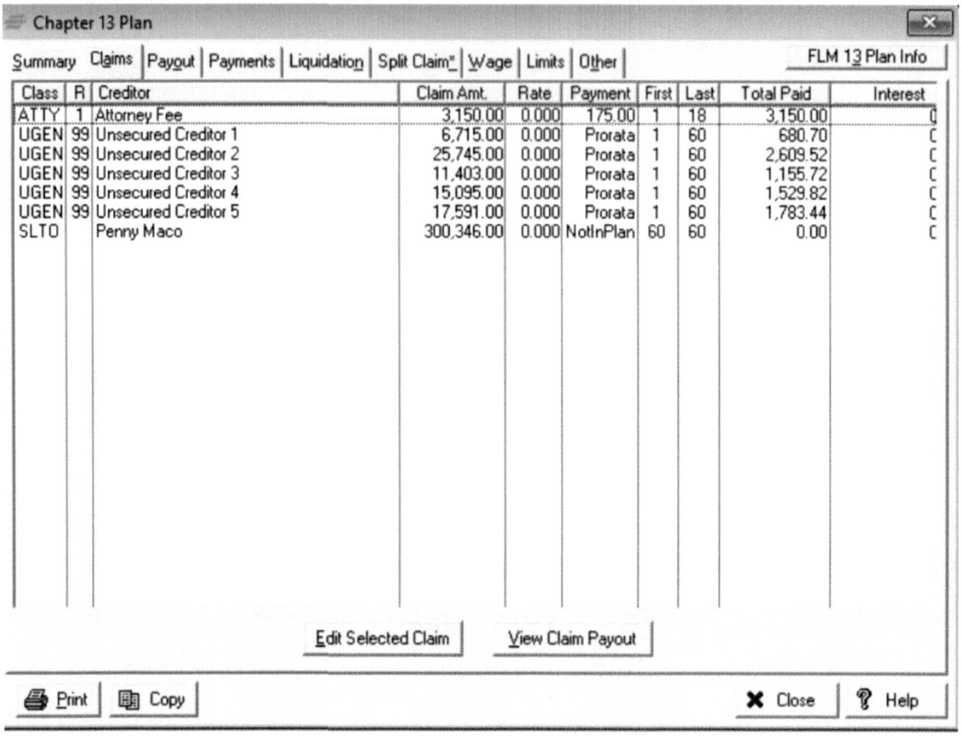

Class	R	Creditor	Claim Amt.	Rate	Payment	First	Last	Total Paid	Interest
ATTY	1	Attorney Fee	3,150.00	0.000	175.00	1	18	3,150.00	0
UGEN	99	Unsecured Creditor 1	6,715.00	0.000	Prorata	1	60	680.70	0
UGEN	99	Unsecured Creditor 2	25,745.00	0.000	Prorata	1	60	2,609.52	0
UGEN	99	Unsecured Creditor 3	11,403.00	0.000	Prorata	1	60	1,155.72	0
UGEN	99	Unsecured Creditor 4	15,095.00	0.000	Prorata	1	60	1,529.82	0
UGEN	99	Unsecured Creditor 5	17,591.00	0.000	Prorata	1	60	1,783.44	0
SLTO		Penny Maco	300,346.00	0.000	NotInPlan	60	60	0.00	0

Best Case®

This next case took longer to confirm as there were various issues such as cramdowns, substantial mortgage arrears, and various objections. Unlike our first case, the over-exempt amount is minimal at approximately $180.00. The arrears on the first mortgage was $50,031.21, there are two vehicles, each secured by a lien, and the balance of attorney's fees is $3,675.00. The regular monthly payment on the mortgage is $800.87.

In the figure below (please note certain parts have been whited out for privacy), we see that the petition was filed along with the credit counseling certificate, the debtor's pay stubs, and the attorney's compensation form. However, notice Docket #8 (Notice of Incomplete Filings) was filed by the clerk of court. Remember, the plan must be submitted within 14 days of filing.[14] The clerk's notice serves as a reminder to file the plan by a specific date. The trustee has also filed a list of required documents (Docket #10).

14 Supra, note 9.

Query Reports Utilities Logout

#	Docket Text
1 (52 pgs)	Chapter 13 Voluntary Petition . [Fee Amount $310]
2	Statement of Debtor(s) Social Security Number(s) [*Document Image Available ONLY to Court Users*] Filed by Debtor
3 (4 pgs)	Chapter 13 Statement of Your Current Monthly Income and Calculation of Commitment Period for 3 Years Form 122C-1. Disposable Income Is Not Determined Filed by Debtor
4 (1 pg)	Disclosure of Compensation by Attorney
5 (1 pg)	Certification of Budget and Credit Counseling Course by Debtor Filed by Debtor
6 (7 pgs)	Payment Advices by Debtor Filed by Debtor
	Receipt of Voluntary Petition (Chapter 13) [misc,volp13a] (310.00) Filing Fee. Receipt number Fee amount 310.00. (U.S. Treasury)
7 (1 pg)	Certification of Compliance and Request for Confirmation of Ch. 13 Plan Filed by Debtor
8 (1 pg)	Notice of Incomplete Filings Due. Chapter 13 Plan due by
9 (1 pg)	Request for Notice Filed by Creditor Synchrony Bank.
10 (8 pgs)	Trustee's Certificate of Service of Trustee's Notice of Required Documents

…tificate of Mailing (Re: 8 Notice of Incomplete Filings Due. Chapter 13 Plan due by 3/9/2020 [Incomplete Filings due by 3/9/2020]) Notice Date 02/27/2020. (Admin.)

CM/ECF

It seems the plan wasn't filed because the attorney was short on time. The mortgage arrears are substantial, and in reviewing the civil court docket, the mortgage lender had already filed a default against the debtor in a foreclosure action. So, the attorney quickly filed the petition and notice of the bankruptcy filing to take advantage of the automatic stay and stall the foreclosure.[15]

To make up for the deficiency filing, the debtor's attorney filed a motion for extension of time to file the plan, requesting an additional 15 days (Docket #12, see the next figure). The extension was granted by the court two days later (Docket #13). Now the debtor's attorney can take a deep breath, relax, and start crunching numbers.

11 (3 pgs)	BNC Certificate of Mailing (Re: 8 Notice of Incomplete Filings Due. Chapter 13 Plan due by
12 (1 pg)	*Ex Parte* Motion to Extend Time to File Plan, Filed by Debtor
13 (1 pg)	Order Granting Motion to Extend Time to File Schedules/Plan/Required Information. Deadline Extended through
14 (1 pg)	Certification of Completion of Instructional Course Concerning Personal Financial Management by Debtor ONLY Filed by Debtor
15 (1 pg)	Certification of Compliance and Request for Confirmation of Ch. 13 Plan Filed by Debtor
16 (3 pgs)	Chapter 13 Plan Filed by Debtor
17 (6 pgs; 2 docs)	Meeting of Creditors to be Held on Last Day to Oppose Discharge or Dischargeability is Proofs of Claim due by Confirmation Hearing to be Held on at C. Clyde Atkins U.S. Courthouse, 301 N Miami Ave Courtroom 8 (LMI), Miami, FL 33128. Objection to Confirmation Deadline:
18 (5 pgs)	BNC Certificate of Mailing (Re: 17 Meeting of Creditors to be Held on at 51 SW First Ave Room 102, Miami. Last Day to Oppose Discharge or Dischargeability is Proofs of Claim due by Confirmation Hearing to be Held on at C. Clyde Atkins U.S. Courthouse, 301 N Miami Ave Courtroom 8 (LMI), Miami, FL 33128. Objection to Confirmation Deadline:
19 (5 pgs)	BNC Certificate of Mailing - PDF Document (Re: 17 Meeting of Creditors to be Held on at 51 SW First Ave Room 102, Miami. Last Day to Oppose Discharge or Dischargeability is . Proofs of Claim due by . Confirmation Hearing to be Held on at 01:30 PM at C. Clyde Atkins U.S. Courthouse, 301 N Miami Ave Courtroom 8 (LMI), Miami, FL 33128. Objection to Confirmation Deadline: Notice Date
20 (2 pgs)	Amended Meeting of Creditors. Meeting of Creditors to be Held on . by TELEPHONE [See Meeting Notice for details]. Last Day to Oppose Discharge or Dischargeability is Proofs of Claim due by .Confirmation Hearing to be Held on at 01:30 PM by TELEPHONE. To participate call CourtCall (888) 882-6878. Objection to Confirmation Deadline:

CM/ECF

15 Official Form 309I. Notice of Chapter 13 Bankruptcy Case.

Twenty-two days after the petition had been filed, the debtor completed the financial management course (Docket #14). The plan was filed on the final day it was due per the court's order (Docket #16) as well as the Certification of Compliance and Request for Confirmation of the Chapter 13 Plan (Docket #15).[16] For months one through five, the original plan had $735.00 per month as attorney's fees and the mortgage arrears payment at $139.35. Months six through 60 had $897.54 per month applied to the mortgage arrears, and $4.55 per month was available for unsecured general creditors. Remember, the non-exempt assets were minimal in this case.

Because of the motion to extend the time to file the plan, the Meeting of Creditors was rescheduled 59 days after the petition had been filed (Docket #17), but then it was rescheduled almost a month later for a total of 87 days since the day of filing (Docket #20). The rescheduling was most likely because the trustee needed additional time to review the petition and the plan.

The rescheduling of the creditors' meeting resulted in the Confirmation Hearing also being rescheduled (Docket #21, see the next figure). A total of 94 days have passed since the petition was filed, so the attorney has strategically taken advantage of the automatic stay by delaying the foreclosure for more than three months. Granted, during this time, the debtor did have to make plan payments.[17] Now that the trustee has viewed the file, the trustee filed a Notice of Deficiency (Docket #22). The trustee's deficiency notice highlighted several issues. Each one will be discussed.

21 (4 pgs)	BNC Certificate of Mailing (Re: 20 Amended Meeting of Creditors. Meeting of Creditors to be Held on by TELEPHONE [See Meeting Notice for details]. Last Day to Oppose Discharge or Dischargeability is Proofs of Claim due by . .Confirmation Hearing to be Held on by TELEPHONE. To participate call CourtCall (888) 882-6878. Objection to Confirmation Deadline:
22 (1 pg)	Chapter 13 Trustee's Notice of Deficiency for Confirmation
23 (2 pgs)	Chapter 13 Trustee's Notice of Deficiency for Confirmation
24 (2 pgs)	Motion to Value and Determine Secured Status of Lien on Personal Property Held by
25 (1 pg)	Notice of Hearing by Filer (Re: 24 Motion to Value and Determine Secured Status of Lien on Personal Property Held by Chapter 13 Hearing scheduled for by TELEPHONE. To participate call Court Solutions (917) 746-7476.
26 (1 pg)	Certificate of Service Filed by Debtor (Re: 24 Motion to Value and Determine Secured Status of Lien on Personal Property Held by , 25 Notice of Hearing by Filer filed by Debtor
27	**FILLABLE DOCUMENT - RESTRICTED**First Amended Chapter 13 Plan (Re:16 Chapter 13 Plan filed by Debtor
28 (1 pg)	Notice to Withdraw Document Filed by Debtor (Re: 27 Amended Chapter 13 Plan).
29 (3 pgs)	First Amended Chapter 13 Plan (Re:16 Chapter 13 Plan filed by Debtor
30 (3 pgs)	Certificate of Service Filed by Debtor (Re: 29 Amended Chapter 13 Plan filed by Debtor
31 (1 pg)	Motion to Waive Wage Deduction Order Filed by Debtor

CM/ECF

One issue was that the attorney was cramming down one of the vehicles, but not only has the cramdown not been approved by the judge, but the motion also had yet to be filed!

16 Local Form 67, revised December 1, 2009; Local Rule 3015-3(B)(2).

17 11 U.S.C. §1326(a)(1).

The attorney responded by filing a Motion to Value and Determine Secured Status of Lien on Personal Property (Docket #24). The Notice of Hearing (Docket #25) and Certificate of Service were filed (Docket #26). The judge granted the motion (Docket #41, see the next figure). Note that docket entries make references. For example, here, there is a reference to Docket #24, which was the motion.

Query	Reports Utilities Logout
32 (1 pg)	Notice of Hearing by Filer (Re: 31 Motion to Waive Wage Deduction Order Filed by Debtor Chapter 13 Hearing scheduled for TELEPHONE. To participate call Court Solutions (917) 746-7476.
33 (3 pgs)	Certificate of Service Filed by Debtor (Re: 31 Motion to Waive Wage Deduction Order filed by Debtor , 32 Notice of Hearing by Filer filed by Debtor
34 (5 pgs)	Objection to Claim of [# 06], Filed by Debtor
35 (1 pg)	Notice of Hearing by Filer (Re: 34 Objection to Claim of Mortgage Filed by Debtor Chapter 13 Hearing scheduled for by TELEPHONE. To participate call Court Solutions
36 (1 pg)	Certificate of Service Filed by Debtor (Re: 34 Objection to Claim of filed by Debtor 35 Notice of Hearing by Filer filed by Debtor
37 (4 pgs)	Notice of Postpetition Mortgage Fees, Expenses, and Charges (No Proof of Claim Filed) with Certificate of Service Filed by Creditor
38 (1 pg)	Chapter 13 Trustee's Notice of Deficiency for Confirmation
39 (1 pg)	Order Granting Motion To Waive Wage Deduction Order (Re: # 31)
40 (1 pg)	Order Sustaining Objection to Claim(s) (Re: # 34).
41 (2 pgs)	Order Granting Motion To Value and Determine Secured Status of Lien on Personal Property (Re: # 24).
42 (2 pgs)	Order Continuing Confirmation Hearing (Re: 29 Amended Chapter 13 Plan filed by Debtor Confirmation Hearing to be Held on by TELEPHONE. To participate call Court Solutions

CM/ECF

Docket #27 was the First Amended Plan, but due to an error, a request was made to withdraw it (Docket #28), and the corrected First Amended Plan was filed (Docket #29). There are three differences between the original and First Amended Plan. In the trustee's deficiency notice, a box was not checked off, confirming that association dues and payments for the second vehicle were being paid outside of the plan. Note that a cramdown was not sought on the second vehicle because the debt was incurred within 910 days.[18] The second issue is that the mortgage company filed a proof of claim, and the address listed for notice was different than the address listed in the plan. Finally, the arrears in the original plan was \$50,031.21, but it wasn't until the Second Amended Plan was filed that arrears were corrected to reflect \$50,800.53.

The next deficiency was that a Wage Deduction Order was not provided, so plan payments could be withdrawn from the debtor's pay stub. In response, the attorney filed a motion to have it waived (Docket #31).

The hearing for the waiver of the Wage Deduction Order was scheduled (Docket #32, see the next figure), the Certificate of Service filed (Docket #33), and the order was granted (Docket #39). Wage Deduction Orders facilitate receiving timely payments since the withdrawals are made by the employer and sent directly to the trustee. But requesting a waiver is also common, as is the granting of that request. The waiver request is usually because a debtor doesn't want anybody to "know their business." Since bankruptcy can be considered

18 11 U.S.C.A. §506.

a private matter and even an embarrassing situation, the fewer people know, the better. I don't remember ever losing a motion to waive the Wage Deduction Order, but it's also fact-specific. For example, what if the debtor works remotely and doesn't speak or even know who is in human resources. I teach remotely, and I can guarantee that HR has no idea who I am, so it may be challenging to win the motion based on those facts. But, what if it is a small company? Imagine a dental office that may have a couple of hygienists and a receptionist. Could the results be different? I would argue yes, and since a bankruptcy filing is a public record, nothing prevents the employee in charge of payroll from telling others, no matter how unprofessional that may be.

Docket #34 includes an objection by the debtor's attorney on the monthly mortgage amount. The mortgage company claimed that payments were $1,127.28 per month, but the attorney objected and filed the mortgage statement confirming the payment amount of $800.87. The hearing was held the same day as that of the Wage Deduction Order and motion for cramdown. The debtor's attorney's objection was sustained (Docket #40), and the Confirmation Hearing was continued (Docket #42).

As a result of the hearing, the mortgage arrears were determined to be $50,800.53, which required amending the plan (trustee's deficiency notice, Docket #43, see the next figure). The trustee's deficiency notice also referenced the order on the cramdown was not specific as to the balance on the secured and unsecured portion of the debt. An amended order was filed to correct the error (Docket #44). The lender also agreed to reduce the claim/loan balance to $6,000.00 with 5.25% interest, for a total of $6,834.95, the same amounts in the original plan. The original claim was for $21,382.00, but the cramdown caused $16,510.09 to become a general unsecured claim. That resulted in savings to the client of $15,382.00 plus interest, and the car will be paid off in five years! The third plan (Second Amended Plan) was filed (Docket #45).

Query	Reports Utilities Logout
43 (1 pg)	Chapter 13 Trustee's Notice of Deficiency for Confirmation
44 (2 pgs)	Amended Order (Re: 41 Order on Motion to Value and Determine Secured Status of Lien on Personal Property).
45 (3 pgs)	Second Amended Chapter 13 Plan (Re:29 Amended Chapter 13 Plan filed by Debtor
46 (3 pgs)	Certificate of Service Filed by Debtor (Re: 45 Amended Chapter 13 Plan filed by Debtor
47 (2 pgs)	Notice of Continued Confirmation Hearing Filed by Trustee (Re: 45 Amended Chapter 13 Plan). Confirmation Hearing to be Held on TELEPHONE through CourtSolutions LLC.
48 (1 pg)	Chapter 13 Trustee's Notice of Deficiency for Confirmation
49 (2 pgs)	Notice of Continued Confirmation Hearing Filed by Trustee (Re: 45 Amended Chapter 13 Plan). Confirmation Hearing to be Held on TELEPHONE through CourtSolutions LLC.
50 (3 pgs)	Third Amended Chapter 13 Plan (Re:45 Amended Chapter 13 Plan filed by Debtor Filed by Debtor
51 (3 pgs)	Certificate of Service Filed by Debtor (Re: 50 Amended Chapter 13 Plan filed by Debtor
52 (1 pg)	Chapter 13 Trustee's Notice of Deficiency for Confirmation
53 (1 pg)	Amended Chapter 13 Trustee's Notice of Deficiency for Confirmation
54	Trustee's Request for Entry of Order Confirming Chapter 13 Third Amended Plan After Confirmation Hearing [Confirmation Hearing Date:

CM/ECF

In Docket #37, the mortgage company did file a motion for post-petition fees. This could have been due to several factors, but in this case, it was about reviewing the plan and additional documents. Since the lender sought an additional $450.00, the trustee filed another deficiency notice (Docket #48). The lender's request was reasonable, and since the parties reached an agreement, the Third Amended Plan was filed (Docket #50) that included a total of $950 in post-petition fees. The trustee followed up with another deficiency notice (Docket #52), where the trustee wanted to distinguish between mortgage arrears and post-petition fees. When the trustee realized that the Third Amended Plan clarified this issue, the deficiency notice was amended (Docket #53) and submitted the plan to the court for confirmation.

From the date of filing till the day of confirmation was a total of 238 days. Below is the comparison between each plan.

ORIGINAL PLAN

Months	Attorney's fees	Mortgage arrears payment	Car payment	Unsecured creditors
1–5	$735.00	$139.35	$139.35	–
6–60	–	$897.54	$111.61	$4.55

* Mortgage arrears at $50,031.21.

FIRST AMENDED PLAN

Months	Attorney's fees	Mortgage arrears payment	Car payment	Unsecured creditors
1–5	$735.00	$139.35	$139.35	–
6–60	–	$897.54	$111.61	$4.55

* Same figures as original plan, but mortgage lender's address updated.

SECOND AMENDED PLAN

Months	Attorney's fees	Mortgage arrears payment	Car payment	Unsecured creditors
1–5	$735.00	$151.62	$151.62	–
6–60	–	$909.87	$110.49	$17.88

* Mortgage arrears increased to $50,800.53

THIRD AMENDED PLAN

Months	Attorney's fees	Mortgage arrears payment	Car payment	Unsecured creditors
1–5	$735.00	$151.62	$151.62	–
6–6	–	$909.87	–	–
6–60	–	–	$110.49	17.88
7–60	–	$927.47	–	–

* Mortgage arrears remained at $50,800.53, but $950 in post-petition fees were added for a total of $51,1750.53.

Note that in the third amended plan, which by now included the correct amount of mortgage arrearages and post-petition fees on behalf of the mortgage lender, there was a separate pay period for month six, and then another for the remaining months, hence, a step plan.

SUMMARY

The first step in a Chapter 13 case is to classify the debts as either secured, priority unsecured, or unsecured. Next, confirm the amount of the trustee's fee in your district and adjust the percentage if necessary. Note that payments will be either fixed, pro-rata, or not included in the plan.

Calculating the plan for a Chapter 13 requires flexibility, imagination, and the ability to crunch numbers. Each case is unique. In one case, attorney's fees can be paid in ten months, but in another case, attorney's fees are extended to qualify the debtor and sufficiently fund the plan. This may include using a step plan which results in payments of varying amounts.

The plan, which is due within 14 days of filing the petition, will likely be modified several times before a case is confirmed. The reasons for amending plans vary, such as additional proof of claims filed by creditors, incorrect arrearage amounts, cramdown, or the stripping of a mortgage. At times, even though a cramdown is allowed, number-crunching proves that the secured debt can't be paid before the plan is completed.

KEYWORDS AND TERMS

- Deficiency filing
- Suggestion of bankruptcy
- Step plan
- Wage Deduction Order

DISCUSSION QUESTIONS

1. What is the amount of the trustee fee in your district?
2. Give three examples of a Notice of Deficiency filing.

PRACTICE QUESTIONS AND EXERCISES

1. Where did you find the fee for the trustee in your district? Provide the link.
2. If the trustee fee in your district is different from the standard ten percent fee, update it in the case jurisdiction feature.
3. Draw a timeline of a Chapter 13 case.
4. Prepare a petition and plan that includes a second mortgage being stripped off.
5. Prepare a step plan.

REFERENCES

11 U.S.C. §341.

11 U.S.C. §506.

11 U.S.C. §522.

11 U.S.C. §707.

11 U.S.C. § 1326.

Fed. R. Bankr. P. 3015.

Local Form 67, revised 12/1/2009.

Local Rule 3015-3.

Official Form 106D. Schedule D: Creditors Who Hold Claims Secured By Property (Individuals).

Official Form 106 E/F. Schedule E/F: Creditors Who Have Unsecured Claims (Individuals).

Official Form 106G. Schedule G: Executory Contracts and Unexpired Leases (Individuals).

Official Form 106I. Schedule I: Your Income (Individuals).

Official Form 106J. Schedule J: Your Expenses (Individuals).

Official Form 113. Chapter 13 Plan.

Official Form 122A-1. Chapter 7 Statement of Your Current Monthly Income.

Official Form 309I. Notice of Chapter 13 Bankruptcy Case.

CHAPTER 24

Chapter 20 Bankruptcy

Strategies, Winning by Losing, and Financial Purgatory

COMBINING BANKRUPTCY STRATEGIES

In this chapter, we're going to discuss strategies that can be used in and outside of bankruptcy, especially when neither a Chapter 7 nor 13 benefits the debtor. Remember the debt limits for Chapter 7? Correct, there are none. What about for Chapter 13? Don't remember? That's okay. See 11 U.S.C. §109.

What happens if a debtor owns a home with a second mortgage that is underwater? The first option you should be considering is *lien stripping* with Chapter 13. Unfortunately, between medical bills and a foreclosure on non-homestead property, the debtor's unsecured debt total exceeds the Chapter 13 debt limits. The debtor still has the option of filing Chapter 7, but there's nothing that could be done about the underwater mortgage.

Chapter 11 is another option, but considering the complexity and costs, it's not recommended unless the debtor has substantial assets and debts. Too bad we can't take the sections of the Code we like and combine them to make another chapter, or can we? What if the debtor filed for Chapter 20? "*What? There's no Chapter 20 bankruptcy in the Code!*" You are correct. But who mentioned the Code? "*So, I am about to learn about a chapter in bankruptcy that doesn't exist? This will be interesting.*" It is, but all you have to know is the answer to this question: what is seven plus 13?

Since the debtor qualifies for Chapter 7, the slate could be wiped clean. But as you already know, Chapter 7 isn't going to allow for the cramdown of a car loan or strip off a second mortgage or buy more time to handle non-dischargeable debts, but Chapter 13 can. So the debtor files Chapter 7 first to eliminate the unsecured debt, then Chapter 13 to strip junior liens.

Of course, Chapter 20 doesn't apply in most cases, and in some jurisdictions, it's prohibited, but that's where local knowledge comes into play. Also, the trustee could object as a "bad faith" filing. Another downside is if Chapter 13 wasn't filed four years after Chapter 7, the debtor isn't entitled to a discharge, but depending on the jurisdiction, the debtor could still strip the mortgage or get the cramdown. Worst case scenario, the debtor could always wait four years. Considering the financial benefits, it's worth the wait.

DOI: 10.4324/9781003203278-25

WINNING BY LOSING

Let's continue with the contradictions. "*How can you win by losing? Next thing you are going to tell me is to dismiss a Chapter 13 case on purpose, and by doing so, the debtor wins.*" You read my mind! That's exactly what I am saying!

We know the advantages of filing Chapter 13, and one of those benefits is allowing the debtor to catch up on arrears for secured debt. Once the debtor is current with arrears, the unsecured creditors start to receive their pro-rata share, which at a minimum, is the same amount that would have been received in a liquidation of a Chapter 7 case. Go back to the first case from the previous chapter where the debtor had $200 per month in disposable income. In that case, the unsecured creditors were receiving more than had the debtor filed for Chapter 7. However, if the debtor stops making plan payments, the case gets dismissed, and the balance is owed to the unsecured creditors. How does this help the debtor?

Suppose that an unsecured creditor was to receive $10 per month for 20 months, a total of $200 through the plan. There's a good chance the creditor is willing to settle with a lump sum payment instead of receiving $200 spread out over almost two years. If the creditors don't want to negotiate, that's fine because the debtor still has the protection of Chapter 13.

The fact is, the faster that a debtor can get out of bankruptcy, the faster they can return to financial normalcy. Dismissals are common and used strategically to pay off creditors quicker. However, notice the dismissal doesn't have to be solely by missing payments. It could be requested as well.[1] For example, if the lender is willing to extend a home equity line of credit or refinance the mortgage, the funds could be used to pay off the unsecured creditors. Unsecured creditors aren't going to object to receiving their money today versus two years from now. Besides dismissal, there's also the option of converting from Chapter 13 to 7 or vice-versa.[2]

FINANCIAL PURGATORY

Unfortunately, there will be clients for whom neither Chapter 7 nor 13 is a viable option. They are stuck somewhere in the middle. For example, in North Carolina, the homestead exemption is $35,000 for a single person.[3] If that person has minimal income or is disabled, they may not qualify for Chapter 13 and risk losing their home with Chapter 7. In Florida, while the homestead exemption is probably one of the most generous in the country, it also has its limits. When I resided in Miami, owning a half-acre lot was unheard of, but it's more common in northern Florida. I've had clients living in mobile homes that should be condemned, have limited income, or are disabled but live on a one-acre lot. They will lose their land with Chapter 7, and they don't earn enough to fund a Chapter 13 plan. Even recently,

1 11 U.S.C.A. §349.
2 11 U.S.C.A. §348
3 N.C. Gen. Stat. Ann. § 1C-1601.

in the Middle District of Florida, a court ruled in favor of a trustee that a resident of Florida for more than two decades could not claim homestead exemption because the debtor had no legal immigration status.[4] So, how do we handle these cases?

The only option left for debtors is to negotiate a debt settlement. Non-profit organizations can assist clients in this regard, and it's a good option if there are multiple creditors. The payment plans offered by the non-profits are usually 60 months, like Chapter 13. Sometimes, this may even be a better option for the debtor to begin with because they skip the expense of attorney's fees and the consequences of filing for bankruptcy and up to five years where a debtor has limited financial mobility.

FINANCIAL PURGATORY 2.0

If there's a topic that's sure to lead to debate and leave debtors in financial limbo, it's student loans, which have become a social, political, and financial issue. Student loan debt is a $1.73 trillion hole that keeps growing by the day and is second in household debt to mortgages.[5] The issue is whether student loans should be discharged in bankruptcy, canceled by executive order, Congressional action, or nothing done at all.

More than 44 million Americans have student loans, and pre-pandemic levels had more than 11 percent in default by more than 90 days, which, of course, does horrors to credit scores.[6] The average college student graduates with $28,950.00 in student loan debt, but as the student climbs the educational ladder, so does the debt.[7] The average debt amount is $201,490 for medical school graduates, $292,169 for dental school graduates, $179,514 for pharmacy school graduates, $149,877 for veterinary school graduates, and $82,800 for graduate students.[8] These figures don't even factor in other forms of debt, such as credit card debt and secured debt like a car loan.

If the average household has $57,520 in student loan debt, that's $57,520 less available toward the purchase of a new home, car, and retirement.[9] It means having children later in life when finances are hopefully more stable. It means mortgages take longer to pay off if paid off at all, and nest eggs will be smaller come retirement. It means that employment may be denied, especially by the federal government, if the loans are in default. As credit scores tumble, it also means being denied loans or paying a higher interest rate.

4 In re de Bauer, 6:20-BK-04228-KSJ, 2021 WL 912678 (Bankr. M.D. Fla. Mar. 10, 2021).

5 Anna Helhoski and Ryan Lane. Student Loan Debt Statistics: 2021. Nerdwallet.com, May 13, 2021, retrieved on May 19, 2021. www.nerdwallet.com/article/loans/student-loans/student-loan-debt#:~:text=2020%20Student%20Loan%20Debt%20Statistics%201%20Average%20student,Income-driven%20repayment%20use.%20...%207%20FAFSA%20completion.%20.

6 A Look at the Shocking Student Loan Debt Statistics for 2021. Retrieved on July 23, 2021. https://studentloanhero.com/student-loan-debt-statistics/.

7 Supra note 5.

8 Id.

9 Id.

Just as worrisome, parents of student loan borrowers are co-signing loans or borrowing independently, so if the borrower defaults, the lender sues the parents. As parents near retirement, they may have substantial assets that aren't exempt in bankruptcy. The consequences are either the older generation filing for bankruptcy in record numbers or working past retirement age to make ends meet. Fourteen percent of parents have an estimated $37,200 in federal parent PLUS loans.[10]

So, I ask you: is the United States facing a student loan debt crisis? You may answer no because those saddled by student loan debt have the same options as everyone else: bankruptcy. Well, not really. For a student loan to be discharged in bankruptcy, the debtor is required to prove it would cause an "undue hardship."

The *Brunner* Test

What is an "undue hardship?" We don't know because Congress failed to define the term under §523, which has been left to the courts to decide, resulting in inconsistent rulings. However, at least the majority of courts have defined "undue hardship" according to the standard outlined in *Brunner v. N.Y. State Higher Educ. Servs. Corp.*, 831 F.2d 395, 396 (2d Cir. 1987).

Known as the *Brunner* test, the debtor must prove three things:

(1) The debtor cannot maintain, based on current income and expenses, a "minimal" standard of living for himself and his dependents if forced to repay the loans.
(2) Additional circumstances exist indicating that the debtor's inability to pay is likely to persist for a significant portion of the repayment period of the student loans.
(3) The debtor has made good faith efforts to repay the loans.[11]

The *Brunner* test has been adopted in the U.S. Courts of Appeals for the Second, Third, Fourth, Fifth, Sixth, Seventh, Ninth, Tenth, and Eleventh Circuits, including the U.S. Bankruptcy Court for the District of Columbia.[12] The First and Eighth Circuit have adopted the "totality-of-the-circumstances test."[13]

In the First Circuit, "all relevant evidence" is considered and includes factors such as the debtor's income and expenses, health, age, education level, the amount of the payments, the ability to find a higher-paying job, and other circumstances such as the number of dependents.[14]

10 Supra, note 5.
11 Brunner, 831 F.2d at 396.
12 Congressional Research Service. *Bankrupty and Student Loans*. July 18, 2019. https://crsreports.congress.gov. https://fas.org/sgp/crs/misc/R45113.pdf
13 Id. at pp. 32–33.
14 Id., citing *Schatz v. U.S. Dep't of Educ.* (In re Schatz), 584 B.R. 1, 7-9 (Bankr. D. Mass. 2018).

The Eighth Circuit considers the debtor's dependents and reasonable living expenses, as well as the debtor's past, present, and reasonably reliable future financial resources.[15] In addition, a laundry list of other relevant factors is considered.[16]

At best, the *Brunner* standard is vague and highly subjective. What's a minimal standard of living? I would love to live in an RV, but if someone had no choice but to live in one, is that a minimal standard of living? How can you predict if someone's financial situation is likely to remain the same throughout the repayment period? How many years of payments are required to show a "good faith effort?" If the debtor couldn't afford payments and sought forbearances, does that show a lack of good faith, or does making minimal payments help? Add this all up, and what do you get? Inconsistency and the inability to discharge student loans in bankruptcy. So what option does the debtor have? For a debtor to attempt to discharge student loans in bankruptcy, the first step is filing an adversary which is found in Part VII of the Federal Rules of Bankruptcy Procedure. The adversary process is reviewed in Chapter 27.

SUMMARY

While bankruptcy is usually the last resort for clients, the fact remains that bankruptcy isn't always in the client's best interests and sometimes will cause more harm than good. When faced with that situation, clients still have other options available.

One option is for clients to file for Chapter 7 to eliminate unsecured debt, then Chapter 13 to strip a mortgage or cram down a vehicle. This tactic is known as Chapter 20. Another strategy is walking away altogether from a pending Chapter 13 to have it dismissed or file for dismissal. This strategy works best when the creditors are willing to negotiate a settlement.

Finally, some clients never even make it to bankruptcy. For example, the equity in their homestead isn't protected. In these cases, clients should seek to negotiate with creditors individually or retain a non-profit organization/debt management company that will assist the debtor with a payment plan to settle the debts. Others have non-dischargeable debts like student loans that require the debtor to file an adversary.

KEYWORDS AND TERMS

- Adversary proceeding
- *Brunner* test
- Chapter 20 bankruptcy
- Converting
- Debt management company

15 Id., citing *Andrews v. S.D. Student Loan Assistance Corp.* (In re Andrews), 661 F.2d 702 (8th Cir. 1981).
16 Id., see *Andrews* at 553.

DISCUSSION QUESTIONS

1. Explain a Chapter 20 bankruptcy to a classmate who is acting as a client.
2. When should a case be dismissed versus converted?

PRACTICE QUESTIONS AND EXERCISES

1. Prepare a motion to convert a Chapter 13 to a Chapter 7 and another motion converting from Chapter 7 to 13.
2. Prepare a motion to dismiss a Chapter 13.
3. Complete the Adversary Proceeding Cover Sheet (Form 1040).
4. Find online an adversary complaint that was filed, and use it as a template to prepare one for discharging student loans.
5. Summarize the deadlines for initiating a complaint to determine dischargeability of a debt or an objection to the debtor's discharge?

REFERENCES

11 U.S.C. §109.

11 U.S.C. §348.

11 U.S.C. §349.

11 U.S.C. §523.

11 U.S.C. §727.

"A Look at the Shocking Student Loan Debt Statistics for 2021." https://studentloanhero.com/student-loan-debt-statistics/.

Andrews v. S.D. Student Loan Assistance Corp. (In re Andrews), 661 F.2d 702 (8th Cir. 1981).

Anna Helhoski and Ryan Lane, "Student Loan Debt Statistics: 2021" (Nerdwallet.com, May 13, 2021). www.nerdwallet.com/article/loans/student-loans/student-loan-debt#:~:text=2020%20Student%20Loan%20Debt%20Statistics%201%20Average%20student,Income-driven%20repayment%20use.%20...%207%20FAFSA%20completion.%20.

Brunner v. N.Y. State Higher Educ. Servs. Corp., 831 F.2d 395, 396 (2d Cir. 1987).

Congressional Research Service, "Bankruptcy and Student Loans" (July 18, 2019). https://crsreports.congress.gov.

In re de Bauer, 6:20-BK-04228-KSJ, 2021 WL 912678 (Bankr. M.D. Fla. Mar. 10, 2021).

N.C. Gen. Stat. Ann. §1C-1601.

Schatz v. U.S. Dep't of Educ., 584 B.R. 1, 7-9 (Bankr. D. Mass. 2018).

CHAPTER 25

Filing a Bankruptcy Petition

You made it! But before you file your first bankruptcy petition, it's time for a quick review. Check the "notes" section or case file. Does anything remain pending? Were all the required documents provided?

After each section of the petition has been reviewed, double-check for mistakes, but this time in PDF format. The different look makes finding errors easier. To convert the petition to PDF, it's the same steps as for filing the petition.

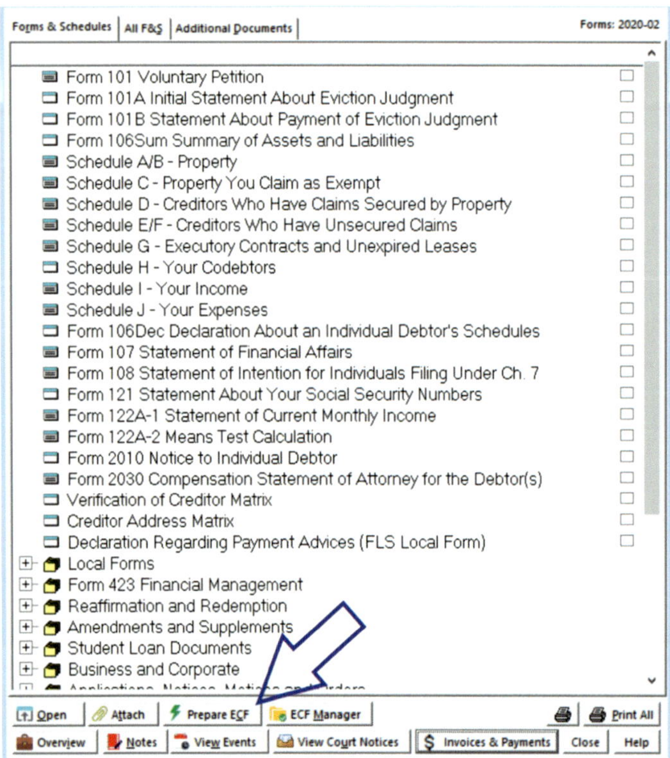

Best Case®

DOI: 10.4324/9781003203278-26

Upon clicking "Prepare ECF," you have the option of filing a complete petition or a "bare-bones" petition. I've never filed a bare-bones petition, but for some attorneys, it seems common practice. Sometimes the attorney may file a deficient petition because the bankruptcy filing is only to take advantage of the automatic stay. Since the attorney knows the client isn't proceeding with the bankruptcy and is only looking to buy time, the thought is why bother doing all the work. Personally, I don't buy into that school of thought. I reason that I want to defeat every argument before it even starts. Clients who complain, ask for a refund, or file a bar complaint result in interruptions and more time working on a file. Clients can always argue that they didn't understand what was being filed or that the procedure wasn't explained. Filing a bare-bones petition opens the door to these issues, but if a completed petition is filed, then at a minimum, the attorney's fee was earned. Plus, you never know if a judge is going to start cracking down on bare-bones petitions that have been filed to take advantage of the automatic stay, which in and of itself is considered a bad faith filing.[1] Some attorneys file a bare-bones petition as a way to not draw too much attention from the U.S. Trustee's Office since the debtor has a substantial amount of unsecured debt, then amend the schedules later.

However, there are valid reasons for filing a bare-bones petition – for example, being retained at the last second with a pending sale date on a foreclosure, as in the real case in Chapter 23. But, as a general rule, I avoid filing a bare-bones petition because the lazy man works double. The petition at some point has to be amended, which takes up more time and work, plus amending some schedules requires additional costs.

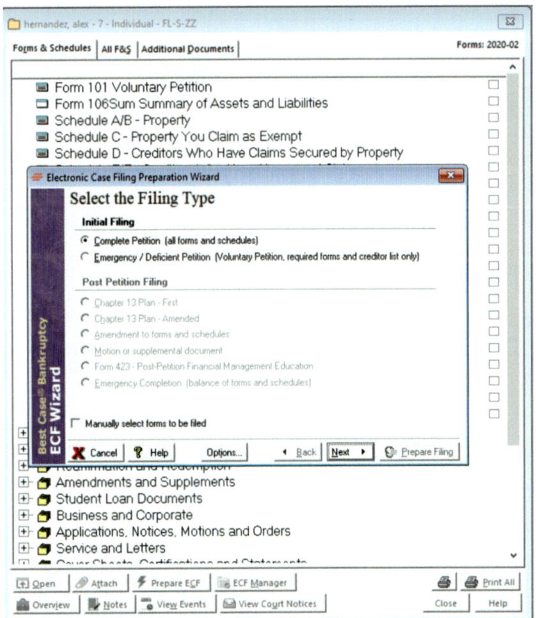

Best Case®

1 See In re: Maurice Symonette, Case 18-15891 BKC-LMI, Chapter 12.

Upon clicking the "next" button, the program converts the petition into a PDF format. All documents filed with the clerk's office are required to be in PDF format. The option also exists to only print specific schedules or sections of the petition. If the petition has not been properly completed, any errors or potential issues are highlighted. In this example, the means test is outdated.[2]

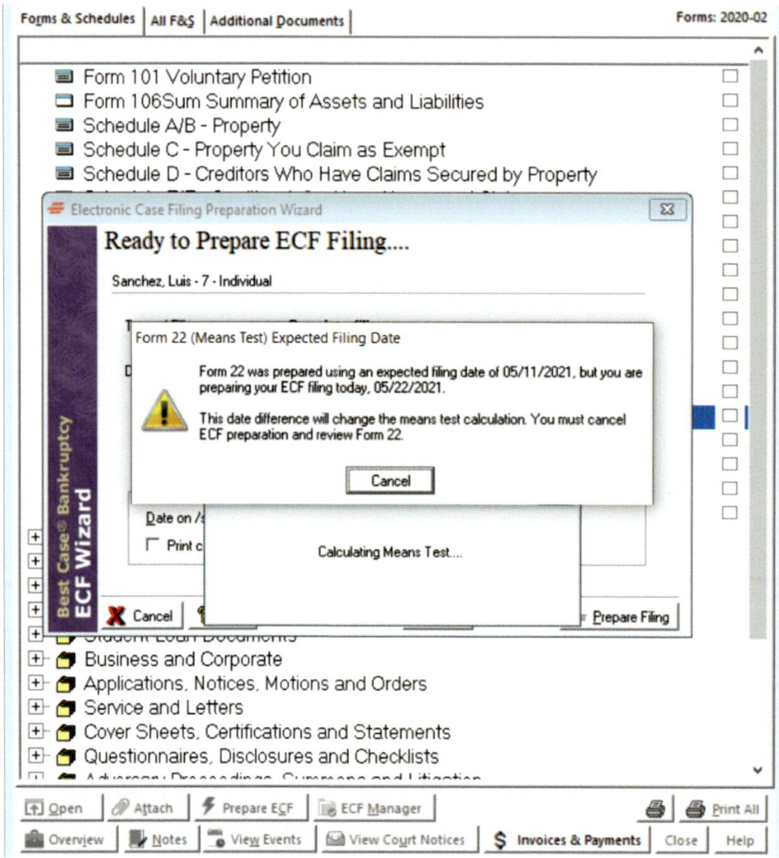

Best Case®

Once converted to PDF, click the petition to review it. The PDF version can be saved or, depending on the law firm's computer network, the petition can also be accessed through the ECF file folder and attached in an email. This will save you considerable time since you won't need to print the petition, scan it, then email it to the client. Remember to click "Erase Files," as that deletes previous versions of the petition. If you click "Delete File," that is only deleting that specific document. As a result, the information won't update, and a previous draft is being filed.

2 Official From 122A-1. Chapter 7 Statement of Your Current Monthly Income.

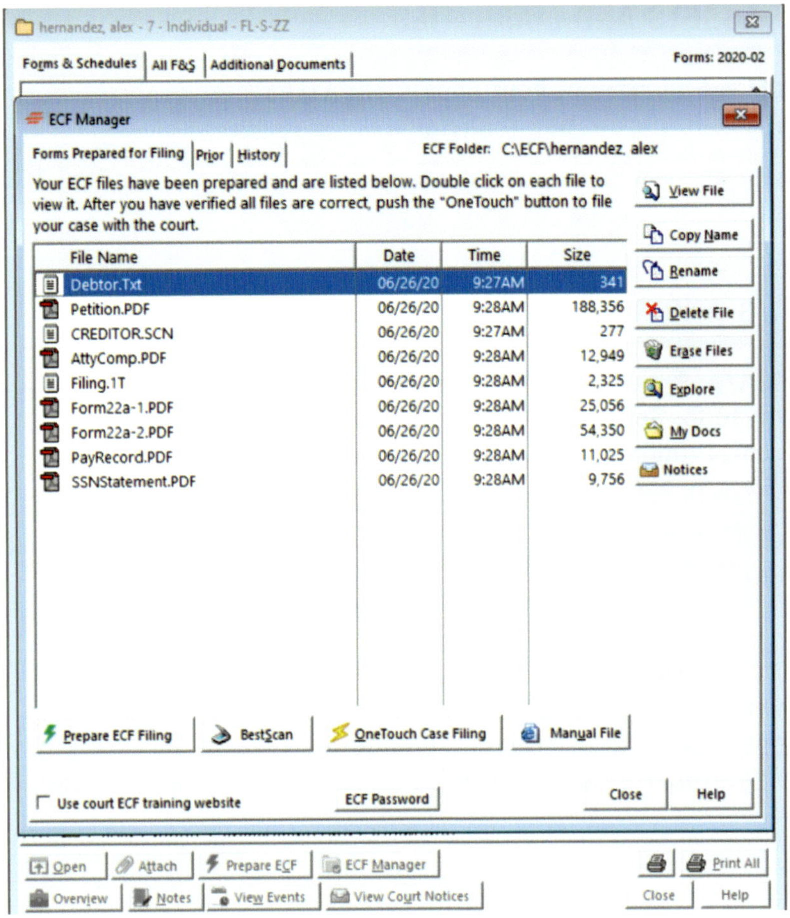

Best Case®

Below is a summary of some of the key sections to review for common errors.

Official Form 101: Voluntary Petition for Individuals Filing for Bankruptcy

1. Make certain the client's name and address match with other forms of identification. If the credit reports list other names used in the past, include those names as well.
2. List previous bankruptcies and confirm there are no issues with refiling.
3. Confirm the credit counseling certificate hasn't expired and matches the date listed on the petition. Verify the same for a joint filing.

SUMMARY OF ASSETS AND LIABILITIES

Official Form 106: A Summary of Your Assets and Liabilities and Certain Statistical Information (Individuals)

1. Review the summary, look for anything that seems out of place, whether substantial assets, liabilities, income, expenses, especially disposable income.

SCHEDULES A/B AND SCHEDULE C

Official Form 106A/B: Schedule A/B: Property (Individuals) and Official Form 106C: Schedule C: The Property You Claim as Exempt (Individuals)

1. Confirm all of the debtor's assets have been listed, including personal property.
2. Compare Schedules A/B to Schedule C. Were the assets given a fair market value and exempted on Schedule C? Identify that the correct exemption statute was applied.

LIABILITIES: SCHEDULES D, E/F, AND G

Official Form 106D: Schedule D: Creditors Who Hold Claims Secured By Property (Individuals)

1. Lien information from assets listed on Schedules A/B also belongs on Schedule D. Update the balances if need be.
2. Remember to choose the debtor's intent (Official Form 108 Statement of Intention for Individuals Filing Under Chapter 7). If the debtor is surrendering the asset, it's marked non-exempt. If the debtor keeps the asset, the three R's apply: retain, redeem, or reaffirm.
3. If the debtor didn't pass the means test, additional debt information is required, including the monthly payment amount and the months left on the debt, which is a maximum of sixty months.[3]

Official Form 106E/F: Schedule E/F: Creditors Who Have Unsecured Claims (Individuals)

1. Include in Schedule E outstanding tax liabilities, domestic support obligations, or personal injury claims while intoxicated. Remember to calculate domestic support obligations for Chapter 13 cases.

3 Official Form 122A-2. Chapter 7 Means Test Calculation.

2. Schedule F includes unsecured creditors such as credit cards, hospital bills, and personal loans. Verify the creditor's address is correct, the debt is categorized correctly, and co-debtors are listed.

Official Form 106G: Schedule G: Executory Contracts and Unexpired Leases (Individuals)

1. Leases are included in Schedule G, and choose whether it will be assumed or rejected. Since there is no ownership interest, the collateral isn't listed in Schedules A/B.

SCHEDULE I: INCOME

Official Form 106I: Schedule I: Your Income (Individuals)

1. When reviewing Schedule I, be aware of the filing date and when income was calculated last, especially if filing on a Thursday or Friday.
2. If it's the beginning of the month, the prior month is included in the means test, and income for the current month is estimated based on previous paystubs.[4]
3. Remember to differentiate between the income of a non-filing spouse and household contributions.
4. Review paystubs and verify the deductions are listed on Schedule I.

SCHEDULE J: EXPENSES

Official Form 107J: Schedule J: Your Expenses (Individuals)

1. Compare the expenses listed on Schedule J to the income on Schedule I for the disposable income amount.
2. If dependents are listed, verify the dependents reside with the debtor.
3. Double-check that paystub deductions haven't been duplicated on Schedule J.

THE MEANS TEST

Official From 122A-1: Chapter 7 Statement of Your Current Monthly Income and Official Form 122A-2: Chapter 7 Means Test Calculation

1. Confirm that paychecks earned from all jobs during the last six months were included in the calculations.

4 Supra, note 2.

2. If it's the beginning of the month, remember to update the months included in the means test calculations.[5]
3. If the debtor's income exceeds the state median, proceed to Form 122A-2, making sure to include all secured debt and allowable deductions.

THE CHAPTER 13 PLAN

Official Form 113: Chapter 13 Plan

If the debtor is filing Chapter 13, review the plan and file it simultaneously with the petition or within 14 days to avoid dismissal. Confirm that the debts were categorized correctly.

STATEMENT OF FINANCIAL AFFAIRS

Official Form 107: Your Statement of Financial Affairs for Individuals Filing for Bankruptcy (individuals)

Review the 28 sections of SOFA, even though most sections may not apply. Issues to keep an eye out for include:

1. The marital status of the debtor since that affects household income and expenses.
2. If the debtor has prior out-of-state addresses, verify there are no domicile or residency issues.
3. Include income for the last two years by reviewing the debtor's tax returns, including income for the year (YTD).
4. If there have been transfers of assets, whether to creditors or insiders, analyze how this may affect the case. Pending lawsuits are listed and can affect when the filing takes place because of the automatic stay.
5. Include fees paid by the client and verify that it matches the amount listed on Official Form 2030: Disclosure of Compensation of Attorney For Debtor.

Once the petition is ready to be filed, click "One Touch Case Filing." The bankruptcy software logs into CM/ECF and completes the filing process. Remember to file the credit counseling certificate, pay stubs if required in your district, and pay the required filing fee, which can be done via ACH debit, debit, or credit card. Online training with CM/ECF is available with your local court.[6]

5 Supra, note 2.
6 Electronic Filing. CM/ECF. www.uscourts.gov/court-records/electronic-filing-cmecf.

PRACTICE TIP

As a matter of preference and security issues, I don't pay the filing fee directly from my trust account because I'm responsible for the funds. I was a victim of fraud with my trust account, and per bar rules, I had to file a police report and notify the incident to the Florida Bar. Since there were minimal funds in the account, the bank quickly replaced the funds while they conducted their investigation. However, what if there is a substantial amount of funds in the IOTA account?

A few months after that incident, I settled a personal injury case for a married couple, and the settlement was substantial. I was checking the trust account multiple times a day, fearful of the same situation happening again because if the amount is considerable, the bank won't replace the funds immediately until their investigation is complete, which could take several months. Most state bars will prohibit the attorney from practicing law until the funds have been replaced.

While I cannot attribute my situation to an online filing, the fact is I rarely write checks from my IOTA account. I prefer to pay the filing fee with my credit card, transfer the funds from my IOTA account to my operating account, then reimburse myself the filing fee by paying the credit card.

REAL CASES

During the real estate boom, a title company may have performed hundreds of closings per month. Even if a title company only closed on ten properties monthly, if the average closing was $200,000 and that's going low, that's $2 million in the trust account at any given time. An attorney came to see me about bankruptcy because a married couple working as paralegals in her office wiped out her IOTA account. As a result, the Florida Bar investigated and confirmed the attorney was not involved as she was a victim of theft. The problem is that the Florida Bar concluded, as it always does, that the clients and/or victims have to be reimbursed, and until that time, she was prohibited from practicing law. Of course, the lawyer did not have $2 million, so her law career was abruptly cut short.

To avoid problems, I've always kept my IOTA checks at home. Otherwise, there are too many variables, whether it's new staff or the janitorial crew. As the paralegal, there's no need to place yourself in the line of fire. I've even known paralegals to have quit their positions with law firms when they've realized the lawyer has been dipping into the trust account.

SUMMARY

The bankruptcy petition is converted into PDF format before a case is filed via the Case Management/Electronic Case Files (CM/ECF) system. PDF format is required for documents filed. Once converted to PDF, this serves as an excellent opportunity to review the petition to check for errors and required updates. Confirm there have not been additional pay dates since the income was last calculated. If so, update Schedule I, and if it's the beginning of the month, the applicable six-month period for the means test also changes. Review the disposable income and update accordingly. Once the petition has been reviewed, obtain approval from the client. Once the petition is filed, include the credit counseling certificate and pay stubs if required in your district.

The final step is paying the required filing fee. Remember that fees and costs are separate. Fees are earned, and the funds are deposited in the firm's operating account, while costs belong in the trust account. Costs belong to the client, not the firm. It's recommended that the paralegal not handle the trust account considering the liability issues.

KEYWORDS AND TERMS

- PDF format
- Trust accounts

PRACTICE QUESTIONS AND EXERCISES

1. Convert your petition to PDF format. Review it for any errors and update it accordingly. If it's Thursday or Friday, or the first week of the month, update Schedules I and J, the means test, and the Chapter 13 Plan.
2. Forward an email to the client that includes the petition as an attachment. Schedule a consultation with the client to review the petition.
3. Scan a credit counseling certificate or any available document and convert it to PDF format.

REFERENCES

Electronic Filing. CM/ECF. www.uscourts.gov/court-records/electronic-filing-cmecf.

In re: Maurice Symonette, Case 18-15891 BKC-LMI.

Official Form 101. Voluntary Petition for Individuals Filing for Bankruptcy.

Official Form 106. A Summary of Your Assets and Liabilities and Certain Statistical Information (Individuals).

Official Form 106A/B. Schedule A/B: Property (Individuals).

Official Form 106C. Schedule C: The Property You Claim as Exempt (Individuals).

Official Form 106D. Schedule D: Creditors Who Hold Claims Secured by Property (Individuals).

Official Form 106E/F. Schedule E/F: Creditors Who Have Unsecured Claims (Individuals).

Official Form 106G. Schedule G: Executory Contracts and Unexpired Leases (Individuals).

Official Form 106I. Schedule I: Your Income (Individuals).

Official Form 107J. Schedule J: Your Expenses (Individuals).

Official Form 107. Your Statement of Financial Affairs for Individuals Filing for Bankruptcy (Individuals).

Official Form 108. Statement of Intention for Individuals Filing Under Chapter 7.

Official Form 113. Chapter 13 Plan.

Official Form 122A-1. Chapter 7 Statement of Your Current Monthly Income.

Official Form 122A-2. Chapter 7 Means Test Calculation.

Official Form 2030. Disclosure of Compensation of Attorney for Debtor.

CHAPTER 26

Post-Petition Filing

Once the bankruptcy petition is filed, the court clerk will send notice of the filing to the email address registered with CM/ECF. Depending on the district, the bankruptcy clerk may generate the hearing notice the same day or within a few days. When the hearing notice is docketed, CM/ECF emails the notice to the law firm, and the clerk sends a copy via regular mail to the debtor. The notice should be forwarded to the client as soon as possible since it contains the case number which is required to register for the financial management course.

Make a notation in the file that the second class remains pending to avoid dismissal pursuant to §727.[1] Clients should be advised to complete the financial management course within the next seven days, even though §727 allows for 60 days from the first scheduled Meeting of Creditors to file the certificate.

Providers of the debtor education or financial management class, just like the credit counseling class, are approved by the U.S. Trustee's Office. The list of approved agencies is available on the U.S. Department of Justice website.[2] Some agencies will offer to file the certificate with the court, but the practitioner must opt in for this service.

If the case was dismissed for failing to complete the second bankruptcy class or file the certificate, the debtor could still receive a discharge under §349.[3] However, court approval is required to reopen the case.[4] Local rules may allow for the reopening of a case ex-parte to file the financial management certificate. Recall that a dismissal is different from a discharge. A dismissal means the bankruptcy court did not enter the discharge. Simply put, the case wasn't finalized, and the court did not approve the bankruptcy. While a discharge means the case was approved, closed, and the bankruptcy estate has been fully administered.[5]

1 11 U.S.C.§727 (a)(1).
2 U.S. Department of Justice. List of Approved Provers of Personal Financial Management Instructional Courses (Debtor Education) Pursuant to 11 U.S.C. §111. www.justice.gov/ust/list-approved-providers-personal-financial-management-instructional-courses-debtor-education.
3 11 U.S.C. §349.
4 11 U.S.C. §350(b).
5 11 U.S.C. §350.

DOI: 10.4324/9781003203278-27

BANKRUPTCY TRUSTEE

Depending on the bankruptcy trustee, a document request will be sent via email or mail approximately one week after filing. Likewise, how the documents are provided to the trustee will be included in that request. Some trustees still prefer snail mail, while others prefer documents to be uploaded directly through their website or emailed. However, most trustees favor receiving documents through secured sites that require registration for first-time users. Documents should be provided to the trustee as soon as possible to avoid a continuance or dismissal, but no less than ten days before the Meeting of Creditors.

REAFFIRMATION AGREEMENTS

If there are secured creditors such as car loans or mortgages, the creditors may require a Reaffirmation Agreement. While rare, a Reaffirmation Agreement can also apply to unsecured debt. For a Reaffirmation Agreement to be valid, several requirements must be complied with under §524.

1. A cover sheet is required under Fed. R. Bankr. P. 4008(a).[6] The agreement must be in writing and entered into before the entry of the discharge.[7] This includes filing the Reaffirmation Agreement within 60 days of the first scheduled Meeting of Creditors.[8] This is important because if the hearing is rescheduled, the issue of the validity of the Reaffirmation Agreement would be based on the first scheduled date of the creditor's meeting, whether it took place or not. A Reaffirmation Agreement is also invalid if rescinded by the debtor before discharge or within 60 days from the date the agreement was filed.[9] Once filed, the creditor will file a motion to approve the Reaffirmation Agreement.[10]
2. Reaffirmation Agreements also have a laundry list of required disclosures so that debtors can make informed choices about keeping dischargeable debts.[11] See Part A, Official Form B-2400A/B.[12]
3. If the attorney assisted the debtor with the Reaffirmation Agreement, the attorney must sign a declaration stating that the debtor was fully informed and signed voluntarily.[13] The debtor was also advised of the consequences of a default.[14] Finally, the attorney is

6 Official Form 427. Cover Sheet for Reaffirmation Agreement.

7 11 U.S.C. §524(c)(1).

8 11 U.S.C. §524(c)(3)(A) to (C).

9 11 U.S.C. §524(c)(4).

10 Official Form 2400B. Motion For Approval of Reaffirmation Agreement. See also Official Form 2400C. Order on Reaffirmation Agreement.

11 11 U.S.C. §524(k).

12 Official Form 2400A/B. Reaffirmation Agreements.

13 11 U.S.C. § 524(c)(3)(A).

14 11 U.S.C. § 524(c)(3)(C).

confirming that the Reaffirmation Agreement doesn't impose an undue hardship on the debtor.[15] If there is an undue hardship, but the debtor still wishes to reaffirm the debt, an additional statement in writing is required.

During the consultation, Reaffirmation Agreements should be explained to the client and detailed in the Retainer Agreement. Review the sample Retainer Agreement in Chapter 28.

As a general rule, the bankruptcy practitioner charges extra for the Reaffirmation Agreement, whether a hearing is required or not, which depends on the local rules and a particular judge's preference. Even without a hearing, additional time is spent working on the client's case.

While Reaffirmation Agreements are common with secured debts, it's not always requested by the creditor. You may encounter situations where the client has two cars financed with the same lender, yet the lender only requests a reaffirmation on one of the vehicles. For this reason, the additional fees aren't charged up front since it's unknown when a creditor will require a Reaffirmation Agreement. However, since the client was made aware of the possibility of additional fees, there's plenty of time for the client to prepare financially.

As always, be aware of the local rules. For example, in the Southern District of Florida, an attorney automatically represents a debtor in Reaffirmation Agreements, even if not retained by the client.[16] Depending on the local rules of your district, some bankruptcy judges require a brief evidentiary hearing where the attorney and client are present. However, if the client is self-represented or if the attorney didn't sign/certify the Reaffirmation Agreement, a hearing is guaranteed.[17] A hearing is also likely if there is a presumption of undue hardship.

When reviewing the Reaffirmation Agreement with the client, confirm the balance, the monthly payment amount, and interest rate. It should be no different than the current terms, although the terms could be negotiated. However, for certain types of secured debt such as car loans and mortgages, a modification is unlikely, but it's common for debts secured by personal property such as furniture and electronics.

During the foreclosure crisis, mortgage lenders were willing to modify the mortgage terms, including reducing the mortgage balance since a debtor was unlikely to sign a Reaffirmation Agreement where the mortgage far exceeded the property's value. Lenders collectively had their backs up against the wall since litigating a foreclosure would take between one to three years, and throughout that time, the debtor was living for free in the house. Once the foreclosure was finalized, the debtor would file for bankruptcy, eliminating any financial responsibility to the lender. So, homeowners had nothing to lose while mortgage lenders were paying a steep price if an agreement could not be reached.

Unlike mortgages, it's common to reduce the balance, sometimes even the interest rate, with secured personal property. If the personal property was purchased recently, the trustee

15 11 U.S.C. §524(c)(3)(B).
16 United States Bankruptcy Court Southern District of Florida, Local Rule 4008-1(d).
17 11 U.S.C. §524(c)(5),(6), and (d).

might object, so it may be prudent to be proactive and contact the lender for a Reaffirmation Agreement, especially since the terms offered by the creditor will likely be more reasonable than that of the trustee.

However, depending on the age and condition of the personal property, sometimes a Reaffirmation Agreement should be avoided, especially if the trustee is not likely to object. Of course, the creditor will send numerous emails stating that they will seek to repossess the personal property, but that's when bankruptcy poker is played. For example, what is the furniture worth? What are the costs to the lender to file a motion in court, then spend additional monies to pick up the furniture, clean and fix it, then return it to the showroom floor? Most of the time, it's not worth it financially to the creditor, but again, it depends on the facts.

Explain the specifics of the Reaffirmation Agreement to the client. For one, and most important is that the debt is dischargeable, so the debtor isn't obligated to keep the secured asset. But, be clear with clients that the security interest isn't eliminated if the client keeps the asset. Clients confuse discharging debt with lien stripping and may believe the debt is eliminated while keeping the asset.

The most important part of reaffirming debts is the consequences. If the client can't afford to pay back the debt and defaults, the balance on the debt is owed. The creditor can file a lawsuit to collect on the debt and take back the property, whether it's a car or home. It's as if bankruptcy was never filed. The debtor is back to square one.

Issues to Be Aware of with Reaffirmation Agreements

Numerous times throughout this text, I have referenced the effect of the coronavirus pandemic. Today it's the coronavirus pandemic; tomorrow, it's another pandemic or global recession. As situations change, so will your response to these issues.

The latest issue I've experienced is lenders not providing Reaffirmation Agreements because the client has deferred payments or is in forbearance status. As a response to the coronavirus shutdown, lenders offered to postpone payments on credit cards, personal loans, car payments, and mortgages. The skipped payments were added to the end of the loan. For example, if the client had ten years left on the mortgage and accepted a six-month deferment or forbearance, now there are ten years and six months left on the mortgage. Simple enough and a much-needed financial lifesaver for those who were furloughed or laid off during the pandemic. However, when it comes to bankruptcy, this presents two issues.

If the client is not making payments on secured loans, with a significant expense such as a mortgage eliminated, albeit temporarily, the disposable income increases, preventing the client from qualifying for Chapter 7. This issue can be resolved easily by advising the client to resume payments. The second issue is more complicated.

What happens if the client deferred mortgage payments for three months but resumed payments to include the expense on Schedule J and the client wants to reaffirm the mortgage?[18] Well, lenders are saying because the loan is in arrears, it can't be reaffirmed. Chapter 7 isn't an

18 Official Form 106J. Schedule J: Your Expenses (Individuals).

option if a debtor is behind on secured debt payments and the intent is to keep the property. So lenders are equating deferred payments and forbearance with late. In discussing this with one lender, I advised the lender to look up the meaning of all three words. I then asked the lender to confirm if a debtor's car can be repossessed or mortgage foreclosed on while in deferment or forbearance status. Of course, the answer was no because it's not considered late in those circumstances, just late for purposes of the Reaffirmation Agreement. Huh?

So, how is the client who filed for Chapter 7 bankruptcy and is six months in arrears due to a forbearance protected from foreclosure? In communicating with the bank, it was made clear that a Reaffirmation Agreement would not be provided, but their policy was that a foreclosure wouldn't take place during the forbearance period. In essence, they said, "trust us." Author's note: don't trust creditors! The lender agreed to commit to writing that foreclosure wouldn't be initiated so long as the client was current with her payments, regardless of the arrears. I know; it's all contradictory language. But, the letter is better than nothing and protects the client if a foreclosure occurs. Make sure to keep a copy in the file.

The other issue is how the forbearance or deferment is referenced in the client's credit report. Clients should take the extra precaution of reviewing their credit report regularly to confirm the mortgage isn't listed as late. It should also be confirmed if interest continues to accrue for the months that were deferred.

PRACTICE TIP

Reaffirmation Agreements are prepared by the creditor and generally sent via email in PDF format. Therefore, it's essential to review the email spam box regularly. Occasionally, creditors are slow in providing Reaffirmation Agreements, so calendar a date to contact the creditor. Also, calendar a second date for filing the reaffirmation. If deadlines are missed, creditors are quick to blame the bankruptcy attorney.

Once, I received via email the Reaffirmation Agreement on the fifty-ninth day from the initially scheduled date of the 341 Meeting of Creditors.[19] The email was also sent late in the day. On the sixtieth day, the client was unable to schedule a same-day visit at the office. So on the sixty-first day, the Reaffirmation Agreement was signed and returned via email. Of course, that's the same day the Order of Discharge was filed. I advised the creditor's attorney of the situation, who responded by saying it was my obligation to reopen the case. The rest of our discussion did not go well, as you can imagine.

First, why would I have to perform the extra-legal work of reopening the case and paying the reopening fee? I provided the creditor's attorney with a timeline, which he was already aware of. Still, the response was the same until I replied that I would file a motion to reopen and seek reimbursement for my fees, costs, and sanctions against the attorney and the creditor. Needless to say, the problem was resolved.

19 11 U.S.C. §341.

The second time this happened to me, the legal assistant titled the email "urgent" and made clear in the email that the Order of Discharge had been docketed, so I'm not sure why the reaffirmation was sent if it lacked validity. Of course, I was to blame again. Interestingly enough, the creditor even sent my client an invoice for $125.00 in attorney's fees for preparing the invalid Reaffirmation Agreement. That's a first.

As always, things change from one district to another. In the Southern District of Florida, I generally receive Reaffirmation Agreements before the creditors' meeting. This is convenient since it can be reviewed, signed and fees collected at that time. In the Middle District of Florida, time moves slower, so Reaffirmation Agreements are received after the creditors' meeting. This results in an office appointment that takes up more time. A follow-up email is sent a few days later after the Reaffirmation Agreement is returned to the creditor because time is running short.

Another issue with Reaffirmation Agreements is BAPCPA's attempt to make attorneys liable. Remember, BAPCPA caused a lot of confusion initially, so for a while, attorneys were performing asset searches to make sure debtors were disclosing all assets, including transfers. Liability was taken a step further by requiring certification by the attorney that the consequences of signing a Reaffirmation Agreement were explained to the client, even though that's already detailed in the agreement under the bold heading "**reaffirming a debt is a serious financial decision**."[20] Form B2400 A/B, §524(k)(5)(b) reads as follows:

> Part C: Certification by Debtor's Attorney (If Any). "I hereby certify that (1) This agreement represents a fully informed and voluntary agreement by the debtor; (2) this agreement does not impose an undue hardship on the debtor or any department of the debtor; and (3) I have fully advised the debtor of the legal effect and consequences of this agreement and any default under this agreement. Signature of Debtor's Attorney: Date:"[21]

If there's a presumption of undue hardship, the attorney can still certify that the debtor can afford the payments. Part C of the Reaffirmation Agreement reads as follows: "a presumption of undue hardship has been established with respect to this agreement. In my opinion, however, the debtor is able to make the required payment."

Income from Schedule I and expenses from Schedule J are duplicated in Reaffirmation Agreements.[22] A presumption of undue hardship exists when the debtor's income is less than the monthly expenses. However, the presumption of undue hardship does not bar the debtor from reaffirming the debt if the debtor provides a statement to the court's satisfaction on how the debtor can afford to make the payments. This burden is usually overcome if a parent or domestic partner agrees to make the payment. However, what happens if the debtor fails to comply with the terms? Does it matter whether there is a presumption of undue hardship or

20 Form B 2400 A/B ALT (12/15), page 4.

21 Part IV, Form 2400 A/B ALT (12/15).

22 Official Form 106I. Schedule I: Your Income (Individuals). Also, supra note 18.

not? Since the attorney signed the certification, is the attorney liable? To whom? The client? The creditor? To the court? Everyone?

As the mysteries of BAPCPA continues, lawyers have become hesitant to assist clients with Reaffirmation Agreements, whether it's for an underwater mortgage or a car loan since car values depreciate quickly. At times it is challenging to explain to clients the concept of negative equity. For example, I may ask a client to assign a value to anything in my office. If the client says my desk is worth $100.00, then my response is my desk is worth $100.00 more than your house or car. While that may seem absurd to them at first, once the client understands that the asset has a negative value, they agree, and this helps simplify explaining the Reaffirmation Agreement.

To this day, I receive calls from potential clients telling me that their bankruptcy attorney refused to sign the certification on the Reaffirmation Agreement because, in their opinion, it wasn't a "good deal." Assuming the bankruptcy attorney was correct, what other options exist for the client? With bad credit, can the client get another car? Does the ride-through option exist in that jurisdiction? Even if it does, a default could result in the client's car being repossessed, putting the client in a worse position than when this started.

PRACTICE TIP

If a client is taking advantage of the ride-through option and has been making timely mortgage payments since the bankruptcy was finalized, they may believe their credit score has improved. However, it's common for lenders not to report payments to the credit bureaus without a Reaffirmation Agreement, arguing that to do so is a violation of the Fair Debt Collection Practices Act.[23] That's when I get calls from potential clients saying they wish to sue their lawyer for malpractice, even though it's not the lawyer's fault. Sometimes debtors already know this from prior communications with the lender who is trying to force the debtor into committing to a Reaffirmation Agreement. The only way to resolve this is by the debtor disputing that the debt isn't listed with the credit reporting bureaus. Hopefully, that resolves the issue.

Personally, I've never rejected a client's request to proceed with a Reaffirmation Agreement. Does it mean there are possible consequences for me? Maybe, although it's never happened to me or anyone that I know of, but I'm sure in other jurisdictions, bankruptcy attorneys have horror stories to tell. By the same token, I believe it's a conflicting situation between BAPCPA's intent and the reality of leaving a client hung out to dry. My ethical responsibility is to my client, nothing more, nothing less. Let the bankruptcy chips fall where they may. While BAPCPA does require reviewing the Reaffirmation Agreement in detail with a client, that is something an attorney should do anyway, even though you will learn that's not always the case. I note their reasons for signing the Reaffirmation Agreement. It's common for a client to conclude that while they agree to keep a home with negative equity,

23 15 U.S.C.A. § 1692.

the costs of renting are the same, if not more. For example, I find it reasonable that the client doesn't want to vacate a three-bedroom, two-bath house for a two-bedroom apartment, especially if the client has minor children and pets. At the end of the day, clients decide how to proceed after being informed by the attorney. The key is being clear and honest with the client. Also, know what the office policies are regarding Reaffirmation Agreements.

In the case I mentioned where the lender billed my client $125 for the Reaffirmation Agreement, my client is taking advantage of the ride-through option. So long as he continues to make payments on his mortgage, the lender will continue to cash the checks. In this case, since the client has equity in his homestead property, I also advised him to refinance the mortgage with another lender since he wasn't happy either with the lender's stunt of actually charging him for an invalid Reaffirmation Agreement.

SUMMARY

Once a bankruptcy petition is filed, the clerk of court sends notice electronically to the email registered with CM/ECF. The clerk also sends notice of the 341 meeting to the client via regular mail, but it should be forwarded via email to the client since the hearing notice contains the case number, which is needed to register for the second bankruptcy class.

Once the trustee is assigned, the trustee will request certain documents, and that request should be complied with immediately to avoid a continuance and/or dismissal of the case. Most secured creditors will also request that the debtor reaffirms the debt. Reaffirmation of debt is voluntary.

For a Reaffirmation Agreement to be valid, it must be in writing and signed by the creditor and debtor. If the attorney represented the debtor with the Reaffirmation Agreement, the attorney must also sign. Disclosures are reviewed with the client, and if a presumption of undue hardship exists, a statement must be provided as to how the debtor can still afford to make payments on the debt. Reaffirmation agreements must be filed within 60 days of the first 341 Meeting of Creditors and before the discharge.

However, there will be situations when a creditor won't offer a Reaffirmation Agreement, and as a result, this has created confusion and conflicting opinions in the district courts as to what options exist for a debtor. Depending on the jurisdiction, there's the "ride-through" option where so long as the debtor continues to make payments on the secured debt, the debtor keeps the property. But some districts have ruled that amendments to BAPCPA have eliminated the "ride-through" option. If the "ride-through" option is available, the debtor has the best of both worlds because the property is kept without the financial consequences of a Reaffirmation Agreement. However, with or without a Reaffirmation Agreement, the creditor has the right to take back the asset if the debtor defaults on payments.

When the debtor hasn't signed a Reaffirmation Agreement, creditors react more swiftly with a default. As a general rule, a debtor is not likely to have a car repossessed quickly. Typically, banks seek to repossess a vehicle around the 90-day mark. The same holds true for debtors that have signed a Reaffirmation Agreement because lenders realize the debtor's intent is/was to keep the vehicle. If not, an agreement wouldn't have been signed in the first place. Hence, the Reaffirmation Agreement works as an insurance policy, guaranteeing the lender that the debtor will comply and continue making payments. But, when there is no Reaffirmation Agreement in place, creditors tend to be more aggressive and act swifter in repossession actions, sometimes with one payment being enough for a creditor to react.

KEYWORDS AND TERMS

- Attorney certification
- Deferred payments
- Ex parte
- Forbearance
- Form B2400A/B
- Reaffirmation Agreement
- Undue hardship

DISCUSSION QUESTIONS

1. Describe the process of reaffirming a debt to the client.
2. By when should a Reaffirmation Agreement be filed?

PRACTICE QUESTIONS AND EXERCISES

1. Complete two Reaffirmation Agreements. One with a presumption of undue hardship and one without.
2. Prepare a motion to reopen to file a Reaffirmation Rgreement.
3. Review and complete the Retainer Agreement. What changes would you suggest?
4. Prepare a suggestion of bankruptcy to be filed in a civil case.

REFERENCES

11 U.S.C. §111.

11 U.S.C. §341.

11 U.S.C. §349.

11 U.S.C. §350.

11 U.S.C. §524.

11 U.S.C. §727.

15 U.S.C.A. §1692.

Fed. R. Bankr. P. 4008(a).

Official Form 106I. Schedule I: Your Income (Individuals).

Official Form 106J. Schedule J: Your Expenses (Individuals).

Official Form B427. Cover Sheet for Reaffirmation Agreement.

Official Form 2400A/B. Reaffirmation Agreements.

Official Form B 2400 A/B ALT (12/15).

Official Form 2400B. Motion for Approval of Reaffirmation Agreement.

Official Form 2400C. Order on Reaffirmation Agreement.

United States Bankruptcy Court Southern District of Florida, Local Rule 4008-1(d).

U.S. Department of Justice. List of Approved Provers of Personal Financial Management Instructional Courses (Debtor Education). www.justice.gov/ust/list-approved-providers-personal-financial-management-instructional-courses-debtor-education.

CHAPTER

27

The 341 Meeting of Creditors

Before, During, and After

BEFORE THE 341 MEETING

Since this may be a client's first time being involved in a legal issue, it's common for them to experience anxiety. Clients will even want to get into details about the Meeting of Creditors during the final review of the petition. But considering that between the filing date and the date of the hearing is 30-plus days, it's best to prepare the client the day before or day of the hearing. Prepping the client as close as possible to the 341 meeting puts the client at ease, leading to increased retention of the information.[1]

I start by advising clients that if they have ever been part of a litigated case such as a divorce or even seen a trial in person or on TV, to delete it from memory because a Meeting of Creditors in no way resembles that. There is no judge or jury, and the hearing isn't even held in a courtroom. There's also no aggressive cross-examination by the trustee, but the same basic questions for everyone. In addition, the attorney may not say another word after stating their name to confirm their appearance on the record. Once clients understand that the setting and process are different, arguably informal, they become more relaxed.

When reviewing questions that the trustee may ask, the first point to get across is to answer the question. While this seems like overstating the obvious, some people, when nervous, speak more than is necessary. Each trustee is different, and while some have the patience of a saint, others do not. The last thing you want is for the trustee to be frustrated and flustered by asking more questions or with a more aggressive tone, as this will only increase the client's nervousness. If the trustee starts to see the same pattern with other debtors, they will conclude your office doesn't properly prepare clients.

To illustrate the point of answering questions correctly, I always start with the same question: "what color is your shirt?" If the shirt is blue, then that's the answer; blue. Yes, it's an oversimplification, but it works well as an example because some clients may volunteer more information, whether as a force of habit or nervousness. Either way, this usually leads to complications. By asking, "what color is your shirt," the question isn't about the shirt's

1 11 U.S.C. §341.

DOI: 10.4324/9781003203278-28

material, where the shirt was purchased, was it on sale, or why blue was chosen instead of red! The question is simply, what color is the shirt? If the trustee wants more information about the shirt, the trustee will ask more questions.

DURING THE 341 MEETING

The day has arrived. What happens at the creditors' meeting? Well, let's start from the beginning, and by that, I mean the old-school way of doing things. And by the way, old school dates back to the beginning of 2020, before the coronavirus pandemic. For now, the hearings are held telephonically, but that may change, or we may have a hybrid model in the future. Regardless, I will start with in-person hearings.

Entering the federal courthouse requires valid identification, both for the client and the attorney. Certain federal courthouses could be busier such as the Claude Pepper building in Miami, Florida, because it also houses the passport and the IRS offices, so a client should have a copy of the hearing notice to gain admittance into the building. The attorney usually presents his driver's license and state bar card.

Policies vary per jurisdiction on whether debtors can have cell phones inside the courtroom, but the general rule is that attorneys are exempt. The use of a cell phone in the courtroom is always prohibited, and the same rule applies to the Meeting of Creditors. Review the court's website for policies and, at a minimum, make sure the client puts the phone in silence mode. Clients should also be warned that federal courthouses have strict security policies, and something as simple as nail clippers will be considered a weapon and not allowed inside the building. Since security isn't likely to store any items and lockers aren't available, the client has two choices at this point: leave the item outside, and hopefully, no one decides to take ownership or return to their car, but if they are running short of time, the latter option may not be possible.

Now, I mentioned federal courthouses, but a creditors' meeting may not even be heard at a courthouse. Smaller jurisdictions may only have one federal bankruptcy court in the entire state, versus large districts like the Southern District of Florida which has three. So, depending on the size of the district, a creditors' meeting could be conducted at other locations. For example, in New Mexico, one district holds the Meeting of Creditors at a college campus.

At the Meeting of Creditors, the trustee will request the driver's license and the original Social Security card to confirm it matches the Social Security number listed on the petition. If the client doesn't provide the original Social Security card, the hearing is likely to be rescheduled as most trustees won't accept copies or tax returns as a substitute.

For in-person hearings, confirm any additional requirements such as wearing a mask and social distancing with the court's website as these policies continue to be updated frequently. If a client is infirm, contact the trustee's office promptly and request that the hearing be held by telephone. Last but not least, make sure your notice letter to the client states to dress appropriately. With time, you will be surprised at what some clients wear to meet with the attorney. If the client requires a translator, there's a free translation service where the translator appears via telephone. Some jurisdictions may have a translator present, but there's likely a fee.

341 MEETING OF CREDITORS VIA TELEPHONE/VIRTUALLY

Because we live in unprecedented times, courts are taking steps towards being virtual at the state and federal levels. However, the U.S. Trustee and bankruptcy trustee have the discretion to have an in-person hearing.[2] For years, bankruptcy courts have been handling appearances by telephone for simple matters through a service called Court Solutions.[3] While there is a $50.00 service charge, considering the costs of transportation, parking, and amount of drive time which easily could amount to a few hours, it's money well spent, especially now to help reduce the spread and/or catch the coronavirus. Many bankruptcy experts and attorneys believe that all 341 meetings will ultimately be held virtually, or at least the trustee will have the option.[4] Even the Consumer Bankruptcy Reform Act of 2020 proposed remote hearings.[5]

To access a telephonic hearing, the notice of hearing contains a PIN. The phone should be muted until the debtor's name is called. Depending on the trustee, the attorney may need to confirm that the debtor's Social Security card and driver's license match the petition's information. Other trustees may have requested a copy of the debtor's identification in advance and confirmed everything matches on the record. Remember, creditors' meetings are recorded electronically.

Whether the Meeting of Creditors is held in person or via telephone, the client should be present early to see/hear how the meeting is conducted. This will familiarize them with the process and provide an increased level of comfort.

QUESTIONS OFTEN ASKED AT THE 341 MEETING OF CREDITORS

The questions asked by trustees are somewhat standard, regardless of the jurisdiction. Granted, some debtors may be asked different questions based on their responses or what's listed in the petition.

For in-person hearings, make sure the client has their driver's license and original Social Security card readily available. I prefer to have my clients provide me with their identification before the hearing, and I hand it directly to the trustee or the assistant. I do this because

2 The U.S. Department of Justice. Local 341 Meeting Status. Important Notice. U.S. Trustee Program Extends Telephonic or Video Section 341 Meetings. Updated August 28, 2020. www.justice.gov/ust/Local_341_Meeting_Status. Retrieved on August 2, 2021.

3 Court Solutions. Participating Courts. https://court-solutions.zendesk.com/hc/en-us/articles/203820285-Participating-Courts. Retrieved August 2, 2201.

4 Supra, note 1.

5 Consumer Bankruptcy Reform Act of 2020, S.4991, 116th Congress, www.congress.gov/bill/116th-congress/senate-bill/4991.

nervous clients will start looking through their purses and pockets anxiously, forgetting where they put them. Once a client becomes nervous, it may be difficult for them to ease back into a level of comfort.

The trustee will confirm the client's identity and that the forms of identification match the information provided on the bankruptcy petition. If addresses don't match, the trustee may require that the information be updated. The trustee may also inquire about the different addresses.

After the client is sworn in, the trustee will begin asking questions. The following are some of the standard questions.

1. Please state your name and address for the record.
   After the debtor answers, the trustee will ask for the attorney to make their appearance. *"Alexander Hernandez on behalf of the debtor(s)."*
2. Did you have a chance to review your bankruptcy petition with your attorney before signing it?
   See why the petition is reviewed with the client? If an interpreter is translating, the trustee will ask if the bankruptcy petition was translated for them.
3. Did you sign the bankruptcy petition freely and voluntarily?
   Even though debtors no longer sign a separate declaration because of online filing, old habits die hard, so trustees continue with the same choice of words. Regardless, the petition would have been reviewed and approved by the client.
4. Did you list all your assets and liabilities in your bankruptcy petition?
5. Do you need to make any changes to your bankruptcy petition?
6. Have you filed for bankruptcy before?
   Even if the client filed for bankruptcy more than eight years ago, trustees may ask which chapter was filed and if a discharge was received.
7. Why did you file for bankruptcy?
   Most answers to the trustee's questions are yes, and no. This is one of the few opened-ended questions that the trustee will ask. Every debtor has a different reason, whether job loss, illness, or divorce. A brief explanation will suffice.
8. Did you provide a true and correct copy of your tax returns?
9. Are you involved in any lawsuits, such as a car accident where you expect to receive money?
10. Are you the beneficiary of a will or expecting to receive an inheritance?
    This question is also open-ended since the trustee does not provide a time frame. The client may be the beneficiary of a will, but the trustee is trying to confirm if there will be a substantial change in the client's immediate financial future. So even though the client is a beneficiary of the rich uncle's will, it's not relevant unless the uncle is on his deathbed.
11. Does anybody owe you money?
12. Are you current on your mortgage or car payments?

13. Do you wish to keep your house or car?

    If there's no equity or a bankruptcy exemption protects either, the trustee will state they abandon their interest in the car or home.
14. Medical bills – if there are medical bills listed on Schedule F, the trustee will ask if those bills are related to an accident such as a personal injury lawsuit.[6]
15. Furniture, jewelry, electronics – if there are creditors listed such as furniture stores, jewelry stores, or electronic stores, depending on the amount, the trustee will also ask questions to confirm the debt wasn't incurred recently. This information should have been known in the initial client consultation.
16. Tax refunds – if the tax refund isn't exempt, the trustee will provide specific instructions on the steps to take once the funds are received.
17. Have you transferred any assets to friends or family or sold any assets in the last two years?
18. Have you made any payments to creditors that total more than $600.00 in the ninety (90) days before filing for bankruptcy?

    Note, for questions 17 and 18, trustees may ask the questions without specifics as to dates or amounts.
19. Are there any creditors present? This concludes the Meeting of Creditors.

    When a couple has filed for bankruptcy, the questions are the same other than the trustee will ask if the parties are legally married. The parties will then take turns answering the questions. For example, once the question is asked, one spouse answers, then the other.

PRACTICE TIP

As a paralegal, nothing beats first-hand experience. A paralegal should attend multiple creditors' meetings with different trustees to learn the style and preferences of individual trustees and better explain the process to the client.

POST–341 MEETING OF CREDITORS

Depending on the facts of the case, once the Meeting of Creditors has concluded, there may be nothing else to do except wait for the Order of Discharge.[7] The same applies for Chapter 13 once the case is confirmed.[8] At this stage, remember the client should have completed the financial management course, and Reaffirmation Agreement should have been returned to the creditors.

Post–341 meeting, the following may occur:

6 Official Form 106 E/F. Schedule E/F: Creditors Who Have Unsecured Claims (Individuals).

7 Official Form B318. Discharge of Debtor in a Chapter 7 Case.

8 Official Form B3180W. Chapter 13 Discharge.

1. If lawsuits were pending in state court, most creditors file for voluntary dismissal at this stage for Chapter 7 or file proofs of claim for Chapter 13.
2. The petition is amended or additional documents provided to the trustee.
3. If there are over-exempt assets, negotiations begin with the trustee to settle the bankruptcy estate.
4. A 2004 Examination or adversary proceeding is filed.

AMENDING THE PETITION

At the Meeting of Creditors, new information may be discovered that requires amending the petition. For example, a closed bank account wasn't disclosed, or a creditor was omitted. Note that the bankruptcy petition can be amended at any time before the case is closed, and it requires notifying the trustee and all creditors.[9]

If the petition was filed with an incorrect Social Security number, trustees normally require that notice be sent to the three major credit reporting bureaus: Equifax, Experian, and Transunion. While not required, sending the notice with a letter of explanation via postal mail certified return receipt is worth the extra expense. Imagine the complications if someone is buying or selling a house or applying for credit and it appears that they are in bankruptcy proceedings. By shifting the responsibility to the credit agencies, liability will be reduced.

SETTLEMENT OF THE BANKRUPTCY ESTATE

The Following is an example of settling the bankruptcy estate with the trustee's office using Florida exemption limits.

PRIVILEGED – FOR SETTLEMENT PURPOSES ONLY

The Trustee believes the following issues are present in this matter: (a) the 2007 Escalade is undervalued, the low NADA is $9200; (b) the Household goods and furnishings (HHG) are undervalued – especially when reviewing the Debtor's creditors (Best Buy, Brandsmart, Rooms to Go); (c) the Trustee asserts that the debtor had more cash on had than scheduled based on the withdrawal of her tax refund in order to shield cash from creditors. Notwithstanding, the Trustee offers settlement as follows: $8,000/12 months of $6500 lump sum payable on or before April 1, 2020.

ASSET DESCRIPTION	Scheduled value	
2007 Cadillac Escalade	$	9,200.00
MZ Motorcycle	$	1,000.00
HHG	$	315.00
Cash	$	40.00
Regions	$	27.75
2019 taxes	$	1,245.00
withdrawal	$	4,900.00
Total	**$**	**16,727.75**
Exemptions	$	6,000.00
Over-exempt	**$**	**10,727.75**

9 Fed. R. Bankr. P. 1009.

The total value of the bankruptcy estate was estimated at $10,727.75. However, since I believed the vehicle's value was far below the estimated value via NADA, I requested other appraisal options from the trustee. Some trustees may refer debtors to an auction house, but in this case, the trustee agreed to an onsite appraisal from a reputable auto dealership. The appraised value would be multiplied by 30 percent (retail sale price) to arrive at the final figure.

WITH A NEW APPRAISAL IN HAND, THE VEHICLE'S VALUE WAS REDUCED TO $4,095, PLUS THE 30 PERCENT INCREASE OF $1,755, FOR A TOTAL OF $5,850, REDUCING THE BANKRUPTCY ESTATE BY $3,350.

The Trustee offers settlement of $5,000.00 payable over 10 months or $4,000 lump sum.

ASSET DESCRIPTION	Scheduled value	
2007 Cadillac Escalade	$	5,850.00
MZ Motorcycle	$	1,000.00
HHG	$	315.00
Cash	$	40.00
Regions	$	27.75
2019 taxes	$	1,245.00
withdrawal	$	4,900.00
Total	$	13,377.75
Exemptions	$	6,000.00
Over-exempt	$	7,377.75

The trustee countered with $5,000 over ten months or a $4,000 lump sum. We settled on a lump sum of $4,000 payable in 60 days. Note that while Chapter 13 has a 36-to-60-month plan, ten to 12 months is common for Chapter 7 cases. The stipulation could be reviewed in Chapter 28.

2004 EXAMINATION

The best comparison to a 2004 Examination is a deposition as part of the fact-finding process during the discovery phase. A creditor or trustee can file for a 2004 Examination.[10] While

10 Fed. R. Bankr. P. 2004.

usually, it's the debtor that is examined, it could also be a third party. In the example of the condominium that was transferred from my client to the son, the trustee could have also examined the son. To proceed with a 2004 Examination, a motion is filed with the court.[11] A sample notice of a 2004 Examination is available in Chapter 28.

ADVERSARY PROCEEDINGS

Consider the adversary process no different than any case in any area of law that's litigated. The debtor can initiate an adversary proceeding, a creditor, or the trustee.[12] Part VII of the Federal Rules on Bankruptcy Procedure, which is almost identical to the Federal Rules of Civil Procedure, provides guidance on the procedural aspects of adversary proceedings.

Note that in the Retainer Agreement available in Chapter 28, a 2004 Examination or adversary proceeding requires additional fees, and the attorney of record is not automatically retained. Even the compensation form excludes adversary proceedings.[13]

A cover sheet is required with the adversary complaint.[14] Since the bankruptcy is being litigated, there is no specific form or template as each case is different. The facts will vary from case to case, just like they would in a civil case. The next step is to serve the defendant with the complaint, who in turn files a response, and most likely a motion to dismiss. If the debtor can survive the motion to dismiss, there's the discovery process, and if a settlement isn't reached, the final step is an evidentiary hearing, similar to a trial.

ORDER OF DISCHARGE

Congratulations! You're done with your first case! It's been approximately 60 days since the creditors' meeting, and there have been no objections.[15] The bankruptcy judge has signed the Order of Discharge which will be received via email from the clerk's office. The next step is to forward the order to the client and close the file according to the firm's policies.

For Chapter 7, the discharge is received under 11 U.S.C. §727 and §1328 for Chapter 13. The court's standard form order provides general information about the discharge, including a list of non-dischargeable debts.[16] Also, the order mentions that creditors cannot collect on debts that have been discharged, nor can the debtor be contacted. While true legally, that's not what usually happens because one hand doesn't know what the other hand is doing. For example, because a debt collection agency recently purchased the debt, it wasn't aware of the bankruptcy. However, the client should advise the debt collector that the debt was

11 Fed. R. Bankr. P. 2004(a).
12 Bankruptcy Rule 4007(c).
13 Official Form 2030B. Disclosure of Compensation of Attorney for Debtor.
14 Official Form B1040. Adversary Proceeding Cover Sheet.
15 Fed. R. Bankr. P. 4004.
16 Supra, notes 7 and 8. See also Official Form 3180WH. Chapter 13 Hardship Discharge.

discharged. Some agencies want the debtor to do all the work and request proof, but that's their job, not the clients. That information is readily available online for debt collection agencies. If the debt collector continues contacting the client, they should be advised in writing that they're violating the Fair Credit Reporting Act and Debt Collection Practices Act which could lead to filing a lawsuit.[17]

PRACTICE TIP

Note that it's common to receive calls from former clients several years after the case was closed. Usually, the client applied for a car or home financing, and the lender wants to confirm the bankruptcy was approved. Real estate title companies are notorious for requesting a copy of the Order of Discharge and petition on the same day of the closing. When a request is made, the first issue is confirming the client's identity since some documents contain confidential information. If it's a public record, then anyone can obtain the document via the clerk's office. Regardless of who has made the request, the attorney should charge for obtaining that information as that requires additional time. The contractual obligation of representing the client ended with the discharge. Clients are typically surprised by this and state, "but you're my attorney." The correct answer is "was your attorney." As always, confirm the firm's policy in accessing closed files.

SUMMARY

While the questions are similar from one trustee to the next, clients should be prepared for the 341 meeting. This includes a review of the bankruptcy petition and highlighting any potential issues. The closer the review is held to the 341 meeting, the better for the client as they will not be able to retain the information if the review is held far in advance. The client should also appear at the hearing early or call in sooner to become familiar with the process.

Depending on the trustee's preference, issues may be resolved prior to the 341 meeting. For example, if there are over-exempt assets, the trustee's office may communicate in advance to confirm a settlement on behalf of the bankruptcy estate. Other trustees that feel comfortable working with the debtor's attorney may request a settlement at the hearing. Also, trustees do request additional information or documents after the 341 meeting.

Once the initial 341 Meeting of Creditors is concluded, the case remains pending the Order of Discharge if no further action is required. During this time, confirm that the financial management certificate was filed and the status of any Reaffirmation Agreement.

Post–341 meeting, if the petition needs to be amended, review the local rules for the procedure and forms. If non-exempt assets require settlement on behalf of the bankruptcy estate, negotiations will occur with the trustee's office. Finally, a 2004 Examination may be

17 15 U.S.C. §1692.

filed if the bankruptcy trustee has further inquiries, or an adversary proceeding if there have been fraudulent transfers or the dischargeability of a debt is being argued.

The Order of Discharge signals the end of the bankruptcy case. The clerk's office sends copies of the discharge via email to the law firm and regular mail to the client. Since clients may contact the law firm years after the case was closed, check with the state bar regarding the rules on the retention of client files.

KEYWORD AND TERMS

- Adversary proceedings
- Deposition
- Order of Discharge
- Rule 2004 Examination
- Stipulation
- Voluntary dismissal

DISCUSSION QUESTIONS

1. Confirm in your jurisdiction if 341 meetings are heard telephonically. If so, listen in on a 341 meeting for a Chapter 7 and Chapter 13 case.
2. What restrictions are in place for entering the building?
3. Role-play with a classmate asking the questions likely to be asked at the 341 meeting and properly responding to the trustee's questions.
4. Because of a transfer of personal property, the trustee will proceed with a 2004 Examination. Explain the process to the client.

PRACTICE QUESTIONS AND EXERCISES

1. Prepare an email notifying the client of the 341 Meeting of Creditors. Advise the client to arrive early, the required forms of identification, and to dress accordingly. If the hearing is by telephone, advise the client on how to access the hearing. Include a reminder on completing the second bankruptcy class in the email.
2. Obtain the information from your district court's website on amending the petition. Add an unsecured creditor using the local forms.
3. Prepare an email for the client that includes a copy of the Order of Discharge. It's good practice to include a "thank you" in the email and advise the client of other areas of law the firm handles.
4. Research the requirements in your state for retaining files. This information is usually available on the state bar association's website. Provide a summary, including how files are required to be stored (see Figure 27.1).

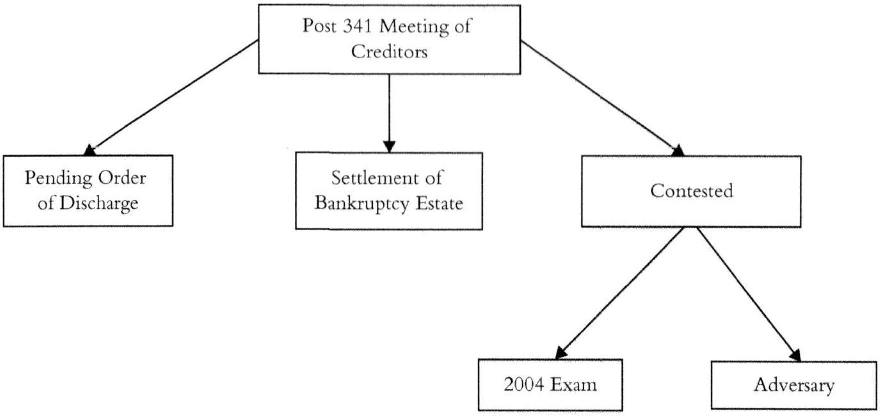

FIGURE 27.1 An overview of post–341 Meeting of Creditors.

REFERENCES

11 U.S.C. §341.

11 U.S.C. §727.

11 U.S.C. §1328.

15 U.S.C. §1692.

Consumer Bankruptcy Reform Act of 2020, S.4991, 116th Congress. www.congress.gov/bill/116th-congress/senate-bill/4991.

Court Solutions. Participating Courts. https://court-solutions.zendesk.com/hc/en-us/articles/203820285-Participating-Courts.

Fed. R. Bankr. P. 1009.

Fed. R. Bankr. P. 2004.

Fed. R. Bankr. P. 4004.

Fed. R. Bankr. P. 4007.

Official Form 106 E/F. Schedule E/F: Creditors Who Have Unsecured Claims (Individuals).

Official Form B318. Discharge of Debtor in a Chapter 7 Case.

Official Form B3180W. Chapter 13 Discharge.

Official Form 3180WH. Chapter 13 Hardship Discharge.

Official Form 2030B. Disclosure of Compensation of Attorney for Debtor.

Official Form B1040. Adversary Proceeding Cover Sheet.

Official Form 2030B. Disclosure of Compensation of Attorney for Debtor.

The U.S. Department of Justice. Local 341 Meeting Status. Important Notice. U.S. Trustee Program Extends Telephonic or Video Section 341 Meetings. www.justice.gov/ust/Local_341_Meeting_Status.

CHAPTER 28

Forms

1. Bankruptcy Intake.
2. Chapter 7 Retainer Agreement.
   a. Notice Required by 11 U.S.C. § 342(b) for Individuals Filing for Bankruptcy (Form 2010).
   b. 11 U.S.C. § 527(a)(2) Disclosure.
   c. 11 U.S.C. Section 527(b) Disclosure.
3. Chapter 13 Retainer Agreement.
   a. Notice Required by 11 U.S.C. § 342(b) for Individuals Filing for Bankruptcy (Form 2010).
   b. 11 U.S.C. § 527(a)(2) Disclosure.
   c. 11 U.S.C. Section 527(b) Disclosure.
4. Trustee's Notice of Rule 2004 Examination Duces Tecum of Debtor.
5. Stipulation for Compromise and Settlement Regarding Valuation and Repurchase of Debtor's Non-Exempt Assets.

DOI: 10.4324/9781003203278-29

Bankruptcy Lawyers R' Us Law Firm, P.A.
179 Broke Lane
Miami, Florida 32232

Date: ______________________ Referred By: ______________________

Client Information Sheet for Bankruptcy

SECTION 1

Marital Status: Single Married Separated Divorced Domestic Partnership

Debtor	Spouse Filing or Non-Filing
Name : ______________________	______________________
A/K/A : ______________________	______________________
Home Address:	
______________________	______________________
______________________	______________________
______________________	______________________
Mailing Address:	
______________________	______________________
______________________	______________________
(Work #) ______________________	*(Work #)* ______________________
(Home #) ______________________	*(Home #)* ______________________
(Cell #) ______________________	*(Cell #)* ______________________
Email ______________________	Email ______________________
Social Security Number: ______________	Social Security Number: ______________

Number of Members: __________

Household Members: ______________________

____

____

Any mail received at your home from a non-household member? Yes No

If yes, elaborate: ______________________

Dependents: Yes No

Name: ______________________________ ______________________

____

Age: ______________________________ ______________________

Relationship: ______________________ ______________________

SECTION 2

Florida Residency Requirements:

List all the addresses where have you resided in the last two years:

1. ____

2. ____

SECTION 3

Domestic Support Obligations – Alimony and/or Child Support

Is there a court order? Yes No

Amount paid monthly: $ ________

Are you current? Yes No Arrears amount? ____________

SECTION 4

Any Prior Bankruptcies? Yes When/Where: ______________________________

Result: ______________________________

Type of Bankruptcy: Chapter 7 Joint or Individual/ Chapter 13 Joint or Individual/Business

SECTION 5

Criminal History: ____

SECTION 6

Properties:

Own *or* *Rent*

Do you reside on the property? Yes No

Type: *Single Family* *Townhome* *Duplex* *Lot size* ________________

Date Purchased: ______________________________

Purchase Price: ______________________________

Fair Market Value: ______________________________

Who Is on Title: ______________________________

Did you sell a prior home to purchase your current home?

When: ________________ Amount of Proceeds: ______________

Buyer known or unknown: ______________

SECTION 7

First Mortgage Information:

Mortgage Company: ____

Address: ____

____

Account Number: ____

Total Amount Owed: $________________

Market Value of Property: $________________

Property Address: Same as Mailing Address Yes No

If no, list address: ______________________________

Regular Monthly Payments: ______________________

Arrears: ________________

Second Mortgage Information (if applicable):

Mortgage Company: ________________________________

Address: ________________________________

____

Account Number: ________________________________

Total Amount Owed: $____________

Market Value of Property: $____________

Property Address: Same as Mailing Address Yes No
If no, list address: ______________________________

Regular Monthly Payments: ______________________
Arrears: ____________

SECTION 8

Property Taxes:
Included in Mortgage: Yes No
Amount Due Annually: $ ______________________
Are you current? Yes No
If not, how much are the arrears and what years: $ ______________________

SECTION 9

Homeowners Insurance:
Included in Mortgage: Yes No
Amount Due Annually: $ ____________________
Are you current? Yes No
If not how much arrears and what years: $ ______________________
Other types of insurance:
Flood insurance, etc. ______________________________
Amount paid: ____________________

SECTION 10

Homeowners Association: Yes or No
Name: ______________________________
Address: ______________________________
Regular Monthly Payment: ______________________________
Arrears: ______________________________
Does it include: Homeowners Insurance, Property Tax, Water ____________
Other/Special Assessment: ______________________________

SECTION 11

Other Real Properties You Own or Holding for Someone Else (timeshares, cemetery lots, vacant land):

Owned By: ____________________
Address: ____________________
Type of Property: ____________________
Mortgage Holder: ____________________
Address: ____________________
Account #: ____________________
Total Balance: ____________
Regular Monthly Payments: ____________
Arrears: ________
Property Insurance: $____________
Property Taxes: $____________
Is Property Rented: Yes No
Rental Income: $ ____________________

SECTION 11(A)

Have You Owned, Sold, or Transferred Any Other Real Estate in the Last 10 Years?

Explain:

____

____

____

SECTION 12

Vehicles:

#1 Own Lease Paid in Full Date of Purchase ________
Do you want to SURRENDER or KEEP/REAFFIRM? ____________
Make: ________ Model ________ Year: ________
Miles: ________ Condition: ____________
Lien Holder/Lender: ____________________
Address: ____________________
Account Number: ____________

Total Amount Owed: $ ________________________________
Market Value of Property: $ ____________________________
Regular Monthly Payments: $ ___________________________
Are you current on the payments: YES NO, arrears and months behind $ ________
____

#2 Own Lease Paid in Full Date of Purchase ________________
Do you want to SURRENDER or KEEP/REAFFIRM? __________________
Make: ________________ Model ______________ Year: ________________
Miles: ________________ Condition: _________________________________
Lien Holder/Lender: ____
Address: ____
Account Number: ______________________________________
Total Amount Owed: $ ________________________________
Market Value of Property: $ ____________________________
Regular Monthly Payments: $ ___________________________
Are you current on the payments: Yes No, arrears and months behind $ ________

#3 Own Lease Paid in Full Date of Purchase ______________
____

Car or Motorcycle
Do you want to SURRENDER or KEEP/REAFFIRM? ______________________
Make: ________________ Model ____________________ Year: ______________
Miles/Hours: __________________
Condition: __________________

Lien Holder/Lender:
____

Address:
____

Account Number: ______________________________________
Total Amount Owed: $ ________________________________

Market Value of Property: $ ____________________

Regular Monthly Payments: $ ____________________

Are you current on the payments: YES NO, arrears and months behind $ __________
____

SECTION 13

Cash on hand: $ ____________

Name of Your Bank ______________ Type of Account ______________
____

Account # ____________________ Balance $ ____________

Name of Your Bank ______________ Type of Account ______________

Account # ____________________ Balance $ ____________

Bank Safe Deposit Box: ____________

Closed Bank Account(s):

Name of the Bank ______________ Type of Account ______________
____

Account # ____________________ Date Closed: ____________

Amount in the Account: $ ________ Funds Went to: ______________

Rental Security Deposit: $ ____________

Retirement Accounts Yes No

401K $ ____________

IRA $ ____________

Pension $ ____________

Investment Stocks $ ____________

Interest in Corporation: Yes No

Does Your Spouse Own a Business? Yes No

Name: ____________

Ownership Interest: $ ____________ or % ____________

Fair Market Value: $ ____________

How Long Owned: ____________

Do you have accounts or sell online with companies such as Poshmark, PayPal, Amazon, or eBay? If so, provide additional details.

____

____

____

____.

Any additional accounts or information please detail below:

Personal Property
Jewelry, Household Goods, and Furnishings

Living Room/Family Room	Date of Purchase	Estimated Value Today
Sofas/love seat		
Recliners		
End table		
Coffee table		
Wall unit		
Lamps		
Misc. Decorations		

Kitchen	Date of Purchase	Estimated Value Today
Dinette table/chairs		
Microwave		
Coffee maker		
Toaster, electric grill		
Dishwasher		
Refrigerator		
Stove		
Dishes, pots/pans		
Silverware		

Bedroom 1 Furniture	Date of Purchase	Estimated Value Today

Bedroom 2 Furniture	Date of Purchase	Estimated Value Today

Bedroom 3 Furniture	Date of Purchase	Estimated Value Today

Electronic Equipment – TV (size), computers, printer, DVR	Date of Purchase	Estimated Value Today

Jewelry	Date of Purchase	Estimated Value Today

Miscellaneous – Sporting equipment, firearms, outdoor furniture, lawn maintenance equipment	Date of Purchase	Estimated Value Today

Do you own anything else having a value of $500.00 or more?

Any additional items, please describe below:

Employer, Income, and Expenses

SECTION 14

Employer: ______________________________
Address: ______________________________
Position: ______________ How Long: ______________

Paid: Weekly Bi-weekly Semi-monthly Monthly

Spouse's Employer: ______________________________
Address: ______________________________
Position: ______________ How Long: ______________

Paid: Weekly Bi-weekly Semi-monthly Monthly

List all former employers and/or sources of income in the last 6 months?

1. ______________________________.
2. ______________________________.
3. ______________________________.

Income Tax:

Total Income (list last 3 years):

$ ______________
$ ______________
$ ______________

Did you receive a Tax Refund last year: Yes, how much: $ ______________ No
IRS Debt: $ ______________ Years: ______________

Other Income: ______________________________
Rental: ______________________________
Investments: ______________________________

SECTION 15: CURRENT MONTHLY INCOME AND EXPENSES

Current monthly gross wages: $ ____________________

Deductions:
Type: ____________________ $ ____________________
Type: ____________________ $ ____________________
Type: ____________________ $ ____________________

Insurance(s):
Type: ____________________ $ ____________________
Type: ____________________ $ ____________________
Type: ____________________ $ ____________________

Retirement:
Type: ____________________ $ ____________________
Type: ____________________ $ ____________________

Other: ____________________ $ ____________________
Other: ____________________ $ ____________________

Commissions: $ ____________________

Net Monthly Income $ ____________________

Current Monthly Expenses

_______ Check if a joint petition is filed and debtor's spouse maintains a separate household.

Rent or Mortgage payment (include lot rented for mobile home) $ ____________________
Are real estate taxes included? Yes No
Is property insurance included? Yes No
Utilities: Electricity and heating fuel $ ____________________
Water and sewer $ ____________________
Telephone $ ____________________
Cable $ ____________________
Alarm/security system $ ____________________
Other: ____________________ $ ____________________

Home maintenance (repairs and upkeep) $ ____________
Food $ ____________
Clothing $ ____________
Laundry and dry cleaning $ ____________
Medical and dental expenses $ ____________
Transportation (not including car payment) $ ____________
Recreation, clubs and entertainment, newspapers, magazines, etc. $ ____________
Charitable contributions $ ____________
Insurance (not deducted from wages or included in home mortgage payments)
Homeowner's or renter's $ ____________
Life $ ____________
Health $ ____________
Auto $ ____________
Other: ____________________ $ ____________

Taxes (not deducted from wages or included in home mortgage payments)
(Specify) ____________________ $ ____________

Installment payments:
Auto #1 ____________________ $ ____________
Auto #2 ____________________ $ ____________
Personal Loan ____________________ $ ____________
Student Loans ____________________ $ ____________

Domestic Support Obligations (Alimony/Child Support)
(Is It Court Ordered?) Yes No $ ____________

Payments for support of additional dependents not living at your home
(Is It Court Ordered?) Yes No $ ____________
Regular expenses from operation of business, profession, or farm
(attach detailed statement) $ ____________

Other:

Cell Phone	$ ______________
Childcare	$ ______________
Grooming	$ ______________
Tolls	$ ______________
Other ______________	$ ______________
Other ______________	$ ______________
Other ______________	$ ______________
Total Monthly Expenses	**$** ______________

SECTION 16

Liabilities:

Credit Cards: Cash Advances: $ ________________ When: ________________________

Date Last Used: ____

Items purchased: ____

____

SECTION 17

Lawsuits: Are you suing or are entitled to sue someone?

Description:

____

Personal injury/Accident:

____

Repossessions:

____

Foreclosures: ____

Payments to any creditors greater than $600.00 within last 90 days:

Date: ________________ Amount: $ ____________________

Date: ________________ Amount: $ ____________________

SECTION 19

List of Creditors

Creditor/Address ____
____

Account # ____________________
Balance $ ____________________
Date Opened/Stopped Making Payments ________________/______________
Type of Debt _________________________

Creditor/Address ____
____

Account # ____________________
Balance $ ____________________
Date Opened/Stopped Making Payments ________________/______________
Type of Debt _________________________

Creditor/Address ____
____

Account # ____________________
Balance $ ____________________
Date Opened/Stopped Making Payments ________________/______________
Type of Debt _________________________

Creditor/Address ____
____

Account # ____________________
Balance $ ____________________
Date Opened/Stopped Making Payments ________________/______________
Type of Debt _________________________

Creditor/Address ____
____

Account # ________________
Balance $ ________________
Date Opened/Stopped Making Payments ____________/__________
Type of Debt ____________________

***Note: List all outstanding debts. This office cannot be responsible for any omissions.**

Bankruptcy Lawyers R' Us Law Firm, P.A.

179 Broke Lane

Miami, Florida 32232

Retainer Agreement for Chapter 7

This agreement is executed on this ______________ day of ____________, 202 _____ by Able the Attorney, (hereinafter the "Attorney") and Carla the Client, hereinafter "Client." The parties agree as follows:

1. **Type of Bankruptcy**
   The Client retains the Attorney to file a Chapter 7 bankruptcy. However, if the Client wishes to file a Chapter 13 bankruptcy at a later date, the parties shall execute a new fee contract setting forth the terms of such representation.

2. **Standard Services Provided by the Attorney**
   Contingent upon being paid for the services as specified below, the Attorney shall provide the following legal services for the Client:
   - Analysis of the Client's financial situation to determine the applicable relief under the Bankruptcy Code whether Chapter 7 or 13;
   - Advise the Client as to the availability of exemptions and how it applies to personal and real property;
   - Advise and assist the Client in assembling all the documents required to file a petition under the Bankruptcy Code;
   - Prepare the bankruptcy petition for electronic filing with the clerk of court;
   - Review and prepare the Client for the *341 Meeting of Creditors*;
   - Attend the *341 Meeting of Creditors* and all court hearings (except as otherwise excluded in this *Retainer Agreement*) with the Client;
   - Assisting the Client with *Reaffirmation Agreements*, if applicable;
   - Assisting with the enforcement of the automatic stay, if required;
   - Communicate with the bankruptcy trustee and creditors, as necessary, including providing the trustee documents timely.

3. **Client Responsibilities**
   The Client agrees to the following:
   - Discuss with the Attorney the Client's objectives in filing the case;
   - To provide the Attorney with full, accurate, and timely information. This includes the *Bankruptcy Intake* and the *List of Required Documents*.
   - The Client shall cooperate with the Attorney in preparing all required bankruptcy papers and documents, thoroughly reviewing drafts of documents, and promptly advising the Attorney of corrections or additions needed;

- To provide any information required by the Chapter 7 trustee, the U.S. Trustee, or any other party in the case, unless the Court rules that the Client is not obligated to provide the information.
- To provide immediate notification in writing of any change in address or telephone number;
- To appear on time at the meeting of creditors or any other hearings that may be scheduled, with a valid government identification card and original Social Security card;
- To comply with all court orders;
- To complete the required credit counseling and financial management courses;
- Documents can be submitted via email or delivered on a jump drive, however, all documents must be submitted in PDF format NOT photos or any other format. In addition, each document is to be submitted as a separate attachment. For example, if you are emailing tax returns, each year of your tax return is separate. Do not scan all the documents together or scan each page separately. If documents are to be delivered in person, please note documents are destroyed once scanned for security purposes.
- Office hours are from 9 a.m. to 5 p.m., Monday through Friday. Please note that email is the preferred method of communication as text messaging is time-consuming. All emails and documents should be sent to bankruptcylawyersrus @law.com. Documents sent in any other format or text messages are deleted automatically.
- Failure of the Client to cooperate fully may result in the Attorney terminating the representation with the Client.
- The Attorney will also cease representation immediately if the Client exhibits aggressive behavior, threatens, curses, or disrespects the Attorney and/or staff. There is a zero-tolerance policy for such behavior.

4. **Fees and Costs**

The base fee for the filing of the bankruptcy is $_______________ which includes filing fees, credit reports if available through AnnualCreditReport.com, one credit counseling class, and one financial management class. Attorney fees are non-refundable. The fee is based on the following assumptions:

a. The Client has provided the Attorney with complete and accurate information.
b. The Client pays the fees and costs within the payment plan period. Failure to do so could result in additional fees at a rate of $50 per month.
c. An additional $250.00 applies if the meeting of creditors is rescheduled due to the Client's fault.
d. *Reaffirmation Agreements* are billed at $150.00 for the first *Reaffirmation Agreement* and $125 for each additional *Reaffirmation Agreement*. Payment is due upon signing the *Reaffirmation Agreement*.
e. *Suggestions of Bankruptcy* are billed at $150.00 and are due before filing.
f. There is an additional fee of $75.00 for each appointment that is not canceled at least 3 hours in advance.

g. There could be an additional charge of $10 per creditor if there are more than fifteen creditors per debtor.
h. Stop payments and checks for insufficient funds will be billed to the Client at costs plus a $75 administrative fee.
i. There are additional fees and costs to obtain documents on a case that has been closed.

5. **Terms of Payment (All Fees Paid are Non-Refundable Except Costs)**
   a. The fees and costs shall be paid in full before the filing of the bankruptcy.
   b. Client has paid **$**_______________ as a retainer fee. This amount has been earned upon receipt by the Attorney and is non-refundable.
   c. If the Debtor decides not to file for bankruptcy, costs will be refunded.
   d. The payment plan is as follows: ______________________________
   ____.

6. **Compensation For Services Not Covered Under Base Fee**
   The Attorney may require an additional retainer for services not covered under the base fee. The Attorney is under no obligation to provide additional services without first having received the additional retainer. The services set out below are not provided under the base fee.
   a. *Adversarial Proceedings*, *2004 Examinations*, depositions, interrogatories, or other discovery proceedings;
   b. *Reaffirmation Agreements*;
   c. Defending Claims;
   d. Discharge Litigation;
   e. Motions whether filing or defending;
   f. Motions to Reopen;
   g. Defending matters arising from the Client's failure to disclose any material fact or false statements in connection with the bankruptcy petition;
   h. Amendments to the petition once filed;
   i. Additional document request by the bankruptcy trustee or the U.S. Trustee's Office;
   j. Any other services not included under the base fee;
   k. Excessive communications initiated by the Client.

   The Client shall compensate the Attorney for these services as follows:

   a. The fees for *2004 Examinations* shall be at an hourly fee of $250.00 per hour, with a minimum of two (2) hours to be paid in advance. The fees and costs for an *Adversary Proceeding* shall be determined on a case-by-case basis.
   b. All motions shall have a flat fee of $500.00 per motion, plus any applicable court costs and/or other costs involved;

7. **Termination of Attorney's Representation**
The Client may terminate the Attorney's representation at any time. The Attorney may terminate representation with the Client's consent, or for cause, including:
   - The Client's failure to pay fees when due;
   - The Client is in breach of this *Retainer Agreement*, is unresponsive or uncooperative; or
   - Circumstances would render the Attorney's continuing representation unlawful or unethical.

   Once the bankruptcy case is filed, the Attorney's representation of the Client continues until the Client receives a discharge (except regarding violations of the permanent injunction as provided for in 11 USC §524), the case is dismissed, the case is converted, or the Bankruptcy Court approves the Attorney's withdraw from representation.

8. **Acknowledgement of Receipt of Disclosures**
The Client acknowledges receiving copies of all disclosure documents attached to this Retainer Agreement. These documents include:
   - Notice to Individual Consumer Debtor under §342(b).
   - Disclosure according to §527(a)(2).
   - Disclosure according to §527(b).

9. **Entire Agreement and Signatures**
The entire agreement between the Attorney and the Client is contained in this Retainer Agreement. The undersigned agrees to all the terms and conditions set forth herein and acknowledges that they have read and understand this agreement.

THE BANKRUPTCY CODE REQUIRES Bankruptcy Lawyers R' Us Law Firm, P.A, TO EXPLICITLY AND CONSPICUOUSLY INFORM YOU THAT:

WE ARE A DEBT RELIEF AGENCY. WE HELP PEOPLE FILE FOR BANKRUPTCY RELIEF UNDER THE BANKRUPTCY CODE

Dated: ________________

____
Client

____
Bankruptcy Lawyers R' Us Law Firm, P.A

Notice Required by 11 U.S.C. § 342(b) for Individuals Filing for Bankruptcy (Form 2010)

This notice is for you if:

You are an individual filing for bankruptcy,
and

Your debts are primarily consumer debts.
Consumer debts are defined in 11 U.S.C.
§ 101(8) as "incurred by an individual primarily for a personal, family, or household purpose."

The types of bankruptcy that are available to individuals

Individuals who meet the qualifications may file under one of four different chapters of Bankruptcy Code:

- Chapter 7 – Liquidation
- Chapter 11 – Reorganization
- Chapter 12 – Voluntary repayment plan for family farmers or fishermen
- Chapter 13 – Voluntary repayment plan for individuals with regular income

You should have an attorney review your decision to file for bankruptcy and the choice of chapter.

Chapter 7: Liquidation

	$245	filing fee
	$78	administrative fee
+	$15	trustee surcharge
	$338	total fee

Chapter 7 is for individuals who have financial difficulty preventing them from paying their debts and who are willing to allow their non-exempt property to be used to pay their creditors. The primary purpose of filing under Chapter 7 is to have your debts discharged. The bankruptcy discharge relieves you after bankruptcy from having to pay many of your pre-bankruptcy debts. Exceptions exist for particular debts, and liens on property may still be enforced after discharge. For example, a creditor may have the right to foreclose a home mortgage or repossess an automobile.

However, if the court finds that you have committed certain kinds of improper conduct described in the Bankruptcy Code, the court may deny your discharge.

You should know that even if you file Chapter 7 and you receive a discharge, some debts are not discharged under the law. Therefore, you may still be responsible to pay:

- most taxes;
- most student loans;
- domestic support and property settlement
- obligations;

- most fines, penalties, forfeitures, and criminal restitution obligations; and
- certain debts that are not listed in your bankruptcy papers.

You may also be required to pay debts arising from:

- fraud or theft;
- fraud or defalcation while acting in breach of fiduciary capacity;
- intentional injuries that you inflicted; and
- death or personal injury caused by operating a motor vehicle, vessel, or aircraft while intoxicated from alcohol or drugs.

If your debts are primarily consumer debts, the court can dismiss your Chapter 7 case if it finds that you have enough income to repay creditors a certain amount. You must file *Chapter 7 Statement of Your Current Monthly Income* (Official Form 122A–1) if you are an individual filing for bankruptcy under Chapter 7. This form will determine your current monthly income and compare whether your income is more than the median income that applies in your state.

If your income is not above the median for your state, you will not have to complete the other Chapter 7 form, the *Chapter 7 Means Test Calculation* (Official Form 122A–2).

If your income is above the median for your state, you must file a second form – the *Chapter 7 Means Test Calculation* (Official Form 122A–2). The calculations on the form – sometimes called the *Means Test* – deduct from your income living expenses and payments on certain debts to determine any amount available to pay unsecured creditors. If your income is more than the median income for your state of residence and family size, depending on the results of the *Means Test*, the U.S. trustee, bankruptcy administrator, or creditors can file a motion to dismiss your case under § 707(b) of the Bankruptcy Code. If a motion is filed, the court will decide if your case should be dismissed. To avoid dismissal, you may choose to proceed under another chapter of the Bankruptcy Code.

If you are an individual filing for Chapter 7 bankruptcy, the trustee may sell your property to pay your debts, subject to your right to exempt the property or a portion of the proceeds from the sale of the property. The property, and the proceeds from property that your bankruptcy trustee sells or liquidates that you are entitled to, is called *exempt property*. Exemptions may enable you to keep your home, a car, clothing, and household items or to receive some of the proceeds if the property is sold.

Exemptions are not automatic. To exempt property, you must list it on *Schedule C: The Property You Claim as Exempt* (Official Form 106C). If you do not list the property, the trustee may sell it and pay all of the proceeds to your creditors.

Chapter 11: Reorganization

	$1,167	filing fee
+	$571	administrative fee
	$1,738	total fee

Chapter 11 is often used for reorganizing a business, but is also available to individuals. The provisions of chapter 11 are too complicated to summarize briefly.

Read These Important Warnings

Because bankruptcy can have serious long-term financial and legal consequences, including loss of your property, you should hire an attorney and carefully consider all of your options before you file. Only an attorney can give you legal advice about what can happen as a result of filing for bankruptcy and what your options are. If you do file for bankruptcy, an attorney can help you fill out the forms properly and protect you, your family, your home, and your possessions.

Although the law allows you to represent yourself in bankruptcy court, you should understand that many people find it difficult to represent themselves successfully. The rules are technical, and a mistake or inaction may harm you. If you file without an attorney, you are still responsible for knowing and following all of the legal requirements.

You should not file for bankruptcy if you are not eligible to file or if you do not intend to file the necessary documents.

Bankruptcy fraud is a serious crime; you could be fined and imprisoned if you commit fraud in your bankruptcy case. Making a false statement, concealing property, or obtaining money or property by fraud in connection with a bankruptcy case can result in fines up to $250,000, or imprisonment for up to 20 years, or both. 18 U.S.C. §§ 152, 1341, 1519, and 3571.

Chapter 12: Repayment plan for family farmers or fishermen

	$200	filing fee
+	$78	administrative fee
	$278	total fee

Similar to Chapter 13, chapter 12 permits family farmers and fishermen to repay their debts over a period of time using future earnings and to discharge some debts that are not paid.

Chapter 13: Repayment plan for individuals with regular income

	$235	filing fee
+	$78	administrative fee
	$313	total fee

Chapter 13 is for individuals who have regular income and would like to pay all or part of their debts in installments over a period of time and to discharge some debts that are not paid. You are eligible for Chapter 13 only if your debts are not more than certain dollar amounts set forth in 11 U.S.C. § 109.

Under chapter 13, you must file with the court a plan to repay your creditors all or part of the money that you owe them, usually using your future earnings. If the court approves your plan, the court will allow you to repay your debts, as adjusted by the plan, within 3 years or 5 years, depending on your income and other factors.

After you make all the payments under your plan, many of your debts are discharged. The debts that are not discharged and that you may still be responsible to pay include:

- domestic support obligations,
- most student loans,
- certain taxes,
- debts for fraud or theft,
- debts for fraud or defalcation while acting in a fiduciary capacity,
- most criminal fines and restitution obligations,
- certain debts that are not listed in your bankruptcy papers,
- certain debts for acts that caused death or personal injury, and
- certain long-term secured debts.

Warning: File Your Forms on Time

Section 521(a)(1) of the Bankruptcy Code requires that you promptly file detailed information about your creditors, assets, liabilities, income, expenses and general financial condition. The court may dismiss your bankruptcy case if you do not file this information within the deadlines set by the Bankruptcy Code, the Bankruptcy Rules, and the local rules of the court.

For more information about the documents and

their deadlines, go to:http://www.uscourts .gov/forms/bankruptcy-forms

Bankruptcy crimes have serious consequences

- If you knowingly and fraudulently conceal assets or make a false oath or statement under penalty of perjury – either orally or in writing – in connection with a bankruptcy case, you may be fined, imprisoned, or both.
- All information you supply in connection with a bankruptcy case is subject to examination by the Attorney General acting through the Office of the U.S. Trustee, the Office of the U.S. Attorney, and other offices and employees of the U.S. Department of Justice.

Make sure the court has your mailing address

The bankruptcy court sends notices to the mailing address you list on *Voluntary Petition for Individuals Filing for Bankruptcy* (Official Form 101). To ensure that you receive information about your case, Bankruptcy Rule 4002 requires that you notify the court of any changes in your address.

A married couple may file a bankruptcy case together – called a *joint case*. If you file a joint case and each spouse lists the same mailing address on the bankruptcy petition, the bankruptcy court generally will mail you and your spouse one copy of each notice, unless you file a statement with the court asking that each spouse receive separate copies.

Understand which services you could receive from credit counseling agencies

The law generally requires that you receive a credit counseling briefing from an approved credit counseling agency. 11 U.S.C. § 109(h). If you are filing a joint case, both spouses must receive the briefing. With limited exceptions, you must receive it within the 180 days ***before*** you file your bankruptcy petition. This briefing is usually conducted by telephone or on the Internet.

In addition, after filing a bankruptcy case, you generally must complete a financial management instructional course before you can receive a discharge. If you are filing a joint case, both spouses must complete the course.

You can obtain the list of agencies approved to provide both the briefing and the instructional course from:

http://www.uscourts.gov/services-forms/bankruptcy/credit-counseling-and-debtor-education-courses.

In Alabama and North Carolina, go to:

http://www.uscourts.gov/services-forms/bankruptcy/credit-counseling-and-debtor-education-courses.

If you do not have access to a computer, the clerk of the bankruptcy court may be able to help you obtain the list.

11 U.S.C. § 527(a)(2) Disclosure

Per the requirements of Section 527(a)(2) of the Bankruptcy Code, please be advised of the following:

1. All information you're required to provide with the bankruptcy petition and while the case remains pending shall be complete, accurate, and truthful.
2. All of your assets and liabilities must be completely and accurately disclosed. You're also required to list the replacement value of each asset as defined in Section 506 of the Bankruptcy Code after reasonable inquiry to establish such value.
3. Your current monthly income as specified in the "Means Test" under Section 707(b)(2), and if filing Chapter 13, disposable income in accordance with Section 707(b)(2), shall be stated after reasonable inquiry.
4. The information you provide during your bankruptcy case may be audited. Failure to provide such information may result in dismissal of the case or other sanctions, including a criminal sanction.

11 U.S.C. Section 527(b) Disclosure

"IMPORTANT INFORMATION ABOUT BANKRUPTCY ASSISTANCE SERVICES FROM AN ATTORNEY OR BANKRUPTCY PETITION PREPARER.

"If you decide to seek bankruptcy relief, you can represent yourself, you can hire an attorney to represent you, or you can get help in some localities from a bankruptcy petition preparer who is not an attorney. THE LAW REQUIRES AN ATTORNEY OR BANKRUPTCY PETITION PREPARER TO GIVE YOU A WRITTEN CONTRACT SPECIFYING WHAT THE ATTORNEY OR BANKRUPTCY PETITION PREPARER WILL DO FOR YOU AND HOW MUCH IT WILL COST. Ask to see the contract before you hire anyone.

"The following information helps you understand what must be done in a routine bankruptcy case to help you evaluate how much service you need. Although bankruptcy can be complex, many cases are routine.

"Before filing a bankruptcy case, either you or your attorney should analyze your eligibility for different forms of debt relief available under the Bankruptcy Code and which form of relief is most likely to be beneficial for you. Be sure you understand the relief you can obtain and its limitations. To file a bankruptcy case, documents called a Petition, Schedules, and Statement of Financial Affairs, and in some cases a Statement of Intention, need to be prepared correctly and filed with the bankruptcy court. You will have to pay a filing fee to the bankruptcy court. Once your case starts, you will have to attend the required first meeting of creditors where you may be questioned by a court official called a 'trustee' and by creditors.

"If you choose to file a chapter 7 case, you may be asked by a creditor to reaffirm a debt. You may want help deciding whether to do so. A creditor is not permitted to coerce you into reaffirming your debts.

"If you choose to file a Chapter 13 case in which you repay your creditors what you can afford over 3 to 5 years, you may also want help with preparing your Chapter 13 plan and with the confirmation hearing on your plan which will be before a bankruptcy judge.

"If you select another type of relief under the Bankruptcy Code other than Chapter 7 or chapter 13, you will want to find out what should be done from someone familiar with that type of relief.

"Your bankruptcy case may also involve litigation. You are generally permitted to represent yourself in litigation in bankruptcy court, but only attorneys, not bankruptcy petition preparers, can give you legal advice."

Bankruptcy Lawyers R' Us Law Firm, P.A.
179 Broke Lane
Miami, Florida 32232

Retainer Agreement for Chapter 13

This agreement is executed on this ______________ day of ________________, 202 ____ by Able the Attorney, (hereinafter the "Attorney") and Carla the Client, hereinafter "Client." The parties agree as follows:

1. **Type of Bankruptcy**
   The Client retains the Attorney to file a Chapter 13 bankruptcy. However, if the Client wishes to file a Chapter 7 bankruptcy at a later date, the parties shall execute a new fee contract setting forth the terms of such representation.

2. **Standard Services Provided by the Attorney**
   Contingent upon being paid for the services as specified below, the Attorney shall provide the following legal services for the Client:
   - Analysis of the Client's financial situation to determine the applicable relief under the Bankruptcy Code whether Chapter 7 or 13;
   - Advise the Client as to the availability of exemptions and how it applies to personal and real property;
   - Advise and assist the Client in assembling all the documents required to file a petition under the Bankruptcy Code;
   - Prepare the bankruptcy petition including the Chapter 13 Plan for electronic filing with the clerk of court;
   - Review and prepare the Client for the *341 Meeting of Creditors*;
   - Attend the *341 Meeting of Creditors* and all other court hearings (except as otherwise excluded in this *Retainer Agreement*) with the Client;
   - Negotiate with creditors and the trustee to present a confirmable plan to the bankruptcy court;
   - Assisting the Client with *Reaffirmation Agreements*, if applicable;
   - Assisting with the enforcement of the *automatic stay*, if required;
   - Communicate with the bankruptcy trustee and creditors, as necessary, including providing the trustee documents timely.

3. **Client Responsibilities**
   The Client agrees to the following:
   - Discuss with the Attorney the Client's objectives in filing the case;
   - To provide the Attorney with full, accurate, and timely information. This includes the *Bankruptcy Intake* and the *List of Required Documents*
   - The Client shall cooperate with the Attorney in preparing all required bankruptcy papers and documents, thoroughly reviewing drafts of documents, and promptly advising the Attorney of corrections or additions needed;

- To provide any information requested by the Chapter 13 trustee, the U.S. Trustee, or any other party in the case, unless the Court rules that the Client is not obligated to provide the information.
- To provide immediate notification in writing of any change in address or telephone number;
- To appear on time at the meeting of creditors or any other hearings that may be scheduled, with a valid government identification card and original Social Security card;
- To make plan payments as required;
- To notify the Attorney immediately of any tax refunds, bonuses, or other lump-sum payments and turn it over if required by the Chapter 13 plan or court order;
- To comply with all court orders;
- To notify the Attorney immediately of any changes in financial circumstances that may affect the Chapter 13 plan;
- To complete the required credit counseling and financial management courses;
- Documents can be submitted via email or delivered on a jump drive, however, all documents must be submitted in PDF format NOT photos or any other format. In addition, each document is to be submitted as a separate attachment. For example, if you are emailing tax returns, each year of your tax return is separate. Do not scan all the documents together or scan each page separately. If documents are to be delivered in person, please note documents are destroyed once scanned for security purposes.
- Office hours are from 9 a.m. to 5 p.m., Monday through Friday. Please note that email is the preferred method of communication as text messaging is time-consuming. All emails and documents should be sent to bankruptcylawyersrus@law.com. Documents sent in any other format or text messages are deleted automatically.
- Failure of the Client to cooperate fully may result in the Attorney terminating the representation with the Client.
- The Attorney will also cease representation immediately if the Client exhibits aggressive behavior, threatens, curses, or disrespects the Attorney and/or staff. There is a zero-tolerance policy for such behavior.

4. **Fees and Costs**

The base fee for the filing of the bankruptcy is $______________ which includes filing fees, credit reports if available through AnnualCreditReport.com, one credit counseling class, and one financial management class. Attorney fees are non-refundable. The fee is based on the following assumptions:

a. The Client has provided the Attorney with complete and accurate information.
b. The Client pays the fees and costs within the payment plan period. Failure to do so could result in additional fees at a rate of $50 per month.
c. An additional $250.00 applies if the meeting of creditors is rescheduled due to the Client's fault.
d. *Reaffirmation Agreements* are billed at $150.00 for the first *Reaffirmation Agreement* and $125 for each additional *Reaffirmation Agreement*. Payment is due upon signing the Reaffirmation Agreement.

e. *Suggestions of Bankruptcy* are billed at $150.00 and are due before filing.
f. There is an additional fee of $75.00 for each appointment that is not canceled at least 3 hours in advance.
g. Stop payments and checks for insufficient funds will be billed to the Client at costs plus a $75 administrative fee.
h. There are additional fees and costs to obtain documents on a case that has been closed.

5. **Terms of Payment (All Fees Paid are Non-Refundable Except Costs)**
   a. The Client has paid **$__________________** as a retainer fee, and the balance of attorney's fees will be collected through the Chapter 13 plan. This amount has been earned upon receipt by the Attorney and is non-refundable.
   b. If the Debtor decides not to file for bankruptcy, costs will be refunded.
   c. The payment plan is as follows: ______________________________________
   ____.

6. **Compensation For Services Not Covered Under Base Fee**
   The Attorney may require an additional retainer for services not covered under the base fee. The Attorney is under no obligation to provide additional services without first having received the additional retainer. The services set out below are not provided under the base fee.
   a. *Adversarial Proceedings*, *2004 Examinations*, depositions, interrogatories, or other discovery proceedings;
   l. *Reaffirmation Agreements*;
   m. Defending Claims;
   n. Discharge Litigation;
   o. Motions whether filing or defending;
   p. Motions to Reopen;
   q. Defending matters arising from the Client's failure to disclose any material fact or false statements in connection with the bankruptcy petition;
   r. Amendments to the petition once filed;
   s. Additional document request by the bankruptcy trustee or the U.S. Trustee's Office;
   t. Any other services not included under the base fee;
   u. Excessive communications initiated by the Client.

   The Client shall compensate the Attorney for these services as follows:

   c. The fees for *2004 Examinations* shall be at an hourly fee of $250.00 per hour, with a minimum of two (2) hours to be paid in advance. The fees and costs for an *Adversary Proceeding* shall be determined on a case-by-case basis.
   d. All Motions shall have a flat fee of $500.00 per motion, plus any applicable court costs and/or other costs involved;

7. **Termination of Attorney's Representation**
The Client may terminate the Attorney's representation at any time. The Attorney may terminate representation with Client's consent, or for cause, including:
– The Client's failure to pay fees when due;
– The Client is in breach of this *Retainer Agreement*, is unresponsive or uncooperative; or
– Circumstances would render the Attorney's continuing representation unlawful or unethical.

Once the bankruptcy case is filed, the Attorney's representation of Client continues through the time Client receives a discharge (except regarding violations of the permanent injunction as provided for in 11 USC § 524), the case is dismissed, the case is converted, or the Bankruptcy Court approves the Attorney's withdraw from representation.

8. **Acknowledgement of Receipt of Disclosures**
The Client acknowledges receiving copies of all disclosure documents attached to this Retainer Agreement. These documents include:
– Notice to Individual Consumer Debtor under §342(b)
– Disclosure according to §527(a)(2)
– Disclosure according to §527(b)

9. **Entire Agreement and Signatures**
The entire agreement between Attorney and Client is contained in this Retainer Agreement. The undersigned agrees to all the terms and conditions set forth herein and acknowledges that they have read and understand this agreement.

THE BANKRUPTCY CODE REQUIRES Bankruptcy Lawyers R' Us Law Firm, P.A, TO EXPLICITLY AND CONSPICUOUSLY INFORM YOU THAT:

WE ARE A DEBT RELIEF AGENCY. WE HELP PEOPLE FILE FOR BANKRUPTCY RELIEF UNDER THE BANKRUPTCY CODE

Dated: ________________

____

Client

____

Bankruptcy Lawyers R' Us Law Firm, P.A

Notice Required by 11 U.S.C. § 342(b) for Individuals Filing for Bankruptcy (Form 2010)

This notice is for you if:

You are an individual filing for bankruptcy,
and

Your debts are primarily consumer debts.
Consumer debts are defined in 11 U.S.C.
§ 101(8) as "incurred by an individual primarily for a personal, family, or household purpose."

The types of bankruptcy that are available to individuals

Individuals who meet the qualifications may file under one of four different chapters of Bankruptcy Code:

- Chapter 7 – Liquidation
- Chapter 11 – Reorganization
- Chapter 12 – Voluntary repayment plan for family farmers or fishermen
- Chapter 13 – Voluntary repayment plan for individuals with regular income

You should have an attorney review your decision to file for bankruptcy and the choice of chapter.

Chapter 7: Liquidation

	$245	filing fee
	$78	administrative fee
+	$15	trustee surcharge
	$338	total fee

Chapter 7 is for individuals who have financial difficulty preventing them from paying their debts and who are willing to allow their non-exempt property to be used to pay their creditors. The primary purpose of filing under Chapter 7 is to have your debts discharged. The bankruptcy discharge relieves you after bankruptcy from having to pay many of your pre-bankruptcy debts. Exceptions exist for particular debts, and liens on property may still be enforced after discharge. For example, a creditor may have the right to foreclose a home mortgage or repossess an automobile.

However, if the court finds that you have committed certain kinds of improper conduct described in the Bankruptcy Code, the court may deny your discharge.

You should know that even if you file Chapter 7 and you receive a discharge, some debts are not discharged under the law. Therefore, you may still be responsible to pay:

- most taxes;
- most student loans;
- domestic support and property settlement
- obligations;

- most fines, penalties, forfeitures, and criminal restitution obligations; and
- certain debts that are not listed in your bankruptcy papers.

You may also be required to pay debts arising from:

- fraud or theft;
- fraud or defalcation while acting in breach of fiduciary capacity;
- intentional injuries that you inflicted; and
- death or personal injury caused by operating a motor vehicle, vessel, or aircraft while intoxicated from alcohol or drugs.

If your debts are primarily consumer debts, the court can dismiss your Chapter 7 case if it finds that you have enough income to repay creditors a certain amount. You must file *Chapter 7 Statement of Your Current Monthly Income* (Official Form 122A–1) if you are an individual filing for bankruptcy under Chapter 7. This form will determine your current monthly income and compare whether your income is more than the median income that applies in your state.

If your income is not above the median for your state, you will not have to complete the other Chapter 7 form, the *Chapter 7 Means Test Calculation* (Official Form 122A–2).

If your income is above the median for your state, you must file a second form – the *Chapter 7 Means Test Calculation* (Official Form 122A–2). The calculations on the form – sometimes called the *Means Test* – deduct from your income living expenses and payments on certain debts to determine any amount available to pay unsecured creditors. If your income is more than the median income for your state of residence and family size, depending on the results of the *Means Test*, the U.S. trustee, bankruptcy administrator, or creditors can file a motion to dismiss your case under § 707(b) of the Bankruptcy Code. If a motion is filed, the court will decide if your case should be dismissed. To avoid dismissal, you may choose to proceed under another chapter of the Bankruptcy Code.

If you are an individual filing for Chapter 7 bankruptcy, the trustee may sell your property to pay your debts, subject to your right to exempt the property or a portion of the proceeds from the sale of the property. The property, and the proceeds from property that your bankruptcy trustee sells or liquidates that you are entitled to, is called *exempt property*. Exemptions may enable you to keep your home, a car, clothing, and household items or to receive some of the proceeds if the property is sold.

Exemptions are not automatic. To exempt property, you must list it on *Schedule C: The Property You Claim as Exempt* (Official Form 106C). If you do not list the property, the trustee may sell it and pay all of the proceeds to your creditors.

Chapter 11: Reorganization

	$1,167	filing fee
+	$571	administrative fee
	$1,738	total fee

Chapter 11 is often used for reorganizing a business, but is also available to individuals. The provisions of chapter 11 are too complicated to summarize briefly.

Read These Important Warnings

Because bankruptcy can have serious long-term financial and legal consequences, including loss of your property, you should hire an attorney and carefully consider all of your options before you file. Only an attorney can give you legal advice about what can happen as a result of filing for bankruptcy and what your options are. If you do file for bankruptcy, an attorney can help you fill out the forms properly and protect you, your family, your home, and your possessions.

Although the law allows you to represent yourself in bankruptcy court, you should understand that many people find it difficult to represent themselves successfully. The rules are technical, and a mistake or inaction may harm you. If you file without an attorney, you are still responsible for knowing and following all of the legal requirements.

You should not file for bankruptcy if you are not eligible to file or if you do not intend to file the necessary documents.

Bankruptcy fraud is a serious crime; you could be fined and imprisoned if you commit fraud in your bankruptcy case. Making a false statement, concealing property, or obtaining money or property by fraud in connection with a bankruptcy case can result in fines up to $250,000, or imprisonment for up to 20 years, or both. 18 U.S.C. §§ 152, 1341, 1519, and 3571.

Chapter 12: Repayment plan for family farmers or fishermen

	$200	filing fee
+	$78	administrative fee
	$278	total fee

Similar to Chapter 13, chapter 12 permits family farmers and fishermen to repay their debts over a period of time using future earnings and to discharge some debts that are not paid.

Chapter 13: Repayment plan for individuals with regular income

	$235	filing fee
+	$78	administrative fee
	$313	total fee

Chapter 13 is for individuals who have regular income and would like to pay all or part of their debts in installments over a period of time and to discharge some debts that are not paid. You are eligible for Chapter 13 only if your debts are not more than certain dollar amounts set forth in 11 U.S.C. § 109.

Under chapter 13, you must file with the court a plan to repay your creditors all or part of the money that you owe them, usually using your future earnings. If the court approves your plan, the court will allow you to repay your debts, as adjusted by the plan, within 3 years or 5 years, depending on your income and other factors.

After you make all the payments under your plan, many of your debts are discharged. The debts that are not discharged and that you may still be responsible to pay include:

- domestic support obligations,
- most student loans,
- certain taxes,
- debts for fraud or theft,
- debts for fraud or defalcation while acting in a fiduciary capacity,
- most criminal fines and restitution obligations,
- certain debts that are not listed in your bankruptcy papers,
- certain debts for acts that caused death or personal injury, and
- certain long-term secured debts.

> **Warning: File Your Forms on Time**
>
> Section 521(a)(1) of the Bankruptcy Code requires that you promptly file detailed information about your creditors, assets, liabilities, income, expenses and general financial condition. The court may dismiss your bankruptcy case if you do not file this information within the deadlines set by the Bankruptcy Code, the Bankruptcy Rules, and the local rules of the court.
>
> For more information about the documents and
>
> their deadlines, go to:http://www.uscourts.gov/forms/bankruptcy-forms

Bankruptcy crimes have serious consequences

- If you knowingly and fraudulently conceal assets or make a false oath or statement under penalty of perjury – either orally or in writing – in connection with a bankruptcy case, you may be fined, imprisoned, or both.
- All information you supply in connection with a bankruptcy case is subject to examination by the Attorney General acting through the Office of the U.S. Trustee, the Office of the U.S. Attorney, and other offices and employees of the U.S. Department of Justice.

Make sure the court has your mailing address

The bankruptcy court sends notices to the mailing address you list on *Voluntary Petition for Individuals Filing for Bankruptcy* (Official Form 101). To ensure that you receive information about your case, Bankruptcy Rule 4002 requires that you notify the court of any changes in your address.

A married couple may file a bankruptcy case together – called a *joint case*. If you file a joint case and each spouse lists the same mailing address on the bankruptcy petition, the bankruptcy court generally will mail you and your spouse one copy of each notice, unless you file a statement with the court asking that each spouse receive separate copies.

Understand which services you could receive from credit counseling agencies

The law generally requires that you receive a credit counseling briefing from an approved credit counseling agency. 11 U.S.C. § 109(h). If you are filing a joint case, both spouses must receive the briefing. With limited exceptions, you must receive it within the 180 days ***before*** you file your bankruptcy petition. This briefing is usually conducted by telephone or on the Internet.

In addition, after filing a bankruptcy case, you generally must complete a financial management instructional course before you can receive a discharge. If you are filing a joint case, both spouses must complete the course.

You can obtain the list of agencies approved to provide both the briefing and the instructional course from:

http://www.uscourts.gov/services-forms/bankruptcy/credit-counseling-and-debtor-education-courses.

In Alabama and North Carolina, go to:

http://www.uscourts.gov/services-forms/bankruptcy/credit-counseling-and-debtor-education-courses.

If you do not have access to a computer, the clerk of the bankruptcy court may be able to help you obtain the list.

11 U.S.C. § 527(a)(2) Disclosure

Per the requirements of Section 527(a)(2) of the Bankruptcy Code, please be advised of the following:

1. All information you're required to provide with the bankruptcy petition and while the case remains pending shall be complete, accurate, and truthful.
2. All of your assets and liabilities must be completely and accurately disclosed. You're also required to list the replacement value of each asset as defined in Section 506 of the Bankruptcy Code after reasonable inquiry to establish such value.
3. Your current monthly income as specified in the "Means Test" under Section 707(b)(2), and if filing Chapter 13, disposable income in accordance with Section 707(b)(2), shall be stated after reasonable inquiry.
4. The information you provide during your bankruptcy case may be audited. Failure to provide such information may result in dismissal of the case or other sanctions, including a criminal sanction.

11 U.S.C. Section 527(b) Disclosure

"IMPORTANT INFORMATION ABOUT BANKRUPTCY ASSISTANCE SERVICES FROM AN ATTORNEY OR BANKRUPTCY PETITION PREPARER.

"If you decide to seek bankruptcy relief, you can represent yourself, you can hire an attorney to represent you, or you can get help in some localities from a bankruptcy petition preparer who is not an attorney. THE LAW REQUIRES AN ATTORNEY OR BANKRUPTCY PETITION PREPARER TO GIVE YOU A WRITTEN CONTRACT SPECIFYING WHAT THE ATTORNEY OR BANKRUPTCY PETITION PREPARER WILL DO FOR YOU AND HOW MUCH IT WILL COST. Ask to see the contract before you hire anyone.

"The following information helps you understand what must be done in a routine bankruptcy case to help you evaluate how much service you need. Although bankruptcy can be complex, many cases are routine.

"Before filing a bankruptcy case, either you or your attorney should analyze your eligibility for different forms of debt relief available under the Bankruptcy Code and which form of relief is most likely to be beneficial for you. Be sure you understand the relief you can obtain and its limitations. To file a bankruptcy case, documents called a Petition, Schedules, and Statement of Financial Affairs, and in some cases a Statement of Intention, need to be prepared correctly and filed with the bankruptcy court. You will have to pay a filing fee to the bankruptcy court. Once your case starts, you will have to attend the required first meeting of creditors where you may be questioned by a court official called a 'trustee' and by creditors.

"If you choose to file a chapter 7 case, you may be asked by a creditor to reaffirm a debt. You may want help deciding whether to do so. A creditor is not permitted to coerce you into reaffirming your debts.

"If you choose to file a Chapter 13 case in which you repay your creditors what you can afford over 3 to 5 years, you may also want help with preparing your Chapter 13 plan and with the confirmation hearing on your plan which will be before a bankruptcy judge.

"If you select another type of relief under the Bankruptcy Code other than Chapter 7 or chapter 13, you will want to find out what should be done from someone familiar with that type of relief.

"Your bankruptcy case may also involve litigation. You are generally permitted to represent yourself in litigation in bankruptcy court, but only attorneys, not bankruptcy petition preparers, can give you legal advice."

UNITED STATES BANKRUPTCY COURT
SOUTHERN DISTRICT OF FLORIDA
www.flsb.uscourts.gov

In re: Benny the Barber, Debtor. ______________________/	Case No. 20-010101-GBK Chapter 7

TRUSTEE'S NOTICE OF RULE 2004 EXAMINATION *DUCES TECUM* OF DEBTOR

Mike the Trustee, as Chapter 7 Trustee (the "Trustee") for the bankruptcy estate of the **Benny the Barber**, (the "Debtor"), by and through her undersigned counsel, pursuant to Fed.R.Bankr.P. 2004 and Local Rule 2004-1, will examine the Debtor (also referred to as the "Examinee"), under oath on **October 10, 2021 at 4 PM** at the **Offices of Trustee, 1155 N.W. Examination Blvd., Suite 1451, Miami, FL 33196.**

The examination was scheduled with Debtor's counsel and may continue from day to day until completed. If the Examinee receives this notice less than seven (7) days prior to the scheduled examination date, the examination will be rescheduled upon timely request to a mutually agreeable date and time.

The examination is being conducted pursuant to Fed. R. Bankr. P. 2004 and Local Rule 2004-1, and will be taken before an officer authorized to stenographically record the testimony. The scope of the examination shall be as described in Fed. R. Bankr. P. 2004. Pursuant to Local Rule 2004-1, no order or subpoena shall be necessary, and to the extent that a request for production of documents under this rule may be construed as a request under Bankruptcy Rule 7034, the time to respond is shortened to 14 days.

If the Debtor requires language interpretation at the examination, arrangements must be made directly and in advance of the scheduled examination, at the Debtor's expense.

The Examinee is further requested to produce all of the documents described on the attached **Exhibit "A"** no later than **October 1, 2021** to the **Offices of Trustee, 1181 N.W. Examination Blvd., Suite 1451, Miami, FL 33196.**

CERTIFICATE OF SERVICE

I CERTIFY that a true and correct copy of the foregoing was served by U.S. Mail on the 1st day of September 2021, upon the Debtor and scheduled secured creditors:

Benny the Barber, Debtor	**Scheduled Secured Creditors**
64 Haircut Lane,	(None)
Miami, FL 33333	

I CERTIFY that a true and correct copy of the foregoing was served via Notice of Electronic Filing (CM/ECF) on the 1st day of September 1, 2021, upon all registered users in this case, including:

- **Mike the Trustee** miketrustee@trusteepa.com
- **Benny's Lawyer**, bennys_laywer@lawyer.com
- **Office of the U.S. Trustee** USTPRegion00.ABCDE.ECF@office.gov

Trustee Law, P.A.
Attorneys for Mike the Trustee
1155 N.W. Examination Blvd., Suite 1451
Miami, FL 33196.
TEL: 444-555-5252
Email: miketrustee@trusteepa.com
By: /s/ Mike the Trustee, Esq.
Mike the Trustee, Esq.
Florida Bar No. 021547422425

Copy: Johnson and Kennedy Court Reporter

EXHIBIT "A"

I. DEFINITIONS AND INSTRUCTIONS

Unless the context of a specific request requires otherwise, the following definitions and instructions shall apply to these requests:

1. "And" and "Or" as used herein are terms of inclusion and not of exclusion and shall be construed either disjunctively or conjunctively as necessary to bring within the scope of the request for production of documents any document or information that might otherwise be construed to be outside its scope.
2. Where the word "any" is used in a request, it includes all documents so described.
3. "Communication" means all written or oral communications however informal, including without limitation to the foregoing, correspondence, memoranda, notes, telegraphs, telephone conversations, negotiations, meetings or other oral communications, which are in any manner evidenced by, or referred to in a document, whether prepared in anticipation of, during, or subsequent to such communications.
4. "Creditor" shall mean any person or entity to whom the Debtor owes money or is due performance of any other contractual obligation.
5. "Debtor", "Examinee", "You" and "Your" shall mean **Benny the Barber.**
6. "Describe," "discuss," "analyze," "describing," "discussion," or "analyzing," mean any document that, in whole or in part, characterizes, delineates, explicates, deliberates, evaluates, appraises, assesses or provides a general explanation of the specified subject.
7. "Document" or "documents" as used herein shall mean the original and any copy, regardless of its origin and location, of all writings of any kind whatsoever including, but not limited to, all abstracts, accounting journals, accounting ledgers, advertisements, affidavits, agendas, agreements or proposed agreements, analyses, appointment books, appraisals, articles of incorporation, balance sheets, bank checks, bank deposit or withdrawal slips, bank credit or debit memoranda, bank statements, blue prints, books, books of account, budgets, bulletins, bylaws, canceled checks, charts, checks, codes, communications, communications with government bodies, computer data or printouts, conferences, contracts, correspondence, data processing cards, data sheets, desk calendars, details, diagrams, diaries, disks or data compilations from which information can be obtained or translated, drafts, drawings, electromagnetic tapes, files, films, financial calculations, financial projections, financial statements, graphs, handwritten notes or comments however produced or reproduced, indexes, insertions, instructions, internal accounting records, interoffice communications, invoices, ledgers, letters, lists, logbooks, manuals, memoranda, microfilm, minutes of meetings, motion pictures, newspaper or magazine articles, networks, nonconforming copies which contain deletions, notations or records of meetings, notes, notices of wire transfer of funds, outlines, pamphlets, papers, passbooks, periodicals, photocopies, photographs, pictures, plans, preliminary drafts, press releases, proposals, publications, punch cards, raw and refined data, receipts, recommendations, records, records of conferences or conversations or

meetings, records of payment, reports, resolutions, results of investigations, schedules, schematics, sepia, shipping papers, slides, specifications, speeches, statements of account, studies, summaries, surveys, tape recordings, tax returns, telegrams, telephone logs and records, telephone and other conversations or communications, teletypes, telexes, transcripts, transcripts of tape recordings, video tapes, voice records, vouchers, work papers, worksheets, written notations, and any and all other papers similar to any of the foregoing. Any document containing thereon or attached thereto any alterations, comments, notes or other material not included in the copies or originals or referred to in the preceding definition shall be deemed a separate document within said definition. Any document shall include all exhibits, schedules or other writings affected by or referenced in any such document or other writings necessary to complete the information contained therein or make it not misleading.

8. "Person" means any natural person, corporation, partnership, company, sole proprietorship, association, institute, joint venture, firm, governmental body, or other legal entity, whether privately or publicly owned or controlled, for profit or non-for-profit, or partially or fully government owned or controlled.
9. "Petition Date" shall mean **July 30, 2021.**
10. "Relate to" and "relating to" mean to make a statement about, refer to, discuss, describe, reflect, contain, comprise, identify, or in any way to pertain to, in whole or in part, or otherwise to be used, considered, or reviewed in any way in connection with, the specified subject. Thus, documents that "relate to" a subject also include those which were specifically rejected and those which were not relied or acted upon.
11. "Year" means calendar year unless otherwise specified.
12. The singular form of a noun or pronoun shall be considered to include within its meaning the plural form of the noun or pronoun, and vice versa. The masculine form of a noun or pronoun shall be considered to include within its meaning the feminine form of the noun or pronoun, and vice versa.
13. Regardless of the tense employed, all verbs shall be read as applying to the past, present and future as is necessary to make any paragraph more, rather than less, inclusive.

II. INSTRUCTIONS

1. With respect to this request for documents, the following instructions shall apply:

    (1) This request for documents is continuing and Examinee is requested to supplement its responses hereto.
    (2) Examinee is hereby notified that its duty to respond includes the duty to supply all documents and materials in Examinee's physical possession, as well as those which can be obtained from additional sources, pursuant to Rule 7036 of the Federal Rules of Bankruptcy Procedure.
    (3) In the event that any document called for by a request is withheld on the basis of claim of privilege, please identify that document by stating: (a) any addressor or

addressee; (b) matter, number of pages, and attachments or appendices; (c) all persons to whom the document was distributed, shown or explained: (d) its present custodian; and (e) the nature of the privilege asserted.

(4) In the event that any document requested herein is not presently in your possession or subject to your control, please identify each person you have reason to believe had or has knowledge of its contents.

(5) In the event that any document called for by a request has been destroyed or discarded, please identify that document by stating: (a) any address or any addressee; (b) any indicated or blind copies; (c) the document's date, subject matter, number of pages, and attachments or appendices; (d) all persons to whom the document was distributed, shown or explained; (e) its date and destruction or discard, manner of destruction or discard, and reason for destruction or discard; and (f) the persons authorizing or carrying out such destruction or discard.

(6) In producing documents requested herein, you shall produce documents in full, without abridgment, abbreviation, and expurgation of any sort.

(7) All documents shall be segregated in accordance with the numbered and lettered paragraphs and subparagraphs herein, and produced pursuant to the provisions of Fed. R. Civ. P. 45, made applicable in bankruptcy cases by Fed. R. Bankr. P. 9016.

III. DOCUMENTS TO BE PRODUCED

1. Provide copies of closing statements, deeds, mortgage or loan applications, mortgage or promissory notes, and proof of ownership for all **real property** not listed under Debtor's **Schedule A** in the Debtor's possession, custody or control for the 48 months prior to the Petition Date.
2. Provide a copy of the application and closing statement for any refinancing or loan modifications that took place within the 48 months prior to the Petition Date and a copy of all current mortgage statements showing the outstanding balances for real property detailed in Item 1 above, including a full accounting of any proceeds received as a result of the refinancing.
3. Provide a copy of the closing statement for any real property that was sold or transferred by the Debtor within the 48 months prior to the Petition Date including a full accounting of any proceeds received from any transaction.
4. Provide a copy of the homeowner's or renter's insurance policy for all real property under Item 1.
5. Provide a copy of any lease or rental agreement or proof of income derived from all real property under Item 1.
6. Provide copies of statements and original cancelled checks for all bank accounts from January 1, 2018, through and including June 30, 2021, that are in the name or joint name of the Debtor, or where the Debtor is an authorized signer or an interested party of any kind.
7. Provide any and all documentation the security deposit as listed in **Schedule B, Item 4**.

8. Provide a copy of the bank statement for Bank 1, Account Number -1055 for the month of June, 2021.
9. Provide copies of statements and original cancelled checks for any and all closed financial accounts from January 1, 2018, through and including June 30, 2021, that are in the name or joint name of the Debtor, or where the Debtor is an authorized signer or an interested party of any kind.
10. Provide support for any and all deposits, withdrawals, and checks that are $500.00 or higher in any bank accounts that are or were in the name or joint name of the Debtor, or where the Debtor is or was an authorized signer or an interested party of any kind, for the period from January 1, 2018, through and including June 30, 2021.
11. Provide a detailed list and documentation to support the value of $950.00 as listed for the "Household Goods and Furnishings" on **Schedule B, Item 4**, including clear photographs of all of these items and their location.
12. Provide a detailed list and documentation to support the value of $125.00 as listed for "Clothing" on **Schedule B, Item 6**, including clear photographs of all of these items.
13. Provide a detailed list and documentation to support the value of $250.00 as listed for "Jewelry" on **Schedule B, Item 7**, including clear photographs of all of these items.
14. Provide any and all documentation regarding the education IRA as listed in **Schedule B, Item 11**.
15. For the 48 months prior to the Petition Date, provide documentation supporting the Debtor's ownership interest in or acquisition of all vehicles including those listed under **Schedule B, Item 25** including, but not limited to, registrations, proof of insurance, proof of purchase, proof of lease, lienholder information, co-owner information, primary driver information, and proof of sale or transfer including consideration, full name and address, date of transfer:
    a. 2019 Nissan Sentra (39,000 miles);
    b. 2019 Suzuki Motorcycle (18,500).
16. Provide a full accounting of all cash advances taken from any credit card or line of credit as listed on **Schedule F** including a detailed description of what the money was used for.
17. Provide any and all documentation regarding the taxes and certain other debts owed to government units listed in **Schedule E**.
18. Provide any and all documentation regarding the payments to creditors including but not limited to Best Friend #1 and Best Friend #2, listed under **Statement of Financial Affairs, Item 3(a)**.
19. Provide copies of the receipts or detailed statements for all purchases made within the last five (5) years from the creditors as listed on **Schedule F**.
20. Provide copies of any and all **applications (for credit)** that were submitted to any party by the Debtor for the 48 months prior to the Petition Date.
21. Provide any and all documentation regarding any and all **transfers** of money, property, loans, investments, gifts over $500, for the forty-eight (48) months up to and including the Petition Date.
22. Provide any and all documentation regarding any and all joint debt of any kind.
23. Provide a copy of a recent credit report for the Debtor.

24. Provide signed copies of your **Personal Income Tax Returns** for 2018, 2019, 2020 and 2021 as submitted to the IRS including supporting documents used to prepare these returns (i.e., Forms W-2, 1099, 1098, K-1, etc.).
25. Provide any and all documentation regarding the domestic partner contribution as listed in **Schedule I**.
26. Provide any and all documentation regarding any and all college and/or education expenses paid by you on behalf of your three (3) children listed under **Schedule J**, including but not limited to names of institutions, current contact information for the institutions, and total payments made by each in the twelve (12) months prior to the Petition Date.
27. Provide any and all documentation regarding any transfers, support payments, or expenses paid by you on behalf of your children listed under **Schedule J**.
28. Provide any and all documentation regarding any and all equitable or future interests, life estates, and rights or powers exercisable for the benefit of the Debtor.
29. Provide any and all documentation regarding any and all life insurance policies and/or annuities in the name of or for the benefit of the Debtor and/or Debtor's estate.
30. Provide any and all documentation regarding corporate information within six (6) years immediately preceding the Petition Date including, but not limited to, formation documents, dissolution documents, transfer documents, stock certificates, names of current officers and directors, names of previous officers and directors, business licenses, payroll records, payroll tax returns, business tax returns, profit and loss statements, general ledgers, accounts receivable, inventory and assets, accounts payable, bank statements, websites, and credit card or merchant account statements, including virtual accounts such as PayPal and Western Union, for:
    a. Benny the Barber, Inc.
31. Provide any and all documentation that would support and/or establish the value of the entities listed under Item 30.
32. Provide a detailed list of all real property, equipment, machinery or inventory held by the Debtor including the location of the property with respect to the entities listed under Item 30.
33. Provide a USB flash-drive, portable drive, or disc containing the accounting data for the entities listed under Item 30 including the name of the software used and the passwords required to access the data.
34. Provide copies of financing statements, factoring agreements, financing agreements, partnership agreements, contracts, leases including storage unit or warehouse leases, and financial statements for the entities listed under Item 30.
35. Provide any and all documentation regarding business ventures or assets held with any individuals within six (6) years immediately preceding the Petition Date.

UNITED STATES BANKRUPTCY COURT
MIDDLE DISTRICT OF FLORIDA
ORLANDO DIVISION

In re: CASE NO.: 2020-00000-BKC-ABC
Chapter 7

Carla the Chef,
Debtor.
______________________/

STIPULATION FOR COMPROMISE AND SETTLEMENT REGARDING VALUATION AND REPURCHASE OF DEBTOR'S NON-EXEMPT ASSETS

Terry the Trustee, as Chapter 7 Trustee, and the Debtor, Carla the Chef (the "Debtor"), enter into this Stipulation for Compromise and Settlement Regarding Valuation and Repurchase of Debtor's Non-Exempt Assets (the "Stipulation"). The Trustee and the Debtor agree upon the following terms and conditions:

1. This case commenced with the filing of a voluntary Chapter 7 Petition on October 1, 2020. Terry the Trustee is the duly appointed Chapter 7 Trustee.
2. The Schedules list certain property (collectively, the "Scheduled Property"). In addition, the Debtor may receive a Federal Income Tax Refund for the period through the Petition Date (the "Refund") (the Scheduled Property and the Refund shall be collectively referred to as the "Property").
3. The Debtor has claimed a portion of the Property as exempt.
4. Based on a review of the documents provided and other salient information, the Trustee asserts that a portion of the Property may be undervalued.
5. The Debtor disputes certain aspects of the Trustee's analysis.

<u>THE SETTLEMENT</u>

6. The Trustee and the Debtor agree to compromise the valuation and repurchase of the non-exempt interest in the Property for $4,000 (the "Settlement Amount").
7. The Trustee and the Debtor(s) agree that the Settlement Amount provides for the repurchase of the Debtor(s)' interest in the following:

ASSET DESCRIPTION	PRORATION %	SETTLED VALUE OF ASSET
Cadillac Escalade	55.74%	$2,229.51
Motorcycle	10%	$385.73
Bed/mattress, dresser, 1 nightstand (2014). Value based on debtor's opinion after considering age, condition, and original purchase price.	1%	$57.86
Samsung Tablet (2014).	0%	$11.57
Value based on debtor's opinion after considering age, condition, and original purchase price.		
32 inch TV (2013). Value based on debtor's opinion after considering age, condition, and original purchase price.	0%	$15.43
Used clothing and shoes.	1%	$28.93
Value based on debtor's opinion after considering age, condition, and original purchase price.		
Costume jewelry.	0%	$7.71
Value based on debtor's opinion after considering age, condition, and original purchase price.		
Regions Checking Account	0%	$11.57
2019 tax refund	12%	$480.23
Cash	19%	$771.46

8. The Trustee and the Debtor agree that the Settlement Amount of $4,000.00 shall be paid in full on or before ____________, 2020.
9. Each payment shall be in the form of a money order or cashier's check, made payable to "Terry the Trustee," Trustee, for the Estate of Debtor 1, Case No.: 2020-00000-BKC-ABC, shall be delivered to: Terry the Trustee, at 123 Main Street, Orlando, FL 33030.
10. The Debtor represents and warrants that: (1) all information contained in the Debtor's Bankruptcy Petition, Schedules, SOFA, and all amendments thereto (collectively, the "Pleadings"), are true and correct, (2) the Pleadings contain no material misrepresentations or omissions, (3) all information and documentation provided to the Trustee (collectively, the "Documents"), are true and correct and (4) the Documents contain no material misrepresentations or omissions. To the extent that the Debtor(s) has failed to disclose any assets, this Stipulation shall not affect the Estate's right to seek turnover of such assets or to avail itself of the remedies provided under the Bankruptcy Code.
11. In the event that the Debtor fails to comply with the terms of this Stipulation, or should any of the Debtor's representations and warranties contained herein be untrue, the Trustee may proceed against any and all assets of the Debtor including, but not limited to, the Property the Debtor has claimed as exempt for the remainder of the amount

due and owing as set forth herein. In addition, the Trustee shall be entitled to interest, which shall accrue at the statutory rate, attorneys' fees and costs. Further, the Trustee may file a Notice of Default and submit an Order to the Court revoking the Debtor's discharge. Pursuant to the terms stated herein, and the provisions of 11 U.S.C. §727(a)(10), the Debtor agrees to waive any procedural requirements prior to the entry of an order revoking discharge. However, the Debtor's discharge will not be revoked without a hearing.

12. This Stipulation represents the entire understanding and agreement between the parties hereto with respect to the subject matter hereof and cannot be amended, supplemented or modified except by an instrument in writing signed by the party or parties against whom enforcement of any amendment, supplement or modification is sought. A waiver by a party of any breach of any provision of this stipulation shall not be construed to be a waiver by any such party of any succeeding breach of such provision or a waiver by such party of any breach of any other provision.
13. This Stipulation may be executed in counterparts, which, when combined, shall be deemed to constitute one original and binding document. The parties further agree that facsimile signatures shall be treated in all manner and respects as original signatures.
14. This Stipulation is subject to approval of the United States Bankruptcy Court, Southern District of Florida.

SIGNATURES ON FOLLOWING PAGE

Dated this ____ day of ________, 2020.

____

Clara the Chef
123 Bankruptcy Lane
Orlando, FL 33333

Dated this ____ day of ________, 2020.

____

Terry the Trustee
123 Main Street
Orlando, FL 33030

Dated this ____ day of ________, 2020.

____

Able the Attorney, Esq.
Attorney for Clara the Chef
123 Lawyer Lane
Orlando, FL 33300

REFERENCES

11 U.S.C. §101.

11 U.S.C. §109.

11 U.S.C. §342.

11 U.S.C. §521.

11 U.S.C. §524.

11 U.S.C. §527.

11 U.S.C. §707.

11 U.S.C. §727.

18 U.S.C. §152.

18 U.S.C. §1341.

18 U.S.C. §1519.

18 U.S.C. §3571.

Fed. R. Bankr. P. 2004.

Fed. R. Bankr. P. 7034.

Fed. R. Bankr. P. 9016.

Fed. R. Civ. P. 45.

Official Form B2010. Notice Required by 11 U.S.C. § 342(b) for Individuals Filing for Bankruptcy (Form 2010).

Official Form 101. Voluntary Petition for Individuals Filing for Bankruptcy.

Official Form 106C. Schedule C: The Property You Claim as Exempt (Individuals).

Official Form 122A-1. Chapter 7 Statement of Your Current Monthly Income.

Official Form 122A-2. Chapter 7 Means Test Calculation.

Answers to End of Chapter Questions

CHAPTER 1

Discussion Questions

1. The answer to whether judges should serve lifetime appointments versus limited terms is debatable. But lately, this has become an issue, especially with the concept of "court-packing" and increasing the number of judges at the U.S. Supreme Court level.
2. This is a trick question because bankruptcy is not an option at the state level.
3. This question requires the student to research Chapter 9 cases in their city/state.
4. The largest municipal bankruptcy was the city of Detroit, Michigan, on July 18, 2013.
5. Credit counseling may reduce the number of bankruptcy cases filed, but it won't necessarily reduce indebtedness. The general consensus, which would be surprising to the student, is that most bankruptcies are filed because of medical bills and health-related issues, divorce, and unemployment.

6–7. Historically, creditors were "loose" with giving consumers credit. Restrictions on the amount that consumers could borrow would likely have reduced bankruptcy filings.

8. This question requires the student to research bankruptcy fraud statistics which are readily available through the U.S. Trustee's Office/Department of Justice.
9. The student will learn that fraud doesn't only occur with the debt amount but also with concealment of transfers of assets. Real cases are cited throughout the text. The issue isn't necessarily the amount owed as there could be substantial medical bills, but how the debtor used credit cards and personal loans at or near the time of filing bankruptcy.

CHAPTER 2

Discussion Questions

1. This question requires the student to use online resources to continue to learn and become familiar with the available bankruptcy resources. The best source of this information is the Department of Justice website, the U.S. Trustee's Office division, and the court's website for their district.

DOI: 10.4324/9781003203278-30

2. The U.S. Trustee works under the umbrella of the Department of Justice, while a bankruptcy trustee is a private individual, usually a lawyer, that handles the administration of the bankruptcy case/estate.
3. Section 101(12A) defines a "debt relief agency" as "any person who provides any bankruptcy assistance to an assisted person in return for the payment of money or other valuable consideration." In this case, the attorney at some point worked for a bankruptcy law firm, but there's no indication that the attorney currently represents debtors or accepts payment from debtors, so it's unlikely that the reporting requirements of BAPCPA apply.
4. Answers will vary, but the focus is for the student to begin to feel comfortable discussing bankruptcy.
5. Section (4A) defines "bankruptcy assistance" as "any goods or services sold or otherwise provided to an assisted person with the express or implied purpose of providing information, advice, counsel, document preparation, or filing, or attendance at a creditors' meeting or appearing in a case or proceeding on behalf of another or providing legal representation with respect to a case or proceeding under this title."

   This is debatable and subject to interpretation. For this reason, it's recommended throughout the text to avoid discussing details over the phone with a debtor that hasn't retained the firm. This helps avoid the appearance of an attorney–client relationship. In addition, paralegals are prohibited from giving legal advice.

CHAPTER 3

Discussion Questions

1. The purpose of an exemption is to protect a debtor's assets to a certain extent. The amount varies per state and whether the state uses state or federal exemptions.
2. The intent of Congress with the means test was to create uniformity for all debtors since Congress was concerned that debtors were abusing the bankruptcy system. Creating the means test eliminated the discretion to depend solely on disposable income with the intent of pushing more debtors towards Chapter 13.
3. This question requires research by the student, and answers vary depending on the state.

CHAPTER 4

Discussion Questions

1. The purpose of diversity of citizenship was to avoid local courts being prejudiced against out-of-state litigants.
2. The Federal Rules of Bankruptcy Procedure, almost a duplicate of the Federal Rules of Civil Procedure, would supersede a local rule.

   Questions 3 and 4 require independent research, and the answers will vary per state.

5. The student should perform independent research to find out information about their district court, or use the resources chapter.

CHAPTER 5

The Discussion Questions and Practice Questions will have varying answers. The Discussion Questions are based on the student's personal experiences, while the Practice Questions prepare the paralegal for issues they are likely to face when handling clients.

CHAPTER 6

The Discussion Questions and Practice Questions will have varying answers, but it prepares the paralegal for issues they are likely to face when handling clients. For Question 5, there are software programs that provide conflict checks.

CHAPTER 7

Introductory Section

Answers will vary depending on the state.

Section 1

1. If the client is not cooperating, at the minimum, a notation should be made in the file and the attorney advised of the situation. The paralegal could also search online through the clerk's office to confirm the status of the divorce case.
2. If the client moved, it's unlikely the new address would be updated with creditors. However, if the client is married, at issue then is if the parties are separated, or the client is only pretending to be separated for purposes of qualifying for bankruptcy. The client's driver's license should reflect the current residence.
3. If there are multiple car payments, the client should confirm if he's in possession of all the vehicles as maybe one vehicle or more was surrendered. If the client is a co-signer on the car loan, then the schedules should reflect that a third party is making the car payments.
4. The client's relationship with the boyfriend could affect the case if they live together since that may affect her monthly expenses. If the client does reside with the boyfriend, any household contributions are reflected on Schedule I, but not on the means test.

Section 2

1. The purpose of residency requirements is to prevent debtors from forum shopping, which is seeking more favorable jurisdictions.

2. The difference between residency and domicile depends on the debtor's intent since a debtor can reside in more than one place but could only have one domicile. This is a fact-based issue, so it depends on where the debtor intends to live permanently.

Section 3

1. There are multiple reasons why the automatic stay doesn't apply to family law cases. For example, whether Chapter 7 or 13, any delays in support would affect the other party financially, preventing the receiving spouse from paying rent, mortgage, utilities, groceries, etc.
2. To confirm the client's monthly child support obligation, review bank statements, paystubs, or request from the client any court order.
3. A priority claim is an unsecured debt that entitles the creditor to receive any distributions from the bankruptcy estate before other types of unsecured claims. Section 507(a) lists the different levels of claim priorities.

Section 4

1. A dismissal means the case wasn't completed and closed before a discharge was received. A discharge means the bankruptcy case was concluded and the dischargeable debts were eliminated, while non-dischargeable debts cannot be eliminated in bankruptcy.
2. Whether Chapter 7 or 13, a case is dismissed for six months with prejudice unless the judge shortens the time frame. If the debtor received a discharge in a Chapter 7 case, the debtor needs to wait eight years to file another. If the debtor previously filed Chapter 13, there's a six-year waiting period to file Chapter 7, unless 100 percent of the unsecured claims were paid or 70 percent, and the plan was made in good faith, and the debtor did their best effort to comply with the plan. If the debtor previously filed Chapter 13, there's a two-year waiting period to file another Chapter 13 or four years if a discharge was received in another bankruptcy.

Section 5

1. If an insurance company or individual is listed as a creditor, confirm the reason for the debt. For example, suppose it was a car accident. In that case, the issue is whether it's a negligence case where the debt is dischargeable or non-dischargeable because the client was charged with driving while intoxicated.
2. John can still file for bankruptcy as his prior felony conviction is unrelated to the bankruptcy filing.

CHAPTER 8

Section 6

Discussion Questions

1. This question requires the student to research the relevant statute in their state.
2. With a divorce case pending and possible settlement, the issue is what is the likely outcome at mediation with marital assets since assets protected during the marriage may be non-exempt after divorce. In this case, the new property becomes the client's homestead property, so an exemption doesn't protect the marital home.

Practice Questions and Exercises

1. The email should focus on the fact that a homestead exemption protects neither the timeshare nor the cemetery plot.

Section 7

1. The student's answer should focus on lien stripping and the fact that filing for bankruptcy won't automatically cause a junior lien to become an unsecured debt, especially if Chapter 7 was filed. To lien strip, a motion would have to be argued before the court.
2. Laws will vary per state on deficiency judgments and foreclosures.

Sections 8 and 9

Discussion Questions

1. If the taxes and insurance aren't escrowed, the annual property tax bill and insurance policy are required to determine the amounts paid since they won't be reflected in the mortgage statement. If the client is behind on his property taxes, he can file for Chapter 13 to cure the arrears.
2. If there is a shortage in the escrow account, the client has to make up the difference. The client may have to file Chapter 13 to cure the deficiency.
3. If there is an overage in the client's escrow account, the lender will refund that amount. Unless protected by an exemption, the escrow overage is part of the bankruptcy estate.
4. Because Harriet the Homeowner's mortgage is interest-only, the issue is when does she have to start paying principal and interest as that will affect the monthly calculations.

Practice Questions and Exercises

1. Calculations monthly are as follows:

   $1,175 monthly mortgage
   $207.33 property taxes
   $207.33 insurance
   $47.41 flood insurance

Section 10

1. If there is a homeowner's association, the client should be advised of the special treatment HOA's receive under §523(a)(16).

Section 11

1. Timeshares are fractional ownership, and likewise, with cemetery lots, a parcel of land is owned.
2. In this case, it should be confirmed if the client owns a cemetery plot. If so, the issue is the equity, so the value and balance owed on the cemetery plot are required. With the timeshare, it likely has minimal value, so the trustee is likely to abandon any interest, but make sure to not deduct the expense on Schedule J and have any automatic withdraws from the client's bank account cease.
3. If the client has continued to make payments on the timeshare and cemetery plot, the issue is the equity. The client should provide an updated statement.
4. If the cemetery plot was sold, questions should focus on when, to whom, and the net proceeds. If the timeshare was returned to the lender, the balance owed is listed as unsecured debt on Schedule F.
5. If the cemetery plot was sold to a family member, the issue is how long ago was the sale and the amount of the net proceeds. This is to determine if there are issues with fraudulent transfers to an insider. With net proceeds, the issue is always the same; how much was received and what the funds were used for. If the cemetery plot was sold back to the funeral service provider, ask the client how much was received, and how were the funds spent?

Section 11(a)

1. Any issues with the client paying back a loan to his brother depend on when the bankruptcy is going to be filed. The more time that has passed since that transaction, the better. However, if the bankruptcy is being filed soon, then the trustee may seek the $3,000 as part of the bankruptcy estate. The client will have to pay back the $3,000 to the trustee, or the trustee has the authority to file a lawsuit (adversary proceeding) against the brother to collect the funds on behalf of the bankruptcy estate.
2. While a sale to an insider could potentially be an issue, the value of the asset sold is of utmost importance. In this case, the value and sale amount is reasonable considering the client's financial difficulties. Because child support is a domestic support obligation, there likely isn't going to be an issue. Likewise, the trustee isn't likely to pursue the issue of the apartment and fees paid to the divorce attorney.
3. Here, considering how underpriced the motorcycle was sold for, the trustee is likely to void the transaction.

Section 12

1. This is a common issue where clients' needs are in conflict with bankruptcy law. Usually, the client knows someone who filed for bankruptcy and kept the car, but either the over-exempt amount was paid to the bankruptcy estate, or the car had little to no equity. One comparison that I've been successful with is to tell the client that bankruptcy means they can't afford to pay back their debts, but at the same time, they have $7,500 in cash that could be used towards negotiating with creditors. Clients usually agree in that scenario that the money should be used towards paying the debt. The fact is that everyone needs $7,500, but unfortunately, the money isn't protected by an exemption. The vehicle's equity is no different from the cash; it's just the asset is in a different form. The client may have to file Chapter 13 to pay back the over exempt amount through the plan.

Section 13

1. The client should provide the corporation documents, usually available online, that will confirm if she also has an ownership interest (shares) in the corporation.
2. For clients that withdraw their paycheck from their bank account or cash their check, there's usually more cash on hand to list in Schedule A/B of the petition. Also, the income listed on Schedule I when compared to Schedule J's expenses should result in minimal disposable income.

CHAPTER 9

Discussion Questions

1. With medical expenses, the concern is if the bills are due to a personal injury case where a settlement will result in non-exempt funds. If it's health-related, then it's not an issue.
2. Whether debt collectors, creditors, or monthly payments with a debt settlement company, it can be difficult to stop automatic withdrawals. Not only is the client not supposed to be paying unsecured creditors if bankruptcy is the next step but it's also a waste of money to do so. If the payments don't stop, the client should close the original checking account and open a new one.

Practice Questions and Exercises

1. Here, the paralegal should address the issues of over-exempt assets because of the large tax refund.
2. The email drafted to the client should focus on an additional revenue stream such as a gig economy job or a side business selling items that will increase both income and disposable income.

CHAPTER 10

Section 16

1. For Questions 1 and 2, both fact patterns could be argued as an exception to §523 since it's only presumed that the debt is non-dischargeable. But the intent is to have the paralegal start to spot issues and analyze fact patterns while learning the applicable statute and summarizing issues for the attorney.

Section 17

1. There are times that a bankruptcy cannot be filed immediately. In this case, the client can avoid a settlement at mediation, which would result in substantial delays since a trial date won't likely be imminent. But if it was, the client can reach an agreement at mediation, and when the case is ready to be filed, stop paying a few months in advance.
2. For Question 2, the student is to become familiar with using online resources in their county/jurisdiction.

Section 18

3. Disputes can be submitted directly to the credit reporting bureau through their website.
4. It is better to err on the side of caution. Even if the client doubts the debt listed in a credit report is theirs, it's better to include it in the petition.

CHAPTER 11

Discussion Questions

1. When a client is served with a lawsuit, depending the status of the case will determine when the bankruptcy should be filed. For example, if a default judgment was entered, the client's wages may be garnished soon, so delays in filing should be avoided.
2. This question requires the student to research the rules of civil procedure in their state. Another alternative is to search for a summons on the clerk's website or state government sites since the summons has that information. Generally, a response is required within 20 to 30 days.

CHAPTER 12

Discussion Questions

1. The first issue with a prior bankruptcy filing is whether the bankruptcy was dismissed or a discharge received. If dismissed, the client can refile Chapter 7 or 13. If discharged,

then the client must comply with the requirements of §727 or §1328 as discussed in Chapter 7. Regardless, due diligence requires confirming if there have been prior filings through CM/ECF.

2. If there is an eviction pending, the client may have to file Official Form 101A and B, depending on whether a judgment was entered, and if the client wishes to take advantage of the automatic stay.

CHAPTER 14

Discussion Questions

1. The bankruptcy might be affected because a reduction in expenses will increase disposable income, possibly resulting in the client filing for Chapter 13 instead of 7.
2. The client should be advised to file the tax returns before filing for bankruptcy since the trustee will require it. An exception is that the client earned minimal income and is not required to file per IRS rules.
3. The first issue is what amount of the tax refund is exempt as the Child Tax Credit. If the client is still over-exempt, the refund will belong to the bankruptcy estate. If the client wishes to keep the refund, the filing should be delayed until the refund has been spent on reasonable ongoing expenses.

CHAPTER 15

Part 2 Discussion Questions

1. Because an insurance company is listed as a creditor, confirm if the debt is related to a car accident and if the debtor filed a personal injury claim since any funds received from a settlement will belong to the bankruptcy estate.
2. If a local chiropractor is listed as a creditor, the issue is the same as in Question 1: confirmation that the client doesn't have a personal injury claim pending.

Schedule G Discussion Questions

1. If the bankruptcy is filed before the creditor repossesses the car, the automatic stay will buy the debtor more time. But, the creditor may seek to lift the automatic stay or wait till the bankruptcy is completed to repossess the vehicle. Also, the debt should be listed on Schedule F as a deficiency judgment.
2. If the client buys the car before the bankruptcy is filed, then the issue is if there is any non-exempt equity in the vehicle. In addition, since the car is no longer leased, it's listed as an asset on Schedules A/B, and the debt is listed on Schedule D (secured).

Schedule H Discussion Questions

1. The best way to determine if a party is a co-borrower or authorized user is to contact the creditor directly as sometimes that information is mixed up on credit reports.
2. When in doubt, DON'T LEAVE IT OUT. The credit reporting system isn't perfect, so it's better to list debts that appear on a credit report, even if it doesn't belong to the debtor.

CHAPTER 16

Discussion Questions

1. Even though the employer categorizes the $1,500 as a gift, it's still considered income, no different than a year-end bonus. The $1,500 at the minimum would leave a substantial amount of disposable income for Schedule I, but it may also affect means testing.
2. Depending on the amount of overtime, it may not only affect Schedule I, leaving disposable income, but it may also affect means testing, especially if the extra income is for a few months. The client will either have to eliminate overtime from his paystubs or delay the filing until clean paystubs are provided.
3. Similar to Questions 1 and 2, the additional income could affect Schedule I and the means test. The issue is further complicated because while PTO increases the client's disposable income, eliminating the extra pay from the client's paystubs will affect the client's finances and household income. But if the PTO results in Chapter 13, once the client uses up his PTO, he won't earn sufficient income to fund the plan, so either the case gets dismissed or converted to Chapter 7. The client most likely should eliminate the PTO and file for Chapter 7 immediately.

CHAPTER 17

Discussion Questions

1. Not paying child support will reduce the client's expenses and increase the amount of disposable income. The client should proceed to continue to pay child support to deduct the $400 expense.
2. Yes, the client can proceed to file Chapter 7 because the expense of the roofing company cancels out the increased income. While the client is getting into more debt, considering the facts, it's a legitimate and reasonable expense.
3. The roofing company will place a lien on the property until payment is received in full. Therefore, as a secured debt, it's listed on Schedule D and the expense on Schedule J.
4. No, the debt with the roofing company won't be eliminated since it's a secured debt.

CHAPTER 18

Discussion Questions

1. Any balance left on the car loan is treated as an unsecured debt, no different than a repossession, so the debt is listed on Schedule F. A notation can be made as well.
2. Depending on the balance of costs per the retainer agreement, the difference subtracted from the $750 is fees and listed in SOFA. The $750 is deposited first in the IOTA account, and once the funds clear, fees can be transferred to the operating account.

Practice Questions and Exercises

1. The debt should be listed in Schedule F since it's an unsecured debt, and since the bank account was seized, that information should be listed in Section 10 of SOFA as well.

CHAPTER 20

Discussion Questions

1. A spouse's income, whether filing or not, is included in both Schedule I and the means test, while a domestic partner's household contributions are added to Schedule I.
2. A divorce can affect the means test in various ways. One way is that income is excluded from Schedule I and the means test if the parties no longer reside together. It may also result in increased expenses in Schedule J if the client is solely maintaining the household expenses. It will also affect exemptions issues for Schedule C, especially if there's property to be divided.

CHAPTER 21

While there are no specific answers for Questions 1 and 2, the student should now know how the means test can be affected by secured debt and delaying filing to eliminate a high-income month.

CHAPTER 22

Discussion Questions

1. Chapter 13, known as a reorganization, is a payment plan that lasts between 36 and 60 months. Chapter 13 is common when a debtor fails the means test or wishes to keep over-exempt property or has fallen behind on secured debt payments.

2. Whether Chapter 7 or 13, the debtor has the option of surrendering the non-exempt asset or keeping it and paying back the asset's value (minus exemptions) to the trustee. The difference with Chapter 7 is that the trustee will extend payments for a maximum of ten to 12 months, while with Chapter 13, payments last between 36 and 60 months.
3. A cramdown reduces secured debt to the asset's value, but a cramdown isn't automatic. A motion must be filed and approved by the bankruptcy judge. If so, the plan is amended to add the amount the debt was reduced by as an unsecured debt.

CHAPTER 24

Discussion Questions

1. Answers will vary, but the student should explain that it is a combination of Chapter 7 and 13 and that it's prohibited in some jurisdictions.
2. When a case should be dismissed or converted depends on the facts. However, suppose the debtor is paying the unsecured portion of the plan. In that case, consideration can be given to either one, especially if a lump sum payment can be agreed to with the creditors.

CHAPTER 26

Discussion Questions

1. Answers will vary, but the student should explain the basics of a reaffirmation agreement. This includes that reaffirming secured debt is voluntary since the client has the option of surrendering the asset. Issues concerning negative equity should be addressed, and the consequences of defaulting on the payments. Depending on the jurisdiction, the ride-through option should also be discussed.
2. The reaffirmation agreement should be filed within 60 days of the first 341 meeting of creditors and before the discharge.

CHAPTER 27

Discussion Questions

4. While answers will vary, the student should be able to compare a 2004 examination to a deposition in a criminal or civil case. At this point in the student's education, they should be familiar with the discovery process.

Index

Note: Page numbers in *italics* indicate figures.

For Product Safety Concerns and Information please contact our EU representative GPSR@taylorandfrancis.com Taylor & Francis Verlag GmbH, Kaufingerstraße 24, 80331 München, Germany

Batch number: 10722134

Printed by Printforce, the Netherlands